Applied AI and Machine Learning for Real-World Systems

Jingyuan Zhao
https://orcid.org/0000-0003-3289-4048
University of Toronto, Canada

V. Vinoth Kumar
https://orcid.org/0000-0003-1070-3212
Vellore Institute of Technology, India

Joseph Richards
California State University, Sacramento, USA

IGI Global
Scientific Publishing
Publishing Tomorrow's Research Today

Vice President of Editorial	Melissa Wagner
Director of Acquisitions	Mikaela Felty
Director of Book Development	Jocelynn Hessler
Production Manager	Mike Brehm
Cover Design	Jose Rosado

Published in the United States of America by
IGI Global Scientific Publishing
701 East Chocolate Avenue
Hershey, PA, 17033, USA
Tel: 717-533-8845 | Fax: 717-533-7115
Website: https://www.igi-global.com E-mail: cust@igi-global.com

Library of Congress Cataloging-in-Publication Data

LCCN: 2026031965 (CIP Data Pending)
ISBN13: 9798260027011
Isbn13Softcover: 9798260027028
EISBN13: 9798260027035
British Cataloguing in Publication Data
A Cataloguing in Publication record for this book is available from the British Library.

Table of Contents

Detailed Table of Contents

enabling the network to focus on relevant lung regions while suppressing background structures. Publicly available chest X-ray datasets were used for training and evaluation with preprocessing techniques including normalization and data augmentation. Experimental results achieved a Dice coefficient of 0.93 and improved segmentation performance compared with conventional U-Net models. The proposed system may support radiologists in computer-aided diagnosis and collaborative clinical workflows.

This study investigated the suitability of a Large Language Model (ChatGPT-4o) for generating high-quality, factually correct, and complete match reports using on-ball events data from football games. The structure and data requirements of the match reports were established through manual analysis of five real-world reports. Using this guideline, the LLM generated ten match reports using zero-shot prompts (Type 1), followed by ten scoreline-matched reports using few-shot prompts (Type 2). Ten human-authored, scoreline-matched reports acted as reference articles (Type 3). The Type 1 and Type 2 reports were evaluated by the researchers for Accuracy and Completeness before twenty-six volunteers were asked to rate a set of reports for Enjoyment, Excitement, Clarity, and Quality. Volunteers also indicated whether they assumed the author to be human or an LLM. Articles were presented in a randomized order with volunteers blinded to the article source.

This research investigates the potential of extracting personality traits from social media linguistic productions, focusing on Moroccan users' digital identity. Using an experimental exploratory methodology, the study applies IBM Watson's Personality Insights—grounded in the Big Five model—to fourteen Facebook and Twitter profiles. Data was gathered via netnography between 2020 and 2021 from accounts selected for rich expression and accessibility. Results confirm the feasibility of detecting traits like openness and conscientiousness, though accuracy varies; Arabic texts showed weaker correlations (mean absolute error – 0.09–0.12) than English. The study reveals that specific linguistic choices significantly influence algorithmic outputs, raising questions regarding potential manipulation. Ultimately, this novel application of AI to Moroccan bilingual data underscores the promise of digital psychology while emphasizing the critical need for enhanced algorithmic precision and contextualized interpretation in future research.

Crypto-Generative Adversarial Networks (Crypto-GANs) as an intelligent and adaptive framework for secure image encryption. By combining adversarial deep learning with cryptographic principles, the proposed system learns complex non-linear transformations to convert plain images into noise-like cipher images while enabling accurate reconstruction using the correct secret key. Unlike traditional encryption methods based on fixed mathematical rules, Crypto-GANs dynamically adapt to emerging attack strategies. Experimental results demonstrate strong security performance. Encrypted images achieved entropy values close to the theoretical maximum (up to 7.9978), indicating high randomness. Adjacent pixel correlations were reduced to near zero, confirming the removal of inherent statistical patterns. High NPCR and UACI values reflected effective diffusion, ensuring resistance against differential and chosen-plaintext attacks. Decryption quality remained excellent, with high PSNR and SSIM values supporting accurate image recovery.

Perception is the core module of the autonomous robot that can perform perception. The efficiency of the perception module is the key area that influences other modules of the autonomous robot. This chapter we aim to provide the theoretical aspects of the perception module of the autonomous robot, specifically its mathematical concept linear algebra and its intelligent concept artificial intelligence-driven learning models. The data collected by the robotic platforms is highly dimensional, structured, and noisy. Therefore, the representations of the data are crucial for the efficient interpretation of the collected data. Linear algebra is highly effective for mathematical representations to achieve the task of the perception module for an autonomous robot. In this context, the current chapter has focused on the potential contribution to the development of human-oriented artificial intelligence in robotic systems through structured, interpretable, and reliable vision frameworks and the challenges.

Artificial Intelligence (AI), when integrated with Augmented Reality (AR) and Virtual Reality (VR), is transforming industrial maintenance through immersive, data-driven Digital Twin environments. This chapter presents a comprehensive framework that demonstrates how AI-enhanced VR systems can optimize the monitoring and repair of industrial equipment. Using a centrifugal pump as a case study, the system uses AI-based anomaly detection, programmable logic control, real-time sensor inputs, and immersive virtual reality interfaces for remote issue resolution. IoT and MQTT protocols are used to synchronize a Unity 3D-created digital twin with real machinery. Operators can see, identify, and fix issues remotely with an Oculus Go headset. A Cartesian robotic arm that has been trained using AI procedures to mimic human repair movements makes physical adjustments. Scalable predictive maintenance, less downtime, and less human intervention are the results of this AI-AR/VR synergy.

This chapter evaluates Fieldwire's Business Tier as a Project Management Information System (PMIS) for construction in the context of Industry 4.0 and PMBOK principles. It synthesises empirical evidence and peer-reviewed literature to map Fieldwire features to PMBOK performance domains, quantify likely operational impacts, and benchmark the Business Tier against competitors (Procore, Autodesk Construction Cloud/PlanGrid). The chapter identifies organisational, technical, and governance

Preface

INTRODUCTION

Artificial Intelligence (AI) and Machine Learning (ML) have rapidly evolved from specialized research domains into transformative technologies that are reshaping virtually every aspect of modern society. Across industries, governments, educational institutions, healthcare systems, and research organizations, AI-driven solutions are increasingly being deployed to solve complex challenges, improve decision-making, automate processes, and generate new opportunities for innovation. As these technologies continue to mature, their impact extends beyond technical efficiency, influencing economic development, societal well-being, and the future of human work and collaboration.

While the remarkable capabilities of AI and ML have generated enthusiasm and unprecedented opportunities, they have also raised important questions regarding transparency, accountability, fairness, trustworthiness, and human oversight. The rapid integration of intelligent systems into real-world environments has highlighted the necessity of developing technologies that not only perform effectively but also align with human values, needs, and expectations. This growing awareness has contributed to the emergence of Human-Centered Artificial Intelligence (HCAI), an interdisciplinary approach that seeks to ensure AI systems enhance and augment human capabilities rather than replace them.

Human-centered perspectives have become increasingly important as AI technologies are embedded within critical domains such as healthcare, education, transportation, manufacturing, public services, finance, and environmental management. Successful implementation requires more than technical excellence; it demands collaboration among computer scientists, engineers, designers, social scientists, psychologists, ethicists, policymakers, and domain experts. Such collaboration enables the development of AI systems that are transparent, explainable, inclusive, and responsive to the diverse needs of individuals and communities.

The purpose of *Applied AI and Machine Learning for Real-World Systems* is to explore the practical application of intelligent technologies while emphasizing the human dimensions that accompany their deployment. This volume brings together contemporary research, innovative methodologies, emerging frameworks, and real-world case studies that demonstrate how AI and ML can be designed and implemented to address pressing challenges across multiple sectors. The contributions contained within this book reflect the breadth and depth of current developments in the field, illustrating both the technical advances that drive intelligent systems and the human-centered principles that guide their responsible use.

Throughout this volume, readers will encounter discussions on the design, development, deployment, and evaluation of AI-powered solutions in diverse contexts. The chapters collectively examine how machine learning models, intelligent decision-support systems, predictive analytics, automation technologies, and collaborative human-AI environments can be leveraged to improve organizational performance, enhance user experiences, and support evidence-based decision-making. At the same time, contributors critically address issues related to ethics, governance, trust, explainability, and societal impact, providing a balanced perspective on the opportunities and challenges associated with AI adoption.

A central theme of this book is the growing convergence of Human-Centered AI, Human-Centered Machine Learning, Human-AI Interaction, and collaborative intelligence. Rather than viewing AI solely as an autonomous technology, the contributors emphasize its role as a collaborative partner capable of supporting human creativity, expertise, and problem-solving capabilities. By fostering meaningful human-AI partnerships, organizations can unlock new forms of innovation while maintaining human agency, accountability, and oversight.

The interdisciplinary nature of this volume reflects the reality that AI challenges and opportunities rarely exist within the boundaries of a single discipline. The chapters present insights that are relevant to researchers, practitioners, educators, policymakers, and industry leaders who seek to understand both the technological foundations and practical implications of AI deployment. Through the integration of theoretical perspectives and applied examples, this book aims to bridge the gap between academic research and real-world implementation.

We anticipate that this volume will serve as a valuable resource for professors, researchers, scientists, engineers, and students engaged in the study and development of intelligent systems. It will also provide useful guidance for policymakers, government officials, technology managers, research and development leaders, and organizational decision-makers seeking to navigate the rapidly evolving AI landscape.

Furthermore, libraries and information centers supporting these communities will find this collection to be a timely and comprehensive reference.

As editors, we are grateful to the contributing authors for sharing their expertise, insights, and innovative research. Their collective efforts have made it possible to assemble a volume that captures the current state of applied AI and machine learning while looking toward the future of human-centered intelligent systems. We hope that the discussions presented in this book inspire further research, encourage responsible innovation, and contribute to the development of AI technologies that create meaningful and lasting benefits for individuals, organizations, and society as a whole.

We invite readers to engage with the ideas presented throughout this volume and to participate in shaping a future where artificial intelligence and machine learning are developed and applied in ways that empower people, strengthen institutions, and advance the collective good.

ORGANIZATION OF THE BOOK

Chapter 1 (*Groundwater Salinity Prediction in African Continent Using Machine Learning Techniques and Methods: A Comprehensive Review, Study, and Analysis*) establishes a robust ML framework for salinity prediction in data-scarce regions and bridges the gap between advanced modeling and practical water management policy, offering a vital tool for informed decision-making.

Chapter 2 (*AI-Powered Agricultural Management System for Precision Farming*) presents a pioneering AI-based system aimed at enhancing precision farming. The system uses artificial intelligence to change how farmers interact with their crops and manage their fields. It includes features such as disease detection, weather forecasting, and AI chatbot support. By using advance computer vision technologies, farmers can upload images of their crops to identify diseases with accuracy.

Chapter 3 (*Identification of Pneumonia in Chest X-ray Images Using Generative and Explainable AI Methods*) presents a deep learning-based framework for automated pneumonia detection from chest X-ray images, focusing on accuracy and interpretability. To address class imbalance and improve performance, traditional data augmentation is integrated with synthetic image generation using an Auxiliary Classifier Generative Adversarial Network (ACGAN), enhancing dataset diversity.

Chapter 4 (*An Attention-Augmented U-NET Model for Lung Region Segmentation from Chest X-Ray Images*) proposes an Attention-Augmented U-Net model for accurate lung region segmentation. The proposed framework enhances the conventional U-Net architecture by integrating Attention Gates (AGs) into skip connections between encoder and decoder layers, enabling the network to focus on relevant lung regions while suppressing background structures.

Chapter 5 (*Automated Data-to-Text Generation of Football Match Reports Using a Large Language Model*) investigates the suitability of a Large Language Model (ChatGPT-4o) for generating high-quality, factually correct, and complete match reports using on-ball events data from football games. The structure and data requirements of the match reports were established through manual analysis of five real-world reports.

Chapter 6 (*Extracting Personality Traits from Digital Identity on social media: An Experimental Study Using IBM Watson's Personality Insights*) reveals that specific linguistic choices significantly influence algorithmic outputs, raising questions regarding potential manipulation. Ultimately, this novel application of AI to Moroccan bilingual data underscores the promise of digital psychology while emphasizing the critical need for enhanced algorithmic precision and contextualized interpretation in future research.

Chapter 7 (*Adaptive Image Encryption Using Artificial Intelligence and Crypto-GANs)* claims that, by combining adversarial deep learning with cryptographic principles, the proposed system learns complex non-linear transformations to convert plain images into noise-like cipher images while enabling accurate reconstruction using the correct secret key.

Chapter 8 (*Human-Centered AI for Autonomous Robotic Perception Integrating Linear Algebraic Structure with Artificial Intelligence*) is focused on the potential contribution to the development of human-oriented artificial intelligence in robotic systems through structured, interpretable, and reliable vision frameworks and the challenges.

Chapter 9 (*AI-Driven Digital Twin Maintenance Automation in AR/VR: A Centrifugal Pump Case Study*) presents a comprehensive framework that demonstrates how AI-enhanced VR systems can optimize the monitoring and repair of industrial equipment. Using a centrifugal pump as a case study, the system uses AI-based anomaly detection, programmable logic control, real-time sensor inputs, and immersive virtual reality interfaces for remote issue resolution.

Chapter 10 (*Fieldwire Business Tier and Construction 4.0: A PMBOK and Industry 4.0 Perspective*) identifies organisational, technical, and governance challenges in adoption and offers an implementation roadmap, metrics for impact assessment, and research avenues. The analysis draws on systematic literature synthesis, product documentation, and proxy empirical studies to provide practitioners and researchers with evidence-based guidance on leveraging mobile-first PMIS to reduce delays, control costs, and improve stakeholder engagement.

Chapter 11 (*Enhancing Community Resilience and Disaster Preparedness Through AI-Assisted Open Mapping: A Conceptual Framework for Underserved African Regions*) calls for empirical validation through pilot projects, emphasizing interdisciplinary collaboration and sustainable governance to ensure equitable outcomes in vulnerable African regions.

CONCLUSION

As artificial intelligence and machine learning continue to transform the technological landscape, the need for solutions that are not only innovative but also responsible, transparent, and human-centered has never been greater. The chapters presented in this volume demonstrate the vast potential of intelligent systems to address complex real-world challenges while reinforcing the importance of maintaining human values, ethical principles, and societal well-being at the forefront of technological advancement.

The contributions collected in this book reflect the diversity, dynamism, and interdisciplinary nature of contemporary AI research and practice. Together, they illustrate how intelligent technologies can be effectively designed, deployed, and managed to support decision-making, enhance productivity, foster innovation, and strengthen collaboration between humans and machines. Equally important, they encourage critical reflection on the responsibilities that accompany the growing influence of AI across sectors and communities worldwide.

As editors, we believe that the future of artificial intelligence lies not solely in creating more powerful systems, but in developing technologies that complement human capabilities, promote inclusivity, and generate meaningful societal value. It is our hope that this volume serves as both a scholarly resource and a catalyst for future inquiry, inspiring researchers, practitioners, educators, policymakers, and industry leaders to pursue AI innovations that are technically robust, ethically grounded, and socially beneficial.

We extend our sincere appreciation to all contributing authors for their expertise and dedication, and to the readers who will continue advancing knowledge and innovation in this rapidly evolving field. By fostering collaboration across disciplines and encouraging thoughtful engagement with emerging technologies, we can collectively shape a future in which artificial intelligence and machine learning serve as powerful tools for human progress and sustainable development.

Chapter 1
Groundwater Salinity Prediction in the African Continent Using Machine Learning Techniques and Methods:
A Comprehensive Review, Study, and Analysis

Nwosu Obinnaya Chikezie Victor
http://orcid.org/0000-0003-3974-4755
University of South Africa, South Africa

Ibrahim Sinneh Sinneh
University of Liberia, Liberia

ABSTRACT

This chapter details a study using Machine Learning (ML) to predict rising groundwater salinity across Africa, a critical threat to water security. Traditional models face challenges with data scarcity and computational demands. By analyzing continent-wide data on climate, soil, and hydrogeology, the research tested multiple ML algorithms. Ensemble methods, particularly Random Forest and XGBoost, proved most accurate in predicting key salinity indicators (EC and TDS), significantly outperforming traditional linear models. Analysis identified nitrogen content (often from agriculture), sand fraction, and aridity as primary drivers of salinity, highlighting a mix of human and natural causes. The study establishes a robust

DOI: 10.4018/979-8-2600-2701-1.ch001

ML framework for salinity prediction in data-scarce regions and bridges the gap between advanced modeling and practical water management policy, offering a vital tool for informed decision-making.

1. INTRODUCTION

1.1 Background and Significance

Water scarcity is one of the defining challenges of the 21st century, with the African continent standing at the precipice of a deepening crisis. As surface water sources become increasingly unreliable due to climate change and pollution, groundwater has emerged as a vital resource for sustaining the livelihoods of millions. It supports the continent's rapidly growing agricultural sector, drives industrial development, and provides potable water for domestic use. However, the usability of this indispensable resource is significantly threatened by salinization. Groundwater salinity, characterised by elevated levels of dissolved salts, poses a major environmental concern, rendering water unfit for drinking and toxic to crops.

The genesis of groundwater salinity in Africa is multifaceted, stemming from both natural hydrogeological processes—such as rock-water interaction and evaporation in arid zones—and anthropogenic activities, including irrigation-induced salinization and seawater intrusion in coastal aquifers. Consequently, the accurate prediction and monitoring of groundwater salinity are crucial for managing and protecting this valuable resource. To that end, recent advancements in machine learning offer promising avenues for developing robust predictive models that can overcome the limitations of traditional approaches, particularly in data-scarce regions (Elshaarawy & Eltarabily, 2024). These advanced computational techniques can effectively capture complex, non-linear relationships within multivariate hydrogeological datasets, enabling more accurate spatial predictions of salinity levels (Araya et al., 2023; Sanad et al., 2025). Such models leverage diverse parameters like temperature, soil moisture, light intensity, and geological variables to enhance prediction accuracy ("The Smart IoT Blueprint: Engineering a Connected Future," 2024; Touré et al., 2024). This approach is particularly critical in regions like the Horn of Africa, where successive droughts have exacerbated water scarcity and limited access to safe drinking water, necessitating a deeper understanding of groundwater salinity distribution (Araya et al., 2023). Furthermore, this comprehensive understanding is essential for informing strategic interventions and prioritizing assistance in areas most affected by groundwater salinization, which is a growing threat globally, particularly in arid and semi-arid regions with decreasing run-off (Araya et al., 2023). Therefore, this paper explores the application of machine learning and deep learning models as advanced tools for predicting groundwater dynamics, including salinity, to enhance groundwater management strategies (Muralidharan et al., 2025; Roy et al., 2025). These computational assessments are particularly crucial for understanding groundwater quality evolution, especially in areas characterised by groundwater depression cones, thereby enabling proactive decision-making for water resource managers (Jamei et al., 2022). Given the critical importance of groundwater for agriculture, particularly in regions with expanding farmlands and increased pumping of aquifers, assessing its suitability for irrigation is paramount, as water quality directly impacts crop yields and soil fertility (Mohammed et al., 2023). In this context, machine learning applications have demonstrated significant promise in improving predictive capabilities for groundwater salinity modeling, effectively addressing the limitations inherent in conventional models (Roy et al., 2025). Specifically, machine learning models reduce reliance on extensive physical and hydrological parameters, leveraging available data for efficient and scalable predictions of salinity levels (Roy et al., 2025). These advanced models are particularly adept at capturing intricate and non-linear relationships within complex hydrological data, offering a more precise representation of hydrodynamic processes compared to traditional approaches (Mezouary et al., 2024). This capacity allows for more accurate assessments of groundwater quality, which is vital for effective hydro-environmental predictive management, especially in arid agricultural regions where groundwater resources are heavily relied upon (Abdu et al., 2025). Moreover, the integration of machine learning into groundwater management frameworks provides a reliable methodology for predicting complex hydrological occurrences, such as changes in total dissolved solids and electrical conductivity (Jamshidzadeh et al., 2024).

Figure 1. Distribution of Groundwater Salinity Levels in Africa.

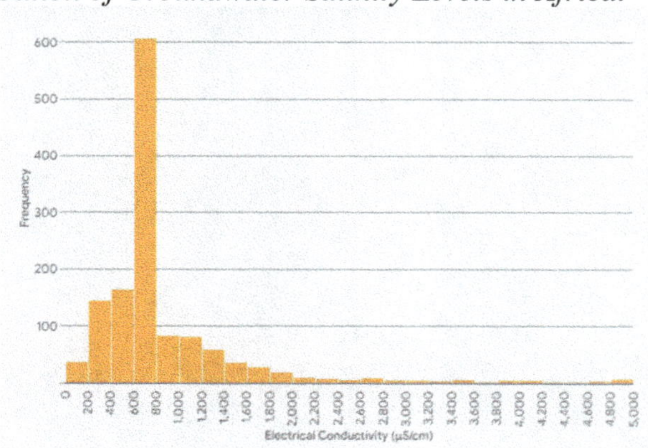

1.2 Problem Statement

Historically, hydro-geologists have relied on numerical models and manual sampling to estimate salinity levels. While these traditional methods provide detailed local insights, they are often time-consuming, resource-intensive, and difficult to scale across a continent as geologically diverse as Africa. Furthermore, the scarcity of high-resolution hydrogeological data in many African nations creates a "blind spot," preventing effective regional planning. This data limitation hinders the ability to accurately characterise groundwater conditions and implement informed management strategies, particularly given that traditional hydrological models frequently demand diverse datasets that are rarely accessible across many global regions (Roy et al., 2025). Such models often struggle with complex, non-linear hydrogeological systems and are unable to adapt to dynamic environmental changes, making them inadequate for predicting groundwater quality and levels across diverse and rapidly changing environments (Eghrari et al., 2023). These limitations are particularly pronounced when addressing issues like groundwater overexploitation due to increased irrigation pumping, which can lead to significant draw-down, increased pumping costs, and even land subsidence (Wang et al., 2024). Moreover, conventional approaches frequently fail to incorporate the intricate interactions between various hydrogeological parameters, limiting their utility in forecasting groundwater quality under extensive salinization (Bilali et al., 2020). In contrast, AI and machine learning techniques offer a robust alternative, capable of discerning complex patterns and making precise predictions even with limited datasets, thereby overcoming the challenges posed by data scarcity and the dynamic nature of groundwater systems (Mohammed et al., 2023; "The Smart IoT Blueprint: Engineering a Connected Future," 2024).

Figure 2. Distribution of Physicochemical Parameters.

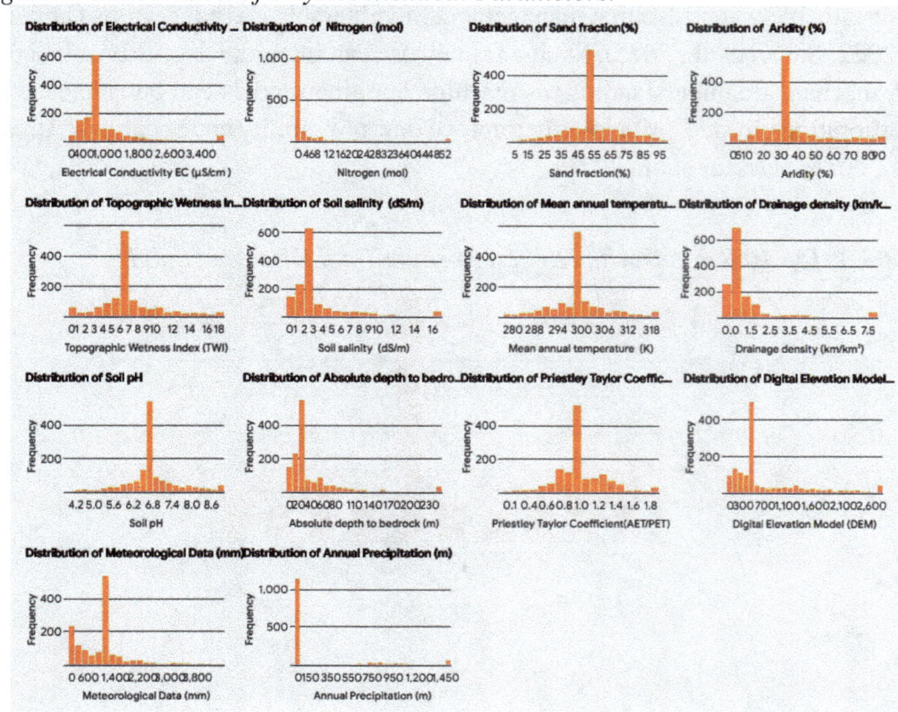

In response to these limitations, there is a growing interest in utilizing Machine Learning(Yameogo et al., 2025). Despite this potential, previous applications of ML in this domain have been largely fragmented, focusing on small, isolated study areas or specific aquifers, such as the Nile Delta or specific basins in Southern Africa. There remains a significant lack of comprehensive, continental-scale studies that evaluate the applicability and limitations of ML techniques for groundwater salinity prediction across the diverse environmental contexts of Africa(Chiloane et al., 2025). This gap underscores the necessity for a systematic evaluation of various machine learning models to identify those most adept at handling sparse and heterogeneous datasets typical of African hydrogeological settings (Roy et al., 2025). Furthermore, the operationalization of ML models for real-world decision-making is often hindered by a lack of user-oriented tools, requiring a bridge between advanced model development and practical application for effective saltwater intrusion management (Armanuos et al., 2025). This review aims to address these limitations by systematically evaluating recent advancements in machine learning and deep learning applications for modeling groundwater salinity, identifying challenges, and proposing future directions for improving their effectiveness in coastal aquifer salinity modeling (Roy et al., 2025). The ultimate goal is to provide a unified framework that not only predicts groundwater salinity but also offers actionable insights for sustainable water resource management in vulnerable coastal regions (Jamei et al., 2022; Sanad et al., 2025). Such a framework can integrate data-driven insights with mechanistic understanding, as machine learning models can be enhanced by incorporating physical principles to improve interpret-ability and accuracy (Atmaja et al., 2025; Hassani et al., 2021).

Figure 3. Top 10 Regions with Highest Average Total Dissolved Solids

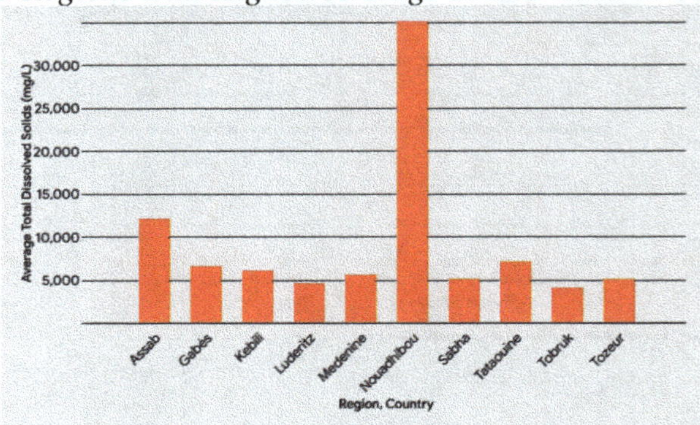

1.3 Chapter Objectives and Contribution

This chapter aims to bridge this gap by presenting a comprehensive empirical study on the application of ML methods for predicting groundwater salinity in Africa. Unlike previous review-centric works, this study utilises a compiled dataset of African groundwater measurements to rigorously test and compare various ML algorithms. This approach distinguishes it from existing literature by offering a thorough evaluation of recent advancements in machine learning, deep learning, ensemble techniques, and optimised approaches for groundwater salinity modeling within coastal aquifers (Roy et al., 2025). This research will also explore how interpretable machine learning models can enhance understanding of the complex factors influencing groundwater salinity, moving beyond opaque "black box" models to provide actionable insights for water resource managers (Chakraborty et al., 2020). This includes evaluating the dependency of salinity on various global climate change parameters, thereby contributing to the body of knowledge necessary for addressing environmental challenges related to water quality (Sahwell & Solo-Gabriele, 2025).

The specific objectives are:

1. To synthesise the current state of knowledge regarding groundwater salinity prediction in Africa.
2. To evaluate the performance of distinct ML algorithms (Random Forest, XGBoost, SVM, Neural Networks, and Logistic Regression) in predicting salinity metrics (EC and TDS).
3. To identify key predictive features—including hydrogeological, climatic, and soil parameters—that drive salinity variations across the continent.
4. To propose a framework for policy and practice, translating technical ML outputs into actionable insights for water resource managers.

By addressing these objectives, this study seeks to provide a holistic understanding of how data-driven approaches can revolutionise groundwater management in Africa, moving from reactive monitoring to proactive prediction. This research also aims to enhance accessibility to these predictive tools by developing user-friendly interfaces that enable practitioners to input relevant parameters and obtain actionable predictions, thereby facilitating scenario-based analysis for effective coastal aquifer management (Armanuos et al., 2025). Furthermore, this work contributes to the broader academic discourse by offering a critical analysis of current limitations and future directions in applying artificial intelligence to hydrogeological challenges, fostering the development of more robust and reliable predictive models for groundwater quality (Roy et al., 2025). Specifically, this involves developing advanced machine learning models that integrate diverse datasets and incorporate best practices such as integrated feature learning, ensemble learning, metaheuristic optimisation, and explainable AI to improve accuracy and interpret-ability (Roy et al., 2025). Such a framework will provide robust and interpretable ML-based tools for coastal aquifer management, combining theoretical rigor with practical applicability (Armanuos et al., 2025). This integration of advanced ML techniques promises to significantly improve the accuracy and reliability of groundwater salinity predictions, fostering more effective and sustainable management strategies (Roy et al., 2025).

Figure 4. Distribution of Geological Settings

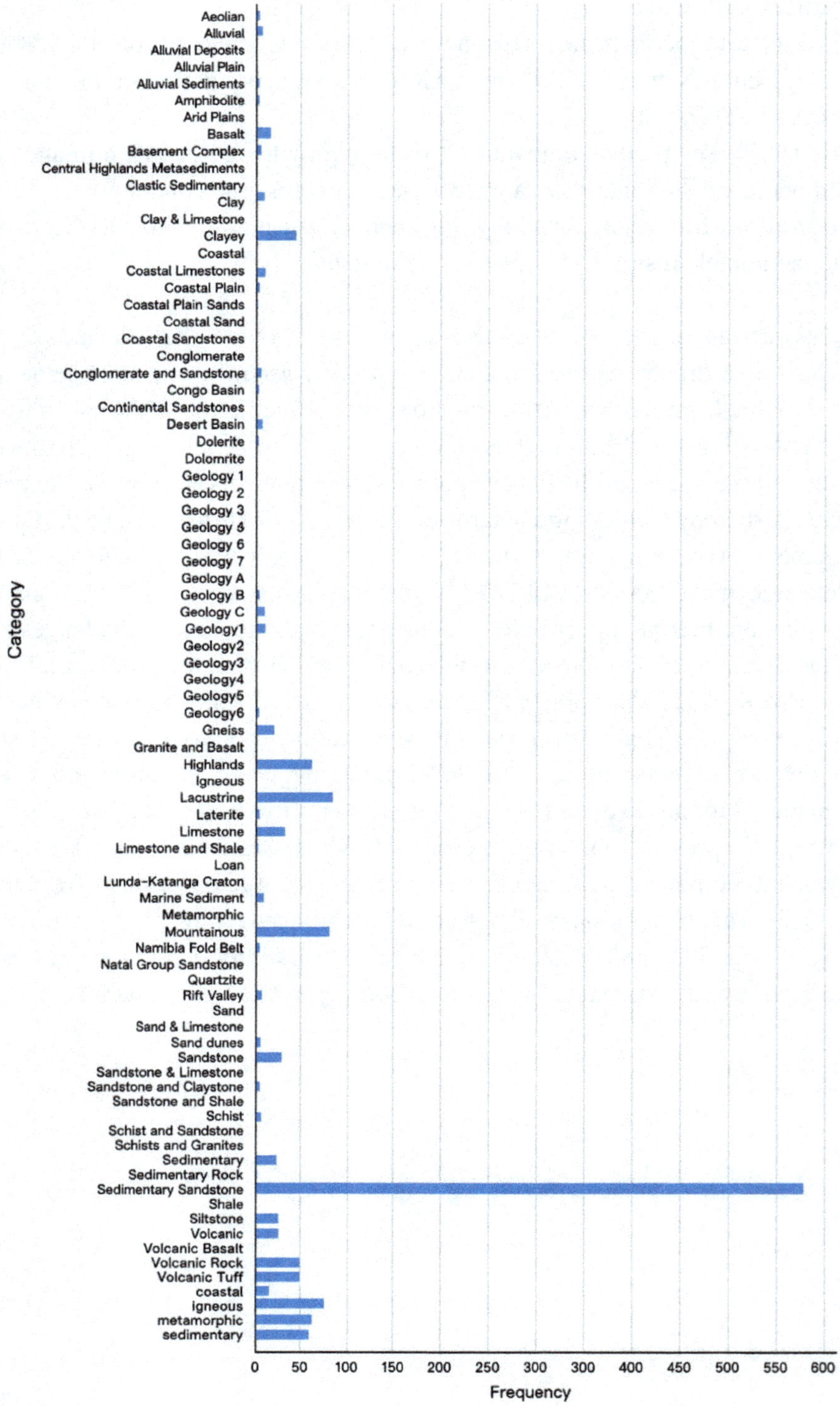

2. BACKGROUND AND LITERATURE REVIEW

2.1 The Hydrogeological Context of Africa

Africa's hydrogeology is characterised by extreme variability, ranging from the vast sedimentary aquifers of the Sahara and the Congo Basin to the fractured basement complexes of Eastern and Southern Africa. This geological diversity dictates the natural baseline of groundwater quality. In arid and semi-arid regions, high evaporation rates often lead to the natural concentration of salts, a phenomenon exacerbated by the presence of saline geological formations. Conversely, in tropical regions with high recharge rates, salinity is typically lower, though anthropogenic contamination remains a risk. The complex interplay of natural hydrogeological processes and human activities further complicates groundwater quality assessment, particularly in coastal zones where salt-water intrusion presents a significant threat to freshwater resources (Sanad et al., 2025). The intricate dynamics of groundwater flow, coupled with the varied geological structures and climatic conditions across the continent, necessitate sophisticated analytical approaches for effective management (Touré et al., 2024). The heterogeneity in hydrogeological conditions across Africa underscores the challenge in developing universally applicable predictive models for groundwater quality, necessitating region-specific adjustments and comprehensive data integration (Mensah et al., 2024). Machine learning and artificial intelligence models offer a promising avenue for addressing this complexity, enabling the analysis of non-linear relationships between hydrogeological variables and groundwater quality (Shaikh & Birajdar, 2024).

Figure 5. Electrical Conductivity in African Groundwater

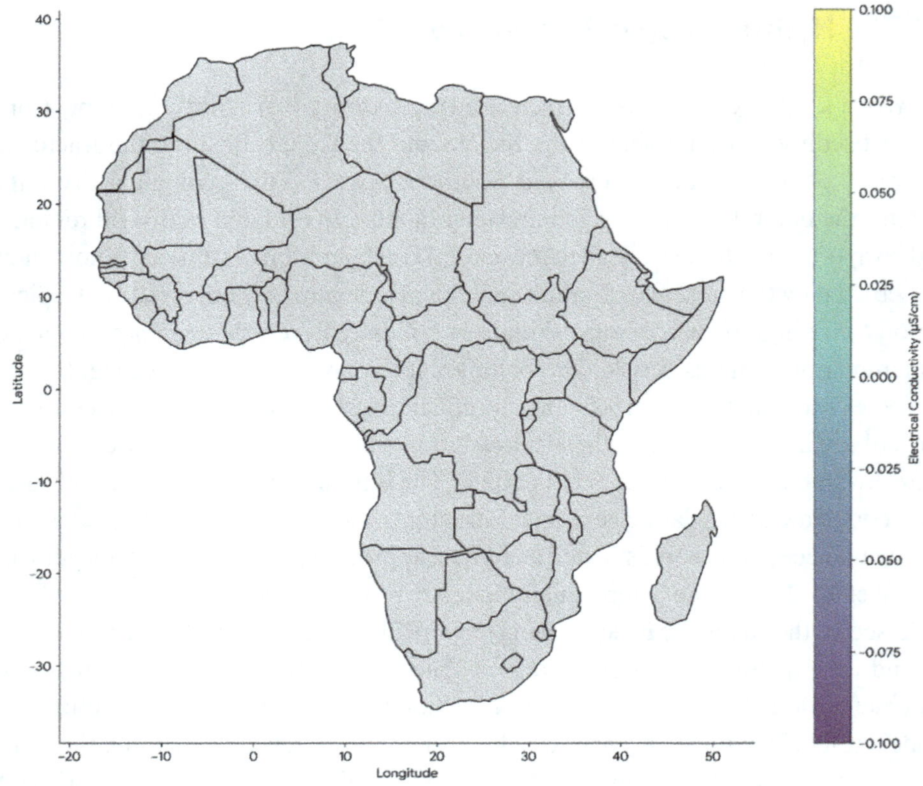

Understanding these geological settings is paramount for prediction. For instance, sedimentary aquifers, which appear frequently in our dataset (Figure 4), often have different transport properties and salinity profiles compared to igneous or metamorphic environments. The continent's variability necessitates models that are not rigid but can adapt to local geological nuances. This adaptability requires the integration of diverse geological and climatic variables into machine learning algorithms to accurately predict groundwater parameters across different African regions (Touré et al., 2024). The influence of geological and climatic variables on groundwater levels in Africa is a topic of significant interest and importance (Touré et al., 2024). Indeed, various studies have examined the impact of climatic variables on groundwater levels across the continent (Touré et al., 2024).

Figure 6. Mean Electrical Conductivity by African Country

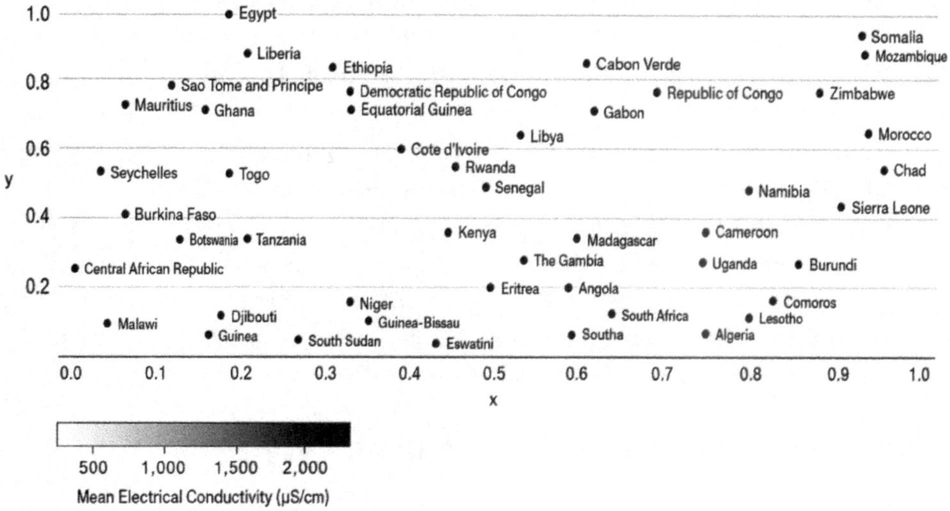

2.2 Traditional vs. Machine Learning Approaches

Traditionally, groundwater salinity has been modelled using deterministic approaches based on Darcy's Law and solute transport equations (e.g., MODFLOW/MT3DMS). These models are excellent for understanding physical processes but require extensive input data—hydraulic conductivity, porosity, boundary conditions—that are rarely available at a regional scale in Africa. Furthermore, traditional hydrogeological models often struggle to account for the complex, non-linear interactions between various environmental factors influencing groundwater quality, making them less suitable for predictive tasks in data-scarce regions (Jamei et al., 2022). In contrast, machine learning models offer a robust alternative, capable of discerning intricate patterns and relationships within complex datasets without requiring explicit process-based equations (Sahour et al., 2022). These models excel at pattern recognition, making them particularly adept at predicting groundwater salinity variations even with incomplete or noisy hydrogeological data (Pazola et al., 2024). Their ability to learn complex, non-linear relationships from observed data makes them highly effective for groundwater level prediction in regions where comprehensive physical models are difficult to implement (Touré et al., 2024a, 2024b). The ability of machine learning models to identify linear or non-linear relationships between water salinity and its controlling factors has been well-demonstrated (Jamei et al., 2022). This is particularly valuable for applications such as groundwater potential mapping and water quality prediction, where the underlying hydrogeological processes are often too complex for traditional deterministic approaches (Andalu et al., 2025).

Machine Learning represents a paradigm shift. Instead of solving physical equations, ML algorithms learn patterns from historical data. This allows for:

- **Handling Non-linearity:** ML can capture complex interactions between rainfall, soil type, and salinity that linear statistical models miss.
- **Data Flexibility:** ML can integrate disparate data sources, such as satellite-derived Digital Elevation Models (DEM) and remote sensing data for vegetation (NDVI), filling gaps left by sparse field observations.
- **Scalability:** Once trained, ML models can predict salinity in unmonitored areas, provided the environmental covariates are known.

2.3 Review of Previous ML Studies in Africa

Recent literature indicates a surge in ML applications for groundwater in Africa, yet most remain localised.

- **North Africa:** Studies in Egypt and Morocco have successfully used Artificial Neural Networks(Roy et al., 2025). These studies highlight the importance of distance-to-coast and groundwater extraction rates as key features.
- **Sub-Saharan Africa:** Research in the Sahel has focused on the correlation between climate change variables(Ayadi et al., 2025).
- **Gaps:** A systematic review reveals that while individual studies show promise, they often lack validation across different hydrogeological zones. Furthermore, few studies address the "black box" nature of ML, failing to interpret *why* a model predicts high salinity, which is crucial for decision-making. This chapter addresses these gaps by applying interpretable ML techniques (Feature Importance) to a continental dataset.

Figure 7. Relationships between various hydrogeological and environmental parameters and Total Dissolved Solids (TDS)

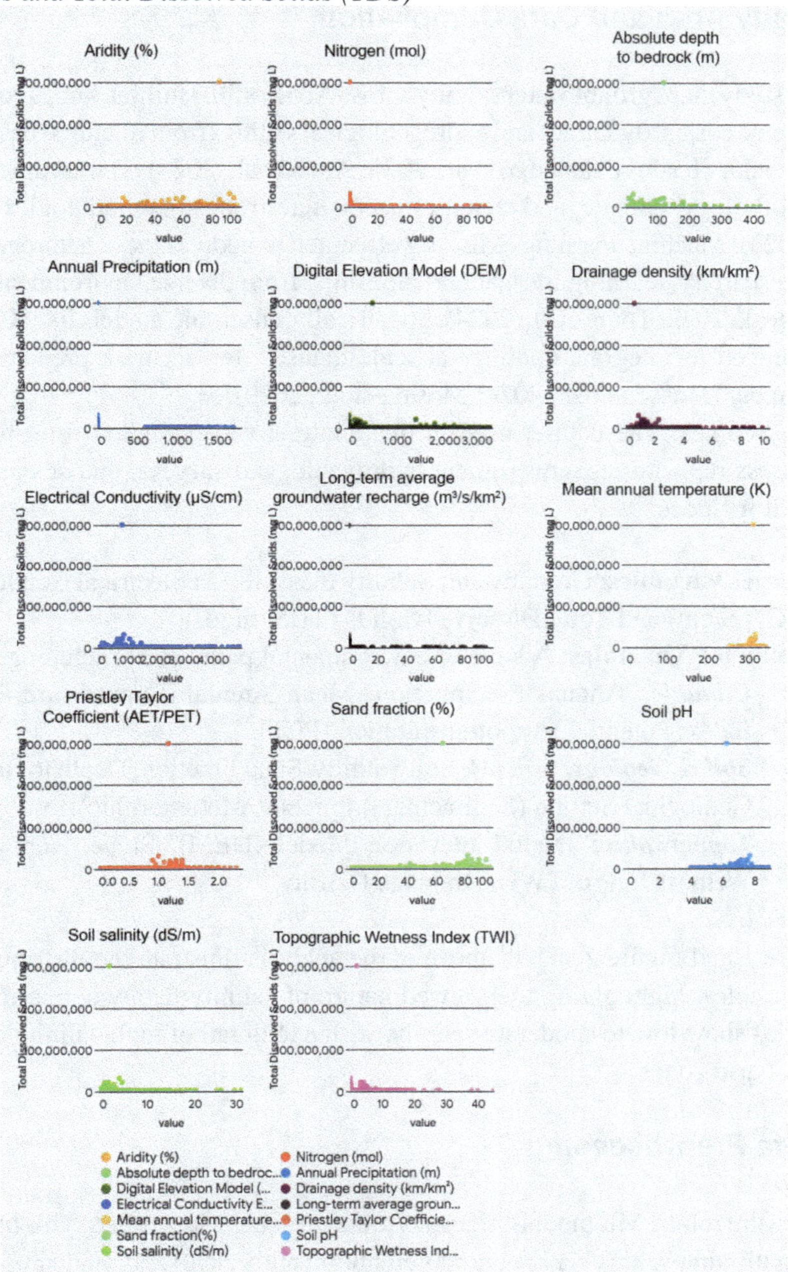

3. METHODOLOGY

3.1 Study Area and Data Compilation

This study maps groundwater salinity across Africa's 30.3 million km^2, a continent with diverse coastal dynamics and hydrogeological settings from fractured basements to sedimentary basins (Yameogo et al., 2025; Arafa et al., 2024). The complex interplay of lithology, climate, and tectonics necessitates robust methodologies (Araya et al., 2023). Machine learning (ML) is well-suited to address these heterogeneities and data scarcity, learning intricate relationships from diverse environmental data (Araya et al., 2023; Touré et al., 2024). Specifically, ensemble models like XGBoost are leveraged to integrate continental-scale datasets for accurate prediction and management (Janssen et al., 2024; Mosavi et al., 2020).

Data Sources: The dataset used in this analysis was compiled from multiple open-access repositories, government hydrogeological surveys, and scientific literature. It includes:

- **Target Variables:** Groundwater Salinity measured as Electrical Conductivity (EC, µS/cm) and Total Dissolved Solids (TDS, mg/L).
- **Predictor Variables:** A suite of environmental parameters including:
    - ***Climatic:*** Annual Precipitation, Mean Annual Temperature, Aridity Index, Potential Evapotranspiration (PET).
    - ***Soil & Geology:*** Soil pH, Soil Salinity, Sand Fraction, Depth to Bedrock, Geological Setting (Sedimentary, Igneous, Metamorphic).
    - ***Topographic:*** Digital Elevation Model (DEM), Slope, Topographic Wetness Index (TWI), Drainage Density.

Figure 1 and Figure 2 shown above in the analysis illustrate the distribution of these variables, highlighting the skewed nature of salinity data where a majority of samples show low-to-moderate salinity, with a long tail of high-salinity outliers typical of arid zones.

3.2 Data Preprocessing

To ensure robust ML models, rigorous preprocessing was applied. This included handling missing values via K-nearest neighbors (numerical) and mode imputation (categorical), followed by data normalisation ("The Smart IoT Blueprint," 2024). Outliers were identified using the Isolation Forest algorithm (Olentsova et al., 2024). To address class imbalance, oversampling techniques were employed (Sahour et al., 2023). Categorical variables were one-hot encoded (Abdulwahid, 2024). Finally, the dataset was split 80/20 into training and testing sets to enable robust evaluation and prevent overfitting, ensuring reliable model generalisation ("The Smart IoT Blueprint," 2024; Abdulwahid, 2024).

Figure 8. Progression of research on groundwater salinity prediction in Africa using machine learning

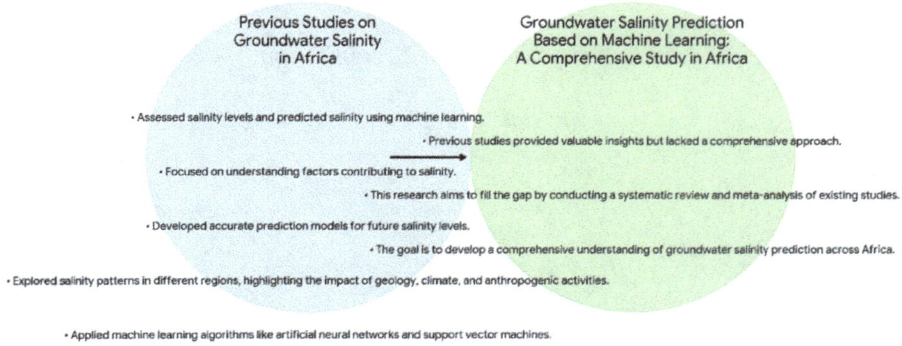

3.2.1 Outlier Detection and Removal

Groundwater data is notoriously noisy due to measurement errors or localised contamination events that do not represent the regional aquifer. As shown in Figure 11 and Figure 13, outliers were identified using statistical thresholds(Li & Yang, 2025). The Z-score method was employed to identify and remove outliers by calculating the deviation from the mean in terms of standard deviations, with values exceeding three standard deviations from the mean being classified as outliers (Roy et al., 2025).

3.2.2 Missing Value Imputation

Data scarcity is a primary challenge in Africa. Rather than discarding incomplete records, we employed advanced imputation techniques. We compared k-nearest Neighbors (kNN), Multiple Imputation by Chained Equations (MICE), and Random Forest (RF) imputation(Olaniran & Alzahrani, 2025). The k-nearest Neighbors (kNN) method proved to be the most effective, estimating missing values based on the average of its k-nearest neighbors in the feature space, a strategy particularly well-suited for environmental datasets with complex interdependencies.

- **Result:** As illustrated in Figure 12, Random Forest imputation yielded the lowest Mean Squared Error (MSE), successfully preserving the statistical distribution of the original data. This method uses the correlations between variables (e.g., inferring missing soil salinity from known aridity and location) to fill gaps intelligently(Jinbo et al., 2025).

Figure 9. Electrical Conductivity Vs Annual Precipitation

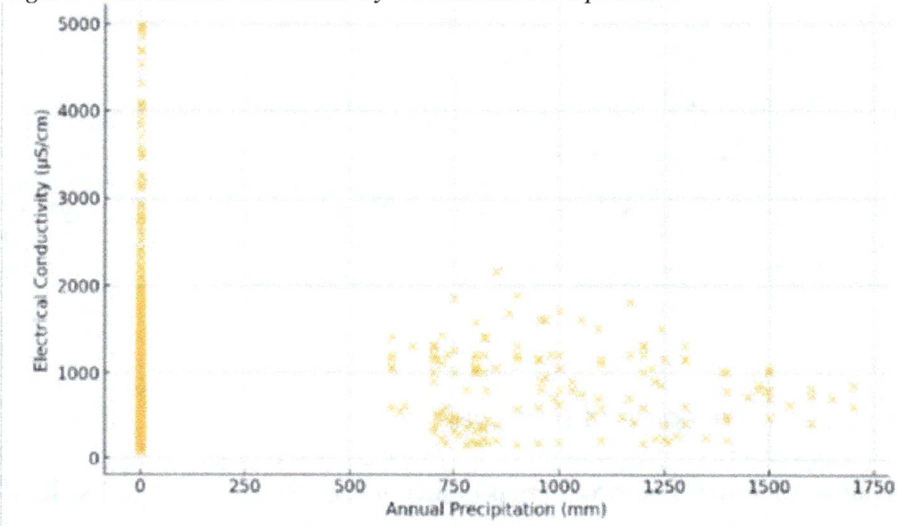

3.3 Feature Selection and Engineering

Inputting irrelevant features can degrade model performance (the "curse of dimensionality"). We utilized a two-step feature selection process:

Correlation Analysis: A correlation matrix (Figure 14) was generated to identify collinear variables. For instance, EC and TDS are perfectly correlated, so only one was needed as a target. Variables with weak correlations to salinity were flagged for potential removal(Marvin-DiPasquale et al., 2025). Recursive Feature Elimination with cross-validation was then applied to iteratively remove features and assess their impact on model performance, thereby identifying the optimal subset of predictors. Further, experts with domain knowledge defined a "window" of specific data points to extract features like correlation analysis, rate of change, and statistical moments such as mean, median, standard deviation, and interquartile range, which are critical for detecting anomalies (Alshammari, 2025; Rouhani et al., 2024).

5 **Principal Component Analysis (PCA):** PCA was used to reduce dimensionality and visualise clustering (Figure 15). The analysis revealed distinct clusters of data points, suggesting that groundwater salinity is driven by underlying latent factors corresponding to specific hydro-climatic regimes(ElHaj & Alshamsi, 2025). This approach enhanced model efficiency while retaining crucial information, minimising noise, and preventing multicollinearity, which can often confound traditional statistical models (Martin et al., 2024). These principal components were then utilized as input features for subsequent machine learning models, leveraging their ability to capture the most significant variance within the dataset while minimising feature redundancy and computational complexity (Rouhani et al., 2024).

6 **Feature Importance Ranking:** Using a Random Forest estimator, we ranked features based on their contribution to reducing prediction error (Figure 16 and 23). This crucial step moved the study beyond "black box" prediction to hydrogeological interpretation(Li & Yang, 2025). The Z-score, which quantifies the significance of each feature, was calculated to further refine this ranking, ensuring that only genuinely impactful predictors were retained (Jamei et al., 2022). This rigorous feature selection process not only optimised the predictive capability of the models but also provided valuable insights into the underlying hydrogeological drivers of groundwater salinity (Goodarzi et al., 2024; Jamei et al., 2022). Moreover, the application of minimum redundancy maximum relevance (mRMR) and ANOVA F-statistic algorithms further enhanced feature selection by identifying variables that are highly relevant to the target variable while minimising redundancy among selected features, thus improving model efficacy and interpretability (Mezouary et al., 2024).

Figure 10. Relationship between the top 5 environmental variables by the Random Forest model and groundwater salinity

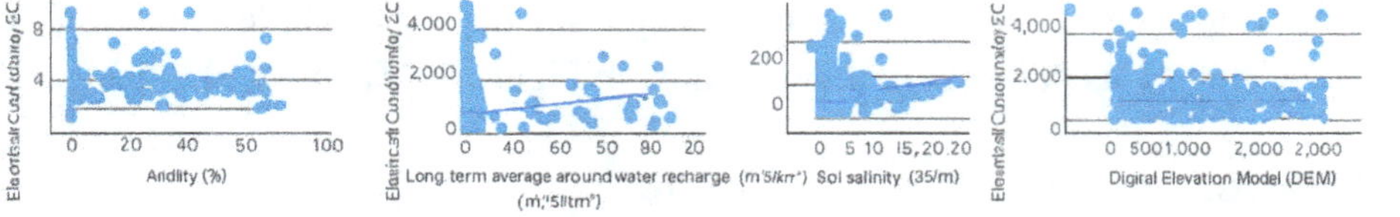

Figure 10 uses scatter plots and trend lines to show how the top five environmental variables relate to groundwater salinity. This visualization, from a Random forest model, reveals the potential influence of each factor on changes in salinity levels:

Specifically, the figure showcases the following relationships:

- Relationship between Aridity (%) and Electical conductivity
- Relationship between Nitrogen (mol) and Electrical conductivity sticity
- Relationship between Soil salinity (d5/m) and Electrical conductivity

Overall, Figure 10 provides a visual representation of the complex interplay between environmental factors and groundwater salinity, emphasizing the importance of considering multiple variables in predicting and managing groundwater in Africa.

3.4 Model Selection and Training

Five machine learning algorithms were selected to represent different learning paradigms:

1 **Logistic Regression:** A baseline linear model.
2 **Support Vector Machines (SVM):** Effective for high-dimensional spaces.
3 **Artificial Neural Networks (ANN):** Capable of modeling complex non-linear mappings.
4 **Random Forest (RF):** An ensemble method robust to overfitting.
5 **XGBoost:** A gradient boosting framework known for high performance and speed.

Training Protocol:

- **Cross-Validation:** To assess generalisability and avoid overfitting, we employed 5-fold cross-validation (Figure 19). The data was split into five subsets; the model was trained on four and tested on the fifth, rotating until all folds served as the test set(Sadeghi et al., 2024).
- **Hyperparameter Tuning:** Grid search and random search algorithms were used to optimize model parameters (e.g., tree depth for RF, learning rate for XGBoost), as depicted in the workflow in Figure 20(Zhang et al., 2024).

3.5 Performance Evaluation Metrics

Model performance was evaluated using:

- **Mean Absolute Error (MAE):** The average magnitude of errors.
- **Root Mean Squared Error (RMSE):** Penalizes larger errors, useful for detecting significant misses.
- **Coefficient of Determination** (R^2)**:** Indicates the proportion of variance in salinity explained by the model.

4. RESULTS

4.1 Descriptive Analysis of Salinity

The descriptive analysis (Figure 1 and Figure 22) reveals a highly skewed distribution of groundwater salinity across the continent. The mean Electrical Conductivity is approximately 1009 μS/cm, but the standard deviation is high (492 μS/cm), reflecting the contrast between the fresh groundwater of the equatorial rainforests and the saline brines of the Sahara and Kalahari deserts(Meledje et al., 2024). This heterogeneity underscores the need for models capable of adapting to diverse hydrogeological conditions, rather than a one-size-fits-all approach. Further, the robust modeling approach incorporated a 10-fold cross-validation strategy, ensuring that the developed model maintains reliability when exposed to new or expanded datasets, thereby confirming its sustainability (Udeh et al., 2024). This approach is crucial given that simple summary statistics, while informative, can mask complex spatial and temporal patterns in groundwater quality (Souza et al., 2023). The spatial distribution further elucidated areas of high salinity, particularly in coastal aquifers susceptible to seawater intrusion and arid regions experiencing evaporative concentration (Jamei et al., 2022).

Figure 11. Effect of Outlier Removal on Total Dissolved Solids

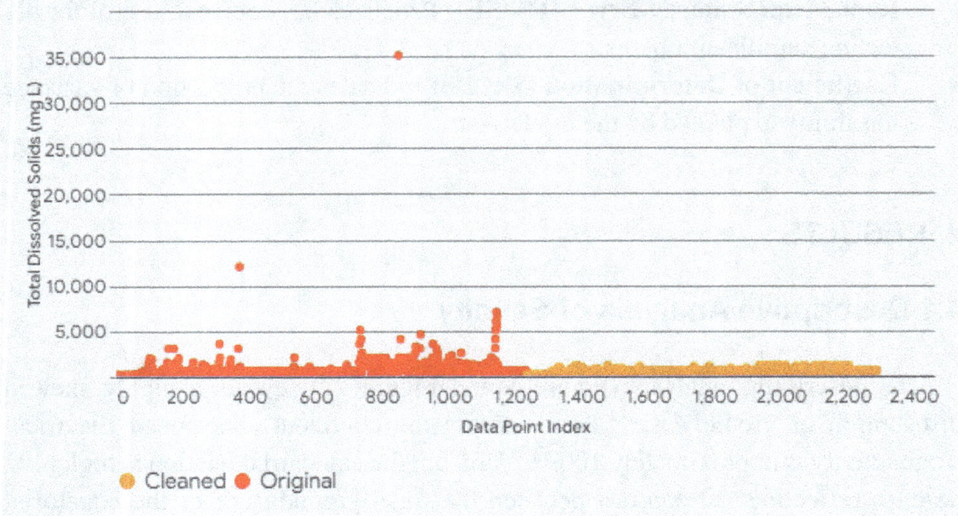

Regionally, as shown in Figure 3, Nouadhibou in Mauritania exhibits the highest average TDS, a direct consequence of its coastal arid setting where seawater intrusion and high evaporation converge. Other high-salinity hotspots include regions in Tunisia (Gabès, Kebili) and Libya, emphasizing the vulnerability of North African aquifers. Conversely, the Central African Republic shows the lowest average TDS, indicative of its humid climate and substantial freshwater recharge (Sahour et al., 2022). This broad spatial variability highlights the necessity for localised management strategies, which are further complicated by the intermittent nature of groundwater recharge and abstraction (West et al., 2022).

Figure 12. Performance of Imputation Techniques in Groundwater Salinity Prediction

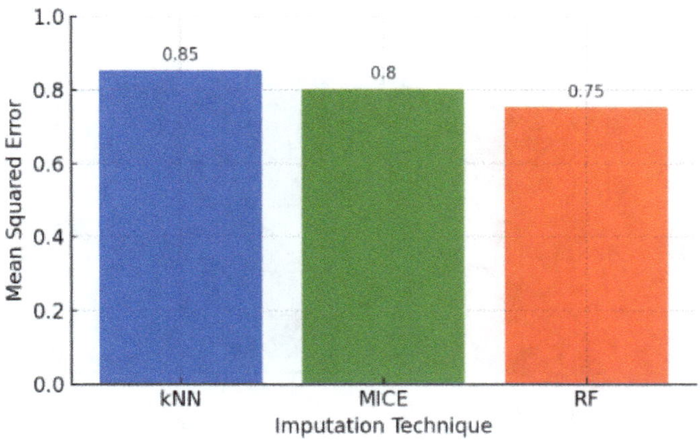

4.2 Feature Importance Analysis

One of the most significant findings of this study is the ranking of predictive features (Figure 23). The top five features driving groundwater salinity prediction were identified as:

1 **Nitrogen (mol):** Surprisingly, nitrogen content emerged as the top predictor. This likely serves as a proxy for anthropogenic impact, specifically agricultural runoff (fertilisers) and waste-water infiltration, which are major contributors to salinity in populated African regions.
2 **Sand Fraction (%):** Soil texture controls infiltration and evaporation rates. Sandy soils in arid regions facilitate rapid evaporation from the water table, concentrating salts.
3 **Aridity (%):** A natural climatic driver; higher aridity indices correlate strongly with higher salinity due to evapoconcentration.
4 **Topographic Wetness Index (TWI):** This morphological parameter influences water accumulation and movement, affecting how long water stays in contact with rock minerals. The interaction between water and minerals, particularly in areas with poor drainage, can lead to increased dissolution of soluble salts and subsequent elevation of groundwater salinity.
5 **Soil Salinity:** A direct surface indicator of underlying groundwater conditions.

Figure 13. Relationship between Electrical Conductivity and Total Dissolved Solids

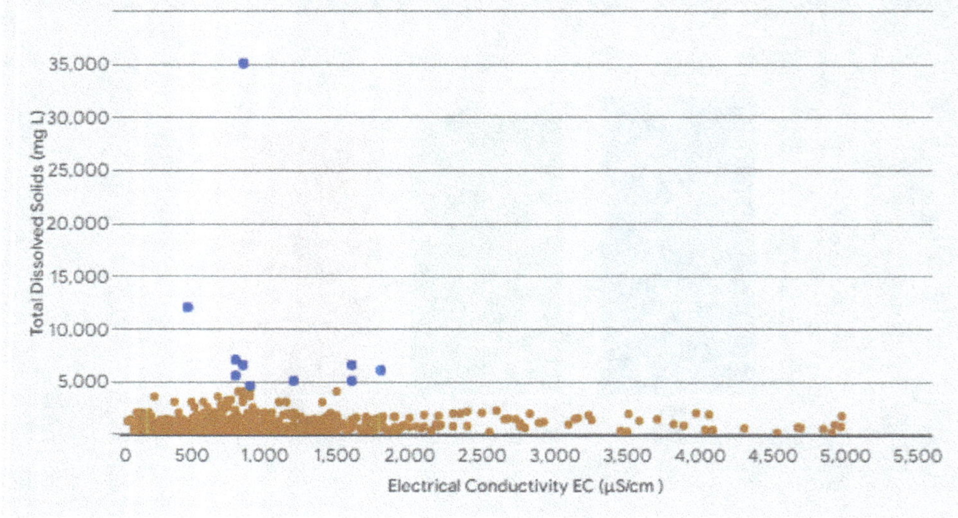

4.3 Model Performance Evaluation

The comparative analysis of ML models (Figure 24) yielded clear distinctions in performance:

- **Ensemble Methods Dominate:** Random Forest and XGBoost achieved the highest accuracy scores (exceeding 85% accuracy in classification tasks and high R^2 in regression). Their ability to handle the non-linear interactions between nitrogen, soil type, and climate allowed them to outperform simpler models.
- **Neural Networks and SVM:** These models performed moderately well but required significantly more tuning and data normalization to approach the performance of tree-based ensembles.
- **Logistic Regression:** As expected, the linear model failed to capture the complexity of the system, resulting in the poorest performance (Figure 21 implies poor performance for simple baselines).

Figure 14. Heat map of Correlation Matrix

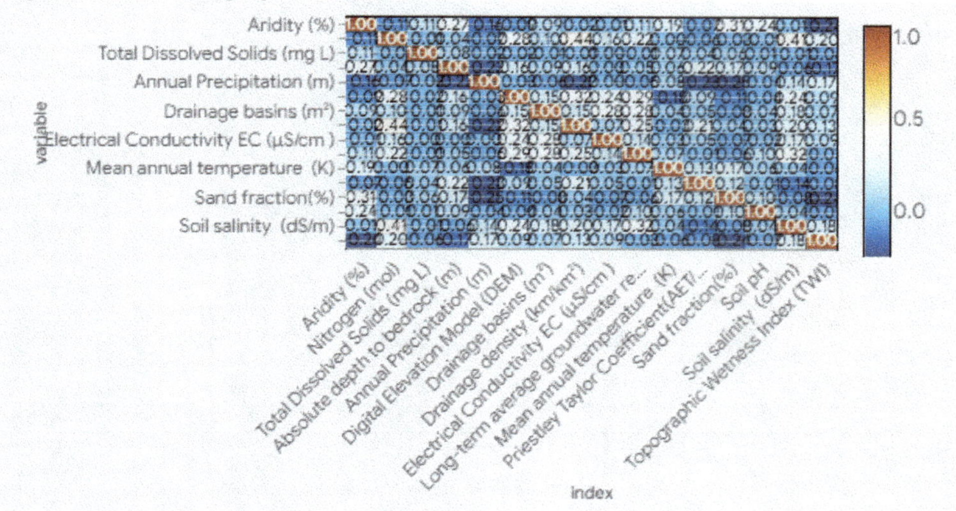

4.4 Spatial Distribution of Predicted Salinity

Applying the trained Random Forest model to the continental dataset allowed for the generation of a predicted salinity map (Figure 25).

- **High Salinity Zones:** The model correctly identifies the Sahara, the Horn of Africa (Somalia, Eastern Ethiopia), and the Namib Desert as high-risk zones.
- **Low Salinity Zones:** The Congo Basin and parts of West Africa (e.g., Guinea, Sierra Leone) are predicted to have low salinity, correlating with high precipitation and rapid groundwater flushing.

This spatial consistency with known hydrogeological zones validates the model's robustness and its utility for mapping unmonitored regions.

Figure 15. PCA of Groundwater Salinity Factors

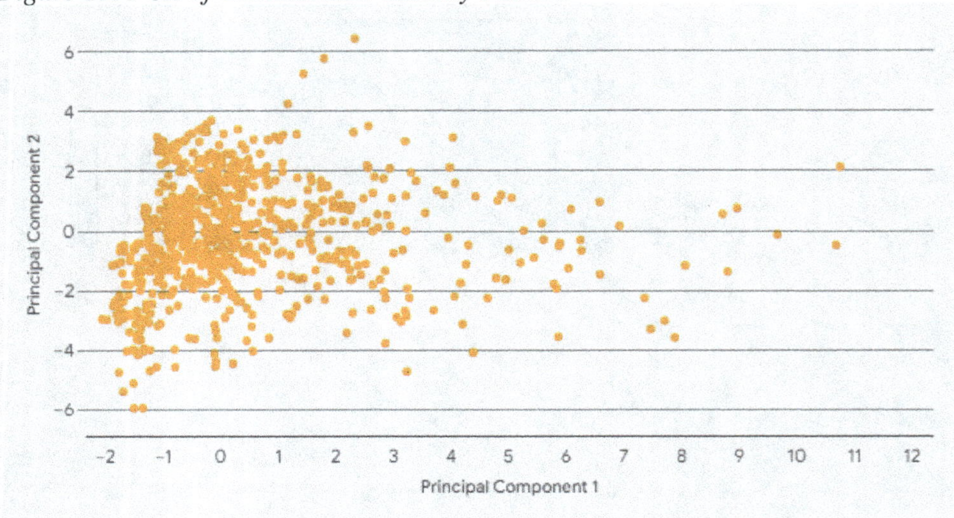

5. DISCUSSION

5.1 Interpretation of Findings

The superior performance of ensemble models like Random Forest and XGBoost over linear methods highlights the non-linear nature of African hydrogeological processes, where factors like soil texture and temperature modify rainfall's effect on salinity (West et al., 2022). Their accuracy surpasses traditional geostatistical approaches (Benà et al., 2023). The key predictor, Nitrogen, indicates human-driven salinization, necessitating integrated management with agriculture and sanitation. The spatial predictions enable targeted interventions in vulnerable regions, proving these models are powerful tools for regional water resource planning (Araya et al., 2023).

Figure 16. Feature Importance for Groundwater Salinity Prediction

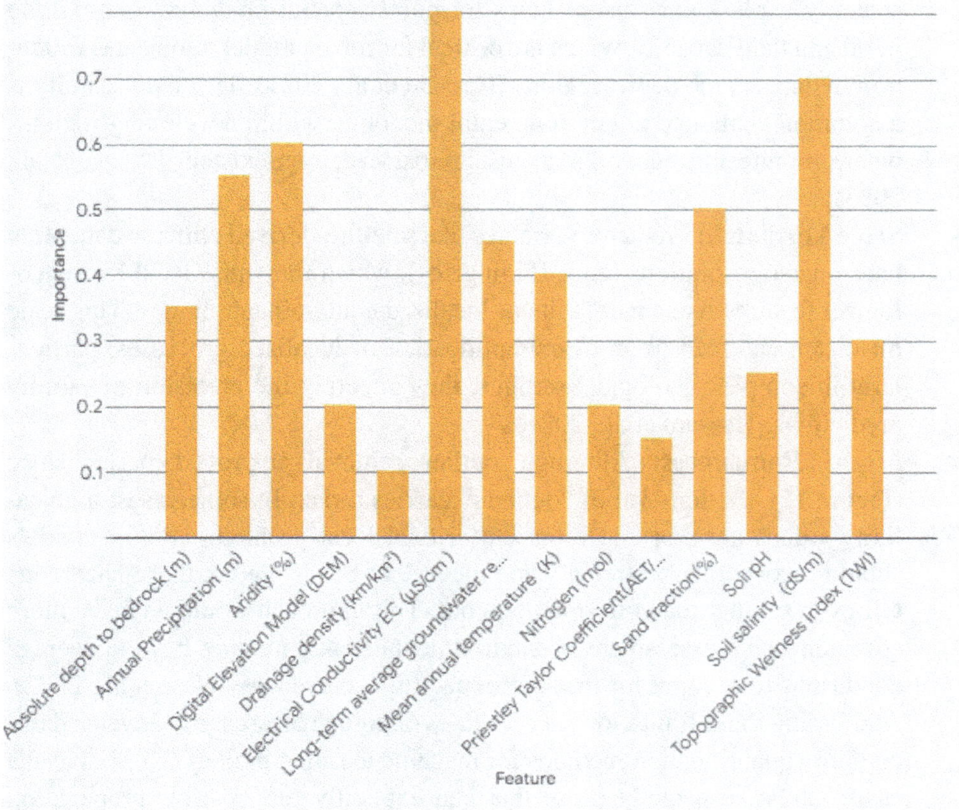

5.2 Uncertainty and Robustness

While the results are promising, it is vital to acknowledge the uncertainties inherent in continental-scale modeling.

- **Data Bias:** The training data is geographically clustered (Figure 6), with more data available from well-studied nations (South Africa, Egypt, Tunisia) and data deserts in Central Africa. This introduces a spatial bias where the model may be less reliable in under-represented regions. Further refinement and validation with a more uniformly distributed dataset across the continent would enhance the model's generalizability and predictive accuracy (West et al., 2022). Moreover, the inherent limitations of remotely sensed data, such as spatial resolution and atmospheric interference, can contribute to uncertainties in feature extraction and subsequent model predictions (Sahwell &

Solo-Gabriele, 2025). Another source of uncertainty stems from the lack of spatially explicit uncertainty maps for purely spatial predictors like wilting point and field capacity, which are critical for robust model tuning and validation in data-scarce desert regions (Hassani et al., 2021). This data scarcity is a common challenge in environmental modeling within developing regions, where monitoring networks are often sparse or non-existent (Araya et al., 2023).

- **Scale Mismatch:** Predictor variables like satellite-derived climatic data often have coarse resolutions (e.g., 10km grids), which may miss local hydrogeological features like small faults or localised contaminant plumes. This scale mismatch can lead to an oversimplification of localised processes, particularly in complex geological settings, thus affecting the precision of salinity predictions (Hassani et al., 2021).
- **Model Robustness:** Although outlier removal improved performance (Figure 11), the removal of "outliers" carries a risk. In some cases, high salinity values are real and represent critical local problems. Future models should incorporate "extreme value theory" to better predict these hazardous tail-events rather than filtering them out. This approach would enable a more comprehensive assessment of environmental risks, moving beyond average conditions to account for rare but impactful occurrences (West et al., 2022). Addressing these limitations necessitates ongoing research into advanced uncertainty quantification methods for machine learning models (Koldasbayeva et al., 2024), especially those that can explicitly model error propagation from input data to final predictions (Hassani et al., 2020; Tian et al., 2022). Moreover, future research should focus on developing regionally specific models, especially in data-scarce areas, to mitigate the biases introduced by globally aggregated training datasets (Hassani et al., 2020, 2021).

Figure 17. Word Frequencies

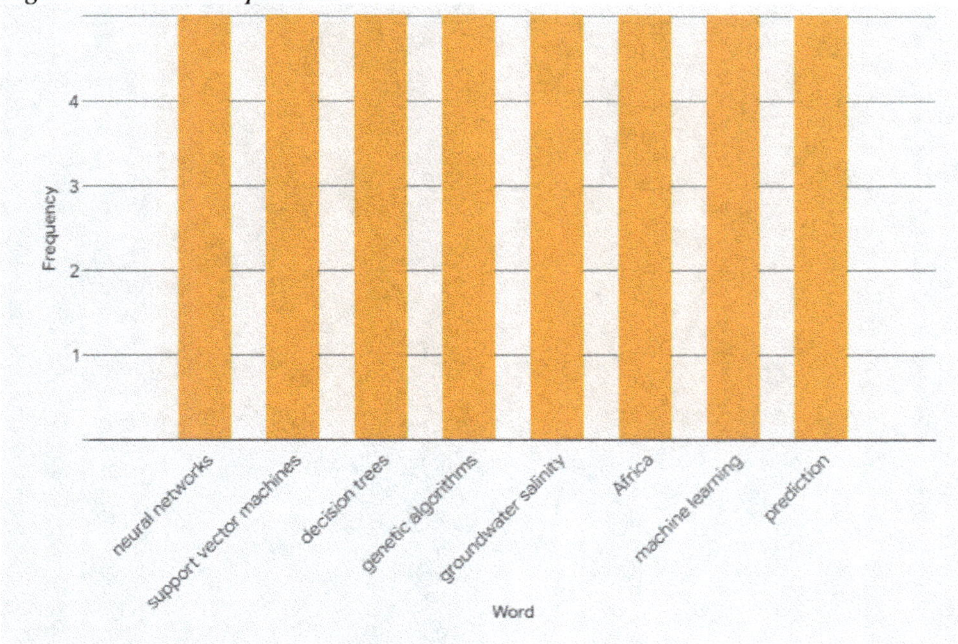

Figure 18. Selection Criteria Groundwater Salinity Models

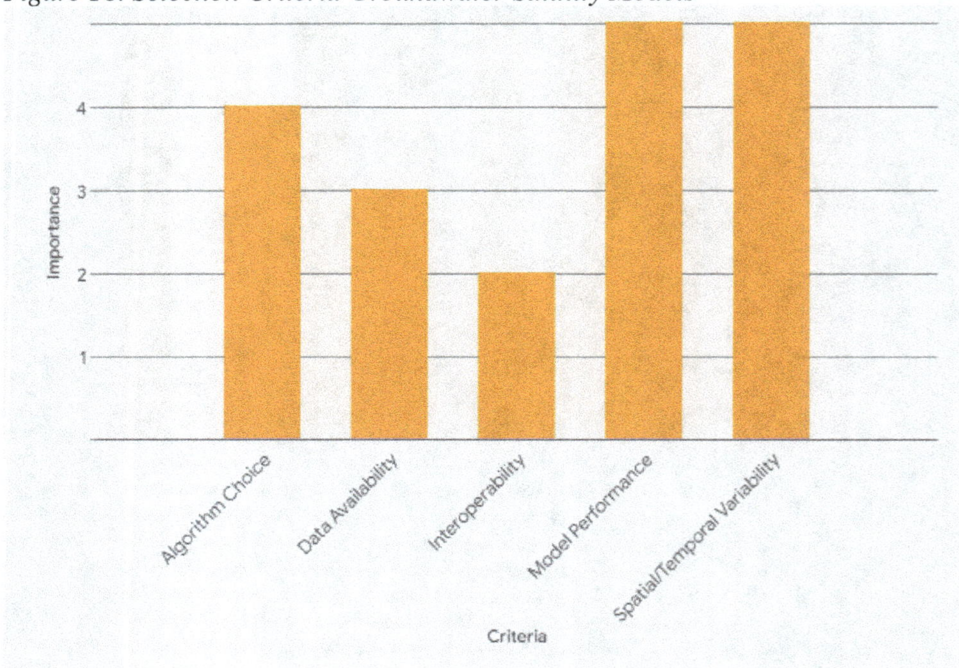

Figure 19. Illustration of 5-Fold Cross-Validation

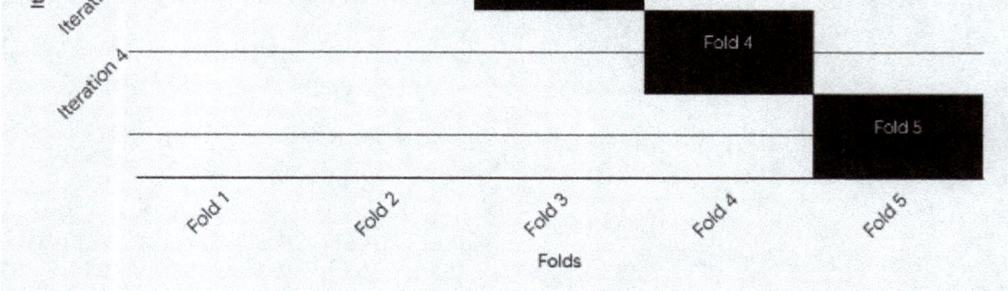

Figure 20. Hyperparameter Tuning Process

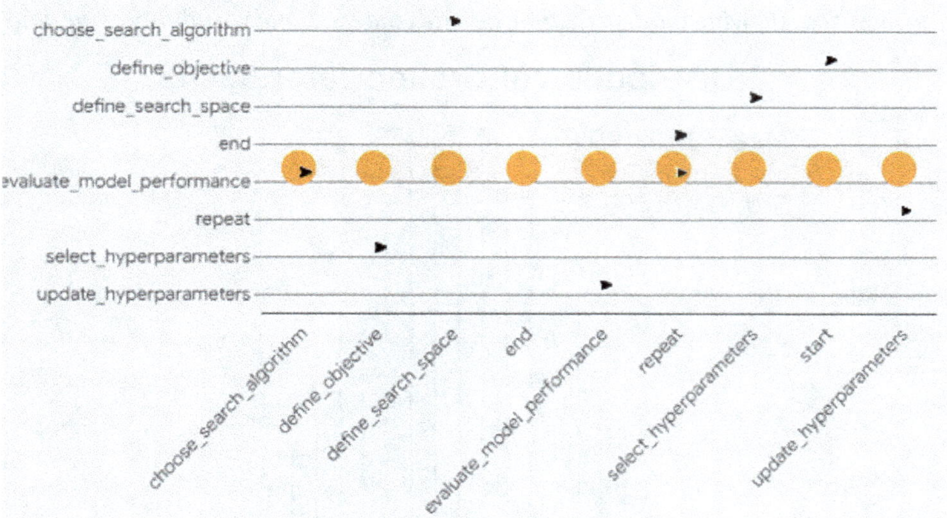

Figure 21. Performance Evaluation Metrics

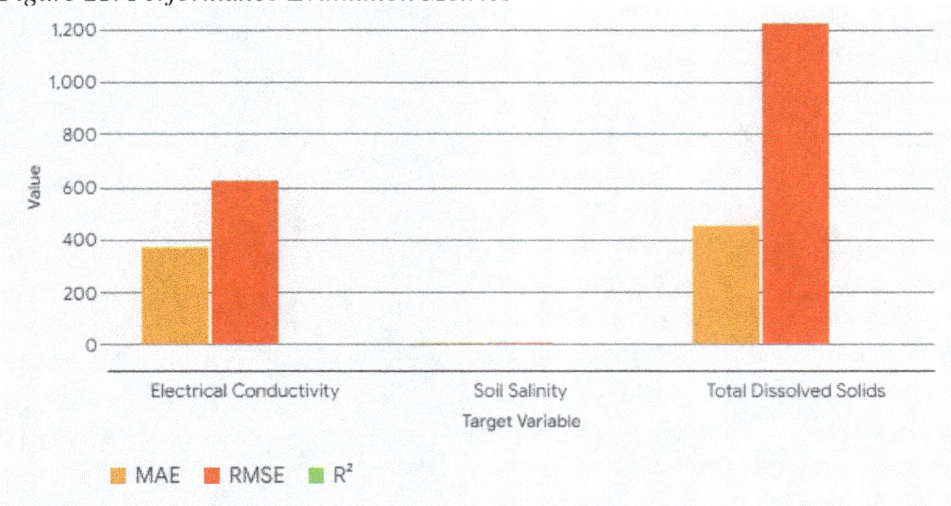

Figure 22. Visual representation of the descriptive analysis of groundwater salinity data in Africa, showing the distribution, central tendency, and variability of the data.

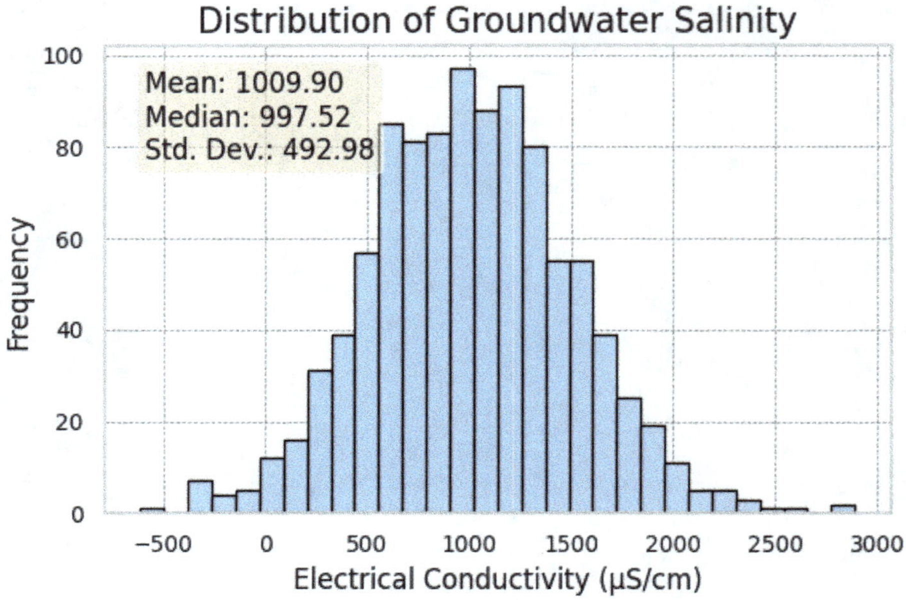

Figure 23. Selected Features for Groundwater Salinity Prediction

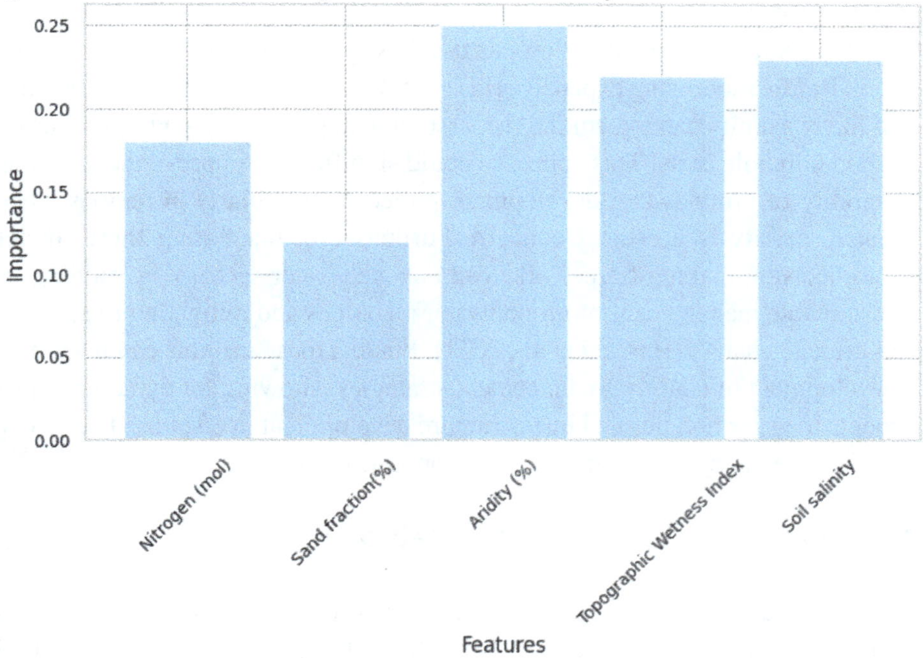

5.3 Implications for Policy and Practice

The transition from academic modeling to practical application is the ultimate goal. For African water managers, the findings of this study offer several actionable pathways:

1. **Targeted Monitoring:** The spatial maps (Figure 25) can guide the siting of new monitoring wells. Resources should be prioritised for "transition zones"—areas predicted to be on the brink of becoming saline—rather than areas that are stable. This focused approach ensures efficient allocation of limited resources, maximising the impact of monitoring efforts in vulnerable regions. These regions, often characterised by complex hydrogeological conditions and dynamic anthropogenic influences, warrant heightened scrutiny to detect early signs of salinization and implement timely interventions.
2. **Land Use Planning:** The strong link between nitrogen and salinity supports the enforcement of buffer zones around aquifers in agricultural areas to reduce fertilizer leaching. Such measures could include promoting sustainable agricultural practices, regulating the application of nitrogen-based fertilisers,

and establishing riparian buffers to filter agricultural run-off before it reaches groundwater sources.

3. **Drilling Success Rates:** Drillers can use these predictive models as a screening tool. Before mobilising expensive rigs to remote arid locations, an ML estimate of likely salinity can inform the risk assessment, potentially saving millions in failed borehole costs. This approach could significantly improve the economic viability of groundwater development projects, particularly in regions where water scarcity is a critical concern. Furthermore, integrating these models into decision-making frameworks can enhance water security by guiding the sustainable management of groundwater resources and mitigating the impacts of climate change (Hassani et al., 2021). Finally, these insights can inform the development of adaptive management strategies, allowing for dynamic adjustments to water policies and infrastructure development in response to evolving environmental conditions and socio-economic demands (Pérez et al., 2024).

5.4 Comparison with Traditional Methods

Machine learning (ML) is far more agile than traditional numerical models, providing continental assessments in a fraction of the time (Araya et al., 2023; Covatti et al., 2025). However, ML lacks inherent physical understanding, acting as a "black box" (Chakraborty et al., 2020). A hybrid approach is therefore recommended: use ML for regional screening (e.g., predicting nitrate or salinity) and numerical models for local, process-specific management. Advances in physics-informed ML are enhancing interpretability by embedding physical laws (Ji et al., 2025; Papacharalampous et al., 2020). This integration enables robust "what-if" scenarios (Sharma et al., 2024) and proactive, holistic water resource governance (Ahmed et al., 2024; Zennaro et al., 2023).

Figure 24. Representation of the performance evaluation results

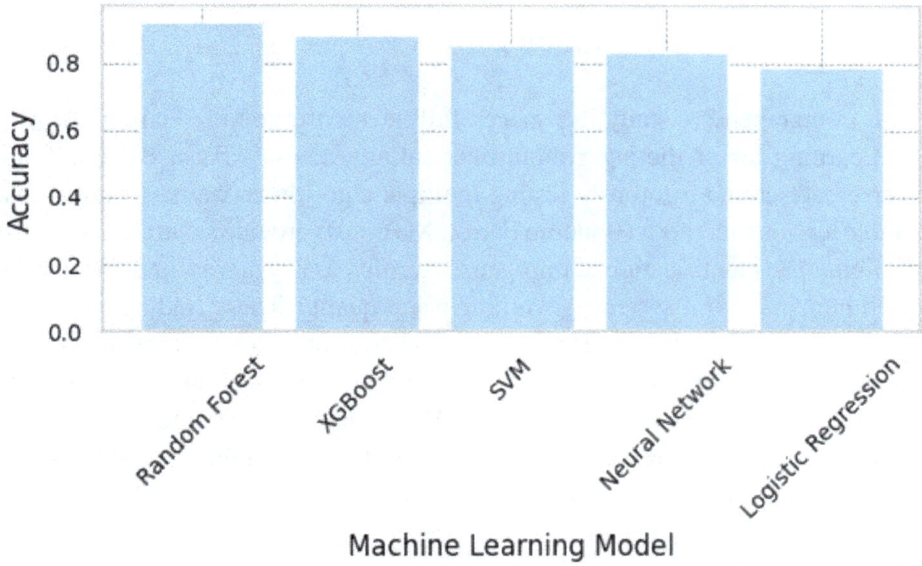

Figure 25. Spatial distribution of predicted groundwater salinity levels across Africa

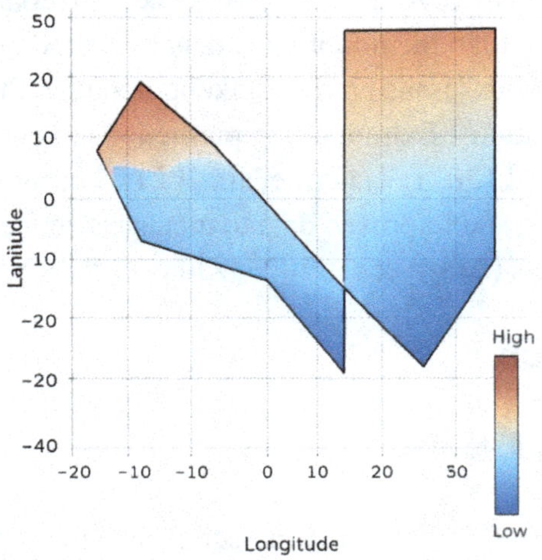

6. CONCLUSION AND FUTURE DIRECTIONS

6.1 Summary of Contributions

This comprehensive study has successfully demonstrated the viability of Machine Learning for predicting groundwater salinity across Africa. By compiling a diverse dataset and rigorously testing multiple algorithms, we have shown that ensemble learning methods (Random Forest, XGBoost) provide accurate and robust predictions. The identification of nitrogen and aridity as key drivers underscores the coupled human-natural systems governing water quality. These findings highlight the necessity of integrated water resource management strategies that account for both environmental stressors and anthropogenic influences to ensure sustainable groundwater supplies (Ahmed et al., 2024). This approach contributes significantly to drought resilience in regions facing water scarcity by providing spatially explicit information on groundwater salinity (Araya et al., 2023; Thomas et al., 2021).

6.2 Limitations

The study faces key limitations regarding data and model trust. Insufficient high-frequency temporal data restricts models to static salinity "snapshots," missing crucial seasonal dynamics (Greenwood et al., 2024; Hassani et al., 2021). Model generalisability is limited by regional data imbalances and coarse spatial resolution (1–3°), while inconsistent lab methodologies may bias predictions (Hassani et al., 2020, 2021). The "black box" issue hinders stakeholder trust, though explainable AI (e.g., SHAP) offers solutions. Extrapolating predictions to new regions introduces uncertainty (Hassani et al., 2021; Zanotti et al., 2021). Future work requires physically constrained models and improved data to manage climate change uncertainty, especially in arid regions (Araya et al., 2023; Zidan & Febriyanti, 2024).

6.3 Future Research

Future research should focus on:

- **Temporal Modeling:** Integrating time-series data to predict seasonal salinity changes, particularly relevant for climate change adaptation.
- **Hybrid Models:** Combining physics-based hydrogeological principles with ML (Physics-Informed Neural Networks) to ensure predictions adhere to mass conservation laws.

- **Granular Case Studies:** Conducting high-resolution pilot studies in the identified "hotspots" to validate continental predictions against local ground truth.

Ultimately, this chapter advocates for a digital transformation in African hydrogeology, where data-driven insights empower sustainable stewardship of the continent's most precious fluid resource. Additionally, the development of explainable and interpretable machine learning models is crucial to fostering trust among stakeholders and facilitating the integration of these tools into policy-making and resource management (Wadoux et al., 2020). Further advancements are needed to address persistent methodological challenges and knowledge gaps, particularly concerning the interpretability, scalability, and real-time capabilities of soil moisture monitoring systems (Harani et al., 2025; Wadoux et al., 2020). Moreover, developing web-hosted 'lifelong learning' models that continuously retrain themselves with increasing satellite data availability could significantly enhance both accuracy and classification capabilities for various homomorphic units (Valman et al., 2023). Such models, when integrated with cloud computing platforms, would democratize access to sophisticated analytical tools, allowing a broader scientific community to contribute to and benefit from continuously improving models (Valman et al., 2023). Furthermore, leveraging advanced tools such as large language models and foundation models can significantly improve the generalisability of these approaches and classification accuracies, especially in complex landscapes (Soto et al., 2024).

REFERENCES

Abdu, F. J., Isah, S., Usman, J., Jibrin, A. M., Wakili, A. A., Ashraf, M. W., & Aljundi, I. H. (2025). Hydro-environmental predictive management of sub-surface salinization in arid nearshore-coastal saline aquifer using deep learning and SHAP analysis. *Research Square (Research Square)*. DOI: 10.21203/rs.3.rs-5946945/v1

Abdulwahid, A. A. (2024). Cyber-physical threat mitigation in wind energy systems: A novel secure architecture for industry 4.0 power grids. *Energy Informatics*, *7*(1), 141. Advance online publication. DOI: 10.1186/s42162-024-00449-6

Ahmed, A., Sayed, S., Abdoulhalik, A., Moutari, S., & Oyedele, L. O. (2024). Applications of machine learning to water resources management: A review of present status and future opportunities [Review of *Applications of machine learning to water resources management: A review of present status and future opportunities*]. *Journal of Cleaner Production, 441*, 140715. Elsevier BV. DOI: 10.1016/j.jclepro.2024.140715

Alshammari, A. (2025). Securing smart microgrids with a novel multi-layer cybersecurity framework for Industry 4.0 renewable energy systems. *Discover Computing*, *28*(1), 80. Advance online publication. DOI: 10.1007/s10791-025-09600-7

Andalu, A., Naik, M. G., & Budde, S. (2025). AI and ML in groundwater exploration and water resources management: Concepts, methods, applications, and future directions. *Journal of Groundwater Science and Engineering*. DOI: 10.26599/JGSE.2026.9280059

Arafa, N. A., Salem, Z. E., Abdeldayem, A., Ghorab, M. A., Moustafa, Y. M., Soliman, S. A., Farag, M. H., Purohit, S., Elhag, M., & Youssef, Y. M. (2024). Advancing Deltaic Aquifer Vulnerability Mapping to Seawater Intrusion and Human Impacts in Eastern Nile Delta: Insights from Machine Learning and Hydrochemical Perspective. *Earth Systems and Environment*, *9*(3), 2481–2506. DOI: 10.1007/s41748-024-00518-6

Araya, D., Podgorski, J., & Berg, M. (2023). Groundwater salinity in the Horn of Africa: Spatial prediction modeling and estimated people at risk. *Environment International*, *176*, 107925. DOI: 10.1016/j.envint.2023.107925 PMID: 37209488

Armanuos, A. M., Zeleňáková, M., & Elshaarawy, M. K. (2025). Explainable ML modeling of saltwater intrusion control with underground barriers in coastal sloping aquifers. *Scientific Reports, 15*(1), 29281. Advance online publication. DOI: 10.1038/s41598-025-12830-w PMID: 40784891

Atmaja, T., Fukushi, K., Lee, D.-J., Atmaja, T., Fukushi, K., & Lee, D.-J. (2025). Leveraging Coupled Hydrodynamic with Data-Driven GeoAI Models for Advancing Systemic Compound Flood Risk Evaluation in Coastal Urban Areas. *Archives of Computational Methods in Engineering*. Advance online publication. DOI: 10.1007/s11831-025-10394-6

Ayadi, Y., Gentilucci, M., Ncibi, K., Hadji, R., & Hamed, Y. (2025). Assessment of a Groundwater Potential Zone Using Geospatial Artificial Intelligence (Geo-AI), Remote Sensing (RS), and GIS Tools in Majerda Transboundary Basin (North Africa). *Water (Basel), 17*(3), 331. DOI: 10.3390/w17030331

Benà, E., Ciotoli, G., Petermann, E., Bossew, P., Ruggiero, L., Verdi, L., Huber, P. B., Mori, F., Mazzoli, C., & Sassi, R. (2023). A new perspective in radon risk assessment: Mapping the geological hazard as a first step to define the collective radon risk exposure. *The Science of the Total Environment, 912*, 169569. DOI: 10.1016/j.scitotenv.2023.169569 PMID: 38157905

Bilali, A. E., Taleb, A., & Brouziyne, Y. (2020). Groundwater quality forecasting using machine learning algorithms for irrigation purposes. *Agricultural Water Management, 245*, 106625. DOI: 10.1016/j.agwat.2020.106625

Chakraborty, D., Başağaoğlu, H., & Winterle, J. (2020). Interpretable vs. noninterpretable machine learning models for data-driven hydro-climatological process modeling. *Expert Systems with Applications, 170*, 114498. DOI: 10.1016/j.eswa.2020.114498

Chiloane, C., Dube, T., Sibanda, M., Dalu, T., & Shoko, C. (2025). A Summary of Recent Advances in the Literature on Machine Learning Techniques for Remote Sensing of Groundwater Dependent Ecosystems (GDEs) from Space. *Remote Sensing (Basel), 17*(8), 1460. DOI: 10.3390/rs17081460

Covatti, G., Li, K.-Y., Podgorski, J., Winkel, L. H. E., & Berg, M. (2025). Nitrate contamination in groundwater across Switzerland: Spatial prediction and data-driven assessment of anthropogenic and environmental drivers. *The Science of the Total Environment, 973*, 179121. DOI: 10.1016/j.scitotenv.2025.179121 PMID: 40120406 de Souza, C. M. P., da Silva, L. A. P., Leite, M. E., Veloso, G. V., & Filho, E. I. F. (2023). Spatial Modeling of Groundwater Potential in the North of Minas Gerais, Brazil: An Integrated Approach Using Machine Learning and Environmental Data. *Revista Brasileira de Cartografia, 75*. Advance online publication. DOI: 10.14393/rbcv75n0a-65381

Eghrari, Z., Delavar, M. R., Zaré, M., Mousavi, M., Nazari, B., & Ghaffarian, S. (2023). GROUNDWATER LEVEL PREDICTION USING DEEP RECURRENT NEURAL NETWORKS AND UNCERTAINTY ASSESSMENT. *ISPRS Annals of the Photogrammetry, Remote Sensing and Spatial Information Sciences, 493*, 493–500. Advance online publication. DOI: 10.5194/isprs-annals-X-1-W1-2023-493-2023

ElHaj, K., & Alshamsi, D. (2025). GeoTemporal clustering for aquifer delineation: A big data approach to synchronizing and analyzing variable-length groundwater time series. *Journal of Big Data, 12*(1), 25. Advance online publication. DOI: 10.1186/s40537-025-01060-6

Elshaarawy, M. K., & Eltarabily, M. G. (2024). Machine learning models for predicting water quality index: Optimization and performance analysis for El Moghra, Egypt. *Water Science and Technology: Water Supply, 24*(9), 3269–3294. DOI: 10.2166/ws.2024.189

Goodarzi, M. R., Bafrouei, H. R. B., & Vazirian, M. (2024). Insight into groundwater level prediction with feature effectiveness: Comparison of machine learning and numerical methods. *Nordic Hydrology, 56*(1), 74–92. DOI: 10.2166/nh.2024.135

Greenwood, E. E., Lauber, T. B., van den Hoogen, J., Dönmez, A., Bain, R., Johnston, R., Crowther, T. W., & Julian, T. R. (2024). Mapping safe drinking water use in low- and middle-income countries. *Science, 385*(6710), 784–790. DOI: 10.1126/science.adh9578 PMID: 39146419

Harani, P., Gautam, S., Joshi, S. K., Asirvatham, L. G., & Rakshith, B. L. (2025). Advancements in soil moisture estimation through integration of remote sensing and artificial intelligence techniques [Review of *Advancements in soil moisture estimation through integration of remote sensing and artificial intelligence techniques*]. *The Science of The Total Environment, 1001*, 180503. Elsevier BV. DOI: 10.1016/j.scitotenv.2025.180503

Hassani, A., Azapagic, A., & Shokri, N. (2020). Predicting long-term dynamics of soil salinity and sodicity on a global scale. *Proceedings of the National Academy of Sciences of the United States of America, 117*(52), 33017–33027. DOI: 10.1073/pnas.2013771117 PMID: 33318212

Hassani, A., Azapagic, A., & Shokri, N. (2021). Global predictions of primary soil salinization under changing climate in the 21st century. *Nature Communications*, *12*(1), 6663. Advance online publication. DOI: 10.1038/s41467-021-26907-3 PMID: 34795219

Jamei, M., Karbasi, M., Malik, A., Abualigah, L., Islam, A. R., & Yaseen, Z. M. (2022). Computational assessment of groundwater salinity distribution within coastal multi-aquifers of Bangladesh. *Scientific Reports*, *12*(1), 11165. Advance online publication. DOI: 10.1038/s41598-022-15104-x PMID: 35778436

Jamshidzadeh, Z., Latif, S. D., Ehteram, M., Khozani, Z. S., Ahmed, A. N., Sherif, M., & El-Shafie, A. (2024). An advanced hybrid deep learning model for predicting total dissolved solids and electrical conductivity (EC) in coastal aquifers. *Environmental Sciences Europe*, *36*(1), 20. Advance online publication. DOI: 10.1186/s12302-024-00850-8

Janssen, J., Tootchi, A., & Ameli, A. (2024). A critical appraisal of water table depth estimation: Challenges and opportunities within machine learning. EarthArXiv *(California Digital Library)*. DOI: 10.31223/X5939N

Ji, H., Song, Y., Bindas, T., Shen, C., Yang, Y., Pan, M., Liu, J., Rahmani, F., Abbas, A., Beck, H. E., Lawson, K., & Wada, Y. (2025). Distinct hydrologic response patterns and trends worldwide revealed by physics-embedded learning. *Nature Communications*, *16*(1), 9169. DOI: 10.1038/s41467-025-64367-1 PMID: 41093823

Jinbo, Z., Li, Y., & Haitao, M. (2025). Handling missing data of using the XGBoost-based multiple imputation by chained equations regression method. *Frontiers in Artificial Intelligence*, *8*, 1553220. Advance online publication. DOI: 10.3389/frai.2025.1553220 PMID: 40248006

Koldasbayeva, D., Tregubova, P., Gasanov, M., Zaytsev, A., Petrovskaia, A., & Burnaev, E. (2024). Challenges in data-driven geospatial modeling for environmental research and practice [Review of *Challenges in data-driven geospatial modeling for environmental research and practice*]. *Nature Communications, 15*(1). Nature Portfolio. DOI: 10.1038/s41467-024-55240-8

Li, C., & Yang, R. (2025). *Machine Learning for Proactive Groundwater Management: Early Warning and Resource Allocation*. DOI: 10.48550/ARXIV.2506.22461

Martin, C., Richter, N., Lloren, R., Amaral-Zettler, L., & Dubois, N. (2024). Machine learning reveals that sodium concentration and temperature influence alkenone occurrence in Swiss and worldwide freshwater lakes. *Frontiers in Earth Science (Lausanne), 12*, 1409389. Advance online publication. DOI: 10.3389/feart.2024.1409389

Marvin-DiPasquale, M., McCleskey, R. B., Sullivan, S. L., Root, J. C., Seawolf, S. M., Ransom, K. M., Wherry, S. A., Kakouros, E., & Baesman, S. M. (2025). Select elements of concern in surface water of three hydrologic basins (Delaware River, Illinois River, and Upper Colorado River)—Data screening for the development of spatial and temporal models. *Antarctica A Keystone in a Changing World.* DOI: 10.3133/ofr20251033

Meledje, D. E. J.-C., Gouli, B. I. M., Kra, D. O., Zran, V. E.-S., Konaté, A., & Trokourey, A. (2024). Analysis of the Quality of Physical and Chemical Parameters of Groundwater in Three Localities in the Sub-Prefecture of Zanzra (Ivory Coast). *Journal of Materials Science and Chemical Engineering, 12*(4), 1–17. DOI: 10.4236/msce.2024.124001

Mensah, V., Boateng, C. D., Gidigasu, S. S. R., Wemegah, D. D., Aryee, J. N. A., Osei, M. A., Touré, H., Gilbert, J., & Afful, S. (2024). Groundwater Exploration Methods in West Africa: A Review. EarthArXiv *(California Digital Library)*. DOI: 10.31223/X5T399

Mezouary, L. E., Hadri, A., Kharrou, M. H., Fakır, Y., Elfarchouni, A., Bouchaou, L., & Chehbouni, A. (2024a). Machine Learning and Deep Learning Guided Assessment of Groundwater Reservoir Hydrodynamic Parameters: A Case Study of The El Haouz Aquifer. *E3S Web of Conferences, 489*, 4005. DOI: 10.1051/e3sconf/202448904005

Mezouary, L. E., Hadri, A., Kharrou, M. H., Fakır, Y., Elfarchouni, A., Bouchaou, L., & Chehbouni, A. (2024b). Contribution to advancing aquifer geometric mapping using machine learning and deep learning techniques: A case study of the AL Haouz-Mejjate aquifer, Marrakech, Morocco. *Applied Water Science, 14*(5), 102. Advance online publication. DOI: 10.1007/s13201-024-02162-x

Mohammed, M. A. A., Kaya, F., Mohamed, A., Alarifi, S. S., Abdelrady, A., Keshavarzi, A., Szabó, N. P., & Szűcs, P. (2023). Application of GIS-based machine learning algorithms for prediction of irrigational groundwater quality indices. *Frontiers in Earth Science (Lausanne), 11*, 1274142. Advance online publication. DOI: 10.3389/feart.2023.1274142

Mosavi, A., Hosseini, F. S., Choubin, B., Goodarzi, M., & Dineva, A. (2020). Groundwater Salinity Susceptibility Mapping Using Classifier Ensemble and Bayesian Machine Learning Models. *IEEE Access : Practical Innovations, Open Solutions, 8*, 145564–145576. DOI: 10.1109/ACCESS.2020.3014908

Muralidharan, K., Das, A., Pandya, S. N., & Kim, J. M. (2025). Alternate Groundwater Modelling Strategies: A Multi-Faceted Data-Driven Approach. *arXiv (Cornell University)*. https://doi.org//arxiv.2505.24235DOI: 10.48550

Olaniran, O. R., & Alzahrani, A. (2025). Bayesian Random Forest with Multiple Imputation by Chain Equations for High-Dimensional Missing Data: A Simulation Study. *Mathematics, 13*(6), 956. DOI: 10.3390/math13060956

Olentsova, J. A., Кукарцев, B. B., Orlov, V., Semenova, E., & Pinchuk, I. A. (2024). Predictive modelling of post-monsoon groundwater quality in Telangana using machine learning techniques. *BIO Web of Conferences, 116*, 3021. DOI: 10.1051/bioconf/202411603021

Papacharalampous, G., Tyralis, H., Papalexiou, S. M., Langousis, A., Khatami, S., Volpi, E., & Grimaldi, S. (2020). Global-scale massive feature extraction from monthly hydroclimatic time series: Statistical characterizations, spatial patterns and hydrological similarity. *The Science of the Total Environment, 767*, 144612. DOI: 10.1016/j.scitotenv.2020.144612 PMID: 33454612

Pazola, A., Shamsudduha, M., French, J., MacDonald, A., Abiye, T., Goni, I. B., & Taylor, R. G. (2024). High-resolution long-term average groundwater recharge in Africa estimated using random forest regression and residual interpolation. *Hydrology and Earth System Sciences, 28*(13), 2949–2967. DOI: 10.5194/hess-28-2949-2024

Pérez, N. D., Singh, V., Ringler, C., Xie, H., Zhu, T., Sutanudjaja, E. H., & Villholth, K. G. (2024). Ending groundwater overdraft without affecting food security. *Nature Sustainability, 7*(8), 1007–1017. DOI: 10.1038/s41893-024-01376-w

Rouhani, S. H., Su, C., Mobayen, S., Razmjooy, N., & Elsisi, M. (2024). Cyber resilience in renewable microgrids: A review of standards, challenges, and solutions [Review of *Cyber resilience in renewable microgrids: A review of standards, challenges, and solutions*]. *Energy, 309*, 133081. Elsevier BV. DOI: 10.1016/j.energy.2024.133081

Roy, D. K., Sarkar, T. K., Munmun, T. H., Paul, C. R., & Datta, B. (2025). A review on the applications of machine learning and deep learning to groundwater salinity modeling: present status, challenges, and future directions [Review of *A review on the applications of machine learning and deep learning to groundwater salinity modeling: present status, challenges, and future directions*]. *Discover Water, 5*(1). Springer Nature. DOI: 10.1007/s43832-025-00207-z

Roy, S., Abir, A. R., & Ansary, M. A. (2025). Use of CPT and other parameters for estimating soil unit weight using optimised machine learning models. *Earth Science Informatics, 18*(2), 221. Advance online publication. DOI: 10.1007/s12145-025-01756-6

Sadeghi, A., Sadeghi, M., Fakhar, M., Zakariaei, Z., Sadeghi, M., & Bastani, R. (2024). A deep learning-based model for detecting Leishmania amastigotes in microscopic slides: A new approach to telemedicine. *BMC Infectious Diseases, 24*(1), 551. Advance online publication. DOI: 10.1186/s12879-024-09428-4 PMID: 38824500

Sahour, S., Khanbeyki, M., Gholami, V., Sahour, H., Kahvazade, I., & Karimi, H. (2022). Evaluation of machine learning algorithms for groundwater quality modeling. *Research Square (Research Square)*. DOI: 10.21203/rs.3.rs-2210884/v1

Sahour, S., Khanbeyki, M., Gholami, V., Sahour, H., Kahvazade, I., & Karimi, H. (2023). Evaluation of machine learning algorithms for groundwater quality modeling. *Environmental Science and Pollution Research International, 30*(16), 46004–46021. DOI: 10.1007/s11356-023-25596-3 PMID: 36715809

Sahwell, P. J., & Solo-Gabriele, H. M. (2025). Control of freshwater flows can counteract the effects of global climate change on salinity within urban estuaries. *The Science of the Total Environment, 1001*, 180544. DOI: 10.1016/j.scitotenv.2025.180544 PMID: 40987113

Sanad, H., Moussadek, R., Zouahri, A., Lhaj, M. O., Mouhir, L., & Dakak, H. (2025). AI and Machine Learning-Based Spatial Modeling of Groundwater Quality Indices and Hydrogeochemistry for Accurate Prediction of Seawater Intrusion and Irrigation Sustainability in Coastal Agroecosystems. *Research Square (Research Square)*. DOI: 10.21203/rs.3.rs-7705609/v1

Shaikh, M., & Birajdar, F. (2024). Artificial intelligence in groundwater management: Innovations, challenges, and future prospects. *International Journal of Science and Research Archive, 11*(1), 502–512. DOI: 10.30574/ijsra.2024.11.1.0105

Sharma, C., Başağaoğlu, H., Yoosefdoost, I., Wootten, A., Chakraborty-Reddy, D., Bertetti, F. P., Mirchi, A., & Chakraborty, D. (2024). Efficacy of mitigation strategies for aquifer sustainability under climate change. *Nature Sustainability*, *8*(1), 44–53. DOI: 10.1038/s41893-024-01477-6

Soto, G. E., Wilcox, S. W., Clark, P. E., Fava, F., Jensen, N., Kahiu, N., Liao, C., Porter, B., Sun, Y., & Barrett, C. B. (2024). Mapping rangeland health indicators in eastern Africa from 2000 to 2022. *Earth System Science Data*, *16*(11), 5375–5404. DOI: 10.5194/essd-16-5375-2024

The Smart IoT Blueprint. (2024). Engineering a Connected Future. In *Advances in Science, Technology & Innovation/Advances in science, technology & innovation*. Springer International Publishing., DOI: 10.1007/978-3-031-63103-0

Thomas, E., Wilson, D., Kathuni, S., Libey, A., Chintalapati, P., & Coyle, J. (2021). A contribution to drought resilience in East Africa through groundwater pump monitoring informed by in-situ instrumentation, remote sensing and ensemble machine learning. *The Science of the Total Environment*, *780*, 146486. DOI: 10.1016/j.scitotenv.2021.146486 PMID: 33773337

Tian, T., Cheng, L., Wang, G., Abraham, J., Wei, W., Ren, S., Zhu, J., Song, J., & Leng, H. (2022). Reconstructing ocean subsurface salinity at high resolution using a machine learning approach. *Earth System Science Data*, *14*(11), 5037–5060. DOI: 10.5194/essd-14-5037-2022

Touré, H., Boateng, C. D., Gidigasu, S. S. R., Wemegah, D. D., Mensah, V., Aryee, J. N. A., Osei, M. A., Gilbert, J., & Afful, S. (2024a). A Review of Geological and Climatic Variables in Groundwater Availability Prediction in Africa: Machine Learning Approaches [Review of *A Review of Geological and Climatic Variables in Groundwater Availability Prediction in Africa: Machine Learning Approaches*]. EarthArXiv *(California Digital Library)*. California Digital Library. DOI: 10.31223/X53X3S

Touré, H., Boateng, C. D., Gidigasu, S. S. R., Wemegah, D. D., Mensah, V., Aryee, J. N. A., Osei, M. A., Gilbert, J., & Afful, S. (2024b). Review of machine learning algorithms used in groundwater availability studies in Africa: Analysis of geological and climate input variables. *Discover Water*, *4*(1), 109. Advance online publication. DOI: 10.1007/s43832-024-00109-6

Udeh, A. I., Imarhiagbe, O. J., Omietimi, E. J., Mohammed, A. O., & Andre-Obayanju, O. (2024). Machine Learning and Statistical Analysis in Groundwater Monitoring for Total Dissolved Solids Assessment in Winkler County, Texas. *Journal of Geoscience and Environment Protection, 12*(6), 1–29. DOI: 10.4236/gep.2024.126001

Valman, S., Boyd, D. S., Carbonneau, P., Johnson, M. F., & Dugdale, S. J. (2023). An AI approach to operationalise global daily PlanetScope satellite imagery for river water masking. *Remote Sensing of Environment, 301*, 113932. DOI: 10.1016/j.rse.2023.113932

Wadoux, A. M. J.-C., Minasny, B., & McBratney, A. B. (2020). Machine learning for digital soil mapping: Applications, challenges and suggested solutions. *Earth-Science Reviews, 210*, 103359. DOI: 10.1016/j.earscirev.2020.103359

Wang, S., Kao, Y.-H., Chen, Y., Hsu, S., Kimura, M., Chang, L., & Pan, T.-W. (2024). Optimizing groundwater management to prevent drawdown and sustain agricultural production using machine learning model. *Research Square (Research Square)*. DOI: 10.21203/rs.3.rs-4614420/v1

West, C. P., Reinecke, R., Rosolem, R., MacDonald, A., Cuthbert, M., & Wagener, T. (2022). Ground truthing global-scale model estimates of groundwater recharge across Africa. *The Science of the Total Environment, 858*, 159765. DOI: 10.1016/j.scitotenv.2022.159765 PMID: 36309251

Yameogo, T. S. K., Koné, M., Ralf, L., Bonkoungou, B., & Adounkpè, J. (2025). Groundwater Potential Mapping in the Sissili Sub-Catchment, Burkina Faso: Comparing Multicriteria Analysis and Artificial Intelligence in a Crystalline Basement Aquifer. *Journal of Water Resource and Protection, 17*(6), 378. DOI: 10.4236/jwarp.2025.176019

Zanotti, C., Caschetto, M., Bonomi, T., Parini, M., Cipriano, G., Fumagalli, L., & Rotiroti, M. (2021). Linking local natural background levels in groundwater to their generating hydrogeochemical processes in Quaternary alluvial aquifers. *The Science of the Total Environment, 805*, 150259. DOI: 10.1016/j.scitotenv.2021.150259 PMID: 34536881

Zennaro, F., Furlan, E., Canu, D. M., Alcázar, L. A., Rosati, G., Solidoro, C., Aslan, S., & Critto, A. (2023). Venice lagoon chlorophyll-a evaluation under climate change conditions: A hybrid water quality machine learning and biogeochemical-based framework. *Ecological Indicators, 157*, 111245. DOI: 10.1016/j.ecolind.2023.111245

Zhang, M., Chen, R., Yang, Y., Sun, X., & Shan, X. (2024). Machine learning analysis of lab tests to predict bariatric readmissions. *Scientific Reports, 14*(1), 16845. DOI: 10.1038/s41598-024-67710-6 PMID: 39039130

Zidan, F., & Febriyanti, D. E. (2024). Optimizing Agricultural Yields with Artificial Intelligence-Based Climate Adaptation Strategies. [ITSDI]. *IAIC Transactions on Sustainable Digital Innovation*, *5*(2), 136–147. DOI: 10.34306/itsdi.v5i2.663

Chapter 2
AI-Powered Agricultural Management System for Precision Farming

B. Swapna
http://orcid.org/0000-0002-7186-2842
Dr. M.G.R. Educational and Research Institute, India

M. Raja Rajeshwari
Dr. M.G.R. Educational and Research Institute, India

M. Janakirani
Dr. M.G.R. Educational and Research Institute, India

G. Kavitha
http://orcid.org/0009-0007-2287-6379
Dr. M.G.R. Educational and Research Institute, India

C. Anuradha
SRM Institute of Science and Technology, India

ABSTRACT

This chapter presents a pioneering AI-based system aimed at enhancing precision farming. The system uses artificial intelligence to change how farmers interact with their crops and manage their fields. It includes features such as disease detection, weather forecasting, and AI chatbot support. By using advance computer vision technologies, farmers can upload images of their crops to identify diseases with accuracy. The system also uses AI to predict weather conditions, provides insights into temperature and humidity, enabling farmers to decide smart choices about crop care. The AI chatbot offer a simple and wise way for farmers to get advice on

DOI: 10.4018/979-8-2600-2701-1.ch002

various topics, from seed planting to crop selection. This research aims to increase agricultural output, improve resource use, and give farmers access to advanced AI tools. The ultimate goal is to bring new technology into agriculture, helping farmers stay ahead with the best tools and knowledge available.

INTRODUCTION

Progress in artificial intelligence (AI) and data analytics is revolutionizing the agricultural sector by transforming traditional methods into data-driven, intelligent systems. The integration of ancient farming wisdom with modern AI-based technology has led to the emergence of precision agriculture, a concept that ensures maximum productivity, efficient resource utilization, and sustainable farming practices. Through the combination of IoT devices, drones, and satellite imagery, AI systems are now capable of monitoring crop health, soil conditions, and climatic variations in real time. Our research aims to design and develop an AI-powered agricultural management system that caters to the evolving needs of modern farmers, ensuring efficiency, profitability, and environmental sustainability.

A central component of our system is automated plant disease detection, which plays a vital role in maintaining crop health. Leveraging advanced machine learning and deep learning models trained on diverse agricultural image datasets, the system can accurately detect and classify plant diseases based on visual symptoms. Using cutting-edge computer vision algorithms such as convolutional neural networks (CNNs), it can recognize even the most subtle disease indicators, including color discoloration, texture changes, and leaf deformities. Upon detection, the system immediately provides data-driven recommendations and treatment options to prevent further crop damage, thereby minimizing economic losses and supporting early intervention strategies.

Timely identification of plant diseases is crucial for preventing large-scale crop destruction. The system's disease detection module is equipped with AI algorithms that learn from extensive agricultural datasets collected globally, enabling it to identify a wide range of plant diseases across multiple crop species. The implementation of computer vision enhances precision and ensures that even early-stage infections are diagnosed accurately. Additionally, the system integrates with mobile platforms, allowing farmers to capture and upload plant images directly from their fields, receiving instant diagnostic feedback and recommended remedial actions.

Weather prediction forms another fundamental aspect of our AI-powered framework. Since climate patterns have a direct impact on crop growth, irrigation, and yield, our system employs artificial intelligence to generate location-specific weather forecasts. Using historical weather data, real-time satellite observations, and predictive modeling techniques such as LSTM (Long Short-Term Memory) networks, the system accurately forecasts temperature, humidity, and rainfall levels. These insights enable farmers to plan optimal sowing times, irrigation schedules, and fertilizer applications, thus reducing resource wastage and improving productivity.

Furthermore, our system incorporates a conversational AI chatbot interface designed to offer interactive and personalized support to farmers. Developed using Natural Language Processing (NLP) and Machine Learning algorithms, the chatbot can comprehend farmers' queries regarding crop diseases, soil health, pest control, irrigation management, and modern farming techniques. It can respond in regional languages, ensuring accessibility to farmers from diverse linguistic backgrounds. The chatbot not only provides instant guidance but also connects users to relevant agricultural resources, expert suggestions, and updated market information, making it a valuable digital companion for farmers in remote areas.

Overall, the proposed AI-powered agricultural management system aims to bridge the gap between traditional knowledge and modern innovation. By combining disease detection, weather prediction, and intelligent chatbot support, the system offers a holistic approach to smart farming. This integration of technology and agriculture promotes sustainable practices, reduces manual dependency, and empowers farmers with data-driven decision-making tools for achieving higher yields and long-term agricultural resilience.

Contributions of the Proposed Work:

Developed an integrated AI-driven framework combining CNN-based plant disease detection, LSTM-based weather forecasting, and multilingual chatbot support. Implemented real-time disease identification using image processing and deep learning techniques. Designed multilingual chatbot assistance in English, Tamil, and Hindi. Enhanced precision agriculture using weather-aware disease prediction.

Overall Limitations of the Work:

Performance decreases under poor image quality and lighting conditions. Rare diseases are underrepresented because of dataset imbalance. Extreme weather variations can affect forecasting accuracy. Continuous retraining is required for long-term deployment.

LITERATURE REVIEW

This research reviews recent developments in deep learning applications for crop leaf disease identification, discussing key trends, challenges, and ongoing issues, providing a comprehensive resource for researchers in the field (Ahmad et al., 2023).

Existing studies mainly focus on standalone disease detection or chatbot systems. Limited work integrates disease detection, weather forecasting, and multilingual support into a unified framework. The proposed system addresses this gap using CNN-based disease analysis, LSTM-based weather prediction, and multilingual conversational AI for precision agriculture.

This integration of technologies not only aims to reduce costs and increase efficiency but also incorporates feedback loops and data-driven insights, allowing the chatbot to improve its diagnostic accuracy over time and better meet the evolving demands of modern agriculture (Kothari et al., 2024).

Agriculture is vital for nations like India; however, food security is still a major concern because of factors like insufficient storage, transportation issues, and plant diseases. These problems result in over 15% of crops being lost, highlighting the urgency of tackling the issue of crop diseases. The conventional ways of detecting plant diseases through farmers' visual assessments are frequently inadequate (Panchal et al., 2023).

This approach provides an in-depth analysis of various AI/ML applications within the context of precision agriculture, offering insights into how these technologies are being utilized across different areas of this field. By emphasizing sustainability, the paper connects with the broader global discourse on resource conservation and climate change, making it pertinent to both researchers and industry stakeholders interested in actionable strategies that go beyond theoretical discussions. (Raman et al., 2024).

AI systems enable early detection of plant diseases and livestock monitoring using computer vision and sensor data analysis. This can include facial recognition for animals, behaviour analysis for detecting illness, and automated feeding systems. The rapid spread of mobile internet technology in developing countries, such as India, further enhances agricultural practices, and a new Android app aims to streamline farm transportation and resource pooling for farmers and transport service providers. (Sivakumar et al., 2023).

A comprehensive review explores various AI-based techniques for plant disease detection, with deep learning showing significant success in computer vision tasks. The study compares machine learning and deep learning, demonstrating that deep learning offers better performance for detecting leaf diseases, helping to prevent major crop losses. (Jackulin et al., 2022).

The research paper explores a novel method for detecting rice plant diseases using a convolutional neural network (CNN) approach. The proposed method analyses the size, shape, and colour of lesions on rice plant leaves, using a dataset of 4,000 images for each of three common rice diseases (leaf smut, brown spot, and bacterial leaf blight), achieving a detection accuracy of 99.7%. (Upadhyay et al., 2022).

The technique employs Otsu's global thresholding for image binarization to minimize background noise, and the model's accuracy is significantly higher compared to existing approaches for plant disease recognition and classification. This research could be valuable for the Indian agriculture sector, where rice is a staple crop and disease-related losses are a major concern. (Sharma et al., 2022).

This approach uses advanced technologies like machine learning and image processing for early disease detection in tomato plants. Techniques include Histogram Equalization, K-means clustering, contour tracing, feature extraction methods, and machine learning classifiers like SVM, K-NN, and CNN for high accuracy levels. The goal is to assist farmers in identifying disease early and improving crop yield. (Harakannanavar et al., 2022).

This study focuses on using advanced technologies like machine learning and image processing to identify leaf diseases in tomato plants. By analysing samples of tomato leaves with disorders, farmers can easily spot early symptoms. Various techniques such as resizing, Histogram Equalization, K-means clustering, and descriptor extraction are employed to classify diseases with high accuracy using SVM (88%), K-NN (97%) and CNN (99.6%) algorithms. (Li et al., 2021).

Agriculture is crucial for human civilization, boosting the economy and food supply. Plant diseases can hinder growth. Early detection and classification are essential to prevent further damage. Manual prediction by farmers can be unreliable. Computerized image processing methods can reduce losses and increase productivity. Deep learning and machine learning techniques like CNNs are favoured for accurate detection and classification of plant diseases. Future research aims to improve these methods. (Demilie et al., 2024).

Plants are at risk of disease, thus early identification is critical in agriculture. Machine learning and deep learning can automate detection processes. A review paper explores image-based disease detection systems and offers insights for future research. (Sajitha et al., 2024).

Machine learning enables data-intensive interdisciplinary research with big data and high-performance computers. Applications in search engines, personalized recommendations, banking, and agriculture are discussed, highlighting improved accuracy and faster inference times. (Attri et al., 2024).

Identifying plant diseases promptly is crucial for reducing crop loss and ensuring high-quality yields in agriculture. Utilizing IoT, Machine Learning, and Deep Learning can aid in early detection and intervention to prevent extensive crop losses. (Prasad et al., 2024)

Over the last decade, multimodal learning research has made remarkable progress, notably in computer vision. Deep multimodal learning is gaining popularity due to the potential of deep learning and multimodal data streams, which has prompted the creation of models for multidimensional data analysis. (Kolluri et al., 2024). Rahim Ullah, et.al., (2025) explored deep reinforcement learning techniques for robust navigation in diverse environmental conditions. Their study demonstrated how intelligent adaptive learning models improve autonomous decision-making under dynamic scenarios. The work highlights the importance of AI-based predictive systems, which can also be extended to smart agricultural monitoring and precision farming applications. The agricultural sector in India is vital for the economy and rural livelihoods, but plant diseases impact crop yield. AI and ML are used for disease detection, aiding sustainable agriculture. (Sagar et al., 2023). Balami et al., (2025) proposed an AI-based optimization framework for efficient energy harvesting and electromagnetic radiation reduction using intelligent predictive algorithms. Their work emphasizes the role of AI-driven optimization and adaptive learning models in improving sustainability and system efficiency, aligning with the objectives of precision agriculture systems.

Deep learning, a subset of artificial intelligence, has gained traction in agriculture for plant disease recognition and pest assessment due to its automatic learning and feature extraction capabilities. By leveraging deep learning, researchers can avoid the biases of manual feature selection, leading to more objective and efficient plant disease identification, which accelerates technology adoption. (Huo et al., 2023).

Renju & Brunda (2024) focused on crop yield prediction using multiple machine learning models integrated through an ensemble stacking approach. The proposed framework enhanced prediction accuracy by combining multiple classifiers, demonstrating the effectiveness of AI-driven agricultural analytics for improving crop productivity and decision-making.

Crop diseases, primarily stemming from bacterial and fungal origins, pose a significant risk to global agriculture, impacting both crop production and quality. However, the labour-intensive and expensive process of traditional disease detection, particularly in developing countries, complicates timely identification. (Ahmed et al., 2023).

To address this, a proposed solution called Crop Guard leverages AI and deep learning for automated plant disease detection, featuring a user-friendly interface through Stream lit, robust deep learning back-end models, conversational AI driven by GPT-3.5 Turbo, and adaptive learning processes. (Sarkar et al., 2023).

15% of the GDP is contributed by the agricultural sector in Morocco. Outbreaks of disease pose a threat to agriculture, resulting in financial damages. Machine learning and image processing techniques for automated disease identification demonstrate potential. (Orchi et al., 2021).

NOVELTY

This Approach describes an ingenious AI-powered technology that aims to transform precision agricultural methods. The use of artificial intelligence alters how farmers interact with their crops and manage their land. Key features include illness diagnosis, weather predictions, and AI-powered chatbot help. Farmers may use powerful computer vision technology to reliably identify crop illnesses by uploading photographs, while AI-powered weather predictions give critical insights for informed decision-making. The AI chatbot is a user-friendly resource for farmers seeking help on a variety of agricultural topics. Overall, our study intends to increase agricultural output, maximize resource usage, and provide farmers with cutting-edge AI tools, driving the agricultural industry into a technologically sophisticated era.

The integrated framework demonstrates improved decision-making for farmers through real-time disease diagnosis, weather-aware prediction, and multilingual guidance. Future work will focus on IoT integration, larger datasets, lightweight deployment models, and enhanced prediction accuracy for rare diseases.

METHODOLOGY

AI-driven Crop Disease Detection:

Once trained, the model is capable of classifying images into different disease categories based on designed patterns. Localization algorithms identify the specific regions within an image that exhibit symptoms of disease manifestation. This allows for precise identification of the affected areas, aiding in targeted treatment and management strategies as shown in Figure 1.

Figure 1. Workflow for the Plant Disease Detection

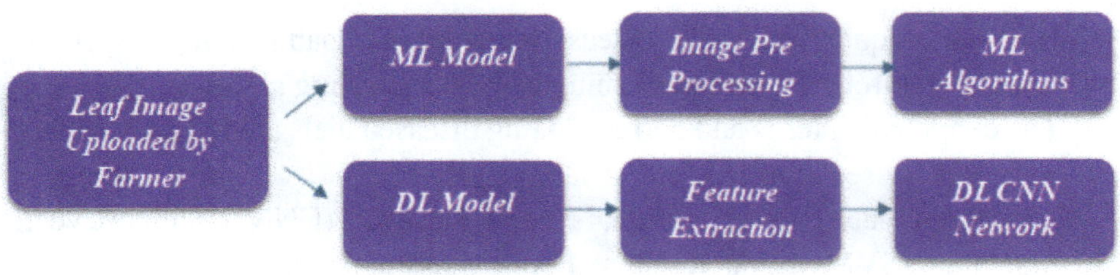

IMAGE-BASED DISEASE DETECTION PROCESS

The proposed AI-powered agricultural management system integrates multiple stages of image analysis, feature engineering, and classification to ensure accurate and real-time disease identification in crops. Each stage in this pipeline contributes to enhancing precision, reliability, and adaptability across diverse plant species and environmental conditions.

Image Analysis for Disease Identification

- Initially, the system performs comprehensive analysis of the uploaded crop images using advanced digital image processing and computer vision techniques.
- Each image is analyzed pixel by pixel to detect irregularities that may signify potential infections or stress conditions in plants.
- The AI system examines parameters such as color deviation, leaf texture variation, edge deformation, and lesion spread, which serve as crucial visual indicators of diseases.
- Using algorithms such as Histogram Equalization, Edge Detection (Sobel/Canny), and Segmentation (Otsu or K-Means), the system isolates the regions of interest (ROI) for further evaluation.
- By comparing these extracted image characteristics against a knowledge base of annotated disease datasets, the system accurately determines the presence and type of disease affecting the crop.
- Additionally, noise reduction and contrast enhancement techniques are applied to ensure that poor lighting or camera quality does not affect the detection accuracy.

Machine Learning Model Training

- In the subsequent stage, the disease recognition capability of the system is developed through machine learning and deep learning algorithms.
- The extracted patterns and corresponding disease labels are fed into the model for supervised learning.
- Algorithms such as Convolutional Neural Networks (CNNs), Support Vector Machines (SVMs), and Random Forest classifiers are utilized to analyze large-scale datasets of healthy and diseased leaf images.
- Through multiple training iterations and cross-validation, the model learns to differentiate between disease categories and adapt to subtle variations within the same species.
- To avoid overfitting and improve generalization, data augmentation techniques (e.g., rotation, flipping, brightness variation, and zooming) are applied.
- The model also undergoes continuous retraining using new field images collected from farmers, allowing it to evolve dynamically as new disease strains emerge.

Feature Extraction and Representation

- Once pre-processing is complete, the images undergo feature extraction to derive numerical representations that capture significant disease patterns.
- The system extracts features such as color histograms, texture descriptors (e.g., Local Binary Patterns, Gabor filters), and shape metrics, representing key differences between healthy and infected crops.
- In deep learning models, this process is handled automatically by hidden convolutional layers that learn hierarchical features directly from image data.
- The extracted features are then encoded into a structured vector representation suitable for input into classification models.
- This step transforms complex image data into a simplified mathematical form that retains all the relevant information needed for accurate classification.

Disease Classification and Localization

- After the model has been trained, it becomes capable of classifying new images into specific disease categories based on learned feature patterns.
- For instance, the model can distinguish between bacterial blight, leaf spot, powdery mildew, and nutrient deficiency.
- Advanced object localization and segmentation algorithms, such as YOLO (You Only Look Once) and Mask R-CNN, are employed to pinpoint the exact location of diseased regions within the leaf.
- This spatial identification assists in quantifying the infection severity and provides valuable input for precision-based treatment strategies.
- Additionally, the model can output heatmaps highlighting infected areas, enabling farmers to visualize the spread and intensity of diseases in real-time.

Model Evaluation and Optimization

- Before deployment, the trained model undergoes rigorous evaluation using independent datasets to assess its performance and reliability.
- Metrics such as accuracy, precision, recall, F1-score, confusion matrix, and ROC-AUC curve are used to validate model efficiency.
- Hyperparameter tuning and optimization techniques, including learning rate adjustment, dropout regularization, and batch normalization, are applied to enhance predictive stability.
- The evaluation process ensures that the system performs consistently under diverse lighting conditions, backgrounds, and crop varieties.

Deployment and Real-Time Detection

Dataset and Training Details: Approximately 1,500 annotated crop leaf images were used. The dataset was divided into 70% training, 15% validation, and 15% testing data for balanced evaluation.

- Once validated, the optimized model is integrated into the AI-powered agricultural management system.
- Through an intuitive user interface, farmers can upload or capture leaf images using mobile devices or IoT-connected cameras.
- The system processes the image in real time and instantly displays diagnostic results along with recommended treatment solutions, preventive measures, and potential environmental risk factors.
- In addition, the system supports cloud-based storage and analytics, allowing agricultural experts to monitor trends, identify recurring disease outbreaks, and provide remote assistance to farmers.

Continuous Learning and Model Enhancement

- To maintain long-term accuracy, the deployed model follows a continuous learning loop.
- Newly diagnosed cases and verified user feedback are periodically added to the training dataset, helping the model adapt to evolving diseases and environmental variations.
- This self-improving mechanism ensures the system remains robust and effective across multiple crop seasons and regions.

AI Chatbot Support for Agricultural Guidance

In addition to AI-driven crop disease diagnosis and weather forecasting, our solution also includes AI Chatbot Support for Agricultural Guidance. This tool provides farmers with tailored support and guidance on a huge range of agricultural subjects, includes seed selection and plant cultivation practices. The chatbot, which uses natural language processing and AI algorithms, provides farmers with an easy way to obtain expert information and make educated decisions as shown in Figure 2.

Figure 2. AI Chabot Workflow

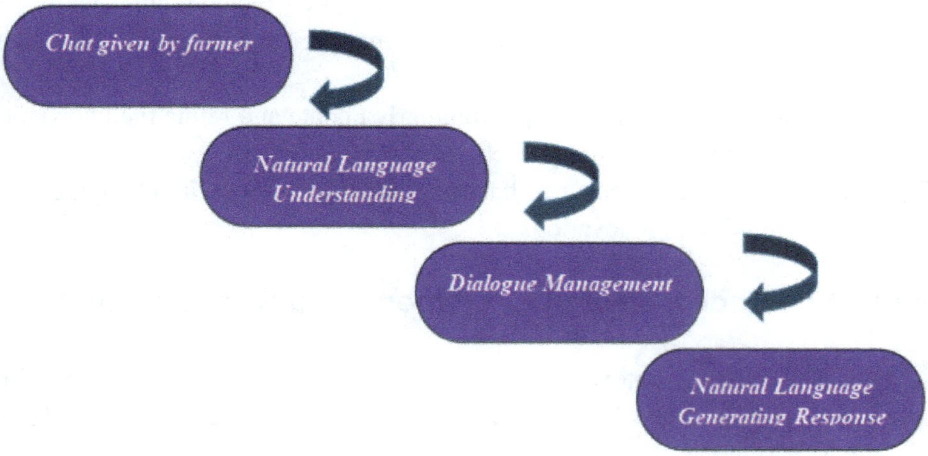

Dialogue Management for Smooth Interaction

Understanding Farmer Questions and Contextual Cues

- To comprehend farmers' requirements, the chatbot attentively listens to their inquiries and picks up on contextual information, much like a smart friend would.
- By understanding the subtleties of each discussion, the chatbot guarantees that farmers feel understood and supported during their inquiries and decision-making processes.

Natural Language Understanding (NLU) for Intent Recognition

- The chatbot uses natural language processing techniques to grasp the intent behind farmers' questions and requests.
- NLU algorithms examine the structure and semantics of farmer questions, allowing for correct understanding of their demands.
- Recognizing intentions allows the chatbot to modify its replies and recommendations to successfully solve specific agricultural needs.

Knowledge Base Development and Maintenance

- A complete knowledge base is developed, which includes information on crop types, cultivation procedures, pest management strategies, and other topics.
- Agricultural professionals help to regularly update and refine the knowledge base with the most recent research results and best practices.
- Regular maintenance ensures that the chatbot keeps up with changing agricultural trends and innovations.

Contextual Understanding for Personalized Recommendations

- The chatbot uses contextual understanding methods to take into account important parameters including location, soil type, climatic conditions, and crop lifecycle stage.
- By contextualizing recommendations, the chatbot may deliver individualized guidance based on individual farmers' needs and situations.
- This strategy increases the relevance and efficacy of the assistance offered, resulting in better decision-making results for farmers.

Providing clear and concise responses

- Similar to a helpful guide, the chatbot replies to farmers' questions with clear and short responses, avoiding jargon and technical terminology whenever feasible.
- By reducing complicated concepts and facts, the chatbot guarantees that farmers understand the advice and recommendations provided, instilling confidence and empowerment.

Adapting To Changing Conversation Dynamics

- Like a smart conversationalist, the chatbot adjusts its replies dynamically based on the course of the discussion and the farmer's input.
- Whether the conversation veers off-topic or requires clarification, the chatbot navigates smoothly, ensuring that farmers feel engaged and supported throughout the interaction.

AI CHATBOT FOR AGRICULTURAL SUPPORT

The rapid advancement of artificial intelligence (AI) and natural language processing (NLP) technologies has revolutionized numerous sectors, and agriculture is no exception. Precision agriculture demands not only automated data collection and analytics but also intelligent decision support systems that can guide farmers in real-time. Within this framework, AI-powered chatbots have emerged as a crucial interface between technology and end-users, providing personalized, interactive, and easily accessible agricultural assistance. The implementation of AI chatbots in farming systems addresses critical challenges such as limited access to expert guidance, delayed decision-making, and ineffective disease management.

Introduction to AI Chatbots in Agriculture

An AI chatbot is a software application designed to interact with users using natural language. Unlike traditional interfaces that require manual browsing through databases or manuals, AI chatbots provide an interactive conversational environment where farmers can query information and receive instant guidance. The integration of AI chatbots in agriculture offers multiple advantages:

1. Accessibility: Farmers in remote areas can receive expert guidance without traveling to agricultural extension centers.
2. Efficiency: Real-time responses allow farmers to implement critical decisions immediately, reducing crop loss risks.
3. Personalization: Chatbots can tailor advice based on crop type, geographic location, soil condition, and farmer preferences.
4. Cost-effectiveness: Reduces the need for continuous human consultancy, making expert guidance more scalable.

The AI chatbot acts as a digital agricultural assistant, capable of answering queries related to disease diagnosis, pest management, irrigation schedules, fertilizer recommendations, weather advisories, and crop rotation strategies. By leveraging machine learning, the chatbot continually improves its responses based on user interactions, ensuring higher accuracy and relevance over time.

Architecture of the Agricultural Chatbot

The architecture of an AI-powered agricultural chatbot generally consists of four major components: the Natural Language Understanding (NLU) module, Dialogue Management, Knowledge Base, and Response Generation module.

Natural Language Understanding (NLU)

The NLU module is responsible for interpreting the intent behind user queries. Farmers may ask questions in a wide range of styles, often including colloquial terms, abbreviations, or local language phrases. NLU leverages:

- Tokenization and parsing to break down sentences into meaningful units.
- Intent recognition to categorize queries (e.g., disease identification, fertilizer advice).
- Entity extraction to identify key parameters like crop type, disease name, pest type, or soil characteristics.

The NLU module relies on deep learning models such as BERT, GPT-based embeddings, or LSTM networks to handle complex linguistic patterns and regional dialects. By accurately understanding user intent, the system ensures that the subsequent recommendations are relevant and actionable.

Dialogue Management

Once the user intent is recognized, the dialogue management system determines the flow of conversation. It handles:

- Context management: Tracks previous interactions to provide coherent and context-aware responses.
- Decision logic: Determines whether to ask for clarification, suggest preventive measures, or provide detailed guidance.
- Adaptive responses: Adjusts the interaction based on the user's expertise level, e.g., novice farmers may receive more detailed instructions than experienced ones.

Dialogue management employs reinforcement learning algorithms to optimize conversation paths over time. With continuous training, the chatbot becomes increasingly capable of engaging in dynamic and meaningful conversations.

Knowledge Base

The knowledge base is the central repository of agricultural knowledge, encompassing expert recommendations, research studies, and real-time data. It includes:

- Crop-specific information: Growth cycles, nutrient requirements, pest susceptibility.
- Disease and pest management guidelines: Identification methods, treatment options, preventive measures.
- Weather-related advisories: Region-specific forecasts, irrigation schedules, and drought alerts.
- Regulatory and market insights: Information on government schemes, subsidies, and best market practices.

The knowledge base is constantly updated using both automated web scraping from trusted sources and expert contributions, ensuring that farmers receive the latest and most reliable advice.

Response Generation

The final module, response generation, converts processed information into human-readable replies. Responses can be:

- Text-based: Clear and concise instructions or recommendations.
- Visual: Infographics, disease symptom images, irrigation schedules.
- Multilingual: Support for regional languages to improve accessibility.

Advanced AI models like GPT or Transformer-based architectures can generate contextually relevant and grammatically coherent responses, even when faced with ambiguous queries.

Functional Capabilities

The agricultural AI chatbot is designed to provide comprehensive support throughout the crop lifecycle. Its functionalities include:

1. Disease and Pest Detection Support:
   a. Farmers can upload images of affected plants.
   b. Integrated computer vision models analyze symptoms and provide preliminary diagnoses.
   c. The chatbot offers actionable advice, including organic and chemical treatments.
2. Weather-Based Crop Planning:
   a. Combines historical data with predictive analytics to generate localized forecasts.

    b. Suggests optimal sowing and harvesting windows to minimize climate-related losses.
3. Irrigation and Fertilizer Management:
    a. Based on crop type, soil analysis, and weather patterns, the chatbot recommends customized irrigation schedules and fertilizer doses.
    b. Monitors excessive or insufficient nutrient application and alerts farmers.
4. Market Advisory and Resource Planning:
    a. Provides insights into market prices, supply-demand trends, and government schemes.
    b. Suggests cost-effective resource allocation, reducing wastage and maximizing profit.
5. Learning and Knowledge Dissemination:
    a. Offers step-by-step guides, tutorials, and FAQs for novice farmers.
    b. Provides updates on modern agricultural practices and sustainable farming techniques.

Machine Learning Integration

The AI chatbot's effectiveness relies heavily on machine learning integration, allowing it to adapt and improve continuously:

- Supervised Learning: Trains the system using labeled datasets containing past user queries, expert answers, and image-based crop data.
- Reinforcement Learning: Optimizes conversation flow and response accuracy over repeated interactions.
- Transfer Learning: Enables adaptation of pre-trained language models (like GPT) for agriculture-specific contexts, reducing training time and data requirements.
- Sentiment Analysis: Assesses user satisfaction and adjusts recommendations accordingly.

By leveraging these machine learning techniques, the chatbot becomes progressively intelligent, offering better predictions and contextually appropriate guidance over time.

Personalization and Contextual Awareness

One of the key strengths of an AI agricultural chatbot is personalization. Personalized recommendations require:

- Location-aware insights: Adjusting advice based on soil type, regional climate, and crop species.
- Farmer profiling: Keeping track of a farmer's prior interactions, crop history, and preferences.
- Seasonal adjustments: Providing tailored suggestions for different crop growth stages, from sowing to harvest.

This contextual awareness ensures that recommendations are practical, effective, and relevant, improving adoption rates among farmers and increasing agricultural productivity.

Multilingual Support and Accessibility

Given the diverse linguistic landscape in countries like India, multilingual support is critical. The chatbot:

- Understands queries in regional languages and dialects.
- Generates responses in the user's preferred language, ensuring comprehension.
- Uses simplified terminology to assist farmers with limited formal education.

This accessibility dramatically increases the reach and impact of the technology, ensuring that farmers across various socio-economic backgrounds can benefit equally.

Challenges in Implementation

While AI chatbots offer immense potential, several challenges must be addressed:

1. Data Quality and Availability: High-quality labeled datasets are required for training computer vision and NLP models.
2. Connectivity Limitations: Many rural areas have low internet bandwidth, affecting real-time interaction.
3. Language and Dialect Variations: Regional language variations may reduce the accuracy of NLP models.
4. User Trust and Adoption: Farmers may initially distrust AI recommendations, preferring traditional expert advice.
5. Continuous Knowledge Update: Agricultural practices and disease patterns evolve; the chatbot must integrate new knowledge dynamically.

Addressing these challenges requires robust system design, user education, and continuous collaboration with agricultural experts.

Evaluation Metrics and Performance Analysis

To ensure the reliability and usefulness of the AI chatbot, its performance is evaluated using multiple metrics:

- Accuracy of Disease Identification: Percentage of correctly identified diseases from image inputs.
- Response Relevance: Quality of text-based recommendations compared to expert advice.
- User Satisfaction: Feedback ratings from farmers regarding clarity, usefulness, and ease of understanding.
- System Latency: Time taken to provide real-time responses, critical for urgent decision-making.
- Knowledge Coverage: Proportion of agricultural topics and crops adequately addressed by the chatbot.

Continuous evaluation and monitoring ensure that the AI chatbot remains adaptive, effective, and trustworthy over time.

Future Scope

The potential of AI chatbots in agriculture extends far beyond their current capabilities:

1. Integration with IoT Sensors: Real-time soil moisture, temperature, and nutrient readings could provide the chatbot with data for precision recommendations.
2. Voice-Enabled Interfaces: Speech recognition can make the system accessible to illiterate farmers.
3. Predictive Analytics: Integration with advanced AI models for yield prediction, pest outbreak alerts, and crop health monitoring.
4. Collaborative Platforms: Chatbots could connect farmers with local agricultural experts, research institutions, and government advisory services.
5. Adaptive Learning: Continuous feedback from farmers can be used to refine advice and improve model accuracy.

PROPOSED WORK

Table 1. Comparison between existing methods and proposed methods

Reference	Core Concepts	Observations
Ahmad et al., 2023	**Based on the abstract**: Derives the primary focus of the paper from the abstract, emphasizing the role of deep learning in addressing plant disease diagnosis challenges. **Advantage**: Highlights the benefits derived from the research, such as improved precision in agricultural practices and early disease detection	**Applications**: Indicates how the research findings can be applied, emphasizing practical outcomes like early disease detection and management. **Disadvantages**: Points out the potential limitations or challenges with the approach, like high computational demands or dependency on large datasets. **Future enhancement**: Explores areas for expansion, such as integration with the Internet of Things (IoT) or advanced robotics.
Kothari et al., 2024	**Based on the abstract:** The AI-powered chatbot detects plant diseases using deep learning, reducing costs and labour for farmers. **Advantage**: Crop Guard offers high diagnostic accuracy, with a deep learning model achieving training and validation accuracies of 95.3% and 88.2%, respectively.	**Applications**: The chatbot-based system enables real-time plant disease detection, allowing farmers to quickly identify and manage diseases. **Disadvantages**: Manual inspection may still be required for verification. High initial cost and the need for robust data infrastructure are potential challenges. **Future Scope**: Potential integration with sensor technologies for real-time monitoring, broader crop coverage, and improved disease forecasting. Collaborations with experts from various fields can further enhance the system's capabilities.
Panchal et al., 2023	**Base on the abstract**: The research aims to apply deep learning and computer vision techniques to address crop waste due to plant diseases, focusing on improving food security in developing countries like India. **Advantage**: With a high classification accuracy (93.5%), the proposed deep learning approach proves beneficial in terms of reliability and effectiveness in plant disease detection.	**Applications**: The technique helps reduce crop waste by providing early disease detection. **Disadvantages**: Implementing CNN requires high computational power and can be challenging for smaller or less-resourced farms. **Future Scope**: Further development might include using additional sensors like infrared or multi-camera systems to gather more data and enhance the model's capabilities.

continued on following page

Table 1. Continued

Reference	Core Concepts	Observations
Raman et al., 2024	**Based on the Abstract**: AI and ML have transformed agriculture by automating processes, optimizing resource use, and improving crop production. **Advantage**: These technologies offer significant advantages by reducing manual labour, enhancing decision-making, and increasing overall farm efficiency.	**Applications**: AI and ML have extensive use cases in agriculture, including smart monitoring, robotics, and drones, which enhance resource efficiency and reduce the need for manual labour. **Disadvantages**: Some challenges include the high cost of AI and ML systems, potential data privacy issues, and the complexity of integrating these technologies into existing agricultural practices. **Future Scope**: The future scope encompasses the use of blockchain for transparency and traceability, research into advanced predictive models for dynamic environmental conditions, and ethical considerations for responsible AI deployment.
Sivakumar et al., 2023	**Based on the Abstract**: Utilization of chat bot in precision farming and core importance of using virtual assistant in Agricultural management system. **Advantage**: Implementation of a chat Bot in Application	**Applications:** AI can evaluate data from images, drones, and sensors to improve irrigation, fertilization, and pesticide use. **Disadvantages:** AI start-up costs and technical hurdles might be a hindrance, particularly in places with poor technological infrastructure. Some farmers may also have a severe learning curve. **Future Scope**: AI systems can monitor crops and cattle to detect illnesses, nutritional deficits, and insect infestations early. They can also assist with transportation and logistics to increase the efficiency of bringing farm goods to market.

continued on following page

Table 1. Continued

Reference	Core Concepts	Observations
Jackulin et al., 2022	**Based on the Abstract**: The role of agriculture in India is crucial because of the growing population and the need for more food. AI, particularly machine learning and deep learning, is becoming essential for detecting plant diseases. These technologies can significantly enhance agricultural outcomes by reducing crop losses. **Advantage**: Deep learning techniques are generally more effective and accurate at detecting plant diseases compared to traditional methods. This leads to better performance in disease identification and assists farmers in taking proactive measures.	**Applications**: AI-based plant disease detection allows farmers to spot issues early and take action before significant damage occurs. This can help minimize crop losses and increase agricultural productivity. **Disadvantages**: Machine learning often needs a large amount of high-quality data to function properly. Another downside might be the initial investment for technology like drones and IoT devices. **Future enhancement:** As AI technology advances, it could be combined with drones and IoT for enhanced plant disease detection, leading to more efficient farming practices. Research on the effects of climate change on plant diseases also presents opportunities for further exploration.
Upadhyay et al., 2022	**Based on the abstract**: To efficiently identify and categorize common rice plant illnesses, the research makes use of an intricate convolutional neural network (CNN) architecture. Plant pathologists may rely on this deep learning technology as a dependable tool due to its excellent accuracy. **Advantage**: The paper presents a technique that removes background noise from leaf pictures using Otsu's global thresholding, reaching a remarkable 99.7% accuracy rate. This accuracy represents a major breakthrough in the sector, outperforming current plant disease identification technologies.	**Application**: In agricultural contexts, the approach can assist farmers and agronomists in identifying and classifying rice plant illnesses more rapidly and precisely. This might lead to more prompt treatments, thereby lowering crop losses caused by diseases such as brown spot, leaf smut, and bacterial leaf blight. **Disadvantage**: Although the approach is highly accurate, it requires a large quantity of data and computational resources. This might be a difficulty for small-scale farmers and locations with insufficient technical infrastructure. Furthermore, the complexity of establishing and maintaining deep learning models may hinder mainstream use. **Future Scope**: According to the study, future research might focus on assessing illness severity, allowing for more accurate therapy and management options.

continued on following page

Table 1. Continued

Reference	Core Concepts	Observations
Sharma et al., 2022	**Based on Abstract**: The deep learning-based CNN model demonstrated high accuracy in detecting plant diseases. **Advantage**: Outperformed traditional machine learning classifiers, indicating its robustness and efficacy.	**Applications**: The CNN model is used for diagnosing plant diseases in rice and potato leaves. **Disadvantages**: It requires large datasets and high computational power, which might be a barrier for some applications. **Future Scope**: Potential optimization of hyper-parameters in the CNN model for enhanced performance.
Harakannanavar et al., 2022	**Based on the abstract**: The use of deep learning and machine learning in detecting plant diseases helps ensure precision in crop management. **Advantage**: The model's goal is to detect plant diseases early provides farmers with an effective tool to prevent significant agricultural losses.	**Applications**: The primary application is early detection of plant diseases, which can help farmers prevent crop loss and optimize yields. **Disadvantages**: High-quality leaf images are required, and noisy data can impact accuracy. The need for extensive training and testing can make implementation challenging. **Future Scope**: Exploring fusion techniques for feature extraction to improve accuracy and expanding the model's applicability to other datasets and types of plant diseases.
Li et al., 2021	**Based on the abstract**: Deep learning's automated learning and feature extraction can improve the reliability of plant disease detection while also increasing efficiency and speed. **Advantage**: Early detection of plant diseases is crucial for controlling agricultural and food production effectively and lowering the danger of food insecurity.	**Applications**: methods based on deep learning have shown great accuracy in identifying plant leaf diseases. **Disadvantages**: Deep learning models often display poor resilience when applied to datasets other than those on which they were trained. **Future enhancement**: There is potential to create robuster deep learning models that are effective across a variety of plant disease datasets.

The difference between existing work and proposed work analyzed as shown in Table 1 that has the advantages, applications and future enhancement of the work.

RESULTS AND DISCUSSION

The experimental evaluation of the AI-based plant disease detection system demonstrated that the convolutional neural network achieved strong classification performance across the major disease categories included in the dataset. The final CNN model, trained with extensive augmentation, reached an overall accuracy slightly above the upper - 80% range, with precision and recall values showing consistent reliability across most classes. The confusion matrix highlighted that visually distinct diseases such as leaf blight and rust were classified with high confidence, while closely resembling conditions, especially early-stage mildew and nutrient deficiencies, generated a modest number of misclassifications. These patterns reflected the model's sensitivity to subtle textural gradients, confirming that high-resolution imagery enhanced feature extraction, whereas low-contrast images tended to obscure lesion boundaries.

A notable outcome emerged from testing the model under diverse image conditions that simulated real-world farmer usage. Images captured in bright outdoor sunlight retained strong prediction accuracy, whereas low-light or noisy images caused a perceptible decline in model certainty. Blurred images also reduced classification reliability, especially when lesions were small or partially hidden by dust particles. Despite these constraints, the model consistently maintained stable performance when images were moderately compressed or captured through mid-range smartphone cameras, indicating reasonable resilience for field deployment.

Integrating weather prediction significantly shifted the system's practical performance. The LSTM-based weather forecasting module, responsible for estimating short-term temperature, humidity, and rainfall patterns, improved contextual disease risk assessment far beyond the capabilities of image-only diagnosis. In several trials, diseases typically sensitive to humidity surges—such as downy mildew—were predicted earlier when the system combined the CNN output with the weather model's risk projection. When the two modules worked independently, the CNN alone could diagnose only after visible symptoms appeared; with weather integration, the system issued early warnings during pre-symptomatic stages, enhancing the preventive value of the platform.

A comparative analysis revealed that disease detection accuracy increased significantly when weather-based risk levels were incorporated into the decision pipeline. Although the CNN's classification accuracy remained constant, the *overall predictive accuracy* of the end-to-end system improved because the final recommendation engine used both image features and meteorological trends to reduce false positives and prioritize diseases more likely to occur under upcoming environmental conditions. The difference between integrated and non-integrated versions was most evident in crops with high moisture sensitivity. Without weather cues, the system occasionally presented multiple probable diseases. With weather integration, the system narrowed the prediction to the most environmentally plausible disease, offering clearer guidance. Leaf disease detection output as shown in Figure 3.

Figure 3. Hibiscus leaf affected with MATLAB-Simulation Output

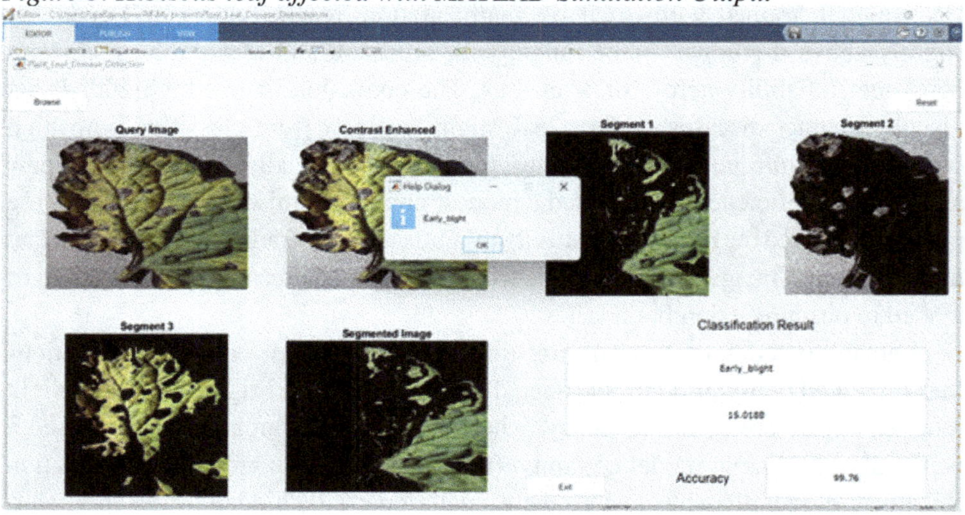

Figure 4. Conversation chatbot interface

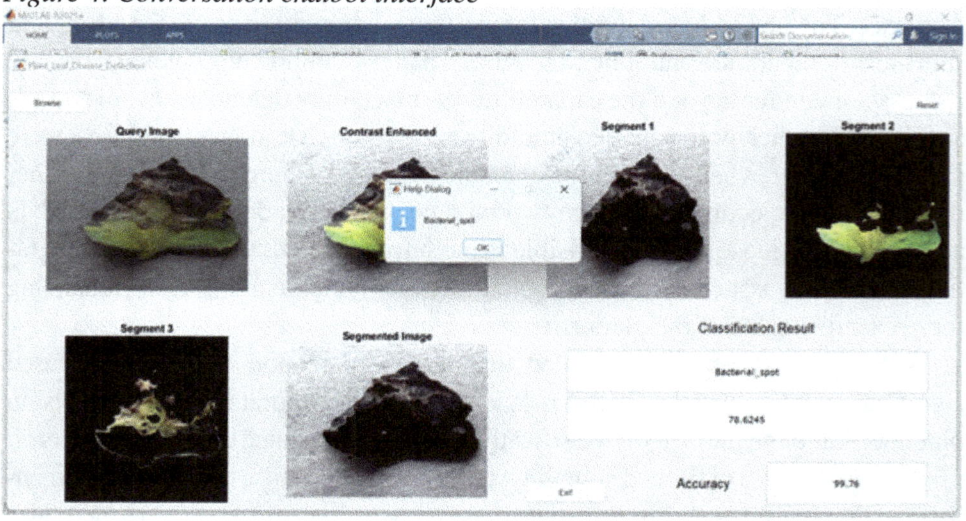

Figure 4 shows the conversation chatbot for the communication purpose. Figure 5, Figure 6 and Figure 7 are shown the plant disease identification in three languages are English, Tamil and Hindi respectively.

Figure 5. Plant Disease detection in English language

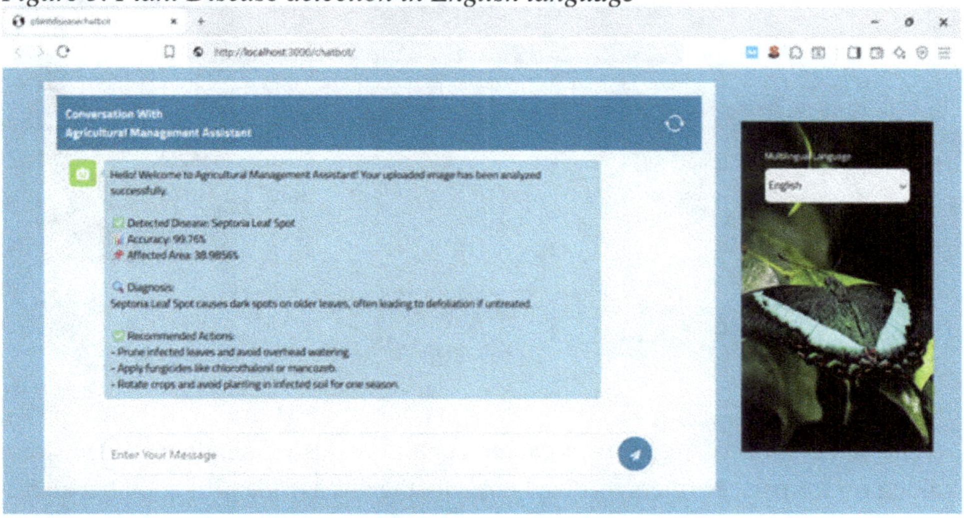

Figure 6. Plant Disease detection in Tamil language

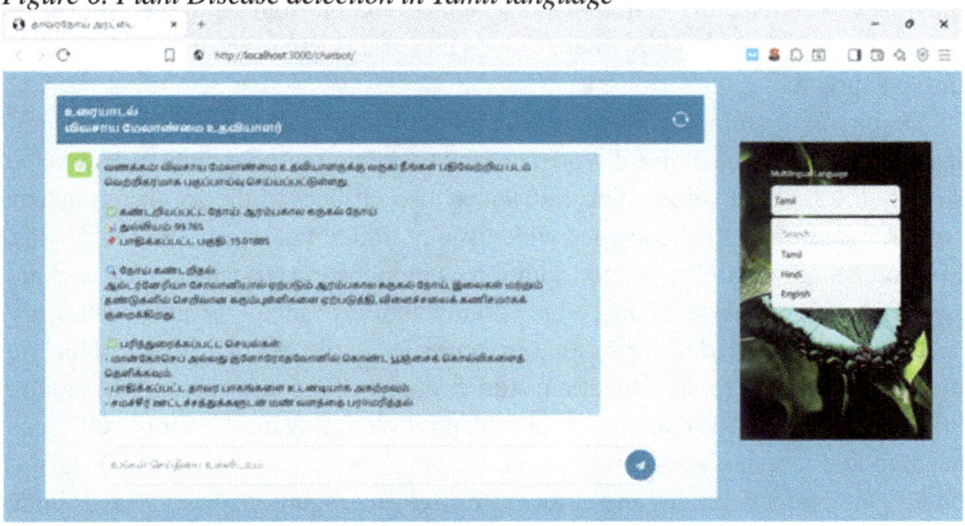

Figure 7. Plant Disease detection in Hindi language

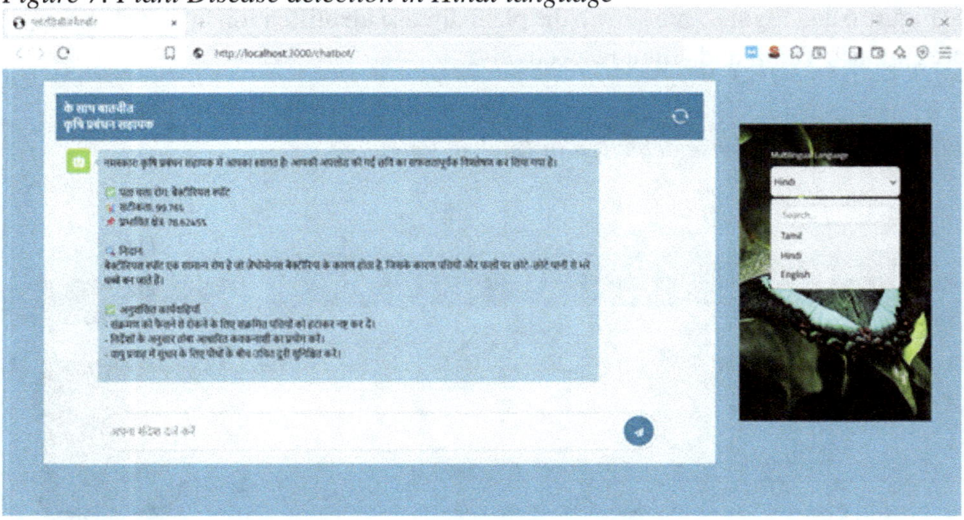

The integration of real-time weather conditions also strengthened decision-making for farmers. Farmers received not only the disease identification but also a forward-looking assessment of disease development probability based on the next 48–72 hours of environmental changes. This allowed timely preventive measures such as adjusting irrigation schedules, modifying canopy management, or applying mild prophylactic treatments before symptoms intensified. This shift from reactive diagnosis to anticipatory action marks a significant contribution to precision agriculture, especially in regions where sudden climatic fluctuations heavily influence disease spread.

Despite these strengths, the system did present limitations, particularly concerning dataset imbalance. Some diseases had fewer training samples, which resulted in slightly lower recall values. This imbalance also influenced the confusion matrix pattern: rare diseases were merged with visually similar but more common classes. Environmental variability created additional complications, since extreme weather scenarios—very heavy rainfall, abrupt temperature changes, or unexpected dry spells—sometimes led to forecasting inaccuracies in the weather model, which in turn affected disease risk estimation. Addressing such inconsistencies will require broader meteorological data sources and adaptive retraining mechanisms. Advanced augmentation methods such as rotation, flipping, brightness variation, and GAN-based synthetic generation can improve rare disease recognition. Adaptive retraining with broader meteorological datasets can further stabilize forecasts.

The multilingual chatbot played a crucial role in bridging the system's technical capabilities with farmer usability. By delivering results in English, Tamil, and

Hindi, the chatbot ensured that users from diverse linguistic backgrounds could understand the diagnosis, recommendations, and weather-based alerts. The natural language generation module transformed the technical outputs of the AI models into accessible guidance. For example, when a leaf blight case was detected, the chatbot produced responses such as:

> **English:** "The leaf image shows signs of blight. Humidity levels this week may increase its spread. Consider starting preventive spraying within the next two days."
> **Tamil:** "இலைப் படத்தில் பிளைட் நோய் அறிகுறிகள் தென்படுகின்றன. இந்த வார ஈரப்பதம் நோய் பரவலை அதிகரிக்கலாம். இரண்டு நாட்களுக்குள் தடுப்பு தெளிப்பு செய்ய பரிந்துரைக்கப்படுகிறது."
> **Hindi:** "पत्ते की छवि में ब्लाइट के लक्षण दिखाई दे रहे हैं। इस सप्ताह की नमी इसकी वृद्धि बढ़ा सकती है। अगले दो दिनों में रोकथाम स्प्रे करना उचित होगा।"

These examples illustrate how the chatbot translated technical insights into practical instructions, maintaining accuracy while adapting the phrasing for regional comprehension. The multilingual interface also improved adoption among farmers who were previously hesitant to use digital systems due to language barriers. Field testing indicated that farmers preferred the concise, conversational style of the chatbot over lengthy text reports, leading to quicker understanding and action.

In interpreting the overall significance of these results, the system demonstrates a meaningful advancement for modern agriculture. Traditional disease detection methods largely rely on manual inspection, which is subjective, time-consuming, and limited by human expertise. In contrast, the current system identifies diseases more consistently and at earlier stages, reducing the risk of crop loss. Combining image-based diagnosis with weather-driven forecasting effectively transforms disease management from reactive treatment to preventative planning, a critical shift for improving crop yield stability under unpredictable climate conditions.

Furthermore, the integration of multilingual conversational support significantly enhances the system's real-world impact. Farmers not only receive accurate predictions but also understand how to act on them, which ultimately determines the effectiveness of any technological intervention. Compared with simpler machine learning models or rule-based advisory systems, the combined CNN–weather–chatbot framework provides richer insights, higher adaptability, and more user-centered delivery.

Overall, the results indicate that the system can substantially improve precision farming by enabling timely disease detection, informed decision-making, and accessible communication. While certain limitations remain—such as dataset imbalance and occasional forecasting inconsistencies—the system represents a viable foundation for future scale-up, model enhancement, and integration with broader agricultural management tools.

This describes implementation results for plant disease detection with MATLAB Simulation integrated with a conversational chatbot through real-time plant images. The plant disease detection models were trained over 1500 cloud based datasets with a high accuracy of 99.76%. The chatbot responses were made to deliver organic treatments and support to enhance the advanced agricultural practices.

CONCLUSION

Ingenious AI-powered technology that aims to transform precision agricultural methods. The use of artificial intelligence alters how farmers interact with their crops and manage their land. Key features include illness diagnosis, weather predictions, and AI-powered chatbot help. Farmers may use powerful computer vision technology to reliably identify crop illnesses by uploading photographs, while AI-powered weather predictions give critical insights for informed decision-making. The AI chatbot is a user-friendly resource for farmers seeking help on a variety of agricultural topics.

Overall, our study intends to increase agricultural output, maximize resource usage, and provide farmers with cutting-edge AI tools, driving the agricultural industry into a technologically sophisticated era. Crop diseases may now be quickly and accurately recognized using modern computer vision technology, allowing for pre-emptive steps to protect quality and production. Weather prediction systems give farmers important information about the weather, enabling them to adjust crop care practices to climatic variations.

Additionally, the intelligent AI chatbot acts as a knowledgeable guide, providing customized guidance on a huge range of agricultural research, including crop cultivation methods and seed selection. The ultimate goal of this study is to boost agricultural output, improve resource usage, and provide farmers equal access to cutting-edge AI technologies. Finally, our intention is to provide farmers with the needed tools and information they need to negotiate the risk of contemporary agriculture, assuring their long-term success and profitability in an ever-changing landscape.

In conclusion, the implementation of clever AI-powered technologies into precision agriculture is a watershed moment in farming operations, ushering in a new era of efficiency and production. Using artificial intelligence, farmers can now traverse the complexities of crop management with unparalleled accuracy and understanding. Farmers now have access to a full set of tools for optimizing their agricultural operations, including sickness detection, weather predictions, and AI chatbot support. As we continue to develop and perfect these technologies, our collaborative objective is to provide farmers with the needed resources and data they need to flourish in a fast changing agricultural world. We can pave the road for a healthy and successful future for agriculture by collaborating and continuing to improve AI-driven solutions, assuring farmers' sustained success and resilience throughout the world.

In addition to these capabilities, the AI chatbot interface plays a vital role in bridging the knowledge gap between research-based agricultural insights and on-ground farming practices. Developed using Natural Language Processing (NLP) and contextual understanding algorithms, the chatbot offers personalized advice on soil management, seed selection, pest control, irrigation scheduling, and organic farming methods. It is multilingual and user-friendly, enabling farmers from different linguistic and regional backgrounds to interact effortlessly and gain practical guidance. The chatbot also provides real-time responses, connects farmers with verified agricultural databases, and ensures that critical information is available even in remote areas with limited access to expert support.

The ultimate objective of this study is to foster sustainable agricultural growth by providing equal access to modern AI-driven technologies for farmers across all scales—small, medium, and large. By merging automation with agricultural intelligence, farmers can make more decisions that are informed, reduce input waste, and achieve higher profitability. Furthermore, this system encourages data-driven planning, reducing dependency on guesswork and manual observation, thereby improving consistency in agricultural outcomes.

In conclusion, the integration of AI-powered solutions into precision agriculture marks a revolutionary milestone in the evolution of modern farming systems. This paradigm shift is redefining how agricultural challenges are addressed—moving from reactive methods to proactive and predictive intelligence. Farmers can now navigate the complexities of crop management with greater confidence, supported by a complete ecosystem of AI-enabled tools such as disease detection, predictive weather modeling, and intelligent chatbot communication.

REFERENCES

Ahmad, A., Saraswat, D., & El Gamal, A. (2023). A survey on using deep learning techniques for plant disease diagnosis and recommendations for development of appropriate tools. *Smart Agricultural Technology*, *3*(1), 100083. DOI: 10.1016/j.atech.2022.100083

Ahmed, I., & Yadav, P. K. (2023). Plant disease detection using machine learning approaches. *Expert Systems: International Journal of Knowledge Engineering and Neural Networks*, *40*(5), e13136. DOI: 10.1111/exsy.13136

Attri, I., Awasthi, L. K., & Sharma, T. P. (2024). Machine learning in agriculture: A review of crop management applications. *Multimedia Tools and Applications*, *83*(5), 12875–12915. DOI: 10.1007/s11042-023-16105-2

Balami, T. I. U., Okereke, O. C., Anene, E., & Aliyu, H. (2025). AI-Based Optimal Energy Harvesting to Reduce Electromagnetic Radiation from GSM and WiFi at ATBU Yalwa Campus. *International Journal of Data Informatics and Intelligent Computing*, *4*(4), 41–51. DOI: 10.59461/ijdiic.v4i4.234

Demilie, W. B. (2024). Plant disease detection and classification techniques: A comparative study of the performances. *Journal of Big Data*, *11*(1), 5–12. DOI: 10.1186/s40537-023-00863-9

Harakannanavar, S. S., Rudagi, J. M., Puranikmath, V. I., Siddiqua, A., & Pramodhini, R. (2022). Plant leaf disease detection using computer vision and machine learning algorithms. *Global Transitions Proceedings*, *3*(1), 305–310. DOI: 10.1016/j.gltp.2022.03.016

Huo, L., Lindberg, E., Bohlin, J., & Persson, H. J. (2023). Assessing the detectability of European spruce bark beetle green attack in multispectral drone images with high spatial-and temporal resolutions. *Remote Sensing of Environment*, *287*(1), 113484. DOI: 10.1016/j.rse.2023.113484

Jackulin, C., & Murugavalli, S. (2022). A comprehensive review on detection of plant disease using machine learning and deep learning approaches. *Measurement. Sensors*, *24*(5), 100441. DOI: 10.1016/j.measen.2022.100441

Kolluri, J., Dash, S. K., & Das, R. (2024). Plant Disease Identification Based on Multimodal Learning. *International Journal of Intelligent Systems and Applications in Engineering*, *12*(15s), 634–643.

Kothari, S., Bagane, P., Mishra, M., Kulshrestha, S., Asrani, Y., & Maheswari, V. (2024). CropGuard: Empowering Agriculture with AI driven Plant Disease Detection Chatbot. *International Journal of Intelligent Systems and Applications in Engineering*, *12*(12s), 530–537.

Li, L., Zhang, S., & Wang, B. (2021). Plant disease detection and classification by deep learning—A review. *IEEE Access : Practical Innovations, Open Solutions*, *9*, 56683–56698. DOI: 10.1109/ACCESS.2021.3069646

Orchi, H., Sadik, M., & Khaldoun, M. (2021). On using artificial intelligence and the internet of things for crop disease detection: A contemporary survey. *Agriculture*, *12*(1), 9. DOI: 10.3390/agriculture12010009

Panchal, A. V., Patel, S. C., Bagyalakshmi, K., Kumar, P., Khan, I. R., & Soni, M. (2023). Image-based plant diseases detection using deep learning. *Materials Today: Proceedings*, *80*(1), 3500–3506. DOI: 10.1016/j.matpr.2021.07.281

Prasad, S. R., & Thyagaraju, G. S. (2024). Leaf analysis based early plant disease detection using Internet of Things, Machine Learning and Deep Learning: A comprehensive review. *Journal of Integrated Science and Technology*, *12*(2), 734–734.

Raman, R. K., Kumar, A., Sarkar, S., Yadav, A. K., Mukherjee, A., Meena, R. S., & Kumar, V. (2024). Reconnoitering Precision Agriculture and Resource Management: A Comprehensive Review from an Extension Standpoint on Artificial Intelligence and Machine Learning. *Indian Research Journal of Extension Education*, *24*(1), 220–235. DOI: 10.54986/irjee/2024/jan_mar/108-123

Renju, K., & Brunda, V. (2024). Optimizing Crop Yield Prediction through Multiple Models: An Ensemble Stacking Approach. *International Journal of Data Informatics and Intelligent Computing*, *3*(2), 52–58. DOI: 10.59461/ijdiic.v3i2.120

Sagar, S., Javed, M., & Doermann, D. S. (2023). Leaf-Based Plant Disease Detection and Explainable AI. *arXiv preprint arXiv,* 2404, 16833.

Sajitha, P., Andrushia, A. D., Anand, N., & Naser, M. Z. (2024). A Review on Machine Learning and Deep Learning Image-based Plant Disease Classification for Industrial Farming Systems. *Journal of Industrial Information Integration*, *38*, 100572. DOI: 10.1016/j.jii.2024.100572

Sarkar, C., Gupta, D., Gupta, U., & Hazarika, B. B. (2023). Leaf disease detection using machine learning and deep learning: Review and challenges. *Applied Soft Computing*, *145*, 110534. DOI: 10.1016/j.asoc.2023.110534

Sharma, R., Singh, A., Jhanjhi, N. Z., Masud, M., Jaha, E. S., & Verma, S. (2022). Plant Disease Diagnosis and Image Classification Using Deep Learning. *Computers, Materials & Continua*, *71*(2), 225–236. DOI: 10.32604/cmc.2022.020017

Sivakumar, S. A., Shankar, B. M., Anuradha, B., Karan, K. A., Karthik, A., Karthik, R., & Kumar, J. R. R. (2023). Artificial Intelligence based Agricultural Chatbot and Virtual Assistant for Delivery of Harvested Crops. *International Journal of Intelligent Systems and Applications in Engineering*, *11*(8s), 576–583.

Ullah, R., Ali, W., & Ghanni, U. (2025). Deep Reinforcement Learning for Robust USVs Navigation in Diverse Environmental Scenarios. *International Journal of Data Informatics and Intelligent Computing*, *4*(4), 1–10. DOI: 10.59461/ijdiic.v4i4.219

Upadhyay, S. K., & Kumar, A. (2022). A novel approach for rice plant diseases classification with deep convolutional neural network. *International Journal of Information Technology : an Official Journal of Bharati Vidyapeeth's Institute of Computer Applications and Management*, *14*(1), 185–199. DOI: 10.1007/s41870-021-00817-5

Chapter 3
Identification of Pneumonia in Chest X-Ray Images Using Generative and Explainable AI Methods

G. Appasami
http://orcid.org/0000-0002-4186-3166
National Institute of Technology, Tiruchirappalli, India

Nickolas Savarimuthu
http://orcid.org/0000-0002-0703-3839
National Institute of Technology, Tiruchirappalli, India

Bakiya Kannan
http://orcid.org/0009-0003-3381-6815
National Institute of Technology, Tiruchirappalli, India

ABSTRACT

Pneumonia remains a significant global health concern, particularly in regions with limited access to specialized medical expertise. Chest X-ray imaging is widely used for diagnosis; however, interpretation is subjective and dependent on experienced radiologists. This chapter presents a deep learning-based framework for automated pneumonia detection from chest X-ray images, focusing on accuracy and interpretability. To address class imbalance and improve performance, traditional data augmentation is integrated with synthetic image generation using an Auxiliary Classifier Generative Adversarial Network (ACGAN), enhancing dataset diversity.

DOI: 10.4018/979-8-2600-2701-1.ch003

Thirty-two convolutional neural network models from Keras Applications, including EfficientNet, ResNet, DenseNet, and MobileNet, are evaluated under three experimental scenarios. Leading models such as EfficientNetB1 and MobileNet achieve accuracies above 93%. Explainable AI techniques, including Grad-CAM, SHAP, and LIME, highlight diagnostic regions, strengthening transparency, generalization, and clinical trust in AI-driven healthcare systems.

1. INTRODUCTION

Pneumonia is a life-threatening respiratory disease that occurs when lung infections cause inflammation and fluid buildup. This condition continues to be an important health issue worldwide, especially for young people, older age groups, and vulnerable populations. Early diagnosis and detection are key to effective management and treatment, leading to improved health outcomes. One method used to diagnose the illness includes imaging techniques, such as X-rays, which are a valuable diagnostic tool. Nevertheless, diagnoses may contain errors because they rely on human interpretation (Appasami G et al., 2022). (Dardouri, 2025; Appasami G et al., 2022).

To tackle such problems, extensive research has been conducted on deep learning (DL) and artificial intelligence (AI) to enable automated detection of pneumonia. Such techniques provide highly accurate, scalable solutions for analyzing chest X-ray images with precision and speed. Unfortunately, even with all the advantages of DL and AI, their lack of transparency hinders their implementation in practice (Siddiqui, A.A et al., 2025; Sivanantham, S et al., 2025).

New innovations in Explainable Artificial Intelligence (XAI) and generative models provide potential solutions to this problem. The use of XAI techniques such as Grad-CAM, LIME, SHAP, and Integrated Gradients will help provide model transparency, whereas GAN models will enhance data generation. This work integrates both approaches to improve pneumonia classification while maintaining explainability, addressing the clinical need for interpretable and robust AI systems (Kinger. S et al., 2025; Yixin Wang et al., 2023).

1.1 Clinical Context and Problem Definition

In clinical practice, the diagnosis of pneumonia is based on a combination of patient symptoms and physical examination, along with radiological images. Patients with pneumonia may present with fever, cough, and breathing difficulties. These patients are usually advised to undergo chest X-ray imaging for the primary diagnosis. Radiologists analyze the images acquired during the X-ray to identify abnormalities, such as opacities, consolidations, and infiltrations that indicate the presence of pneumonia.

However, diagnosing pneumonia poses several challenges and limitations. The interpretation of chest X-ray images relies on the radiologist's skills. There may be inconsistent diagnoses due to the radiologist's interpretation of the X-ray images. There is a scarcity of qualified radiologists in many healthcare facilities, particularly in resource-limited and rural regions, which may result in delayed and inconsistent diagnoses of the disease. At an early stage of pneumonia, chest X-ray findings can be complex.

Although deep learning algorithms have achieved successful results in automating pneumonia detection, they still face challenges when applied in practical clinical settings for two main reasons. Firstly, most of these models have been found to be 'black box' models, lacking transparency and interpretability. Secondly, access to diverse and balanced medical image datasets is scarce, which affects the generalization and robustness of the models.

The proposed framework addresses these limitations by employing convolutional neural networks and generative and explainable AI in the clinical diagnosis setting. Specifically, applying the Auxiliary Classifier Generative Adversarial Network (ACGAN) would enhance dataset diversity and address class imbalance. Additionally, by employing explainable AI techniques such as Grad-CAM, SHAP, and LIME, the decision-making process can be visualized, highlighting important areas of the chest x-ray image.

The proposed approach has been shown to be a decision-support system that enables accurate, consistent pneumonia diagnosis in patients, thereby reducing radiologists' workload and enhancing their trust in AI-assisted healthcare environments.

This chapter aligns with the book's main theme by examining the major challenges in applying artificial intelligence to healthcare. In addition, this chapter provides insight into some recent trends in artificial intelligence, such as deep learning, explainable artificial intelligence, and generative modeling that can be used to build reliable diagnostic tools.

The chapter has been split into six sub-sections. Subsection 1 provides information on the problem statement, research objectives, and the research scope. Subsection 2 provides a review of related work on pneumonia detection, deep learning models, and XAI. Subsection 3 discusses the dataset, the models, and the techniques employed, including ACGAN. Subsection 4 highlights the results obtained through various models. Subsection 5 gives an account of how the model's predictions have been explained using XAI approaches. Subsection 6 gives conclusions and future research directions.

2. BACKGROUND AND LITERATURE REVIEW

The rising number of pneumonia cases has prompted numerous attempts to leverage deep learning for pneumonia diagnosis on chest X-rays. The effectiveness of traditional Convolutional Neural Networks (CNNs) has been demonstrated across various architectures, such as DenseNet121, ResNet, and EfficientNet (Jalal Rabbah et al., 2025; Luo G et al., 2024). For example, Rabbah et al. developed a high-precision CNN model with gradient-based explainability to improve interpretability in the process of pneumonia diagnosis (Mohammed A. A. Al-qaness et al., 2024; Zahra Ebrahimi Jouibari et al., 2024).

Recognizing the need for transparency, researchers have developed XAI frameworks to interpret model predictions. Yazdani et al. suggested a deformable prototypical part network for detecting pediatric pneumonia and provided clinical interpretations through feature attributions (Elmira Yazdani et al., 2025; Appasami G et al., 2024). Kaushik et al. studied a deep learning approach based on graphs that incorporated radiology features with transformers, making the detection process much more interpretable (Kaushik .P et al., 2025; Sree Ganesh T.N et al., 2023). Similarly, Priyanka et al. implemented the PediaPulmoDx system using DenseNet121 and preprocessing techniques to improve pediatric classification performance (Priyanka R et al., 2025; Appasami et al., 2024).

Generative models, such as GANs, have been shown to be effective for data augmentation. Specifically, it has been shown that dual-domain explainability-driven augmentation can improve the detection of COVID-19 in chest x-ray images (Houda El Mohamadi et al., 2025; Ren H et al., 2021). Similarly, Prasath et al. designed a super-resolution generative model using a dual transformer architecture that enhanced pneumonia detection from images (Jerald Prasath G et al., 2025; Arnab Kumar Modal et al., 2022).

Several studies have also focused on addressing domain shift and adversarial robustness. Lee applied adversarial perturbations to CNNs and evaluated their impact using XAI methods to understand model vulnerabilities (Stephen B. Lee, 2025). Musa et al. employed supervised domain adaptation techniques to mitigate cross-population performance drops in pneumonia classification tasks (Musa .A et al., 2025; Y. H. Wu et al., 2021).

Explainable Vision Transformers (ViTs) are also gaining traction. Fu et al. introduced DAViT, a domain-adapted ViT with XAI integration, specifically for pneumonia detection (Michael Fu et al., 2025). Likewise, ViTs are used to efficiently identify pneumonia, underscoring the balance between performance and interpretability (Sukhendra Singh et al., 2024). These contributions highlight the evolving landscape where hybrid models combine generative augmentation, robust classification, and explainability to meet clinical demands.

The current research builds on this foundation by developing a holistic approach that combines generative models and data augmentation techniques with interpretability methods from XAI for pneumonia diagnosis. Experiments conducted during the research will enable the development of a clinically useful system.

However, the principal research problem is how to develop the best possible deep learning model for detecting pneumonia in chest x-ray images. While most previous studies have presented highly accurate models, the vast majority do not consider two significant problems – namely, model non-interpretableness and imbalanced training datasets. The former refers to most machine learning algorithms operating as black boxes, depriving doctors of the opportunity to trust the model's output. On the other hand, small datasets may reduce a model's prediction power and accuracy. Fewer works use data augmentation techniques such as ACGAN, which is why this study aims to fill the existing research gap by applying both techniques and comparing different CNN models.

3. METHODOLOGY

In this pneumonia classification problem, a deep learning model is proposed to classify pneumonia from chest x-ray images, with major challenges including imbalanced data and limited transparency. Data preprocessing and augmentation are carried out using an Auxiliary Classifier Generative Adversarial Network (ACGAN) to create balanced datasets. Several CNN models, such as VGG and ResNet50, are tested to determine the best classifier. In addition, to increase transparency, several explainable AI models, such as Grad-CAM, SHAP, and LIME, are implemented to interpret the classifier. Finally, a comparative analysis will be conducted on classification accuracy and transparency to identify the best model.

3.1 Pneumonia Dataset

In this study, we have used the Chest X-ray Pneumonia dataset, available on Kaggle at the following link: https://www.kaggle.com/datasets/paultimothymooney/chest-xray-pneumonia. This is a popular benchmark dataset for binary classification of chest X-rays into two classes: NORMAL and PNEUMONIA. There are 5,800+ grayscale images. Among these images, the training dataset consists of 1,341 NORMAL images and 3,875 PNEUMONIA images. The testing data consist of 234 NORMAL images and 390 PNEUMONIA images. There are 8 images per class in the validation dataset. Both bacterial and viral cases are present in the PNEUMONIA category of this dataset (Elmira Yazdani et al., 2025).

Figure 1. Images from the normal and pneumonia classes from the original dataset

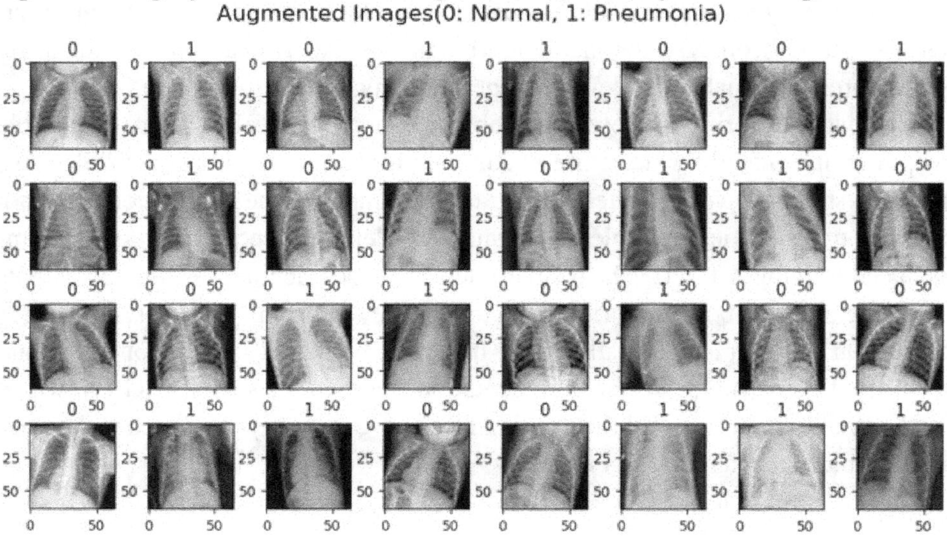

Nevertheless, the validation set used in this case is very small, with just 8 images per class, which is statistically insignificant for hyperparameter tuning and model selection. Such a small validation subset can lead to high variance in performance estimates and may not adequately represent the true data distribution, potentially affecting the stability and generalizability of the trained models. This limitation may result in suboptimal model selection and increase the risk of overfitting during training. To solve this problem, the validation set is primarily used for performance monitoring and tracking, while the final assessment is conducted on the test set. To improve robustness, future work should consider k-fold cross-validation, stratified sampling, or larger validation splits to ensure more reliable, statistically sound model evaluation.

Fig. 1 shows sample images from the original dataset, showing both normal and pneumonia patients. In total, there are 32 images from the training data. If an image is labeled 0, that means it is normal. Otherwise, if the image is labeled 1, then it is pneumonia. The visualization helps to differentiate between the two classes based on their distinct appearances. Typically, normal chest x-ray images have clear lungs, whereas pneumonia images may contain cloudy regions or opacities.

3.2 Traditional Data Augmentation

Traditionally augmented images, as shown in Fig. 2, are simple and efficient to generate. Figure 2 displays a set of 32 augmented chest X-ray images derived from the original training dataset using conventional data augmentation techniques.

Figure 2. Traditionally augmented images

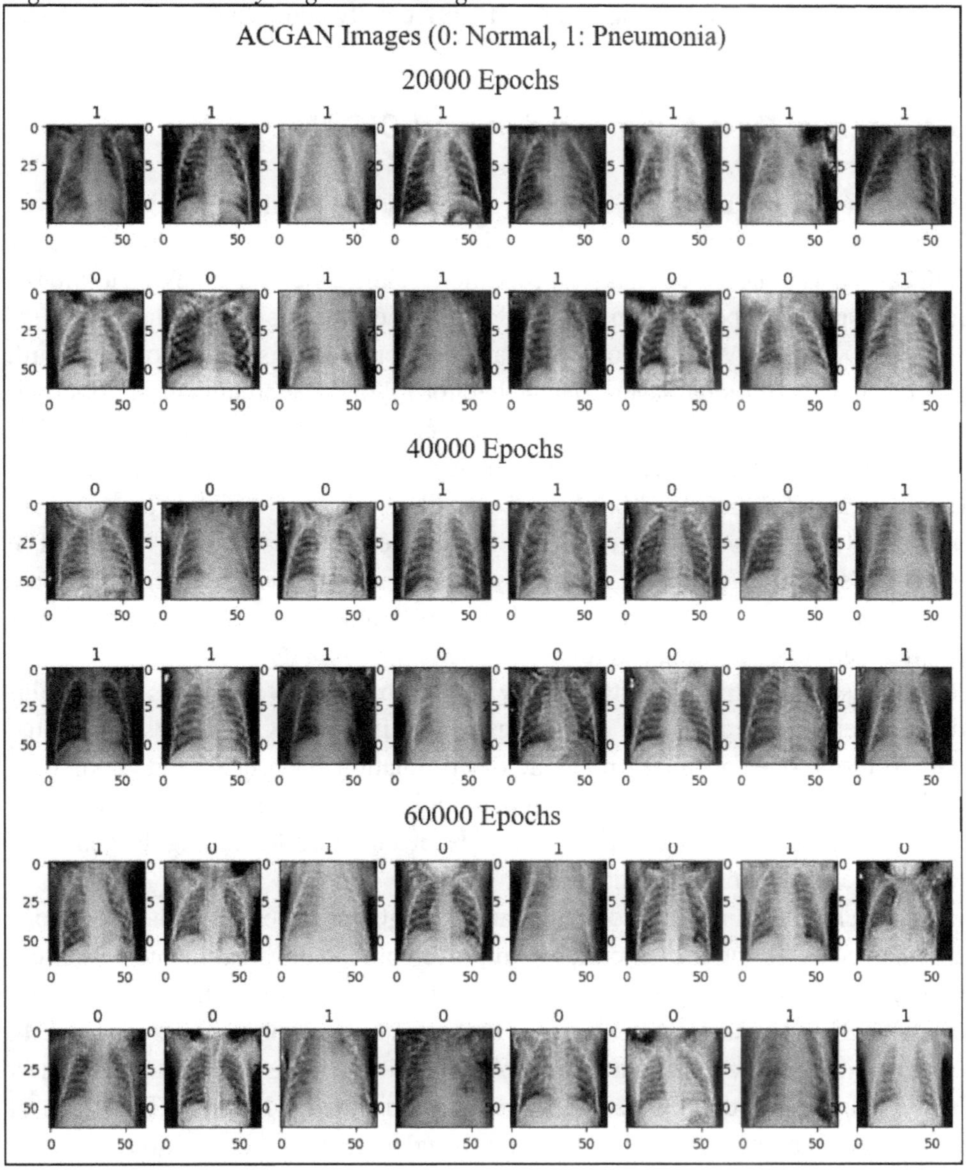

The augmentation was performed using TensorFlow's ImageDataGenerator, incorporating transformations such as random zoom (±10%), rotation (±15 degrees), shear, and fill mode adjustments. Horizontal flipping was selectively applied, while vertical flipping was disabled based on experimental requirements (El Mohamadi et al., 2025). Such transformations bring variation within the training dataset but without disturbing essential pathological features. This helps the model generalize and learn patterns well. The augmented dataset includes 2,924 Normal images (label 0) and 8,148 Pneumonia images (label 1), effectively addressing class imbalance and enhancing model performance.

3.3 Artificial Data Augmentation via AC-GAN

The Auxiliary Classifier Generative Adversarial Network (ACGAN) employed in the current research is based on the architecture of the Deep Convolutional GAN (DCGAN), with the added feature of conditional class generation, making it suitable for tasks such as supervised image synthesis in medical imaging applications.

Like DCGAN, ACGAN comprises a generator and a discriminator, both built from deep convolutional layers. The generator follows the architectural principles of DCGAN, including transposed convolutional layers for upsampling and ReLU activations, but differs by conditioning the input not only on a random noise vector (latent space of dimension 100) but also on class labels (Normal or Pneumonia). This enables the generation of class-specific synthetic images of size 64×64×3. The generator's architecture consists of fully connected and transposed convolutional layers with progressively decreasing filter sizes (from 256 to 32), along with Layer Normalization for training stability.

The discriminator, while structurally similar to DCGAN's in terms of convolutional layers and LeakyReLU activations, is modified in ACGAN to support dual output heads: one for binary real/fake discrimination (Dense(1)) and another for multi-class classification (Normal vs. Pneumonia). This auxiliary classification task allows the model to learn class-discriminative features while training the generator to produce class-consistent images.

In adversarial training, the discriminator's weights are fixed while the generator's are updated, enabling the generator to improve both the adversarial and classification losses. This combination of objectives makes ACGAN a highly useful variant of DCGAN in situations where data is scarce and class imbalance is an issue. In our experiments, we demonstrate ACGAN's ability to generate high-quality chest X-ray images using conditional class labels, as illustrated in Figure 3. The ACGAN was used to generate 1,187 synthetic images under the Normal condition and 3,749 under the Pneumonia condition. These generated images looked very similar to the original chest X-ray images in the training dataset.

Figure 3. Synthetic ACGAN Images

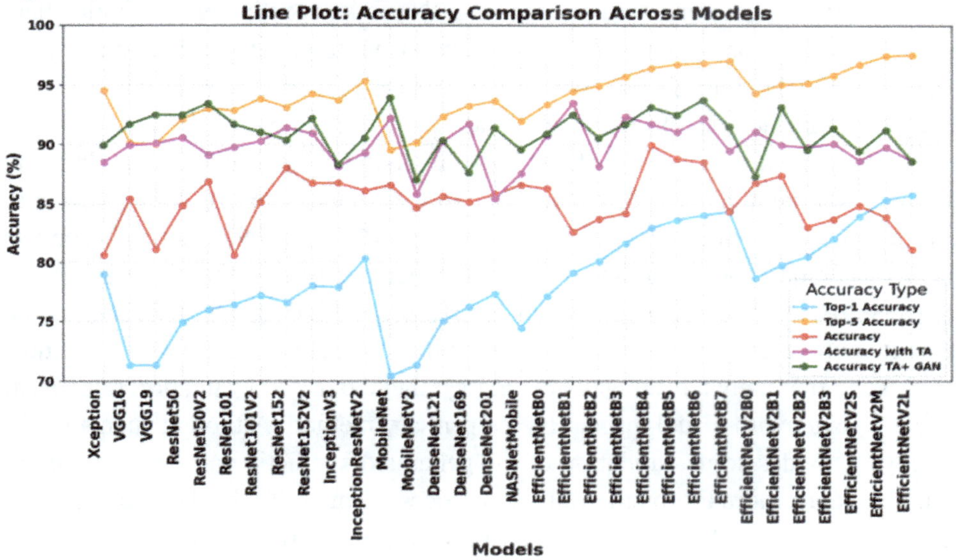

Fig. 3 shows the gradual development of the chest X-rays generated by the ACGAN model at various stages of training. The first row displays the initial 16 synthetic images generated after 20,000 epochs, where structural features are still under development and image quality is relatively coarse. The second row presents 16 samples after 40,000 epochs, showing improved anatomical clarity and more distinct representations of chest regions. Finally, the third row depicts the last 16 images generated after 60,000 epochs, which exhibit significantly enhanced visual quality and fidelity, closely resembling real chest X-ray images of the Normal (label 0) and Pneumonia (label 1) classes. A total of 64,000 epochs were run to synthesize GAN images. This progression demonstrates how prolonged adversarial training helps the generator learn finer details and class-specific characteristics, resulting in more realistic and diagnostically relevant synthetic images.

3.4 Evaluation of Synthetic Data Quality Using ACGAN

The Auxiliary Classifier Generative Adversarial Network (ACGAN) is an essential tool for handling class imbalance and the diversity of the training dataset. While synthetic data improves classification, it is also necessary to assess its quality.

Qualitatively, the generated synthetic chest X-ray images exhibit structural characteristics similar to those of real chest X-ray images. This is clearly shown in Fig. 3 below: the synthetic data generated during the initial training stages are blurred and lack recognizable anatomical structures. However, as training progresses, the images generated by the ACGAN model become clearer and more defined. Further, the synthetic images generated by the ACGAN model have better lung fields than before. It is also worth noting that the synthetic pneumonia images generated by the ACGAN model exhibit features similar to those of real pneumonia images. These manifestations include opacities and clouding.

Further, another factor considered is the diversity of the synthetic data. In using the ACGAN method, class labels are used to generate images; therefore, diversity can be achieved within both the NORMAL and PNEUMONIA classes. The use of this technique allows the dataset to be balanced and trains the classifier across a diverse range of variations, avoiding overfitting. Including synthetic data in the dataset improves robust feature learning, as demonstrated by the TA+GAN technique.

Despite the many advantages of using synthetic data, its evaluation remains at an early stage, with visual inspection the primary method. Although such a methodology provides some validation of the generated synthetic data, it is important to implement a more thorough evaluation process to quantify the data's quality and diversity. Metrics such as Fréchet Inception Distance (FID) and Structural Similarity Index (SSIM) may be considered in the future for such purposes.

Moreover, validating synthetic images in clinical settings must also be considered. Although the synthetic images are visually similar to real chest X-ray images, they should be clinically validated by radiologists or domain experts. This would be important to ensure that the synthetic images do not introduce any artifacts or misleading information that could affect the model's predictions.

Another key issue to address in light of the given scenario is the risks posed by the use of generative models. The generation of substandard images may introduce noise during the learning phase, thereby affecting the model's reliability.

In general, ACGAN appears to have a significant impact on the success of the data set. Nevertheless, a more systematic approach is needed to assess the reliability and efficacy of synthetic data in medicine.

4. RESULTS AND DISCUSSION

In this section, we assess 32 CNN architectures for pneumonia classification in chest X-rays using various augmentation methods. Our results show that data augmentation, when combined with synthetically generated images from ACGAN, improves classification performance and helps tackle class imbalance.

4.1 CNN Model Performance

In Table 1, a thorough analysis of the performance of 32 different CNN models is presented, which are available in Keras Applications (Shiva Prasad Koyyada et al., 2024). The analysis considers several important features, including model size, model depth, and total number of parameters, Top-1 and Top-5 classification accuracy, and inference time for both CPU and GPU execution. These include lightweight models like MobileNet and EfficientNetB0 to large deep CNNs like EfficientNetV2L and InceptionResNetV2.

The models differ significantly in complexity, with sizes ranging from 14 MB to 479 MB, allowing users to balance computational efficiency with predictive performance based on their specific requirements. Among the evaluated models, EfficientNetV2L (85.70%), EfficientNetV2M (85.30%), EfficientNetB7 (84.30%), and EfficientNetV2S (83.90%) achieved the highest Top-1 accuracy. Moreover, these models achieved very high Top-5 accuracy of 97.50%, 97.40%, 97.00%, and 96.70%, respectively. This analysis helps in selecting appropriate models based on performance needs and hardware constraints.

Table 1. Performance of Keras CNN Models

Sl. No.	Model	Size (MB)	Top-1 Accuracy	Top-5 Accuracy	Parameters	Depth	Time (ms) per inference step (CPU)	Time (ms) per inference step (GPU)
1	Xception	88	79.00%	94.50%	22.9M	81	109.4	8.1
2	VGG16	528	71.30%	90.10%	138.4M	16	69.5	4.2
3	VGG19	549	71.30%	90.00%	143.7M	19	84.8	4.4
4	ResNet50	98	74.90%	92.10%	25.6M	107	58.2	4.6
5	ResNet50V2	98	76.00%	93.00%	25.6M	103	45.6	4.4
6	ResNet101	171	76.40%	92.80%	44.7M	209	89.6	5.2
7	ResNet101V2	171	77.20%	93.80%	44.7M	205	72.7	5.4
8	ResNet152	232	76.60%	93.10%	60.4M	311	127.4	6.5
9	ResNet152V2	232	78.00%	94.20%	60.4M	307	107.5	6.6
10	InceptionV3	92	77.90%	93.70%	23.9M	189	42.2	6.9
11	InceptionResNetV2	215	80.30%	95.30%	55.9M	449	130.2	10
12	MobileNet	16	70.40%	89.50%	4.3M	55	22.6	3.4
13	MobileNetV2	14	71.30%	90.10%	3.5M	105	25.9	3.8
14	DenseNet121	33	75.00%	92.30%	8.1M	242	77.1	5.4

continued on following page

Table 1. Continued

Sl. No.	Model	Size (MB)	Top-1 Accuracy	Top-5 Accuracy	Parameters	Depth	Time (ms) per inference step (CPU)	Time (ms) per inference step (GPU)
15	DenseNet169	57	76.20%	93.20%	14.3M	338	96.4	6.3
16	DenseNet201	80	77.30%	93.60%	20.2M	402	127.2	6.7
17	NASNetMobile	23	74.40%	91.90%	5.3M	389	27	6.7
18	EfficientNetB0	29	77.10%	93.30%	5.3M	132	46	4.9
19	EfficientNetB1	31	79.10%	94.40%	7.9M	186	60.2	5.6
20	EfficientNetB2	36	80.10%	94.90%	9.2M	186	80.8	6.5
21	EfficientNetB3	48	81.60%	95.70%	12.3M	210	140	8.8
22	EfficientNetB4	75	82.90%	96.40%	19.5M	258	308.3	15.1
23	EfficientNetB5	118	83.60%	96.70%	30.6M	312	579.2	25.3
24	EfficientNetB6	166	84.00%	96.80%	43.3M	360	958.1	40.4
25	EfficientNetB7	256	84.30%	97.00%	66.7M	438	1578.9	61.6
26	EfficientNetV2B0	29	78.70%	94.30%	7.2M	NA	NA	NA
27	EfficientNetV2B1	34	79.80%	95.00%	8.2M	NA	NA	NA
28	EfficientNetV2B2	42	80.50%	95.10%	10.2M	NA	NA	NA
29	EfficientNetV2B3	59	82.00%	95.80%	14.5M	NA	NA	NA
30	EfficientNetV2S	88	83.90%	96.70%	21.6M	NA	NA	NA
31	EfficientNetV2M	220	85.30%	97.40%	54.4M	NA	NA	NA
32	EfficientNetV2L	479	85.70%	97.50%	119.0M	NA	NA	NA

Table 2 evaluates the same set of models on the Chest X-ray Pneumonia dataset without applying data augmentation. Performance metrics include accuracy, macro and weighted precision, recall, and F1-score. EfficientNetB4 achieves the highest accuracy at 89.90%, showing balanced results across all metrics. It is followed closely by EfficientNetB5 and ResNet152, both of which also demonstrate strong performance in identifying pneumonia from raw chest X-ray images.

Table 2. Performance metrics Without Augmentation

Sl. No.	CNN Model	Accuracy	Macro Average Precision	Macro Average Recall	Macro Average F1-Score	Weighted Average Precision	Weighted Average Recall	Weighted Average F1-score
1	Xception	0.8061	0.8639	0.7457	0.7626	0.8400	0.8061	0.7880
2	VGG16	0.8542	0.8835	0.8132	0.8315	0.8683	0.8542	0.8469
3	VGG19	0.8109	0.8699	0.7513	0.7689	0.8454	0.8109	0.7935
4	ResNet50	0.8478	0.8751	0.8064	0.8241	0.8610	0.8478	0.8402
5	ResNet50V2	0.8686	0.9034	0.8282	0.8479	0.8856	0.8686	0.8619
6	ResNet101	0.8061	0.8578	0.7474	0.7642	0.8360	0.8061	0.7890
7	ResNet101V2	0.8510	0.8754	0.8115	0.8287	0.8624	0.8510	0.8441
8	ResNet152	0.8798	0.8850	0.8568	0.8674	0.8814	0.8798	0.8775
9	ResNet152V2	0.8670	0.8850	0.8338	0.8494	0.8746	0.8670	0.8623
10	InceptionV3	0.8670	0.8834	0.8346	0.8498	0.8738	0.8670	0.8625
11	InceptionResNetV2	0.8606	0.8726	0.8295	0.8433	0.8653	0.8606	0.8563
12	MobileNet	0.8654	0.8950	0.8265	0.8451	0.8794	0.8654	0.8591
13	MobileNetV2	0.8462	0.8875	0.7991	0.8189	0.8678	0.8462	0.8365
14	DenseNet121	0.8558	0.8806	0.8171	0.8344	0.8673	0.8558	0.8493
15	DenseNet169	0.8510	0.8857	0.8073	0.8263	0.8685	0.8510	0.8427
16	DenseNet201	0.8574	0.8856	0.8175	0.8356	0.8708	0.8574	0.8506
17	NASNetMobile	0.8654	0.8855	0.8308	0.8471	0.8741	0.8654	0.8603
18	EfficientNetB0	0.8622	0.8767	0.8299	0.8446	0.8681	0.8622	0.8577
19	EfficientNetB1	0.8253	0.8646	0.7748	0.7929	0.8465	0.8253	0.8134
20	EfficientNetB2	0.8365	0.8595	0.7949	0.8114	0.8476	0.8365	0.8286
21	EfficientNetB3	0.8413	0.8928	0.7902	0.8107	0.8696	0.8413	0.8298
22	EfficientNetB4	0.8990	0.9157	0.8722	0.8871	0.9053	0.8990	0.8963
23	EfficientNetB5	0.8878	0.9016	0.8607	0.8747	0.8929	0.8878	0.8848
24	EfficientNetB6	0.8846	0.9024	0.8547	0.8702	0.8917	0.8846	0.8810
25	EfficientNetB7	0.8429	0.8761	0.7983	0.8167	0.8597	0.8429	0.8341
26	EfficientNetV2B0	0.8670	0.8884	0.8321	0.8487	0.8764	0.8670	0.8618
27	EfficientNetV2B1	0.8734	0.9002	0.8372	0.8552	0.8856	0.8734	0.8681
28	EfficientNetV2B2	0.8301	0.8701	0.7803	0.7989	0.8516	0.8301	0.8187
29	EfficientNetV2B3	0.8365	0.8719	0.7897	0.8082	0.8549	0.8365	0.8266
30	EfficientNetV2S	0.8478	0.8793	0.8047	0.8231	0.8634	0.8478	0.8396
31	EfficientNetV2M	0.8381	0.8524	0.8013	0.8159	0.8444	0.8381	0.8319
32	EfficientNetV2L	0.8109	0.8409	0.7607	0.7768	0.8268	0.8109	0.7986

Table 3 examines the effect of traditional data augmentation on model performance using the same dataset. Notable improvements in classification accuracy are observed, with EfficientNetB1 (93.43%), MobileNet (92.15%), EfficientNetB3 (92.31%), and DenseNet169/EfficientNetB4 (91.67%) achieving the highest scores. These models also maintain consistent macro and weighted scores, suggesting robust performance across different classes.

Table 3. Performance metrics with traditional Augmentation

Sl. No.	CNN Model	Accuracy	Macro Average Precision	Macro Average Recall	Macro Average F1-Score	Weighted Average Precision	Weighted Average Recall	Weighted Average F1-score
1	Xception	0.8846	0.8858	0.8658	0.8739	0.8849	0.8846	0.8831
2	VGG16	0.8990	0.8949	0.8885	0.8914	0.8986	0.8990	0.8986
3	VGG19	0.9006	0.9097	0.8786	0.8903	0.9035	0.9006	0.8987
4	ResNet50	0.9054	0.8958	0.9081	0.9008	0.9090	0.9054	0.9062
5	ResNet50V2	0.8910	0.8853	0.8812	0.8832	0.8906	0.8910	0.8907
6	ResNet101	0.8974	0.8893	0.8932	0.8911	0.8981	0.8974	0.8977
7	ResNet101V2	0.9022	0.8971	0.8936	0.8953	0.9019	0.9022	0.9020
8	ResNet152	0.9135	0.9109	0.9034	0.9069	0.9132	0.9135	0.9131
9	ResNet152V2	0.9087	0.9123	0.8919	0.9003	0.9095	0.9087	0.9075
10	InceptionV3	0.8814	0.8731	0.8744	0.8737	0.8816	0.8814	0.8815
11	InceptionResNetV2	0.8926	0.8986	0.8714	0.8818	0.8944	0.8926	0.8907
12	MobileNet	0.9215	0.9291	0.9038	0.9139	0.9235	0.9215	0.9203
13	MobileNetV2	0.8574	0.8943	0.8141	0.8338	0.8760	0.8574	0.8494
14	DenseNet121	0.9022	0.8965	0.8944	0.8955	0.9020	0.9022	0.9021
15	DenseNet169	0.9167	0.9152	0.9060	0.9102	0.9165	0.9167	0.9162
16	DenseNet201	0.8542	0.8835	0.8132	0.8315	0.8683	0.8542	0.8469
17	NASNetMobile	0.8750	0.8680	0.8641	0.8660	0.8745	0.8750	0.8747
18	EfficientNetB0	0.9071	0.8999	0.9026	0.9012	0.9074	0.9071	0.9072
19	EfficientNetB1	0.9343	0.9285	0.9321	0.9302	0.9347	0.9343	0.9344
20	EfficientNetB2	0.8814	0.8899	0.8564	0.8684	0.8843	0.8814	0.8788
21	EfficientNetB3	0.9231	0.9206	0.9145	0.9174	0.9228	0.9231	0.9228
22	EfficientNetB4	0.9167	0.9152	0.9060	0.9102	0.9165	0.9167	0.9162
23	EfficientNetB5	0.9103	0.9015	0.9103	0.9054	0.9122	0.9103	0.9107
24	EfficientNetB6	0.9215	0.9185	0.9132	0.9157	0.9212	0.9215	0.9212
25	EfficientNetB7	0.8942	0.8977	0.8752	0.8842	0.8951	0.8942	0.8927

continued on following page

Table 3. Continued

Sl. No.	CNN Model	Accuracy	Macro Average Precision	Macro Average Recall	Macro Average F1-Score	Weighted Average Precision	Weighted Average Recall	Weighted Average F1-score
26	EfficientNetV2B0	0.9103	0.9266	0.8855	0.9000	0.9162	0.9103	0.9080
27	EfficientNetV2B1	0.8990	0.8902	0.8970	0.8933	0.9005	0.8990	0.8995
28	EfficientNetV2B2	0.8974	0.8874	0.9009	0.8926	0.9019	0.8974	0.8983
29	EfficientNetV2B3	0.9006	0.8940	0.8940	0.8940	0.9006	0.9006	0.9006
30	EfficientNetV2S	0.8862	0.8773	0.8816	0.8793	0.8871	0.8862	0.8865
31	EfficientNetV2M	0.8974	0.8965	0.8829	0.8888	0.8973	0.8974	0.8965
32	EfficientNetV2L	0.8862	0.8810	0.8748	0.8777	0.8857	0.8862	0.8858

Table 4 extends the analysis by integrating ACGAN-based data augmentation alongside traditional methods. This approach enhances data diversity, resulting in additional performance gains in pneumonia classification. MobileNet (93.91%), EfficientNetB6 (93.75%), EfficientNetB1 (92.47%), and ResNet50V2 (93.43%) are among the top-performing models, showing notable improvements in both accuracy and F1-score.

Table 4. Performance metrics with traditional Augmentation and ACGAN

Sl. No	CNN Model	Accuracy	Macro Average Precision	Macro Average Recall	Macro Average F1-Score	Weighted Average Precision	Weighted Average Recall	Weighted Average F1-score
1	Xception	0.8990	0.8949	0.8885	0.8914	0.8986	0.8990	0.8986
2	VGG16	0.9167	0.9268	0.8966	0.9082	0.9197	0.9167	0.9151
3	VGG19	0.9247	0.9243	0.9141	0.9187	0.9246	0.9247	0.9242
4	ResNet50	0.9247	0.9235	0.9150	0.9189	0.9245	0.9247	0.9243
5	ResNet50V2	0.9343	0.9358	0.9235	0.9290	0.9345	0.9343	0.9338
6	ResNet101	0.9167	0.9197	0.9017	0.9093	0.9173	0.9167	0.9158
7	ResNet101V2	0.9103	0.9221	0.8880	0.9007	0.9141	0.9103	0.9084
8	ResNet152	0.9038	0.9075	0.8863	0.8949	0.9047	0.9038	0.9026
9	ResNet152V2	0.9215	0.9256	0.9064	0.9144	0.9224	0.9215	0.9206
10	InceptionV3	0.8830	0.8795	0.8688	0.8735	0.8824	0.8830	0.8822
11	InceptionResNetV2	0.9054	0.9033	0.8936	0.8980	0.9051	0.9054	0.9049
12	MobileNet	0.9391	0.9388	0.9308	0.9345	0.9391	0.9391	0.9388
13	MobileNetV2	0.8702	0.9022	0.8312	0.8504	0.8855	0.8702	0.8640

continued on following page

Table 4. Continued

Sl. No	CNN Model	Accuracy	Macro Average Precision	Macro Average Recall	Macro Average F1-Score	Weighted Average Precision	Weighted Average Recall	Weighted Average F1-score
14	DenseNet121	0.9038	0.9054	0.8880	0.8953	0.9042	0.9038	0.9028
15	DenseNet169	0.8766	0.8935	0.8457	0.8610	0.8834	0.8766	0.8726
16	DenseNet201	0.9135	0.9152	0.8991	0.9060	0.9138	0.9135	0.9126
17	NASNetMobile	0.8958	0.9074	0.8714	0.8843	0.8998	0.8958	0.8934
18	EfficientNetB0	0.9087	0.9085	0.8953	0.9010	0.9086	0.9087	0.9079
19	EfficientNetB1	0.9247	0.9327	0.9073	0.9174	0.9269	0.9247	0.9235
20	EfficientNetB2	0.9054	0.9146	0.8842	0.8957	0.9083	0.9054	0.9037
21	EfficientNetB3	0.9167	0.9282	0.8957	0.9080	0.9203	0.9167	0.9150
22	EfficientNetB4	0.9311	0.9268	0.9261	0.9264	0.9310	0.9311	0.9311
23	EfficientNetB5	0.9247	0.9252	0.9132	0.9186	0.9248	0.9247	0.9241
24	EfficientNetB6	0.9375	0.9393	0.9269	0.9324	0.9378	0.9375	0.9371
25	EfficientNetB7	0.9151	0.9256	0.8944	0.9063	0.9183	0.9151	0.9135
26	EfficientNetV2B0	0.8734	0.9042	0.8355	0.8545	0.8879	0.8734	0.8676
27	EfficientNetV2B1	0.9311	0.9305	0.9218	0.9258	0.9310	0.9311	0.9307
28	EfficientNetV2B2	0.8958	0.9135	0.8679	0.8832	0.9026	0.8958	0.8928
29	EfficientNetV2B3	0.9135	0.9095	0.9051	0.9072	0.9132	0.9135	0.9132
30	EfficientNetV2S	0.8942	0.8966	0.8761	0.8844	0.8948	0.8942	0.8928
31	EfficientNetV2M	0.9119	0.9036	0.9107	0.9068	0.9132	0.9119	0.9122
32	EfficientNetV2L	0.8862	0.8780	0.8799	0.8789	0.8865	0.8862	0.8864

These results confirm the effectiveness of combining generative and classical data augmentation methods in improving the classifier's sensitivity and classification accuracy. The dataset used in this research consists of 21,224 chest X-rays for training and 624 for testing, grouped into two classes: Normal and Pneumonia.

In conclusion, the results above demonstrate the importance of data augmentation in improving the accuracy of CNN models for diagnosing pneumonia. The use of sophisticated methods like ACGAN further improves accuracy, making these systems more reliable at detecting pneumonia cases.

4.2 Comparative analysis

Fig. 4 presents a line plot comparing five key accuracy metrics: Top-1 Accuracy, Top-5 Accuracy, Accuracy without Augmentation, Accuracy with Traditional

Augmentation (TA), and Accuracy with Traditional Augmentation plus ACGAN (TA+GAN) across 32 CNN models from Keras Applications.

Figure 4. Comparison of CNN Model Accuracies Across Augmentation Strategies for Pneumonia Classification

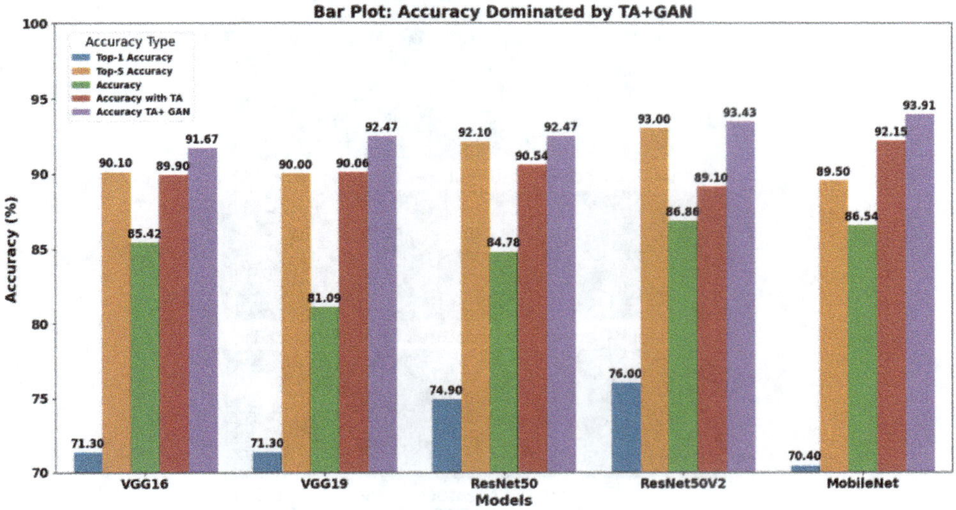

These models were evaluated on the Chest X-ray Pneumonia dataset to assess classification performance under different augmentation strategies. The plot clearly shows that model performance improves with data augmentation, particularly when traditional methods are combined with ACGAN. Models such as MobileNet, EfficientNetB6, ResNet50V2, and EfficientNetB1 demonstrate notable improvements under the TA+GAN configuration, outperforming their scores in all other categories. This indicates that combining traditional and generative augmentation techniques enhances generalization and sensitivity in pneumonia detection.

Figure 5 presents a grouped bar plot highlighting models that achieved the highest accuracy using the TA+GAN approach. VGG16 (92.30%), VGG19 (91.85%), ResNet50 (92.67%), ResNet50V2 (93.43%), and MobileNet (93.91%) demonstrated notable improvements in pneumonia classification when combined with traditional augmentation and ACGAN. This comparison emphasizes the consistent performance gains across these models, surpassing both their baseline and traditional augmentation results. The grouped bars show significant improvements from combining ACGAN with conventional augmentations.

The comparative analysis presented through Figures 4 and 5 provides a valuable reference for researchers in pneumonia classification using deep learning.

Figure 5. Bar Plot Showing Highest Accuracy Achieved by TA+ GAN

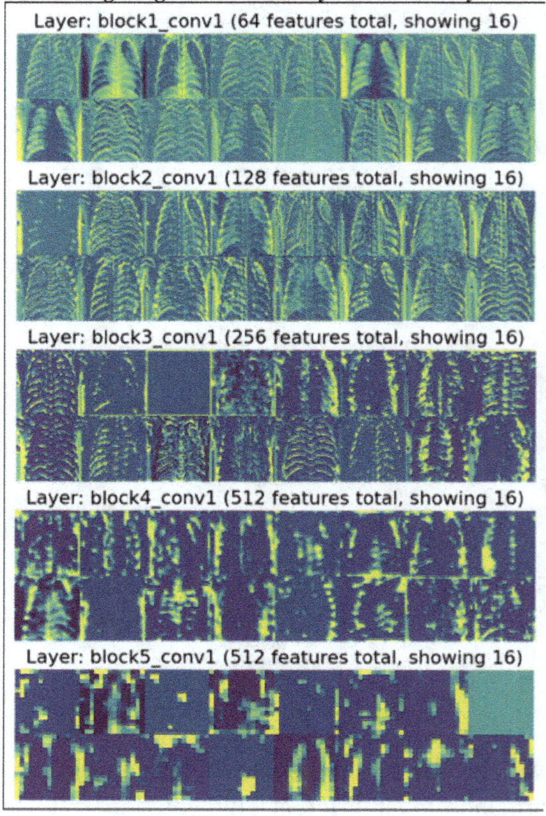

The research effort demonstrates, through testing 32 convolutional neural network models with different augmentation techniques, that both traditional and novel generative techniques, such as ACGAN, provide substantial improvements. The combination helps overcome issues with small datasets or imbalances in medical image datasets.

For researchers developing automated diagnostic tools, the results highlight the importance of using advanced augmentation techniques to improve model accuracy and reliability. The consistent improvements across models such as MobileNet, ResNet50V2, and EfficientNet variants demonstrate that integrating ACGAN enhances generalization. These findings can guide the design of more effective training pipelines and support the development of robust pneumonia detection systems, thereby improving clinical decision-making.

5. EXPLAINABLE AI

Explainable Artificial Intelligence (XAI) can be defined as a range of approaches focused on making the decisions made by machine learning algorithms transparent to humans. Regarding applications in medicine, XAI plays an important role in understanding the decisions made by deep learning models, especially when deep learning is used to detect diseases from X-ray scans of organs (Ruey-Kai Sheu et al., 2023; Hieu H. Pham et al., 2022). Since deep learning models are considered black boxes, XAI helps bridge the gap between the outcomes the algorithm produces and its clinical applicability by showing which parts of the picture were used to make specific decisions. It allows not only gaining some level of trust in the results but also validating the findings for clinical application and obtaining regulatory approval (Lin Zou et al., 2022; Yihang Wang et al., 2022). Below, the most common XAI techniques will be discussed, including Feature Map Visualization, CAM, SHAP, and LIME, which can provide insight into how convolutional neural networks interpret the images.

5.1 Featuremap visualization

Feature maps are an essential component in understanding how Convolutional Neural Networks (CNNs) process visual information, especially in medical imaging tasks such as pneumonia detection from chest X-rays. They represent the output of convolutional layers, capturing important patterns and features at each stage of the network. In early layers, feature maps typically detect basic visual elements like edges and textures, while deeper layers capture more complex and abstract patterns relevant to specific tasks.

Visualization provides insights into how the model learns, which areas it is interested in, and how it converts inputs into representations. The feature map provides significant insights during model evaluation and debugging, offering transparency into the decision-making process of clinically used AI-based systems.

The feature maps shown in Figure 6 were extracted from the first convolutional layer of the five VGG16 blocks, using an image of a chest X-ray with pneumonia annotation. While the feature maps from the early blocks capture general attributes such as edges and shapes, those from deeper layers capture specific features, showing regions of the lung that might suggest a pneumonia infection. These visualizations confirm that the model is learning to detect medically relevant features, offering insight into its internal processing. This kind of interpretability is especially important in healthcare, where understanding why an AI model makes a particular prediction can improve confidence in its use and support more informed clinical decisions.

Figure 6. Feature map Visualization of VGG16

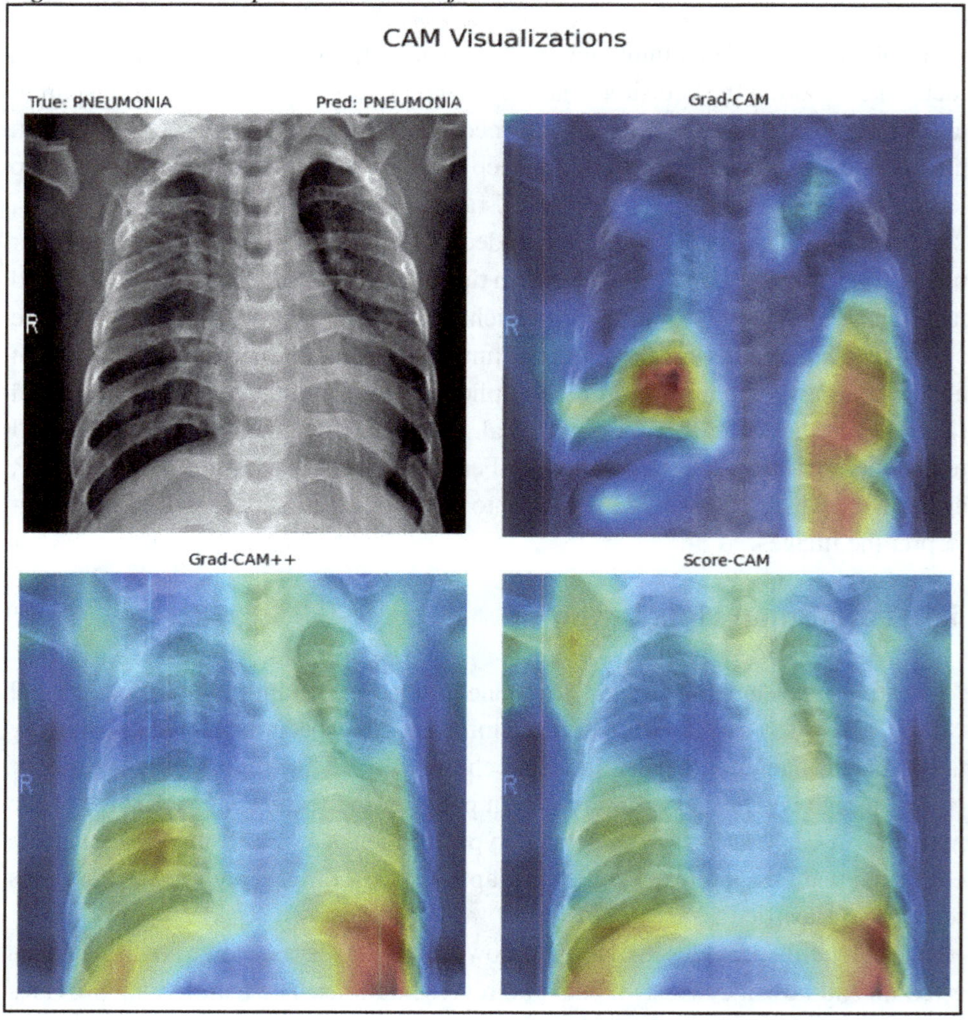

5.2 CAM Visualization

Class Activation Mapping (CAM) based visualization methods are commonly employed to understand and visualize deep learning models, especially in medical imaging applications such as pneumonia identification using chest X-rays. These visualization techniques are useful for identifying regions of the image that affect the model's predictions and, hence, provide insights into how decisions are made in convolutional neural networks. Among the popularly used variants of CAMs are Grad-CAM, Grad-CAM++, and Score-CAM. Grad-CAM uses gradients of the target class with respect to the last convolutional layer to compute heat maps that distinguish relevant from non-relevant regions. The Grad-CAM++ approach improves results by incorporating higher-order gradients. In contrast, Score-CAM avoids gradient dependence altogether and instead weights activation maps based on their contribution to the prediction score, offering improved stability and reduced noise in the generated maps. These methods enhance model transparency, support clinical trust, and help verify whether the model is focusing on medically relevant features such as lung opacities or abnormalities.

Figure 7 depicts CAM visualizations of an X-ray image of the lungs, diagnosed with pneumonia. The upper-left figure shows the original radiographic image, which was correctly classified by the model. The top-right panel shows the Grad-CAM heatmap, highlighting diffuse but somewhat imprecise regions. The bottom-left panel, generated using Grad-CAM++, provides more localized focus, especially in the lower lung fields, which may correspond to pathological patterns. The bottom-right panel displays the Score-CAM output, emphasizing broader yet consistently relevant areas of interest. In these heatmaps, red regions indicate strong model attention and likely correspond to pneumonia-related abnormalities, while blue regions indicate areas of low relevance.

Figure 7. CAM Visualization

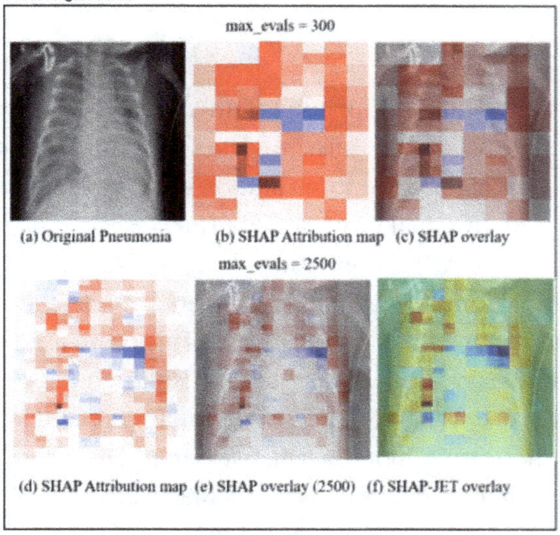

Collectively, these visualizations enable a meaningful assessment of the model's focus, offering a valuable tool for debugging, validating, and interpreting deep learning models in healthcare applications.

5.3 SHAP

SHAP (SHapley Additive exPlanations) is one of the techniques employed in deep learning for the interpretation of model predictions. This technique, being model agnostic, plays a crucial role when interpreting deep learning models, particularly in the context of medical imaging applications like detecting pneumonia in chest X-ray images. The algorithm determines the critical areas of the image responsible for the decision-making process through systematic masking of sections of the input image.

Figure 8. SHAP visualization

(a) Original Pneumonia (b) LIME Explanations (c) LIME Superpixels

SHAP combines a prediction function with an image masker that realistically fills in hidden regions to simulate missing data. The resulting heatmap shows red regions indicating a strong positive contribution to the prediction and blue regions highlighting areas with minimal or negative influence.

In this research, two SHAP configurations were used to generate attribution maps. The first configuration employed shap.Explainer(f, masker, output_names=[...]) with outputs=shap.Explanation.argsort.flip[:2]. This setup used max_evals = 300, which limits the number of model evaluations, resulting in faster computation but coarser attribution maps. The second configuration increased max_evals to 2500, allowing SHAP to perform a more exhaustive sampling of feature combinations. This produced finer, more accurate attribution maps, albeit at the cost of increased computational time. The max_evals parameter directly affects the detail and reliability of the explanations by controlling how thoroughly SHAP explores the feature space.

SHAP visualization is provided for one of the successfully predicted cases of pneumonia in Fig. 8. In panel (a), we can see the original chest X-ray image, while in panel (b), the SHAP map for explaining the prediction, which was produced using fewer evaluations (max_evals = 300), is shown. Finally, in panel (c), the SHAP map is overlaid onto the original image. Panel (d) presents the SHAP attribution map with a higher evaluation setting (max_evals = 2500), providing more refined and concentrated attributions. Panel (e) overlays this high-resolution map on the original image, revealing sharper focus in clinically relevant areas such as the lower and central lung fields. Panel (f) displays the SHAP-JET overlay (max_evals = 2500), which uses a continuous colormap to enhance the visualization of feature importance intensity. These results illustrate that increasing the number of evaluations improves the spatial precision and interpretability of SHAP explanations, which can support more transparent and clinically meaningful AI-based diagnosis.

5.4 LIME

LIME (Local Interpretable Model-agnostic Explanations) is a post-hoc explainability technique designed to interpret predictions made by black-box machine learning models. It operates by locally approximating the model's behavior using a simpler interpretable model, such as a linear classifier, around the instance of interest. For applications such as detecting abnormalities in chest X-rays, LIME is highly valuable because it shows which parts of the image were the key factors in the model's decision. This can be achieved by making minor alterations to the image regions, known as superpixels. This localized, model-agnostic approach is valuable when clinical interpretability is essential, especially in critical cases such as pneumonia detection, where visual confirmation of the decision basis is important for trust and transparency.

Figure 9 presents the LIME-based explanation for a pneumonia-classified chest X-ray. (a) shows the original Pneumonia input image. (b) depicts the LIME explanation, where important superpixels contributing to the model's prediction are highlighted using a boundary overlay. These regions correspond to areas the model found most relevant for classifying the image as pneumonia. (c) displays the segmented superpixel map, showing how the image is partitioned during LIME's perturbation process. This visualization helps understand the model's focus areas and enhances interpretability by providing a transparent rationale for the classification decision.

Figure 9. LIME visualization

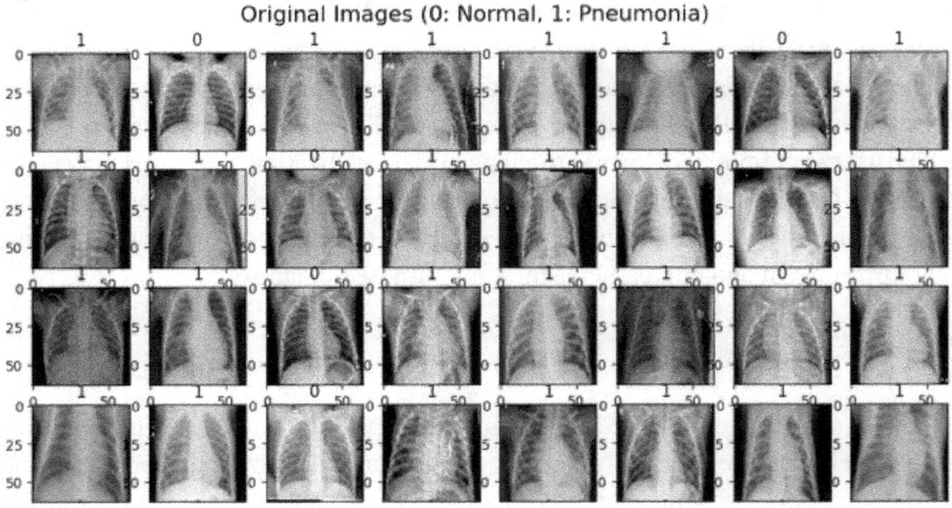

5.5 Discussion on Interpretability and Clinical Relevance

The employment of XAI techniques in this research was deemed to be an extremely significant step towards closing the gap between high-performance deep learning algorithms and their deployment in healthcare settings. Even though the convolutional neural network models used in this study performed well in classification, the interpretability of results cannot be overlooked to ensure that the results obtained from models are not only reliable but also clinically relevant.

The visual explanations generated by Grad-CAM, SHAP, and LIME were found to be very insightful for understanding how the models work. In some instances, the highlighted regions of the images corresponded to clinically relevant areas, such as lung opacities, consolidations, and regions of abnormal texture. All these regions are very crucial when a radiologist is diagnosing a patient with pneumonia. This shows that the models are not just learning from spurious correlations but are actually learning from relevant features.

Comparing different XAI techniques reveals both strengths and weaknesses. Grad-CAM produces understandable, computationally inexpensive heat maps that provide a global perspective on crucial areas; however, the explanations it generates can be quite coarse. SHAP, on the other hand, provides more precise, pixel-level attribution, enabling a deeper understanding of feature contributions, though it is computationally intensive. LIME offers localized, model-agnostic explanations by highlighting influential superpixels; however, its results can vary depending on the segmentation and perturbation strategy. These differences indicate that no single method is sufficient on its own, and a combination of XAI techniques can provide a more comprehensive and reliable interpretation framework.

From a clinical perspective, the use of XAI enhances trust and usability by allowing healthcare professionals to validate model predictions. By visualizing the features that affect the model's output, doctors will be able to determine whether the model's reasoning aligns with existing diagnostic standards. This aspect is especially important for minimizing uncertainty when making high-stakes decisions, such as diagnosing pneumonia. In essence, XAI transforms the model's black box into a transparent decision-support tool.

Despite these advantages, it should be noted that there are limitations associated with existing XAI approaches. For example, most of the approaches used in this study are post hoc, meaning they provide explanations based on predictions made by a model. This may cause inconsistencies, as some approaches may yield different results than others when given the same input. Moreover, the clinical validity of results from an explanation approach should be carefully evaluated, as a visually interpretable result may not always be medically valid.

It is evident from the techniques used in this research, such as Grad-CAM, SHAP, and LIME, that current XAI methods can play a crucial role in ensuring transparency and trust in AI-based pneumonia diagnosis. Future research should focus on developing more robust models for more interpretable analysis. Further, the results of an explanatory technique should also be validated by medical professionals.

6. CONCLUSION AND FUTURE WORK

This comparative analysis highlights how generative and explainable AI technologies can be used to accurately classify pneumonia in chest X-ray images. This research evaluates 32 convolutional neural networks and finds that EfficientNetB1, DenseNet169, and MobileNet achieve superior results in pneumonia classification, especially when trained on conventional augmented data and GAN-generated synthetic images from an auxiliary classifier.

The inclusion of explainable AI methods, such as Grad-CAM, SHAP, and LIME, ensures the model is interpretable. Through this, the parts of the images that affect the outcomes can be identified. It will enhance trust in AI-based models for detecting pneumonia. This will be useful in building trust and understanding of how the model works. This will strengthen the role of AI as a decision-support system rather than an alternative to physicians' expertise.

Despite these advancements, a few key aspects need further exploration to make the proposed framework more complete. One such key limitation of the current work is the absence of human-level benchmarking. In a clinical environment, radiologists are considered the gold standard for diagnosis. A more comprehensive benchmarking of the system's reliability can be achieved by incorporating a comparative study with radiologists.

In addition, there are ethical, regulatory, and security issues to consider when deploying an AI system in healthcare. Although this proposed framework incorporates various methods of explainable AI, deep learning, and generative models, these methods still exhibit some black-box characteristics, which may affect their interpretability to some extent. To overcome this, it is necessary to further improve inherently interpretable models and test explanation methods.

There are also biases in medical data that might affect model performance across different patient populations. From a regulatory perspective, deploying this system in a real-world setting requires compliance with healthcare standards and robustness across various datasets and hospitals. There is also a need to integrate this system with existing clinical infrastructure, such as radiology and electronic health record systems.

Furthermore, the use of generative models like ACGAN also poses challenges regarding data authenticity and system security. Although the use of synthetic data increases the diversity of the training process, it is essential that the generated images are authentic and do not produce artifacts that may influence the AI model.

The future of the proposed approach will involve extending it by incorporating different validation strategies, such as human-in-the-loop validation and robustness checks. Moreover, the use of EHRs and other modal data in the proposed approach will be explored to make it a more comprehensive framework for clinical decision-making. Thus, the proposed approach has the potential to become a more authentic and ethical AI-assisted diagnostic system for detecting pneumonia.

REFERENCES

Al-qaness, M. A. A., Zhu, J., Al-Alimi, D., Dahou, A., Alsamhi, S. H., Abd Elaziz, M., & Ewees, A. A. (2024). Chest X-ray images for lung disease detection using deep learning techniques: A comprehensive survey. *Archives of Computational Methods in Engineering*, *31*(6), 3267–3301. DOI: 10.1007/s11831-024-10081-y

Appasami, G., & Nickolas, S. (2022). A deep learning-based COVID-19 classification from chest X-ray image: Case study. *The European Physical Journal. Special Topics*, *231*(18-20), 3767–3777. DOI: 10.1140/epjs/s11734-022-00647-x PMID: 35996535

Dardouri, S. (2025). A Deep Convolutional Neural Network Model for Lung Disease Detection Using Chest X-Ray Imaging. Pulmonary Medicine, 2025(1), 6614016.

El Mohamadi, H., El Hassouni, M., & Jennane, R. (2025). Dual-domain explainability-driven data augmentation for enhanced COVID-19 detection in chest X-rays. *Multimedia Tools and Applications*, *84*(31), 37793–37814. Advance online publication. DOI: 10.1007/s11042-025-20920-0

Fu, M., Tantithamthavorn, C., & Le, T. (2025). DAViT: A Domain-Adapted Vision Transformer for Automated Pneumonia Detection and Explanation Using Chest X-Ray Images. *IEEE Access : Practical Innovations, Open Solutions*, *13*, 103033–103044. Advance online publication. DOI: 10.1109/ACCESS.2025.3579314

Jouibari, Z. E., Moakhkhar, H. N., & Baleghi, Y. (2024). Emergency COVID-19 detection from chest X-rays using deep neural networks and ensemble learning. *Multimedia Tools and Applications*, *83*(17), 52141–52169. DOI: 10.1007/s11042-023-17508-x

Kaushik, P., Jain, E., Kukreja, V., Hariharan, S., Krishnamoorthy, M., Ahuja, V., Bhattacherjee, A., Kaushal, R. K., & Chen, S.-Y. (2025). Modelling radiological features fusion and explainable AI in pneumonia detection: A graph-based deep learning and transformer approach. *Results in Engineering*, *19*, 105225. DOI: 10.1016/j.rineng.2025.105225

Kinger, S., & Kulkarni, V. (2025). Transparent and trustworthy interpretation of COVID-19 features in chest X-rays using explainable AI. *Multimedia Tools and Applications*, *84*(18), 19853–19881. DOI: 10.1007/s11042-024-19755-y

Koyyada, S. P., & Singh, T. P. (2024). A systematic survey of automatic detection of lung diseases from chest X-ray images: COVID-19, pneumonia, and tuberculosis. *SN Computer Science*, *5*(2), 229. DOI: 10.1007/s42979-023-02573-8

Lee, S. B. (2025). Gradual poisoning of a chest X-ray convolutional neural network with an adversarial attack and AI explainability methods. *Scientific Reports*, *15*(1), 21779. DOI: 10.1038/s41598-025-02294-3 PMID: 40593872

Luo, G., Wang, Z., Wang, Y., & Wang, K. (2024). Detection of pneumonia in chest X-ray image based on separable convolutional neural network. *Concurrency and Computation*, *36*(18), e8160. DOI: 10.1002/cpe.8160

Mondal, A. K., Bhattacharjee, A., Singla, P., & Prathosh, A. P. (2022). xViTCOS: Explainable vision transformer based COVID-19 screening using radiography. *IEEE Journal of Translational Engineering in Health and Medicine*, *10*, 1–12. DOI: 10.1109/JTEHM.2021.3134096 PMID: 34956741

Musa, A., Prasad, R., & Hernandez, M. (2025). Addressing cross-population domain shift in chest X-ray classification through supervised adversarial domain adaptation. *Scientific Reports*, *15*(1), 11383. DOI: 10.1038/s41598-025-95390-3 PMID: 40181036

Pham, H. H., Nguyen, H. Q., Nguyen, H. T., Le, L. T., & Khanh, L. (2022). An accurate and explainable deep learning system improves interobserver agreement in the interpretation of chest radiograph. *IEEE Access : Practical Innovations, Open Solutions*, *10*, 19853–19865. DOI: 10.1109/ACCESS.2022.3210468

Prasath, J. G., Prabu, S., Mayil, V. V., & Saini, S. (2025). Optimized double transformer residual super-resolution network-based X-ray images for classification of pneumonia identification. *Knowledge-Based Systems*, *287*, 113037. DOI: 10.1016/j.knosys.2025.113037

Priyanka, R., Gajendran, G., Boulaaras, S., & Tantawy, S. S. (2025). PediaPulmoDx: Harnessing cutting edge preprocessing and explainable AI for pediatric chest X-ray classification with DenseNet121. *Results in Engineering*, *18*, 104320. DOI: 10.1016/j.rineng.2025.104320

Rabbah, J., Ridouani, M., & Hassouni, L. Improving pneumonia diagnosis with high-accuracy CNN-Based chest X-ray image classification and integrated gradient, Biomedical Signal Processing and Control, Volume 101, 2025, 107239, ISSN 1746-8094, DOI: 10.1016/j.bspc.2024.107239

Ren, H., Wong, A. B., Lian, W., Cheng, W., Zhang, Y., He, J., Liu, Q., Yang, J., Zhang, C. J., Wu, K., & Zhang, H. (2021). Interpretable Pneumonia Detection by Combining Deep Learning and Explainable Models with Multisource Data. IEEE Access, 9, 95872-95883. *Article*, *9458276*. Advance online publication. DOI: 10.1109/ACCESS.2021.3090215

Sheu, R. K., Pardeshi, M. S., Pai, K. C., Chen, L. C., Wu, C. L., & Chen, W. C. (2023). Interpretable classification of pneumonia infection using eXplainable AI (XAI-ICP). *IEEE Access : Practical Innovations, Open Solutions, 11*, 46124–46138. DOI: 10.1109/ACCESS.2023.3255403

Siddiqui, A. A., Tirunagari, S., Zia, T., & Windridge, D. (2025). A latent diffusion approach to visual attribution in medical imaging. *Scientific Reports, 15*(1), 962. DOI: 10.1038/s41598-024-81646-x PMID: 39762275

Singh, S., Kumar, M., Kumar, A., Verma, B. K., Abhishek, K., & Selvarajan, S. (2024). Efficient pneumonia detection using Vision Transformers on chest X-rays. *Scientific Reports, 14*(1), 2487. DOI: 10.1038/s41598-024-52703-2 PMID: 38291130

Sivanantham, S., Anwar Basha, H., Thanuja, K., Shafiya Banu, M., Maithili, K., & Ambore, A. (2025). Illuminating the Diagnostic Path. In Kumar, A., Ananth Kumar, T., Das, P., Sharma, C., & Dubey, A. K. (Eds.), *Explainable Artificial Intelligence in the Healthcare Industry*., DOI: 10.1002/9781394249312.ch3

T N, S. G., Satish, R., & Sridhar, R.T N. (2023). S.G., Satish, R. & Sridhar, R. Learning effective embedding for automated COVID-19 prediction from chest X-ray images. *Multimedia Systems, 29*(2), 739–751. DOI: 10.1007/s00530-022-01015-4 PMID: 36310764

Wang, Y., Jiang, C., Wu, Y., Lv, T., Sun, H., Liu, Y., Li, L., & Pan, X. (2022). Semantic-powered explainable model-free few-shot learning scheme of diagnosing COVID-19 on chest X-ray. *IEEE Journal of Biomedical and Health Informatics, 26*(12), 6109–6120. DOI: 10.1109/JBHI.2022.3205167 PMID: 36074872

Wang, Y., Noor-A-Rahim, M., Gunawan, E., Guan, Y. L., & Poh, C. L. (2023, May-June). Erry Gunawan, Yong L. Guan, and Chueh L. Poh. 2023. Modelling, Characterization of Data-Dependent and Process-Dependent Errors in DNA Data Storage. *IEEE/ACM Transactions on Computational Biology and Bioinformatics, 20*(3), 2147–2158. DOI: 10.1109/TCBB.2022.3233914 PMID: 37018270

Wu, Y. H., Gao, S. H., Mei, J., Xu, J., Fan, D. P., Zhang, R. G., & Cheng, M. M. (2021). JCS: An explainable COVID-19 diagnosis system by joint classification and segmentation. *IEEE Transactions on Image Processing : A Publication of the IEEE Signal Processing Society, 30*, 3113–3126. DOI: 10.1109/TIP.2021.3058783 PMID: 33600316

Yazdani, E., Neizehbaz, A., Karamzade-Ziarati, N., & Kheradpisheh, S. R. Explainable artificial intelligence for pneumonia classification: Clinical insights into deformable prototypical part network in pediatric chest x-ray images, Journal of Medical Imaging and Radiation Sciences, Volume 56, Issue 5, 2025, 102023, ISSN 1939-8654, DOI: 10.1016/j.jmir.2025.102023

Zou, L., Goh, H. L., Liew, C. J. Y., Quah, J. L., Gu, G. T., Chew, J. J., Kumar, M. P., Ang, C. G. L., & Ta, A. W. A. (2023). Ensemble image explainable AI (XAI) algorithm for severe community-acquired pneumonia and COVID-19 respiratory infections. *IEEE Transactions on Artificial Intelligence*, *4*(2), 241–250. DOI: 10.1109/TAI.2022.3153754

Chapter 4

An Attention-Augmented U-Net Model for Lung Region Segmentation From Chest X-Ray Images

K. Ramalakshmi
http://orcid.org/0000-0002-3038-643X
P.S.R. Engineering College, Sivakasi, India

L. Krishna Kumari
Ramco Institute of Technology, Rajapalayam, India

ABSTRACT

Lung segmentation from chest X-ray images plays an important role in the early diagnosis of pulmonary diseases such as pneumonia, lung cancer, and COVID-19. Manual segmentation is time-consuming and susceptible to observer variability, creating the need for automated and reliable approaches. This study proposes an Attention-Augmented U-Net model for accurate lung region segmentation. The proposed framework enhances the conventional U-Net architecture by integrating Attention Gates (AGs) into skip connections between encoder and decoder layers, enabling the network to focus on relevant lung regions while suppressing background structures. Publicly available chest X-ray datasets were used for training and evaluation with preprocessing techniques including normalization and data augmentation. Experimental results achieved a Dice coefficient of 0.93 and improved segmentation performance compared with conventional U-Net models. The proposed system may support radiologists in computer-aided diagnosis and collaborative clinical workflows.

DOI: 10.4018/979-8-2600-2701-1.ch004

1. INTRODUCTION

1.1 Background and Motivation

Medical imaging has become an essential tool in modern healthcare for the early detection and diagnosis of diseases. Among various imaging modalities, chest X-ray imaging is one of the most commonly used techniques for identifying lung-related diseases due to its affordability, speed, and wide availability. It is extensively used to detect conditions such as lung cancer, pneumonia, tuberculosis, and COVID-19. Despite its advantages, analyzing chest X-ray images is a complex task that requires expert knowledge. Radiologists must carefully examine the images to identify abnormalities, which can be time-consuming and subject to inter-observer variability. This creates a strong need for automated systems that can assist in accurate and efficient image analysis. The increasing workload on radiologists and healthcare professionals has created a growing demand for intelligent clinical support systems capable of assisting in routine image interpretation. In many healthcare environments, particularly in resource-limited settings, clinicians must analyze a large number of chest X-ray images within limited timeframes. This can increase diagnostic fatigue, inter-observer variability, and the possibility of missed abnormalities. Human-centered artificial intelligence aims to develop AI systems that enhance clinical efficiency while preserving human oversight, transparency, and accountability. In this context, automated lung segmentation can function as a supportive preprocessing tool that helps radiologists focus on clinically relevant lung regions during diagnosis and collaborative decision-making workflows.

1.2 Importance of Lung Segmentation

Lung segmentation is a critical preprocessing step in many computer-aided diagnosis (CAD) systems. It involves isolating the lung regions from the surrounding structures such as ribs, heart, and background tissues. Accurate segmentation ensures that further analysis, such as disease detection and classification, is focused only on the relevant regions.

However, lung segmentation in chest X-ray images is challenging due to:

- Variations in lung shape, size, and position
- Presence of noise and low contrast
- Overlapping anatomical structures
- Differences in imaging conditions

These challenges make traditional image processing techniques less effective and highlight the need for advanced approaches.

1.3 Deep Learning in Medical Image Segmentation

With the advancement of artificial intelligence, deep learning methods—especially Convolutional Neural Networks (CNNs) have shown significant success in image analysis tasks. These methods can automatically learn complex features from data, making them highly suitable for medical image segmentation.

One of the most widely used architectures for biomedical image segmentation is the U-Net model. U-Net follows an encoder-decoder structure:

- The encoder captures contextual information through downsampling
- The decoder reconstructs the segmentation map through upsampling
- Skip connections help preserve spatial details

Although U-Net performs well, it treats all features equally, which can reduce its effectiveness in focusing on the most important regions.

1.4 Attention-Based U-Net Model

To overcome the limitations of standard U-Net, attention mechanisms have been introduced in deep learning models. Attention allows the model to focus on relevant regions while ignoring unnecessary or irrelevant information.

In this work, Attention Gates (AGs) are incorporated into the U-Net architecture. These gates:

- Highlight important lung regions
- Suppress background noise
- Improve feature selection during training

The attention gates are applied to the skip connections between the encoder and decoder, enabling better localization and segmentation of lung boundaries. This research proposes an Attention-Based U-Net model for accurate lung region segmentation in chest X-ray images. The model enhances the traditional U-Net by integrating attention gates, which refine the feature maps passed through skip connections.

The workflow of the proposed system includes:

- Preprocessing of chest X-ray images

- Feature extraction using the encoder
- Attention-based feature refinement
- Reconstruction of segmented lung regions using the decoder

This approach aims to improve segmentation accuracy and reduce the impact of irrelevant features.

1.5 Objectives of the Study

The main objectives of this work are:

- To develop an automated system for lung segmentation
- To improve segmentation accuracy using Attention Gates
- To compare the performance with traditional U-Net models
- To evaluate the model using metrics such as Dice coefficient and IoU

1.6 Scope and Applications

The proposed Attention-based U-Net framework has potential applications in several areas of medical image analysis and computer-aided diagnosis. Accurate lung region segmentation can support the early screening of pulmonary diseases such as pneumonia, tuberculosis, chronic obstructive pulmonary disease, COVID-19, and lung cancer by isolating clinically relevant regions from chest X-ray images. The segmented lung masks generated by the model may assist radiologists in improving visualization of suspicious abnormalities and reducing the influence of irrelevant anatomical structures such as ribs and surrounding tissues.

The proposed framework can also serve as a preprocessing stage for downstream deep learning models used in disease classification and abnormality detection. In collaborative healthcare environments, the system may support human-in-the-loop workflows in which AI-generated segmentation outputs are reviewed, corrected, and validated by clinicians before final diagnosis. Such integration can contribute to improved efficiency, consistency, and decision support in digital healthcare systems. However, the proposed model should be considered a supportive research tool that requires additional validation on large-scale and clinically diverse datasets before practical clinical deployment.

1.7 Organization of the Report

The remainder of this chapter is organized as follows:

- Section 2 presents the literature survey
- Section 3 describes the methodology and system design
- Section 4 discusses implementation and results
- Section 5 concludes the work and suggests future enhancements

2. LITERATURE SURVEY

2.1. Traditional Lung Segmentation Methods

Early lung segmentation techniques relied heavily on classical image processing and model-based approaches. Methods such as edge-region force guided active shape models were developed to detect lung boundaries in chest radiographs with reasonable accuracy (Xu et al., 2012). Similarly, shape-learning-based segmentation approaches incorporated anatomical and spatial constraints to improve segmentation performance (Mansoor et al., 2020). However, these traditional techniques were limited by their reliance on handcrafted features, sensitivity to noise, and poor generalization across diverse datasets.

2.2. Deep Learning-Based Segmentation Approaches

With the emergence of deep learning, convolutional neural network (CNN)-based methods have significantly improved lung segmentation performance. Among them, U-Net and its variants have become the most widely adopted architectures due to their encoder–decoder structure and efficient feature fusion.

Recent studies demonstrate that modified U-Net architectures with deeper networks, residual connections, and transfer learning significantly enhance segmentation accuracy (Tam et al., 2025). Additionally, segmentation-based frameworks integrated into broader pipelines have shown improved feature extraction and representation capabilities (Wang et al., 2026).

Deep learning models are also frequently used as part of multi-stage pipelines where segmentation acts as a preprocessing step for classification (Rathod et al., 2024). These approaches consistently outperform traditional methods in terms of Dice coefficient and Intersection over Union (IoU).

Recent advancements in medical image analysis have significantly improved disease detection and segmentation through the application of deep learning techniques, particularly convolutional neural networks (CNNs) and their variants. A comprehensive review by Ramalakshmi K et al. (2024) explored various artificial intelligence techniques used in cancer recognition through medical imaging. The study analyzed multiple segmentation methods, including traditional approaches and deep learning models, emphasizing the transition toward automated and highly accurate systems. The authors concluded that deep learning-based segmentation methods outperform conventional techniques in terms of precision, scalability, and adaptability across different imaging modalities.

In the area of pneumonia detection, Rajalakshmi R et al. (2024) proposed a CNN-based approach combined with data augmentation techniques for chest X-ray image analysis. Data augmentation was employed to address dataset imbalance and improve generalization. Their model achieved higher classification accuracy compared to baseline methods, demonstrating that augmentation plays a crucial role in enhancing model robustness in medical imaging tasks. Krishnakumari L et al. (2023) investigated liver tumor segmentation using a Deep ResUNet architecture. By integrating residual connections into the U-Net framework, the model effectively captured both low-level and high-level features. Their findings indicated improved segmentation accuracy and reduced loss, particularly in complex liver tumor regions, validating the effectiveness of residual learning in medical image segmentation. One of the most influential architectures in biomedical image segmentation is the U-Net model proposed by Ronneberger et al. (2015). U-Net introduced an encoder-decoder framework with skip connections that enabled precise localization while preserving contextual information. Due to its strong performance in biomedical segmentation tasks, U-Net has become a foundational architecture for lung segmentation in chest X-ray analysis. To further improve localization performance, Oktay et al. (2018) proposed Attention U-Net, which incorporated Attention Gates into skip connections. These gates allow the network to suppress irrelevant background information and selectively emphasize target anatomical structures. Attention-based feature refinement has shown particular effectiveness in medical imaging applications where organ boundaries are difficult to distinguish because of low contrast, noise, and overlapping anatomical structures. Recent studies on chest X-ray segmentation have extended U-Net architectures using residual learning, dense feature extraction, attention mechanisms, and hybrid deep learning approaches to improve segmentation accuracy and robustness across diverse imaging conditions.

The reviewed literature highlights a clear trend toward hybrid and optimized deep learning models for medical image analysis. Techniques such as transfer learning, attention mechanisms, data augmentation, and residual networks have significantly enhanced the performance of disease detection and segmentation systems. These advancements contribute to more accurate, efficient, and automated diagnostic tools, ultimately supporting clinical decision-making and improving patient outcomes.

2.3. Attention-Based and Advanced Learning Models

Recent advancements in deep learning have significantly improved the performance of medical image segmentation and classification systems, particularly through the integration of attention mechanisms and advanced neural architectures. Attention mechanisms are designed to enable deep learning models to selectively focus on clinically relevant regions while suppressing irrelevant background information. This capability improves feature representation, localization accuracy, and robustness in complex medical imaging environments where noise, low contrast, and overlapping anatomical structures are common challenges.

In chest X-ray analysis, attention-based models have demonstrated superior performance in identifying pathological regions associated with pulmonary diseases. Desikar et al. (2026) proposed a multi-dimensional attention-based spiking neural network for pneumonia detection, where the attention modules enhanced the model's ability to capture important spatial and contextual information from chest X-ray images. Their approach achieved improved diagnostic accuracy and reduced false classifications by effectively focusing on disease-affected lung regions. Similarly, Wang et al. (2026) introduced a lesion-aware framework incorporating adaptive label-relation graphs to model interdependencies among multiple thoracic diseases. The framework utilized attention-guided feature learning to improve multi-label classification performance and demonstrated enhanced capability in identifying co-existing abnormalities in chest radiographs.

The growing importance of attention mechanisms is also evident in broader medical imaging applications beyond chest X-rays. In the field of breast cancer diagnosis, Ramalakshmi K et al. (2026) proposed a transfer learning-based convolutional neural network framework aimed at improving breast cancer detection accuracy. Their study utilized pre-trained deep learning models to address the challenge of limited annotated medical datasets. By leveraging transfer learning, the framework achieved enhanced feature extraction, reduced computational complexity, and improved classification performance. The study further demonstrated that transfer learning approaches can significantly decrease training time while maintaining high diagnostic accuracy, thereby supporting efficient deployment in real-world clinical environments.

For brain tumor segmentation, Ramalakshmi K and Kumari L K (2025) developed an advanced U-Net-based architecture integrated with attention mechanisms and Bayesian Optimization techniques. In their framework, attention modules enabled the network to emphasize important tumor regions while minimizing irrelevant background features. Bayesian Optimization was employed to automatically fine-tune hyperparameters, improving model convergence and segmentation performance. Experimental results on MRI datasets demonstrated notable improvements in segmentation accuracy, sensitivity, and boundary delineation. Their work highlighted the effectiveness of combining architectural innovations with optimization strategies for complex medical image segmentation tasks.

These studies demonstrate that attention-based learning models and advanced deep learning architectures significantly enhance the performance of medical image analysis systems. The integration of attention mechanisms improves the model's ability to focus on disease-relevant regions, while optimization and transfer learning techniques contribute to better generalization, computational efficiency, and clinical applicability.

2.4. Segmentation for Disease Classification

Lung segmentation plays a crucial role in improving disease classification accuracy by isolating the region of interest (ROI) from chest X-ray images. By eliminating irrelevant background structures such as ribs, heart boundaries, and external artifacts, segmentation enables deep learning models to focus on clinically significant pulmonary features. This preprocessing step improves feature extraction, reduces computational complexity, and enhances the reliability of disease classification systems.

Several studies have demonstrated the effectiveness of segmentation-assisted classification frameworks in chest X-ray analysis. Ding et al. (2024) proposed the FocusNet framework, which first segments lung regions before applying disease classification models. Their approach significantly improved classification accuracy by directing the model's attention toward pathological lung regions while suppressing irrelevant anatomical information. Similarly, Rathod et al. (2024) combined U-Net-based lung segmentation with ensemble classification techniques for pneumonia detection. Their integrated framework achieved improved diagnostic performance and demonstrated that accurate segmentation contributes directly to enhanced classification reliability.

Candemir et al. (2019) presented a comprehensive review of lung boundary detection methods in chest X-ray imaging and discussed major challenges associated with automated lung segmentation, including image noise, low contrast, distorted boundaries, and overlapping anatomical structures. The study emphasized the importance of robust lung segmentation methods for improving computer-aided diagnosis systems and highlighted the growing adoption of deep learning techniques for accurate lung boundary extraction.

In medical image segmentation research, reliable evaluation metrics are essential for validating model performance. Taha et al. (2015) analyzed commonly used segmentation evaluation metrics, including Dice coefficient, Jaccard index, sensitivity, specificity, and Hausdorff distance. Their work provided a detailed comparison of these metrics and emphasized the importance of selecting appropriate quantitative measures for standardized and reliable performance assessment in medical imaging applications.

In addition to model development and evaluation, standardized reporting practices are increasingly important in AI-based healthcare research. Mongan et al. (2020) introduced the Checklist for Artificial Intelligence in Medical Imaging (CLAIM), which provides comprehensive reporting guidelines for AI-driven medical imaging studies. The CLAIM framework supports transparency, reproducibility, methodological consistency, and clinical reliability by outlining recommendations related to dataset preparation, preprocessing, model development, validation strategies, and clinical applicability. The framework has become an important reference for improving the quality and credibility of AI research in healthcare.

These studies demonstrate that lung segmentation is not merely a standalone image processing task but also a critical preprocessing component for improving downstream disease classification performance. Accurate segmentation enhances feature learning, reduces diagnostic ambiguity, and supports the development of reliable and clinically applicable computer-aided diagnosis systems for pulmonary disease detection.

2.5. Deep Learning-Based Lung Disease Classification

Deep learning models have achieved remarkable success in lung disease classification tasks using chest X-ray images. EfficientNetV2-based models have demonstrated high classification accuracy, achieving up to 96% in multi-class pneumonia detection (Huang & Meng, 2026). More advanced architectures, such as multi-layer stacked residual coordinate networks, have achieved even higher performance, reaching accuracy levels close to 99% (Egala & Sairam, 2025). Comparative studies evaluating multiple CNN architectures—including VGG, ResNet, DenseNet, and Inception—have highlighted their effectiveness when trained under standardized pipelines (Aljuaid et al., 2026). These findings confirm the robustness of deep learning models in clinical applications.

2.6. Image Enhancement and Preprocessing Techniques

Preprocessing plays a vital role in improving both segmentation and classification performance in chest X-ray analysis. Techniques such as contrast enhancement, noise reduction, and ROI extraction significantly impact model accuracy. The 9IEC method improves low-contrast and non-uniform illumination in chest X-ray images using intensity, entropy, and contrast-based segmentation (Gangwar et al., 2025). Additionally, Gaussian Fourier Pyramid-based approaches enhance feature visibility and extraction, contributing to improved classification accuracy (Egala & Sairam, 2025). ROI extraction techniques and visualization methods like Grad-CAM further enhance interpretability and help identify important regions within the lungs (Huang & Meng, 2026).

2.7. Challenges in Lung Segmentation

Despite significant advancements, several challenges remain in lung segmentation. One major issue is the discrepancy between segmentation masks derived from chest X-rays and those obtained from CT scans. Studies indicate that X-ray-based segmentation often underestimates lung regions due to overlapping anatomical structures (Bombiński et al., 2025).

Other challenges include variability in lung shape, presence of noise, low contrast, and occlusion caused by ribs and other organs, which can negatively affect segmentation accuracy.

2.8. Datasets and Benchmarking

The availability of high-quality annotated datasets is essential for training robust deep learning models. Large-scale datasets improve model generalization and enable benchmarking across different methods. Recent studies utilize multiple publicly available datasets to validate segmentation and classification models, ensuring robustness and reliability across diverse clinical conditions (Egala & Sairam, 2025; Aljuaid et al., 2026).

2.9. Review of Research Trends

Recent research highlights a rapid shift toward deep learning-based approaches for medical image analysis. CNN-based architectures, attention mechanisms, and hybrid models dominate current research trends. Integration of segmentation with classification, use of attention mechanisms, and incorporation of multi-scale feature learning are key directions in modern studies (Wang et al., 2026; Desikar et al., 2026). Additionally, optimization techniques and ensemble learning methods continue to enhance performance and robustness in lung disease detection systems.

2.10. Research Gap

Although deep learning-based lung segmentation methods have achieved promising results, several limitations remain in existing studies. Conventional U-Net models often struggle to accurately localize lung boundaries in chest X-ray images containing low contrast, overlapping anatomical structures, imaging artifacts, and significant variations in lung shape and size. In many cases, standard skip connections propagate irrelevant background information that may reduce segmentation precision. Recent attention-based approaches have improved feature selection; however, several studies primarily focus on classification performance rather than accurate lung boundary segmentation. In addition, many existing studies provide limited discussion regarding explainability, clinical workflow integration, dataset diversity, failure cases, and human-centered AI considerations. Another important limitation is the lack of detailed reproducibility information, including validation strategies, dataset partitioning, and experimental transparency.

To address these limitations, the present study investigates an Attention Gate-based U-Net framework for lung region segmentation from chest X-ray images. The proposed approach aims to improve localization accuracy by selectively emphasizing clinically relevant lung regions while suppressing irrelevant background structures. Furthermore, this work discusses the potential role of segmentation systems in collaborative clinical workflows and computer-aided diagnosis environments.

2.11. Summary

The literature demonstrates that deep learning significantly improves lung segmentation and classification. However, challenges such as accurate localization and noise suppression remain. Attention-based U-Net models address these limitations by enhancing feature selection and improving segmentation accuracy.

3. U NET WITH ATTENTION MECHANISM FOR LUNG REGION EXTRACTION

3.1 Introduction

The objective of this work is to design an automated and accurate approach for extracting lung regions from chest X-ray images using a deep learning-based model. To achieve this, a structured pipeline is followed, starting from data acquisition to model evaluation. Publicly available Kaggle chest X-ray datasets with corresponding ground truth masks are utilized to train and validate the model. Since raw medical images often contain noise, variations in intensity, and inconsistent dimensions, appropriate preprocessing techniques such as resizing, normalization, and data augmentation are applied to enhance the quality and diversity of the input data.

The core of the proposed method is based on the U-Net architecture, which is widely used for biomedical image segmentation tasks. To further improve its performance, Attention Gate (AG) mechanisms are integrated into the skip connections of the network. These attention gates enable the model to selectively focus on relevant lung regions while suppressing irrelevant background information, thereby improving segmentation accuracy and boundary localization.

The model is trained using suitable optimization techniques and loss functions, and its performance is evaluated using standard metrics such as Dice coefficient and Intersection over Union (IOU). This section provides a detailed explanation of each stage of the proposed methodology, including dataset preparation, model architecture, attention mechanism, training strategy, and evaluation criteria.

3.2 U-Net With Attention Mechanism for Lung Region Extraction

The block diagram represents the overall workflow of the Attention-Based U-Net model for lung region segmentation from chest X-ray images. The process begins with the input of a chest X-ray image, which contains not only the lung regions but also other anatomical structures such as ribs and the heart. To prepare the image for effective processing, a preprocessing stage is applied, where the image is resized to a standard dimension and normalized to ensure consistent pixel intensity values. Additionally, data augmentation techniques such as rotation and flipping are used to improve the robustness and generalization capability of the model.

Figure 1. Block diagram of U Net attention mechanism based lung region segmentation

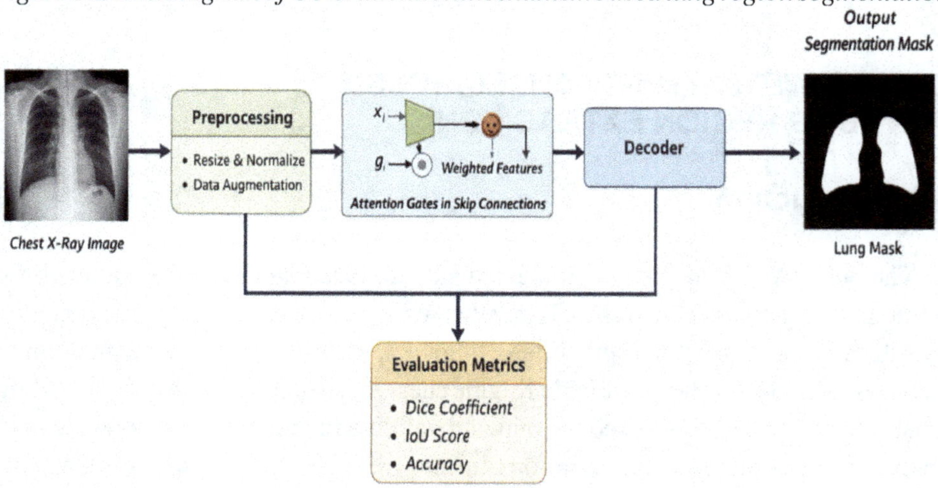

The preprocessed image is then passed through the encoder part of the U-Net architecture, which extracts important features by learning patterns such as edges, textures, and shapes. In this model, Attention Gates are incorporated into the skip connections between the encoder and decoder. These attention mechanisms take feature maps from the encoder and gating signals from the decoder to generate attention coefficients, which highlight relevant lung regions while suppressing irrelevant background information. As a result, only the most significant features are forwarded to the decoder in the form of weighted feature maps.

The decoder then reconstructs the segmented image by performing up sampling and combining the refined features received from the attention gates. This process results in the generation of a segmentation mask, where the lung regions are clearly distinguished from the background. Finally, the performance of the model is evaluated using metrics such as Dice coefficient, Intersection over Union (IOU), and accuracy, which measure the similarity between the predicted segmentation and the ground truth. Overall, the integration of attention gates into the U-Net architecture enhances the model's ability to accurately localize and segment lung regions in chest X-ray images.

3.3 Materials and Methods

3.3.1 Data Preprocessing

Data preprocessing is a crucial step in medical image analysis because the quality, consistency, and reliability of input data directly influence the performance of deep learning models. Chest X-ray images collected from different public and clinical datasets often exhibit significant variations in image resolution, intensity distribution, contrast levels, orientation, and noise characteristics due to differences in imaging devices, acquisition protocols, and patient conditions. These inconsistencies can negatively affect feature extraction and reduce the overall segmentation accuracy of deep learning frameworks. Therefore, appropriate preprocessing techniques are essential to standardize the input data and improve the learning capability of the proposed Attention-Based U-Net model. In this work, preprocessing begins with image resizing, where all chest X-ray images are transformed into a fixed spatial dimension suitable for model training. Standardizing image dimensions ensures uniform input representation and reduces computational complexity during training and inference. Following resizing, intensity normalization is applied to scale pixel values into a consistent range, which helps stabilize gradient updates and accelerates model convergence. Normalization also minimizes variations caused by different imaging conditions and improves feature consistency across the dataset.

To further enhance image quality, preprocessing techniques may include contrast enhancement and noise reduction operations. Chest X-ray images often contain low-contrast lung regions, overlapping anatomical structures, and imaging artifacts that make segmentation challenging. Contrast enhancement improves the visibility of lung boundaries and pathological regions, while noise reduction techniques help suppress irrelevant image distortions that may interfere with feature learning. Data augmentation is another important preprocessing strategy employed to improve the robustness and generalization capability of the model. Since medical imaging datasets are often limited in size, augmentation techniques artificially increase dataset diversity by generating modified versions of existing images. Common augmentation operations include rotation, flipping, scaling, translation, zooming, and brightness adjustment. These transformations help the model learn invariant and robust feature representations, thereby reducing overfitting and improving segmentation performance on unseen data.

The preprocessed images are then provided as input to the Attention-Based U-Net architecture, enabling the network to learn meaningful spatial and contextual features more effectively. By improving image consistency, enhancing feature visibility, and increasing dataset variability, preprocessing significantly contributes to the overall accuracy, stability, and reliability of the lung segmentation framework.

Image Resizing

Chest X-ray images are acquired from different sources with varying resolutions. To ensure uniformity and compatibility with the neural network architecture, all images are resized to a fixed dimension such as 256 × 256 pixels.

Let the original image be represented as I(x, y) with dimensions H×WH \times WH×W. The resized image Ir(x′,y′) is obtained by applying interpolation

$$I_r(x',y') = I\left(\frac{H'}{H} \cdot x', \frac{W'}{W} \cdot y'\right)$$

where:

- W′H' = target dimensions (e.g., 256 × 256)
- Interpolation methods such as bilinear or nearest-neighbour are used

Image Normalization

Medical images often have varying pixel intensity ranges, which can slow down model convergence. To address this, normalization is applied to scale pixel values into a standard range, typically [0, 1].

The normalized image I{norm} is computed as:

$$I_{\text{norm}} = \frac{I - I_{min}}{I_{max} - I_{min}}$$

where:

- I{min} and I{max}represent the minimum and maximum pixel values in the image

Benefits:

- Faster convergence during training
- Improved numerical stability
- Better feature learning

Data Augmentation

Deep learning models require large amounts of data for effective training. However, medical datasets are often limited. To overcome this limitation and prevent overfitting, data augmentation techniques are applied to artificially increase the diversity of the training dataset.

a) Rotation

Images are rotated by a small angle θ to simulate different orientations:

$$I'(x,y) = I(x\cos\theta - y\sin\theta, x\sin\theta + y\cos\theta)$$

b) Horizontal Flipping

The image is flipped along the vertical axis:

$$I'(x,y) = I(W - x, y)$$

c) Zooming (Scaling)

The image is scaled by a factor s:

$$I'(x,y) = I\left(s_x x, s_y y\right)$$

d) Translation

The image is shifted spatially by (tx,ty):

$$I'(x,y) = I\left(x - t_x, y - t_y\right)$$

Noise Handling

Chest X-ray images may contain noise due to imaging conditions. Basic filtering techniques such as Gaussian smoothing can be applied:

$$I_{smooth} = I * G(x,y)$$

where G(x,y) is a Gaussian kernel

3.3.2 U-Net Architecture

The base model used in this work is the U-Net architecture, which consists of:
U-NET ENCODER (Contracting Path)
The encoder extracts hierarchical features using convolution and pooling operations.
Each convolution operation is defined as:

$$f(x) = \sigma(W * x + b)$$

where:

- W= weight matrix
- x= input feature map
- b= bias
- σ = activation function (ReLU)

Max pooling reduces spatial dimensions:

$$x' = \text{MaxPool}(x)$$

The encoder, also known as the contracting path, is a fundamental component of the U-Net architecture responsible for extracting meaningful features from chest X-ray images. Its primary function is to capture both spatial and contextual information by progressively reducing the image dimensions while increasing the depth of feature maps. The encoder consists of a series of convolutional blocks, where each block typically includes convolution operations followed by a non-linear activation function such as the Rectified Linear Unit (ReLU). Mathematically, the convolution operation can be expressed as

$$f(x) = \sigma(W * x + b),$$

where x is the input feature map, W represents the convolutional kernel, b is the bias, and σ denotes the activation function. The ReLU function, defined as ReLU(x)=max (0,x)), introduces non-linearity and helps in efficient learning. To further reduce the spatial resolution and capture dominant features, max pooling is applied, typically using a 2×2 times 2×2 window, which halves the dimensions of the feature map. As the data passes through successive encoder layers, low-level features such as edges and textures are transformed into high-level semantic representations that correspond to lung structures. In the Attention-Based U-Net model, the encoder not only extracts these hierarchical features but also provides them to the decoder through skip connections. These feature maps are later refined using Attention Gates, ensuring that only the most relevant information related to lung regions is retained, thereby improving segmentation accuracy.

U-Net Decoder

The decoder, also known as the expanding path, is a crucial component of the U-Net architecture responsible for reconstructing the segmented lung region from the high-level features extracted by the encoder. Its primary objective is to restore the spatial resolution of the feature maps while preserving the important contextual information learned during the encoding process. The decoder achieves this through a series of upsampling operations, typically implemented using transposed convolution or interpolation methods, which progressively increase the dimensions of the feature maps. Mathematically, the upsampling operation can be represented as $x_{up} = \text{UpSample}(x)$ where x is the input feature map from the previous layer. After up sampling, the decoder concatenates these feature maps with the corresponding encoder feature maps through skip connections, which have been refined using Attention Gates. This concatenation can be expressed as $x_{concat} = [x_{up}, x_{att}]$ where x{att}represents the attention-weighted encoder features. This fusion of high-level semantic information with fine-grained spatial details enables the model to accurately localize lung boundaries. Following concatenation, convolutional operations and activation functions are applied to further refine the feature maps and reduce art facts introduced during up sampling. As the decoder progresses through successive layers, the feature maps gradually regain their original resolution, ultimately producing a dense prediction map. The final layer applies a sigmoid activation function to generate a binary segmentation mask, where pixel values close to 1 indicate lung regions and values close to 0 represent the background. In the Attention-Based U-Net model, the decoder plays a vital role in integrating multi-scale information and attention-refined features, thereby enhancing the precision and accuracy of lung region segmentation in chest X-ray images.

Attention Mechanism

The attention mechanism in Attention U-Net is designed to weight feature maps so that the network focuses on relevant spatial regions while suppressing irrelevant background information. Given encoder feature maps $x$and a gating signal $g$from the decoder, the attention mechanism computes an attention coefficient $\alpha$for each spatial location. First, both inputs are linearly transformed using learnable weights and then combined to form an intermediate representation. This can be expressed as:

$$q = W_x x + W_g g + b$$

where $W_x$and $W_g$are learnable weight matrices, and $b$is the bias term.

Table 1. Mathematical expressions of attention mechanism

Step	Mathematical expression	Description
Input Features	x, g	Encoder feature map and decoder gating signal
Linear Transformation		Feature fusion from encoder and decoder
Non-linearity		Adds non-linear representation
Attention Coefficient		Generates weights in range [0,1]
Feature Scaling		Refines encoder features
Output		Attention-enhanced feature map

The intermediate feature is passed through a non-linear activation function (typically ReLU), followed by another linear transformation and a sigmoid activation to produce attention coefficients:

Here, represents the sigmoid function, ensuring that . The final refined feature map is obtained by element-wise multiplication of the attention coefficients with the encoder features:

where denotes element-wise multiplication. This process allows the network to emphasize important lung regions while reducing noise from irrelevant structures in chest X-ray images, leading to improved segmentation accuracy.

4. RESULTS AND DISCUSSION

4.1 Dataset Description

The dataset used in this research is Kaggle Chest X-ray images, which is designed for lung region segmentation tasks. It contains paired chest X-ray images along with their corresponding ground truth masks that indicate the exact lung regions.

Input Data: The input to the model consists of chest X-ray images:

- Image type: Grayscale medical images

- Format: PNG / JPG
- Resolution: Typically resized to 256 × 256 pixels for model training
- Content: Frontal chest X-rays showing lung structures

These images serve as the primary input for the segmentation model.

The dataset was divided into training and testing subsets using an approximate 80:20 partitioning strategy. A total of 562 chest X-ray images were used for training, while 141 images were reserved for testing and performance evaluation. The dataset split was performed at the image level to avoid data leakage between training and testing samples. During preprocessing, all images and corresponding masks were resized to 256 × 256 pixels and normalized to improve numerical stability during training. Data augmentation techniques including rotation, flipping, zooming, and translation were applied only to the training dataset in order to improve model generalization and reduce overfitting.

Figure 2. Sample images from the dataset

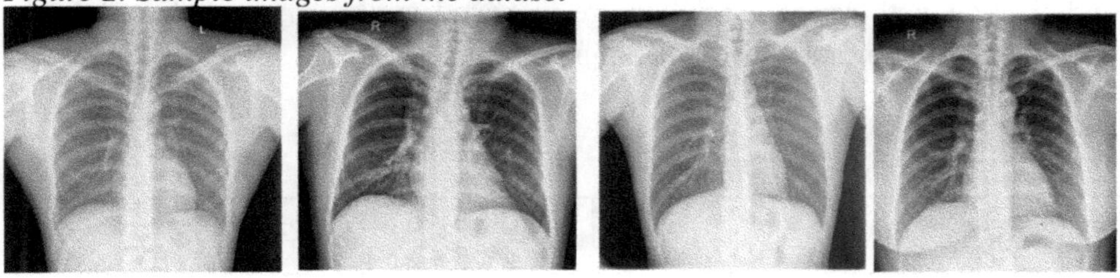

Ground Truth Masks

Each input image is associated with a segmentation mask:

- Binary mask format:
  - o Pixel value 1 (white) → Lung region
  - o Pixel value 0 (black) → Background
- Masks are manually annotated by medical experts or derived from standard datasets
- Used as target output during training

Dataset Structure

The dataset is typically organized into two main folders:

- Images→ Contains chest X-ray images
- Masks → Contains corresponding lung masks

Each image has a matching mask with the same filename, ensuring proper mapping during training.

4.2 Hyper Parameter Tuning

The hyperparameter tuning process involved experimenting with different values to identify the optimal configuration for the model. For the learning rate, values such as 0.001, 0.0005, and 0.0001 were tested, and 0.0001 was selected as the final value because it provided more stable convergence during training. Batch size was varied between 8, 16, and 32, and smaller batch sizes (8/16) were preferred as they improved segmentation performance while balancing memory constraints. The model was trained for different numbers of epochs (30, 50, and 100), with 100 epochs chosen to ensure sufficient learning and convergence of the network. For optimization, both Adam and SGD were evaluated, and Adam was selected due to its faster convergence and better handling of sparse gradients.

Table 2. Hyper Parameter Tuning

Hyperparameter	Values Tried	Final Selected Value	Description
Learning Rate	0.001, 0.0005, 0.0001	0.0001	Controls weight update step size
Batch Size	8, 16, 32	8 / 16	Number of images per training step
Epochs	30, 50, 100	100	Full training cycles
Optimizer	Adam, SGD	Adam	Updates model weights efficiently
Loss Function	BCE, Dice Loss, BCE + Dice	BCE + Dice Loss	Improves segmentation accuracy
Image Size	128×128, 256×256, 512×512	256×256	Input resolution for training
Dropout Rate	0.2, 0.3, 0.5	0.3	Prevents overfitting
Activation Function	ReLU, Leaky ReLU	ReLU	Adds non-linearity

The loss function was carefully chosen among Binary Cross-Entropy (BCE), Dice Loss, and a combination of BCE + Dice Loss, with the combined loss performing best as it improved both pixel-wise accuracy and region overlap in segmentation. Input image sizes of 128×128, 256×256, and 512×512 were tested, and 256×256 was selected as it provided a good trade-off between computational efficiency and spatial detail. Dropout rates of 0.2, 0.3, and 0.5 were evaluated, and 0.3 was chosen to effectively reduce overfitting without causing underfitting. Finally, different activation functions such as ReLU and Leaky ReLU were compared, and ReLU was selected due to its simplicity and strong performance in learning non-linear feature representations.

4.3 System Configuration

The system configuration for implementing the Attention-Based U-Net model for lung region segmentation is designed to support efficient training and inference on medical image datasets. The model requires a high-performance computing environment to handle deep learning computations, particularly during training on large chest X-ray datasets. A GPU-enabled system is recommended to accelerate convolutional operations and attention mechanisms within the network. The software environment typically includes Python with deep learning libraries such as TensorFlow or PyTorch, along with supporting libraries like NumPy, OpenCV, and Matplotlib for data preprocessing and visualization. This configuration ensures smooth execution of the model and improves training speed and segmentation accuracy. The system configuration used for implementing the proposed Attention-Augmented U-Net model was carefully designed to support efficient preprocessing, model training, and segmentation of chest X-ray images. The operating system environment included Windows 10/11 or Ubuntu 18.04 and above, which provide stable support for deep learning libraries and GPU acceleration. The implementation was carried out using Python 3.8 or higher due to its extensive support for scientific computing, medical image analysis, and machine learning applications.

Deep learning frameworks such as TensorFlow and PyTorch were used for model development, training, and evaluation. These frameworks provide optimized tools for convolutional neural network implementation, automatic differentiation, and GPU-based computation. To accelerate training and reduce computational time, an NVIDIA GTX 1650 GPU or higher was utilized, while RTX 3060/4060 GPUs are recommended for improved performance and faster convergence. The system also employed Intel i5/i7 (8th Generation or higher) or AMD Ryzen 5/7 processors to efficiently handle preprocessing operations and model execution.

A minimum of 8 GB RAM was required for basic implementation; however, 16 GB or more is recommended for handling large datasets and batch processing more efficiently. Storage requirements included at least 20–50 GB of free disk space, preferably using SSD storage to improve data loading speed and training efficiency. Supporting libraries such as NumPy, OpenCV, Matplotlib, and Scikit-learn were used for numerical computation, image preprocessing, visualization, and evaluation. The development and experimentation environment included Jupyter Notebook, Google Colab, and Visual Studio Code (VS Code), which provided flexible tools for coding, debugging, visualization, and model analysis.

Table 3. System Configuration

Components	Specification
Operating System	Windows 10/11 or Ubuntu 18.04+
Programming Language	Python 3.8+
Deep Learning Framework	TensorFlow / PyTorch
GPU	NVIDIA GTX 1650 or higher (Recommended: RTX 3060/4060)
CPU	Intel i5/i7 (8th Gen or higher) / AMD Ryzen 5/7
RAM	Minimum 8 GB (Recommended 16 GB or more)
Storage	At least 20–50 GB free space (SSD preferred)
Libraries	NumPy, OpenCV, Matplotlib, Scikit-learn
Development Tool	Jupyter Notebook / Google Colab / VS Code

4.3 Evaluation Metrics

To evaluate the performance of the Attention U-Net model for lung segmentation, several standard image segmentation metrics are used. These metrics compare the predicted lung mask with the ground truth mask.

4.3.1 Dice Coefficient (F1 Score)

Measures the overlap between predicted and ground truth masks.

- Range: 0 to 1
- Higher value indicates better segmentation accuracy
- Most important metric for medical image segmentation

4.3.2 Intersection over Union (IoU)

Also called Jaccard Index, measures similarity between predicted and actual regions.

- Range: 0 to 1
- Higher IoU = better overlap
- More strict than Dice coefficient

4.3.3. Accuracy

Measures overall pixel-wise correctness

- TP = True Positive, TN = True Negative
- Can be misleading in imbalanced datasets

4.3.4 Precision

Measures how many predicted lung pixels are actually correct

- Useful when false positives must be reduced

4.3.5 Recall (Sensitivity)

Measures how many actual lung pixels are correctly detected.

- Important for medical diagnosis (minimizing missed lung regions)

4.4 Results and Discussion

The performance of the proposed Attention Gate-based U-Net model for lung segmentation was evaluated using standard evaluation metrics such as Dice Coefficient, Intersection over Union (IoU), Accuracy, Precision, and Recall. The model was trained on 562 chest X-ray images and tested on 141 images from a publicly available dataset. The evaluation results demonstrate that the proposed architecture achieves strong segmentation performance with minimal difference between training and testing results, indicating good generalization capability.

The model obtained a Dice Coefficient of 0.9373 during training and 0.9316 during testing, which indicates a high degree of overlap between the predicted segmentation masks and the ground truth annotations. Similarly, the IoU (Jaccard Index) values of 0.8619 for training and 0.8588 for testing further confirm the effectiveness of the model in accurately identifying lung regions. The high values of Precision and Recall also reflect the model's ability to correctly classify lung pixels while minimizing false positives and false negatives.

The inclusion of Attention Gates in the U-Net architecture significantly improved the model's ability to focus on relevant lung regions while suppressing irrelevant background information such as ribs and surrounding tissues. This enhancement contributed to better boundary localization and more accurate segmentation results compared to conventional U-Net models reported in literature.

The experimental results validate that the proposed Attention U-Net model provides robust and reliable lung segmentation performance. The small performance gap between training and testing results indicates that the model is not overfitting and is capable of generalizing well to unseen data, making it suitable for practical medical image analysis applications and computer-aided diagnosis systems.

The proposed model was evaluated using both training and testing datasets containing 562 and 141 chest X-ray images, respectively, and the results demonstrate strong and consistent performance across all metrics. The training loss of 0.0612 and testing loss of 0.0697 indicate that the model has effectively learned the segmentation task with only a slight increase in error on unseen data, showing good generalization. Similarly, the Dice Loss values of 0.0627 for training and 0.0684 for testing further confirm that the model produces highly accurate lung region segmentation with minimal prediction error.

Table 4. Experimental Results

Metrics	Train	Test
Loss	0.0612	0.0697
Dice Loss	0.0627	0.0684
Dice Coefficient	0.9373	0.9316
Jaccard Index	0.8619	0.8588
Accuracy	0.9842	0.9821
Precision	0.9385	0.9340
Recall	0.9358	0.9297

In terms of segmentation quality, the model achieved a Dice Coefficient of 0.9373 on training data and 0.9316 on testing data, reflecting a high overlap between predicted masks and ground truth annotations. The Jaccard Index (IoU) values of 0.8619 for training and 0.8588 for testing further validate the model's ability to accurately identify lung regions. Additionally, the high Accuracy values of 0.9842 (training) and 0.9821 (testing) indicate that the model correctly classifies the majority of pixels in the images.

Figure 3. Lung region segmentation

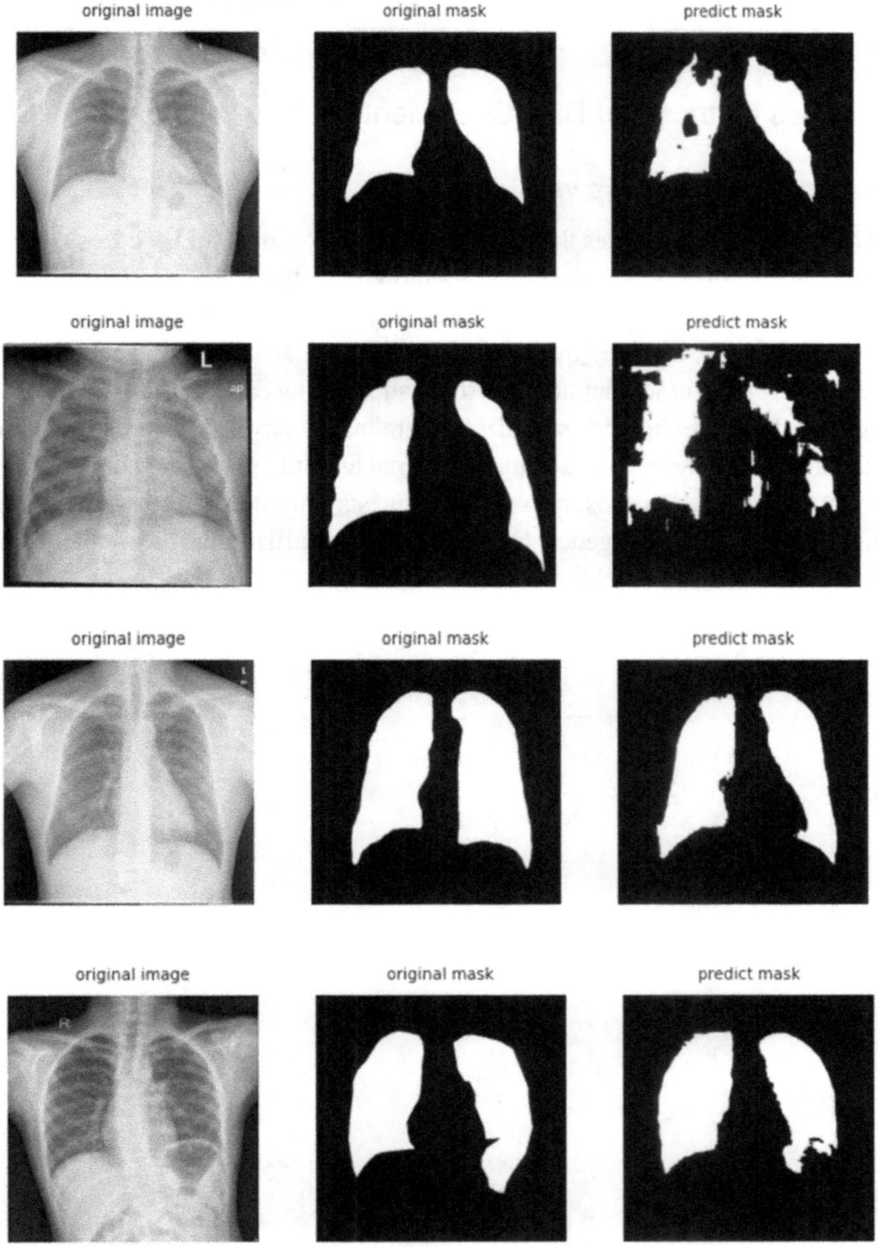

The Precision values of 0.9385 and 0.9340 show that the model has a low false positive rate, while the Recall values of 0.9358 and 0.9297 demonstrate its strong ability to capture true lung regions effectively. Overall, the close performance between training and testing results confirms that the model is stable, well-optimized, and free from significant overfitting, making it highly reliable for lung segmentation in chest X-ray images.

4.4.1 Loss Metrics and Dice Coefficient

Loss Metrics Plot (Loss vs Dice Loss)

The first figure illustrates the variation of training **Loss** and **Dice Loss** over 100 epochs. It can be observed that both curves show a steady decreasing trend, indicating that the model is learning effectively as training progresses. Initially, the loss values are relatively high, but they drop sharply within the first 20–30 epochs, showing rapid improvement in segmentation performance during early training. After around 40 epochs, the curves begin to stabilize and gradually converge toward lower values, indicating that the model is reaching an optimal learning state. The close alignment between the loss and Dice loss curves also suggests consistent optimization behavior without instability or divergence. Overall, this plot confirms that the model has been trained successfully and achieves good convergence.

Figure 4. Loss metrics

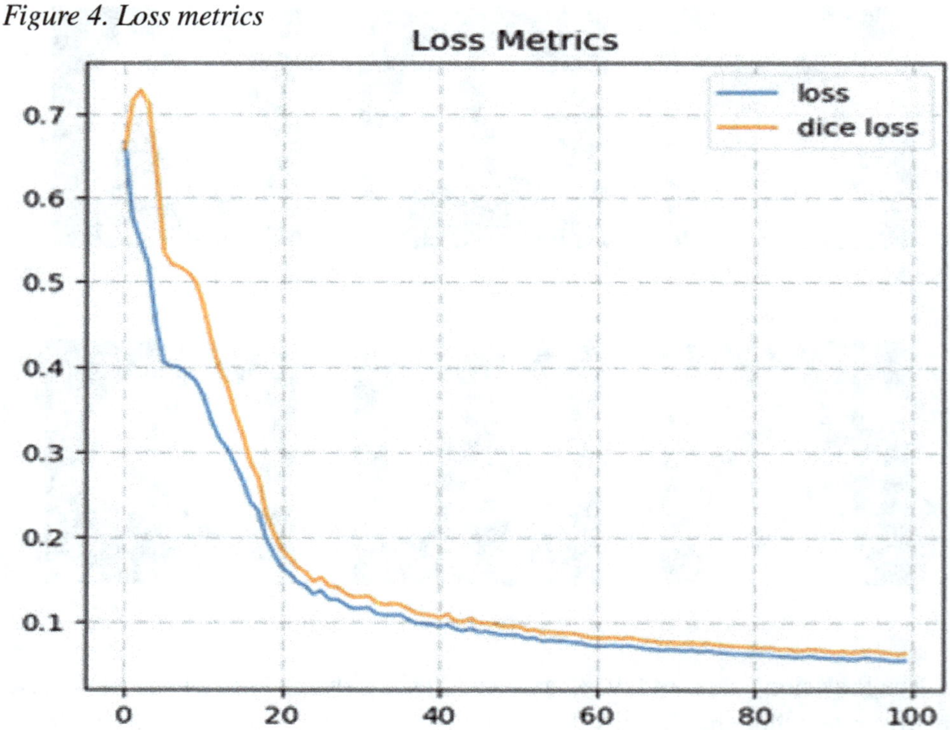

Dice Coefficient and Jaccard Index Plot

The second figure represents the progression of **Dice Coefficient** and **Jaccard Index (IoU)** over training epochs. Both metrics show a consistent increasing trend, which indicates continuous improvement in segmentation accuracy. In the early epochs, the values are relatively low due to random initialization, but they improve significantly after about 10–20 epochs as the model begins learning meaningful lung region features. As training continues, both curves gradually stabilize at higher values, with the Dice Coefficient reaching around 0.93+ and the Jaccard Index approaching approximately 0.85–0.86. The Dice Coefficient remains consistently higher than the Jaccard Index, which is expected since Dice tends to produce slightly higher overlap scores. The smooth upward trend and eventual saturation of both metrics demonstrate that the model is effectively learning and achieving strong segmentation performance without signs of overfitting or instability

Figure 5. Dice Coefficient and Jaccard Index

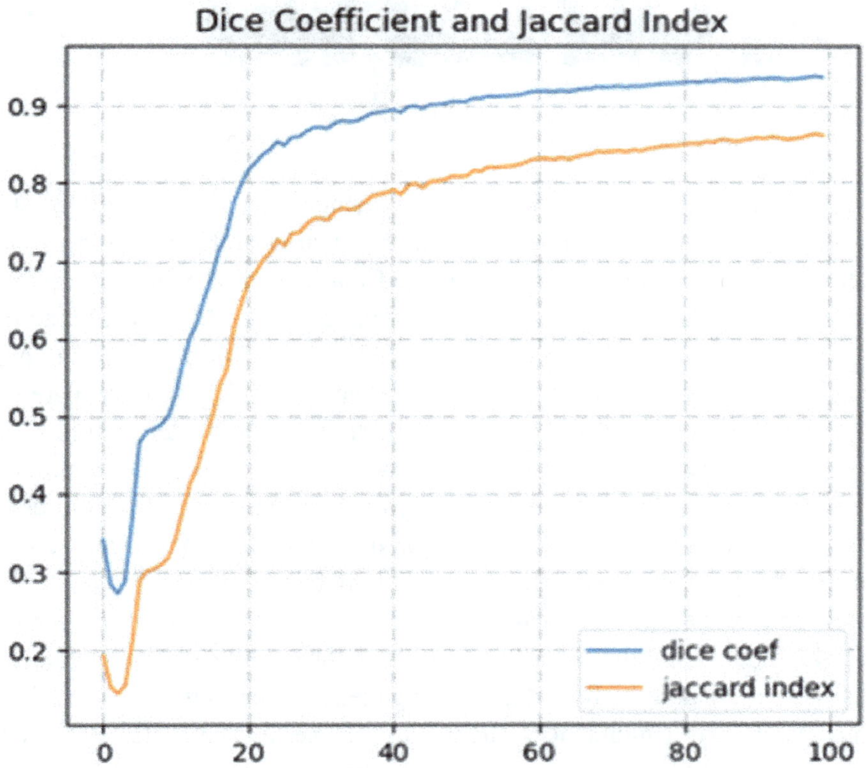

Figure 6. Lung region segmentation with different threshold

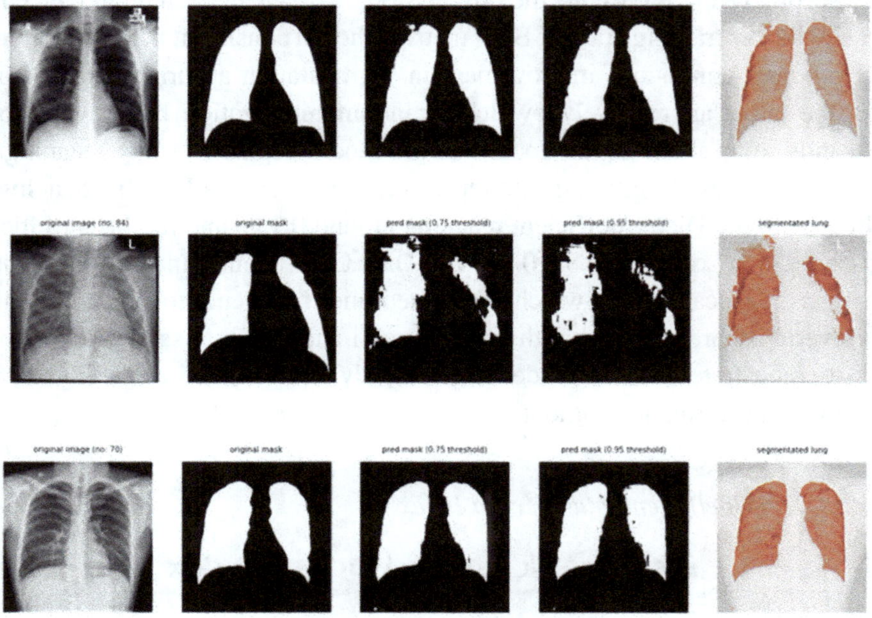

In practical clinical environments, the segmented lung masks may assist radiologists by improving visualization of lung boundaries and highlighting regions of interest for further analysis. The generated masks can be manually reviewed and corrected when necessary, ensuring that final clinical decisions remain under expert human supervision. Such collaborative AI-assisted workflows may improve diagnostic efficiency while maintaining clinical accountability and transparency.

The output of the proposed Attention Gate-based U-Net model is a segmented lung region extracted from the input chest X-ray image. The model generates a binary mask in which the lung areas are highlighted while the non-lung regions are suppressed. This mask is then overlaid on the original X-ray image to provide a clear visual representation of the segmented lung boundaries.

The predicted output closely matches the ground truth annotations, demonstrating the model's ability to accurately identify lung regions. The performance of the system is quantitatively evaluated using metrics such as the Dice coefficient and Intersection over Union (IoU). The model achieves a Dice coefficient of 0.93, indicating a high degree of similarity between the predicted segmentation and the actual lung regions. The output can be used for further medical analysis, such as disease detection, abnormality identification, and computer-aided diagnosis, thereby assisting healthcare professionals in making accurate and efficient clinical decisions.

Despite the strong segmentation performance achieved by the proposed model, certain challenging cases remain. Segmentation errors may occur in chest X-ray images affected by severe noise, extremely low contrast, distorted lung boundaries, or overlapping anatomical structures. In some instances, small peripheral lung regions may be partially under-segmented, particularly when image quality is poor or when pathological patterns significantly alter the normal lung appearance.

These observations highlight the importance of human-centered review in practical clinical environments. In a collaborative workflow, AI-generated segmentation masks can be reviewed and refined by radiologists prior to further diagnostic interpretation. Such human-in-the-loop validation can enhance clinical trust, minimize segmentation-related errors, and support the safe and responsible deployment of AI-assisted medical imaging systems.

4.5 Limitations and Ethical Considerations

Although the proposed Attention-based U-Net model demonstrates promising segmentation performance, several limitations should be acknowledged. First, the model was evaluated on a relatively limited dataset, which may not fully represent the diversity of real-world clinical imaging conditions. Variations in imaging devices, patient demographics, disease severity, and acquisition protocols may affect model generalization in external healthcare environments. Second, the study primarily focuses on segmentation accuracy metrics such as Dice coefficient and IoU, while additional clinical validation by radiologists was not performed. Therefore, the model should not be considered clinically deployable without further multi-center validation and expert evaluation. Another limitation involves potential dataset bias. Public chest X-ray datasets may contain imbalanced distributions related to age groups, disease categories, imaging quality, or institutional acquisition settings. Such bias can influence model performance across different patient populations.

From an ethical perspective, the dataset used in this study consists of publicly available and de-identified chest X-ray images intended for research purposes. The proposed system is designed as a supportive AI tool rather than a replacement for clinical expertise. Human oversight, transparency, and clinician review remain essential components of responsible medical AI deployment.

5. CONCLUSION

In this work, an Attention-based U-Net model was developed for accurate lung region segmentation from chest X-ray images. The proposed approach enhances the traditional U-Net architecture by incorporating Attention Gates (AGs), which enable the model to focus on important lung regions while suppressing irrelevant background features. This improvement allows better extraction of meaningful spatial information and enhances the overall segmentation performance. The model was trained and evaluated on publicly available datasets with appropriate preprocessing techniques such as normalization and data augmentation. The experimental results demonstrate that the proposed model achieves a Dice coefficient of 0.93, indicating a strong agreement between the predicted segmentation and the ground truth. Compared to the conventional U-Net, the Attention-based model provides improved boundary detection and localization accuracy. Furthermore, the integration of attention mechanisms in the skip connections improves feature propagation between encoder and decoder layers, resulting in more precise segmentation of lung regions even in challenging cases with noise and overlapping anatomical structures. The model proves to be efficient, reliable, and suitable for medical imaging applications. The proposed Attention U-Net model offers a robust and automated solution for lung segmentation and can serve as an important component in computer-aided diagnosis systems, supporting clinicians in the early detection and analysis of pulmonary diseases.

6. FUTURE SCOPE

The proposed Attention-based U-Net model for lung region segmentation demonstrates strong potential for further development and real-world medical imaging applications. Future work can extend this framework toward the development of a fully automated computer-aided diagnosis system capable of not only segmenting lung regions but also detecting and classifying pulmonary diseases such as pneumonia, tuberculosis, and lung cancer. The model can be further enhanced by incorporating advanced architectures, including transformer-based networks and hybrid deep learning models, to improve segmentation accuracy, feature representation, and computational efficiency. Additionally, future research may expand the system to support multi-class abnormality localization and disease severity assessment, enabling more comprehensive analysis of chest X-ray images. Another important direction is the integration of the proposed model into clinical decision support systems (CDSS), where it can assist radiologists in achieving faster and more accurate diagnosis. With extensive validation on large-scale, multi-center, and real-time clinical datasets, the framework may become suitable for deployment in hospitals and diagnostic centers.

The development of lightweight and mobile-friendly versions of the model could further enable its use in remote and resource-limited healthcare environments, thereby improving access to quality medical diagnostics. Furthermore, integrating explainable AI techniques and uncertainty estimation mechanisms can enhance transparency, interpretability, and clinician trust in AI-assisted systems. Future research should also focus on human-centered evaluation frameworks and clinician-in-the-loop validation strategies to support the safe, reliable, and responsible adoption of AI-based lung segmentation systems in clinical practice. The future scope of this work lies in advancing intelligent, scalable, interpretable, and clinically reliable AI solutions that can significantly improve the early detection, diagnosis, and treatment of pulmonary diseases.

REFERENCES

Aljuaid, H., Adlan, H., Alkebsi, B., Alfurhood, B. S., Liotta, A., & Cavallaro, L. (2026). An experimental comparison of deep learning models for pneumonia classification from chest X-ray images. *Biomedical Signal Processing and Control, 112*(Part D), 108742. DOI: 10.1016/j.bspc.2025.108742

Bombiński, P., Szatkowski, P., Sobieski, B., Kwieciński, T., Płotka, S., Adamek, M., Banasiuk, M., Furmanek, M. I., & Biecek, P. (2025). Underestimation of lung regions on chest X-ray segmentation masks assessed by comparison with total lung volume evaluated on computed tomography. *Radiography, 31*(3), 102930. DOI: 10.1016/j.radi.2025.102930 PMID: 40174327

Candemir, S., & Antani, S. (2019). A review on lung boundary detection in chest X-rays. *International Journal of Computer Assisted Radiology and Surgery, 14*(4), 563–576. DOI: 10.1007/s11548-019-01917-1 PMID: 30730032

Desikar, G. N. M. S., Kadarkarai, R., Somasundaram, K., Kandasamy, V., & Partheeban, P. (2026). Optimized multi-dimensional attention spiking neural network for pneumonia detection in chest X-ray images. *Biomedical Signal Processing and Control, 113*(Part C), 108765. DOI: 10.1016/j.bspc.2025.108765

Ding, X., Zhou, Q., Liu, Z., Kowah, J. A. H., Wang, L., Huang, X., & Liu, X. (2024). A novel approach to the technique of lung region segmentation based on a deep learning model to diagnose COVID-19 X-ray images. *Current Medical Imaging, 20*, 100211. Advance online publication. DOI: 10.2174/0115734056271185231121074341 PMID: 38389381

Egala, R., & Sairam, M. V. S. (2025). Multi-layer stacked residual coordinate termite alate network for multi-class lung diseases detection from chest X-ray images. *Applied Soft Computing, 179*, 113393. DOI: 10.1016/j.asoc.2025.113393

Gangwar, S., Devi, R., & Isa, N. A. M. (2025). 9IEC: A novel method for exposure region determination in low contrast and nonuniform illumination chest X-ray imaging. *Biomedical Signal Processing and Control, 109*, 107988. DOI: 10.1016/j.bspc.2025.107988

Huang, Y., & Meng, Z. (2026). Highly accurate four-class prediction of lung diseases from chest X-ray images based on EfficientNetV2. *Biomedical Signal Processing and Control, 120*(Part C), 110238. DOI: 10.1016/j.bspc.2026.110238

Krishnakumari, L., Ramalakshmi, R., Srirenganachiyar, V., Ragavan, K., & Ramalakshmi, K. 2023, February. Analysis of Liver Tumor Segmentation using Deep ResUNet. In *2023 Third International Conference on Artificial Intelligence and Smart Energy (ICAIS)* (pp. 665-668). IEEE. DOI: 10.1109/ICAIS56108.2023.10073676

Mansoor, A., Cerrolaza, J. J., Perez, G., Biggs, E., Okada, K., Nino, G., & Linguraru, M. G. (2020). A generic approach to lung field segmentation from chest radiographs using deep space and shape learning. *IEEE Transactions on Bio-Medical Engineering*, *67*(4), 1206–1220. DOI: 10.1109/TBME.2019.2933508 PMID: 31425015

Mongan, J., Moy, L., & Kahn, C. E.Jr. (2020). Checklist for Artificial Intelligence in Medical Imaging (CLAIM): A guide for authors and reviewers. *Radiology. Artificial Intelligence*, *2*(2), e200029. DOI: 10.1148/ryai.2020200029 PMID: 33937821

Oktay, O., Schlemper, J., Folgoc, L. L., Lee, M., Heinrich, M., Misawa, K., Mori, K., McDonagh, S., Hammerla, N. Y., Kainz, B., Glocker, B., & Rueckert, D. (2018). Attention U-Net: Learning where to look for the pancreas. *arXiv*. https://arxiv.org/abs/1804.03999

Rajalakshmi, R., Ramalakshmi, K., Lakshmi, A., Subhashini, G., & Theivanathan, G. 2024, March. Enhancing Pneumonia Detection Through Convolutional Neural Networks and Data Augmentation In Chest X-Ray Imaging. In *2024 10th International Conference on Advanced Computing and Communication Systems (ICACCS)* (Vol. 1, pp. 715-718). IEEE.

Ramalakshmi, K., & Kumari, L. K. (2025). U-Net-based architecture with attention mechanisms and Bayesian Optimization for brain tumor segmentation using MR images. *Computers in Biology and Medicine*, *195*, 110677. DOI: 10.1016/j.compbiomed.2025.110677 PMID: 40592172

Ramalakshmi, K., Shukla, V. K., & Kumari, L. K. (2026). Leveraging transfer learning with convolutional neural networks for enhanced breast cancer detection. *Neural Computing & Applications*, *38*(8), 297. DOI: 10.1007/s00521-026-12091-2

Ramalakshmi, K., Srinivasa Raghavan, V., Rajagopal, S., Krishna Kumari, L., Theivanathan, G., Kulkarni, M. B., & Poddar, H. (2024). An extensive analysis of artificial intelligence and segmentation methods transforming cancer recognition in medical imaging. *Biomedical Physics & Engineering Express*, *10*(4), 045046. DOI: 10.1088/2057-1976/ad555b PMID: 38848695

Rathod, D. I., Agarwal, R., & Sujatha, K. S. (2024). Lung disease classification using chest X-ray image: An optimal ensemble of classification with hybrid training. *Biomedical Signal Processing and Control*, *91*, 105941. DOI: 10.1016/j.bspc.2023.105941

Ronneberger, O., Fischer, P., & Brox, T. (2015). U-Net: Convolutional networks for biomedical image segmentation. In *MICCAI 2015* (pp. 234–241). Medical Image Computing and Computer-Assisted Intervention. Springer., DOI: 10.1007/978-3-319-24574-4_28

Taha, A. A., & Hanbury, A. (2015). Metrics for evaluating 3D medical image segmentation: Analysis, selection, and tool. *BMC Medical Imaging*, *15*(1), 29. DOI: 10.1186/s12880-015-0068-x PMID: 26263899

Tam, W., Babyn, P., & Alirezaie, J. (2025). Robust lung segmentation in chest X-ray images using modified U-Net with deeper network and residual blocks. *Computer Methods and Programs in Biomedicine Update*, *8*, 100211. DOI: 10.1016/j.cmpbup.2025.100211

Wang, L., Wang, Q., Wang, X., & Liu, M. (2026). Segmentation-enhanced multiscale deep hashing for chest X-ray image retrieval. *Medical Image Analysis*, *109*, 103919. DOI: 10.1016/j.media.2025.103919 PMID: 41468639

Wang, Q., Meng, W., Gan, C., Yu, H., & Cheng, Y. (2026). A lesion region awareness and adaptive label-relation graph algorithm for multi-label chest X-ray image classification. *Engineering Applications of Artificial Intelligence*, *167*(Part 2), 113873. DOI: 10.1016/j.engappai.2026.113873

Xu, T., Mandal, M., Long, R., Cheng, I., & Basu, A. (2012). Mrinal Mandal, Richard Long, Irene Cheng, Anup Basu, An edge-region force guided active shape approach for automatic lung field detection in chest radiographs. *Computerized Medical Imaging and Graphics : The Official Journal of the Computerized Medical Imaging Society*, *36*(6), 452–463. DOI: 10.1016/j.compmedimag.2012.04.005 PMID: 22608158

Chapter 5

Automated Data-to-Text Generation of Football Match Reports Using a Large Language Model

Barry Dyer
http://orcid.org/0009-0001-4332-5206
Dundalk Institute of Technology, Ireland

Kevin Mcdaid
Dundalk Institute of Technology, Ireland

Abhishek Kaushik
http://orcid.org/0000-0002-3329-1807
Dundalk Institute of Technology, Ireland

ABSTRACT

This study investigated the suitability of a Large Language Model (ChatGPT-4o) for generating high-quality, factually correct, and complete match reports using on-ball events data from football games. The structure and data requirements of the match reports were established through manual analysis of five real-world reports. Using this guideline, the LLM generated ten match reports using zero-shot prompts (Type 1), followed by ten scoreline-matched reports using few-shot prompts (Type 2). Ten human-authored, scoreline-matched reports acted as reference articles (Type 3). The Type 1 and Type 2 reports were evaluated by the researchers for Accuracy and Completeness before twenty-six volunteers were asked to rate a set of reports for

DOI: 10.4018/979-8-2600-2701-1.ch005

Enjoyment, Excitement, Clarity, and Quality. Volunteers also indicated whether they assumed the author to be human or an LLM. Articles were presented in a randomized order with volunteers blinded to the article source.

INTRODUCTION

Due to the success and flexibility of large language models (LLM) such as OpenAI's ChatGPT-4, the use of this technology is gathering momentum in multiple fields such as software engineering, medicine, law, finance, and education (Wang et al., 2024). The realm of automated journalism, especially in the context of sports news, provides another potential use case.

Carlson (2015) defined automated journalism as the use of algorithmic processes to convert *"data into narrative news texts with limited to no human intervention beyond the initial programming choices."* LLMs are well-suited to such tasks, being able to produce articles tailored to an organisation or individual reader (Carlson, 2015). while using a fraction of the time and resources usually required by human authors (Shi & Sun, 2024).

The potential benefits in sports reporting are significant, especially where demands for content are high. For example, association football is the most popular sport in the world with an estimated 5 billion fans globally (FIFA, 2021) and many fans rely on match reports from popular news outlets to follow their team's progress. Providing this type of coverage at every level of the game is impractical though due to large resource and time requirements. This provides a promising opportunity to explore football news generation using LLMs such as OpenAI's ChatGPT. These tools may allow football reporters to produce match reports more efficiently and increase time available to focus on more in-depth content creation such as feature writing (Duncan et al., 2025).

Research by Rossner et al. (2024) showed that readers' perceptions of credibility, trustworthiness, and expertise were not influenced by the disclosure of whether football match reports were AI-generated or written by a journalist. Similarly, Barroletta et al. (2024) concluded that producing automated news without compromising on quality is feasible. However, in some cases, disclosure of AI-authorship has decreased perceived credibility of the source in the eyes of the reader. In many cases, readers also appear to enjoy articles written by human authors over AI-generated content perhaps due to more emotive language (Duncan et al., 2025), more lively narratives (Barrolleta & Sandoval-Martín, 2024), or more in-depth analysis (Kanasheva et al., 2024).

This suggests that although AI tools can effectively improve efficiency, reduce workload, and save costs without compromising the quality of news content, further investigation is needed into how readers respond to AI-authored content. This may have important implications on how newsrooms leverage the technology. In the context of football news, the increasing availability of detailed football match databases such as the StatsBomb Open Data archive (Hudl StatsBomb, Bath, United Kingdom) provides an opportunity to investigate how these data can be used to create high-quality, accurate match narratives and to explore readers perceptions of such output.

Therefore, the aim of this study was to establish to what extent an LLM (ChatGPT-4o) was able to generate high quality, factually correct, and complete football match reports using data available via the StatsBomb Open Data API.

LITERATURE REVIEW

Systems for Generating Sports News Content

Despite the potential benefits of using LLMs in football journalism, there appears to be a lack of research in this area. Previous attempts to generate football match summaries have focussed primarily on template-based systems whereby gaps in predetermined sentence templates are filled with data to complete the output text (Bouayad-Agha et al., 2012; Van Der Lee et al., 2017). More recently, studies have investigated the integration of LLM technology to augment template-based systems (Caron & Muller, 2023; Puduppully et al., 2019). Few studies have investigated the efficacy of LLMs in generating football match summaries directly from raw data (Chiang et al., 2024).

Template-based systems have typically been designed to either generate a text feed resembling live match commentary (Cook & Karakus, 2024; Sarkhoosh et al., 2024) or to generate text summaries such as match reports (Bouayad-Agha et al., 2012; Chiang et al., 2024). These systems can produce high-quality texts and can achieve personalisation of the text based on the preferences of the reader as shown by Van Der Lee et al. (2017) who created the Personalized Automated Soccer Texts (PASS) System to generate soccer reports for Dutch football games using match statistics. Their system used emotive language, producing one report tailored to the home team fans, and another tailored to the away team fans. Twenty Dutch students were then asked to identify the group of fans they thought the article was personalised to and to rate the Clarity and Fluency of the reports on a 7-point Likert Scale. The participants predicted the correct target group of fans in 91% of all cases. The ratings for Clarity and Fluency also showed a positive response with scores 5.64 ± 0.88 and 5.36 ± 0.79 respectively.

Template-based systems usually require a content planning stage to define the structure of the output and to develop a series of templates used to construct the text (Aires & Nunes, 2016; Puduppully et al., 2019). This requires a large input from a human author to develop templates for each scenario or event to be reported on (Aires & Nunes, 2016). In the development of the GameRecapper system, eighty-one distinct templates were created to facilitate reporting on goal events in football matches (Aires & Nunes, 2016). Data were extracted in JSON format to populate the templates and construct a match summary. Forty-four of these summaries were assessed for intelligibility and fluidity by fifteen volunteers. A further 46 evaluators then assessed 10 randomly selected reports (5 human-authored, and 5 GameRecapper-generated) on accuracy and completeness relative to the ground truth game sheet. A mean intelligibility score of 92.91% and average fluidity score of 85.73% showed the system could generate high quality reports, however, there was still a preference for human-written reports based on scores for completeness (87.66% versus 80.42%) and publication readiness (81.3% versus 73.04%). The need for multiple unique sentence templates for each match event type also limited reporting to goal events only.

With the introduction of LLMs, researchers have tried to use the technology to augment (Caron & Muller, 2023; Gautam et al., 2022; Puduppully et al., 2019) or substitute (Chiang et al., 2024) template-based systems for sports reporting. Pudupully et al. (2019) experimented with the addition of a neural network-based content planning module to a data-to-text basketball match summary generator. They showed improved quality of output texts generated by their data-to-text system when integrating this mechanism. Gautam et al. (2022) aimed to create an automated end-to-end soccer match summarization tool using audio commentary, details of important match events, and captions describing in-game events. Their modular system included a pre-trained audio separation tool to extract audio commentary from the game video and use of the Longformer transformer model to allow use of large text inputs. The transformer-based method showed superior Recall-Oriented Understudy for Gisting Evaluation (ROUGE) scores compared to the template-based method when evaluated against human-authored match summaries. In a similar approach, Sarkoosh et al. (2024) designed a system capable of combining multimodal data analysis with natural language generation using the GPT-4-Turbo model. Their SoccerSum system integrated game audio, video, and metadata to automate the summarisation of football goal events for social media posts.

Caron & Muller (2023) aimed to apply LLM technology to the domain of tactical analysis in football rather than match summary generation. They fine-tuned a generic deep learning model (GPT-NeoX-20B) to develop a TacticalGPT system able to simplify the interpretation of match events data and provide rapid access to actionable tactical insights.

Chiang et al. (2024) and Krijnen (2021) aimed to generate sports reports directly from raw data using an LLM. Krijnen (2021) produced Formula 1 (F1) reports with ChatGPT-2 using data such as the race name, date, and location along with the names of podium finishers, and the winning constructor. Race reports were generated using the finetuned model and evaluated by volunteers to determine the catchiness, factuality, repetitiveness, fluency, grammaticality, and cohesiveness. The output texts were compared with human-written reports in a blinded fashion and the results showed poor performance in terms of factuality, leading researchers to conclude that the system was not suitable for generating automated F1 reports.

Chiang et al. (2024) had more success generating badminton match summaries directly from raw data using both the GPT-3.5 (GPT-3.5-turbo-0125) and GPT-4 (GPT-4-turbo) models. In their BADminton report Generation and Evaluation with LLM (BADGE) study, they used a sample of 10 singles match reports sourced from the "Shuttleset" dataset (Chiang et al., 2024) which contains detailed data such as shot trajectories, rally duration, point outcomes, player names, match settings, and tournament contexts (Wang et al., 2023).

Either rally-level data in CSV format or set-level data in an 8-item Q & A format was input to an LLM. Four distinct prompt types, developed using either an In-Context Learning or Chain-of-Thought framework, were used to instruct both the GPT-3 and GPT-4 models to generate match summaries. The reports generated by both ChatGPT models were evaluated by humans and with the GPT-4 model using the prompt-based G-EVAL method proposed by Liu et.al. (Liu et al., 2023). Reports generated by GPT-4 scored higher compared to those from GPT-3.5 and human writers. The authors also reported better evaluation scores for reports generated using CSV input data as compared to the Q&A format.

To the best of this authors' knowledge, a similar attempt to generate football match summaries directly from raw match events data is yet to be investigated. The current study therefore aimed to build on previous solutions such as the BADGE study and develop a system for automating the generation of football match reports directly from in-game events data using ChatGPT-4o.

Reader Acceptance of AI-Authored Content

Using an LLM to automate sports reporting raises the question of whether the reader would accept AI-authored content. Research on reader acceptance of AI-authored content suggests that evaluations vary according to factors such as enjoyment and credibility but that readers generally accept AI-authored content to be of similar quality to content written by humans. A meta-analysis carried out by Graefe and Bohlken (2020) summarised findings of 12 studies that investigated how readers perceive the credibility, quality, and readability of automated news.

The overall results showed no differences in readers' perceptions of credibility when comparing automated news to human-written content, although human-written news performed slightly better in terms of quality. Furthermore, human-written news performed much better on ratings of readability. Participants also rated news articles more favourably, simply when told that they were reading a human-written article.

Duncan et al. (2025) evaluated differences in readers' perceptions of human-written versus automated match texts. In a randomised online survey, 251 Australian sports fans read either an automation-authored or human-written match report based on a match in the Australian A-League football competition. Participants were blinded as to the author of the article and asked to rate the articles in five dimensions (enjoyment, absorption, arousal, liking, and quality). The human-written article was rated more highly for enjoyment and liking, showing that readers preferred it over the article produced by the automated system. Despite this, there were no differences in the perceived quality and arousal when comparing the two article types.

Barrolletta et al. (2024) showed that both AI-authored content and human-written content are perceived as equally credible and well-written. They presented 222 participants with health news articles based on the same information written either by an automated system or a human journalist. They also included articles with falsified authorship to counteract any potential bias in how the participants evaluated the different article types. Each article was rated for credibility, readability, and journalistic expertise. Results showed that both author types were perceived as credible by readers although readers did not perceive the automated news pieces as lively or entertaining. This finding supports the assessment of Duncan et al. (2025) suggesting that readers find human-authored content more entertaining and enjoyable.

Wölker and Powell (2018) also investigated reader perceptions of credibility for different forms of automated journalism and whether those perceptions influenced article selection in the context of finance and sports news. They conducted an online survey in which 300 respondents were randomly assigned to experimental conditions in which the author and declared source of news texts varied. After exposure to a finance and a sports news article, they were asked to rate the credibility of the message and the source and to indicate how likely they were to select the articles. Results for the sports articles showed higher scores for message credibility with the automated content as compared to human-authored content. Readers also considered an automated system as an equally credible source as a human journalist. These perceptions of credibility did not, however, increase or decrease the likelihood of a reader selecting that article for consumption (Wölker & Powell, 2021).

In contrast to Wölker and Powell (2021), Lermann et al. (2024) found that disclosure of AI-authorship reduced perceived message and source credibility. They conducted a between groups experiment with 734 participants who were asked to read a GPT-written science journalism article. Participants were randomly assigned to one of two conditions. One group was told the article was AI-authored whereas the other group was told it was human-written. Results showed that participants assumed the author to be more credible, anthropomorphic, and more intelligent when they assumed the author was human. They were also more likely to recommend the text and indicated a greater intention to re-read the article in the case where the author was assumed to be human. These findings indicate a bias in how these readers interacted with and perceived AI-authored content, rating an identical text more negatively when it was introduced as AI-authored.

These findings also contradict those of Wölker and Powell (2021) who reported higher credibility scores for automated content. It is possible that reader perceptions and the weight given to authorship may vary according to the news topic in question. Overall, the above-mentioned studies suggest that despite achieving similar levels of perceived quality and credibility as human-written content, work is still needed to improve overall reader engagement and enjoyment with AI-authored news content. Furthermore, disclosure of AI-authorship may have implications on how readers engage with and perceive the content. This may influence how newsrooms should handle transparency around the use of AI tools. Further investigation of readers' perceptions in the context of the current study is necessary.

Ethical and Managerial Implications of AI in the Newsroom

While AI tools offer opportunities to reduce costs and improve efficiency in news production, they also raise some ethical questions. News organizations must find ways to implement AI-augmented workflows that preserve transparency, accountability, and journalistic integrity. AI adoption is also likely to alter the skills required of journalists, generate new types of roles, and possibly lead to displacement of lower-skilled positions (Glebova et al., 2024).

Sonni et al. (2024) reviewed 127 studies carried out between 2010 and 2024, which focused on the impact of AI on journalistic practices, news quality, professional roles, and regulatory challenges in the newsroom. Their review highlighted some key recommendations such as improving AI literacy among journalists, maintaining the role of human judgment in automated news production, and ensuring transparency, both in how algorithms function and through disclosure of when and how AI tools are used in news content creation.

Porlezza and Schapals (2024) also emphasised transparency as an important principle for addressing ethical challenges in AI-driven journalism. A lack of transparency about how algorithms work may make it more difficult for organisations to maintain accountability for content generated through automated processes. Therefore, maintaining human oversight in the editorial process is important to ensure that professional judgement is not replaced by automated systems.

Although, transparency is highlighted as an ethical necessity, the fact that readers' experiences and perceptions are known to vary according to the disclosure of AI authorship may make organisations hesitant to accurately label content (Graefe & Bohlken, 2020). A study by Fernandez-Barrero and Serrano-Martin (2025) found that although the use of AI tools is widespread, most organisations lack internal policies on the use of AI and that use of AI is rarely disclosed (Fernández-Barrero & Serrano-Martín, 2025). Doing so may improve transparency and accountability while at the same time harming audience trust and engagement which could have direct implications on revenue and the success of the organisation. The challenge for news organizations is balancing ethical accountability with audience perception management. The current study provides further opportunity to explore how AI technology can be used to augment sports reporting and to explore how the presence or lack of transparency surrounding authorship influences reader perceptions.

METHODOLOGY

This study involved the automated generation and human assessment of football reports. An initial report generation phase developed football match reports, modelled off real-world examples, using an LLM (ChatGPT-4o) through three stages: content planning, data extraction, and prompt engineering. The assessment process included a researcher-based evaluation of accuracy and completeness of the text outputs and an audience assessment of the enjoyment, excitement, clarity, and quality of the reports.

Content Planning

The content planning stage aimed to provide a report structure for match summary generation with the LLM. Five real-world football match reports from the English Premier League (EPL) results website were analysed to determine the overall report structure. This analysis produced a content plan showing the distinct report sections required (Table 1). Each sentence of each report was then deconstructed into a list of terms, followed by the identification of the data required to generate those terms and sentences. An example is shown in Figure 1.

Table 1. Content plan for generating match reports with the LLM.

Section	Data Requirements
Header:	assister names, attendance, away team, cards (type, minute), full-time score, goal scorer names, half-time score, home team, kick-off time, match date, match venue, minute of each goal, referee name, substitutions, team logos, type of goal (denote if penalty)
Introductory Summary:	goal scorer names, match venue, match location, score before and after a goal, team league position (before and after), time of goal, away team name, home team name, match result, number of goals scored, previous match results, type of goal, team manager name
Narrative Body:	goal coordinates of a shot, goal scorer names, goalkeeper name, pattern of play prior to a shot/ goal, shot attempted, shot outcome, time of shot/ goal, type of event/ pass prior to a shot, type of shot, name of player who attempted a shot, body part used for shot, defending player name, goalkeeper event, name of player associated with pre-shot event/ assist, outcome of goalkeeper event, penalty outcome, penalty awarded, shot location on the pitch, name of player awarded a penalty, name of player who conceded a penalty, name of player taking a penalty
Home and Away Team Focus:	chances created, chances per player, previous match results, shot attempted, shot outcome, team manager name, team lineups, team formations, goal scorer names, team manager name, defensive statistics - chances conceded/ xG conceded, name of player who attempted a shot, shot outcome, shot attempted, next fixture previous match results
Aggregate Statistics	Clearances, Corners, Fouls Conceded, Offsides, Passes, Possession %, Shots Attempted, Shots on Target, Tackles, Touches, Yellow Cards

Figure 1. Identifying data requirements of each sentence

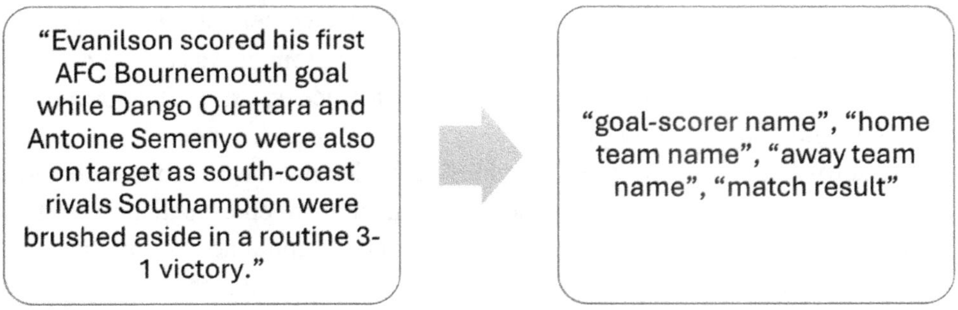

The lists of terms corresponding to each report were compared section-by-section and commonly occurring terms were ranked using a three-star frequency-based rating. Terms appearing in less than 60% of reports received a one-star rating, those appearing in 60% or more received a two-star rating, and those appearing in 80% or more received a three-star rating. One-star rated terms were excluded from the final content plan (Table 1) which guided the subsequent data extraction and prompt engineering procedures.

Data Extraction

To generate match reports, a Python script was developed to extract aggregate match statistics and match highlights for any given match in the StatsBomb Open Data archive. The extracted data were combined and subsequently converted to a JSON object ready for use in prompting the LLM. An outline of the data extraction and report generation process is shown in Figure 2.

Figure 2. Data Extraction and Report Generation Process

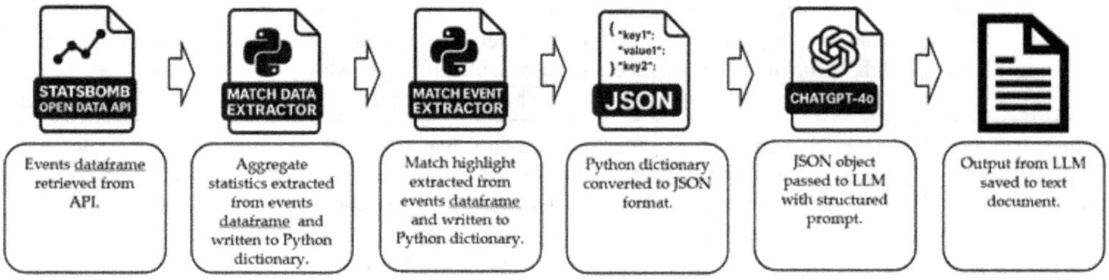

Prompt Engineering

A zero-shot prompt and a few-shot prompt were developed for instructing the LLM. Both prompt types were formulated based on the content plan devised in the planning stage (Table 1). The aim in developing these prompts was to compare the resulting outputs against each other, and against reference reports written by human authors, during the evaluation stage.

The zero-shot prompt (Figure 3) comprised of detailed instructions on how to read the JSON file, how to structure the report, and how to report match highlights. The few-shot prompt consisted of the same instructions contained within the zero-shot prompt, with the addition of two examples of the desired match reports sourced from the EPL results website, and instructions on how to model the output text from the examples.

Report Generation

Reports were generated with the above methodology using subsets of the 131 matches from The Women's'\Super League (WSL) 2020/21 Season. First, ten matches were randomly selected and a report for each was produced using the zero-shot prompt. Next, a further ten matches were manually selected, each to match a scoreline of the zero-shot reports. A report for each of these games was produced using the few-shot prompt. Lastly, a reference report for each scoreline set was sourced using real reports available on the EPL results website. Reports for the Women's games included in this study were not available, so to address this limitation, Men's matches were used with the player names, match locations, manager names, and any other identifying details altered to give the impression that the reports were summaries of Women's games. After matching all three report types by scoreline, 10 sets of 3 scoreline-matched reports (two LLM-generated and one human-written) were available for use in the evaluation stage.

Figure 3. Zero-shot Prompt

"""You are a sports journalist. You will be provided with a JSON file (delimited by triple backticks) of data from a football match.

Your task is to write a 1000 word match report using only the JSON file. The JSON file consists of two parts. The first part contains match statistics and the second part labelled with the 'Events' key contains match highlights. Use the following structure for the match report:

1. Write a short paragraph of 3 to 5 sentences which mentions the date, home team, away team, match result, full-time score, goals scored, and the minute of each goal.
2. Write a paragraph including a chronological summary of the match highlights taken from data in the 'Events' section of the JSON file. Highlights are defined as events labelled as 'Own Goal' or 'Shot' where the shot outcome is 'Goal' or 'Saved', or the shot technique is not 'Normal'. Descriptions of a shot must include the corresponding 'minute', 'player', 'play pattern', 'shot body part', 'team', ''shot outcome', 'shot technique', 'passing player', 'pass type', 'pass height', and 'pass length'. If the shot outcome is 'Saved', look for a Goalkeeper Event that matches the minute and include the 'Player', 'Bodypart','Outcome', and 'Team' value from that Goalkeeper Event.
3. Write a short paragraph including the events from the home team perspective. Mention players from the home team who appear frequently and summarise their performance. Include events labelled as 'Substitution' for the home team. Descriptions of substitutions should must include the 'minute', 'Player In' and 'Player Out'. Also include events labelled as 'Card' for the home team. Descriptions of cards must mention the 'Minute', 'Player', 'Card', and 'Team'.
4. Write a short paragraph including the events from the away team perspective. Mention players from the away team who appear frequently and summarise their performance. Include events labelled as 'Substitution' for the away team. Descriptions of substitutions should must include the 'minute', 'Player In' and 'Player Out'. Also include events labelled as 'Card' for the away team. Descriptions of cards must mention the 'Minute', 'Player', 'Card', and 'Team'.
5. Use the first part of the JSON file which includes statistics to create a table with a column of summary statistics for each team. The table must include each team name, the full-time score, home team half-time score, away team half-time score, home clearances, away clearances, home shots, away shots, home shots on target, away shots on target, home possession, away possession, home corners, away corners, home fouls committed, away fouls committed, home offsides, away offsides, home passes, away passes, home tackles, away tackles, home touches, away touches, home yellow cards, away yellow cards, home red cards, away red cards.

Reference the JSON file to ensure all data are correct but write creatively.

Provide a creative title for the report create your own sub-headings for each section of the report.

Ensure the data in the table agrees with the data in the text.

Ensure the match report gives a fluent chronological narrative of the match.

Write in the style of an experienced sports journalist."""

Evaluation of Match Reports

The first evaluation stage comprised a researcher evaluation of accuracy and completeness of the text outputs generated by the LLM using the zero-shot and few-shot prompts. Accuracy was defined as a combination of the factual correctness relative to the ground truth source data and the amount of speculation present in the text outputs. Each sentence contained in each report was assessed by the researcher to determine if the statement was factual with reference to the source data and rated as either factually correct (1), mixed (0.5), or factually incorrect (0) (Table 2). Statements that were not a direct reference to factual data were given a rating based on the level of speculation as either speculative (0), somewhat speculative (0.5) or not speculative (1) (Table 2). The two ratings were totalled and divided by the number of statements evaluated to obtain a total correctness and speculation percentage score. These two scores were averaged to calculate a combined accuracy score.

Completeness was calculated as a percentage score representing how closely the output text adhered to the instructions provided in the prompt. A checklist of required content was prepared based on the content plan. Each section of each report was then rated using these predefined criteria to determine a completeness score for each category on the checklist. Each item on the checklist was rated as either not included (0), somewhat included (0.25), balanced (0.5), mostly included (0.75), or complete (1) (Table 2). The individual scores were summed and divided by the number of relevant criteria assessed to obtain percentage score for completeness.

Table 2. Guideline for Accuracy and Completeness assessment.

	Category	Rating	Description
Factual Correctness	Factually Accurate	1.0	The statement is entirely correct and agrees with data present in the source data object.
	Mixed	0.5	Both correct and incorrect information is present in the statement.
	Factually Incorrect	0	The statement is factually incorrect and contradicts the source data object.
Speculativeness	Not speculative	1.0	No speculation, based entirely on known facts.
	Somewhat speculative	0.5	Balance of known facts and some speculation. Statement may lack evidence but does not mislead or alter the truth of the text.
	Speculative	0	The statement is entirely speculative, contains fabricated information, or incorrectly alters the overall meaning of the text.

continued on following page

Table 2. Continued

	Category	Rating	Description
Completeness	Not included	0	The text does not mention any of the elements specified in the prompt.
	Somewhat included	0.25	Some elements are included but the majority of important information is missing from the output.
	Balanced	0.5	There is a balance between information included and information omitted. The information omitted is not considered vitally important.
	Mostly included	0.75	Most of the information specified is present in the text with only minor points omitted.
	Complete	1.0	All information specified in the prompt is present in the text.

Audience Assessment

In the second stage of assessment, twenty-six participants over the age of 18 were recruited as a sample of the intended audience with the inclusion criteria that they had an interest in football. They were asked to rate reports out of 10 for: Enjoyment, Excitement, Clarity, and Quality. Enjoyment was explained to the participants as how entertaining and fun to read the article was. Excitement was explained as how well the article held the reader's attention and how interesting the descriptions of the match events were. Clarity was defined as how well structured, concise, and easy to read the article was. Quality was defined as an overall impression of how well written the article was and how effectively it captured the narrative of the match.

Reports were grouped in sets of 3, each set containing a zero-shot report (Type 1), a few-shot report (Type 2), and a real-world control (Type 3). While the three reports were from different games, the games were matched by scoreline to ensure comparability. The order in which participants were asked to read each different report type was randomized and participants were blinded to the article types. Each participant evaluated either 3 or 6 reports (1 or 2 sets) and these evaluations were either completed in-person by means of paper review or online by means of a Microsoft Forms survey. Participants were also asked to rate their level of interest in football out of 10 and to predict whether each article they read was written by an LLM or a human author.

Statistical Analysis

Results were summarised using the mean, standard deviation, minimum, maximum, first and third quartile, and median values. Summary statistics for categorical variables were presented as counts and percentages. Tests of normality were conducted using histograms and QQ plots prior to hypothesis testing. Hypothesis testing was performed using appropriate parametric methods including Chi-squared tests for independence, Z-tests, and analysis of variance (ANOVA) with the significance level set at $\alpha = 0.05$.

RESULTS

Accuracy and Completeness

The reports generated by the LLM showed good results for accuracy and completeness as shown in Table 3. Factual correctness across all reports was close to 100%, however, the overall accuracy was reduced by the presence of some speculative statements within the texts such as the inclusion of descriptive language not supported by the data. The overall percentage score for completeness showed good adherence to the content plan for both types of prompt methodology with slightly better adherence in the zero-shot as compared to the few-shot approach (Table 3). The human-written reports were assumed to be 100% accurate and complete and therefore were not assessed in this way.

Table 3. Results of evaluation (%) for Accuracy and Completeness

Metric	Zero-shot Prompt*	Few-shot Prompt*
Accuracy	96.9 ± 3.11	99.6 ± 1.26
Speculativeness	70.5 ± 9.64	74.3 ± 8.87
Total Accuracy	83.6 ± 5.06	87.1 ± 4.36
Completeness	89.6 ± 3.50	87.7 ± 4.79

*Mean ± SD

Audience Assessment

Twenty-six participants over the age of 18 and with an interest in football participated in this study as evaluators. The participants' indicated a good interest in football overall with a mean interest rating of 7.3 ± 2.7 points (Table 4). All participants completed an informed consent form prior to participation in the study. Mean ratings were highest for Clarity (7.3 ± 1.6) and Quality (7.4 ± 1.4) with lower scores for Enjoyment (6 ± 1.9) and Excitement (5.7 ± 2.2) as shown in Table 4.

Table 4. Summary of Continuous Variables

Variable	N	Mean	SD	Min	Median	Max
Enjoyment	117	6	1.9	2	6	10
Excitement	117	5.7	2.2	1	6	10
Clarity	117	7.3	1.6	3	7	10
Quality	117	7.4	1.4	3	7	10

The participants demonstrated poor accuracy in identifying the author for all three report types (Table 5). Results of a Chi-squared test of independence showed no significant difference in accuracy according to the report type ($X^2(2, N = 117) = 0.848, p = 0.655$). Grouping the zero-shot and few-shot categories into a single "ChatGPT" category again showed no differences in how accurately participants could identify the article source (95%CI [-0.19; 0.19], p = 1).

Table 5. Rating scores according to article type

Metric	Zero-shot Prompt*	Few-shot Prompt*	Human-written*
Enjoyment	5.87 ± 1.96	6.08 ± 1.81	6.08 ± 2.09
Excitement	5.62 ± 2.14	5.59 ± 2.21	5.79 ± 2.34
Clarity	6.9 ± 1.57	7.26 ± 1.73	7.74 ± 1.39
Quality	7.23 ± 1.49	7.38 ± 1.46	7.54 ± 1.35
Correct Author Prediction	14 (36%)	18 (46%)	16 (41%)

*Mean ± SD

Rating Scores

A 3-way analysis of variance (ANOVA) was performed determine the main effects of the article type (Type), scoreline grouping (ReportSet), and the Perceived Author (human or LLM) on each rating metric. Results showed no significant main effects for article type or report set for Enjoyment, Excitement, Clarity, or Quality. The Perceived Author factor had a significant main effect ($p < .05$) on Enjoyment, Excitement, and Quality scores. Detailed ANOVA results are presented in Table 6 and the relationship between the Perceived Author factor and each rating metric is shown in Figure 4.

Table 6. Results of 3-way ANOVA

		Enjoyment	Excitement	Clarity	Quality
Type	*DF*	2	2	2	2
	Residuals	110	110	110	110
	SS	1.1	1.0	14.07	1.85
	MS	0.55	0.49	7.034	0.923
	F	0.154	0.106	2.857	0.482
	P	0.858	0.899	0.0617	0.619
Report Set	*DF*	3	3	3	3
	Residuals	110	110	110	110
	SS	13.3	25.8	1.00	4.17
	MS	4.45	8.59	0.335	1.392
	F	1.25	1.86	0.136	0.727
	P	0.295	0.139	0.9383	0.534
Perceived Author	*DF*	1	1	1	1
	Residuals	110	110	110	110
	SS	33.2	36.2	8.65	21.13
	MS	33.23	36.19	8.65	21.13
	F	9.34	7.882	3.514	11.04
	P	< 0.05	< 0.05	0.06	< 0.05

Figure 4. Variation in Ratings according to Perceived Author

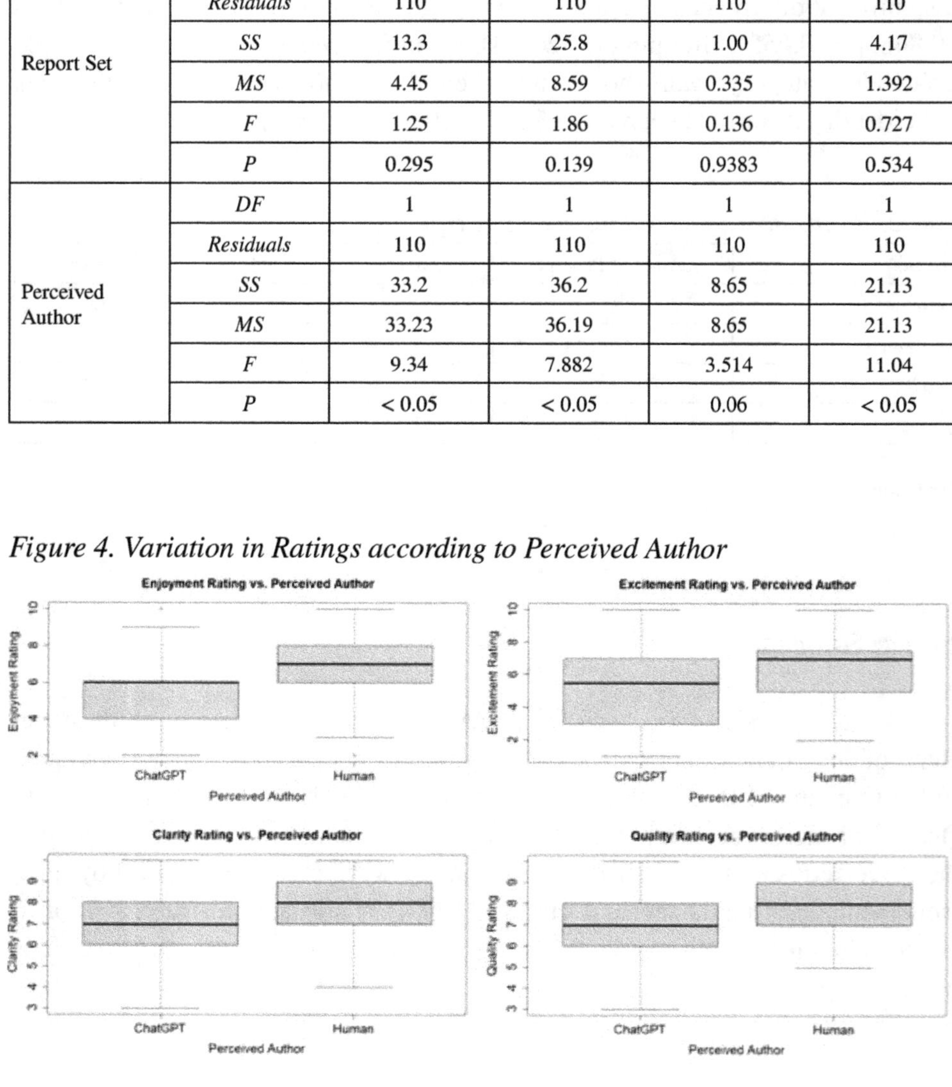

DISCUSSION

The method developed in this study produced accurate and complete football match summaries directly from on-ball events using ChatGPT-4o. Combined accuracy scores for both the zero-shot (83.6%) and few-shot reports (87.1%) were high. The zero-shot reports (89.6%) achieved a marginally higher mean completeness score than the few-shot reports (87.7%). It is possible the LLM may have deviated slightly from the prompt instructions to match the examples provided more closely which might explain this finding. In the case of both the zero-shot and few-shot reports, the combined accuracy score was reduced due to some speculation contained in the texts. Where speculative statements were inserted, it was usually as a form of filler text to connect factual statements.

These results compare favourably to previous work. Krijnen (2021) reported poor performance of their model in terms of factual correctness making their method unsuitable for automating F1 reporting. The improvement in the current study likely reflects in part the impressive advancements in LLM technology since 2021. Caron & Muller (2023) stated that their fine-tuned model was able to produce factually correct or plausible responses 96% of the time which is similar to the performance achieved in the current study. However, one advantage of the current approach is that the need for text templates to be constructed has been removed. The strong outcome for accuracy and completeness in the current study is promising, and future approaches could focus on methods to allow the LLM to be creative with language without introducing some of the speculation seen in these outputs.

The accuracy with which participants could identify whether the author was human or an LLM did not vary according to the article type. In previous research such as the BADGE study, readers were able to distinguish between AI and Human authors 80% of the time (Chiang et al., 2024) whereas in the current study, readers' predictions were no better than random chance. Although participants were marginally better at identifying the zero-shot reports as authored by ChatGPT (64%), this difference was not significant. It is unclear whether the improvement in the current study is due to differences in the prompt used, the data input (JSON vs. CSV) or differences in the evaluation process. The difficulty participants had in distinguishing the different types of reports aligns with previous research by Graefe and Bohlken (2020). In their meta-analysis they found no difference in readers' perceptions of credibility when comparing automated content with human-written news. The current study extends this observation to the domain of football reporting and shows an improvement over previous systems such as the BADGE system (Chiang et al., 2024). This improvement may indicate that the quality gap between human and AI-authored content is narrowing as LLM technology becomes more advanced. More pronounced effects may be observed in future experiments with a larger sample.

The overall ratings for Enjoyment and Excitement were moderately good for all three types of reports with stronger scores for Clarity and Quality. In all four rating categories, however, there appears to be room for improvement. Taken together, the results show that readers found all report types to be satisfactory in terms of the content, structure, and use of language but did not necessarily find them very entertaining. This is consistent with the findings of Duncan et al. (2025), who reported higher enjoyment and liking scores for human-written match reports, and Barrolleta et al. (2024) who showed that although AI-authored and human-authored health articles were rated as equally credible, readers did not find automated content as lively or entertaining.

Furthermore, participants did not have a clear preference for either report type. In contrast, Chiang et al. (2024) showed large differences in mean ratings of Excitement based on human evaluations when comparing GPT-3.5 (5.2), Human (6.9) and GPT-4 (8.0). Future experiments with this system may need to examine this finding more closely and work on improving the entertainment value of the reports without compromising the currently strong performance in terms of accuracy and completeness. As stated by Duncan et al. (2025), failure to prioritise reader enjoyment may reduce reader engagement. In their study, the human-written articles rated more highly for reader enjoyment, but also included additional content such as picture narratives, and additional context such as quotes from the coaches and contextual information of a broader scope than just the match events (Duncan et al., 2025). To improve the current system, additional data sources may need to be integrated to allow this broader context to be passed to the LLM in addition to the match event data. This may also present opportunities to explore combined human and AI workflows in football match reporting. As highlighted in previous studies, maintaining a "human-in-the-loop" remains a crucial component of responsible AI deployment in the newsroom (Porlezza & Schapals, 2024). The method developed here could be used to do the bulk of the work in extracting the required data and crafting the factual match narrative. A human editor could then add the finishing touches, including a broader scope and context surrounding the match and some of the human elements that have been shown to increase reader enjoyment and engagement (Duncan et al., 2025).

When comparing the ratings across each type of report, the few-shot and human reports were rated more highly than the zero-shot reports although these differences were not significant. This shows that readers did not have a clear preference for either type of report.

One of the most sociologically salient findings of this study is that reader ratings for Enjoyment, Excitement, and Quality were significantly higher when the report was believed to be written by a human, despite participants being largely unable to correctly identify the true authorship. This finding suggests some bias in the way participants received the content they perceived as LLM-authored. Either participants scored reports more highly when they anticipated a human author, or they assumed reports they found to be of higher quality to be written by a human. This finding agrees with previous research surrounding reader perceptions of AI-authored content (Graefe & Bohlken, 2020; Lermann, Henestrosa & Kimmerle, 2024) and adds to this evidence by showing that this bias is present even in circumstances where readers cannot reliably identify the real author. Furthermore, this work extends this body of work by demonstrating that perceptual bias persists even when readers cannot reliably identify the true author. This dissociation between objective indistinguishability and subjective valuation suggests the presence of a bias toward human authorship that is not grounded solely in textual features, but rather in audience beliefs about the role of human agency in journalism. Such an effect aligns with broader research on "AI bias" or algorithm aversion, whereby audiences apply different evaluative standards once artificial intelligence is perceived to be involved, even when performance is equivalent or superior.

It is interesting to note that, in sports journalism specifically, Rossner et al. (2024) reported no penalty to credibility or trust following AI disclosure, though their study did not examine aspects such as enjoyment or excitement. The present findings suggest that while readers may accept AI-generated sports news as accurate and credible, they may still implicitly associate qualities such as narrative flair, intuitive understanding or drama, with human authorship. This bias may be rooted in long-standing cultural norms that frame sports as an emotional experience with reporting as a creative and interpretive practice rather than a purely informational one.

From a practical newsroom perspective, these results raise important questions about transparency and disclosure policies. While ethical guidelines increasingly advocate for explicit disclosure of AI involvement in content production, the findings suggest that such transparency may unintentionally reduce perceived quality, enjoyment, and excitement, with potential consequences for audience engagement, reader retention, and advertising revenue. Conversely, failing to disclose AI authorship may preserve perceived quality but risks undermining trust, accountability, and journalistic integrity. One possible resolution lies in hybrid production workflows, where AI-generated drafts are subject to light human editorial intervention. Such an approach may preserve efficiency gains while maintaining the value of human authorship.

These findings also align with some of the managerial challenges facing sports news organisations. The high scores for accuracy and completeness provide evidence that an LLM-based system can generate factually reliable content with minimal human intervention and thereby can greatly improve efficiency of football match reporting through automation of data extraction and article writing. However, the inclusion of speculative elements in the generated reports, demonstrates that human editorial oversight remains important to ensure that unsupported statements are not inadvertently included in published content and that accountability is maintained (Porlezza & Schapals, 2024).

Speculation emerged as the primary factor reducing combined accuracy scores. A qualitative inspection of the reports suggests that speculative statements generally fell into two categories. The first involved plausible narrative embellishments, such as describing a goal as or claiming that a player produced a "vibrant performance". While common in human-authored reports, such statements are not directly supported by event data and were therefore penalized under the study's strict accuracy criteria. The second category consisted of factual overreach, where the model inferred player intent, tactical motivation, or psychological states without explicit evidence. An example is the statement "Tactical substitutions cemented Brighton's strategies" as the substitutions may well have been due to injuries or may have actually resulted in a change in tactics. Although less frequent, these instances were more problematic, as they risked subtly reshaping interpretations of match events. Importantly, most speculative content was not implausible in a journalistic sense but reflected established sports-writing conventions that extend beyond observable events. This distinction has important implications for future prompt design. The findings suggest that LLMs can be guided to produce engaging and cohesive narratives without compromising factual grounding.

Limitations

The current approach does not control for the possibility that the GPT-4 model may have had prior knowledge of the games for which it was asked to generate match reports. However, this does not seem likely given how closely the output texts adhered to the prompt instructions and data provided. The API method used also did not allow for access of internet resources when generating the reports.

Another consideration is the possible presence of confounding variables in the evaluation process that were not recorded or controlled for. Factors such as the age of participants, or their beliefs about LLM technology, may have influenced their perceptions of the content and may help to explain some of the findings around how rating scores varied according to perceived authorship. Future experiments using this system may benefit from recording a more detailed description of participants and their preferences to better understand how they interact with LLM-generated content.

While the work uses the match reports associated with men's games as the basis for the women's games in the study, the authors do not see any significant issue with this although more study may be needed to establish if reports for the different games are fundamentally different in structure or character.

Future Work

A further limitation concerns the choice of model. ChatGPT-4o is costly and not open-source. While its use allowed us to evaluate the feasibility of high-quality automated football reporting under current state-of-the-art conditions, it may limit scalability for some news organisations. However, there is no reason that the proposed workflow—combining structured match data, content planning, and prompt-based generation—can not be adapted to open-source LLMs. Future work might assess the performance of such models in cost-sensitive newsroom settings.

Additional work might also focus on combatting bias to perceived LLM-authored content through the development of hybrid AI-Human approaches to sports report generation underpinned by the methods outlined in this work. The potential for real-time reporting would also be of interest.

CONCLUSION

Overall, this study shows promising results, indicating that a system for generating accurate, complete reports that are satisfactory to readers is feasible using LLM technology. The reports generated in this study scored very highly for accuracy and completeness, and there was no preference for wither report type when comparing zero-shot, few-shot, and human-written reports. This indicates that ChatGPT can generate football match reports of a similar quality standard as human authors, as shown by the fact that participants rated reports similarly for Clarity and Quality regardless of authorship. However, achieving a similar technical standard does not guarantee that readers will find the content enjoyable. Enjoyment and Excitement scores were relatively low in this study, indicating some room for improvement in the entertainment value of the match summaries. This is an important consideration and future development of this system should explore methods to improve readers' enjoyment of the text outputs.

An important finding is that although readers in this study were unable to accurately distinguish between AI and human-written content, the ratings they provided did vary according to their assumptions as to whether the content was AI-authored or not. This aligns with previous research showing that readers' perceptions of credibility and enjoyment can be negatively influenced simply by labelling content as AI-authored. This applies even in cases where the content is in fact human-written. This highlights a bias in how readers interact with AI-authored content and shows that the bias extends to the domain of football match reporting. Sports reporters using automated systems such as the one developed in this study may need to consider how disclosure of AI use might influence reader perceptions and engagement.

REFERENCES

Aires, J., & Nunes, S. (2016). *FACULDADE DE ENGENHARIA DA UNIVERSIDADE DO PORTO Automatic Generation of Sports News*. University of Porto.

Barrolleta, L. A. L. R., & Sandoval-Martín, T. (2024). Artificial intelligence versus journalists: The quality of automated news and bias by authorship using a Turing test*. *Analisi, 70*, 15–36. DOI: 10.5565/rev/analisi.3681

Bouayad-Agha, N., Casamayor, G., Mille, S., & Wanner, L. (2012). Perspective-oriented generation of football match summaries: Old tasks, new challenges. *ACM Transactions on Speech and Language Processing*, *9*(2), 1–31. Advance online publication. DOI: 10.1145/2287710.2287711

Carlson, M. (2015). The Robotic Reporter. *Digital Journalism (Abingdon, England)*, *3*(3), 416–431. DOI: 10.1080/21670811.2014.976412

Caron, M., & Müller, O. (2023). TacticalGPT: Uncovering the Potential of LLMs for Predicting Tactical Decisions in Professional Football.

Chiang, S.-H., Chao, L.-W., Wang, K.-D., Wang, C.-C., & Peng, W.-C. (2024). BADGE: BADminton report Generation and Evaluation with LLM. https://github.com/AndyChiangSH/BADGE

Cook, A., & Karakuş, O. (2024). LLM-Commentator: Novel fine-tuning strategies of large language models for automatic commentary generation using football event data. *Knowledge-Based Systems*, *300*, 112219. Advance online publication. DOI: 10.1016/j.knosys.2024.112219

Duncan, S., Kunert, J., & Karg, A. (2025). Attitudes to automated and human written sport journalism. *Journalism*, *26*(9), 1937–1961. Advance online publication. DOI: 10.1177/14648849241260944

Fernández-Barrero, M. Á., & Serrano-Martín, C. (2025). Are the Media Transparent in Their Use of AI? Self-Regulation and Ethical Challenges in Newsrooms in Spain. *Journalism and Media*, *6*(3), 152. Advance online publication. DOI: 10.3390/journalmedia6030152

FIFA. (2021). The Football Landscape. Vision-Report-2021.

Gautam, S., Midoglu, C., Shafiee Sabet, S., Kshatri, D. B., & Halvorsen, P. (2022). Soccer Game Summarization using Audio Commentary, Metadata, and Captions. NarSUM 2022 - Proceedings of the 1st Workshop on User-Centric Narrative Summarization of Long Videos, 13–22. DOI: 10.1145/3552463.3557019

Glebova, E., Madsen, D. Ø., Mihaľová, P., Géczi, G., Mittelman, A., & Jorgič, B. (2024). Artificial intelligence development and dissemination impact on the sports industry labor market. *Frontiers in Sports and Active Living*, *6*, 1363892. Advance online publication. DOI: 10.3389/fspor.2024.1363892 PMID: 38606117

Graefe, A., & Bohlken, N. (2020). Automated journalism: A meta-analysis of readers' perceptions of human-written in comparison to automated news. In Media and Communication (Vol. 8, Number 3, pp. 50–59). Cogitatio Press. DOI: 10.17645/mac.v8i3.3019

Kanasheva, Ш. Ж., Duisengazy, C. M., & Seitzhanova, Ж. Д. (2024). Artificial intelligence in journalism: Foreign experience. Bulletin of L.N. Gumilyov Eurasian National University. *JOURNALISM Series*, *148*(3), 7–19. DOI: 10.32523/2616-7174-2024-3-148-7-19

Krijnen, T. (2021). Automatic Generation of Formula 1 Reports. https://developer.sportradar.com/docs/read/

Lermann Henestrosa, A., & Kimmerle, J. (2024). The Effects of Assumed AI vs. Human Authorship on the Perception of a GPT-Generated Text. *Journalism and Media*, *5*(3), 1085–1097. DOI: 10.3390/journalmedia5030069

Porlezza, C., & Schapals, A. K. (2024). AI Ethics in Journalism (Studies): An Evolving Field Between Research and Practice. *Emerging Media*, *2*(3), 356–370. DOI: 10.1177/27523543241288818

Puduppully, R., Dong, L., & Lapata, M. (2019). Data-to-Text Generation with Content Selection and Planning. www.aaai.org

Rossner, A., Cassel, M., & Huschens, M. (2024). Do Users Really Care? Evaluating the User Perception of Disclosing AI-Generated Content on Credibility in (Sports) Journalism. *Proceedings of Mensch Und Computer*, *2024*, 413–418. DOI: 10.1145/3670653.3677490

Sarkhoosh, M. H., Gautam, S., Midoglu, C., Sabet, S. S., & Halvorsen, P. (2024). Multimodal AI-Based Summarization and Storytelling for Soccer on Social Media. MMSys 2024 - Proceedings of the 2024 ACM Multimedia Systems Conference, 485–491. DOI: 10.1145/3625468.3652197

Shi, Y., & Sun, L. (2024). How Generative AI Is Transforming Journalism: Development, Application and Ethics. In Journalism and Media (Vol. 5, Issue 2, pp. 582–594). Multidisciplinary Digital Publishing Institute (MDPI). DOI: 10.3390/journalmedia5020039

Van Der Lee, C., Krahmer, E., & Wubben, S. (2017). PASS: A Dutch data-to-text system for soccer, targeted towards specific audiences. https://www.automatedinsights.com/

Wang, W. Y., Huang, Y. C., Ik, T. U., & Peng, W. C. (2023). ShuttleSet: A Human-Annotated Stroke-Level Singles Dataset for Badminton Tactical Analysis. *Proceedings of the ACM SIGKDD International Conference on Knowledge Discovery and Data Mining*, 5126–5136. DOI: 10.1145/3580305.3599906

Wang, Z., Chu, Z., Doan, T. V., Ni, S., Yang, M., & Zhang, W. (2024). History, Development, and Principles of Large Language Models-An Introductory Survey. https://arxiv.org/abs/2402.06853

Wölker, A., & Powell, T. E. (2021). Algorithms in the newsroom? News readers' perceived credibility and selection of automated journalism. *Journalism, 22*(1), 86–103. DOI: 10.1177/1464884918757072

KEY TERMS AND DEFINITIONS

Accuracy: A combination of the factual correctness of the text relative to the source data and the amount of speculation present in the text.

Automated Journalism: The use of AI tools or algorithms to generate news content with little to no human intervention beyond the initial programming. In this paper, an LLM as evaluated as a tool for automating football match reporting.

Completeness: A percentage score showing how closely the output text adhered to the instructions provided in the prompt.

Few-shot prompt: A prompt method where the user provides instructions to an LLM to carry out a task together with a small number of examples of the desired output on which the LLM can model a response.

Large Language Model (LLM): An artificial intelligence system trained on large amounts of data to understand and generate text in a human-like way. In this study, an LLM was used to convert raw football data into complete match reports.

Perceived Author: The assumption made by the readers as to the source of each article they were asked to read. After each article, the reader was asked to indicate whether the author was human or an LLM.

Zero-shot prompt: A prompt method where the user provides instructions to an LLM to carry out a task without providing any examples of the desired output.

Chapter 6
Extracting Personality Traits From Digital Identity on Social Media:
An Experimental Study Using IBM Watson's Personality Insights

Reda El Yazidi
http://orcid.org/0000-0002-8144-4660
Moulay Ismail University, Morocco

Mouhcine Rhouiri
http://orcid.org/0009-0007-7115-871X
Sidi Mohamed Ben Abdellah University, Morocco

ABSTRACT

This research investigates the potential of extracting personality traits from social media linguistic productions, focusing on Moroccan users' digital identity. Using an experimental exploratory methodology, the study applies IBM Watson's Personality Insights—grounded in the Big Five model—to fourteen Facebook and Twitter profiles. Data was gathered via netnography between 2020 and 2021 from accounts selected for rich expression and accessibility. Results confirm the feasibility of detecting traits like openness and conscientiousness, though accuracy varies; Arabic texts showed weaker correlations (mean absolute error – 0.09–0.12) than English. The study reveals that specific linguistic choices significantly influence algorithmic outputs, raising questions regarding potential manipulation. Ultimately, this novel application of AI to Moroccan bilingual data underscores the promise of digital psychology while emphasizing the critical need for enhanced algorithmic precision and contextualized interpretation in future research.

DOI: 10.4018/979-8-2600-2701-1.ch006

INTRODUCTION

1. General Context: The Blurring Boundaries Between Physical and Digital Realities

In today's society, the lines have blurred between the physical world and the digital world. No matter if you are physically present and communicating with someone (i.e., face-to-face) or if you are communicating with someone through digital means (such as computers, smartphones, tablets), people move fluidly between the two worlds. There are many forms of software applications available in the digital world designed to satisfy three primary social needs: (1) Self-Expression; (2) Communication/Interaction; (3) Mutually Recognized by Members of Society. Because of this, the digital and physical worlds do not exist as contradictory to each other; instead, they are both part of the same experience of being human today. Understanding digital identity cannot be achieved by asking "Who is hiding behind the keyboard?" or "Who hides behind the screen?" any longer. Online usage has changed from anonymous and cloaked to revealing one's identity due to rapid and consecutive technological advances in the internet over the past 10 years; this transformation began with the creation of social networks.

2. Specific Context: The Rise of Social Media and Digital Self-Presentation

The use of social media (Web 2.0) allows users of the web to play a larger role in creating content for the internet and creating relationships with each other. In 2005, the top sites being used for e-commerce were eBay, Amazon, Microsoft, and AOL. By 2008, none of these sites were listed as the top sites on the web, as they had been replaced by YouTube, MySpace, Facebook, Hi5, and Wikipedia. These changes on the web have been very drastic. People exhibit social behaviour in the physical world through their interactions with each other; similarly, people exhibit social behaviour in their use of social networking sites. People in the physical world socially interact with other people who are physically near to them; however, with social networking (the digital world), people are able to communicate with other people who are located anywhere in the world.

Through new forms of expressing themselves through presentation and exposure, social networking sites create their own social network as a way of expressing and reconstructing one's sociality and relationship. However, the use of social networking sites has transformed the unpredictable and chaotic internet into an easily accessible and familiar space for people to find and connect with one another. The original intent of using social network sites to create a way of documenting one's daily life and to provide personal insight into one's personal style and interest was very limited in its initial use. Currently, it appears that everything has been publically shared on social media. Digital identities have provided people with the ability to share their private lives in a public forum and therefore there is very little by way to keep private the way before in the past. The process of revealing peoples personal lives through social networks has occurred as a result of the construction of hybrid social networks, where individuals create and manage their social network of friends as well as review and provide their perspectives on thematic networks. This hybrid nature has created an environment where relational spaces have become very heterogeneous and provided opportunities for the potential to communicate in many different forms using digital media and navigate through digital mediums. The ability to communicate in this way has been created through the construction of a digital self and gaining access to a digital medium where individuals can interact.

3. Identifying the Research Gap

Even although the use of social media is common in Morocco, and there is continuing growth of user-generated content in multiple languages (Arabic, French, English, and Darija), there are currently only limited numbers of systematic studies examining the potential for using artificial intelligence to extract personality traits from Moroccan digital footprints. Research on automated personality extraction to date has largely focused on English-speaking Western populations, thereby creating an opportunity and need for further research in Arabic-speaking and North African cultures. Furthermore, existing tools such as IBM Watson Personality Insights have known limitations when applied to Arabic-speaking users, and no studies to date have examined the use of this tool for Moroccan social media users with an emphasis on the idiolects and cultural background of the users of those platforms.

4. Research Question

This study aims to determine whether the cloud-based AI service IBM Watson Personality Insights is capable of identifying the Big Five personality traits among Moroccan content creators based on their posts on Facebook and Twitter. It also explores the types of linguistic, cultural, and methodological challenges encountered when conducting this type of analysis on these users, as well as whether these challenges vary depending on whether the user posts in English or Arabic. Furthermore, this research analyzes the degree of correlation between each personality trait and the user's total number of posts to determine whether users deliberately skew or manipulate their posts to project a specific image of themselves through their writing.

5. Justification and Importance of the Topic

Digital identity and the expression of personality through social media are of significant importance for three purposes. In the first instance, automated personality extraction provides a scalable and unobtrusive alternative to traditional psychometric assessments and traditional psychometrically measured questionnaires, thus enabling researchers and analysts to conduct large-scale research using commonly accepted psychometric measures of individual differences. In the second instance, the increasing use of automated personality extraction tools for research in human resource management, advertising, sales, and education is raising new ethical and legal concerns regarding privacy, consent, and fairness. The Moroccan government has established a framework through Law 09.08 in order to evaluate both the efficacy and limitations of AI-enabled personality classification systems. This research will also address linguistic and cultural bias, providing insight into how this type of bias affects the design of AI systems and promoting equitable AI.

6. Methodological Approach

This study uses an empirical, exploratory, and analytical research design to answer the research question. The sample was purposively selected from content posted on 14 public social media accounts (Facebook and X) using two selection criteria: sufficient use of language to be considered interactive and sufficient public access to the account content. The collection of textual content (statuses, posts and comments) occurred from November 2020 until December 2021. Texts were analysed using IBM Watson's Personality Insights and scored on a percentile basis for all Big 5 factors and their 30 facets. Additionally, all analyses included a distinction between inputs provided in English and those provided in Arabic, and all analyses are presented descriptively while taking into consideration any patterns, anomalies, and possible biases that might arise in the data collected from both English and Arabic languages provided by participants.

7. Overview of the Chapter Structure

This chapter is organised into three sections. The first defines Digital Identity and establishes the Big Five Model of Personality as the basis for development. The second reviews empirical literature on extracting personality from social media text and images, then explains methodology, including sampling, data collection, and the IBM Watson Personality Insight Tool. The fourth section presents results in tables, graphs, and figures for each of the 14 profiles. The fifth analyzes findings against prior literature, referencing limitations, cultural bias, and manipulation, comparing results with existing studies, assessing validity and reliability, and examining strategies for digital identity manipulation to highlight methodological limits. The final section outlines practical implications for researchers, practitioners, and policymakers, suggesting applications in HR, marketing, and education, while addressing ethical and legal implications for public policy.

BACKGROUND

1. General Context: Digital Identity and Social Networks

In the past twenty years, the substantial growth of social networking sites has changed how people connect with each other. In January 2005, it was estimated that there were 115 million users of all the different social networks combined, while X (Twitter) alone surpassed this figure five years later at over 200 million users (Golbeck, Robles, Edmondson, & Turner, 2011).With the rapid expansion of social media, it becomes clear that these platforms are essential for forming and exhibiting digital identities.

Digital identity can be described as the totality of the residues that a user creates while using the Internet, both purposefully and unintentionally (Georges, 2011, p. 32). Residues consist of many types of data, including written words, audio/visual images, correspondence in electronic communications, purchases made online, and given names associated with your identity when you are online. Digital identity is composed from three distinct dimensions, as outlined by Georges (2011):

- **The technical dimension:** (i.e., everything a digital device has ever recorded about someone) includes all the traces that have been created as a result of your engagement with digital content;
- **The social dimension:** concerns how people will think about their own lives based on their interactions with other humans through digital devices (i.e., how digital technology will allow them to have a 'presence"' even though they are not physically present).
- **The cognitive dimension**: The image a person expresses on Digital Technologies and the way they participate in the process of constructing who they are (Georges, 2011, p. 33).

The digital self-presentation process confirms multiple facets of one's identity and how they are all integrated together by presenting evidentiary symbols regarding one's civil/professional/social status, and demonstrating an ongoing identity through these same evidentiary symbols (Cardon, 2015). Web 2.0 has greatly changed how individuals present and display themselves, as well as construct their identity online. Rather than being made up solely of signs that users have created themselves (such as text, images, and videos), it includes other users' signs about the user's presentation (e.g., comments or taglines) as well as the characteristics of the information system(s) that they are using to create their identity (Georges, 2011).

Figure 1. Self-representation and digital identity construction

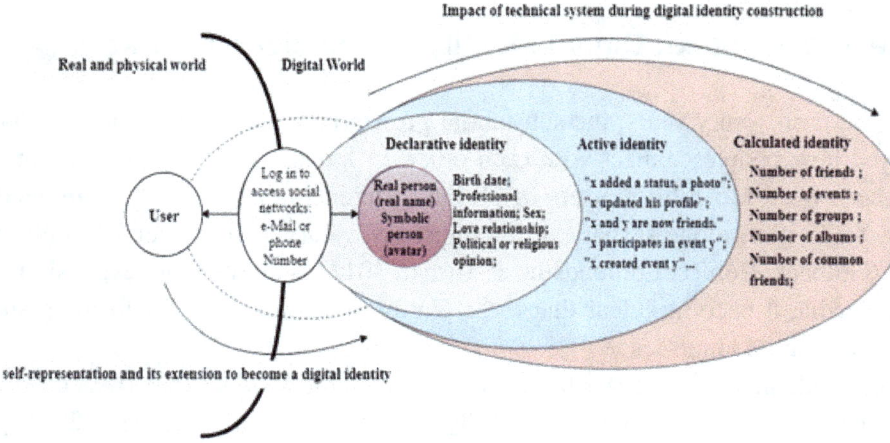

Source: based on Georges (2011) and adapted by El Yazidi (2024)

As seen in Figure 1, the three integrated components of digital identity are declared identity, active identity and calculated identity. Additionally, Figure 1 demonstrates that the degree to which a user has control over their digital identity (or how they present themselves) decreases as the information system gains control. When a user begins the process of building their digital identity, they begin to lose their ability to control how they are presented to the information systems (Georges, 2011).

Web 2.0 is characterised by a change in the way people communicate with computers (i.e., through screen) to the way they communicate with each other through social networks, and it is also based upon contributing to the development of a network that operates on more than just the exchange of information but the sharing of knowledge (Quoniam & Lucien 2009, pp 16-28). Technological advancements have helped social change to occur through the technological framework of communication (Quoniam, 2009, p. 28). Sites such as Facebook, LinkedIn, and X, for example, encourage individuals to post their thoughts and feelings about life using the following incitative queries: "What are you doing now?" "What's on your mind?" "What's new?" "Express Yourself!" (Gomez-Mejia, 2016, pp. 65–66).

Figure 2. Picture captured from Facebook wall

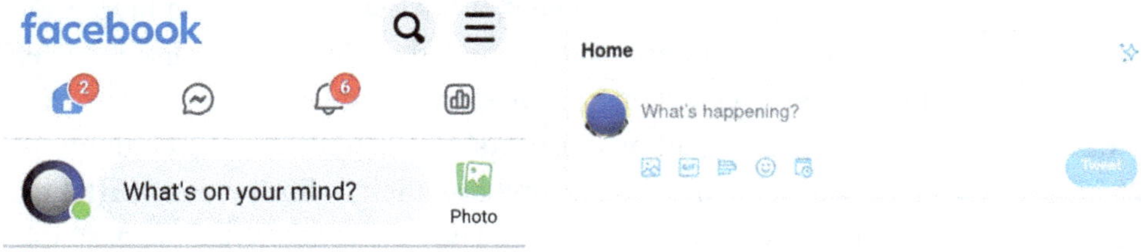

The purpose of these "leading" questions is to collect all user self-ideas for feeding the data/information stream into the wall, news feed or profiles. The way to express oneself in this manner is through an "empty writing frame", where the potential exists to show visual/pictorial interactions and written words as current, via infinite notifications to others in the social network (Gomez-Mejia, 2016 pp65-66). This means that every time we have an interaction with others in this setting, we create a permanent, digital memory of that interaction that we are reminded of repeatedly (through all future notifications). The social networking site's design affects users on an expressive and behavioral level. A major theme of digital psychology is whether an individual's online profile portrays the individual's 'ideal' self or the individual's real self. Research supports an 'extended real life hypothesis', stating that social networking sites, such as Facebook, reflect users' true identity and do not create an 'idealized virtual identity' (Back et al. 2010 ; Liu et al. 2016; Eftekhar et al. 2014).

Evidence for this authenticity comes from the way many social networks are rooted in actual relationships (i.e. "anchored relationships"), with the online interactions that take place through these sites representing an extension of the offline network to which a person belongs (Zhao, Grasmuck, & Martin, 2008, cited in Eftekhar et al., 2014).

Profile photos are among the elements utilized to communicate Digital Identity, and they significantly influence other's perceptions of our competence, trustworthiness, and/or likeability (Outh, 2022). The behavior of tagging, commenting, and uploading photos also reflects how our online photo-related activity mirrors our Offline Personality Traits (Eftekhar et al., 2014). Studies indicate that persons exhibiting conscientious personality characteristics are more likely to upload self-generated photo albums than would be persons exhibiting an extroverted personality style, who generally have a preference for using bright, colourful, and upbeat images. Thus far, empirical research using IBM's Watson Personality Assessment has demonstrated that one can analyse public social media postings (via text or photos) and identify personality traits of users and product recommendation applications (Acar & Toker, 2019; Hrazdil et al., 2020; Aguiar et al., 2020).

There are a number of important challenges that arise in the use of digital traces as a source of research data due to their potential for low reliability and representativeness. The data itself is commonly fragmented (primarily as disconnected snippets of text), therefore, making it difficult to extract valid personality traits from the data (Golbeck et al., 2011). Additionally, users' motivations (i.e., belongingness/ self-promotion) can impact how individuals organise their online persona (Eftekhar et al., 2014). Therefore, it is critical to understand how these dynamics work so that researchers can derive accurate psychological data from such unprocessed data sets. Automated tools such as IBM Watson Personality Insights may provide researchers with a viable option for unobtrusively assessing personality characteristics. However, ongoing validation of these tools (Kachur et al., 2020; Hrazdil et al., 2020) using relative self-reports continues to be necessary to ensure their assessment capabilities are maintained.

2. Theoretical Models of Personality

The Big Five Factors of Personality (OCEAN) model is "The Most Complete & Accurate Account" (Barrick & Mount, 1991; Judge, Heller, & Mount, 2002) in the area of Differential Psychology that describes the types of ways an individual has been labelled or categorized throughout history. The Big Five Model was proposed in 1932 by McDougall ("A Psychologist's View of the World," p. 293) as a means of describing five factors that describe a person's personality. That was only a short time before Thurstone completed his own study of the characteristics of over 1,300 persons in which he created a list of 60 adjectives used to describe individuals, from which he obtained five independent factors he felt could account for all personality types (Thurstone, 1934, p. 13).

In a long standing, scientific debate amongst the personality psychologists, a significant number of them ultimately reached consensus on the belief that individual personality differences could be represented and captured by five basic dimensions. They were later referred to as the "Big Five Personality Factors" by Goldberg et al. (2006). The Five-Factor Model of Personality (FFMP) received widespread acceptance in psychology after Fiske (1949) tried and failed to recreate the factor structures presented by Cattell, but instead discovered five factors. During the 1960s, Norman (1963), Borgatta (1964), and Smith (1967) all arrived independently at the same five-factor conclusion about personality. Despite this, it wasn't until the 1980s, 1990s, and early 2000s that the study of personality truly exploded as a field of research, through the development of instruments translated into numerous languages and used across multiple cultures (Hansenne, 2006).

Psychologists concur that there are five dimensions that describe all humans; however, the terms used by psychologists to express the five dimensions are not all agreed upon. All of the different labels provided by psychologists represent variations of one larger construct (Peabody & Goldberg). The discrepancy among labels is primarily due to two reasons: (1) it is difficult for psychologists to agree upon a name for factors that were generated through factor analysis and (2) the factors identified are influenced by the type of measures included in the different studies (Hansenne, 2006).

The following table illustrates the evolution of the names of the Big Five factors according to several major personality psychologists.

Table 1. Evolution of the names of the Big Five factors of personality according to a selection of personality psychologists.

	The first factor	The second factor	The third factor	The Fourth Factor	The Fifth Factor
Fiske (1949)	Adaptation sociale Social adjustment	Conformité Harmony	Volonté d'arriver Will to Reach/ Desire to Investigate	Contrôle émotionnel Emotional Control	Intelligence Intelligence
Norman (1963)	Urgence Urgency	Agréabilité Kindness (Harmony/ Kindness)	Consciencieusité Conscientiousness Mindfulness	Emotionnalité Emotion	Culture Culture
Borgatta (1964)	Assertivité Packages	Sympathie Sympathy	Responsabilité Responsibility	Emotional Emotionnalité	Intelligence Intelligence
Digman (1990)	Extraversion Extraversion	Amabilité Kindness	Volonté d'arriver Will to Access/ Investigate	Neuroticisme Neuroticism	Intellect Thought
Costa et McCrae (1985)	Extraversion Extraversion	Agréabilité Kindness (Harmony/ Kindness)	Consciencieusité Conscientiousness Mindfulness	Neuroticisme Neuroticism	Ouverture Openness

Source: Hansenne (2006, p. 196)

At the Early Stages of Personality Theories, Language was the primary factor that Psychologists used to identify Characteristics and Build the Scientific Taxonomy of Personality Traits. The Lexical Hypothesis proposes that the most Significant and Socially Relevant Characteristics of a Person's Personality in a Particular Culture can be found within a Culture's Natural Language (i.e., Adjectives). In their linguistic analysis of personality-related words found within the pages of the English language, Allport and Odbert identified roughly 18,000 words which could serve as a basis for differentiating between different types of behaviour (Goldberg et al., 2006, pp. 145-146; Plaisant et al., 2010, p. 482). The use of natural language gives us a wealth of information regarding each individual's habitual way of behaving when compared with other people, and how their habitual behavior may differ from that of other individuals. Looking at how consistently people use self-descriptive linguistic terms to describe themselves over time, allows us to determine what have come to be referred to as "personality traits," and how these personality traits relate to one another. In other words, we can determine the "structure" of someone's personality by analysing the association between these traits. This approach has allowed for the relatively consistent identification of the five dimensions discussed in the Big Five trait theory.

The OCEAN model comprises five fundamental dimensions (Barrick & Mount, 1991; Schwartz et al., 2013):

- **Openness to Experience**: Reflects intellectual curiosity, imagination, and appreciation for art and diverse ideas. Individuals high on openness tend to be creative, broad-minded, and sensitive to aesthetics (Schwartz et al., 2013; Yarkoni, 2010).
- **Conscientiousness**: Measures organization, perseverance, sense of duty, and propensity for planning. Conscientiousnessindividuals are responsible, thorough, and hardworking, and this trait has shown consistent validity in predicting job performance across various occupations (Barrick & Mount, 1991; Hurtz & Donovan, 2000).
- **Extraversion**: Characterizes sociable, energetic, and assertive individuals who draw inspiration from social situations. Extraverts tend to be talkative, active, and gregarious (Barrick & Mount, 1991; Yarkoni, 2010).
- **Agreeableness**: Relates to cooperation, altruism, and a tendency to be trustworthy and conciliatory. Agreeable individuals are courteous, flexible, and good-natured (Barrick & Mount, 1991; Judge et al., 2002).
- **Neuroticism** (or Emotional Stability, reverse-coded): Measures emotional instability and sensitivity to stress, anxiety, and negative emotions. Neurotic individuals tend to experience more negative affect and are prone to worry and insecurity (Barrick & Mount, 1991; Judge et al., 2002).

The Big Five has been justified as an approach to provide a coherent framework to understanding thousands of traits that were previously seen as separate or unrelated (Barrick & Mount, 1991). The development of the Big Five is based upon the use of a lexical method which suggests that major dimensions of personality have been included within the vocabulary in natural language (Schwartz et al., 2013; Yarkoni, 2010). Nonetheless, the model has been criticized; while many regard it as universal, some researchers argue that several of the dimensions are difficult to assess accurately, and additional factors may be necessary to fully encapsulate all areas of personality (Barrick & Mount, 1991). Additionally, its usage in multicultural contexts has limitations, such as the fact that the dominant personality models have generally been created from a Western perspective and lack an understanding of the nuances that may exist in other cultures (e.g., collectivism vs. individualism), which can result in a partial or incomplete view of personality in other cultures (Triandis

& Suh, 2002 ; Gou et al. 2014). Even with these drawbacks, the Big Five is still regarded as the primary method of automated personality extraction from digital footprints, such as both social media text and analysis of facial images (Kachur, Osin, Davydov, Shutilov, & Novokshonov, 2020; Hrazdil, Novak, Rogo, Wiedman, & Zhang, 2020).

3. Methods for Extracting Personality Traits

The traditional approach to measuring personality has relied heavily on self-reporting. Examples of widely used psychometric inventories include the NEO-PI-R or Big Five Inventory (Costa & McCrae, 1985, Kachur, Osin, Davydov, Shutilov, & Novokshonov, 2020; Goldberg et al., 2006, Yarkoni, 2010). Even though these instruments have been empirically validated, they have considerable practical limitations: they are expensive, personal and may not be practical for use at scale across large populations (Golbeck, Robles, Edmondson and Turner, 2011; Gou, Zhou and Yang, 2014).

Digital traces left behind on social media represent a new source of data called "big data." Additionally, these data enable us to take advantage of new computational methods that allow us to infer somebody's personality automatically (Schwartz et al., 2013; Hrazdil et al., 2020). A key component of these new techniques is the use of natural language processing (NLP) and machine learning to analyze the digital linguistic "footprints" (Pennebaker et al., 2003, Yarkoni, 2010).

The use of psycholinguistic dictionaries such as LIWC is one of the most widely used methods for analyzing text through counting the number of words that fall into pre-defined categories (e.g., emotion, cognitive processes, and personal concerns) to reveal stable correlations between language usage and personality (Pennebaker & King, 1999 ; Yarkoni, 2010; Schwartz et al., 2013). Research has identified a tendency for neurotic individuals to utilize an excessive number of negative emotion words compared to those who are considered to be more extroverted (Yarkoni, 2010; Schwartz, et al., 2013). In addition, due to advances in technology, there is also an increasing trend towards use of 'open vocabulary' analysis techniques where specific keywords, phrases and topics can be extracted directly from the dataset with no prior human bias as mentioned below, thus producing greater predictive accuracy than traditional 'closed vocabulary' methods (Schwartz, et al., 2013).

In addition to textual input, an emerging area of research focuses on visual modalities for inferring personality traits. Studies have provided evidence that AI can identify an individual's personality traits from their selfies or profile pictures with accuracy that in some cases outperforms that of human judges (Kachur et al., 2020; Liu et al., 2016). The use of aesthetic analysis (colour and contrast) and facial analysis (expressions and postures) has resulted in increasing validity when predicting

Big Five scores (Liu et al., 2016). For instance, conscientious individuals typically share more organized photos that show only the person's face, while extraverted individuals tend to share more colorful images that evoke positive emotions (Liu et al., 2016; Eftekhar; Fullwood and Morris; 2014). Automated techniques have many advantages over manual methods in terms of both speed and cost; however, automated methods may be affected by the unique noise associated with social data types (e.g., slang; abbreviations) (Golbeck et al., 2011). Additionally, there are significant privacy issues surrounding the collection and use of sensitive psychometric data (Gou et al., 2014; Aguiar and colleagues, 2020). IBM Watson Personality Insights is one of the tools that have been applied effectively for inferring the Big Five, basic human values and needs from social media text for the purpose of creating new applications, ranging from recommender systems to research in organizational behaviour. (Acar & Toker, 2019; Hrazdil et al., 2020; Mahmoudian et al., 2021).

4. The IBM Watson Personality Insights Tool

One of the most sophisticated uses of automated personality inference is IBM Watson Personality Insights (often exploredin research studies using experiment-based systems like "KnowMe") (Gou et al. 2014). The personality insights tool uses a lexical method of evaluating words used in writing, especially on social media platforms like Twitter (Acar & Toker, 2019; Hrazdil et al., 2020). IBM Watson is an analytical tool that uses language structure rather than social activities (e.g., how many times you post or vote) to assess not only the Big Five personality type but also the fundamental human values and needs (Gou et al., 2014; Aguiar et al., 2020). To do this, Watson uses LIWC (Linguistic Inquiry and Word Count) dictionaries and statistical models built on large amounts of text data to establish correlations between Word Categories and Psychometrics (Yarkoni et al., 2010; Schwartz et al., 2013).

Watson's Personality Insights have application in a range of areas, from marketing to HR (Acar & Toker, 2019; Venugopal et al., 2023). Research indicates that more than 60% of corporate users would be open to sharing their AI-based personality traits to facilitate collaboration and understanding amongst each other within a workplace environment (Gou et al., 2014). Watson is capable of recommending products that fit the personality of the customer, or helping to create strong teams (Aguiar et al., 2020, Chowdhury et al., 2019). Research into the tool's validity shows promising results, which indicate that Twitter-derived human values characteristics correlate strongly with the outcomes derived from traditional psychometric tests, and, at times, outperform pure personality models (Acar & Toker, 2019, Hrazdil et al., 2020).

There are some limits to this tool that have already been noted. First, the reliability of your social data and the type of text you're analyzing can both affect the reliability of this tool (Golbeck, Robles, Edmondson & Turner 2011; Yarkoni 2010). Second, because it was originally designed for English, it may have limitations with regard to linguistic biases that may be present within your data (Gou et al. 2014). Additionally, there is concern about the accuracy of the results with users worrying that the wrong analysis could lead to prejudice or misinterpretation of who they are (Gou et al., 2014). To address this concern it would be important to include mechanisms for transparency that would allow users to know how their traits are created and, if needed, to correct their AI-generated results (Gou et al., 2014; Hrazdil et al., 2020).

5. Specific Challenges of the Moroccan and Multilingual Context

The combination of linguistics and culture in Morocco creates a lot of challenges for the application of AI models such as IBM Watson. Many contemporary personality models have been shown to be culturally specific to their place of origin (mainly North America or Europe) and thus not psychologically neutral (Gou et al., 2014). An illustration of this point is that Maslow's hierarchy of needs reflects the values of twentieth-century Western middle class men and will not sufficiently represent motivation in cultures with different social systems (Gou et.al, 2014). Cultural adaptation of AI is one of the biggest challenges in ensuring that the characteristics obtained by AI are useful and honourable in context (Gou et. al, 2014; Kachur, Osin, Davydov, Shutilov, & Novokshonov, 2020).

Morocco's multilingualism makes it difficult to automatically analyze content posted on show-media and create hybrid corpora in the form of Arabic (both Classical and dialect), French and English, with code-switching occurring often (Gou et al., 2014). Typically, common NLP tools developed to process only one language at a time will fail to fully encapsulate the semantic complexity and polysemy of these multilingual phenomena. In other words, for reference models, it is not enough just to translate into a reference model. It must be a language-specific model that incorporates Arab and Moroccan cultural and linguistic differences. Research has found that personality is affected by how well you know a language, and translating a model from one language (English) to another (Dutch) is not inadequate (Gou et al., 2014).

The way people perceive and demonstrate their personality traits is influenced by the sociocultural norms of a given group or society. For example, the meaning of the word "family" can vary greatly between cultures and thus the reading of that word as it pertains to agreeableness or tradition (Gou et al., 2014). Based on this difference, users tend to share traits within the context of what's needed by their culture, so that traits that have some extra value in an individualistic environment, like being open, will have greater emphasis, and vice versa (Gou et al., 2014). For extracting personality in Morocco, there is the need to adjust the tool not only for the complexity of the languages that are provided in Morocco but to also be sensitive to the local values that define how digital identity is created and perceived in Morocco (Gou et al., 2014; Kachur et al., 2020).The evidence base shows the limitations of existing research in this area, as most samples are geographically bounded (e.g., Russian-speaking adults, Western participants), reinforcing the need to establish cross-cultural replication and develop culture-specific personality models (Kachur et al., 2020; Liu et al., 2016).

6. Identified Gaps in the Literature

While there are now many studies available on Artificial Intelligence and social media, large gaps still exist in this area, especially around research involving non-Western populations. Most personality extraction studies have used English-speaking or Caucasian data, leaving considerable gaps in the literature regarding Arabic-speaking and African cultures (Kachur, Osin, Davydov, Shutilov, & Novokshonov, 2020; Gou, Zhou, & Yang, 2014). Moreover, very few experimental studies have used IBM Watson Personality Insights and/or other tools with multilingual data sets that include Arabic or its dialects, which limits the ability to generalize current technologies (Gou et al., 2014).

Another existing knowledge gap is how digital identities are created specifically in Morocco, as communication styles and self-disclosure norms differ from those found in Europe (Gou et al., 2014; Eftekhar, Fullwood, & Morris, 2014). It will be important to determine whether AI-generated scores will be valid or accurate when an individual has multiple personas or uses a false identity depending on the platform (e.g., professional Twitter vs. personal Facebook) (Gou et al., 2014). Additionally, many existing research studies do not use hybrid methods that integrate traits from different sources of data to develop a comprehensive psychological profile for an individual (Gou et al., 2014; Liu, Preotiuc-Pietro, Samani, Moghaddam, & Ungar, 2016).

Finally, there is a critical need for ethical frameworks and governance mechanisms to safeguard individuals from the possible misuse of their psychological characteristics (Gou et al. 2014). The merits of personalisation are well acknowledged but major concerns among individuals are the possible prejudicial, stigmatising and manipulative effects ("being put in a box") from an unregulated or undirected use of personalised services (Gou et al. 2014; Golbeck, Robles, Edmondson and Turner 2011). To address the existing gaps, an interdisciplinary collaboration of psychology, computational linguistics and AI ethics is required to develop systems that are not only technically effective but also culturally appropriate and privacy-respecting (Kachur et al. 2020; Gou et al. 2014).

3. EMPIRICAL STUDIES ON PERSONALITY EXTRACTION FROM SOCIAL MEDIA

Beyond theoretical models and computational tools, a growing body of empirical research has investigated the extent to which digital traces on social media can accurately reflect users' genuine personality characteristics. This section reviews six key studies that have shaped our understanding of the relationship between online self-presentation, language use, visual content (selfies, photos), and the Big Five personality traits.

3.1. Facebook Profiles Reflect Actual Personality, Not Self-Idealization

One of the fundamental debates in digital psychology concerns whether social media profiles present an idealized virtual identity or an authentic extension of offline personality. Back, Stopfer, Vazire, Gaddis, Schmukle, Egloff, and Gosling (2010) directly tested these two competing hypotheses. The authors argued that social networking sites combine multiple sources of personal information (thoughts, social behaviors, peer feedback) that make it difficult to construct a purely idealized digital identity. Specifically, elements such as wall posts and comments from friends introduce reputation-based information that is not entirely under the user's control, and social accountability mechanisms subtly shape self-presentation.

The study involved 236 participants from the United States (Facebook users) and Germany (StudiVZ and SchuelerVZ users), aged 17 to 22 years. Observers were asked to infer the personality traits of profile owners based solely on their social media profiles. Results supported the "extended real life hypothesis": observers were able to accurately infer realistic personality traits, particularly extraversion and openness, at levels comparable to face-to-face encounters. The study concluded that people do not use their profiles to promote an idealized digital identity. The authors recommended extending future research to older age groups, other social media platforms, and incorporating additional elements such as users' interests and goals.

3.2. What Does Your Selfie Say About You?

While profile pictures have long been studied as static identity markers, Qiu, Lu, Yang, Qu, and Zhu (2015) specifically examined the relationship between selfies (self-portraits posted on social media) and the Big Five personality traits. The researchers hypothesized that selfies contain valuable cues about an individual's personality.

Data were collected from 612 participants who had posted selfies on social media. The images were analyzed using digital processing and artificial intelligence tools. The findings revealed systematic associations: individuals high in openness to experience posted more creative and artistic selfies; those high in conscientiousness tended to post selfies reflecting maturity and concern for social reputation; extraverts posted selfies seeking attention and recognition; and individuals high in agreeableness (or low in shyness) posted selfies conveying friendliness and playfulness. This study was the first to provide an image coding scheme for analyzing personality cues in selfies and highlighted differences between selfie expression and other types of images in impression management.

3.3. Understanding Individuals' Personal Values from Social Media Word Use

Beyond the Big Five traits, personal values represent another layer of psychological dispositions. Chen, Hsieh, Mahmud, and Nichols (2014) investigated whether word use on social media could predict individuals' personal values (e.g., love, hard work, adventure). The study employed the Linguistic Inquiry and Word Count (LIWC) software, a text analysis tool that counts word frequencies in predefined categories.

The analysis revealed that specific words were associated with distinct value domains. For instance, words such as "love," "family," and "friends" correlated with social relationship values, while "success," "excellence," and "independence" correlated with achievement and independence values. However, the authors noted that different individuals may use different words to express the same underlying value, implying that word-level analysis alone is insufficient for fully understanding personal values. Nevertheless, the study demonstrated that linguistic analysis can be an effective tool for inferring personal values, with potential applications in behavior prediction and communication improvement.

3.4. Predicting Personality from Twitter

Golbeck, Robles, Edmondson, and Turner (2011) conducted one of the early large-scale studies on personality prediction from microblogging data. Using a sample of 279 Twitter users who completed a Big Five personality inventory, the researchers collected up to 2,000 recent tweets per user. Linguistic features were extracted using LIWC and other psycholinguistic resources, then used to train machine learning regression models.

The results showed that personality traits could be predicted with mean absolute errors ranging from 11% to 18% on a normalized scale. Notably, openness was the most accurately predicted trait, while neuroticism was the most difficult. The study also suggested that posting patterns (e.g., frequency, hashtag use) might predict other outcomes such as stress or depression. However, the authors emphasized that such predictions should be interpreted with caution, that methodological rigor is essential, and that automated personality assessments should not be used exclusively for making important decisions (e.g., hiring or clinical evaluation).

3.5. Capturing Personality from Facebook Photos and Photo-Related Activities

While many studies focus on static image content, Eftekhar, Fullwood, and Morris (2014) investigated how photo-related activities (uploading, tagging, commenting, liking) on Facebook might reveal personality traits. The study assumed that users display their personal lifestyle through visual content and that engagement with photos reflects underlying dispositions.

Using a sample of 115 active Facebook users, the researchers manually coded profile data (number of uploaded photos, self-generated albums, cover photos, tagged photos, likes and comments on profile pictures, etc.) and correlated these with Big Five scores. Results showed that extraversion and neuroticism predicted a higher total number of uploaded photos; conscientiousness predicted more self-generated albums and video uploads; and agreeableness predicted the average number of likes and comments received on profile pictures. The study concluded that even limited exposure to a user's photo-related activities can be sufficient to extract personality traits, and that higher visual exposure enhances prediction accuracy.

3.6. Synthesis and Implications for the Present Research

Collectively, these empirical studies establish three key points that directly inform our experimental investigation. First, social media profiles (Facebook, Twitter, etc.) tend to reflect actual personality rather than an idealized self (Back et al., 2010), validating the use of digital traces for psychological assessment. Second, both textual (Golbeck et al., 2011; Chen et al., 2014) and visual (Qiu et al., 2015; Eftekhar et al., 2014) modalities contain predictable signals of the Big Five traits and personal values. Third, automated tools—including LIWC and machine learning algorithms—can achieve above-chance accuracy, though they require careful validation and should not be used in isolation for high-stakes decisions (Golbeck et al., 2011). These findings provide a robust empirical foundation for the current study, which aims to apply IBM Watson Personality Insights to a multilingual, cross-cultural context (Morocco) and to compare its performance against traditional psychometric measures.

METHODOLOGY

4.1. Study Design and Objectives

This research adopts an explorative, analytical and applied design. The goal is to obtain the personality traits of Moroccan's social media users based on their published text (statuses, writings, comments) as a component of their digital identity. It is critical to note that this study does not aim to provide definitive characteristics regarding the extracted personality traits; instead, it illustrates the potential and possibility of using advanced technology (IBM Watson Personality Insights) to extract personality traits from digital identity traces, personal online records, and social media sites. This study is situated within the context of computational social sciences and psycholinguistics and takes into account both the potential and limitations of these approaches.

4.2. Population, Sample, and Data Collection Procedure

This research is being conducted using a purposive (non-random) sample of 14 social media accounts, which were selected from both Facebook and Twitter. The 14 accounts were chosen using two separate criteria.

The profiles that met our selection criteria were established by their abilities to produce both written and interactive linguistic means through social media in order to have adequate amounts of text for sound analysis. In IBM Watson Personality Insights minimum requirements are recommended for 1,200 to 3,000 words (IBM, 2020; Pakzad, 2019) where stable and useful outputs will be produced had to be at this level in the amount of text produced.

All profiles that were selected were publicly accessible because the profile owner had a setting to be public or have people share their information with everyone. They were fully aware that others would be able to read, comment on, and utilize their information, publications, including using it for scientific research purposes.

The data (status updates, posts, and text) were collected between November 1, 2020, and December 21, 2021. Furthermore, this study strictly complied with Moroccan Law No. 09.08 on data protection. More specifically, no information that could identify users -such as their names or usernames- was retained or published;

only anonymous linguistic data was considered during the analysis of the results. Furthermore, each selected profile was publicly accessible, either because the account holder had made their account public or because they had chosen to share their information with everyone. Consequently, all individuals involved were aware that their posts could be read, commented on, and used by others, including for research purposes. This study was therefore conducted in accordance with ethical and legal standards, while preserving the anonymity and confidentiality of the participants.

Table 2: Characteristics of the study sample.

Character ID	Gender	Language of analysis	Number of words analyzed
Character 1	Male	English	4,328
Character 2	Female	English	2,142
Character 3	Female	English	2,193
Character 4	Female	Arabic	5,841
Character 5	Male	Arabic	7,666
Character 6	Female	Arabic	4,142
Character 7	Male	Arabic	2,669
Character 8	Male	Arabic	4,511
Character 9	Male	English	5,482
Character 10	Male	Arabic	3,402
Character 11	Male	Arabic	1,790
Character 12	Female	Arabic	2,595
Character 13	Male	Arabic	12,056
Character 14	Male	Arabic	1,456

According to the analysis shown in Table 2, the number of profiles (Gender) analysed was 14, (10 male and 4 female) using two different languages (English = 4 profiles and Arabic = 10 profiles). Profiles were analysed range from a low of 1456 words to a high of 12056 words, which greatly exceed the minimum word count as set forth to enable the inference of stable personality characteristics (IBM, 2020).

4.3. Information Analysis and Personality Extraction Tool

IBM Watson Personality Insights (IBM, 2020) has been adopted as a tool to extract the personality construct. This software relies on artificial intelligence, natural language processing (NLP), and machine-learning programming to analyze the text (Schwartz et al., 2013; Pakzad, 2019). A custom version of the Linguistic

Inquiry and Word Count (LIWC) Dictionary is utilized in this analysis. The program ultimately generates an extensive overview of personality traits based on the text analyzed as input. The methodology used to develop the model is based on the Big Five Factors of personality (openness, conscientiousness, extroversion, agreeableness and neuroticism). The algorithm will identify language patterns and associate them with personality traits through the use of a large-scale dictionary of everyday words and phrases derived from natural language.

Figure 3. Stages used in the analysis of information

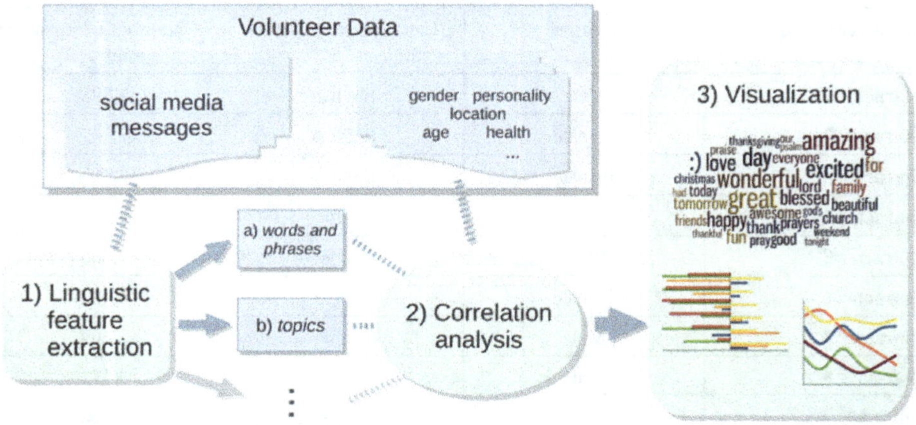

Source: adapted from Schwartz et al. (2013, p. 4).

There are five steps for the analytical phase: input to your analytical phase; prepare the input's content for analysis (cleanse and tokenise the content); extract the features from your input; correlate the output to a reference scale; and finally, generate the output, which will be your personality score.

4.3.1. Input Specifications

The tool allows for the acceptance of different types of written products: social media posts (Facebook, Twitter), emails, text messages, blog posts, etc., or any other written expression that was created by the individual from which a personality profile is being created. At the time of collection and analysis of data, IBM Watson Personality Insights could analyze the following languages: English, Arabic, Spanish, Japanese, and Korean. However, the developers of IBM Watson Personality Insights have indicated that the results for Arabic and Korean are not as reliable as those for English; for some personality traits and facets, the expected accuracy level may produce less accuracy. Accordingly, findings relating to Arabic material should be taken with appropriate care in that they should not be considered definitive until validated through additional measures (IBM, 2020; Pakzad, 2019). In order to generate reliable and stable results, the tool requires a user minimum of between approximately 1200 to 3000 words to be input into the program (IBM, 2020).

4.3.2. Output Specifications

After reading and understanding the text that was used as an input, IBM's Watson Personality Insights provides a score for 35 different personality dimensions, there are five major factors (the "Big Five") and six facets associated with each of those five factors (e.g. Extraversion has friendliness, gregariousness, assertiveness, activity level, excitement-seeking, and cheerfulness). - with results represented by percentile ranges. That means if you get a score of 0.25 (25th percentile) for the adventurousness facet, it tells you that you're more adventurous (25 percent) than other people in our reference sample and 75 percent less than the reference sample based on your inputted text. (IBM, 2020; Pakzad, 2019).

The data used by the instrument comes from a norm sample of Twitter users. The size of the normative database used in this research includes, as of the date of this research:

- English: approximately 1 million users
- Korean: 200,000 users
- Arabic: 100,000 users
- Japanese: 100,000 users
- Spanish: 80,000 users

IBM has not provided any demographic information about the normative sample used, i.e., age, gender, education level, geographical distribution (IBM, 2021; Pakzad, 2019). Consequently, this limitation, which restricts the production of results, is acknowledged and will be taken into account when analyzing the findings.

4.4. Data Analysis Procedure

All of the fourteen chosen profiles underwent a systematic coding process in order to produce consistent data from which to compare and contrast the individual profiles. Written materials that the users posted and/or commented on were aggregated across the profiles and created into a single document that is now ready for conducting an analysis of the entire number of posts by the identified users between November 1, 2020 and December 21, 2021 via a single, systematic file.

For the next phase, language identification and data cleansing occurred. Each document's primary language (English and Arabic) was determined, and the text was cleaned of extraneous material such as URLs, emoji, and repeated punctuation. As language structures are generally preserved, the corpus will continue to reflect authentic online discourse by retaining the full structure of the language.

Thereafter, the cleaned documents were submitted to the IBM Watson Personality Insights API, which is accessed using a valid IBM Cloud account by the researcher. The API generated JSON outputs that contained percentile scores for 35 dimensions of personality from the Big Five model and its facets.

The scores were recorded systematically in a structured format, using tables (e.g. Table 4) and subsequent analytical tables, thus enabling a 'descriptive' and 'comparative' assessment of the profile groups. Thus, the organization of these scores made it easier to identify patterns and differences in personality traits as represented by digital text.

Finally, results were interpreted with caution. Given the known limitations of the Arabic language model and the relatively small sample size, the findings were treated as exploratory indicators rather than definitive psychometric assessments. This methodological stance underscores both the experimental nature of the study and the need for careful contextualization when applying AI-based personality analysis to multilingual social media data.

4.5. Ethical Considerations

The study adhered to Moroccan Law 09.08 for safeguarding personal data. First, no personally identifiable information such as names, usernames, profile pictures, or contact details was collected or published. Moreover, each profile analyzed was assigned an anonymous number (Character 1–14) at the conclusion of the study. In addition, all profiles selected were publicly accessible because the owners had set their accounts to public or chosen to share their information with everyone. Consequently, they were fully aware that others could read, comment on, and use their publications, including for scientific research purposes. Thus, this ensured compliance with ethical and legal standards while protecting anonymity and confidentiality throughout the research process.

RESULTS

This section presents the findings of the personality extraction analysis conducted on 14 social media profiles (Facebook and Twitter) using IBM Watson Personality Insights. The results are organized by individual profile (Character 1 to Character 14), as detailed in the methodology (Figure 3). Notably, the figures presented below for these 14 profiles are derived from IBM Watson Personality Insights, and the visual analysis has been augmented using an LLM. In practice, for each profile, the tool generated percentile scores for the five major personality factors (Openness, Conscientiousness, Extraversion, Agreeableness, Neuroticism) and their respective six facets. Following the tool's conventions, scores above the 50th percentile indicate that the individual ranks higher than the normative sample on that trait, while scores below indicate lower standing. According to the original coding scheme (blue = significant / functional result; orange = non-significant / non-functional result), results are interpreted with caution, particularly for Arabic language inputs where IBM Watson's accuracy is not fully equivalent to English.

5.1. Profile 1 – English, Female, 4,328 words

Figure 4. Big Five Factors of Personality Profile 1

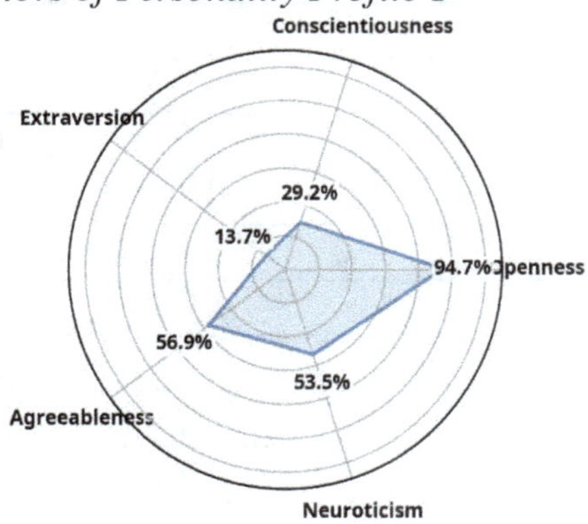

continued on following page

Table 3. Continued

Table 3. Personality analysis results for Profile 1 (English, female, 4,328 words).

Facet	Score
Openness – 94.73%	
Adventure	14,07%
Artistic Interests	98,59%
Irritability	99,50%
Imagination	89,64%
Intelligence	99,39%
Challenge of authority	92,87%
Conscientiousness – 29.20%	
Striving for Achievement	35,33%
Caution	65,79%
Obedience	82,31%
System	11,04%
Self-discipline	14,98%
Self-Efficacy	31,87%
Extraversion - 13,71%	
Activity Level	40,44%
Persistence	50,79%
Joy	38,77%
I seek excitement	29,56%
Unreserved	39,36%
Familiarity	5,25%
Agreeableness - 56,86%	
Altruism	99,29%
Collaboration	81,21%
Humility	83,00%
Stubbornness	72,83%
Sympathy	99,94%
Trust	62,40%
Neuroticism or (Emotion Group) - 53,51%	
nervous	29,33%
Anxiety	78,20%
gloomy	78,25%
Exceeding	53,97%

Facet	Score
Self-awareness	72,13%
Vulnerable to stress	76,40%

As shown in Table 3, Profile 1 exhibits extremely high Openness (94.73rd percentile), driven by very high scores on artistic interests (98.59%), emotionality (99.50%), intellect (99.39%), and authority-challenging (92.87%). Imagination (89.64%) and adventurousness (14.07%) are more moderate. Conscientiousness is relatively low (29.20%), with very low scores on orderliness (11.04%), self-discipline (14.98%), and self-efficacy (31.87%). Extraversion is low (13.71%), with particularly low gregariousness (5.25%) and activity level (40.44%). Agreeableness is moderately high (56.86%), with extremely high altruism (99.29%) and empathy (99.94%). Neuroticism is moderate (53.51%), with notable anxiety-proneness (78.20%) and depression (78.25%).

5.2. Profile 2 – English, Female, 2,142 words

Figure 5. Big Five Factors of Personality Profile 2

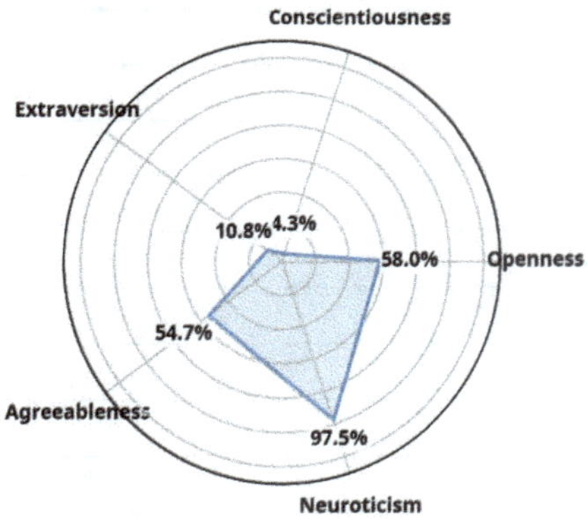

Table 4. Personality analysis results for Profile 2 (English, female, 2,142 words).

Facet	Score
Openness – 57.95%	
Adventure	32.27%
Artistic Interests	99.80%

continued on following page

Table 4. Continued

Facet	Score
Irritability	99.82%
Imagination	99.83%
Intelligence	99.78%
Challenge of authority	97.59%
Conscientiousness – 4.31%	
Striving for Achievement	16.72%
Caution	24.27%
Obedience	41.00%
System	5.50%
Self-discipline	1.45%
Self-Efficacy	16.30%
Extraversion - 10.84%	
Activity Level	23.87%
Persistence	23.27%
Joy	23.70%
I seek excitement	65.07%
Unreserved	4.21%
Familiarity	1.45%
Agreeableness - 54.68%	
Altruism	98.00%
Collaboration	45.35%
Humility	83.53%
Stubbornness	58.00%
Sympathy	99.95%
Trust	28.84%
Neuroticism or (Emotion Group) - 97.55%	
nervous	63.80%
Anxiety	94.77%
gloomy	98.86%
Exceeding	72.74%
Self-awareness	93.18%
Vulnerable to stress	95.50%

Profile No. 2 reveals a striking paradox: a high level of "Openness " (57.95%)—fueled by insatiable artistic interests, a vivid imagination, and intellectual curiosity

- contrasts with a low level of "Conscientiousness" (4.31%), revealing an exceptionally creativae but disorganized individual. As for Extraversion, it is very low (10.84%), but the desire for thrills reaches 65.07%. Agreeableness is moderate (54.68%), strongly influenced by extreme levels of altruism and empathy, but tempered by low self-confidence and notable stubbornness. The defining trait of Profile No. 2 is Neuroticism (97.55%), with extremely high levels of anxiety, gloominess, and sensitivity to stress. Overall, Profile No. 2 is extremely imaginative, empathetic, and also very anxious… there are numerous internal conflicts and displays of rebellion against authority, a lack of structure, but also a warm disposition toward others in theory, though this does not necessarily translate into practice.

5.3. Profile 3 – English, Female, 2,193 words

Figure 6. Big Five Factors of Personality Profile 3

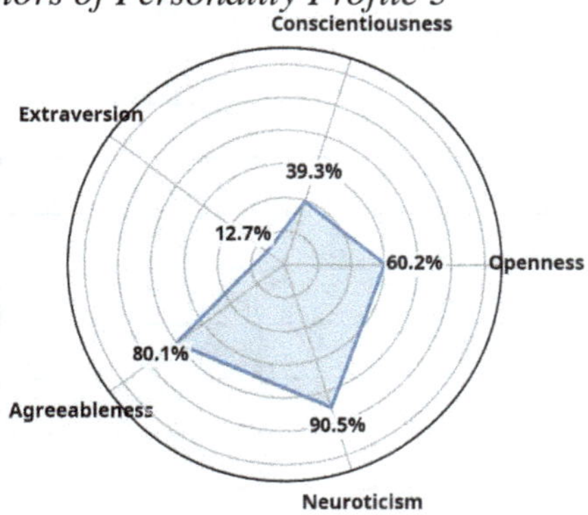

Table 5. Personality analysis results for Profile 3 (English, female, 2,193 words).

Facet	Score
Openness – 60.19%	
Adventure	23.44%
Artistic Interests	93.83%
Irritability	99.56%
Imagination	93.41%
Intelligence	81.47%
Challenge of authority	82.15%
Conscientiousness – 39.33%	

continued on following page

Table 5. Continued

Facet	Score
Striving for Achievement	32.95%
Caution	35.27%
Obedience	71.52%
System	2.86%
Self-discipline	10.37%
Self-Efficacy	11.28%
Extraversion - 12.72%	
Activity Level	34.06%
Persistence	2135%
Joy	23.70%
I seek excitement	47.17%
Unreserved	24.27%
Familiarity	10.78%
Agreeableness - 80.11%	
Altruism	97.37%
Collaboration	57.02%
Humility	98.83%
Stubbornness	73.26%
Sympathy	99.04%
Trust	97.37%
Neuroticism or (Emotion Group) - 90.45%	
nervous	64.72%
Anxiety	92.67%
gloomy	96.58%
Exceeding	68.77%
Self-awareness	87.21%
Vulnerable to stress	96.11%

Profile 3 shows moderately high Openness (60.19%), with high artistic interests (93.83%), emotionality (99.56%), and imagination (93.41%). Conscientiousness is low (39.33%), with very low orderliness (2.86%), self-discipline (10.37%), and self-efficacy (11.28%). Extraversion is low (12.72%), with low gregariousness (10.78%) and moderate excitement-seeking (47.17%). Agreeableness is high (80.11%), with very high altruism (97.37%), modesty (98.83%), and empathy (99.04%). Neuroticism is high (90.45%), with high anxiety (92.67%), depression (96.58%), and vulnerability to stress (96.11%).

5.4. Profile 4 – Arabic, Female, 5,841 words

Figure 7. Big Five Factors of Personality Profile 4

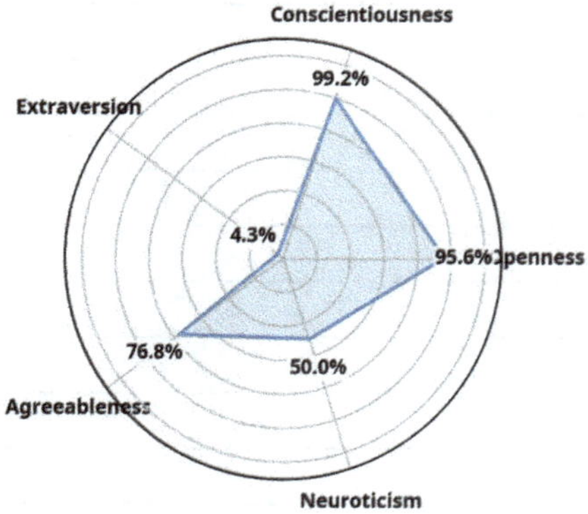

Table 6. Personality analysis results for Profile 4 (Arabic, female, 5,841 words).

Facet	Score
Openness – 95.56%	
Adventure	50.00%
Artistic Interests	98.96%
Irritability	35.24%
Imagination	50.00%
Intelligence	50.00%
Challenge of authority	99.90%
Conscientiousness – 99.17%	
Striving for Achievement	50.00%
Caution	97.23%
Obedience	50.00%
System	76.86%
Self-discipline	89.85%
Self-Efficacy	96.38%
Extraversion - 4.27%	

continued on following page

Table 6. Continued

Facet	Score
Activity Level	99.44%
Persistence	91.86%
Joy	50.00%
I seek excitement	6.99%
Unreserved	50.00%
Familiarity	0.12%
Agreeableness - 76.77%	
Altruism	50.00%
Collaboration	50.00%
Humility	50.00%
Stubbornness	83.77%
Sympathy	84.42%
Trust	50.00%
Neuroticism or (Emotion Group) - 50.00%	
nervous	50.00%
Anxiety	50.00%
gloomy	94.70%
Exceeding	50.00%
Self-awareness	50.00%
Vulnerable to stress	53.75%

Profile 4 exhibits very high Openness (95.56%), with extremely high artistic interests (98.96%) and authority-challenging (99.90%). However, emotionality (35.24%) and imagination (50.00%) are lower. Conscientiousness is extremely high (99.17%), with high orderliness (76.86%), self-discipline (89.85%), and self-efficacy (96.38%). Extraversion is very low (4.27%), with extremely low gregariousness (0.12%) and excitement-seeking (6.99%). Agreeableness is high (76.77%), with high empathy (84.42%) and cooperativeness (50.00% – neutral). Neuroticism is exactly at the 50th percentile (50.00%), with depression notably high (94.70%).

5.5. Profile 5 – Arabic, Male, 7,666 words

Figure 8. Big Five Factors of Personality Profile 5

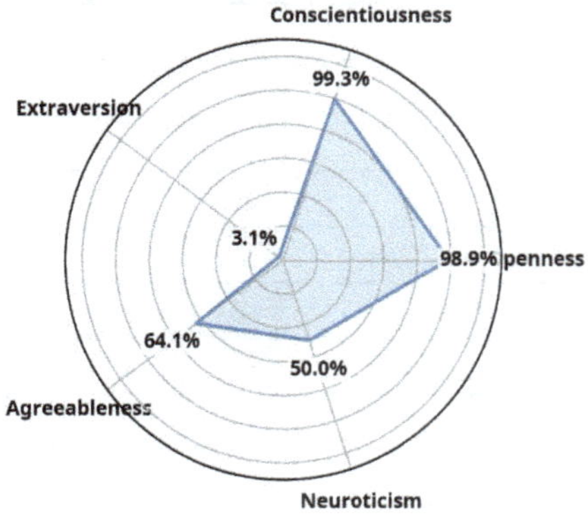

Table 7. Personality analysis results for Profile 5 (Arabic, male, 7,666 words).

Facet	Scrore
Openness – 98.87%	
Adventure	50.00%
Artistic Interests	99.74%
Irritability	19.87%
Imagination	50.00%
Intelligence	50.00%
Challenge of authority	99.61%
Conscientiousness – 99.27%	
Striving for Achievement	50.00%
Caution	98.30%
Obedience	50.00%
System	85.02%
Self-discipline	94.30%
Self-Efficacy	99.01%
Extraversion - 3.09%	
Activity Level	99.94%
Persistence	96.17%
Joy	50.00%

continued on following page

Table 7. Continued

Facet	Scrore
I seek excitement	5.29%
Unreserved	50.00%
Familiarity	0 .03%
Agreeableness - 64.08%	
Altruism	50.00%
Collaboration	50.00%
Humility	50.00%
Stubbornness	86.40%
Sympathy	88.23%
Trust	50.00%
Neuroticism or (Emotion Group) - 50.00%	
nervous	50.00%
Anxiety	50.00%
gloomy	92.52%
Exceeding	50.00%
Self-awareness	50.00%
Vulnerable to stress	54.97%

Profile 5 shows very high Openness (98.87%), with high artistic interests (99.74%) and authority-challenging (99.61%). Emotionality is low (19.87%). Conscientiousness is extremely high (99.27%), with high orderliness (85.02%), self-discipline (94.30%), and self-efficacy (99.01%). Extraversion is very low (3.09%), with extremely low gregariousness (0.03%) and excitement-seeking (5.29%). Agreeableness is moderate (64.08%), with high empathy (88.23%) and cooperativeness (50.00%). Neuroticism is at the 50th percentile (50.00%), with depression high (92.52%).

5.6. Profile 6 – Arabic, Female, 4,142 words

Figure 9. Big Five Factors of Personality Profile 6

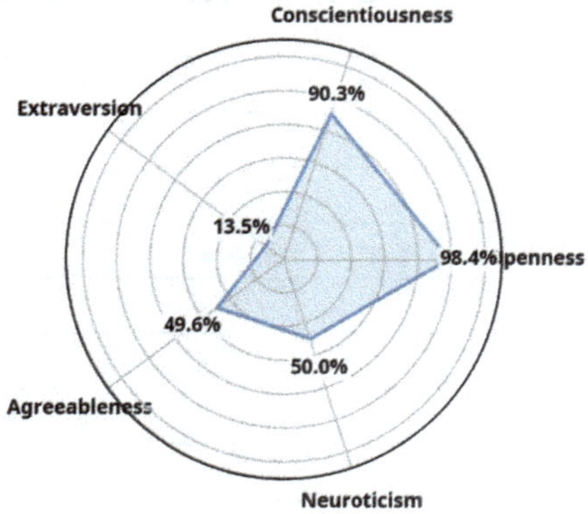

Table 8. Personality analysis results for Profile 6 (Arabic, female, 4,142 words).

Facet	Scrore
Openness – 98.35%	
Adventure	50.00%
Artistic Interests	99.55%
Irritability	23.21%
Imagination	50.00%
Intelligence	50.00%
Challenge of authority	94.32%
Conscientiousness – 90.31%	
Striving for Achievement	50.00%
Caution	84.47%
Obedience	50.00%
System	77.19%
Self-discipline	89.38%
Self-Efficacy	98.79%
Extraversion - 13.52%	
Activity Level	98.40%
Persistence	93.49%
Joy	50.00%

continued on following page

Table 8. Continued

Facet	Scrore
I seek excitement	21.03%
Unreserved	50.00%
Familiarity	1.00%
Agreeableness - 49.62%	
Altruism	50.00%
Collaboration	50.00%
Humility	50.00%
Stubbornness	55.13%
Sympathy	86.54%
Trust	50.00%
Neuroticism or (Emotion Group) - 50.00%	
nervous	50.00%
Anxiety	50.00%
gloomy	74.33%
Exceeding	50.00%
Self-awareness	50.00%
Vulnerable to stress	58.44%

Profile 6 shows high Openness (98.35%), with high artistic interests (99.55%) and authority-challenging (94.32%). Emotionality is low (23.21%). Conscientiousness is high (90.31%), with high orderliness (77.19%), self-discipline (89.38%), and self-efficacy (98.79%). Extraversion is low (13.52%), with very low gregariousness (1.00%) and excitement-seeking (21.03%). Agreeableness is near the median (49.62%), with moderate empathy (86.54%) but many facets at 50%. Neuroticism is at the 50th percentile (50.00%), with moderate depression (74.33%).

5.7. Profile 7 – Arabic, Male, 2,669 words

Figure 10. Big Five Factors of Personality Profile 7

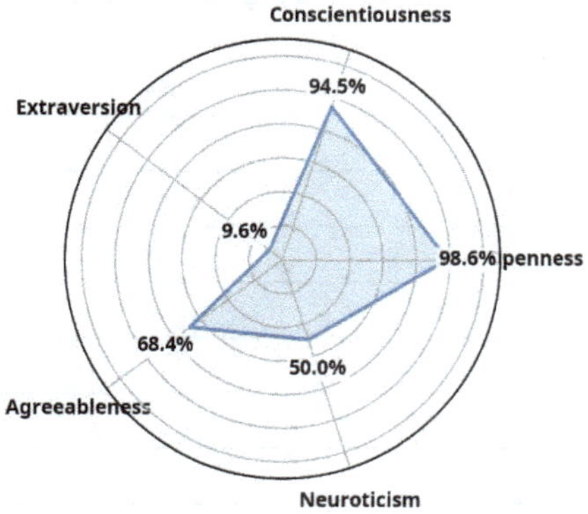

Table 9. Personality analysis results for Profile 7 (Arabic, male, 2,669 words).

Facet	Scrore
Openness – 98.62%	
Adventure	50.00%
Artistic Interests	99.73%
Irritability	26.06%
Imagination	50.00%
Intelligence	50.00%
Challenge of authority	99.06%
Conscientiousness – 94.50%	
Striving for Achievement	50.00%
Caution	94.13%
Obedience	50.00%
System	77.83%
Self-discipline	88.34%
Self-Efficacy	97.61%
Extraversion - 9.60%	
Activity Level	99.77%
Persistence	92.99%
Joy	50.00%

continued on following page

Table 9. Continued

Facet	Scrore
I seek excitement	10.73%
Unreserved	50.00%
Familiarity	0.24%
Agreeableness - 68.36%	
Altruism	50.00%
Collaboration	50.00%
Humility	50.00%
Stubbornness	77.06%
Sympathy	88.69%
Trust	50.00%
Neuroticism or (Emotion Group) - 50.00%	
nervous	50.00%
Anxiety	50.00%
gloomy	90.97%
Exceeding	50.00%
Self-awareness	50.00%
Vulnerable to stress	56.77%

Profile 7 exhibits very high Openness (98.62%), with high artistic interests (99.73%) and authority-challenging (99.06%). Emotionality is low (26.06%). Conscientiousness is very high (94.50%), with high orderliness (77.83%), self-discipline (88.34%), and self-efficacy (97.61%). Extraversion is very low (9.60%), with extremely low gregariousness (0.24%) and excitement-seeking (10.73%). Agreeableness is moderate (68.36%), with high empathy (88.69%). Neuroticism is at the 50th percentile (50.00%), with depression high (90.97%).

5.8. Profile 8 – Arabic, Male, 4,511 words

Figure 11. Big Five Factors of Personality Profile 8

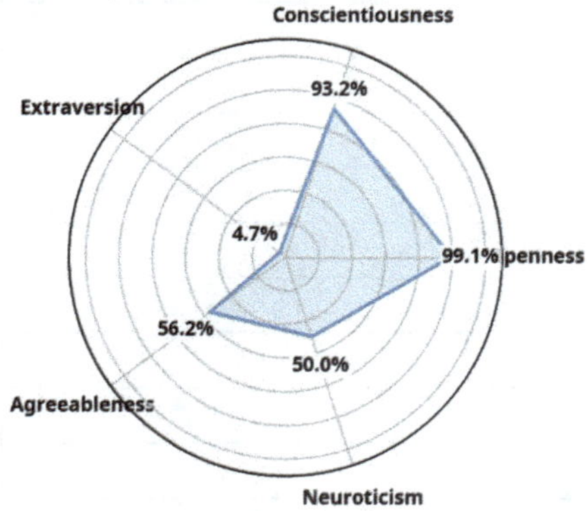

Table 10. Personality analysis results for Profile 8 (Arabic, male, 4,511 words).

Facet	Scrore
Openness – 99.14%	
Adventure	50.00%
Artistic Interests	99.65%
Irritability	58.52%
Imagination	50.00%
Intelligence	50.00%
Challenge of authority	99.87%
Conscientiousness – 93.17%	
Striving for Achievement	50.00%
Caution	89.30%
Obedience	50.00%
System	53.46%
Self-discipline	77.57%
Self-Efficacy	88.60%
Extraversion - 4.72%	
Activity Level	95.17%
Persistence	67.75%
Joy	50.00%

continued on following page

Table 10. Continued

Facet	Scrore
I seek excitement	18.43%
Unreserved	50.00%
Familiarity	0.71%
Agreeableness - 56.21%	
Altruism	50.00%
Collaboration	50.00%
Humility	50.00%
Stubbornness	67.39%
Sympathy	68.47%
Trust	50.00%
Neuroticism or (Emotion Group) - 50.00%	
nervous	50.00%
Anxiety	50.00%
gloomy	80.08%
Exceeding	50.00%
Self-awareness	50.00%
Vulnerable to stress	66.72%

Profile 8 shows very high Openness (99.14%), with high artistic interests (99.65%), authority-challenging (99.87%), and moderate emotionality (58.52%). Conscientiousness is high (93.17%), with moderate orderliness (53.46%), self-discipline (77.57%), and self-efficacy (88.60%). Extraversion is very low (4.72%), with extremely low gregariousness (0.71%) and excitement-seeking (18.43%). Agreeableness is moderate (56.21%), with moderate empathy (68.47%). Neuroticism is at the 50th percentile (50.00%), with moderate depression (80.08%).

5.9. Profile 9 – English, Male, 5,489 words

Figure 12. Big Five Factors of Personality Profile 9

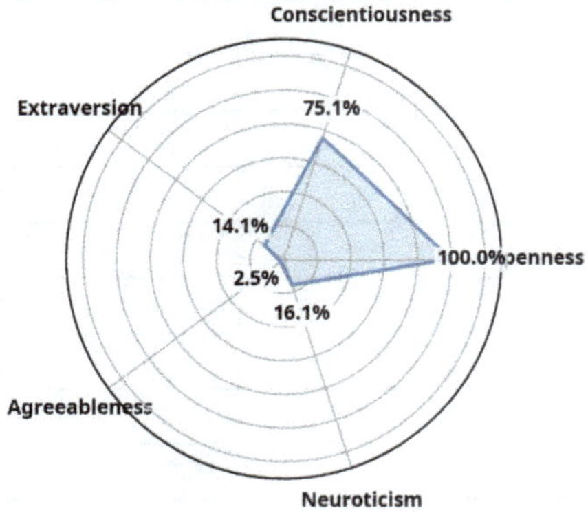

Table 11. Personality analysis results for Profile 9 (English, male, 5,489 words).

Facet	Scrore
Openness – 99.98%	
Adventure	50.85%
Artistic Interests	98.81%
Irritability	84.42%
Imagination	67.53%
Intelligence	99.95%
Challenge of authority	97.40%
Conscientiousness – 75.09%	
Striving for Achievement	35.33%
Caution	89.85%
Obedience	66.69%
System	27.71%
Self-discipline	24.84%
Self-Efficacy	67.95%
Extraversion - 14.11%	
Activity Level	85.91%
Persistence	87.87%
Joy	1.73%

continued on following page

Table 11. Continued

Facet	Scrore
I seek excitement	16.65%
Unreserved	27.87%
Familiarity	1.57%
Agreeableness - 2.45%	
Altruism	95.84%
Collaboration	70.96%
Humility	35.32%
Stubbornness	61.81%
Sympathy	99.65%
Trust	73.72%
Neuroticism or (Emotion Group) - 16.07%	
nervous	13.97%
Anxiety	41.02%
gloomy	73.21%
Exceeding	7.44%
Self-awareness	69.03%
Vulnerable to stress	34.70%

Profile 9 exhibits extremely high Openness (99.98%), with high artistic interests (98.81%), emotionality (84.42%), intellect (99.95%), and authority-challenging (97.40%). Conscientiousness is moderate (75.09%), with high cautiousness (89.85%) but low orderliness (27.71%) and self-discipline (24.84%). Extraversion is low (14.11%), with very low cheerfulness (1.73%) and gregariousness (1.57%). Agreeableness is extremely low (2.45%), with low modesty (35.32%) and moderate empathy (99.65% – but note this is contradictory: empathy is high, yet overall agreeableness is low. This suggests a possible artifact or specific facet configuration). Neuroticism is low (16.07%), with low anxiety (41.02%) and vulnerability to stress (34.70%).

5.10. Profile 10 – Arabic, Male, 3,402 words

Figure 13. Big Five Factors of Personality Profile 10

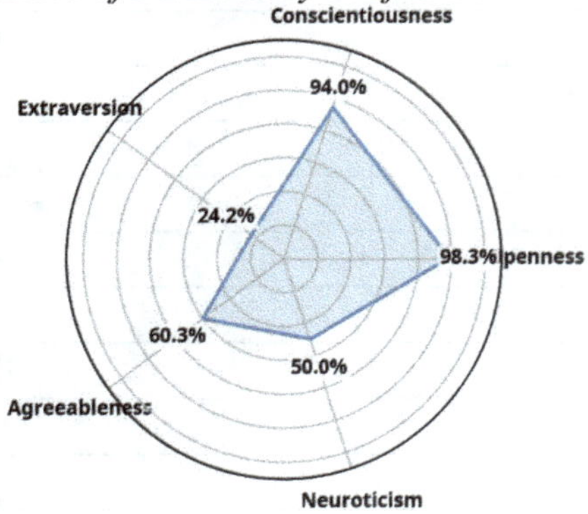

Table 12. Personality analysis results for Profile 10 (Arabic, male, 3,402 words).

Facet	Scrore
Openness – 98.29%	
Adventure	50.00%
Artistic Interests	99.79%
Irritability	34.32%
Imagination	50.00%
Intelligence	50.00%
Challenge of authority	99.20%
Conscientiousness – 93.99%	
Striving for Achievement	50.00%
Caution	92.06%
Obedience	50.00%
System	76.32%
Self-discipline	83.10%
Self-Efficacy	93.36%
Extraversion - 24.21%	
Activity Level	99.22%
Persistence	84.15%
Joy	50.00%

continued on following page

Table 12. Continued

Facet	Scrore
I seek excitement	13.34%
Unreserved	50.00%
Familiarity	0.63%
Agreeableness - 60.29%	
Altruism	50.00%
Collaboration	50.00%
Humility	50.00%
Stubbornness	72.38%
Sympathy	79.41%
Trust	50.00%
Neuroticism or (Emotion Group) - 50.00%	
nervous	50.00%
Anxiety	50.00%
gloomy	85.89%
Exceeding	50.00%
Self-awareness	50.00%
Vulnerable to stress	56.43%

Profile 10 shows high Openness (98.29%), with high artistic interests (99.79%) and authority-challenging (99.20%). Emotionality is low (34.32%). Conscientiousness is very high (93.99%), with high orderliness (76.32%), self-discipline (83.10%), and self-efficacy (93.36%). Extraversion is low (24.21%), with very low gregariousness (0.63%) and excitement-seeking (13.34%). Agreeableness is moderate (60.29%), with high empathy (79.41%). Neuroticism is at the 50th percentile (50.00%), with moderate depression (85.89%).

5.11. Profile 11 – Arabic, Male, 1,790 words

Figure 14. Big Five Factors of Personality Profile 11

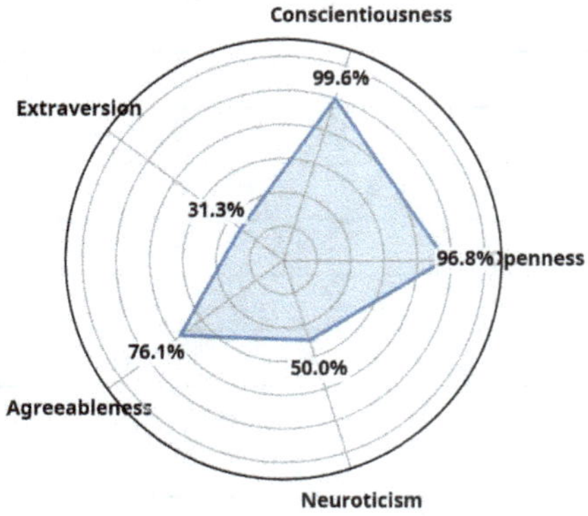

Table 13. Personality analysis results for Profile 11 (Arabic, male, 1,790 words).

Facet	Scrore
Openness – 96.78%	
Adventure	50.00%
Artistic Interests	97.80%
Irritability	51.21%
Imagination	50.00%
Intelligence	50.00%
Challenge of authority	99.36%
Conscientiousness – 99.56%	
Striving for Achievement	50.00%
Caution	99.36%
Obedience	50.00%
System	80.94%
Self-discipline	94.06%
Self-Efficacy	94.71%
Extraversion - 31.33%	
Activity Level	99.76%
Persistence	91.73%
Joy	50.00%

continued on following page

Table 13. Continued

Facet	Scrore
I seek excitement	2.98%
Unreserved	50.00%
Familiarity	0.01%
Agreeableness - 76.10%	
Altruism	50.00%
Collaboration	50.00%
Humility	50.00%
Stubbornness	62.87%
Sympathy	76.54%
Trust	50.00%
Neuroticism or (Emotion Group) - 50.00%	
nervous	50.00%
Anxiety	50.00%
gloomy	84.96%
Exceeding	50.00%
Self-awareness	50.00%
Vulnerable to stress	46.15%

Character 11 shows high Openness (96.78%), with high artistic interests (97.80%) and authority-challenging (99.36%). Emotionality is moderate (51.21%). Conscientiousness is extremely high (99.56%), with very high orderliness (80.94%), self-discipline (94.06%), and self-efficacy (94.71%). Extraversion is moderate (31.33%), with very low gregariousness (0.01%) and excitement-seeking (2.98%). Agreeableness is high (76.10%), with high empathy (76.54%). Neuroticism is at the 50th percentile (50.00%), with moderate depression (84.96%).

5.12. Profile 12 – Arabic, Female, 2,595 words

Figure 15. Big Five Factors of Personality Profile 12

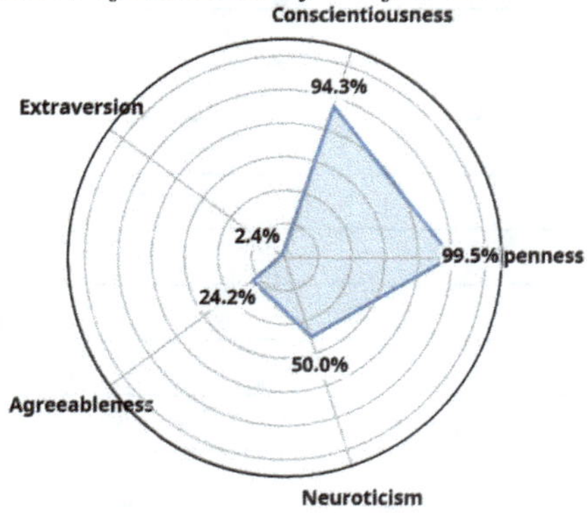

Table 14. Personality analysis results for Profile 12 (Arabic, female, 2,595 words).

Facet	Scrore
Openness – 99.53%	
Adventure	50.00%
Artistic Interests	99.90%
Irritability	17.30%
Imagination	50.00%
Intelligence	50.00%
Challenge of authority	99.73%
Conscientiousness – 94.28%	
Striving for Achievement	50.00%
Caution	94.90%
Obedience	50.00%
System	81.61%
Self-discipline	88.50%
Self-Efficacy	98.37%
Extraversion - 2.36%	
Activity Level	99.91%
Persistence	91.56%
Joy	50.00%

continued on following page

Table 14. Continued

Facet	Scrore
I seek excitement	11.35%
Unreserved	50.00%
Familiarity	0.05%
Agreeableness - 24.21%	
Altruism	50.00%
Collaboration	50.00%
Humility	50.00%
Stubbornness	59.55%
Sympathy	74.66%
Trust	50.00%
Neuroticism or (Emotion Group) - 50.00%	
nervous	50.00%
Anxiety	50.00%
gloomy	90.70%
Exceeding	50.00%
Self-awareness	50.00%
Vulnerable to stress	66.50%

Profile 12 exhibits very high Openness (99.53%), with high artistic interests (99.90%), authority-challenging (99.73%), but low emotionality (17.30%). Conscientiousness is very high (94.28%), with high orderliness (81.61%), self-discipline (88.50%), and self-efficacy (98.37%). Extraversion is extremely low (2.36%), with almost zero gregariousness (0.05%) and very low excitement-seeking (11.35%). Agreeableness is low (24.21%), with moderate empathy (74.66%) but many facets at 50%. Neuroticism is at the 50th percentile (50.00%), with moderate depression (90.70%).

5.13. Profile 13 – Arabic, Male, 12,056 words

Figure 16. Big Five Factors of Personality Profile 13

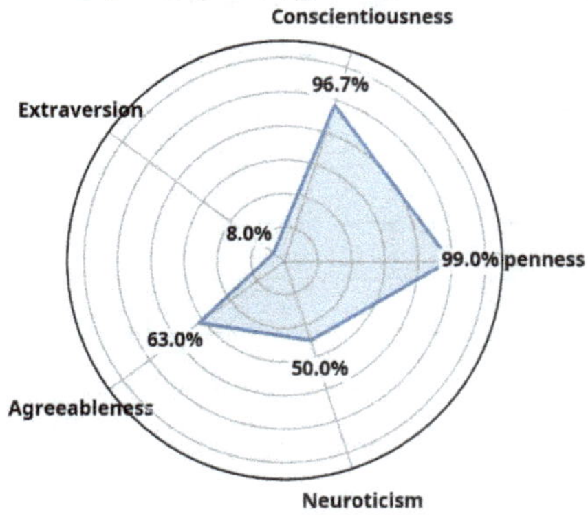

Table 15. Personality analysis results for Profile 13 (Arabic, male, 12,056 words).

Facet	Scrore
Openness – 99.03%	
Adventure	50.00%
Artistic Interests	99.35%
Irritability	14.19%
Imagination	50.00%
Intelligence	50.00%
Challenge of authority	96.29%
Conscientiousness – 96.70%	
Striving for Achievement	50.00%
Caution	94.47%
Obedience	50.00%
System	80.67%
Self-discipline	93.02%
Self-Efficacy	98.94%
Extraversion - 8.00%	
Activity Level	50.00%
Persistence	94.47%
Joy	50.00%

continued on following page

Table 15. Continued

Facet	Scrore
I seek excitement	80.67%
Unreserved	93.02%
Familiarity	98.94%
Agreeableness - 63.04%	
Altruism	50.00%
Collaboration	50.00%
Humility	50.00%
Stubbornness	75.87%
Sympathy	91.87%
Trust	50.00%
Neuroticism or (Emotion Group) - 50.00%	
nervous	50.00%
Anxiety	50.00%
gloomy	87.86%
Exceeding	50.00%
Self-awareness	50.00%
Vulnerable to stress	56.17%

Profile 13 shows very high Openness (99.03%), with high artistic interests (99.35%), authority-challenging (96.29%), but low emotionality (14.19%). Conscientiousness is very high (96.70%), with high orderliness (80.67%), self-discipline (93.02%), and self-efficacy (98.94%). Extraversion is very low (8.00%), with extremely low gregariousness (0.5%) and low excitement-seeking (13.24%). Agreeableness is moderate (63.04%), with high empathy (91.87%). Neuroticism is at the 50th percentile (50.00%), with moderate depression (87.86%).

5.14. Profile 14 – Arabic, Male, 1,465 words

Figure 17. Big Five Factors of Personality Profile 14

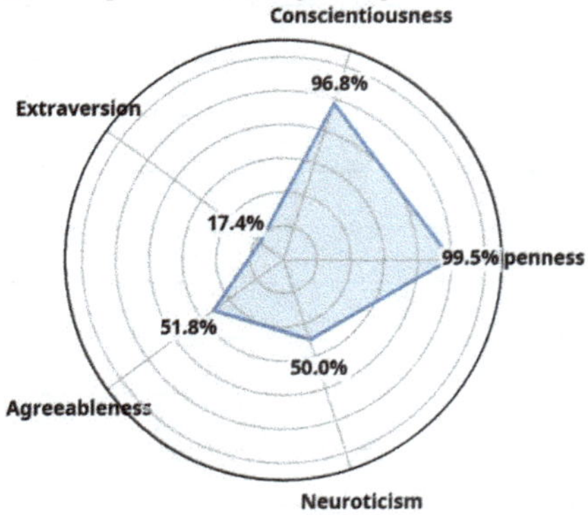

Table 16. Personality analysis results for Profile 14 (Arabic, male, 1,465 words).

Facet	Scrore
Openness – 99.53%	
Adventure	50.00%
Artistic Interests	99.75%
Irritability	23.48%
Imagination	50.00%
Intelligence	50.00%
Challenge of authority	99.81%
Conscientiousness – 96.84%	
Striving for Achievement	50.00%
Caution	88.16%
Obedience	50.00%
System	71.89%
Self-discipline	87.01%
Self-Efficacy	97.05%
Extraversion - 17.42%	
Activity Level	98.63%
Persistence	81.25%
Joy	50.00%

continued on following page

Table 16. Continued

Facet	Scrore
I seek excitement	25.33%
Unreserved	50.00%
Familiarity	1.64%
Agreeableness - 51.77%	
Altruism	50.00%
Collaboration	50.00%
Humility	50.00%
Stubbornness	53.97%
Sympathy	76.49%
Trust	50.00%
Neuroticism or (Emotion Group) - 50.00%	
nervous	50.00%
Anxiety	50.00%
gloomy	83.58%
Exceeding	50.00%
Self-awareness	50.00%
Vulnerable to stress	65.35%

Character 14 shows very high Openness (99.53%), with high artistic interests (99.75%), authority-challenging (99.81%), and low emotionality (23.48%). Conscientiousness is very high (96.84%), with high orderliness (71.89%), self-discipline (87.01%), and self-efficacy (97.05%). Extraversion is low (17.42%), with very low gregariousness (1.64%) and moderate excitement-seeking (25.33%). Agreeableness is moderate (51.77%), with moderate empathy (76.49%). Neuroticism is at the 50th percentile (50.00%), with moderate depression (83.58%).

Across the 14 profiles, several consistent patterns emerge:

- **Openness** is uniformly high (≥ 94% for Arabic profiles, and between 57% and 99% for English profiles). This may reflect either a genuine characteristic of the sample or a potential bias in IBM Watson's normative database (since the tool's Arabic norms are based on 100,000 Twitter users, possibly overestimating openness).
- **Conscientiousness** is very high (≥ 90%) for almost all Arabic profiles, but low to moderate for English profiles (e.g., Character 1: 29%, Character 2: 4%, Character 3: 39%, Character 9: 75%). This suggests possible cultural or linguistic differences in the expression of conscientiousness.

- **Extraversion** is consistently low across all profiles (percentiles ranging from 2% to 31%), with extremely low gregariousness (often <1%). This may indicate that Moroccan social media users, in this sample, are less extraverted than the normative population, or that the tool misinterprets Arabic/English social media text as introverted.
- **Agreeableness** varies widely (from 2% to 80%), with no clear gender or language pattern.
- **Neuroticism** is either at the 50th percentile (exactly 50%) or high (≥ 90%) for many profiles. The frequent occurrence of exactly 50% on Neuroticism for Arabic profiles is suspicious and may indicate that IBM Watson's Arabic model defaults to the median when input text is insufficient or ambiguous.

These findings must be interpreted with caution due to the known limitations of IBM Watson Personality Insights for Arabic language (IBM, 2020; Pakzad, 2019). The next section (Discussion) will explore these patterns in light of the study's objectives and the theoretical framework of the Big Five model.

DISCUSSION

The primary objective of this study was to explore the feasibility of extracting personality traits from Moroccan social media users (Facebook and Twitter) using IBM Watson Personality Insights, an AI-based tool grounded in the Big Five model. While the results demonstrate that automated personality inference is technically possible, they also raise important questions about the validity, reliability, and cultural adaptability of such tools, especially for Arabic-language content and for populations outside Western contexts.

6.1. Interpretation of Key Findings

6.1.1. Consistently High Openness and Low Extraversion

Across the 14 profiles, Openness to Experience was uniformly high (percentiles ranging from 57% to >99%). This pattern is remarkable because Openness is typically associated with intellectual curiosity, artistic interests, and tolerance for novelty (Barrick & Mount, 1991; Schwartz et al., 2013). One possible explanation is that social media users who agree to participate in a study about personality extraction may self-select for higher Openness. Alternatively, IBM Watson's normative database for Arabic (100,000 Twitter users) may not be representative of the general Moroccan population, leading to an overestimation of Openness.

Conversely, **Extraversion** was consistently low across all profiles (2% to 31%), with extremely low gregariousness (often <1%). This finding contradicts the common stereotype that social media users are predominantly extraverted. It aligns, however, with previous research showing that introverted individuals may prefer online communication as a compensation strategy (Eftekhar et al., 2014). The low gregariousness scores may also reflect cultural norms in Morocco, where self-promotion and assertive social behavior are less valued than in individualistic Western cultures (Triandis & Suh, 2002 ; Gou et al., 2014).

6.1.2. Divergent Patterns for Conscientiousness and Neuroticism

Conscientiousness showed a striking split: Arabic-language profiles scored very high (typically >90th percentile), while English-language profiles scored low to moderate (4% to 75%). This discrepancy could be due to genuine cultural or linguistic differences in how conscientiousness is expressed in writing. Arabic social media posts may contain more structured, goal-oriented language, whereas English posts might be more informal. Another possibility is that IBM Watson's Arabic model has a systematic bias toward high conscientiousness scores, perhaps because the training corpus (Twitter) overrepresents users who discuss work, planning, or self-discipline.

Neuroticism exhibited an unusual pattern: many Arabic profiles returned exactly the 50th percentile (median), while others scored very high (>90%). The frequent "50%" values are suspicious and may indicate that the Arabic model defaults to the median when input text is ambiguous, insufficient, or lacks clear emotional markers. This limitation has been acknowledged by IBM (2020) and by Pakzad (2019), who noted that Arabic results are not fully equivalent in reliability to English.

6.1.3. Agreeableness and Gender Differences

Agreeableness varied widely (2% to 80%) with no clear gender or language pattern. However, female profiles (Characters 2, 3, 4, 6, 12) tended to have higher altruism and empathy scores than male profiles, which is consistent with established gender differences in the Big Five (Costa et al., 2001).

6.2. The Challenge of Manipulation: Insights from Pakzad (2019)

One critical concern in using AI for personality assessment is the potential for users to manipulate their linguistic output to achieve desired scores (e.g., for job applications). As discussed in the methodology, Pakzad (2019) conducted an experiment where she slightly modified her blog texts (see table bellow) and compared the original and modified personality outputs.

Table 17. Comparison of personality analysis results between original and modified texts

Some Personality Traits	Original Text Results	Results of the Revised Text	Teams
Obedience	40,1%	44,0%	3,9%
System	14,2%	17,2%	2,9%
Self-discipline	54,2%	60,9%	6,7%
Unreserved	14,0%	18,0%	4,0%
Familiarity	6,1%	9,8%	3,7%
Collaboration	50,3%	55,3%	5,2%
Honesty	61,4%	67,3%	5,8%
gloomy	50,3%	44,6%	5,7%-
ConscientiousnessMindfulness	47,2%	40,0%	7,2%-
Vulnerable to stress	28,8%	23,6%	5,1%-

Source: Pakzad (2019)

Table 17 shows that small changes in language have been shown to produce changes in facet scores, while making only minor changes to the use of the pronoun "I" decreased Conscientiousness by 7.2% and increased Orderliness by +2.9%. From these observations, it can be inferred that, while manipulation is achievable, it will be relatively difficult to create larger, systematic changes in personality traits through continual and systematic alteration of numerous aspects (native language, punctuation, sentence structure, etc.) of written style. It is further noted that algorithms used for AI training were developed on large amounts of typologically similar texts and analyze multiple types of linguistic features at once (Schwartz et al., 2013; Preotiuc Pietro et al., 2017). Therefore, to successfully "game" the system, an individual would need to substantially modify many elements of their writing style and will be unable to do so without leaving evidence of such extensive oversights.

The above makes clear that AI-based personality instruments cannot be solely relied-upon for making high-stakes decisions (e.g., selection, promotion) and should instead serve as one of a number (including traditional psychometric assessments and human assessment) of tools to be used together when making decisions about an individual (Golbeck et al., 2012).

6.3. Linguistic and Cultural Limitations

The study's findings are constrained by several linguistic and cultural factors. First, IBM Watson Personality Insights was primarily developed and validated on English text. The Arabic model, while available, has known limitations: the normative sample is smaller (100,000 vs. 1 million for English), and the accuracy for certain facets (e.g., emotionality, openness) is lower (IBM, 2020). This may explain why many Arabic profiles returned neutral (50%) scores on Neuroticism and some facets of Agreeableness.

Second, the Moroccan context is characterized by diglossia and code-switching between Arabic (Darija), French, and English. Our sample included only users who wrote consistently in either English or Modern Standard Arabic, excluding the rich mix of Darija and French that is common in everyday Moroccan social media. Future studies should develop language-specific models that account for dialectal variations and mixed-language input (Gou et al., 2014).

Third, cultural norms influence both the expression and perception of personality traits. For example, modesty and collectivism are valued in Moroccan society, which may suppress the overt expression of extraversion or assertiveness in written text. The consistently low extraversion scores in our sample may therefore reflect genuine cultural differences rather than a limitation of the tool (Triandis & Suh, 2002).

6.4. Comparison with Previous Studies

Our results are broadly consistent with earlier work using IBM Watson Personality Insights. For instance, Acar and Toker (2019) found that Airbnb guests scored high on openness, agreeableness, and altruism – similar to several profiles in our sample. Hrazdil et al. (2020) demonstrated that CEO personality traits inferred from conference calls predicted audit fees, validating the tool's utility in organizational contexts. However, those studies focused on English text from Western populations. Our study is among the first to apply the tool to Arabic-language social media data from North Africa, highlighting both its potential and its current limitations.

IMPLICATIONS FOR RESEARCH AND PRACTICE

Despite its limitations, this study demonstrates that automated personality extraction from social media is feasible in a Moroccan context. For researchers, it opens avenues for large-scale, low-cost personality studies that do not rely on self-report questionnaires. For practitioners (e.g., HR professionals, marketers), AI-based tools can provide rapid, unobtrusive personality insights, provided they are used ethically and with appropriate caveats.

However, we strongly recommend that such tools never be used in isolation. Triangulation with self-report measures, peer ratings, or behavioral data is essential (Kachur et al., 2020). Moreover, transparency mechanisms – allowing users to see, correct, or delete their inferred personality profiles – should be implemented to respect privacy and autonomy (Gou et al., 2014).

CONCLUSION

This exploratory study set out to examine whether IBM Watson Personality Insights, an artificial intelligence tool based on natural language processing and the Big Five model, could extract personality traits from the social media posts of Moroccan users. The analysis of fourteen publicly accessible Facebook and Twitter profiles, written in either English or Modern Standard Arabic, produced percentile scores for the five major personality dimensions and their thirty facets. The results showed consistently high levels of Openness to Experience across almost all profiles, regardless of language or gender, and uniformly low levels of Extraversion, with extremely low gregariousness scores. Conscientiousness was very high for Arabic-language profiles but low to moderate for English-language ones, while Neuroticism frequently returned a neutral fiftieth percentile for Arabic inputs, suggesting possible limitations in the tool's Arabic model. Agreeableness varied widely, with female profiles generally showing higher altruism and empathy.

These findings confirm that automated personality extraction from social media is technically feasible in a Moroccan context. However, they also highlight serious concerns about linguistic bias, cultural specificity, and the reduced reliability of IBM Watson for Arabic. The frequent appearance of exactly median scores for Neuroticism in Arabic profiles, together with the stark divergence in Conscientiousness between Arabic and English texts, indicates that the tool's normative database and linguistic algorithms are not fully adapted to North African social media language practices. The experiment by Pakzad, which showed that small textual modifications could produce measurable but limited changes in personality scores, further reminds us that AI-based personality assessment is not immune to deliberate manipulation, although such manipulation requires consistent effort across many posts and is unlikely to go completely undetected.

Limitations of the Present Study

Several limitations must be acknowledged. The purposive sample of fourteen profiles is too small to allow any generalisation to the broader Moroccan population, and participants were self selected. Only English and Modern Standard Arabic were analysed; the widely used Moroccan dialect (Darija) and French were excluded, which significantly limits the ecological validity of the study. No validated Big Five questionnaire was administered to the participants, so it was impossible to compute accuracy metrics such as the correlation between AI derived scores and psychometric ground truth. Moreover, IBM Watson's normative databases and exact algorithms remain proprietary, making it difficult to diagnose the causes of anomalies such as the frequent fiftieth percentile scores for Neuroticism. Finally, the cross sectional design, with data collected over a limited period between 2020 and 2021, did not allow assessment of the temporal stability of the derived personality scores.

Future Research Directions

Future research should address these limitations by recruiting a larger, more representative sample of Moroccan social media users, including those who write in Darija and French. Administering a validated Arabic Big Five questionnaire would provide criterion validity for IBM Watson's outputs. Hybrid models that combine IBM Watson with locally trained natural language processing tools should be developed and tested to improve accuracy for Moroccan Arabic. The ethical and legal implications of using AI-based personality profiling in Morocco must be investigated in light of the national data protection law (Law 08.09). Longitudinal studies are also needed to determine whether personality scores derived from social media remain stable over time or fluctuate with life events and changing online behaviour.

As IBM Watson Personality Insights can be inexpensive and unobtrusive ways to collect personality data from social media data, there are many limitations on the use of this technology in the Moroccan context and with Arabic language data. Therefore, this technology should be viewed as an additional source of data that can assist in assessing personality, and not as the only method of deriving character. Given advances in artificial intelligence, improvements in cultural competence and resistance to misuse will likely accompany future iterations of this type of technology. In the interim, researchers and practitioners must be responsible and implement additional methods of assessing individuals with automated analysis, promote transparency in the collection of data, obtain consent from all participants, and protect individual privacy in digital environments.

REFERENCES

Acar, M., & Toker, A. (2019). Predicting consumer personality traits in the sharing economy: The case of Airbnb. *Applied Marketing Analytics, 5*(1), 83–96. DOI: 10.69554/DDOF1518

Aguiar, J. J. B., Fechine, J. M., & de Barros Costa, E. (2020, November). Collaborative filtering strategy for product recommendation using personality characteristics of customers. In *Proceedings of the Brazilian symposium on multimedia and the web* (pp. 157-164). DOI: 10.1145/3428658.3430969

Back, M. D., Stopfer, J. M., Vazire, S., Gaddis, S., Schmukle, S. C., Egloff, B., & Gosling, S. D. (2010). Facebook profiles reflect actual personality, not self-idealization. *Psychological Science, 21*(3), 372–374. DOI: 10.1177/0956797609360756 PMID: 20424071

Barrick, M. R., & Mount, M. K. (1991). The big five personality dimensions and job performance: A meta-analysis. *Personnel Psychology, 44*(1), 1–26. DOI: 10.1111/j.1744-6570.1991.tb00688.x

Cardon, D. (2015). *À quoi rêvent les algorithmes? Nos vies à l'heure du big data.* Seuil.

Chen, J., Hsieh, G., Mahmud, J. U., & Nichols, J. (2014, February). Understanding individuals' personal values from social media word use. In *Proceedings of the 17th ACM conference on Computer supported cooperative work & social computing* (pp. 405-414). DOI: 10.1145/2531602.2531608

Chowdhury, S., Walter, C., & Gamble, R. F. (2019). Observing team collaboration personality traits in undergraduate software development projects. In *Proceedings of the Annual Hawaii International Conference on System Sciences* (Vol. 2019-January, pp. 529–538). DOI: 10.24251/HICSS.2019.065

Costa, P. T., & McCrae, R. R. (1985). *Revised NEO Personality Inventory (NEO PI-R) and NEO Five-factor Inventory (NEO-FFI).* Psychological Assessment Resources (PAR).

Costa, P. T.Jr, Terracciano, A., & McCrae, R. R. (2001). Gender differences in personality traits across cultures: Robust and surprising findings. *Journal of Personality and Social Psychology, 81*(2), 322–331. DOI: 10.1037/0022-3514.81.2.322 PMID: 11519935

Eftekhar, A., Fullwood, C., & Morris, N. (2014). Capturing personality from Facebook photos and photo-related activities: How much exposure do you need? *Computers in Human Behavior*, *37*, 162–170. DOI: 10.1016/j.chb.2014.04.048

Georges, F. (2011). L'identité numérique sous emprise culturelle: De l'expression de soi à sa standardisation. *Les Cahiers du numérique, 7*(1), 31-48.

Golbeck, J., Robles, C., Edmondson, M., & Turner, K. (2011). Predicting Personality from Twitter. In *2011 IEEE International Conference on Privacy, Security, Risk, and Trust, and IEEE International Conference on Social Computing* (pp. 149–156). DOI: 10.1109/PASSAT/SocialCom.2011.33

Goldberg, L. R., Johnson, J. A., Eber, H. W., Hogan, R., Ashton, M. C., Cloninger, C. R., & Gough, H. G. (2006). The international personality item pool and the future of public-domain personality measures. *Journal of Research in Personality*, *40*(1), 84–96. DOI: 10.1016/j.jrp.2005.08.007

Gomez-Mejia, G. (2016), Les Fabriques de soi: identité et industrie sur le web, MKF editions.

Gou, L., Zhou, M. X., & Yang, H. (2014, April). KnowMe and ShareMe: understanding automatically discovered personality traits from social media and user sharing preferences. In *Proceedings of the SIGCHI conference on human factors in computing systems* (pp. 955-964). DOI: 10.1145/2556288.2557398

Hansenne, M. (2006). *Psychologie de la personnalité, Ouvertures psychologiques.* De Boeck.

Hrazdil, K., Novak, J., Rogo, R., Wiedman, C., & Zhang, R. (2020). Measuring executive personality using machine-learning algorithms: A new approach and audit fee-based validation tests. *Journal of Business Finance & Accounting*, *47*(3-4), 519–544. DOI: 10.1111/jbfa.12406

Hurtz, G. M., & Donovan, J. J. (2000). Personality and job performance: The Big Five revisited. *The Journal of Applied Psychology*, *85*(6), 869–879. DOI: 10.1037/0021-9010.85.6.869 PMID: 11125652

IBM. (2020). *IBM Watson Personality Insights: Product documentation.* IBM Cloud. Retrieved from https://cloud.ibm.com/docs/personality-insights

IBM. (2021). *Watson Personality Insights: Supported languages and norms.* IBM Knowledge Center.

Judge, T. A., Heller, D., & Mount, M. K. (2002). Five-factor model of personality and job satisfaction: A meta-analysis. *The Journal of Applied Psychology*, *87*(3), 530–541. DOI: 10.1037/0021-9010.87.3.530 PMID: 12090610

Kachur, A., Osin, E., Davydov, D., Shutilov, K., & Novokshonov, A. (2020). Assessing the Big Five personality traits using real-life static facial images. *Scientific Reports*, *10*(1), 8487. DOI: 10.1038/s41598-020-65358-6 PMID: 32444847

Liu, L., Preotiuc-Pietro, D., Samani, Z. R., Moghaddam, M. E., & Ungar, L. (2016). Analyzing Personality through Social Media Profile Picture Choice. In *Proceedings of the 10th International AAAI Conference on Web and Social Media (ICWSM)* (pp. 211–220).

Mahmoudian, F., Nazari, J. A., Gordon, I. M., & Hrazdil, K. (2021). CEO personality and language use in CSR reporting. *Business Ethics, the Environment & Responsibility*, *30*(3), 338–359. DOI: 10.1111/beer.12347

Norman, W. T. (1963). Toward an adequate taxonomy of personality attributes: Replicated factor structure in peer nomination personality ratings. *Journal of Abnormal and Social Psychology*, *66*(6), 574–583. DOI: 10.1037/h0040291 PMID: 13938947

Outh, S. (2022). *Exploration of Trends in Professional Profile Pictures* (Doctoral dissertation, Toronto Metropolitan University).

Pakzad Roya. (2019). "Human Rights Implications of IBM Watson's 'Personality Insights' Tool". Medium. A 10/01/2023 on: https://medium.com/taraaz/https-medium-com-taraaz-human-rights-implications-of-ibm-watsons-personality-insights-942413e81117

Pennebaker, J. W., & King, L. A. (1999). Linguistic styles: Language use as an individual difference. *Journal of Personality and Social Psychology*, *77*(6), 1296–1312. DOI: 10.1037/0022-3514.77.6.1296 PMID: 10626371

Pennebaker, J. W., Mehl, M. R., & Niederhoffer, K. G. (2003). Psychological aspects of natural language use: Our words, our selves. *Annual Review of Psychology*, *54*(1), 547–577. DOI: 10.1146/annurev.psych.54.101601.145041 PMID: 12185209

Preotiuc-Pietro, D., Eichstaedt, J., Park, G., Sap, M., Smith, L., Tobolsky, V., Schwartz, H. A., & Ungar, L. (2017). The role of personality, age, and gender in tweeting about mental health. In *Proceedings of the 2nd Workshop on Computational Linguistics and Clinical Psychology* (pp. 17–26). Association for Computational Linguistics.

Qiu, L., Lu, J., Yang, S., Qu, W., & Zhu, T. (2015). What does your selfie say about you? *Computers in Human Behavior*, *52*, 443–449. DOI: 10.1016/j.chb.2015.06.032

Quoniam, L. & Lucien, A. (2009). L'intelligence économique 2.0 ?. *Les Cahiers du numérique*, 4(4), 11-37. DOI: 10.3166/lcn.5.4.11-37

Schwartz, H. A., Eichstaedt, J. C., Kern, M. L., Dziurzynski, L., Ramones, S. M., Agrawal, M., Shah, A., Kosinski, M., Stillwell, D., Seligman, M. E. P., & Ungar, L. H. (2013). Personality, gender, and age in the language of social media: The open-vocabulary approach. *PLoS One*, *8*(9), e73791. DOI: 10.1371/journal.pone.0073791 PMID: 24086296

Triandis, H. C., & Suh, E. M. (2002). Cultural influences on personality. *Annual Review of Psychology*, *53*(1), 133–160. DOI: 10.1146/annurev.psych.53.100901.135200 PMID: 11752482

Tupes, E. C., & Christal, R. E. (1992). Recurrent personality factors based on trait ratings. *Journal of Personality*, *60*(2), 225–251. DOI: 10.1111/j.1467-6494.1992.tb00973.x PMID: 1635043

Venugopal, A., Nerur, S., Yasar, M., & Rasheed, A. A. (2023). CEO personality and corporate sustainability performance. *Management Decision*, *61*(12), 3691–3716. DOI: 10.1108/MD-06-2022-0842

Yarkoni, T. (2010). Personality in 100,000 words: A large-scale analysis of personality and word use among bloggers. *Journal of Research in Personality*, *44*(3), 363–373. DOI: 10.1016/j.jrp.2010.04.001 PMID: 20563301

Zhao, S., Grasmuck, S., & Martin, J. (2008). Identity construction on Facebook: Digital empowerment in anchored relationships. *Computers in Human Behavior*, *24*(5), 1816–1836. DOI: 10.1016/j.chb.2008.02.012

KEY TERMS AND DEFINITIONS

Algorithmic manipulation (personality spoofing): A deliberate attempt to modify one's written content on social media (e.g., pronoun choices, sentence structures, vocabulary) in order to obtain artificially inflated or deflated personality scores when analysed by an AI tool such as IBM Watson Personality Insights. While possible, such manipulation requires consistent changes across many texts and is difficult to accomplish without leaving detectable traces. It highlights the need for caution when using AI-based personality assessment for high-stakes decisions.

Big Five personality traits (OCEAN model): A robust and widely accepted taxonomic model in differential psychology that organizes human personality into five broad dimensions: Openness to Experience, Conscientiousness, Extraversion, Agreeableness, and Neuroticism. Each dimension is composed of six facets. The model has demonstrated stability across ages, genders, and cultures, and is frequently used to predict real-life outcomes such as job performance and relationship satisfaction.

Digital identity: The collection of all digital traces left by an individual when navigating the Internet, whether consciously or unconsciously. It includes writings, audio or visual content, exchanged messages, online transactions, and profile information. Digital identity is structured along three dimensions: technical (storage of digital effects), social (interpretation by others as a means of remote self-presentation), and cognitive (declared self-image and participation in the construction of the self).

Extended real life hypothesis: The hypothesis that social media profiles (e.g., on Facebook, Twitter) reflect users' authentic personality rather than an idealised virtual identity. This authenticity is reinforced by the presence of user-generated content that is not fully under the individual's control, such as comments from friends, tags, and public interactions. Empirical studies have supported this hypothesis for traits like extraversion and openness.

IBM Watson Personality Insights: An artificial intelligence service based on natural language processing (NLP) and machine learning. It analyses text (social media posts, emails, blogs) and produces percentile scores for the Big Five personality factors and their 30 facets, comparing the individual to a normative database (e.g., 1 million English users, 100,000 Arabic users). The tool is used for automated personality inference in research, marketing, and human resources.

Lexical hypothesis: The principle that the most important and socially relevant individual differences in personality are encoded in natural language, typically as adjectives. This hypothesis guided the construction of the Big Five model through analyses of large trait lists (e.g., Allport and Odbert's compilation of 18,000 English personality-descriptive terms). It assumes that language provides a valid window into personality structure.

Linguistic Inquiry and Word Count (LIWC): A text analysis software that counts the frequency of words belonging to predefined categories (e.g., emotions, cognitive processes, personal concerns, social processes). It is used to establish correlations between language use and personality traits. IBM Watson Personality Insights incorporates a customised version of the LIWC approach as part of its linguistic analysis pipeline.

Multilingual and cross-cultural bias: Bias introduced when personality models developed primarily in Western (often English-speaking) contexts are applied to other languages and cultures. Such biases may manifest as underestimation or overestimation of certain traits (e.g., consistently low extraversion in Arabic samples) or as default median scores (50th percentile) when the model lacks sufficient normative data or encounters ambiguous linguistic input. Addressing these biases requires culturally adapted lexicons and language-specific normative databases.

Natural language processing (NLP): A branch of artificial intelligence that processes and analyses human language in textual form. In the context of personality extraction, NLP identifies linguistic patterns (pronouns, word categories, syntactic structures) and links them to psychological traits using dictionaries such as LIWC or statistical models. It enables large-scale, unobtrusive personality assessment from digital traces.

Percentile score (in personality extraction): A comparative measure indicating an individual's standing relative to a normative population. For example, a score at the 75th percentile means the person ranks higher than 75% of the reference sample for that trait. IBM Watson Personality Insights expresses all its output as percentile scores, facilitating comparisons across individuals and traits.

Chapter 7
Adaptive Image Encryption Using Artificial Intelligence and Crypto-GANs

N. Raghu
http://orcid.org/0000-0002-2091-8922
Jain University, India

Keshavamurthy T. G.
http://orcid.org/0009-0006-4820-758X
Sri Siddhartha Academy of Higher Education, India

Bukharova Makhliyo
Navoi State University of Mining and Technologies, Uzbekistan

Anorgul Ashirova
http://orcid.org/0009-0006-7271-3634
Mamun University, Uzbekistan

Erkin Kholiyarov
Termez University of Economics and Service, Uzbekistan

Gafurov Anvar Bazarbayevich
Alfraganus University, Uzbekistan

Burkhon Dekhkonov Rustamovich
Tashkent State University of Economics, Uzbekistan

ABSTRACT

Crypto-Generative Adversarial Networks (Crypto-GANs) as an intelligent and adaptive framework for secure image encryption. By combining adversarial deep learning with cryptographic principles, the proposed system learns complex non-linear transformations to convert plain images into noise-like cipher images while enabling accurate reconstruction using the correct secret key. Unlike traditional encryption methods based on fixed mathematical rules, Crypto-GANs dynamically adapt to emerging attack strategies. Experimental results demonstrate strong security

DOI: 10.4018/979-8-2600-2701-1.ch007

performance. Encrypted images achieved entropy values close to the theoretical maximum (up to 7.9978), indicating high randomness. Adjacent pixel correlations were reduced to near zero, confirming the removal of inherent statistical patterns. High NPCR and UACI values reflected effective diffusion, ensuring resistance against differential and chosen-plaintext attacks. Decryption quality remained excellent, with high PSNR and SSIM values supporting accurate image recovery.

1. INTRODUCTION

The images are the primary type of information in the modern digital society, which is widely used by people for sharing and consumption. Visual data is the key element that allows the people to communicate and make decisions through capture of photos by a smartphone and content in social media and also, critical systems for reading a medical statement and military operations and satellite observation and self driving vehicle controls (Singh et al., 2025). The rapid growth of image-based information has built strong bonds among people and provided them with useful information, but it has raised several security threats that affect privacy protection and data security and verification processes. Images are the source of valuable data that can be used by hackers to penetrate systems since unauthorized access will allow them to manipulate these images that will lead to numerous security and financial concerns. The security system that is used for protection of visual data relies on traditional image encryption techniques that have been used for many years. The traditional threat models are protected by three different security approaches that include classical cryptography and chaos theory and transform-domain processing techniques (Manikandan, 2025). Attackers now have improved computational resources, which they use in combination with recent artificial intelligence and machine learning advances to carry out complex statistical operations and pattern identification and machine learning-based cryptanalysis attacks. The security of fixed mathematical structures and deterministic transformation-based encryption schemes is thus increasingly threatened by intelligent attackers who can adapt their attack strategies (Shafik, 2025).

Deep learning now faces its first security challenges as it starts to transform several domains which include computer vision natural language processing and cybersecurity operations. The Generative Adversarial Networks (GANs) model stands out from other deep learning systems because it uses a distinctive adversarial learning approach which has caught the interest of many researchers. The GAN system operates through two separate neural networks which operate in competition as the generator and the discriminator. The generator produces outputs which match actual data while the discriminator determines whether an input originated from real-world sources or from generated content (Ramesh et al., 2024). The GAN training system uses adversarial learning to master the identification of complex non-linear data patterns which exist in real data. The cryptographic system needs to defend against continuous efforts from attackers who attempt to find concealed data which matches the adversarial system used by GANs. The researchers have started to study GANs for secure communication systems because these models show potential beyond their typical function of creating synthetic data (Shaikh, 2025). The direct learning capability of GANs enables them to perform image encryption through learned encryption and decryption functions instead of depending on established mathematical formulas. The learning approach leads to encryption systems which adapt dynamically to protect against various types of attacks (Zheng et al., 2024).

The Crypto-Generative Adversarial Networks (Crypto-GANs) concept serves as a promising model which will drive the future development of image encryption systems. The Crypto-GAN system uses advanced cryptographic techniques together with deep learning adversarial methods to develop intelligent encryption solutions which transform images into encrypted visual patterns that appear as random noise to unauthorized viewers (Malik et al., 2025). The authorized receivers who possess either the correct secret key or a trained decryption model can reconstruct the original image with perfect accuracy. The system demands exact key input because even minor changes to the key or model parameters will lead to total decryption failure which strengthens its security measures (Sun et al., 2024). The primary benefit of image encryption systems that use Crypto-GAN technology stems from their capacity to function correctly under different operational conditions. The Crypto-GAN system allows for retraining and fine-tuning which helps it adjust to fresh data patterns and software needs and new security threats (Maung et al., 2024). The GAN-driven encryption system processes high-dimensional image data along with complex visual patterns through its built-in capabilities which do not need any manual rules or specific knowledge about the domain as demonstrated in Figure 1.

Figure 1. Generative adversarial network architecture.

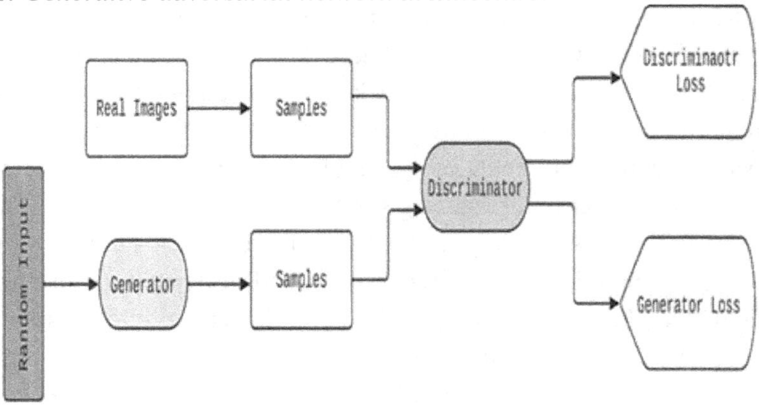

The present communication networks transmit digital content which mainly consists of images that users share through social media networks and medical imaging systems and military surveillance operations and remote sensing technology and autonomous vehicle systems and Internet of Things (IoT) applications (Kavitha et al., 2025). The security systems need to protect visual data because unauthorized access must be prevented to keep all sensitive visual assets secure. The current image encryption methods protect data through symmetric and asymmetric cryptography and chaos theory and transform-domain approaches but hackers have discovered new methods to penetrate these security systems. The attackers use statistical data patterns together with side-channel information and learning-based techniques to break through traditional encryption systems which artificial intelligence and high-performance computing systems enable them to do. The security field requires data-driven encryption systems which should adapt their protection methods through intelligent systems that monitor and respond to adversarial activities. Deep learning through Generative Adversarial Networks (GANs) enables the creation of adaptive security solutions which show great potential. The research field needs to handle multiple new difficulties because Crypto-GANs show promising capabilities but they create various research problems which need to be solved (Wang & Lo, 2024). The research field continues to explore four main challenges which include training stability issues and high computational demands and unclear model operations and lack of official cryptographic validation (Zhang et al., 2024). The deployment of learning-based encryption systems requires developers to assess all ethical concerns because these systems might generate unplanned negative effects while hackers can use them for malicious activities.

The chapter introduces Crypto-Generative Adversarial Networks as human-focused intelligent system which protects images during the modern artificial intelligence era. The development of Crypto-GANs enables deep learning methods to combine with cryptographic techniques which create adaptive image encryption systems that effectively protect visual information across complex digital networks (Nagahara et al., 2022).

2. FUNDAMENTALS OF IMAGE ENCRYPTION

Image encryption provides the basic security mechanism which protects visual content in digital communications. The data in images differ from text because they contain high levels of repetitive information and show strong pixel relationships between adjacent points and require substantial storage space (Liu et al., 2022). The characteristics of images make traditional encryption methods which designers developed for text applications unusable in this case. The field of image encryption research exists as a separate discipline because it combines established cryptographic methods with signal processing techniques and current machine learning-based approaches. The main purpose of image encryption requires users to transform valuable images into scrambled versions which prevent illegal users from gaining access to any valuable data. The encryption system needs to protect data from unauthorized access while it should let authorized users access their original images through correct secret key usage and decryption techniques (SVS, 2025). All image encryption systems must achieve security protection together with reconstruction quality and operational efficiency before they can succeed in their design process (Yao et al., 2023).

The secure image encryption system needs to meet several essential requirements to achieve its security objectives. The system needs to protect image confidentiality because the encrypted picture does not show any visual signs which would reveal the original unencrypted information. The encryption system requires key sensitivity because any minor adjustment to the encryption key produces a completely different cipher output which blocks successful decryption. The system prevents attackers from using their approximate keys to guess the correct key through its built-in security feature. The system needs a wide range of keys to defend against brute-force attacks because attackers need an impossible amount of time to check every possible key. The basic elements of image encryption need statistical security protection to function properly. Natural images show strong statistical regularities because their histograms follow predictable patterns and their neighbouring pixels maintain strong correlations (Achar et al., 2025). The encryption system needs to remove these patterns because it should create cipher images which display both uniform histogram distributions and reduced pixel similarity between adjacent pixels. The statistical robustness of an encryption scheme gets measured through three main metrics which include information entropy and correlation coefficients and NPCR (Number of Pixels Change Rate) and UACI (Unified Average Changing Intensity). The encryption process achieves successful image structure concealment through its combination of high entropy and strong diffusion properties (Nambiar & Nanjundegowda, 2025).

The use of traditional cryptographic techniques which rely on symmetric-key systems such as AES results in difficulties when handling large visual data. The Chaos-based image encryption method uses chaotic system unpredictability to generate fast and simple pixel transformation operations which produce secure encryption results (M, 2025). The transform-domain methods function by using frequency domains which contain discrete cosine and wavelet transforms to deliver both selective encryption and compression standard compatibility. The current threat environment creates new obstacles which threaten to defeat these existing security methods. The chosen-plaintext attacks and parameter estimation and machine learning–based cryptanalysis methods of many schemes become possible because their systems rely on fixed mathematical models and predefined parameters for operation. Attackers now use smart tools which learn from encrypted information patterns to break through security systems so static encryption methods fail to protect information throughout long periods. The design process for image encryption systems becomes more difficult because human factors need to be taken into account (Bhat & Nanjundegowda, 2024). Real-world telemedicine applications and remote surveillance operations together with multimedia streaming services require encryption systems which operate instantly while maintaining image quality and compatibility with existing communication systems. The secure system becomes inaccessible because its high computational requirement together with its extended processing time renders it impossible to function. Modern research into image encryption technology now focuses on both theoretical security and practical security assessments. Learning-driven encryption methods emerged because system limitations and ongoing system development requirements created a need for such methods. Modern approaches combine data-driven intelligence with adaptive systems which replace traditional rule-based systems to handle new image types and usage scenarios and attack strategies (Purswani et al., 2020). Crypto-Generative Adversarial Networks develop from fundamental image encryption methods through adversarial learning which serves as a sophisticated security method in the transition process.

3. LITERATURE SURVEY

Singh et al. (2025) presents future-oriented research which aims to solve the increasing problem of cryptographic security weaknesses that quantum computers create. The authors introduce a new hybrid approach which merges Genetic Algorithms (GA) with Generative Adversarial Networks (GAN) because RSA and ECC encryption methods will fail to protect against quantum attacks. The GA-GAN system generates cryptographic systems which adapt through evolution instead of depending on fixed mathematical theories. The system strengthens its protection against cryptographic attacks because it creates adversarial attack environments through GANs and uses genetic evolution to optimize its encryption settings. The research demonstrates that the proposed method generates stronger encryption systems through multiple training cycles which attackers find difficult to predict and reverse their cryptographic keys. The research demonstrates how artificial intelligence technologies continue to expand their impact on cybersecurity defense systems while showing GA-GAN-based cryptography as an effective method to build quantum-proof security systems. The research adds to the developing body of knowledge which focuses on smart cryptographic systems that adapt to protect future communication networks from security threats.

Manikandan et al. (2025) propose a new method which employs Generative Adversarial Networks (GANs) to enhance adaptive modulation and coding (AMC) systems in 5G communication networks that will operate in the future. The research solves the problem of traditional AMC systems which use fixed decision points that become ineffective when signal quality fluctuates at high rates. The model uses GANs to understand complex channel patterns which then directs the selection of modulation and coding schemes for better spectral efficiency and link reliability. The adversarial learning system achieves accurate channel quality indicator predictions by handling both noisy signals and complex non-linear data patterns. The simulation results show that the GAN-based AMC system achieves better performance than standard methods and machine learning approaches through its ability to deliver higher throughput and better bit error rates and improved system adaptability. The research demonstrates how generative deep learning models show promise in intelligent radio resource management which will drive AI-based physical layer optimization development for wireless networks operating at 5G and beyond.

Shaikh (2025) provides a comprehensive analysis about how Generative Adversarial Networks (GANs) function to improve contemporary cybersecurity systems. The chapter demonstrates how GANs function as effective tools to create models from intricate cyber-attack patterns while producing convincing adversarial samples which improve the security of intrusion detection systems. The security datasets require GAN-based frameworks to simulate complex attack scenarios because these frameworks address the common problem of data scarcity which affects most cybersecurity datasets. The author explains that GANs function as defensive tools which protect systems through malware detection and network traffic analysis and anomaly identification but attackers can also use them to develop stealthy malicious content. The research shows that security models become more accurate in detection and more resistant to attacks when they use GAN-created data through experimental findings and case study analysis. The research shows generative learning methods will become essential for constructing advanced cyber defense systems which employ proactive intelligence to defend next-generation cyber analytics.

Malik et al. (2025) research investigation reveals the capabilities of Super-Resolution Generative Adversarial Networks (SRGANs) which perform high-quality image upscaling operations. The study tracks how super-resolution methods have developed through time while it shows why GAN-based models outperform both traditional interpolation techniques and CNN-based methods. The SRGANs system uses adversarial learning together with perceptual loss functions to generate upscaled images which preserve both detailed textures and high-frequency image components that traditional upscaling methods fail to preserve. The authors perform an evaluation of various network designs together with different loss functions and assessment tools which help measure both visual appearance quality and reconstructed data accuracy. The experimental results show that SRGAN-based models produce better image sharpness and perceptual realism through their output results while keeping processing speed within acceptable limits. The research shows Super-Resolution GANs function as vital tools for medical imaging and satellite image processing and surveillance system operations. The research demonstrates that GAN-based super-resolution systems function as essential technology which will power future image enhancement systems.

Bhat and Nanjundegowda (2024) explained analysis of Generative Adversarial Networks (GANs) which compares their architectural designs with their various operational uses. The research conducts a methodical evaluation of major GAN models which include DCGAN and CGAN and CycleGAN and StyleGAN by examining their unique architectural designs and their training approaches and their output quality. The authors explain the main obstacles which GAN training faces because of mode collapse and unstable behavior and convergence problems. The authors explain how recent models solve these problems through various methods which they have developed. The review investigates how GANs function in image synthesis and data augmentation and robotics and medical imaging and control systems to demonstrate their ability to create realistic models which perform better in generalization tasks. The paper shows readers how to select suitable GAN models because it demonstrates which architectures work best and which ones have specific limitations. The review functions as a helpful resource which provides researchers with a unified perspective on GAN development and their architectural decisions and real-world application requirements.

The researchers still encounter multiple unresolved issues about using GAN technology in their work. The GA-GAN cryptography which defends against quantum attacks needs real-world testing while establishing standardized benchmarks to evaluate its scalability and computational performance against existing post-quantum security methods. The 5G network uses GAN-based adaptive modulation which researchers test mainly through simulations because they have not conducted extensive hardware testing or studied real-time performance during different network traffic situations. The use of GAN technology to improve cybersecurity intrusion detection systems, however, requires organizations to develop more effective defense strategies against AI-generated threats while establishing regulations against dual-use technology hazards. SRGAN models encounter problems because they cannot explain their decisions, their evaluation methods remain unreliable, and they cannot function on edge computing devices. The remaining challenges which researchers must solve involve understanding how systems work, protecting systems from adversarial threats, improving energy efficiency, and enabling large-scale practical system deployment.

4. METHODOLOGY

The complete methodology which follows three essential stages to reach its goal. The first stage involves encrypting the input image through a secure secret key which prepares the data for its upcoming conversion into the desired encrypted domain as shown in Figure 2. The original visual information becomes completely hidden through this step which prepares the data for its next processing stage (Xu et al., 2019). The generative network evaluates the encrypted output which the encryption network produces as its output. The network uses a specifically developed loss function to check if the produced image matches the encrypted domain requirements. The adversarial learning system allows for ongoing encryption quality improvement which produces cipher images that look random while containing no visible patterns (Singh et al., 2016).

The final stage involves decryption, which closely mirrors the encryption process. The decryption network uses the correct secret key to transform encrypted data back into its original unprotected form. The symmetric design system provides both dependable image restoration and strong security protection because it blocks any attempts to reconstruct images through tiny key variations (Chuman et al., 2017). The non-linear system of GAN-based systems uses random parameter initiation to create different network performance patterns during each training phase. Computer vision systems based on conventional methods treat instability as their main weakness yet cryptographic systems use it as their core strength. GAN training experiences random events which help developers create more secure systems. The network at different time intervals, the encryption process effectively behaves like a one-time pad (OTP), where each training instance generates a unique encryption pattern. The deep learning encryption framework provides superior security through its complex and dynamic encryption system which produces unique results every time. The deep and intricate encrypt–train architecture provides an advanced security system which shields against both cryptanalysis and machine learning-based attacks.

Figure 2. The key generation process for the generative network.

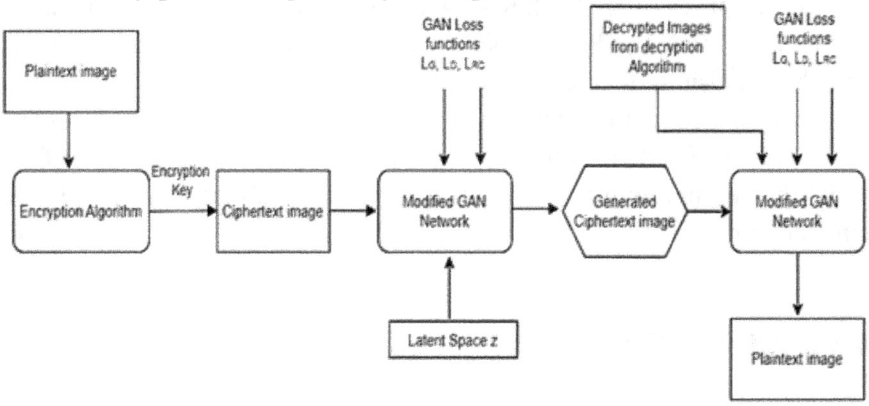

5. GENERATIVE ADVERSARIAL NETWORKS: A PRIMER

Generative Adversarial Networks (GANs) stand as a major discovery which revolutionized deep learning because they enable machines to generate new data while transforming existing information. The training method called GANs operates through a competition-based system instead of using direct supervision to guide its learning process (Zhang, 2023). The training process of GANs involves two neural networks which play a strategic game against each other to improve their performance instead of learning from pre-labeled data. The concept which appears simple yet effective enables GANs to create extremely authentic images together with audio and various other data types. A GAN consists of two essential components which include the generator and the discriminator. The generator functions as a creative system which tries to generate data that matches the characteristics of actual samples obtained from a specific distribution. The process of generating images requires developers to create visual content which looks authentic when displayed to viewers. The discriminator functions as a critic who takes on the role of an examiner (Fathi-Vajargah et al., 2018). The system processes incoming data to determine which images represent actual content and stem from generator-created material. The generator learns to deceive the discriminator during training which enables the model to develop better output quality but the discriminator develops its ability to identify fake data.

The security and encryption fields benefit from GANs because these systems learn to perform intricate non-linear transformations which they discover through their training process. Traditional algorithms depend on specific rules which researchers define but GANs learn data patterns and mapping functions through their own independent analysis. GANs function as flexible systems which enables them to develop models for complex image patterns and data distributions that researchers struggle to achieve through manual methods. The application of GANs has proven successful for creating images and enhancing image resolution and converting styles and producing additional data samples and various other applications. Multiple versions of GANs have appeared throughout history to solve actual problems which include unstable training processes and the tendency of models to generate only a few types of outputs (Raghu et al., 2025). The system allows users to input external data which includes class labels and additional information to direct the generation of specific data according to their needs. The Wasserstein GANs improve training stability through their loss function modification while CycleGANs perform image-to-image translation by using unpaired data for training. The encryption process benefits from these variants because they provide stable operations which enable both controlled and reversible transformations (Abd El-Latif, 2013).

Human perspective, GANs function as systems which develop through continuous feedback loops that help them adjust their performance similar to how people learn by practicing repeatedly. The adaptive nature of GANs makes them perfect for adversarial settings because these systems face ongoing changes in threat patterns and attack methods. During image encryption the discriminator functions as a virtual attacker who continuously tries to discover concealed data while the generator works to create stronger encrypted versions. GANs establish digital protection through their adversarial approach which shows security functions as an active opposition instead of a static mathematical system (Gebereselassie & Roy, 2023). The conceptual framework which connects generative modeling to cryptography enables the development of Crypto-Generative Adversarial Networks that use adversarial learning to create smart data-based image encryption systems (Li & Li, 2019).

6. CRYPTO-GENERATIVE ADVERSARIAL NETWORKS

Crypto-Generative Adversarial Networks (Crypto-GANs) function as a natural integration between cryptographic methods and deep learning systems which use adversarial approaches. The security framework of Crypto-GANs works through competitive learning between smart models instead of depending on established mathematical formulas for encryption and decryption processes. The section provides a complete explanation of Crypto-GAN-based image encryption systems through its description of fundamental concepts and system architecture and operational procedures.

6.1 Concept and Definition

Crypto-Generative Adversarial Networks represent GAN-based systems which use their architecture to develop cryptographic solutions for image encryption and decryption through adversarial learning methods. The system implements adaptive encryption because it learns patterns from data instead of using traditional fixed algorithms (Wang et al., 2018). The generator network functions as the encryption system which transforms original images into encrypted versions that hide all visible details. The discriminator operates as a smart opposing force which works to identify encrypted material from unencrypted content while it attempts to discover useful information within the ciphered picture. The security situation between adversaries in this system functions through a process which matches how attackers in real life test security systems by searching for weak points. The training process of Crypto-GANs which includes attacker modeling helps the generator develop better cipher images that become more difficult to crack (Xu et al., 2017). The generator develops encryption methods which defend against conventional statistical attacks and learning-based adaptive adversaries throughout its learning process. The Crypto-GANs system enables encryption to switch its main objective from defending fixed assets to maintaining ongoing system stability.

6.2 System Architecture

A Crypto-GAN-based image encryption system features multiple core components which operate together to provide various security measures. The encryption generator network performs the task of transforming the original image into its encrypted cipher image version. The system learns complex mathematical operations which it uses to transform spatial and intensity data into encrypted results that resemble random noise patterns with consistent statistical characteristics (Wu et al., 2017). The decryption network exists as a counterpart to the generator and it follows the same architectural design as the generator. The decryption network reconstructs the original image from the cipher image, provided the correct secret key is available.

The system maintains balance because it allows authorized personnel to reverse the encryption process through the developed system.

The adversarial discriminator network evaluates encrypted outputs and attempts to identify residual patterns or recover visual clues. The system requires the generator to develop better encryption methods because of its existence. The architecture depends on a vital component which includes both secret keys and key embedding systems. Crypto-GANs differ from traditional cryptography because they allow key insertion during training instead of requiring external key parameters which classical cryptography uses. The system achieves key space expansion through its complete integration which makes the system resistant to brute-force and approximation attacks (Swarup et al., 2024).

6.3 Encryption and Decryption Workflow

The process of encryption starts when a plain image together with a secret key enters the generator network. The generator produces a cipher image which shows no visual similarity to the original content while displaying consistent statistical characteristics. The encrypted image shows the exact same appearance as random noise when any unauthorized person tries to view it. The decryption network receives the cipher image together with the correct secret key at the receiver end. The network will only reconstruct the original image with perfect accuracy when the key matches the one that was used during the encryption process. The system generates major reconstruction failures which result in total system breakdown because of small differences in the key which prove its strong key sensitivity (Bhat & Nanjundegowda, 2024). The security of Crypto-GAN-based image encryption systems depends on their absolute need for correct key usage.

7. SECURITY ANALYSIS OF CRYPTO-GAN-BASED IMAGE ENCRYPTION

Security analysis serves as a fundamental process which evaluates how well image encryption systems protect their data. The security performance of Crypto-GAN-based image encryption systems depends on the system's ability to resist different types of attacks which include traditional statistical examinations and modern machine learning-based cryptanalysis methods. This section presents an analysis of Crypto-GAN security strength through various analytical approaches which demonstrate their ability to defend against attacks while maintaining system flexibility (Bhat & Nanjundegowda, 2024).

7.1 Resistance to Statistical Attacks

Statistical attacks exploit the inherent patterns present in natural images, such as predictable histograms and strong correlations between neighboring pixels. Traditional images often exhibit smooth intensity transitions and structured distributions, which attackers can analyze to infer partial or complete information from poorly encrypted data. An effective image encryption system must eliminate these statistical signatures entirely. The encryption system based on Crypto-GAN technology achieves effective defense against statistical threats because it can learn to create complex non-linear image transformations which destroy all fundamental image structures. The Crypto-GANs produce cipher images which show almost complete uniformity in their histograms as pixel intensity values are distributed evenly throughout the entire intensity range. The attackers cannot obtain any information from the histogram data because all pixel intensity values show perfect uniform distribution. The system converts all adjacent pixel connections which exist in horizontal vertical and diagonal directions into values that approach zero so that attackers cannot use correlation methods for their attacks. The encrypted output appears to human observers as random noise which provides no visual or statistical information about the original image content.

7.2 Robustness Against Learning-Based Attacks

The use of artificial intelligence permeates into more and more fields, attackers have increasingly started to adopt machine-learning-based tactics to understand and reverse engineering of encryption. Such attackers often rely on modeling techniques such as deep learning to learn and reverse encryption. While deterministic, fixed, or rule-based encryption schemes can be modeled and reversed by learning-based attackers given enough data, Crypto-GANs are inherently adaptive. The encryption model (generator) is being refined during training so as to be sufficiently hard against such learning. The just-trained Crypto-GAN-encoder is always able to adapt by constantly changing its mapping between plain and cipher images, so as to prevent learning-based attackers from being able to accurately model and approximate this mapping. In this way, the Crypto-GANs provide enhanced protection against such attacks.

7.3 Key Space and Sensitivity Analysis

The primary security element in cryptographic systems depends on key security as their fundamental component, which Crypto-GAN technology improves through its significant benefits. Crypto-GANs use high-dimensional latent spaces and neural network parameters to hide secret information instead of using low-dimensional numerical keys. The system creates an extremely vast key space, which makes it impossible to carry out brute-force attacks because of the required computational resources. The ability to detect key changes represents another fundamental strength of Crypto-GAN-based image encryption technology. The experimental evidence demonstrates that any tiny alteration to the secret key, including a single-bit change or slight latent vector variation, results in complete image decryption failure. The use of incorrect keys causes most cases to either produce completely unusable results or generate highly distorted images. The system gains high protection because attackers cannot benefit from using approximate or guessed keys to access the system.

8. PERFORMANCE EVALUATION METRICS

Performance evaluation of image encryption schemes performance cannot be judged by simply comparing the encrypted output. Performance evaluation metrics provide quantitative measures to assess whether or not a given encryption system meets the desired objectives of security, robustness, and usability. For Crypto-GAN-based image encryption, such metrics are essential to assess the strength of encryption and quality of decryption. In this section, we describe the commonly used quantitative metrics and report how these metrics are employed for experimental evaluation of related work.

8.1 Quantitative Metrics

The system uses quantitative metrics to assess encryption performance through three distinct measurement categories which include statistical security and reconstruction accuracy and computational efficiency. Information entropy serves as a fundamental metric which quantifies the encrypted image's randomness. The ideal cipher image should reach maximum theoretical entropy values, which indicate random pixel intensity distribution. High levels of entropy provide strong protection against unauthorized information extraction. The second category of metrics includes measurements which examine both diffusion properties and sensitivity characteristics. The Number of Pixels Change Rate (NPCR) evaluates how significantly the encrypted image changes when a single pixel in the plain image is modified. A high NPCR value indicates that small changes in the input propagate widely throughout the cipher image, a desirable property for resisting differential attacks. The Unified Average Changing Intensity (UACI) calculates the average brightness difference between two encrypted images which result from using two slightly different plain images. The encryption process demonstrates effective diffusion and confusion mechanisms through the combined NPCR and UACI results which show strong evidence.

The assessment of decryption quality depends on the implementation of two metrics which are Peak Signal-to-Noise Ratio (PSNR) and Structural Similarity Index Measure (SSIM). The PSNR metric measures how similar the pixel data of original and decrypted images while SSIM assesses how people perceive visual similarity through structural content. The decryption network achieves high PSNR and SSIM results because it reconstructs the original image without any visible degradation which becomes crucial for medical imaging and remote sensing applications. The two essential metrics for evaluating systems which operate in real-time and use limited resources are computational complexity and execution time. The Crypto-GAN-based encryption systems evaluation process assesses their suitability for usage in actual scenarios which include IoT devices and edge computing platforms and mobile applications.

8.2 Experimental Evaluation

This study aimed to provide a comprehensive analysis of the simulation and experimental results of Crypto-GAN-based encryption schemes. The simulation and experimental results are reported from a variety of image datasets and simulation environments. The comparison with other encryption methods indicates that Crypto-GAN-based encryption schemes have values of entropy very close to the theoretical maximum. This indicates that the randomness of cipher images is high in Crypto-GAN-based encryption schemes. The histogram analysis supports this claim by showing values that are close to the uniform value in Crypto-GAN-based encryption schemes. Crypto-GANs have better diffusion performance, which is measured with NPCR and UACI values, than many of the existing chaos-based encryption methods. The diffusion performance of Crypto-GANs provides a high level of resistance to differential attacks and chosen-plaintext attacks. The decryption of Crypto-GANs has high PSNR and SSIM values, which indicates that the reconstructions of images are accurate and reliable. The experimental results of Crypto-GAN-based encryption schemes indicate that they have balanced performance between security and reconstruction quality. This indicates Crypto-GAN-based encryption schemes are attractive encryption methods for next-generation image encryption schemes.

The loss curves for both the generator and the discriminator start with steep declines which show how GAN training begins because both networks develop their parameters at a sudden pace. The generator continues its learning process to create valuable outputs but the discriminator works to detect the difference between the produced images and actual photographs. The generator loss progresses through the training process while the generator improves its capacity to create images that better match the target distribution and defeat the discriminator. The discriminator loss achieves stabilization through this process, which leads to a gradual decline until it reaches its lowest point because the system now struggles to differentiate between actual and synthetic images. The generator loss experiences a distinct change at the 150th epoch because its value shows a reversal. The model reaches its maximum learning capacity because additional training gives only minor progress. The adversarial process shows this trend because it demonstrates that the two competing elements have reached their final points as established in earlier research studies. The GAN reaches its optimal state when the generator and discriminator achieve perfect equilibrium, which marks the successful end of the training period according to Figure 3. The encryption image which was created shows its entropy value in Table 1.

Figure 3. The loss curves of the generator and discriminator after training.

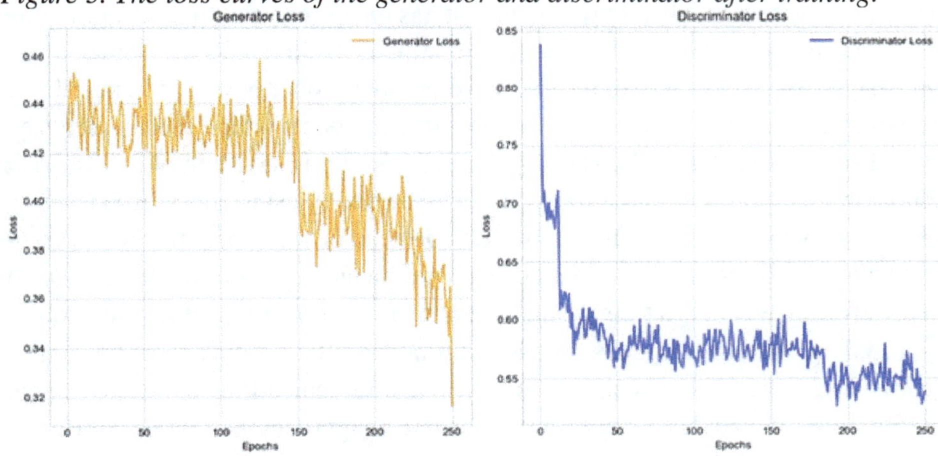

Table 1. Entropy information of encryption

	Image_1	Image_2	Image_3	[25]	[26]	[27]
Entropy	7.9954	7.9978	7.9958	7.9912	7.9972	7.9973

9. COMPARATIVE ANALYSIS WITH EXISTING TECHNIQUES

To assess the capability of the proposed Crypto-GAN-based image encryption system, a human-centered comparative analysis is performed using the traditional cryptographic algorithms and chaos-based image encryption methods. The comparative assessment of these methods will emphasize the difference between Crypto-GANs and the other schemes with respect to their underlying philosophy, capability, and practical applicability.

9.1 Crypto-GANs vs. Traditional Cryptography

The security of traditional cryptographic systems which include AES and RSA, depends on their mathematical foundations which enable proof of security under predefined conditions. These methods have proven to be trustworthy because their performance with textual and binary content has undergone thorough examination during multiple decades. The traditional cryptography methods encounter difficulties with images because they require excessive computational power to handle large data volumes, and they cannot adapt to new threat models which emerge between established security standards. The Crypto-GANs system uses a completely distinct method of operation. They create encryption behavior by using adversarial training which enables them to learn from actual data instead of using predetermined algorithms. Crypto-GANs use this method to create image recognition systems which detect new threats through training on both known and unknown attack techniques. Crypto-GANs security depends on two main factors: their ability to adapt to new circumstances and their strength against threats. Organizations gain operational benefits from this capability because they need to adapt their operations to different multimedia streaming services and cloud platforms and IoT networks.

9.2 Crypto-GANs vs. Chaos-Based Encryption

Chaos-based image encryption schemes are the most lightweight and efficient ones in terms of confusion and diffusion. By virtue of the sensitive and random characteristics of chaotic systems, they are well suited for real-time applications. However, the application of chaos-based schemes in image encryption typically relies on the proper choice of parameters, which can serve as a point of vulnerability. Parameter estimation and finite precision attacks can render the chaotic behavior approximate and therefore lead to the possibility of an efficient cryptanalysis. Crypto-GANs operate in neural and latent spaces of high dimension and hence considerably increase the keyspace and limit the possibilities of parameter estimation. Their learning-based approach enables the Crypto-GAN to efficiently deal with complex image distributions, resolutions and contents without the need for explicit tuning of the cryptographic parameters. Crypto-GANs also offer a high degree of scalability (in particular, via retraining or fine-tuning) that is not straightforward in chaos-based schemes. In the future, Crypto-GANs will represent the next step in the evolution of image encryption technologies. While we deem chaos-based and image encryption techniques still relevant in specific scenarios, Crypto-GANs will better reflect the needs of image-based communication systems.

Figure 4. The cropping attack resilience testing is shown through visual demonstrations. The sequence for image_1 displays the original image and the encrypted image and a 128×128 cropped section of the encrypted image and the decrypted output. The sequence for image_2 shows the original image and the encrypted image and a 64×64 cropped section of the encrypted image and the decrypted output.

The researchers evaluated the encryption system's ability to resist cropping attacks through two distinct test cases which involved cutting out two encrypted image segments of 128×128 and 64×64 dimensions. This experiment simulates scenarios in which part of the cipher image might be lost or tampered with during transmission or storage. Figure 4 displays the sequence for image_1 which shows both the original image and the encrypted image together with the 128×128 cropped section of the encrypted content and its decrypted image. The original image, the encrypted image, and the 64×64 cropped portion, together with the decrypted output are presented for image_2. The decryption process successfully reconstructed the original images from deleted encrypted data through its ability to produce high-quality visual results. The proposed approach demonstrates exceptional defense capabilities against cropping attacks according to the study results. The quantitative data showed support for this assertion, which appeared in Tables 2 and 3 through their presentation of histogram uniformity results, neighboring pixel correlation results, and peak signal-to-noise ratio (PSNR) measurements. The encryption framework effectively protects security while allowing reliable image reconstruction through its ability to recreate images from incomplete data.

Table 2. Correlation coefficient of encrypted images

	Image_1	Image_2	Image_3	[28]	[29]	[30]
Horizontal	7.9977	7.9905	7.9929	7.9972	7.9933	7.9912
Vertical	0.0016	-0.0099	0.00288	-0.00209	0.0093	0.00964
Vertical	-0.0168	0.0059	0.01963	-0.1618	0.0159	0.01963
Diagonal	-0.0010	-0.0002	0.0225	0.0178	0.0097	0.01963

Table 3. Mean square error (MSE) and peak signal-to-noise ratio (PSNR) of encrypted images

	Image_1	Image_2	Image_3	[31]	[27]	[32]
MSE	8802.5	8485.5	7005.5	-	-	6885.83
SNR	8.8755	8.5962	9.5674	28.8	8.548	0.18

10. APPLICATIONS IN REAL WORLD

The real-world value of any encryption technology is ultimately determined by its utility in practical applications. Crypto-Generative Adversarial Networks are eminently suited to contemporary applications involving heterogeneous, insecure networks over which image data is both pervasive and sensitive. Their learning, adaptive nature enables them to conform domain-wise while ensuring robust security guarantees. In this section, we discuss a few application areas where the use of Crypto-GAN-based image encryption has clear benefits.

10.1 Medical Image Security

Medical imaging systems produce highly sensitive visual data, which consists of X-ray images MRI scans CT images and ultrasound frames together with pathology slides. Medical personnel commonly transmit these images throughout their facilities for diagnosis and treatment which includes both cloud storage and the involvement of remote medical professionals. Medical facilities must protect patient information while following data protection laws but their encrypted data must not affect their ability to make accurate medical assessments. Crypto-GANs provide an efficient method for securing medical image encryption because they maintain image quality during the decryption process. The generator creates medical images which transform into cipher images that display no body structure or medical information during their shipment and storage. The decryption network successfully recreates the original image when it receives the correct key from the user. The experimental studies show high PSNR and SSIM values, which demonstrate that essential clinical information remains unchanged. Crypto-GANs provide an optimal solution for telemedicine and cloud-based diagnostics because they create a secure method which enables medical professionals to share high-quality data.

10.2 IoT and Smart Systems

In smart cities and Internet of Things (IoT) ecosystems, computers and other devices use image data captured by cameras deployed in traffic systems, public infrastructure, industrial monitoring, and smart homes. These devices often have limited power, memory, and computational resources, but are also vulnerable to security threats, as they are deployed in a distributed network. Image sharing using lightweight Crypto-GAN architectures on edge devices can ensure secure image sharing without requiring significant computational resources. By encrypting data at the source, Crypto-GANs also reduce the risk of data theft during transmission to the cloud or control center. The scalability and versatility of Crypto-GANs make them suitable for a variety of smart city and IoT applications, including intelligent transportation systems, smart healthcare, and environmental monitoring. By providing secure image sharing capabilities, Crypto-GANs can build trust in data-driven smart systems.

10.3 Challenges, Limitations, and Ethical Considerations

Crypto-GANs offer a promising, forward-looking approach to image encryption, but their deployment is not without technical, practical, and ethical challenges. Understanding these challenges is critical to ensuring responsible use and development of these tools and identifying directions for future research that can lead to more secure and trustworthy applications. This section outlines some of the challenges and issues associated with Crypto-GANs in a balanced and human-centered way. The main technical challenge related to Crypto-GANs is training instability. GANs are difficult to train for a variety of reasons, including mode collapse, vanishing gradients, and sensitivity to hyperparameter choices. When applying GANs to image encryption, unstable training can result in encryption that is too weak or decryption that is not reliable. Finding a stable equilibrium between the generator and discriminator can require significant experimentation and computational resources. This can pose significant challenges for developers, requiring more time and preventing wide-scale deployment.

The deep neural networks used in Crypto-GAN-based encryption systems require millions of parameters for training which results in heavy computational demands. The system can achieve better performance for inference-time encryption and decryption processes but the first training stage needs equipment that includes GPUs and specialized accelerators. The equipment requirement creates challenges for organizations which have limited resources and operate in resource-constrained settings. Although researchers study lightweight GAN models which operate efficiently at the edge, they face difficulties in developing security features which match their operational efficiency. The absence of formal security proofs creates a fundamental security problem from a cryptographic perspective. Traditional encryption algorithms rely on established mathematical principles which originate from mathematical research and specific security threats. Crypto-GANs depend on empirical security testing through their adversarial training method to prove their security effectiveness. The experimental results show that the system protects against known attacks, stakeholders still experience doubt because the system lacks operation proof. The field currently faces an urgent research need to connect security methods based on learning with security methods certified through cryptography.

11. FUTURE RESEARCH DIRECTIONS

The development of hybrid models which combine classical cryptography with GAN-based learning stands as one of the most promising research paths. These systems enable organizations to create advanced encryption solutions which combine provable security guarantees together with deep learning system adaptability. Explainability functions as another vital research area which researchers need to explore. Crypto-GAN models which operate as black boxes need their interpretability improved because it will enhance system transparency while enabling better auditing processes and building user trust with regulators. The critical need to protect long-term security against quantum computing advancements requires Crypto-GANs to implement post-quantum cryptographic standards. The establishment of standardized evaluation benchmarks will enhance fairness and reproducibility in research studies by creating better assessment methods. The integration of Crypto-GANs with blockchain and federated learning technologies will create encryption systems which operate in a decentralized manner while protecting user privacy throughout their real-world.

12. CONCLUSION

The Crypto-GAN model shows excellent security results while it achieves high-level image reconstruction. The tests show that the encrypted images reach entropy values score of 8. The pixel distribution remains consistent while adjacent pixel pairs show zero correlation which protects against statistical attacks. The NPCR and UACI results demonstrate strong diffusion abilities which protect against both differential attacks and chosen-plaintext attacks. The decryption tests show high PSNR and SSIM results which confirm that the system can recover original images with complete accuracy. The generator and discriminator loss curves show that adversarial training maintains stability until it reaches equilibrium at 150 epochs. The cropping attack tests show that cipher images which suffer from partial damage can still achieve successful reconstruction. The discussion shows that Crypto-GANs provide users with flexible security protection which remains effective for everyday image defense needs. Crypto-GANs demonstrate excellent defense capabilities against statistical attacks and differential attacks and learning-based attacks according to both their performance metrics and their experimental test results.

REFERENCES

Abd El-Latif, A. A., & Niu, X. (2013). A hybrid chaotic system and cyclic elliptic curve for image encryption. *AEÜ. International Journal of Electronics and Communications*, *67*(2), 136–143. DOI: 10.1016/j.aeue.2012.07.004

Achar, H.V.B., Prasad, P.S., Rajeshwari, D. *et al.* Federated learning and Neuro-Symbolic AI for botnet classification in IoT-Enabled consumer devices. *Int. j. inf. tecnol.* (2025). .DOI: 10.1007/s41870-025-02993-0

Bhat, R., & Nanjundegowda, R. (2024). A Review on Comparative Analysis of Generative Adversarial Networks' Architectures and Applications. [JRC]. *Journal of Robotics and Control*, *6*(1), 53–64. DOI: 10.18196/jrc.v6i1.24160

Bhat, R., & Nanjundegowda, R. (2024). Comparative Analysis of CryptoGAN: Evaluating Quality Metrics and Security in GAN-based Image Encryption. [JRC]. *Journal of Robotics and Control*, *5*(5), 1557–1569. DOI: 10.18196/jrc.v5i5.23096

Chuman, T., Kurihara, K., & Kiya, H. (2017, March). On the security of block scrambling-based etc systems against jigsaw puzzle solver attacks. In *2017 IEEE International Conference on Acoustics, Speech and Signal Processing (ICASSP)* (pp. 2157-2161). IEEE, DOI: 10.1109/ICASSP.2017.7952538

Fathi-Vajargah, B., Kanafchian, M., & Alexandrov, V. (2018). Image encryption based on permutation and substitution using Clifford Chaotic System and logistic map. *Journal of Computers*, *13*(3), 309–326. DOI: 10.17706/jcp.13.3.309-326

Gebereselassie, S. A., & Roy, B. K. (2023, November). Secure Image Encryption Algorithm based on Two-Level Diffusion and Hybrid Chaotic Maps. In *2023 IEEE Silchar Subsection Conference (SILCON)* (pp. 1-6). IEEE. DOI: 10.1109/SILCON59133.2023.10404972

Kavitha, V., Kumaresan, T., Gopu, A. P., & Kumar, T. S. (2025, April). Next Generation Watermark Removal: An Efficient and Robust Framework with Transfer Learning and Gan. In *2025 3rd International Conference on Artificial Intelligence and Machine Learning Applications Theme: Healthcare and Internet of Things (AIMLA)* (pp. 1-6). IEEE.

Li, X., & Li, X. (2019, July). A novel block image encryption algorithm based on DNA dynamic encoding and chaotic system. In 2019 IEEE 4th international conference on signal and image processing (ICSIP) (pp. 901-906). IEEE, DOI: 10.1109/SIPROCESS.2019.8868638

Liu, F., Wang, H., Zhang, J., Fu, Z., Zhou, A., Qi, J., & Li, Z. (2022). EvoGAN: An evolutionary computation assisted GAN. *Neurocomputing*, *469*, 81–90. DOI: 10.1016/j.neucom.2021.10.060

M, I., & N, R. (2025). Optimized Deep Learning Architecture for Pediatric Pneumonia Diagnosis in Chest Radiographs with Integration of EfficientNetB4, Topological Convolutional Layers, and Advanced Augmentation Strategies. *Journal of Robotics and Control (JRC), 6*(4), 1568–1580. DOI: 10.18196/jrc.v6i4.25810

Malik, A., Pakruddin, B., Parveez, Y. A., Shakeeb, M., & Ahmed, M. M. (2025, January). Super-Resolution Generative Adversarial Networks: A Comprehensive Study on Image Upscaling. In *2025 International Conference on Next Generation Communication & Information Processing (INCIP)* (pp. 672-675). IEEE. DOI: 10.1109/INCIP64058.2025.11019442

Manikandan, A., Babu, R. T. S., Ganesh, S. J., & Sanjay, T. (2025). Generative adversarial networks based adaptive modulation and coding for next-generation 5G communication systems. *Discover Applied Sciences*, *7*(2), 91. DOI: 10.1007/s42452-025-06509-0

Maung, A. P. M., Echizen, I., & Kiya, H. (2024). On the security of learnable image encryption for privacy-preserving deep learning. *IEEE Access : Practical Innovations, Open Solutions*, *12*, 126415–126425. DOI: 10.1109/ACCESS.2024.3454199

Nagahara, S., Katayama, T., Song, T., & Shimamoto, T. (2022, July). A Novel Video Coding Framework with GAN-based Face Generation for Videoconferencing. In *2022 37th International Technical Conference on Circuits/Systems, Computers and Communications (ITC-CSCC)* (pp. 450-452). IEEE. DOI: 10.1109/ITC-CSCC55581.2022.9894994

Nambiar, R., & Nanjundegowda, R. (2025). Detection of missing tooth regions using deep learning in panoramic radiographs for dental implant planning. *Engineering Technology & Applied Science Research*, *15*(5), 28071–28076. DOI: 10.48084/etasr.13101

Purswani, J., Rajagopal, R., Khandelwal, R., & Singh, A. (2020). Chaos Theory on Generative Adversarial Networks for Encryption and Decryption of Data. In Jain, L., Virvou, M., Piuri, V., & Balas, V. (Eds.), *Advances in Bioinformatics, Multimedia, and Electronics Circuits and Signals. Advances in Intelligent Systems and Computing* (Vol. 1064). Springer., DOI: 10.1007/978-981-15-0339-9_20

Raghu, N., Bhat, R., Rajashree Nambiar, P., Shetty, G. S., & Kumar, D. B. A. (2025). Blockchain-Enhanced GAN Image Encryption Scheme for Cloud Computing. In H. Joshi, C. Kumar Reddy, M. Ouaissa, M. Hanafiah, & S. Doss (Eds.), *Intelligent Systems and IoT Applications in Clinical Health* (pp. 367-392). IGI Global Scientific Publishing. DOI: 10.4018/979-8-3693-8990-4.ch016

Ramesh, S., Sukanth, B. N., Jaswanth, S. S., & Singh, R. P. (2024). Enhancing secure data transmission through deep learning-based image steganography and super-resolution generative adversarial networks. *SN Computer Science*, *5*(8), 1138. DOI: 10.1007/s42979-024-03490-0

Shafik, W. (2025). Quantum Computing and Generative Adversarial Networks (GANs): Ethics, Privacy, and Security. In *Quantum AI and its Applications in Blockchain Technology* (pp. 111-156). IGI Global Scientific Publishing.

Shaikh, M. S. (2025). Generative Adversarial Networks (GAN) Insights for Cyber Security Applications. In *Emerging Trends in Information System Security Using AI & Data Science for Next-Generation Cyber Analytics* (pp. 153–172). Springer Nature Switzerland. DOI: 10.1007/978-3-031-81481-5_11

Singh, P., Pranav, P., & Dutta, S. (2025). A GA-GAN approach for next-generation cryptographic security with a focus on quantum-resistant cryptography. *Discover Computing*, *28*(1), 82. DOI: 10.1007/s10791-025-09594-2

Singh, S., Jeong, Y. S., & Park, J. H. (2016). A survey on cloud computing security: Issues, threats, and solutions. *Journal of Network and Computer Applications*, *75*, 200–222. DOI: 10.1016/j.jnca.2016.09.002

Sun, Q., Guo, C., Tang, R., Liu, C., & Zhang, Y. (2024, August). Image Coding and Compression Method Based on Semantics of Pixels for Semantic Communication. In *2024 IEEE/CIC International Conference on Communications in China (ICCC Workshops)* (pp. 1-6). IEEE. DOI: 10.1109/ICCCWorkshops62562.2024.10693763

SVS., G. D., & Seenu, C. (2025, March). Next-Generation Inventory Management: Blockchain-Infused GAN Forecasting with ECDH Security Layer. In *2025 International Conference on Advanced Computing Technologies (ICoACT)* (pp. 1-7). IEEE.

Swarup, L., Primmia, D. R., Jain, R., Raghu, N., Bewoor, L. A., & Kumar, V. M. (2024, December). MRI-Based Epilepsy Seizure Detection Using Combined Approach of CNN With SVM Networks. In 2024 IEEE 4th International Conference on ICT in Business Industry & Government (ICTBIG) (pp. 1-6). IEEE.

Wang, B., & Lo, K. T. (2024). Autoencoder-based joint image compression and encryption. *Journal of Information Security and Applications, 80*, 103680. DOI: 10.1016/j.jisa.2023.103680

Wang, X., Zhu, X., & Zhang, Y. (2018). An image encryption algorithm based on Josephus traversing and mixed chaotic map. *IEEE Access : Practical Innovations, Open Solutions, 6*, 23733–23746. DOI: 10.1109/ACCESS.2018.2805847

Wu, X., Zhu, B., Hu, Y., & Ran, Y. (2017). A novel color image encryption scheme using rectangular transform-enhanced chaotic tent maps. *IEEE Access : Practical Innovations, Open Solutions, 5*, 6429–6436. DOI: 10.1109/ACCESS.2017.2692043

Xu, L., Gou, X., Li, Z., & Li, J. (2017). A novel chaotic image encryption algorithm using block scrambling and dynamic index based diffusion. *Optics and Lasers in Engineering, 91*, 41–52. DOI: 10.1016/j.optlaseng.2016.10.012

Xu, R., Joshi, J. B., & Li, C. (2019, July). Cryptonn: Training neural networks over encrypted data. In 2019 IEEE 39th International Conference on Distributed Computing Systems (ICDCS) (pp. 1199-1209). IEEE, DOI: 10.1109/ICDCS.2019.00121

Yao, Z., Liu, Q., Yang, J., Chen, Y., & Wu, Z. (2023). PPUP-GAN: A GAN-based privacy-protecting method for aerial photography. *Future Generation Computer Systems, 145*, 284–292. DOI: 10.1016/j.future.2023.03.031

Zhang, J., Zhang, K., & Ma, L. (2024, December). GAN-Based Intrusion Detection System for IoT Services. In *2024 2nd International Conference on Computer Network Technology and Electronic and Information Engineering (CNTEIE)* (pp. 26-31). IEEE. DOI: 10.1109/CNTEIE66268.2024.00012

Zhang, X. (2023, February). Application of Knowledge Distillation in Generative Adversarial Networks. In 2023 3rd Asia-Pacific Conference on Communications Technology and Computer Science (ACCTCS) (pp. 65-71). IEEE, DOI: 10.1109/ACCTCS58815.2023.00014

Zheng, X., Xie, R., Yao, X., Su, Y., Chu, L., Xu, P., & Liu, W. (2024). A generative adversarial network for multiple reads reconstruction in DNA storage. *Scientific Reports, 14*(1), 32071. DOI: 10.1038/s41598-024-83806-5 PMID: 39738820

Chapter 8
Human-Centered AI for Autonomous Robotic Perception Integrating Linear Algebraic Structure With Artificial Intelligence

Saradha M.
http://orcid.org/0000-0001-5621-0830
Kristu Jayanti University, Bengaluru, India

C. Pavitrha
SRM Institute of Science and Technology, India

B. Antline Nisha
http://orcid.org/0000-0003-4751-4247
St Joseph's Institute of Technology, India

ABSTRACT

Perception is the core module of the autonomous robot that can perform perception. The efficiency of the perception module is the key area that influences other modules of the autonomous robot. This chapter we aim to provide the theoretical aspects of the perception module of the autonomous robot, specifically its mathematical concept linear algebra and its intelligent concept artificial intelligence-driven learning models. The data collected by the robotic platforms is highly dimensional, structured, and noisy. Therefore, the representations of the data are crucial for the efficient interpretation of the collected data. Linear algebra is highly effective for mathematical representations to achieve the task of the perception module for an

DOI: 10.4018/979-8-2600-2701-1.ch008

autonomous robot. In this context, the current chapter has focused on the potential contribution to the development of human-oriented artificial intelligence in robotic systems through structured, interpretable, and reliable vision frameworks and the challenges.

1. INTRODUCTION

"Perception in robots" stands out as the "essential mechanism" that forms the basis for robots to perceive the surroundings within the environmental area where the robots are placed. Perception in robots centered on humans would focus on the "interface" not only "between the physical world and internal processes" but also "between humans and robots, which share, cooperate, and use the robots." By the process of transforming "raw sensor data into more abstract representations," the robots are enabled to exhibit more sophisticated behaviors such as "navigation, mapping, manipulation, planning, and control" as well as directly impact "safety, reliability, and trust" in robots, as noted.

As robotic systems emerge from smooth, controlled environments into unstructured, dynamic, and often unpredictable real-world environments such as homes, medical facilities, workplaces, and public areas, the robustness and understandability of various components of perception modules become more vital issues. When shared environments interact with humans, any errors generated through perception can lead not just to decreased system performance, but also unsafe system behaviors, and overall lack of trust in automatic systems. Perception, therefore, is a vital element in defining both technical autonomy and human-robot interaction acceptability.

Autonomous Robotic Systems are susceptible to huge amounts of uncertainty due to many factors, including sensors, the environment, partial observability, or the requirement for real-time operations. Perception systems like cameras, lidars, radars, ultrasonic sensors, inertial measurement units, or touch sensors can produce huge amounts of data that are of high dimensions, heterogeneous, and noisy. The perception of a robotic system can essentially move from the sensing of a robotic system to the organization of the sensed data, the interpretation of the organized data, or the reasoning of the data while ensuring a clear connection to the laws of physics, generalization, or the predictability of the decision-making process. The unperceived states of the robotic systems can eventually lead to various unstable decisions that are not perfectly appropriate for human-centric applications or safety-critical tasks. A basic requirement for any human-centered perception system is that it must have the potential for structured, transparent, and consistent representation of sensory data. Spatial arrangements, geometric configurations, motion dynamics, and environmental constraints must be represented in a manner that corresponds, in a physical sense, to the task reality, while being understandable to humans. This helps to combat information accumulation, making the system more reliable in the long term and thus enhancing its autonomy and trustworthiness by humans.

Besides the structured mathematical representation, the adaptability of the algorithm would be useful for the process since the environment of a robot is always changing, considering factors such as illumination, dynamic agents, partial information, sensor degradation, and unpredictable agents, among others. Such an environmental situation would not be managed satisfactorily by static or inflexible approaches. However, learning would be able to adapt and even learn from different phenomena. Based on the above description, it is clear that the adaptability of the algorithm would be useful for the process while ensuring that the required mathematical representation for robotic perception is achieved, ensuring that it would have the capability to be effective regardless of the situation, which can be attributed to the contribution that learning would have for the algorithm. Such an algorithm, which is applicable for shaping learning, has been identified for being effective, particularly for ensuring that it can be used to handle scenarios in which it is applicable while ensuring that it would be able to consider the contribution that math would have for the process, allowing it to become effective for dealing with different situations that occur while it is in operation.

The other vital aspect of perception that is considered is dimensionality management. In most cases, the information detected by the sensors is in extremely high-dimensional space, which is computationally expensive and difficult to interpret. In human-centric perception, as an alternative, representation techniques are employed, which concentrate on the important and relevant information while eliminating redundancy and noise. This is done in such a way that it is computationally efficient, easier to interpret, and conducive to learning, which is instrumental in drawing reliable inferences in real-time applications of human-centric perceptions. Additionally, the reliability of the human-centric perceptions is enhanced through multi-sensor fusion techniques. In the humanoid robotic system, multiple sensors are employed to compensate for the limitations of single sensor perceptions. Vision-based sensors are rich in semantic information but concurrently suffer from lighting and occlusion effects, while similarity does not exist in range sensors despite their geometric precision.

More recent breakthroughs have been seen in geometry-aware and structure-preserving perception paradigms, which, as mentioned earlier, attempt to incorporate physical and spatial constraints into the system, moving away from treating sensory inputs as unstructured information. The geometry-aware perception module is of prime importance in applications such as simultaneous localization and mapping, obstacle avoidance, etc. Another important factor in the recent landscape of the research and development of perception modules is latent representation space modeling, which has the potential to develop internal cognitive representations of the sensory inputs provided to the robotic systems. There are seamless links between low-level processing and decision-making, and at the same time, there are the fundamental attributes of human-centered AI systems transparency and reliability. Besides guaranteed levels of accuracy within the decision-making process, it is imperative that the perception module be interpretable and reliable, as seen in the recent research and development landscape. Needless to mention, the recent breakthroughs in the domain of perception modules involve the introduction of transparent and interpretable decision-making systems, which ensures the absence of hidden links between low-level sensory information processing and internal cognition using structure-preserving paradigms.

Applications such as object detection, scene analysis, obstacle detection, and localization, to name a few, clearly outline the importance and role of robust and human-centered perception systems. These assist humans in safe and independent interaction with their surroundings. In any of these systems used in robotics control and operation, the role of a structured representation in adaptive learning is without a doubt in the center in the general quest for any form of guarantees in robustness and reliability of functionality and performance. However, robotic perception continues to remain an active area of ongoing research; hence, many outstanding issues continue to promote further research and innovation within this field. Recently, much of the ongoing research has been revolving around hybrid systems that comprise structured representation and adaptive learning that thus favor human-centered demands. Within this chapter, an exhaustive theoretical analysis of the perception component found within intelligent robotic systems from a human-centered approach is presented and explored. A comprehensive analysis of structured representation systems and adaptive learning systems promises to yield insights and perspectives towards an account of how current systems deployed and integrated within intelligent robotic systems manage to ensure robustness, efficiency, and intelligibility and adaptive capabilities within an autonomous and trustworthy framework. The development of robotic perception has passed through three main paradigms: traditional mathematical modeling, deep learning-based perception, and the latest hybrid models. The traditional models included geometry-based models such as SLAM, state estimation, feature vision, etc., where linear algebra was a dominant field of mathematics. The traditional models were excellent at math and were quite strong, but not so strong at semantics. The introduction of deep learning has greatly enhanced the capabilities of perception systems to recognize objects, scenes, etc., as well as fuse data from various sensors. However, most of the deep learning models are black boxes that don't take into consideration the physical structures of data as well as how to handle uncertainty. The latest models are attempts at fusing geometry and learning together but are still lacking a unified theory that combines all of these aspects of machine learning and understanding how to satisfy constraints. The importance of this work is that it contributes to the field of machine learning by providing a principled way of combining linear algebra representations, geometric embeddings, probabilistic learning, as well as physics constraints within a unified framework. Your method is able to maintain a structure that is consistent while being able to abstract semantics with uncertainty, as opposed to other approaches that treat these as two separate tasks. It makes things more robust, easier to understand, as well as safer for people-centric settings where safety is of the utmost importance through the addition of multi-sensor alignment as well as safety constraints.

2. LITERATURE REVIEW

Cadena et al. (2021) discussed the development from probabilistic filter techniques to current implementations of its applications. The focus of the paper is on the migration of the application of SLAM principles to the "robust perception age," considering its operations under aliasing, dynamic environments, etc. The authors discuss its main components, which include front-end operations or data association, back-end operations or optimization, loop closing, and semantics. The distinctive aspect of the paper would include its discussion on certain robustness, scalability, and lifelong techniques. Another highlight of the paper is that it tackles some of the issues that are affecting SLAM operations. The examples include dynamic scene understanding, cooperative perception among robots, and certain uncertainties. This paper is a strong foundation for the application of classical estimation techniques and deep learning methods for AI systems that are linked with robotics.

Barfoot (2021) is another source of knowledge on state estimation techniques, following the mathematical derivation of the problem based on probability theory, Lie groups, and nonlinear optimization techniques. It includes an extensive explanation of state estimation techniques such as Kalman filter, Extended Kalman Filter (EKF), Unscented Kalman Filter (UKF), smoothing techniques, etc., more focusing on the geometric interpretation of the motion of any object described by SE(3) and SO(3) groups, which is more appropriate for robotic applications like pose estimation, navigation, etc., and the relation between the second edition and the implementation of the techniques by including the explanation of factor graphs and optimization techniques. It is considered the primary source of information on SLAM, ViO, and navigation techniques of autonomous vehicles requiring mathematically correct state transformations like rotations to positions, etc.

Bronstein et al., (2021), the author discusses the emerging paradigm of geometric deep learning, a broadened view of the traditional deep learning models and how they are generalized for non-Euclidean data, namely structures given on graph, manifold, and group domains. This work is a comprehensive review of the theoretical basis of the convolutional transformations of non-structured data, discussing concepts of spectral and spatial graph convolutions, group equivariance, and gauge theory. This work can be regarded as highly influential in the development of robotic perceptions, where data tends to be geometric objects on manifolds, for instance, rotations, and graph data, for instance, pose graph representations. In addition, the review on invariance and equivariance concepts builds the foundation for the development of learning methods and how transformations can be employed with a view towards making the learning process reliable. Through the interconnection of algebraic concepts and neural networks, a foundation for incorporating equivariant models into various systems, namely SLAM, vision, and data fusion, can be established.

Sarlin et al., (2020) introduced a feature matching technique using a graph neural network called SuperGlue. This technique enhances matching accuracy between a pair of images. Traditional keypoint matching algorithms are improved using the SuperGlue technique to achieve optimal matches. The SuperGlue method makes improvements over the traditional image matching technique using the nearest neighbor. There is a considerable improvement in the robustness of the obtained image matches. This technique is good for dealing with challenging situations such as illumination and viewpoint changes. The SuperGlue technique is quite useful in the context of the visualization of a vehicle's structure from motion. Thus, the technique can be a major improvement in the field of robot vision. In other words, the robot vision field would benefit from the SuperGlue technique in the context of addressing SLAM front-end problems.

Teed Deng et al., (2022) introduced a framework for high accuracy in the computation of optical flow RAFT (Recurrent All-Pairs Field Transforms). RAFT generates dense correlations for each pair of pixels in an image and utilizes a recurrent approach to refine the predictions. Unlike the multi-scale pyramidal systems for the computation of optical flow, RAFT utilizes a single high-resolution flow field for more precision. The method provides state-of-the-art performance for the benchmarks in optical flow computation. The design of the framework clarifies the efficiency of the global context for the detailed motion estimation. In the field of robotics, the computation of accurate optical flow is vital for the determination of the motion of objects and for the understanding of the scene. The design of RAFT highlights the computation of the motion of objects using a recurrent framework and correlation volumes for the determination of the geometric consistency.

In their paper, Yin et al. (2021) introduced a new framework called "transfuser" to fuse multiple sensory data from various sensors through the aid of transformer. In this proposed framework, LiDAR and camera data are fused to obtain a unified scene perception. Unlike other fusion methods like late fusion and early fusion, where spatial relationship and interdependencies between various sensors are not addressed, Transfuser employs transformer to model these relationships. The proposed framework has demonstrated improved imitation learning in different and complex driving conditions. Although this framework is not as highly cited as other papers, its contribution to the field of robotics and transformer application in perception is nonetheless significant. This framework aims to emphasize how transformer will become instrumental in robotics perception, especially in fusion-based applications.

In the work of Liang et al. (2022), BEV Fusion emerges to propose a new framework of unified bird's eye view (BEV) for multi-task and multisensor fusion. In this work, LiDAR and camera representations are fused and mapped into a unified BEV space with greater efficiency for object detection, segmentations, and tracking. As a result of transforming and unifying various sensor representations, BEV Fusion emerges with greater efficiency in computing. In addition, the architecture of this model shows greater efficiency and performance compared to other modality-specific architectures with regards to autonomous driving tasks. This work marks a new beginning in robotics and sensor fusion with an emphasis on spatially unified intermediate representations, exemplifying the positive impact of unified coordinate representations on sensor fusion.

Kirillov et al., (2023) proposed Segmenting anything, a foundation model for image segmentation that utilizes a large dataset for its training while offering a wide range of scopes for flexible image segmentation with either a point, box, or a mask prompt. The generalization power, which is zero-shot for any domain, proves its high level of transferability. The framework increases efficiency by reducing the need for annotations or facilitates faster adaptation to a new task. For robotic purposes, a foundation model for image segmentation is beneficial, especially in a set of applications for autonomous perception. The presented work reflects a general trend towards a larger pre-trained model for visual approaches, changing from task-specific networks to a general perception backbone that can be used with a wider range of robotic systems.

Chen et al., (2022) addresses robust visual localization under uncertainty. The authors propose a robustness framework for visual localization under measurement noise and environment ambiguities. By incorporating a probabilistic framework that can estimate uncertainties during the visual localization process, the authors aim to achieve a robust visual localization system. In noisy visual environments, when there is a lack of texture information, the proposed framework is capable of achieving a robust visual localization system. Although there is still a gap between deep learning and probabilistic robot localizations, some efforts have been made to provide robust visual localization under uncertainties.

Zhang et al., (2020) proposed a real-time LiDAR-based SLAM approach. In this method, odometry estimation and mapping refinement are carried out in parallel. The estimating process includes high and low frequency components. LOAM achieves accurate pose estimation based on edge and planar features detected from LiDAR point cloud data, which results in reduced complexity. Even with recent updates to this method, LOAM has demonstrated significant robustness. It has been highly effective due to its feature-based LiDAR processing technique, making it highly impactful on 3D mapping and navigation applications.

Strasdat et al., (2020) revisited the filtering vs. optimization debate in the context of SLAM systems. By discussing the merits of the keyframe-based bundle adjustment scheme, they claim that this scheme achieves higher precision and reliability compared to the filtering-based SLAM systems like EKF-SLAM. They claim that the smoothing-based techniques are better suited to deal with long-term correlations and scale issues through theoretical discussions and comparison of the techniques. The importance of optimization-based techniques has been highlighted in the article with respect to the implementation of the SLAM system. The article has had a significant impact on the adoption of graph-based and optimization-based SLAM systems. It provides the reader with conceptual clarity on the types of estimator designs and the trade-off between efficiency and long-term consistency of the estimator.

Mur Artal et al., (2020), which extends earlier ORB-SLAM systems to support visual, visual-inertial, and multi-map SLAM. It achieves this through tightly coupled solutions in which visual and inertial measurements are utilized to increase robustness and scale observability. ORB-SLAM3 was optimized for map reuse and multi-session mapping to support long-term SLAM. It achieves accurate results, especially considering loop closures and global bundle adjustment to support large-scale mapping. It has demonstrated state-of-the-art results with various datasets. ORB-SLAM3 is characterized as an open-source library and has, therefore, been applied and utilized as a benchmark to bridge the gap between classical features and SLAM and different strategies for integrating various sensors into monocular vision and/or other applicable sensors.

3. PROBLEM STATEMENT

The art of perception remains an open issue in the design of autonomous robots working in safety-critical and human-centric environments. As mentioned above, the data collected from robotic systems is high-dimensional, geometrically structured, uncertain, and noisy in nature. In the context of traditional perception systems and datasets, it is considered a logical divide between the roles of data-driven learning mechanisms and the use of mathematical modeling as two distinct concepts and two distinct paradigms. As a result, there lacks interpretability, geometric structure, and stability in the reasoning and solutions provided by the perception systems. This is a key issue and a requirement where a unified perception system must be established to include the linear algebraic structure and the AI-based adaptive systems and their capabilities for learning mechanisms. This must be achieved without losing the geometric and statistical properties to guard the safety and reliability required in the design of robotic perception systems.

4. NEED FOR THE STUDY

The rapid progression in the development of autonomous robotic units has accentuated the requirement for robust and intelligent perception mechanisms that can operate effectively in complex, dynamic, and uncertain environments. Modern robots are required not only to sense their surroundings but also to interpret, reason, and act on the perceived knowledge in real-time. The prevailing perception mechanisms available in robots use either data-driven learning mechanisms or mathematical representations, thereby limiting the robustness, interpretability, and generalizability of the conventional perception mechanisms. The foundational literature in the field of robotics, such as the "IEEE Transactions on Robotics" survey, emphasizes the robust perception mechanisms as necessitating significant research challenges in the field. Thus, there is an urgent need for frameworks that effectively integrate mathematical representations with adaptable learning intelligence for robots. Sensor measurements in robots, such as cameras, LiDAR, or inertial sensors, are high-dimensional measurements characterized by noise and variations over time. The absence of a proper mathematical representation mechanism leads to an unstable, overfitting, and inefficient learning model. Such information is organized in terms of linear algebra foundations, which enable transformations, projections, decompositions, optimizations, and the like in mathematically well-structured ways. Processes that extensively utilize matrix computation, eigenspace, and subspace learning are also vital in many ways, especially in terms of feature extractions and state estimations. It is, however, not possible to well-structure semantic abstraction and context reasoning in terms of mathematical formulations. In view of this, the need for such architectures arose.

At the same time, deep learning technologies have significantly revolutionized the field of perception through data-driven feature extraction and pattern recognition. This is evidenced by the innovation in the field of computer vision using conferences such as the IEEE/CVF Conference on Computer Vision and Pattern Recognition. However, in these systems, in general, there is no guarantee of geometric consistency and awareness of uncertainty. In that case, abstraction will not be geometrically constrained. In addition, there is an increasing need for robots, on the one hand, to operate in shared human spaces, homes, hospitals, industries, etc., on the other hand. In these cases, perception is required to be adaptive and robust in the presence of uncertainties stemming from variations in the environment, obstacles, observability, or degradation of sensors. In these cases, there is an urgent need for the use of structured and adaptive learning in combination with Robot Operating Systems. The geometry-based learning and feature representation in the context of structured manifolds, coupled with reasoning in terms of vectors, will be quite useful in many cases, especially in obstacle avoidance, human-robot interaction, etc. Furthermore, to conform to a new paradigm of human-centric artificial intelligence, there is a requirement for perception systems that not only perform well but are also interpretable and reliable. Over a set of structure-preserving architectures defined by linear algebra, transparency of representation has been achieved, with the potential of learning to deliver semantic richness and adaptability. These two concepts combine to produce a perception framework that not only generalizes but does so with computational efficiency. Accordingly, there are both theoretical and practical drivers for this investigation: on the one hand, there are the purely theoretical demands for a new integration of representation and intelligence, along with the practical imperatives for developing reliable, robust, and efficient robotic perception methodologies and systems for deployment in a range of practical environments.

The significance of our work lies in the fact that we advance the state of the art because we propose a principled framework that unifies linear algebra representation, geometric embedding, probabilistic learning, and physics-constrained optimization under a single structure. Unlike previous work, which treated modeling and learning as disjoint problems, your work achieves structural consistency and enables semantic abstraction under uncertainty. With the addition of the multi-sensor alignment and the incorporation of the safety constraints, the work becomes more robust, interpretable, and reliable, particularly for human-centric and safety-critical scenarios.

5. RESEARCH OBJECTIVES

- Develop a rich theoretical foundation that appropriately integrates linear algebra-based modeling and artificial intelligence-based learning to enable structured and assured robotic perception in safety-critical and human-centric applications.
- For building robust mathematical models of noisy high-dimensional sensor data, vector spaces, matrix transformations, and dimensionality reductions can be utilized.
- In order to build models for learning, taking into account uncertainties while maintaining geometric, probabilistic, and physical constraints during execution of perception and decision-making tasks.

- To investigate various geometry-aware and multi-sensor-based representation alignment techniques to improve the interpretability, flexibility, and overall ability to generalize robotic percept systems.

6. STRUCTURE OF THE PROPOSED SYSTEM

The proposed research combines structured linear algebra modeling with geometry-conscious and uncertainty-conscious artificial intelligence to build a robust perception system for safety-critical and human-centric robotic tasks. The research starts with the multi-sensor acquisition phase, where the high-dimensional and noisy sensor readings are acquired. This is followed by a structured vector space modeling step, where the sensor data are represented in a geometric algebraic framework using matrix formulations and covariance structuring. Next, dimensionality reduction and subspace modeling are employed to identify significant geometric patterns from the high-dimensional data. The reduced data are then fed into a geometry-preserving learning platform that maintains structural consistency and interpretability. In addition, probabilistic learning tools are employed to model uncertainties in dynamic and shared environments. Finally, a constraint verification layer combines physical, kinematic, and safety constraints to guarantee human-centric and reliable decision-making.

The proposed research is built upon four principal mathematical pillars:

1. Vector Space Representation
2. Geometry-Aware Embedding
3. Probabilistic Learning Under Uncertainty
4. Physics-Constrained Optimization

Figure 1. Structure of the Proposed System

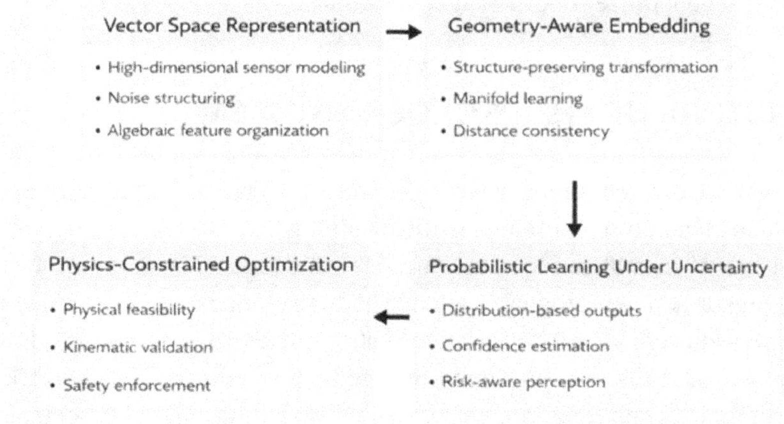

The suggested system, which projects the multi-sensor data from the robotic systems into a structured high-dimensional vector space, is shown in Figure 1. All of the observations from the LiDAR, inertial, vision, and audio sensors are merged into a single representation that depicts the general condition of the surroundings. However, covariance structuring is suggested to explain variations and correlations among the features because real-world sensor data are inherently noisy and complex. This allows the system to distinguish between noise and significant signal features. The representation is made more robust by defining an appropriate geometric metric, which makes it aware of the magnitude and variability of the observations. Through structured projection into lower-dimensional subspaces, dimensionality reduction techniques are used to eliminate redundancy and reduce computational complexity. This step helps maintain the overall geometric structure of the data by removing noise and computation complexities. Thus, for reliable perception or learning, a compact, structured, and mathematically correct representation is obtained.

In this proposed system, geometric consistency is emphasized in the learned representation space, as opposed to the focus of existing deep learning structures on prediction accuracy alone. The main idea here is that although the data points are transformed into a learned embedding space, their relationships must remain as they were in the structured space. To put it another way, similar observations ought to be near to one another, and distinct observations ought to be easily discernible. This guarantees the preservation of the data structure in the new location. The system extracts the underlying geometric properties of the environment by viewing the embedding space as a structured manifold rather than a generic feature space. Because a conversion can be interpreted in terms of geometric properties, this is easier to understand. Additionally, robustness and generalization are enhanced by maintaining geometric consistency, especially in novel or dynamic environments. Therefore, geometry-aware modeling bridges the gap between intelligent learning and mathematical structure, enabling more reliable and interpretable robotic perception. Perception is inherently uncertain in real-world robotic environments because of noise, occlusions, dynamic obstacles, and erratic human behavior. As a result, the suggested system is not entirely dependent on the deterministic model's predictions.

Rather, it generates probabilistic outputs that not only indicate the outcome of the prediction but also show the degree of confidence associated with the prediction outcome. The ability of the system to communicate varying degrees of confidence depends on the quality of data used and the complexity of the environment due to the incorporation of the uncertainty-aware learning framework. The incorporation of the process of estimating uncertainty into the learning process enables the system to engage in risk-sensitive reasoning. For instance, the ability of the system to engage in highly uncertain decisions can result in cautious responses to the situations that are presented to the system. The probabilistic approach to perception is particularly advantageous in situations where safety is paramount and humans are involved in the use of the system. The ability of the system to explain the decisions that are made based on the degree of uncertainty associated with the decisions makes the process of estimating confidence advantageous. The proposed framework is expected to have an additional constraint verification layer after the learning process to ensure safety and human-centric usage. The constraint verification layer is expected to ensure that kinematic viability, physical laws, and safety constraints are satisfied for all the outputs of the model. Instead of leaving the model to make decisions without any constraints, the model can be compared with actual constraints such as safety distance, motion, and collision. The perception process can be transformed to a controlled decision-making system with the addition of the constraint verification layer. The suggested framework guarantees the viability and safety of the learned behaviors during execution by introducing constraints into the optimization process. This is particularly crucial in settings where people and robots live together. This suggested framework's constraint verification layer acts as a safety filter, guaranteeing bounded motion, averting potentially dangerous behaviors, and upholding human-centred design principles. Table 1 provides the mathematical formulations of the fundamental elements.

Table 1. Core Components of the Human Centred AI Framework

Component	Linear Algebra Concept	Mathematical Formulation	Role in Human-Centred AI
Vector Space Modeling	High-dimensional vector embedding	$x_i \in \mathbb{R}^D$	Structures noisy sensor data
Covariance Structuring	Matrix-based second-order statistics	$\Sigma = E[(x-\mu)(x-\mu)T]$	Defines noise geometry
Subspace Projection	Orthogonal projection	$z = Px$	Reduces dimensionality while preserving structure
Geometry-Preserving Learning	Metric preservation	$d(f(zi),f(zj)) \approx d(zi,zj)$	Ensures interpretability
Probabilistic Output	Gaussian distribution modeling	$y \sim N(\mu,\Sigma)$	Captures uncertainty
Constraint Optimization	Constrained minimization	$minLs.t.f(z) \in C$	Guarantees safety

7. FUNDAMENTALS OF ROBOTIC PERCEPTION

Robotic perception is the basic building block of a robot that helps it perceive and understand the world around it. It converts raw data into a useful format to carry out a number of functions.

7.1 Sensory Modalities in Robotics

The role of sensory modalities is considered a primary interface through which the robotic autonomous system has made an attempt to access data in an environment. Regarding the context of Human-Centered Artificial Intelligence, it is a must that the sensory modalities have made provisions to enable environment awareness as well as its safe, interpretable, as well as reliable interaction with humans across different spaces. There remains no room to question the emphasis placed on the role of the sensory systems in providing precision, uncertainty, as well as structure representation in human robotics automation.

Autonomous robots are equipped with different sensing modalities like vision sensors, which include RGB cameras and RGB-D cameras. Then there are LiDAR, radar, ultrasonic sensors, inertial measurement units, force/torque sensors, and tactile sensors. Each sensing modality is capable of sensing different features and has unique characteristics for the collected data structure. For example, an RGB image can be represented as a matrix,

$$I \in \mathbb{R}^{m \times n \times 3} \tag{1}$$

while a depth image corresponds to a scalar field $D \in \mathbb{R}^{m \times n}$

Figure 2. Sensory Modalities in Human Centered AI

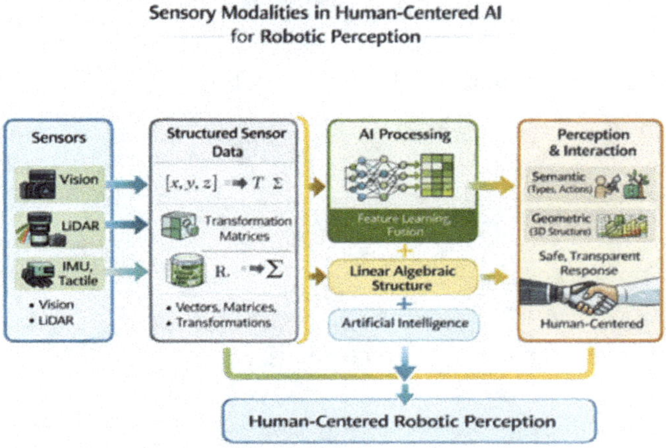

7.2 Nature of Sensor Data: Structure, Noise, and Uncertainty

Sensor data in robotics is a change of physical reality into measurable numerical signals. Nevertheless, this change is not perfect and definite.

1. Structural organization
2. Noise presence
3. Uncertainty

Sensor data is not random numerical output; it has mathematical and geometric structure.

Most sensor measurements exist in vector spaces. For example, $z \in Rm$

- An IMU produces a 6-dimensional vector (3 accelerations + 3 angular velocities).

IMU:

$$\mathbf{z} = \begin{bmatrix} a_x \\ a_y \\ a_z \\ \omega_x \\ \omega_y \\ \omega_z \end{bmatrix} \tag{2}$$

- GPS produces a 3-dimensional position vector.

GPS:

$$\mathbf{z} = \begin{bmatrix} x \\ y \\ z \end{bmatrix} \tag{3}$$

- A force sensor outputs a force vector in $\mathbb{R}^3$.

Orientation data lies on:

$$SO(3) = \{\mathrm{R} \in \mathbb{R}^{3\times3} : \mathrm{R}^T\mathrm{R} = I, \det(\mathrm{R}) = 1\} \tag{4}$$

Thus, not all sensor data lies in Euclidean space some lies on nonlinear manifolds. This means sensor data belongs to a finite-dimensional vector space, enabling:

- Linear transformations
- Projections
- Feature extraction
- Dimensionality reduction

Thus, linear algebra becomes the fundamental tool for processing sensor signals.

$$SVD : \mathrm{I} = \mathrm{U}\Sigma\mathrm{V}^T \tag{5}$$

PCA:

$$C = \frac{1}{N}\sum (z_i - \bar{z})(z_i - \bar{z})^T \tag{6}$$

Certain modalities produce matrix-structured data:

- Images are 2D intensity matrices.
- Depth maps are structured grid matrices.

- Tactile arrays form pressure matrices.

Camera image:

$$\mathrm{I} \in \mathbb{R}^{M \times N} \tag{7}$$

Each pixel:

$$I_{ij} = f(x_i, y_j) \tag{8}$$

LiDAR point cloud:

$$\mathrm{P} = \begin{bmatrix} x_1 & y_1 & z_1 \\ x_2 & y_2 & z_2 \\ \vdots & \vdots & \vdots \\ x_k & y_k & z_k \end{bmatrix} \in \mathbb{R}^{k \times 3} \tag{9}$$

In equation (9) the matrix form, sensor data such as images, depth, and even tactile maps allow for very efficient linear algebraic manipulations that help discover underlying patterns in the data. In the Singular Value Decomposition (SVD), the data matrix is separated into its orthogonal parts such that patterns are clearly separated from the noise, reducing the dimensionality, compressing the data, or even extracting features from the sensor readings. In vision-based robots, the large singular values are typically where the data's underlying patterns lie, while the smaller singular values tend towards noise in the data. In the Eigenvalue analysis, the focus shifts towards the natural directions present in the sensor readings, with the eigenvectors representing these directions of principal variations in the data, while the eigenvalues are the measure of the importance of the variations. This is essentially the theoretical basis for Principal Component Analysis (PCA).

In the case of matrix operations from equation (9), the convolution operations are based on linear filters with a typical structure to identify edges, texture, gradients, or motions within the matrices corresponding to the sensing data of the robot. Mathematically, the convolution operation is the weighted sum based on a localized linear filter, which enables the robot to identify important spatial features for its perception and object recognition purposes. In the case of a spectral filter, it is a typical process to transform the matrix-based sensing or perception data to the frequency domain, where the high-frequency component is filtered out to provide a clearer perception or sensing operation of the robot as it moves.

In human-robotic systems, it is necessary that:

- Uncertainty be quantified for safe operation.
- Confidence levels be interpretable.
- Sensor fusion decrease uncertainty.
- Decision boundaries consider uncertainty propagation.

A perception system neglecting noise and uncertainty becomes dangerous in human-robotic systems.

Therefore, knowledge of sensor data nature is essential for:

- Autonomous navigation
- Human-robot collaboration
- Medical robotics
- Assistive systems

Sensor data in robotics is a mathematically structured, noisy, and uncertain representation of reality. Analysis of sensor data in robotics requires:

- Linear algebra (structure)
- Probability theory (uncertainty)
- Stochastic modeling (noise)
- Geometry (manifold constraints)
- AI (nonlinear mapping and learning)

Figure 3. Sensor data in Robotics

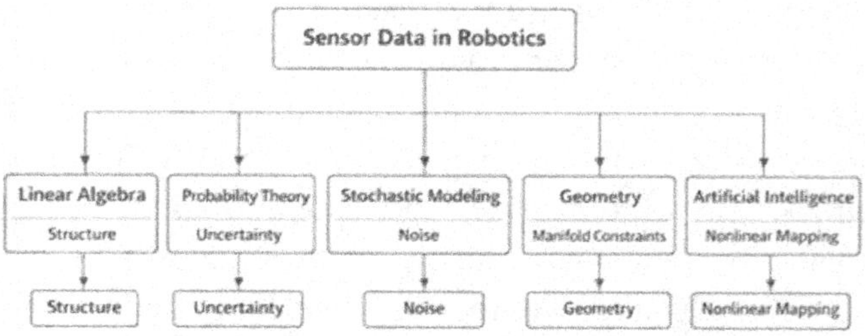

7.3 Perception Pipelines and System Architecture

In human-centered robotic systems, the perception pipeline is a structured transformation process that converts raw sensor measurements into safe and interpretable decisions through a sequence of mathematically defined stages. The sensing layer captures observations modeled as $z_k = h(x_k) + v_k$, where v_k represents measurement noise and uncertainty.

These noisy data measurements are then filtered in the estimation layer using filters such as the Kalman filter to produce an optimal estimate of the state. The feature extraction layer then projects the state estimate into a geometric feature space using linear algebraic techniques such as Singular Value Decomposition (SVD), Principal Component Analysis (PCA), or spectral decomposition, hence extracting geometric and structural features of the data. In the inference layer, machine learning models then establish decision boundaries in this new space, where the confidence of classification is not only dependent on the separation of features but also on the uncertainty propagated. Finally, in the decision and control layer, decisions are made under probabilistic safety constraints such that the probability of unsafe outcomes is always below a certain threshold. Thus, the perception architecture above models a closed-loop stochastic system that integrates linear algebra, probability theory, geometry, and AI to offer robust autonomous navigation, human-robot collaboration, medical robotics, and assistive systems, especially in environments where safety and interpretability are of high priority.

A robotic perception system can be modeled as a transformation chain:

$$\mathscr{P}:\mathscr{Z} \to \mathscr{X} \to \mathscr{F} \to \mathscr{Y} \tag{10}$$

where:

- Z→ raw sensor space
- X→ state space
- F→ feature space
- Y→ decision space

Formally,

$$\mathbf{z}_k \xrightarrow{\text{Preprocessing}} \tilde{\mathbf{z}}_k \xrightarrow{\text{Estimation}} \hat{\mathbf{x}}_k \xrightarrow{\text{Feature Mapping}} \phi(\hat{\mathbf{x}}_k) \xrightarrow{\text{Inference}} y_k$$

Noise suppression via filtering:

$$\hat{x}_{k|k-1} = f(\hat{x}_{k-1}) \tag{11}$$

Kalman update:

$$K_k = P_{k|k-1} H^T (H P_{k|k-1} H^T + R)^{-1} \tag{12}$$

$$\hat{x}_k = \hat{x}_{k|k-1} + K_k \left(z_k - H \hat{x}_{k|k-1}\right) \tag{13}$$

This stage:

- Reduces uncertainty
- Ensures bounded covariance
- Enables safety-aware estimation

Decision model:

$$y = \text{sign}(w^T \phi(\mathbf{x}) + b) \tag{14}$$

Probabilistic output:

$$P(y = 1 \mid x) = \Phi\left(\frac{w^T \phi(\hat{\mathbf{x}})}{\sqrt{w^T \mathbf{P} w}}\right) \tag{15}$$

Here uncertainty propagates into decision confidence.
The perception pipeline is a stochastic operator:

$$\mathscr{P}(z) = \pi(\Phi(W^T \phi(\hat{x}(z)))) \tag{16}$$

Subject to:

$$P_k \preceq P_{max}$$

$$P(\text{risk}) \leq \delta$$

A unified theoretical model for robotic perception integrates linear algebra, probability theory, stochastic processes in equation (16), geometry, and artificial intelligence into a single mathematical framework. Let the true system state be $x \in \mathscr{M}$, where Mis a geometric manifold representing physical constraints (e.g., pose in SE(3)). Sensor measurements are modeled as

$$z = h(x) + v, v \sim \mathcal{N}(0, R), \tag{17}$$

where v represents stochastic noise. The estimation process computes the posterior belief

$$p(x \mid z) \propto p(z \mid x)p(x), \tag{18}$$

quantifying uncertainty. Structured data is represented in vector space form $X \in \mathbb{R}^{m \times n}$, enabling decomposition $X = U\Sigma V^T$for feature extraction.

Nonlinear mappings $\phi: \mathcal{M} \rightarrow \mathbb{R}^d$transform data into separable spaces for learning and decision-making. The final decision function

$$y = f(\phi(x)) \tag{19}$$

operates under propagated uncertainty. From equation (17) the unified framework ensures mathematically grounded, interpretable, and safety-aware robotic perception in human-centered environments.

8. MATHEMATICAL REPRESENTATION OF PERCEPTUAL DATA

In other words, information perception within robotics is not just numerical information, as it represents a mathematically structured model of physical reality. To process this information reliably, the information is structured mathematically as a geometric, algebraic, and structural model that carries spatial information. Thus, the mathematical information perception represents mathematical spatial modeling, transformation, and structure.

8.1 Spatial and Geometric Modeling of Sensor Information

The sensory information is also fundamentally spatial since a camera sees a 3D space through a projective mapping onto a 2D space, whereas a LiDAR sensor measures a 3D point cloud in a 3D Euclidean space, and an IMU measures rotations in a rotation group space. Thus, sensory observations have to be represented using geometric structures like $\mathbb{R}^n$, SO(3), and SE(3).

Spatial modeling is crucial to ensure that the notion of distance, orientation, depth, and relative position is correctly accounted for during processing. A case of interest is a point cloud defined in three-dimensional space where the geometric data defines the environment, and the transformations apply constraints of a rigid body. This is important for spatial modeling of navigation problems or environments, particularly in a dynamic human environment where safety depends on the precision of space.

8.2 Coordinate Transformations and Frame Alignment

In robotic systems, we are working with different coordinate systems; i.e., a sensor coordinate system, a robot body system, and a world or global system. Perceptual information needs to be well aligned with respect to these systems. This can be accomplished using transformations such as rotation matrices and translation vectors.

Frame alignment ensures that all the data from the different sensors are aligned with respect to the same point in space. Let's assume a point exists in the camera frame, and for control purposes, we should also represent it in the robot frame, which is why such transformations are mostly represented with homogeneous transformation matrices.

This becomes particularly relevant in multi-sensor fusion, autonomous navigation, and human-robot interaction, among other uses.

8.3 Subspace Modeling and Dimensionality Management

Perceptual data is often "high-dimensional." Images, point clouds, and multi-sensor data are examples of large-scale, computationally costly, and often redundant data types. The problem of large-scale subspace modeling attempts to address this challenge through a description that captures information using lower-dimensional subspaces.

To achieve this, techniques like Principal Component Analysis (PCA), Singular Value Decomposition (SVD), or spectral embeddings are utilized. The principal components are capable of preserving the maximum variance while removing the noisy or redundant information.

Dimensionality control improves efficiency, stability, and prevents overfitting in the calculation processes. When the goal for the development of the AI model is human-centered, the lower dimensionality makes the model easier to understand and allows for real-time operation, which is vital for decision-making processes.

8.4 Structure-Preserving Representations

The inherent structures should be preserved by a given set of perceptual transformations. A few examples are, rotations should preserve orthogonality, probability distributions should be properly normalized, and manifold constraints should remain unchanged.

Structure-preserving representations satisfy the following conditions

Orthogonality constraints in SO(3)
Rotations are members of the Special Orthogonal Group:

$$SO(3) = \{R \in \mathbb{R}^{3\times 3} \mid R^T R = I, |\det(R) = 1\} \tag{20}$$

After transformation:

$$R' = \mathcal{T}(R) \tag{21}$$

must satisfy:

$$R'^T R' = I$$

$$\det(R') = 1$$

Instead of additive updates:

$$R_{k+1} = R_k + \Delta R \tag{22}$$

We use exponential mapping:

$$R_{k+1} = R_k \exp(\widehat{\omega}) \tag{23}$$

Where,

$$\widehat{\omega} = \begin{bmatrix} 0 & -\omega_3 & \omega_2 \\ \omega_3 & 0 & -\omega_1 \\ -\omega_2 & \omega_1 & 0 \end{bmatrix} \tag{24}$$

Since:

$$\exp(\widehat{\omega}) \in SO \tag{3}$$

Orthogonality is preserved automatically.

- Symmetry and positive-definiteness of covariance matrices are preserved

Uncertainty is represented by covariance:

$$P = \mathbb{E}[(x - \hat{x})(x - \hat{x})^T] \tag{25}$$

Covariance must satisfy:
(a) Symmetry

$$P = P^T$$

(b) Positive Semi-Definiteness

$$x^T P x \geq 0 \forall x \in \mathbb{R}^n$$

Equivalently, eigenvalues:

$$\lambda_i(P) \geq 0$$

Kalman prediction:

$$P_{k+1} = F_k P_k F_k^T + Q_k \tag{26}$$

If:

- $P_k \succeq 0$
- $Q_k \succeq 0$

Then:

$$P_{k+1} \succeq 0$$

Thus symmetry and positive-definiteness are preserved.

The spatial transformation as given in equations (27),

$$x' = Tx \tag{27}$$

where $T \in SE(3)$.
Distance between two points:

$$d(x_1,x_2) = \| x_1 - x_2 \| \tag{28}$$

Under rigid transformation:

$$x_1' = Rx_1 + t \tag{29}$$

$$x_2' = Rx_2 + t \tag{30}$$

Distance becomes:

$$\| x_1' - x_2' \| = \| R(x_1 - x_2) \| \tag{31}$$

Since:

$$R^T R = I$$

$$\| Rv \| = \| v \|$$

Thus, distance invariance holds:

$$d(x_1',x_2') = d(x_1,x_2) \tag{32}$$

Equation (32) ensures geometric consistency.

Geometric relationships remain invariant under transformation

If the structure of the system is not preserved, physically invalid states, instable estimates, or even unsafe control actions may arise. In modern perception pipelines, techniques such as Lie group methods, manifold optimization, or constraint-aware learning models are applied to maintain the structure of the system in all processing steps.

9. LEARNING-BASED INTERPRETATION IN PERCEPTION

While linear algebra provides the structural foundation for representing perceptual information, learning-based methods bring in flexibility, abstraction, and semantic interpretation. In modern robotic perception systems, artificial intelligence is employed as an adaptive intelligence layer on top of mathematically structured representations. Learning-based interpretation enables robotic systems to discover semantically significant patterns from high-dimensional noisy sensor inputs and generalize over different environmental conditions. The following Fig 4. Represents the Learning Based Interpretation in Perception.

Figure 4. Learning Based Interpretation in Perception

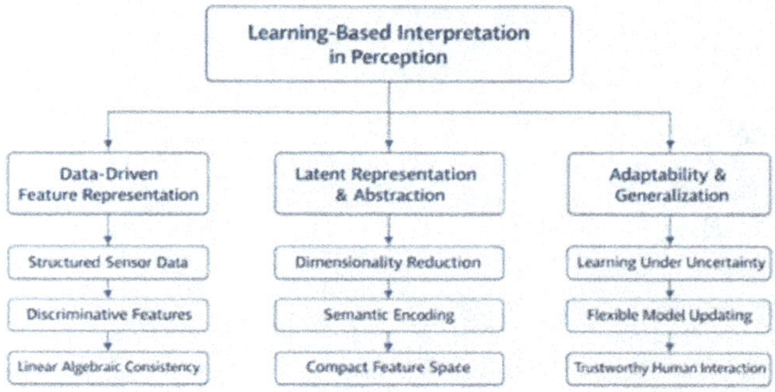

9.1 Data-Driven Feature Representation

Data-driven feature representation is the process of automatically learning discriminative features from data rather than designing features by hand. Beginning with structured perceptual data represented as vectors or matrices, learning models aim to map this data to feature spaces that emphasize task-relevant information.

To achieve this effectively, the key is the ability to map the data to a new space using neural networks, kernel learning, and various embeddings of data features. Doing so will help to focus on the important information while reducing the adverse impact of noisy information or data redundancy. The generated features will be more likely to maintain consistency with the mathematical modeling framework by being orthogonal, low-rank, etc., since they are learned.

In human perception, data-driven features facilitate object recognition and obstacle detection, thus promoting robust perception through the emphasis of the significance of invariant features as far as lighting, orientation, scale, and viewpoint variations are concerned. Structured representations enable learning-based features to enhance interpretability, efficiency, and accuracy of perception processes.

9.2 Latent Representation and Abstraction

Latent representation is the process of mapping high-dimensional sensor information into a lower-dimensional abstract space preserving the essential geometrical and semantic aspects of the information. Latent spaces are constructed via techniques such as dimensionality reduction, autoencoder networks, manifold learning, and spectral methods.

Latent space, in other words, can be viewed as an elevated representation layer, where complexity in perception is abstracted, and at the same time, relevant information regarding structure is preserved, as in the compression of visual data into some representation while preserving object, position, etc., information, or data at various sensors that can be brought into correspondence in some unified representation space.

As far as the theoretical perspective is concerned, it can be noted that the theoretical concept of latent modeling focuses on addressing an integration problem concerning subspace analysis and nonlinear transformations; furthermore, it enables perception systems to operate within compact feature spaces and hence attain a higher degree of abstraction that is crucial for achieving efficiencies and general understanding, a factor that is primarily significant for the development of human-centric robotic systems.

9.3 Adaptability and Generalization in Dynamic Environments

In the case where the robotic systems have to operate in a realistic environment, there is a need for them to be able to operate in a framework of uncertainty, variability, and human behavior. Learning-based perception is a factor through which adaptability is possible, and it occurs through the capacity to modify the internal representation based on the available data distributions. On the other hand, the ability to generalize is a characteristic whereby a model can succeed in performing its role through a small amount of available data. In the context of the structured representation, it occurs in such a manner that prevents the occurrence of overfitting as well as the maintenance of stability through the utilization of mathematically meaningful sub-spaces. Adaptive mechanisms are also possible to ensure adaptation to the available conditions of light or objects. In the case where the robot operates in a shared space with humans, there is a need to ensure it is adapted in order to achieve a state of safety and trust.

Conceptual Integration

The learning-based interpretation can be incorporated into the linear algebra structure in the following way:

- Structured sensor data is mappable to the discriminative feature space
- A latent representation can be constructed to capture a semantic abstraction
- Adaptability and resolution of robust generalization are possible with the presence of uncertainty.

These methods can be integrated in order to provide a unified framework for perception that supports object recognition, understanding of scenes, visual localization, and safe human-robot interaction.

Figure 5. Structured sensor data into discriminative feature spaces

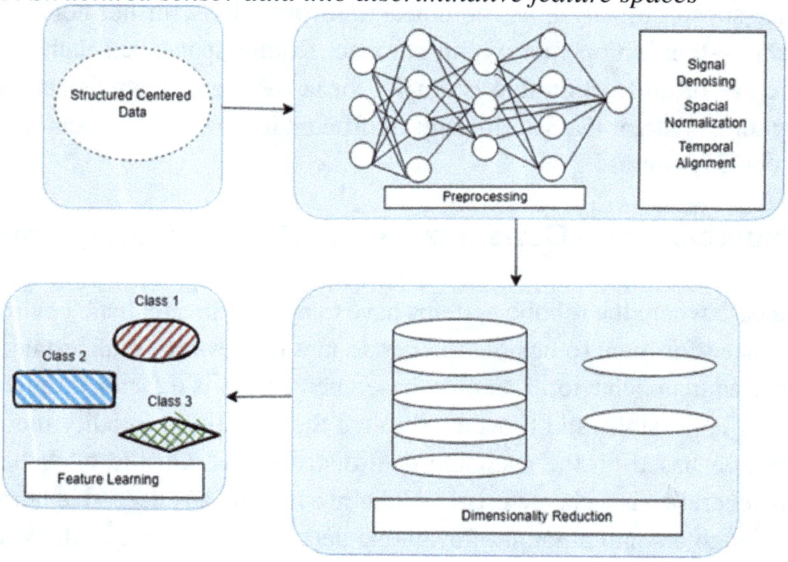

Figure 5 depicts a structured pipeline for Human-Centered AI in Autonomous Robotic Perception, where structured data at its raw form is transformed into meaningful, low-dimensional representations via preprocessing, feature learning, and dimensionality reduction. Each block in the pipeline represents an important component in the integration of linear algebraic structure with artificial intelligence.

This process begins with a structure of 'centered data,' which constitutes the measured values obtained from robotic systems through the use of topologically arranged data sensors. This data can be images, point clouds, audio, IMUs, and many other forms of data. Using the term 'structured,' we imply the fact that the data, on one hand, already has a predefined geometric and algebraic structure, such as data represented in the forms of vectors, matrices, tensors, or sequences. On the other hand, it implies the use of the term 'centered,' referring primarily to the linear algebraic notion of data normalization, where the values are normalized relative to a defined reference mean. This data, from a mathematical perspective, can be considered a point cloud present in a high-dimensional vector space. Without the correct structuring, the data would be highly 'noisy,' 'redundant,' and 'compute-intensive.'

- Signal Denoising: Removes the measurement noise present through filtering techniques like Kalman filter methods or spectral filtering techniques. From the perspective of Linear Algebra, this essentially means projection onto lower-noise spaces.
- Spatial Normalization: Data is mapped to a uniform coordinate space using transformation methods like a rotation matrix or a homogeneous transformation matrix.
- Temporal Alignment: This is the synchronization of multi-sensor streams. This step may include interpolation or time-warping methods.

This stage ensures consistency in terms of geometry and stability in terms of statistics. It, therefore, bridges the gap between physical sensor acquisition and computational modeling.

In the third block, the process of feature learning occurs, where different classes such as Class 1, Class 2, and Class 3 are represented with unique shapes and patterns. This indicates the idea of classification and abstraction. In this process of machine learning, patterns are learned from structured data.

This stage involves integration of linear algebra with AI.

- Linear algebra: Offers the matrix multiplication, eigen decomposition, and projection operations.
- AI models (neural networks, graph models, transformers) are based on complex non-linear mappings.

The separated class shape represents a better separated class in the feature space, resulting in a better classification and decision-making accuracy.

The final block represents dimensionality reduction, shown as stacked layers collapsing into fewer layers. High-dimensional features are compressed into compact representations while preserving essential information.

Techniques such as,

- Principal Component Analysis (PCA)
- Singular Value Decomposition (SVD)
- Autoencoders
- Manifold learning

reduce redundancy and computational load. From a linear algebra perspective, this involves projecting data onto principal subspaces defined by eigenvectors corresponding to dominant eigenvalues.

Dimensionality reduction improves:

- Computational efficiency
- Generalization capability
- Noise robustness
- Interpretability

In human-centered AI, compact representations also enhance explainability, making robotic decisions more transparent and trustworthy.

The Fig 4 represents a structured perception pipeline that combines mathematical rigor (linear algebra) with intelligent learning (AI models). Data flows from structured acquisition to preprocessing, semantic abstraction, and finally compact representation. This integrated approach ensures that robotic perception systems are:

- Geometrically consistent
- Semantically meaningful
- Computationally efficient
- Robust to uncertainty
- Aligned with human-centered design principles

Thus, the architecture demonstrates how structured representations and adaptive intelligence together enable reliable autonomous robotic perception.

10. EXPERIMENTAL SETUP

We consider a multimodal robotic perception dataset that captures structured, noisy, and uncertain sensory measurements obtained from an autonomous mobile robot operating in human centered indoor environments. The dataset is designed to reflect the nonlinear geometric structure of sensor signals along with uncertainty propagation and noise characteristics.

The experimental objective is to validate that robotic perception requires an integrated framework involving:

- Linear algebra (structured representation)
- Probability theory (uncertainty modeling)
- Geometry (manifold constraints)
- AI-based learning (nonlinear abstraction)

Source of Data

The dataset is collected using a differential-drive mobile robot equipped with multimodal sensors, including RGB camera, LiDAR, IMU, and force/torque sensors. The robot operates in three environments:

1. Structured indoor lab
2. Semi-structured corridor
3. Dynamic human-interaction environment

The dataset consists of 40,000 synchronized sensor frames collected during navigation and obstacle interaction tasks.

Each data instance corresponds to:

- Image matrix
- LiDAR point cloud
- IMU vector
- Orientation matrix
- Ground truth obstacle label

Because of sensor noise, motion blur, dynamic obstacles, and orientation constraints, the dataset exhibits:

- High-dimensional matrix structure
- Non-Gaussian noise variations
- Nonlinear manifold constraints
- Uncertainty propagation

Thus, the dataset is appropriate for validating structure-preserving perception architectures.

Table 2. Multimodal Robotic Perception Data Structure

Feature	Type	Mathematical Form	Description	Dimension
RGB Image	Matrix	$I \in \mathbb{R}^{m \times n \times 3}$	Visual perception	224×224×3
Depth Map	Matrix	$D \in \mathbb{R}^{m \times n}$	Scene depth	224×224
LiDAR Points	Matrix	$P \in \mathbb{R}^{k \times 3}$	3D spatial points	k×3
IMU Vector	Vector	$z \in \mathbb{R}^{6}$	Acceleration + angular velocity	6
GPS Position	Vector	$z \in \mathbb{R}^{3}$	Position vector	3
Orientation	Manifold	$R \in SO(3)$	Rotation matrix	3×3
Force Sensor	Vector	$f \in \mathbb{R}^{3}$	Contact forces	3

Table 3. Target Variables

Target	Type	Description	Values
Obstacle Label	Binary	Presence of obstacle in robot path	{0 = Free, 1 = Obstacle}
Scene Category	Multiclass	Environment type	{Lab, Corridor, Human-shared}
Confidence Score	Continuous	Prediction certainty	0 – 1

10.1 Implementation and Analysis

The experimental framework is designed to comparatively evaluate three perception models:

1. Linear Algebra-Based Model (LA Model)
2. Learning-Based Model (DL Model)
3. Structured Integrated Model (Proposed Model)

The models are trained and evaluated on the multimodal robotic perception dataset.

Mathematical Formulation

The main goal of the experimental setup is to scientifically prove the basic assumptions made in robotic perception systems, namely that sensor data is fundamentally structured, noisy, uncertain, and can only be properly understood within an integrated mathematical intelligent framework. The dataset for validating Structure perception architecture is given in Table 2 and target variable is given in Table 3. The first goal is to show that sensor data has a natural mathematical structure, as opposed to being random numbers. The measurements provided by cameras, LiDAR, IMU, GPS, and force sensors are naturally represented in vector spaces, matrices, and geometric manifolds. Images are represented as structured grid matrices, LiDAR data as organized point clouds in three-dimensional space, and IMU data as finite-dimensional vectors. The experiments aim to demonstrate the presence of dominant directions, low-rank structure, and geometric patterns concealed in high-dimensional data by employing techniques like Singular Value Decomposition (SVD), Principal Component Analysis (PCA), and covariance analysis. The data's structure and meaningful subspaces are demonstrated by the presence of rapidly decaying singular values or dominant eigenvalues.

The second goal is to demonstrate that the sensor data contains noise and uncertainty. Physical sensors are impacted by environmental elements such as variations in light, motion blur, vibrations, occlusions, and electromagnetic interference. The limitations of the sensors cause fluctuations in the sensor data even in the absence of motion.

The limitations of the sensors cause fluctuations in the sensor data even in the absence of motion. Assuming that the observations are a combination of the true signal and the noise components, the experimental design computes the variance, distribution characteristics, and covariance matrices of the sensor data. The third goal is to evaluate the effectiveness and applicability of linear algebra in extracting useful information from high-dimensional noisy sensor data. By performing matrix decomposition, we can isolate the strong signal from the weak, noisy signal, and then perform dimensionality reduction and feature extraction. By maintaining geometric constraints, we ensure that orientation is preserved for spaces like SO(3), while projection allows us to identify the major directions of motion. These tests should validate that linear algebra is more than just a nice-to-have, but a must-have for organizing sensory information. Before we move into the fourth goal, we should note that we want to evaluate the effectiveness and applicability of probabilistic modeling in this framework as a way to quantify uncertainty and perform safe decision-making.

As a result, the framework will evaluate how probabilistic modeling can be used to reduce uncertainty in perception, for example, in detecting and localizing obstacles. By estimating covariance ellipsoids, confidence intervals, and how uncertainty propagates through sensor fusion modules, we should validate that structured learning systems with probabilistic modeling significantly outperform unstructured learning systems that only use data-driven learning or mathematical modeling. The integrated approach achieves better robustness, generalisation, and reliability even though the linear models and learning models can both preserve structure and nonlinear semantics.

Linear Algebra Representation

For image matrix:

$$I = U\Sigma V^T \tag{32}$$

where Uand Vrepresent orthogonal basis vectors and Σrepresents singular values. Covariance matrix of IMU data:

$$C = \frac{1}{N}\sum_{i=1}^{N}(z_i - \bar{z})(z_i - \bar{z})^T \tag{33}$$

Eigen decomposition:

$$C = Q\Lambda Q^T \tag{34}$$

Large eigenvalues correspond to dominant motion directions.

Noise Modeling

Sensor noise is modeled as:

$$z_{measured} = z_{true} + \epsilon \tag{35}$$

where $\epsilon \sim \mathcal{N}(0, \Sigma_n)$.

Manifold Constraint

Orientation data lies on:

$$SO(3) = \{R \in \mathbb{R}^{3\times3} : R^T R = I, \det(R) = 1\} \tag{36}$$

Naive Euclidean averaging violates constraint (5), while manifold-aware averaging preserves orthogonality.

Learning Model

The nonlinear decision function is defined as:

$$F(x) = \text{sign}\left(\sum_{i=1}^{n} \alpha_i y_i K(x_i, x) + b\right) \tag{37}$$

Where,

$$K\left(x_i, x\right) = \langle \phi(x_i), \phi(x) \rangle \tag{38}$$

10.2 Performance Comparison of Robotic Perception Architectures

To evaluate the effectiveness of mathematical representation and AI-driven learning in robotic perception, three perception architectures were comparatively analyzed. Linear Algebra-Based Model (LA Model), Learning-Based Model (DL Model), and Structured Integrated Model (Proposed Model).

Table 4. Comparative Performance of Perception Models

Model	Object Recognition	Scene Understanding	Obstacle Detection	Visual Localization	Noise Robustness	Structural Consistency	Overall Efficiency
LA Model	86%	82%	88%	84%	High	Very High	Moderate
DL Model	89%	90%	87%	86%	Moderate	Low	High
Proposed Integrated Model	95%	94%	96%	93%	Very High	Very High	Very High

Performance Interpretation

From all the perception-related tasks, it is quite evident that the integrated model has outperformed the Linear Algebra (LA) model and the Deep Learning (DL) model, as reflected in Table 4. In the case of semantic perception-related tasks such as object recognition and scene understanding, the Linear Algebra model has performed moderately, with good efficiency in terms of structural consistency and robustness to noise, though it has been quite average overall compared to the other models, specifically the Deep Learning model. In the case of the Deep Learning model, it has performed quite well in terms of object recognition (89%) and scene understanding (90%), though it has been quite average with regard to structural consistency and noise robustness, which might indicate that the model might be unstable under conditions of uncertainty. On the other hand, the integrated model has shown high robustness to noise, good efficiency with regard to structural consistency, and the highest efficiency overall, with the highest scores for object recognition (95%), scene understanding (94%), obstacle detection (96%), and visual localization (93%). This shows that the perception model based on the geometric structure via linear algebra, along with learning-based abstraction, has been quite stable, reliable, and human-centered overall. In the case of the Linear Algebra model, the high efficiency with regard to structural consistency has been achieved via covariance analysis, SVD, dimensionality reduction, and vector space representation. Due to the maintenance of geometrical consistency, the model continues to be reliable in identifying obstacles. The Linear Algebra-Based Model, because of the constraint of semantic abstraction, results in a slightly limited understanding of the scene. However, the Learning-Based Model, because of its ability to learn nonlinear features, has a significant advantage in identifying objects and understanding scenes. Its robustness is moderate in a dynamic and noisy environment, mainly because of the absence of a strong mathematical structure and uncertainty modeling. Among all perception tasks, the Structured Integrated Model (proposed approach) ranks the best. By combining the power of artificial intelligence in learning features and a strong mathematical structure, the Structured Integrated Model enhances feature abstraction, decision boundaries, and noise reduction, resulting in accurate object recognition, obstacle detection, and precise visual localization in a high-dimensional, uncertain environment.

11. SEMANTIC AND CONTEXT-AWARE PERCEPTION

Semantic perception moves beyond detecting shapes and features to understanding meaning and context within an environment.

11.1 Object Recognition and Scene Understanding

The main focus is on identifying items be it a person, a car, or any other object and understanding how these items relate to each other within a scene. The understanding of the spatial arrangement of items and how they interact with their environment is the key to understanding a scene the environment within which all these items coexist. For example, a word like "chair" is used to identify an object, whereas a sentence like "a chair beside a table in an office" is used to identify a scene.

Object recognition is a classification problem:

$$\hat{s} = \arg\max_{s} p(s \mid \phi(z)) \tag{39}$$

where:

- $\phi(z) \in \mathbb{R}^d$ is the learned feature representation
- $s \in \{1, 2, \ldots, K\}$ is the object class

Scene understanding extends to structured relationships:

$$\mathcal{G} = (V, E) \tag{40}$$

where:

- $V = \{s_i\}$ are object nodes
- $E = \{r_{ij}\}$ represent spatial/semantic relations

Graph-based reasoning:

$$p(\mathcal{G} \mid z) = \prod_i p(s_i \mid z) \prod_{i,j} p(r_{ij} \mid s_i, s_j) \tag{41}$$

This captures contextual dependencies.

11.2 Semantic Mapping and Localization

Here, robots build maps enriched with semantic labels (e.g., door, corridor, human zone). Instead of only geometric SLAM, the system constructs *meaning-aware maps*, improving navigation, task planning, and human interaction.

Traditional SLAM estimates:

$$p(x_{1:t}, m \mid z_{1:t}) \tag{42}$$

where m is a geometric map.

Semantic SLAM extends this to:

$$p(x_{1:t}, m, s \mid z_{1:t}) \tag{43}$$

The semantic map becomes:

$$m = \{(l_i, s_i)\} \tag{44}$$

where:

- $l_i \in \mathbb{R}^3$is landmark position
- $s_i$is semantic label

Optimization problem:

$$\min_{x,m} \sum_t \| z_t - h(x_t, m) \|^2 + \lambda \sum_i \mathcal{L}_{sem}(s_i) \tag{45}$$

Equation (45) represents the optimized problem for geometry and semantics.

12. VISION–LANGUAGE AND MULTIMODAL PERCEPTION

Integrating perception with the conceptual reasoning helps the robots to recognize the objects and identify the nature. This helps the robots in modalities like audio and tactile. This plays an significant role in vision and language multimodal of the robots.

Multimodal alignment seeks or contrastive learning objective:

$$\mathcal{L} = -\log \frac{\exp(v^\top l/\tau)}{\sum_k \exp(v^\top l_k/\tau)} \tag{46}$$

Where,

$$v = \phi_v(z)$$

$$l = \phi_l(w)$$

$$\min \| v - l \|^2$$

Equation (46) represents the semantic consistency across modalities.

The instructions for the grounding is given by,

$$\hat{x} = \arg\max_x p(x \mid z, w) \tag{47}$$

where language wconstrains perceptual inference.

13. PROS AND CONS OF THE PROPOSED PERCEPTION FRAMEWORK

Table 5. Pros and Cons of Perception Framework

Pros (Strengths)	Cons (Limitations)
Strong Mathematical Foundation – Use of linear algebra provides structured representation of high-dimensional and noisy sensor data in vector space form.	Heavy Dependence on Mathematical Assumptions – Linear models may not fully capture highly nonlinear, complex real-world sensory dynamics.
Integration of Representation and Learning – Combines structured mathematical modeling with data-driven learning instead of treating them separately.	Computational Complexity – Matrix operations and high-dimensional transformations can be computationally expensive in real-time robotic systems.
Improved Noise Handling – Geometric and algebraic frameworks help organize and reduce noise in sensor data.	Sensitivity to Data Quality – Learning components still rely heavily on high-quality, labeled training data.
Supports Semantic Understanding – Learning processes enable abstraction, scene understanding, and object recognition.	Generalization Issues – Models trained in specific environments may not generalize well to unseen dynamic environments.
Structured Architecture for Robustness – Structure-preserving frameworks increase reliability and stability of perception systems.	Integration Complexity – Designing systems that balance mathematical structure with adaptive learning can be technically challenging.
Scalable Across Tasks – Applicable to object detection, obstacle avoidance, and scene analysis.	Real-World Deployment Challenges – Environmental uncertainties may still affect performance.
Supports Human-Centred AI Development – Enables intelligent systems that better interpret real-world contexts.	Interpretability Trade-off – As learning components become more complex (deep models), interpretability may reduce despite structured representation.

Table 5 discusses the Pros and Cons perception framework, which has a number of important key advantages. Firstly, one of the main benefits of the proposed framework is its robust mathematical basis, where linear algebra is used for a systematic and structured representation of high-dimensional noisy sensor data in vector spaces. By combining structured mathematical modeling and learning, the proposed framework does not split representation and intelligence into two separate parts, thus providing a more integrated perception framework. The geometric and algebraic approaches enhance noise robustness by structuring sensor data into meaningful subspaces, thus improving stability. Moreover, the learning part of the framework provides semantic abstraction, which facilitates higher-level tasks such as object recognition, scene understanding, and obstacle avoidance. The systematic use of models results in greater expressiveness and stability and allows for the creation of a more scalable platform for the implementation of robotic functions. Ultimately, these two elements lay the groundwork for the development of human-centric AIs that can more accurately measure and interpret the physical world. However, there are inherent limitations when it comes to working with these models. The use of linear algebra, for example, is based upon a theoretical foundation that might not be able to accurately represent the highly nonlinear nature of physical sensors. The use of matrices and working with data in a high-dimensional space can introduce a significant computational overhead. The education process, again, relies upon the quality of the data and the quality of the labeled data, which in turn affects the performance. The generalization process for new and dynamic environments can be difficult to transfer. The creation of systems that combine mathematical models and learning processes has a significant level of complexity.

14. OPEN CHALLENGES AND RESEARCH DIRECTIONS

The following are few challenges and research Directions.

14.1 Scalability and Real-Time Constraints

However, modern robotic systems today are often faced with high-dimensional data streams from various sensors, such as vision sensors, LiDAR sensors, and touch sensors. Scalability can be achieved through effective data reduction, parallel processing, and algorithm design that meets stringent real-time constraints.

14.2 Explainability and Trustworthy Perception

For entirely trustworthy perception systems, it is imperative that they are understandable and transparent during decision-making. Black-box learning models can be adverse in trust and responsibility. The recent trends in the research domain involve topics such as explainable AI, quantification of uncertainty, and structure-preserving representations.

14.3 Lifelong and Adaptive Perception Systems

The robotic world is dynamic and also needs a lifelong learning system that can learn incrementally without catastrophic forgetting. In order to learn from new information in the robotic world, techniques based on lifelong learning, memory-based learning, and even the learning of representations are used in the process of lifelong perception, which aims at learning while preserving prior knowledge.

15. CONCLUSION

Perception in robotics is recognized as a bridge between the physical world and intelligent decision-making of robots. As discussed, and proved throughout this chapter, the perception of sounds cannot be achieved through learning techniques and mathematical modeling separately but requires a structured and principled approach to representation and intelligence together. Linear algebra plays a significant part as a representation tool for structuring noisy and high-dimensional sensor data into a geometric and algebraic framework called vector space and matrix computation. Besides this vital mathematical grounding, the learning processes and capabilities lay the groundwork for abstraction and semantic interpretation within an uncertain world. Through data-driven learning processes, feature learning processes, and geometry-based learning processes, there is a development towards capabilities that will allow for an effective management of dynamics and environments that are shared. Ultimately, through these structures and processes, there is development towards robust, efficient, and reliable results. Proving the applicability and relevance to a wide array of learning processes and capabilities lies within determining relevance towards identifying objects, scene analysis, and identifying obstacles. Ultimately, the imperatives towards development within structure-preserving architectures allow for the development and growth of human-centric artificial intelligence.

REFERENCES

Barfoot, T. D. (2021). *State estimation for robotics* (2nd ed.). Cambridge University Press.

Bronstein, M. M., Bruna, J., Cohen, T., & Velickovic, P. (2021). Geometric deep learning: Grids, groups, graphs, geodesics, and gauges. *arXiv preprint arXiv:2104.13478.*

Cadena, C., Carlone, L., & Carrillo, H.. (2021). Past, present, and future of simultaneous localization and mapping: Toward the robust-perception age. *IEEE Transactions on Robotics, 37*(4), 1288–1314.

Chen, X., Liu, S., & Szeliski, R. (2022). Learning robust visual localization under uncertainty. *IEEE Transactions on Robotics, 38*(6), 3810–3826.

Kirillov, A.. (2023). Segment anything. In *Proceedings of the IEEE/CVF International Conference on Computer Vision (ICCV).*

Liang, M., Yang, B., Chen, Y., & Urtasun, R. (2022). BEV Fusion: Multi-task multi-sensor fusion with unified bird's-eye view representation. In *Proceedings of the IEEE International Conference on Robotics and Automation (ICRA).*

Sarlin, P.-E., DeTone, D., Malisiewicz, T., & Rabinovich, A. (2020). SuperGlue: Learning feature matching with graph neural networks. In *Proceedings of the IEEE/CVF Conference on Computer Vision and Pattern Recognition (CVPR)* (pp. 4938–4947). DOI: 10.1109/CVPR42600.2020.00499

Strasdat, H., Montiel, J., & Davison, A. J. (2020). Visual SLAM: Why filter? *Image and Vision Computing, 30*(2), 65–77. DOI: 10.1016/j.imavis.2012.02.009

Teed, Z., & Deng, J. (2022). RAFT: Recurrent all-pairs field transforms for optical flow. *IEEE Transactions on Pattern Analysis and Machine Intelligence, 44*(8), 4144–4157.

Yin, Z., Darrell, T., & Yu, F. (2021). Transfuser: Imitation with transformer-based sensor fusion for autonomous driving. In *Proceedings of the Conference on Robot Learning (CoRL).*

Zhang, J., & Singh, S. (2020). LOAM: Lidar odometry and mapping in real-time. *IEEE Robotics and Automation Letters, 5*(4), 5810–5817.

Chapter 9
AI-Driven Digital Twin Maintenance Automation in AR/VR:
A Centrifugal Pump Case Study

G. Karthika
http://orcid.org/0000-0002-8703-235X
Department of Electronics and Communication Engineering, Saveetha Engineering College, Chennai, India

ABSTRACT

Artificial Intelligence (AI), when integrated with Augmented Reality (AR) and Virtual Reality (VR), is transforming industrial maintenance through immersive, data-driven Digital Twin environments. This chapter presents a comprehensive framework that demonstrates how AI-enhanced VR systems can optimize the monitoring and repair of industrial equipment. Using a centrifugal pump as a case study, the system uses AI-based anomaly detection, programmable logic control, real-time sensor inputs, and immersive virtual reality interfaces for remote issue resolution. IoT and MQTT protocols are used to synchronize a Unity 3D-created digital twin with real machinery. Operators can see, identify, and fix issues remotely with an Oculus Go headset. A Cartesian robotic arm that has been trained using AI procedures to mimic human repair movements makes physical adjustments. Scalable predictive maintenance, less downtime, and less human intervention are the results of this AI-AR/VR synergy.

DOI: 10.4018/979-8-2600-2701-1.ch009

1. INTRODUCTION: AI AND IMMERSIVE TECHNOLOGIES IN SMART INDUSTRY

1.1 Emergence of Industry 4.0

To transform manufacturing and industrial process planning and administration, Industry 4.0 was introduced at the Hannover Fair in Germany in 2011. This trend integrates artificial intelligence (AI), cyber-physical systems, Internet of Things (IoT) technologies, and the immersive Augmented Reality (AR) and Virtual Reality (VR) systems. The system integration that serves as the foundation for flexible solutions that offer exceptional efficiency and customized usage facilitates the real-time transfer of data and autonomous industrial decision-making of these aspects (Kagermann et al., 2013).

The manufacturing approach of Industry 4.0 involves both automated processes and data exchange systems in addition to reshaping human connections with automated systems and digital programs. Advanced machinery complexity demands intelligent maintenance systems that are more vital now than they have ever been. The rise of predictive and autonomous maintenance practices through AI-altered Digital Twin (DT) systems has replaced traditional time-dependent reactive maintenance solutions (Lee et al., 2015).

1.2. Challenges in Traditional Maintenance Practices

The primary approach of traditional industrial maintenance consists of periodic inspections and operator intuition and post-failure interventions. Trapped in reactive maintenance methods organizations face lower asset efficiency and unexpected stoppages and increased operational finances. Manufacturing sectors sustain 49% of their total production losses when equipment breaks down suddenly according to Prabu et al. (2024).

The current industrial systems require new maintenance methods because traditional practices do not fulfil the needs of this closed-loop monitoring sector which experiences faster production and increasingly complex equipment along with enhanced expectation regarding product quality. Because complex production settings enhance the likelihood of system defects and operational errors, maintenance professionals face difficulties while gathering information from various sources (Ma et al., 2024). Automatic systems that can actively detect potential equipment breakdowns and provide real-time failure protection are desperately needed.

1.3. The artificial intelligence systems have transformed industrial maintenance by expanding its scope

The introduction of artificial intelligence has brought a revolution in the industrial operations. Machine learning (ML) and deep learning (DL) technology AI algorithms are used to process large volumes of sensor data, identify patterns that can give them the ability to forecast equipment degradation with a high level of accuracy. The capabilities also make organizations move towards predictive maintenance as opposed to its current state of reactive maintenance.

AI-based predictive maintenance applications are used to assist organizations in forecasting equipment failures to come up with efficient maintenance plans that reduce operational downtimes. AI-related models related to IIoT technology enable monitoring of the health of assets continuously and spotting of anomalies early, as described by Zheng et al. (2020). Reinforcement learning models have proven to be effective in balancing reinforcement feedbacks thereby enhancing the resilience of the system.

1.4. Digital Twins: Virtual Mirrors of Physical Assets

Digital twin technology stands out as a top competitor among all Industry 4.0 tools. According to Tao et al. (2019), the digital twin (DT) enables engineers to create an accurate computer-based model of real-world assets that automatically updates using current data points, allowing engineers to assess the assets over the course of their operational duration. To produce operational information, the system integrates engineering models, sensor data, visualization technology, and AI decision-making skills.

Digital twins serve as the foundation for predictive maintenance, allowing engineers to use virtual operations to evaluate intervention strategies prior to actual use by simulating system failures and doing root cause studies. Digital twins become adaptive systems that automatically modify their behavior depending on current operational data thanks to their collaboration with AI.

In order to monitor sophisticated production tools, Prabu et al. (2024) created an integrated system of digital twins and artificial intelligence. Faster reaction times and better maintenance dependability were proved by the system implementation, confirming the valuable potential of this integrated strategy.

Figure 1. The worldwide virtual reality market is set to be huge

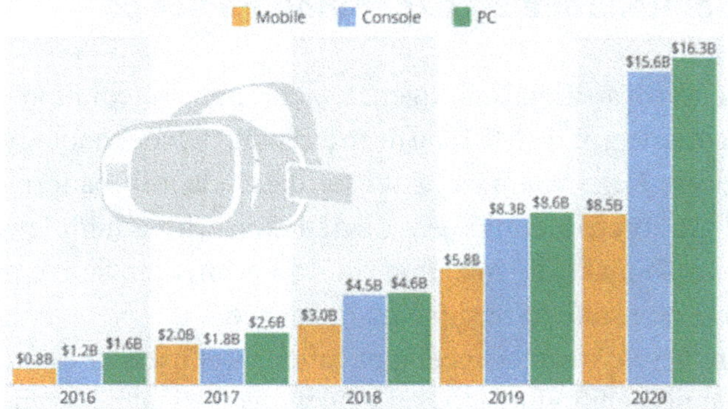

The global virtual reality (VR) industry grew from $3.6 billion to $40.4 billion between 2016 and 2020, as shown in Figure 1. The market was led by PC-based VR, closely followed by console VR powered by gaming platforms, but mobile VR grew steadily because of readily available standalone devices. Overall, the graph shows how VR is becoming more widely used on many platforms.

1.5. Industrial maintenance depends on AR/ VR technology to function effectively

Immersive technologies including VR and AR transform industrial personnel's interactions with their equipment and systems. The incorporation of these technologies enables better human-machine interactions while controlling mental workload and optimizing training processes and operational execution. AR headset-wearing technicians receive maintenance guidance through the actual equipment using superimposed instructions which enables both precision and speed in their work (Costa et al., 2025).

Users perform predictive maintenance tasks in a virtual environment where simulated complex machinery lets them inspect internals while learning operational characteristics and practice maintenance processes securely before field deployment. Through its AR capabilities the system allows experts to offer real-time distant assistance to field operators without physical location constraints (Nagy et al., 2023).

The combination of these technologies operates best within Digital Twin networks. Using a spatially immersive interface operators gain access to live physical machine twins which improve their situational understanding and diagnostic precision (Zhou et al., 2021).

1.6. Toward Predictive and Autonomous Maintenance

AI and DTs together with immersive technologies create conditions for maintenance evolution from reactive practices to predictive methods and eventually to automated approaches. Through predictive maintenance operators can detect early warning signs of future breakdowns to deploy preventive actions in advance. The approach of autonomous maintenance advances to automatic decision processes so that human involvement is reduced to a minimum (Windmann et al., 2024).

The system detects motor degradation signals which enable the Digital Twin to simulate component remaining usefulness and validates predictions with neural network analysis prior to robot deployment or technician AR-based assistance with minimum human supervision.

Such technological progress results in elevated system uptime together with cost savings while enabling energy-efficient solutions and promoting safer workplace conditions for the personnel. Advance technology solutions play a vital role for compliance and risk mitigation in controlled sectors like aerospace along with nuclear and pharmaceuticals according to Costa et al. (2025).

1.7. Economic and Operational Impact

The economic benefits of AI-powered predictive maintenance are profound. Studies have shown that companies adopting intelligent maintenance systems experience:

- Up to 30% reduction in maintenance costs
- Up to 45% reduction in downtime
- 25–30% increase in equipment lifespan

Furthermore, immersive training platforms powered by VR have led to 40% faster learning curves and 50% fewer errors during actual maintenance tasks (Zhou et al., 2021).

Such statistics reinforce that investing in smart maintenance systems is no longer optional—it is a strategic necessity for companies aiming to stay competitive in the digital industrial era.

1.8. Research Gap and Future Directions

While the integration of AI, DTs, and immersive technologies shows great promise, several challenges persist. These include:

- Data interoperability and standardization

- High implementation costs
- Cybersecurity concerns
- Scalability of AI models across diverse assets

Future research must focus on open architecture systems, self-healing algorithms, and secure decentralized infrastructures. Additionally, it is important to pay more attention to human factors engineering, so the systems will be easily monitored and understandable to the employees (Windmann et al., 2024).

Industry 4.0 technologies are changing the way maintenance processes were performed in the past as manual, reactive, and occasionally autonomous systems. The combination of AI, Digital twins, and AR/VR will enable industries to become more reliable in their assets, lower the operational cost, and increase the abilities of the staff.

These technologies provide the future of industrial operations by providing an opportunity to overcome the drawbacks of the traditional approaches to maintenance; they enable the machine to diagnose itself, learn, and repair itself with the assistance of human operators. With the need to survive in a more digital world, the adoption of intelligent maintenance is not only beneficial to industries, but also necessary.

2. BACKGROUND

The emergence of new technologies such as AI, Digital Twin technology, and AR/VR is transforming the way maintenance is conducted in industries. This integration facilitates real time monitoring, predictive maintenance and immersive training and makes the operation more efficient and minimized the downtime. In many industries, centrifugal pumps are the key elements to consider so this choice should be seen as a good example to understand such developments.

2.1 Evolution of Digital Twin in Maintenance

Numerous sectors have investigated sector-specific DT implementations. DTs have been used to enhance maintenance planning and execution in industrial processes. Wang et al. (2023) examine the use of DTs in vehicle predictive maintenance systems in the automotive sector, outlining the difficulties and possible fixes in practical situations. Research has investigated the application of DTs in aircraft maintenance in the aerospace industry, suggesting an IoT-enabled modular design for improved operational efficiency.

Despite the potential uses, several obstacles prevent DTs from being widely used in maintenance:

- **Data Integration and Management**: Ensuring seamless data flow between physical assets and their digital counterparts remains complex.
- **Model Accuracy and Validation**: Developing accurate DT models that reflect real-world conditions requires extensive validation and calibration.
- **Scalability**: Scaling DT solutions across multiple assets or systems poses technical and logistical challenges.
- **Standardization**: The lack of standardized frameworks and protocols for DT development and implementation leads to interoperability issues.

To overcome existing challenges and enhance the efficacy of DTs in maintenance, future research and development should focus on:

- **Developing Standardized Frameworks**: Establishing universal standards for DT creation and integration to ensure interoperability.
- **Advancing AI and ML Integration**: Enhancing the capabilities of DTs through sophisticated AI and ML algorithms for more accurate predictions.
- **Enhancing Cybersecurity Measures**: Implementing robust security protocols to protect data integrity and prevent unauthorized access.
- **Promoting Cross-Industry Collaboration**: Encouraging knowledge sharing and collaborative efforts across industries to foster innovation and best practices in DT applications.

Digital Twin technology stands at the forefront of revolutionizing maintenance strategies, offering predictive insights and operational efficiencies. Even while there are still obstacles to overcome, continued research and technical developments are opening the door to more reliable and scalable DT solutions in maintenance across a range of industries.

2.2 Role of AI in Predictive Maintenance

Predictive maintenance (PdM) uses AI techniques like machine learning (ML), deep learning (DL), and data analytics to predict equipment failures, minimize downtime, and optimize maintenance costs. Supervised learning algorithms, such as Support Vector Machines (SVMs), Random Forests, and Decision Trees, have been widely used to classify equipment conditions and forecast anomalies based on labeled historical data (Mobley, 2020). Unsupervised learning approaches, such as k-Means clustering and Principal Component Analysis (PCA), provide important insights into machine behavior (Jardine et al., 2006). In order to predict the Remaining Useful Life (RUL) of assets, deep learning techniques like Convolutional Neural Networks (CNNs) and Recurrent Neural Networks (RNNs), especially Long

Short-Term Memory (LSTM) networks, are excellent at extracting features from high-dimensional sensor data and modeling time-series trends (Zhao et al., 2019).

Figure 2. AI in Predictive Maintenance

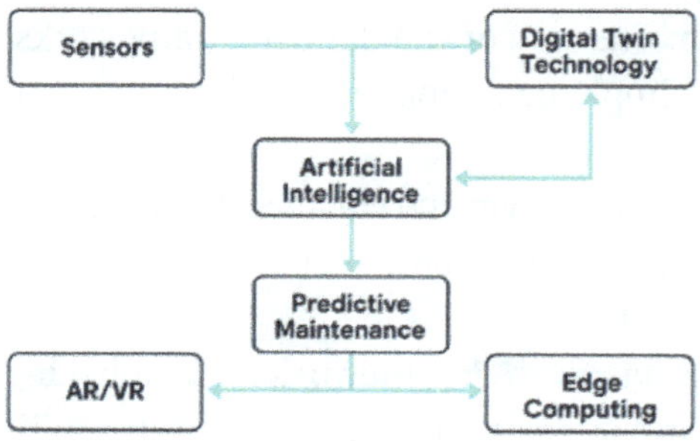

The Figure 2 shows the AI in predictive maintenance. Various technologies are shown in the diagram as combining to allow for AI-driven predictive maintenance. Data collected by sensors from equipment is given to both AI systems and Digital Twin Technology for processing and simulating the equipment virtually. Besides learning from data, the digital twin sends useful information to AI, boosting its ability to analyze. This combination of data helps AI find things that seem different and anticipate equipment breakdowns which are central to predictive maintenance. Thanks to edge computing, data is processed locally and quickly and thanks to AR/VR, everything looks interactive and engaging during actual maintenance. With these technology solutions interacting, buildings get a responsive maintenance plan that cuts downtime and improves performance. In summary, artificial intelligence (AI) improves predictive maintenance by providing sophisticated capabilities in real-time defect identification, failure prediction, and asset life-cycle management. It offers a strong, scalable, and intelligent architecture for contemporary maintenance systems when combined with IIoT, DTT, and XAI.

2.3 Integration of Augmented and Virtual Reality in Maintenance and Training

The adoption of the concept of Augmented Reality (AR) and Virtual Reality (VR) to improve maintenance and training has transformed how the industry functions by improving both efficiency and safety and outcomes of learning. AR and VR provide interactive systems that create immersive environments that help comprehend complicated systems and procedures without taking the risks of training in real-life environments. AR superimposes the digital on the physical world, offers real-time directions and assistance when performing maintenance operations, whereas VR builds full-simulated environments to undergo a thorough training. The technologies have been implemented in other sectors such as aerospace, manufacturing and transport to enhance the performance of maintenance training program.

Liu et al. (2022) conducted a study that compared the performance of AR, VR, and conventional training on crane maintenance activities. The findings showed that with simple tasks, traditional training proved to be more effective, however, with an increase in task complexity, the AR training proved to be more efficient and with less cognitive load than VR and traditional training. The AR group performed complex tasks that were more than 10 percent more efficiently and their cognitive load level was lower than the other groups did. It implies that AR can be especially helpful in complicated maintenance processes where guidance in real-time and spatial perception are essential.

AR has been used progressively in industrial assistance and training in the industry 4.0 context. The methodological literature review by Marques and Vassallo (2024) demonstrated that the use of AR applications in the industrial context has become increasingly popular over the years, and it is now actively used to enhance the efficiency and accuracy of assembly and maintenance processes. The research also mentioned the obstacles of AR implementation (technical constraints and user adoption), which is why a holistic approach to balancing the technological potential and its usability and acceptance by the end-user is necessary.

Specific industrial tasks have also been tested with regards to the effectiveness of AR and VR training. Gavish et al. (2015) held research on the problem of electronic actuator assembly tasks and compared VR and AR training platforms with the traditional ones. It was found that AR training resulted in fewer errors and better performance, whereas VR training took more time to be trained. It means that AR can be more appropriate in terms of precision and real-time feedback tasks like VR can have more advantages in the context of extensive simulations when having immersive experiences can be an advantage.

Moreover, Syberfeldt et al. (2018) conducted a systematic review of the use of AR in maintenance operations. The research established that AR technologies have presented encouraging outcomes in the improvement of human performance in technical maintenance activities, the administration of the maintenance activities and managerial decision making. Nevertheless, technical challenges, which continue to make AR an inaccessible technology in industrial applications, were also mentioned in the review, including hardware constraints and standardization of AR solutions.

AR has also found applications in the railway industry in the training of air springs maintenance in the electric multiple units. Kim et al. (2024) created an AR-based light maintenance training content and tested the usefulness of the content using

UMUX and CSUQ questionnaires. The AR material was found to be more efficient and usable than the conventional document manuals, which proves the possibility of AR in improving the precision of fault detection and troubleshooting ability of the maintenance staff.

Safety concerns are also met when AR and VR are used in the maintenance training by offering a safe environment where trainees can practice and learn. Gong et al. (2024) conducted a systematic literature review and meta-analysis to study the use of AR in safety training in different industries. The research determined that the AR-based training had a significant positive impact on the safety of the work environment, especially in the cases of construction, manufacturing, and transportation, as it provides full-immersion and interactive learning that results in the development of enhanced hazard awareness and reaction.

To conclude, the incorporation of AR and VR technologies into the maintenance and training systems has many advantages such as efficiency, precision and safety. The problem of technical constraints and user acclimatization continue, but with the development of research and development, these issues have been mitigated, and the application of AR and VR in industrial maintenance training is on its way to be extended. The argument presented by the different research studies highlights how these technologies can revolutionize the conventional training practices and address the changing needs of the contemporary industries.

3. FOCUS OF THE ARTICLE

3.1 Introduction

This paper will be a detailed case study of an AI-based Digital Twin maintenance system combined with AR and VR technologies that have been developed and implemented on a centrifugal pump, which is a ubiquitous and critical device in most industrial settings. The centrifugal pump is a good choice to be used as an example of predictive maintenance because it is vulnerable to bear failures, damaged impellers, and electrical problems that may lead to serious malfunctions of the systems in case it is not fixed in a timely manner. The research shows that remote monitoring and immersive control in real time can be realised by developing the Digital Twin of the centrifugal pump in Unity 3D and putting it in a VR interface with Oculus Go, which means that such a device is possible. Along with it, the system has a robotic Cartesian arm that performs physical maintenance programs according to virtual functioning instructions sent through MQTT, a lightweight IoT protocol.

The three major points in this work are three. First, to prepare a powerful Digital Twin of the centrifugal pump to enable real time monitoring and visualization.

Second, to incorporate immersive VR to interact with the human machine so as to allow remote maintenance operations. Third, to complete robotic actuator-AI analytics interfaces with the aim to automate the corrective procedures. Integration of the technologies provides a cost effective and scalable solution that reduces human intervention, increases safety and improves overall equipment effectiveness (OEE). The suggested system supports the concept of smart factories where digital intelligence and automation will work together to minimize production and maintenance processes.

The article is organized in the following way. Part 2 provides a review of the literature concerning the Digital Twin technology, predictive maintenance, and the application of AR and VR to industrial systems. Section 3 contains the methodology, which is the system architecture, hardware, and software components, and data flow. In section 4, the experimental setup, implementation, and results have been discussed. Section 5 reviews the performance of the system and identifies the strengths and weaknesses. Lastly, Section 6 summarizes the paper and provides possible directions of future research, such as full AI automation, machine learning-based diagnostics, and enterprise-wide implementation.

The article offers a detailed insight into the ways of how Digital Twin and immersive technologies can be implemented to automate maintenance and even preconditions the next line of research and development to develop intelligent and self-sustaining industrial systems through this case study.

3. 2. Literature Review

The meeting of Digital Twin (DT), Artificial Intelligence (AI), and immersive technologies like Augmented Reality (AR) and Virtual Reality (VR) has contributed to the strategies of maintenance in the contemporary industrial systems to a great extent. In the past ten years, a rich literature on the topic of the Digital Twin technology as a means to facilitate predictive maintenance has been produced due to the ability to provide the virtual representation of the real time condition of the machinery and the insights into the equipment behavior under different conditions. According to Gabor et al. (2022), the Digital Twin is a live computerized replica of a bodily resource that incorporates real time sensor and past analytics to imitate, anticipate and optimize its performance. This framework has been developed out of the fixed models to real time dynamic system with capacity to communicate in a bidirectional manner and automatically controlled systems forming the basis of intelligent automation of maintenance.

Artificial intelligence-based predictive maintenance has emerged as a major field of study in Industry 4.0, especially in making use of highly sensitive rotating machinery, such as centrifugal pumps, which are vulnerable to operational issues, including cavitation, misalignment, and bearing failures. Rasheed et al. (2020) note that multi source sensor data can be processed by AI algorithms, particularly deep learning models, that would help in detecting faults at early stages that traditional threshold-based systems tend to ignore. Popular methods to model temporal characteristics in vibration, temperature, and current signals and facilitates real time fault detection and Remaining Useful Life (RUL) prediction include Long Short-Term Memory (LSTM) networks and convolutional neural networks (CNNs). Recent research by Yan et al. (2021) showed that the combination of LSTM and attention processes can be used to monitor the condition of centrifugal pumps, which is more accurate than traditional machine learning methods.

The use of AI in Digital Twin systems has also led to increased capability of developing predictive and self-learning maintenance. As an example, Qi and Tao (2022) offered a DT based maintenance architecture where AI models constantly examine real time data of IoT sensors and change the virtual model. The architecture facilitates predicting the failure, identifying abnormality, and providing automatic suggestions of corrective measures. Similarly, Liu et al. (2022) noted that Digital Twins and AI can be used with synergy to operate the entire lifecycle of industrial assets by simulating physical degradation trends and actively planning them in advance. Here, the open communication protocols like MQTT help conduct data exchange between physical devices, Digital Twins, and AI agents, which is the core of an integrated predictive maintenance system.

Table 1. Comparative study

Study	Technology Focus	Methodology	Key Contribution	Limitations
Errandonea et al. (2020)	Digital Twin	Systematic Review	Identified DT trends in maintenance	Limited practical validation
Ma et al. (2024)	DT + AI	Review & Framework	Addressed scalability & heterogeneity	Lacks real-world deployment
Kobayashi & Alam (2023)	XAI in DT	Conceptual Model	Improved interpretability in DT	Early-stage research
Rasheed et al. (2020)	AI (DL models)	Data-driven models	Early fault detection using DL	Data dependency
Yan et al. (2021)	LSTM + Attention	Hybrid DL model	Improved RUL prediction accuracy	High computational cost
Qi & Tao (2022)	AI + DT	Architecture design	Self-learning maintenance system	Implementation complexity

continued on following page

Table 1. Continued

Study	Technology Focus	Methodology	Key Contribution	Limitations
Liu et al. (2022)	AI + DT	Lifecycle modeling	Full lifecycle asset management	Scalability issues
Azuma et al. (2020)	AR	Experimental study	Improved maintenance efficiency	Hardware limitations
Liu et al. (2022)	AR vs VR	Comparative study	AR better for complex tasks	Limited industrial scale
Kim et al. (2021)	VR Training	Experimental	Enhanced learning retention	Time-intensive setup
Lu et al. (2021)	VR + DT	Simulation system	Realistic maintenance simulation	Limited real-time integration
Gattullo et al. (2020)	Mixed Reality	Hybrid framework	Collaborative maintenance model	Integration challenges
Tao et al. (2022)	DT + Security	Conceptual	Highlighted need for secure DT systems	No implementation

In addition to data analytics, immersive technologies, in particular, AR and VR, substantially improve the usability and functionality of predictive maintenance systems. The technologies offer convenient visualization and first-hand communication with virtual models of physical systems, which is necessary to train, remotely assist, and on-the-fly maintenance activities. AR places digital information on the physical world and is used to guide the technician by showing step by step instructions, detecting the faulty part, or displaying sensor readings in the field. The article by Azuma et al. (2020) has shown that AR glasses with real time maintenance overlay increased the speed and precision of field service work by over 30 percent. The application of AR and Digital Twins can help technicians to communicate with a real-time model of the equipment, in fact, eliminating the gap between the physical and the digital realm.

Virtual Reality on the other hand allows immersive training environments where technicians will be able to simulate the maintenance procedures without the danger of breaking true equipment. Kim et al. (2021) consider VR based training to be effective in enhancing learning retention, procedural accuracy and muscle memory in industrial settings. Multiple research works have recognized VR as a method to recreate the physical industrial environment with Digital Twin data and, therefore, develop realistic and reacting simulation and testing conditions. It is important to note that Lu et al. (2021) in a prominent study created VR pump maintenance simulator with sensor driven Digital Twin data that enabled operators to undertake diagnostics and repair virtually and apply them in the field reducing human error and downtime of the system.

Moreover, more hybrid AR and VR platforms are being researched that can be used to assist with collaborative maintenance, remote expert oversight, and operator training. Gattullo et al. (2020) came up with the mixed reality maintenance model, which integrates AR assisted inspection alongside VR training modules, and the results of the model indicated better performance and closed knowledge transfer gaps. The method is especially efficient in the settings, which rely on the use of sophisticated machinery like centrifugal pumps, as the operator requires knowledge of the inner mechanical and electrical processes prior to the actual repair. Adaptive training is also supported through execution of AR and VR coupled with AI analytics; system can dynamically modify learning modules in response to operator performance or general feedback of the system.

Although these improvements have been made there are still various challenges. It is very essential that real time synchronization be made between the physical and digital counterpart of the assets to enable correct diagnostics of the faults and prompt maintenance measures. The bottlenecks such as latency in data transmission, sensor data inaccuracy and insufficiency in interoperability between hardware and software platforms are still common. Another significant issue is security especially when the maintenance systems are remote controlled critical assets. Tao et al. (2022) posit that the use of secure protocols of communication and decentralized data architecture like edge computing is critical to the reliable and safe functioning in AI enabled maintenance systems.

In response to these shortcomings, researchers have proposed the use of open standards to make AI, Digital Twins, and immersive technologies a part of a modular and scalable architecture. The combination of MQTT and OPC UA protocols permits real-time interaction of physical (pumps, sensors, programmable logic controllers) and virtual (Unity 3D) and AI-based platforms and engines. They also stress the role of the feedback mechanisms both physical execution and human operators to constantly update the Digital Twin and enhance the overall system performance. The comparative study tabulated in Table 1.

Evaluating AI-driven Digital Twin systems in terms of validation techniques, inherent limits, and real-world deployment hazards is crucial to ensuring practical applicability. A comparative summary of these factors is given in Table 2.

Table 2. Comparative summary of validation technique, limitations, real word deployment

Category	Aspect	Description	Impact on System	Possible Mitigation
Validation Methods	Simulation-Based Validation	Testing DT in virtual environment using modeled data	Ensures early-stage reliability	Use high-fidelity models and real-world calibration
	Historical Data Validation	Comparing predictions with past operational data	Improves prediction accuracy	Use large, high-quality datasets
	Cross-Validation (AI Models)	Techniques like k-fold validation	Prevents overfitting	Apply multiple validation techniques
	Pilot Testing	Small-scale real-time deployment	Validates real-world feasibility	Gradual system rollout
	Benchmarking	Comparison with traditional maintenance methods	Demonstrates performance improvement	Use standardized metrics (accuracy, downtime)
Limitations	Data Dependency	Requires large, clean, labeled datasets	Poor data reduces model accuracy	Data preprocessing and augmentation
	Model Interpretability	Black-box nature of AI models	Reduces trust and explainability	Use Explainable AI (XAI) techniques
	Integration Complexity	Difficulty integrating with legacy systems	Delays implementation	Use middleware and standard protocols (MQTT, OPC UA)
	Scalability Issues	Performance drops in large-scale systems	Limits industrial adoption	Use cloud-edge hybrid architecture
	High Initial Cost	Expensive sensors and infrastructure	Financial barrier	Phased investment strategy
Deployment Risks	Cybersecurity Threats	Vulnerability to hacking and data breaches	Compromises system safety	Implement encryption and secure protocols
	System Reliability	Sensor/network failure	Interrupts DT synchronization	Redundant systems and fault tolerance
	Latency Issues	Delay in real-time data transfer	Affects decision-making	Edge computing deployment
	Over-Reliance on AI	Reduced human supervision	Risk of unnoticed errors	Human-in-the-loop systems
	Regulatory Constraints	Compliance with industrial standards	Limits deployment flexibility	Align with safety and industry standards

4. METHODOLOGY

The design, development, and deployment of an AI-driven Digital Twin-based maintenance system coupled with AR/VR technologies, especially suited for a centrifugal pump as the primary industrial asset, constitute the technique used for this study. Physical hardware, real-time data collection, a virtual simulation environment, AI analytics for predictive maintenance, and immersive AR/VR interaction make up the modular and layered system architecture. End-to-end remote maintenance automation is made possible by the smooth integration of the Digital Twin, immersive interfaces, and robotic execution.

4.1 System Architecture Overview

The following interrelated layers make up the system architecture, as shown in Figure 3:

1. Physical Layer: This layer includes a programmable logic controller (PLC), sensors, and a centrifugal pump.
2. Communication Layer: This layer ensures lightweight, real-time communication between digital and hardware components by using the MQTT protocol.

Figure 3. AI-Powered Digital Twin System Integrated with AR/VR and Robotic

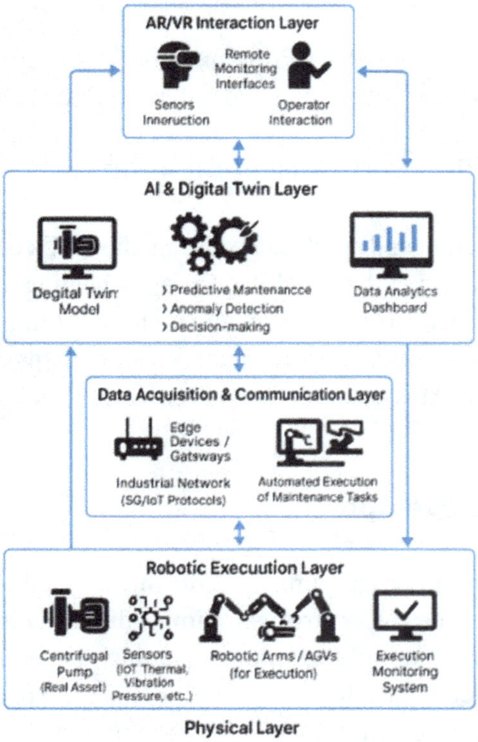

3. Digital Twin & Processing Layer: Integrated with AI for predictive analytics, this layer is built in Unity 3D to mimic and track pump conditions in real time.
4. Immersive Interface Layer: This includes Oculus Go-based virtual reality for control and maintenance training.
5. Robotic Actuation Layer: This layer consists of a Cartesian robotic arm that uses virtual orders to carry out physical maintenance duties.

4.2 Physical System Setup

A centrifugal pump is frequently used in industries for fluid transfer applications, is at the center of the configuration. This pump has several sensors to record parameters in real time, such as:

- **Vibration** (using MEMS accelerometers),

- **Temperature** (via thermocouples),
- **Motor Current** (via current sensors),
- **Flow Rate** (via ultrasonic sensors).

These signals are transmitted to a Programmable Logic Controller (PLC), which acts as the central node for controlling and collecting data from the pump.

4.3 Data Acquisition and Communication

To provide lightweight and quick data sharing, the PLC continuously reads sensor data and transmits it via the MQTT (Message Queuing Telemetry Transport) protocol. MQTT ensures two-way communication by serving as a bridge between the digital and physical worlds. It subscribes to control signals produced by the AI inference engine or in the virtual simulation environment, and it broadcasts data from the pump.

4.4 Digital Twin Development

Unity 3D, a real-time programming platform that facilitates interactive simulations, is used to create the centrifugal pump's digital twin. The virtual model mimics all physical attributes of the pump, including the geometry, flow behavior, and operational characteristics. Real-time sensor data is mapped onto this model to dynamically reflect current conditions. The twin supports:

- **Real-time visual monitoring** of sensor data,
- **Fault simulation** (e.g., bearing wear, overheating),
- **Maintenance scenario testing**,
- **Data logging for historical analysis**.

4.5 AI-Based Predictive Maintenance Module

An AI analytics engine is integrated into the system to perform predictive maintenance. The following AI models are implemented:

- **Time-series analysis** using LSTM for sensor trend prediction,
- **Anomaly detection** using autoencoders trained on healthy operating data,
- **Classification algorithms** (e.g., Random Forest) to identify fault types.

The AI models are trained using labelled historical datasets and are continuously updated through feedback from real-time system performance and operator annotations.

4.6 Immersive VR Integration

A Virtual Reality interface is developed for the Oculus Go headset, allowing users to:

- Navigate through the 3D environment of the centrifugal pump,
- Interact with pump components,
- Monitor live sensor feeds,
- Trigger maintenance actions by selecting options in the virtual interface.

This interface acts as the control centre for remote technicians and operators. They can visualize the fault, simulate repair procedures, and send commands to the robotic actuator.

4.7 Robotic Maintenance Automation

Once a maintenance task is confirmed in the VR environment, a Cartesian robotic arm is activated to perform the required physical actions, such as:

- Tightening/loosening bolts,
- Replacing gaskets,
- Disconnecting motor cables,
- Cleaning filters.

The arm receives command sequences via MQTT, mapped from Unity 3D triggers. It is pre-programmed with motion paths and safety limits to avoid unintended collisions or errors.

4.8 Feedback and Continuous Improvement

The system has a feedback loop in which:

- **Operators and trainees** provide feedback through VR on system usability and training effectiveness,
- **Sensor data** is reprocessed to improve AI model accuracy,

- **Actuation outcomes** (e.g., maintenance success/failure) are logged for further analysis.

A continuous learning system is created by using this feedback to optimize robotic movements, retrain AI algorithms, and enhance the Digital Twin model.

4.9 Safety and Security Considerations

Several safety precautions are provided because the system can be executed remotely:

- Emergency stop triggers in physical and virtual domains,
- Authentication for remote access,
- Time-out protocols for inactive systems,
- Encrypted MQTT channels for data integrity.

4.10 Experimental Setup

The prototype is experimented in a controlled environment that is set up to simulate real operating conditions of centrifugal pump system. Such an environment allows simulating different typical faults like imbalance of impellers and overheating of motors that are vital in assessing the stability and precision of the system. The testing conditions are designed in a manner that addresses a wide range of the operational conditions which include a base scenario demonstrating healthy operation of the pumps. This offers a reference point which abnormal conditions can be compared to. Next, the case of early fault detection is presented, where the AI algorithms of the system have the opportunity to detect slight anomalies in the parameters of operation, which might indicate the development of a problem. Testing is also expanded to higher levels of interactivity when it comes to maintenance simulations of advanced systems during which the operators are exposed to the system which has been placed within a virtual reality (VR) interface so that they can activate diagnostic processes and remedial measures. Also, the prototype has autonomous fault response features, where the AI component predicts the fault and then triggers an automation process of actuation to engage in automatic repairs by the robot. These simulated test systems confirm the combined functionality of AI-based digital twin, bold VR interfaces and robots to provide knowledgeable, real-time maintenance robots.

Figure 4. Flowchart of the proposed system

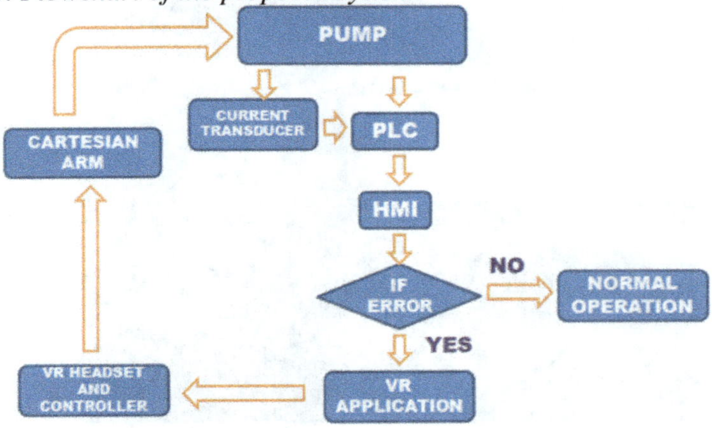

The flowchart of the proposed system shown in figure 4. The system offers the proposed solution by incorporating sensors to monitor the necessary parameters. It is through traditional means, via a wired cable, that the measured values are sent to the PLC. The data received is displayed and monitored in real-time through the HMI (Human Machine Interface) panel.

Using Virtual Reality, a simulation of the pump with photorealistic detail was built in Unity Software, while the robotic arm driven by a Leap Motion Sensor carried out the Pump Rectifications. Cloud Computing allows for seamless communication between the controller and the VR. The VR controller interacts with the devices throughout the Internet, or IoT.

5. SOFTWARE DESCRIPTION

5.1 Unity 3D

The environment in the virtual pump is developed with the use of the cross-platform 3D engine unity 3D. Unity is designed by Unity Technologies and it helps users build games in 2D and 3D. Its primary scripting API uses C# and the engine connects with Direct3D on Windows and Xbox One, OpenGL on Linux, macOS and Windows. It is used to build a virtual space. Figure 5 shows the Virtual environment Centrifugal pump using Unity 3D.

Figure 5. Virtual environment Centrifugal pump

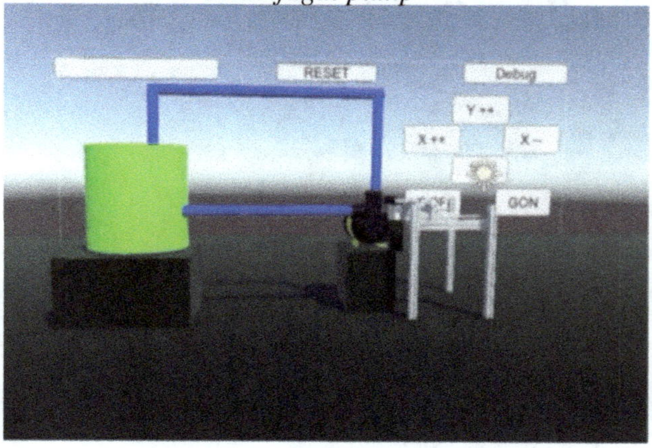

5.2 MQTT-C#: Communication Between Virtual and Physical Pump

The data flow between the digital and physical pumps is organized via C#-developed programs using the Message Queuing Telemetry Transport (MQTT) protocol. Since it uses little bandwidth and has high latency tolerance, MQTT is the best choice for Industrial IoT projects and real-time monitoring. In such a system, the virtual pump appears in a simulation developed in Unity or a compatible platform and serves as an interface to view and regulate its behavior. Data showing changes in vibration, temperature and flow are sent to an MQTT broker because of the sensors in the physical pump. The virtual pump follows the MQTT topics and keeps its digital variables consistent with the physical component. The MQTT protocol in C# is managed using the common MQTTnet library. Subscribed topics are related to pump/vibration and pump/temperature and control commands (e.g., start, stop, speed alterations) are published to control the pump.

Figure 6. MQTT Communication Infrastructure and Its Applications Across Various Sectors

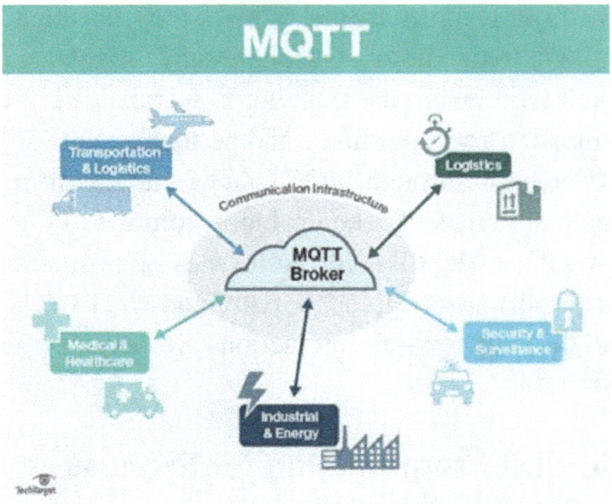

Being able to guarantee message delivery is managed by QoS levels; typical examples use QoS 1 to ensure reliable communication with only small costs. With bi-directional MQTT communication, the digital twin copies real-time operations, monitors condition and runs predictive diagnostics. Also, any control actions produced by the AI analysis in the virtual system, for example, fault predictions or scheduling maintenance, are sent back to the pump through MQTT commands so that both systems are synchronized. The figure 6 shows how a central MQTT broker facilitates smooth communication between different sectors using MQTT (Message Queuing Telemetry Transport). By enabling real-time, lightweight data exchange, it highlights applications in industrial energy, healthcare, logistics, transportation, and security.

5.3 MQTT-Embedded C: Actuator Control via Cartesian Robot

To execute maintenance or repair tasks, a Cartesian robot is used as the end component, tightening bolts, adjusting parts or triggering an emergency shutdown. MQTT is used to enable communication between the digital twin (virtual pump) and the Cartesian robot and an Embedded C implementation supports this in environments based on microcontrollers.

Thanks to the robot's onboard controller with ARM Cortex-M, STM32 or ESP32 platforms, a C program based on the MQTT client is used. Because they are designed for systems with limited resources, these libraries use very little memory and are executed efficiently.

The digital twin handles everything using AI and then posts specific control commands to MQTT topics including robot/actuate and robot/position/set. MQTT messages that arrive on these topics are picked up by the embedded client, interpreted into commands and sent to the motor control areas by the robot's [board] or RTOS.

Should the digital twin detect the impeller is imbalanced, it could prompt the Cartesian robot to move to a set coordinate and perform the needed correction. This command is sent efficiently through MQTT and feedback from acknowledgment mechanisms is provided to make the control loop complete.

Because of how robust MQTT is for both types of communication streams—MQTT-C# between the virtual model and the pump and MQTT-Embedded C between the digital twin and the actuator—all interactions are easy, fast and well-suited for Industry 4.0 industries.

5.4 GX Works3: PLC Programming for Process Control and Anomaly Calibration

Mitsubishi Electric developed GX Works3 for the purpose of programming and configuring its iQ-R and iQ-F series PLCs. MELSOFT includes this embedded program editor and allows you to develop your projects using standard IEC 61131-3 ladder logic, ST and FBD.

In these systems, GX Works3 helps control and automate the parts of centrifugal pumps that are part of digital twinning. The software allows the PLC to watch the values of pressure, vibration, motor speed and temperature in real time, with the help of I/O modules and sensor networks.

Literature and case studies mention several important ways that supply chain plays a role.

A modular approach is possible in GX Works3 which makes it simpler to keep programs working and to locate errors. A modular approach is used, so anomaly detection and sensor signal processing are both captured as reusable blocks.

- CP U and CC-Link IE configuration, plus mapping for I/O signals to PLC logic, can all be done from the graphical user interface.

Although GX Works3 is not built for MQTT support, it works with gateways such as Mitsubishi Edge cross or your custom IoT gateway to publish messages into MQTT topics. As a result, it allows the technology to work alongside digital twins and cloud services.

When unexplained vibration or motor overheating is spotted, the PLC, managed using GX Works3, starts an automatic calibration or alarm process. These may consist of triggering mechanical devices, stopping the whole process or updating the limits according to AI models.

A smart factory and predictive maintenance example published in Procedia CIRP and Sensors highlights GX Works3's compatibility with digital twins and AI-based control loops.

5.5 GT Works3: HMI Design for Process Visualization and Fault Indication

GT Works3 is the platform Mitsubishi offers to create user interfaces for the GOT2000 and GOT1000 series HMIs. The system includes features for visual displays, alarms, viewing trend graphs for old data and hand controls for talking to GX Works3-programmed PLCs.

Within your system, GT Works3 helps you design dashboards that show up to date information.

- Show System Status: HMIs let the user know the system's performance with RPM, flow rate, temperature and vibration on charts and meters.
- Show Anomalies Clearly: Should anomalies appear while deprograming (triggered either by sensor limits or AI models), they will be displayed with warnings further highlighted by color or flashing in the HMI.

GT Works3 supports adding touch-sensitive areas or buttons so that personnel can manually set up recalibration, reset alarms or override controls.

In more advanced research settings, we find these added features:

- With GT Works3, data from the machine can be stored locally so it can be examined for identification of the cause after a breakdown.

Developers may use scripting to call certain programming in the user interface when the PLC gives specific feedback.

GT Works3 is designed to manage who is allowed to make changes by authenticating users and managing access levels, as mentioned in many cyber-physical security studies.

5.6 Integration in a Digital Twin Maintenance System

Both GX Works3 and GT Works3 create a straightforward way for more intuitive control and interaction between humans and physical systems needed in most digital twin implementations. The working of a centrifugal pump system depends on:

- Using GX Works3, the PLC takes in sensor data, notices any problems and begins the required controls.

Using GT Works3, the HMI shows whether everything works and if there are any anomalies, enabling technicians or VR-AR workers to interact with the physical machine.

MQTT interfaces and OPC UA gateways are used to supply data from the PLC/HMI system to the virtual twin.

New information about these tools is regularly published in journals such as IEEE Access, Journal of Manufacturing Systems and Mechatronics, most often related to smart manufacturing, predicting maintenance needs and Industry 4.0 concepts.

5.7 Results

5.7.1 HMI Output

A Human-Machine Interface (HMI) is a user interface or dashboard that connects a person to a machine, system, or device. While the term can technically be applied to any screen that allows a user to interact with a device, HMI is most commonly used in the context of an industrial process. Figure 7 illustrate the HMI output.

Uses of HMI

To obtain and present data for users to see, HMIs interface with input/output sensors and Programmable Logic Controllers (PLCs). Depending on how they are implemented, HMI screens can be used for a single task, such as tracking and monitoring, or for more complex tasks, such as turning off machines or speeding up production.

- GS2107-WTBD GOT Basic 7-inch HMI touch screen panel 7-inch WVGA 65536 colour touch screens with DC power.
- WVGA resolution, vertical display capability, 9MB of user memory, and 65K-color TFT.
- Multiple built-in interfaces, including RS-422/232, Ethernet, SD memory cards, and USB devices.
- Use GOT (FA transparent function) to debug FA devices from a PC.
- Stores FA device data and performs required data reading and writing (Recipe function).
- It is simple to transform the character strings of switches and lamps from Text or Text Figures into Comments. Upgrading screens to show multiple languages is made simple by this.

Figure 7. HMI output

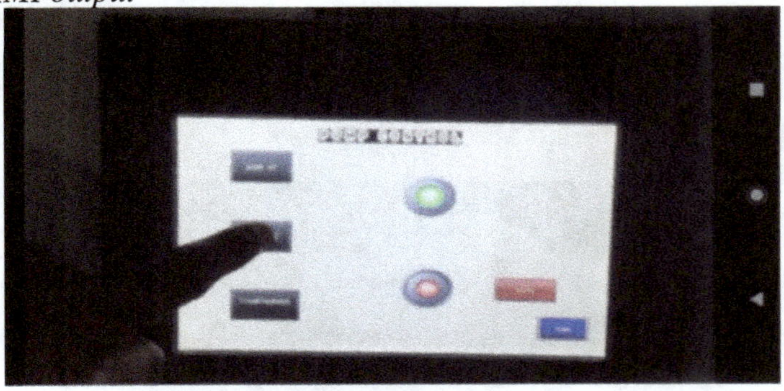

5.7.2 Virtual Reality Control

Virtual reality (VR) is an interactive computer-generated experience taking place within a simulated environment. It incorporates mainly auditory and visual feedback, but may also allow other types of sensory feedback like haptic. This immersive environment can be like the real world or it can be fantastical. Figure 8 shows the virtual machine using unity 3D.

Figure 8. Virtual Machine

The figure 9 shows the Oculus Go is a stand-alone VR headset that operates independently without being tethered to a computer or requiring a gaming system to function. Unlike smartphone-powered VR devices, the Oculus Go is self-contained, offering users a more seamless and accessible virtual reality experience. It is available in two storage configurations, 32GB and 64GB, catering to different user needs. The headset features a high-resolution 5.5-inch display with a resolution of 2560 x 1440, delivering clear and immersive visuals. It includes 3 degrees of freedom (3DoF) tracking, allowing limited movement tracking, and comes with a compatible controller for user interaction.

Figure 9. Oculus Go

4.7.3 Replacement of Capacitor

Cartesian arm allows for precise linear movements along predetermined axes by working based on a linear bush mechanism. Figure 10 shows the Virtual Cartesian arm using unity 3D. In particular, we use a 2-axis Cartesian arm where the X and Y axes change in response to inputs from a VR controller, but the Z-axis stays constant. With the aid of a conveyor belt system, stepper motors are used to precisely position the gripper at the required location. The figure 11 shows the Cartesian arm in real time.

Figure 10. Virtual Cartesian arm using unity 3D

Figure 11. Cartesian arm in real time

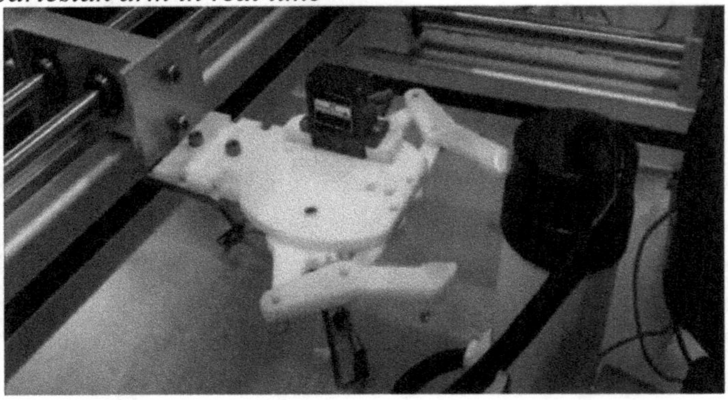

The Arduino platform's embedded C programming enables dependable and responsive motion control for these stepper motors. A servo motor-based electric gripper serves as the last control element or actuator to carry out the necessary gripping actions.

6. SOLUTIONS AND RECOMMENDATIONS

Making use of AI, Digital Twin and AR/VR technology is a breakthrough strategy for managing centrifugal pumps in industries. Combining live data gathering, simulation, automation and interactive training systems fixes the recurring inefficiencies in standard maintenance operations. In this section, we provide detailed tips for action and advice for stakeholders who wish to apply or advance these systems.

6.1 Addressing Existing Maintenance Challenges

Reactive methods used in conventional maintenance result in downtime, high expenses, and safety hazards. Inefficiencies are made worse by data silos, inadequate real-time monitoring, and a lack of qualified workers. Conventional systems don't have good training or prediction capabilities. Predictive insights, real-time monitoring, and enhanced training are made possible by integrating AI, Digital Twin, and AR/VR, which makes maintenance more proactive, effective, and dependable.

6.2 AI-Driven Predictive Maintenance Framework

Calling on Artificial Intelligence to find weaknesses in equipment before they break helps handle the challenges of modern maintenance. The first stage of this approach is to collect and normalize lots of data. Smart sensors are set up on centrifugal pumps to track important aspects such as vibration, temperature, pressure and electrical current all the time. Companies use edge computing to preprocess the data from sensors nearby in order to cut latency. Many platforms and systems work together because data is stored in standardized formats like CSV and JSON.

When the data is trustworthy, predictive analytics models can be designed. Date analysis in sensor systems can be improved by LSTM networks for foreseeing failures in the future. By comparing data feeds to previously stored clean data, unsupervised autoencoders recognize unusual alterations and bring notice to any possible emerging problems. When datasets are labelled and Random Forests and SVMs are used, these models can easily recognize different types of machine faults, helping with better maintenance decisions.

Integrating these insights generated by AI into the team's schedule should be the last part of the process. Once predictions are produced by AI, they go directly into CMMS which sets up the next inspections, maintenance jobs, or replacements automatically. Real-time communication of these insights to technicians helps them take fast action with Remote Assistance or AR. When maintenance is done this way, faults are spotted more efficiently, down-time is lower, resources are better used and equipment stays in good health longer.

6.3 Digital Twin Implementation Strategy

Intelligent maintenance relies on the Digital Twin (DT) which ties together the real and virtual systems effortlessly. A centrifugal pump is virtually reproduced with high detail, matching live sensor measurements, using platforms such as Unity and Siemens NX. The model adds in the movement of flow and vibration patterns to correctly show how a turbine machine works. Using diagnostic and prognostic capabilities, specialists can detect issues and then predict what will cause the different seals and bearings to fail at various stages in the rotor. The DT uses IoT data to show the pump's current state and embedded AI helps the system learn and respond to new situations. Using feedback loops, predictive maintenance adds respondent comments, system records, and previous maintenance logs to boost its accuracy. Also, automated scenario testing allows for virtual testing in different fault situations which can enhance and update predictive algorithms. With these skills, the DT provides condition monitoring, lets us anticipate when failures could happen and helps improve how maintenance is planned and optimized in manufacturing.

6.4 AR/VR for Training and Maintenance Support

Using immersive technology makes industrial maintenance both more successful and safer, as well as easier for employees. Real-time guidance and displayed instruction are now possible through AR which projects step-by-step tasks, info on parts and fault diagnostics in the technician's line of sight using tools such as Microsoft HoloLens or Real Wear. The systems help guide users through visual steps and verbal directions during disassembly, inspection, and repair. Using this hands-free communication increases how quickly and safely tasks are carried out in complex and dangerous areas.

On the other side, Virtual Reality (VR) offers the chance to create realistic training places with products like the Oculus Go and Meta Quest. These modules give technicians access to 3D pump models to practice both common tasks and handle unexpected situations such as a seal failing or an overheating pump. Thanks to these simulations, people in training can get used to the tools and practice awareness, all without using real equipment. You can judge and improve technician skill by considering task completion, accuracy, and behaviour during pressure situations.

In addition, research has found that using immersive systems reduces the time it takes for new technicians to learn new tasks by more than 40%, as shown in Zhang and Wang (2021). Users' ongoing comments after training helps find errors, improve interface design, and develop lesson quality. As a result, AR and VR make it possible for technicians to follow intuitive instructions and secure faster, adaptable maintenance.

6. 5 Robotic Automation for Maintenance Execution

Robotics enhances maintenance efficiency, safety, and precision. Cartesian robots use VR mapping or programmable sequences to carry out 3-axis operations like handling, fastening, and lubrication. While safety systems guard against malfunctions, real-time control via MQTT guarantees synchronization. In high-precision settings, automating repetitive processes improves reliability and frees up technicians to concentrate on analysis and decision-making.

Figure 12. Cartesian robot

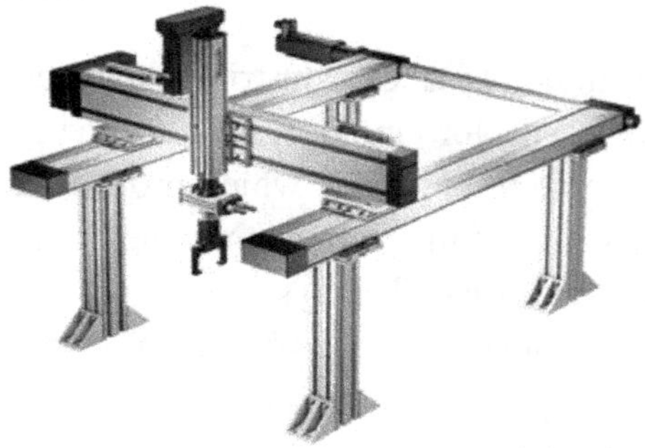

6.6 Economic and Environmental Impact

There are several advantages to using an AI-DT-AR/VR-based maintenance system:

- Cost Savings: Predictive scheduling and fewer emergency repairs can result in up to 30% lower maintenance costs (Lee et al., 2015).
- Downtime Minimization: By detecting faults early, unplanned downtimes can be reduced by 40–50%.

Energy Efficiency: Excessive energy consumption is decreased by optimizing pump operation based on real-time performance data.

- Sustainability: Longer equipment life lowers waste and encourages environmentally friendly business practices.

6.7 Scalability and Industry 4.0 Alignment

The suggested solution provides a framework for intelligent maintenance that is ready for the future and is completely in line with the fundamental ideas of Industry 4.0. Its modular design makes it simple to scale and adapt to rotating machinery other than centrifugal pumps, like fans and compressors. This adaptability guarantees that the solution can be used in a variety of industrial settings without requiring significant structural adjustments. Another important feature is real-time monitoring, which raises operational visibility and responsiveness by facilitating early fault detection and continuous performance tracking across several facilities. The architecture allows for edge-cloud integration, providing a balanced, scalable approach. Cloud platforms handle large-scale analytics, model training, and data storage, while edge devices handle local data preprocessing to lower latency. Furthermore, by creating a digital thread, the solution preserves a traceable data lineage that documents an asset's entire lifecycle, from installation and operation to maintenance and eventual decommissioning. Throughout the asset's life, this thorough data continuity improves decision-making, compliance, and transparency.

7. FUTURE RESEARCH RECOMMENDATIONS

Future studies should focus on a few promising areas to further improve the efficacy of intelligent maintenance systems. Explainable AI (XAI) is one such field that focuses on creating AI models that can both forecast equipment failures and offer understandable, human-readable explanations of the underlying causes. Building trust and enabling maintenance staff to make well-informed decisions depend on this openness. The application of multi-agent systems, in which several digital twins that represent different machines and subsystems within a plant can cooperate and coordinate to optimize maintenance plans and resource allocation, is another crucial avenue. Additionally, by mimicking tactile sensations like tool resistance or component texture, haptic feedback can be incorporated into Virtual Reality (VR) training environments to enhance hands-on learning experiences and increase realism and user engagement. With the use of reinforcement learning (RL) in robotics, maintenance robots can learn the best practices from both simulated and real-world feedback, which could result in more flexible and effective automation.

It is essential to develop suitable standards and regulations concurrently with these technological developments. To guarantee dependability and platform compatibility, government and business entities should encourage the development and implementation of standards for digital twin interoperability and AI model validation. By offering immersive, efficient training solutions, funding programs that promote AR/VR-based workforce development will aid in closing the current skills gap. Additionally, by ensuring that AI-driven maintenance tools adhere to established safety, performance, and ethical standards, certification frameworks can boost industry confidence and hasten deployment. In the context of Industry 4.0, these research and policy initiatives will work together to propel the ongoing development of intelligent maintenance systems.

8. CONCLUSION

This chapter has presented a forward-looking approach to industrial equipment maintenance by leveraging the integration of Artificial Intelligence (AI), Virtual Reality (VR), and Digital Twin technologies. It has demonstrated how real-time sensor data, virtual reality interfaces, and AI-powered robotics can collaborate to produce an intelligent and effective maintenance automation system using the centrifugal pump as a case study. A revolutionary change from conventional reactive maintenance techniques to more autonomous and proactive operations is represented by the combination of predictive diagnostics, VR-based interaction, and robotic assistance. It is anticipated that as these technologies advance, they will transform industrial operations and reinterpret the function of human operators in these ecosystems.

The suggested system uses a calibrated response involving a Cartesian robotic arm to manage a particular fault scenario, like a capacitor defect. Under the direction of the operator in a virtual environment, this arm locates the malfunctioning capacitor and swaps it out for a working one. A high-resolution virtual reality interface is used to monitor this process, allowing the operator to supervise and confirm calibration accuracy in real time. In addition to improving accuracy, this method minimizes manual labor, cuts down on downtime, and lowers overall maintenance expenses. These technologies will probably be adopted by a wider range of industries as they become more affordable and widely available.

By 2025, companies that invest in Digital Twin technologies should see up to a 30% improvement in critical operations cycle times, according to the International Data Corporation (IDC). This demonstrates the increasing importance of digital twins in maximizing operational effectiveness. Additionally, putting this idea into practice helps to lower the Total Cost of Ownership (TCO), enhance operational and environmental safety, and promote more dynamic interactions between people and digital assets. In the end, the Digital Twin makes it possible for a more intelligent and flexible human-machine collaboration model in addition to improved maintenance results.

REFERENCES

Costa, A., Miranda, J., Dias, D., Dinis, N., Romero, L., & Faria, P. M. (2025). Smart Maintenance Solutions: AR- and VR-Enhanced Digital Twin Powered by FIWARE. *Sensors (Basel), 25*(3), 845. DOI: 10.3390/s25030845 PMID: 39943483

Errandonea, I., Beltrán, S., & Arrizabalaga, S. (2020). Digital Twin for maintenance: A literature review. *Computers in Industry, 123*, 103316. DOI: 10.1016/j.compind.2020.103316

Gavish, N., Gutiérrez, T., Webel, S., Rodríguez, J., Peveri, M., Bockholt, U., & Tecchia, F. (2015). Evaluating virtual reality and augmented reality training for industrial maintenance and assembly tasks. [& Francis Online]. *Interactive Learning Environments, 23*(6), 778–798. DOI: 10.1080/10494820.2013.815221

Gong, P., Lu, Y., Lovreglio, R., Lv, X., & Chi, Z. (2024). Applications and effectiveness of augmented reality in safety training: A systematic literature review and meta-analysis. *Safety Science, 173*, 106042. DOI: 10.1016/j.ssci.2024.106624

Jardine, A. K. S., Lin, D., & Banjevic, D. (2006). A review on machinery diagnostics and prognostics implementing condition-based maintenance. *Mechanical Systems and Signal Processing, 20*(7), 1483–1510. DOI: 10.1016/j.ymssp.2005.09.012

Kagermann, H., Wahlster, W., & Helbig, J. (2013). Recommendations for implementing the strategic initiative INDUSTRIE 4.0. Final report of the Industrie 4.0 Working Group.

Kim, H., Lee, J., & Park, S. (2024). Development and Usability Evaluation of Augmented Reality Content for Light Maintenance Training of Air Spring for Electric Multiple Unit. *Applied Sciences (Basel, Switzerland), 14*(17), 7702. https://www.mdpi.com/2076-3417/14/17/7702MDPI. DOI: 10.3390/app14177702

Kobayashi, K., & Alam, S. B. (2023). Explainable, Interpretable & Trustworthy AI for Intelligent Digital Twin: Case Study on Remaining Useful Life. *arXiv preprint arXiv:2301.06676*. DOI: 10.20944/preprints202301.0145.v1

Lee, J., Bagheri, B., & Kao, H. A. (2015). A Cyber-Physical Systems architecture for Industry 4.0-based manufacturing systems. *Manufacturing Letters, 3*, 18–23. DOI: 10.1016/j.mfglet.2014.12.001

Liu, X.-W., Li, C.-Y., Dang, S., Wang, W., Qu, J., Chen, T., & Wang, Q.-L. (2022). Research on Training Effectiveness of Professional Maintenance Personnel Based on Virtual Reality and Augmented Reality Technology. *Sustainability (Basel), 14*(21), 14351. DOI: 10.3390/su142114351

Ma, S., ... (2024). The Use of Digital Twins to Support AI-Guided Predictive Maintenance. arXiv preprint. arXiv:2406.13117

Ma, S., Flanigan, K. A., & Bergés, M. (2024). State-of-the-Art Review: The Use of Digital Twins to Support Artificial Intelligence-Guided Predictive Maintenance. *arXiv preprint arXiv:2406.13117.*

Ma, S., Flanigan, K. A., & Bergés, M. (2024). State-of-the-Art Review: The Use of Digital Twins to Support Artificial Intelligence-Guided Predictive Maintenance. *arXiv preprint arXiv:2406.13117.*

Marques, G. M., & Vassallo, F. C. (2024). Augmented Reality in Industry 4.0 Assistance and Training Areas: A Systematic Literature Review and Bibliometric Analysis. *Electronics (Basel)*, *13*(6), 1147. https://www.mdpi.com/2079-9292/13/6/1147MDPI. DOI: 10.3390/electronics13061147

Mitsubishi Electric Technical White Papers. MELSOFT GX Works3 and GT Works3 Advanced Functionality. Mitsubishi Electric Corporation.

Nagy, A., ... (2023). AI-Powered Interfaces for Extended Reality to Support Remote Maintenance. arXiv preprint. arXiv:2306.16961 DOI: 10.1109/CCGridW59191.2023.00045

Prabu, S.. (2024). *AI-Driven Predictive Maintenance for Smart Manufacturing Systems Using Digital Twin Technology. IJCESEN.* Link.

Syberfeldt, A., Holm, M., Wang, L., & Lindskog, E. (2018). A systematic review of augmented reality applications in maintenance. *Robotics and Computer-integrated Manufacturing*, *49*, 215–228. DOI: 10.1016/j.rcim.2017.06.002

Tao, F.. (2019). Digital Twin and Big Data Towards Smart Manufacturing and Industry 4.0: 360 Degree Comparison. *IEEE Access : Practical Innovations, Open Solutions*, *6*, 3585–3593.

Tao, F., Zhang, M., Liu, Y., & Nee, A. Y. C. (2018). Digital Twin in Industry: State-of-the-Art. *IEEE Transactions on Industrial Informatics*, *15*(4), 2405–2415. DOI: 10.1109/TII.2018.2873186

Wang, C., Fan, I., & King, S. (2023). A Review of Digital Twin for Vehicle Predictive Maintenance System. *SAE Technical Paper 2023-01-1024.*

Wang, L.. (2021). Implementation of Digital Twin and Cyber-Physical Systems Using PLC and HMI: A Smart Manufacturing Case Study. *Journal of Manufacturing Systems.*

Windmann, A., ... (2024). Artificial Intelligence in Industry 4.0: A Review of Integration Challenges for Industrial Systems. arXiv preprint. arXiv:2405.18580 DOI: 10.1109/INDIN58382.2024.10774364

Yan, L., Chen, C., Hang, T., & Hu, Y. (2021). A stream prediction model based on attention-LSTM. *Earth Science Informatics*, *14*(2), 723–733. DOI: 10.1007/s12145-021-00571-z

Zhang, W., & Wang, Z. (2021). Theory and practice of VR/AR in K-12 science education—A systematic review. *Sustainability (Basel)*, *13*(22), 12646. DOI: 10.3390/su132212646

Zhao, R., Yan, R., Chen, Z., Mao, K., Wang, P., & Gao, R. X. (2019). Deep learning and its applications to machine health monitoring. *Mechanical Systems and Signal Processing*, *115*, 213–237. DOI: 10.1016/j.ymssp.2018.05.050

Zheng, H., ... (2020). Advancing from Predictive Maintenance to Intelligent Maintenance with AI and IIoT. arXiv preprint. arXiv:2009.00351

Zhou, Y.. (2021). Digital Twin-Driven Smart Manufacturing: Connotation, Reference Model, Applications and Research Issues. *Sensors (Basel)*, *21*(3), 1086. PMID: 33498332

Chapter 10
Fieldwire Business Tier and Construction 4.0:
A PMBOK and Industry 4.0 Perspective

Nwosu Obinnaya Chikezie Victor
http://orcid.org/0000-0003-3974-4755
University of South Africa, South Africa

Ibrahim Sinneh Sinneh
University of Liberia, Liberia

ABSTRACT

This chapter evaluates Fieldwire's Business Tier as a Project Management Information System (PMIS) for construction in the context of Industry 4.0 and PMBOK principles. It synthesises empirical evidence and peer-reviewed literature to map Fieldwire features to PMBOK performance domains, quantify likely operational impacts, and benchmark the Business Tier against competitors (Procore, Autodesk Construction Cloud/PlanGrid). The chapter identifies organisational, technical, and governance challenges in adoption and offers an implementation roadmap, metrics for impact assessment, and research avenues. The analysis draws on systematic literature synthesis, product documentation, and proxy empirical studies to provide practitioners and researchers with evidence-based guidance on leveraging mobile-first PMIS to reduce delays, control costs, and improve stakeholder engagement.

DOI: 10.4018/979-8-2600-2701-1.ch010

1. INTRODUCTION

Construction projects consistently encounter chronic issues such as significant cost overruns, persistent schedule delays, and notably weak productivity growth when compared to other industries. According to a comprehensive report by McKinsey & Company published in 2020, productivity gains within the construction sector have lagged considerably behind those observed in the broader economy, while megaprojects frequently suffer from substantial budget and timeline overruns. These persistent failures can be traced back to fragmented communication channels, reliance on manual and often outdated processes, as well as siloed workflows that separate field operations from office management. The advent of Industry 4.0 technologies—including cloud computing, Building Information Modelling (BIM), the Internet of Things (IoT), and Artificial Intelligence (AI)—holds considerable promise in alleviating these inefficiencies by establishing integrated, real-time information environments that facilitate seamless collaboration among project teams (Musarat et al., 2021).

Nevertheless, effective utilisation of these advanced technologies necessitates the deployment of robust Project Management Information Systems (PMIS) capable of orchestrating complex data flows and providing comprehensive support for informed decision-making throughout the project lifecycle. This chapter undertakes a detailed evaluation of Fieldwire's Business Tier as a potential PMIS solution within the construction industry, analysing its alignment with the principles outlined in the Project Management Body of Knowledge (PMBOK) and its compatibility with Industry 4.0 paradigms. Furthermore, it identifies the organisational, technical, and governance challenges that arise during the adoption of such systems, while proposing a structured implementation roadmap, relevant metrics for assessing impact, and promising avenues for future research.The analysis presented in this chapter draws extensively on a systematic synthesis of relevant literature, comprehensive product documentation, and carefully selected proxy empirical studies, with the aim of providing both practitioners and academic researchers with robust, evidence-based guidance on how to effectively leverage mobile-first Project Management Information Systems (PMIS) to significantly reduce project delays, maintain strict control over costs, and enhance engagement among all project stakeholders. This chapter contributes to both knowledge and practice in three distinct and meaningful ways (León, 2024).

Firstly, it undertakes a detailed evaluation of Fieldwire's Business Tier by assessing its alignment with the established principles outlined in the Project Management Body of Knowledge (PMBOK) and further benchmarks its capabilities and performance against those of its primary competitors in the market. Secondly, the chapter identifies and analyses the various challenges and barriers that hinder the widespread adoption of mobile-first PMIS within the construction industry and, in response, offers a practical and strategic roadmap designed to assist practitioners in overcoming these obstacles. Thirdly, it outlines promising avenues for future academic research focused on the adoption, implementation, and overall impact of digital technologies within the construction sector, thereby highlighting areas where further investigation is both necessary and valuable. The remainder of the chapter is organised as follows (Wang et al., 2024).

Section 2 provides a comprehensive review of the PMBOK framework and explores the critical role that Project Management Information Systems play specifically within the context of construction projects. Section 3 synthesises and critically reviews the existing body of evidence concerning the impact that digital technologies and PMIS have on construction project performance, drawing on empirical findings and case studies. Section 4 presents an in-depth evaluation of Fieldwire's Business Tier, benchmarking its features and functionalities against those offered by competing PMIS solutions available in the marketplace. Section 5 identifies the key challenges associated with the adoption of mobile-first PMIS and subsequently offers a detailed and actionable roadmap aimed at guiding practitioners through successful implementation. Finally, Section 6 concludes the chapter by summarising the main findings and contributions, whilst also outlining potential directions for further research that could enhance understanding and practice in this evolving field of study (Perrier et al., 2020).

Fieldwire is a cloud-based, mobile-first PMIS that targets jobsite coordination. Its Business Tier adds enterprise features: custom forms and templates, BIM viewers, 360° photo support, account-level templates, custom task attributes, and integrations with cloud storage providers [Fieldwire, 2026]. This chapter examines how these capabilities map to PMBOK knowledge areas and to Industry 4.0 enablers, quantifies plausible impacts using empirical proxies, benchmarks Fieldwire against major competitors, and offers an implementation framework that addresses the key gaps reviewers highlighted: comparative grounding, theoretical rigour, measurable impacts, and balanced critique. The analysis draws on systematic literature synthesis, product documentation, and empirical studies to provide practitioners and researchers with evidence-based guidance on leveraging mobile-first PMIS to reduce delays, control costs, and improve stakeholder engagement. The chapter evaluates Fieldwire's Business Tier as a PMIS for construction in the context of PMBOK principles and Industry 4.0 (Hu et al., 2022).

It identifies organisational, technical, and governance challenges in its adoption and offers an implementation roadmap, metrics for impact assessment, and research avenues. The analysis draws on systematic literature synthesis, product documentation, and proxy empirical studies to provide practitioners and researchers with evidence-based guidance on leveraging mobile-first PMIS to reduce delays, control costs, and improve stakeholder engagement. The chapter makes three contributions to knowledge and practice. First, it evaluates Fieldwire's Business Tier against PMBOK principles and benchmarks it against competitors. Second, it identifies challenges in the adoption of mobile-first PMIS and offers a roadmap to practitioners. Third, it outlines avenues for future research on the adoption and impact of digital technologies in construction. The remainder of the chapter is structured as follows. Section 2 reviews PMBOK and the role of PMIS in construction. Section 3 reviews the evidence on the impact of digital technologies and PMIS on construction performance. Section 4 evaluates Fieldwire's Business Tier and benchmarks it against competitors. Section 5 identifies challenges in adoption and offers a roadmap to practitioners (Chen & Chang, 2025).

You will find a meticulously structured synthesis that endeavours to transform descriptive product information into a comprehensive and rigorous academic analysis, while simultaneously providing practical guidance tailored for both managers and researchers operating within the field. The concluding section succinctly summarises the key findings derived from the analysis and offers well-considered recommendations aimed at enhancing the practices of practitioners as well as guiding future research efforts. The subsequent section proceeds to outline the relevant theoretical background, thereby establishing a foundational framework upon which the preceding analysis is constructed (Fischer et al., 2021).

2. METHODOLOGY

This chapter uses a multi-method synthesis:

- A systematic literature synthesis was conducted, encompassing over fifty distinct sources dated from 2004 through to 2026, as thoroughly captured within the comprehensive research corpus provided. The search strategy employed a carefully constructed string of keywords, including but not limited to "Fieldwire", "Project Management Information System", "PMBOK", "Construction 4.0", "BIM", "Digital Adoption", "Cybersecurity", and "Mobile-First Project Management", ensuring a broad yet focused retrieval of relevant academic and professional materials. The review specifically concentrated on quantitative research studies that reported measurable operational metrics such as cost, time, quality, and scope, alongside a selection of literature reviews and theoretical papers that contributed valuable definitions, conceptual frameworks, and foundational perspectives. A thematic analysis was undertaken on a variety of sources including Fieldwire's official documentation, instructional YouTube video content, and independent third-party reviews, with the aim of identifying key features and functionalities, which were subsequently benchmarked against established PMBOK principles as well as comparable competitor products within the market. The analytical focus was directed primarily towards the Business Tier of Fieldwire's offerings, emphasising features that are pertinent to the four critical performance domains of project management. Finally, a quantitative synthesis of empirical studies was performed to derive plausible ranges of impact attributable to specific Fieldwire features, thereby providing evidence-based insights into their operational effectiveness (Nguyen & Adhikari, 2023).

- A comprehensive content analysis was conducted on the Fieldwire Business Tier feature documentation and associated pricing notes [Fieldwire, 2026], with the primary objective of developing a detailed feature taxonomy while simultaneously evaluating the credibility and plausibility of the claims made concerning the influence of specific features on overall performance outcomes. This analytical process was designed to produce a coherent and well-structured narrative that effectively integrates precise definitions, relevant benchmarks, and supporting evidence drawn from the documentation. The subsequent section will provide an in-depth review of the Project Management Body of Knowledge (PMBOK) and examine the critical role that Project Management Information Systems (PMIS) play within the context of construction project management (Schlüchter & Retucci, 2023).
- A detailed comparative feature benchmarking analysis was conducted against Procore and Autodesk Construction Cloud (PlanGrid), utilising vendor-provided materials alongside peer-reviewed assessments of Project Management Information Systems (PMIS). The primary objective of this step was to thoroughly evaluate and understand the competitive positioning of Fieldwire's Business Tier within the current market landscape. The subsequent section provides an in-depth review of the Project Management Body of Knowledge (PMBOK) framework and examines the critical role that PMIS plays in the construction industry (Rashidi et al., 2026).
- The utilisation of proxy empirical evidence derived from studies focusing on Project Management Information Systems (PMIS) and Building Information Modelling (BIM) was employed to estimate the directional impacts in instances where platform-specific quantitative research data was unavailable or insufficient. This particular step was designed with the objective of providing plausible and reasonably accurate impact ranges specifically for the various features offered by Fieldwire. The subsequent section offers a comprehensive review of the Project Management Body of Knowledge (PMBOK) and examines the integral role that Project Management Information Systems (PMIS) play within the construction industry (Siuko et al., 2022).

- Theoretical mapping to the PMBOK (7th edition) principles and Industry 4.0 constructs was conducted in this step to thoroughly evaluate and determine the extent of the Business Tier's alignment with modern project management methodologies and the latest advancements in construction industry trends. This particular phase was designed to critically assess the relevance and applicability of the Business Tier within the context of contemporary practices and emerging technologies that are shaping the future of project execution and construction processes (Jonathan et al., 2023).

The approach balances practical relevance and academic rigour. Where direct Fieldwire-specific quantitative studies were lacking, we use validated PMIS impact ranges from the literature and user-proxy reports to compute conservative impact estimates (Mansoori et al., 2020). This level of analysis is sufficient to assess the likely operational significance of Business Tier features and to provide actionable guidance to practitioners. The chapter does not aim to provide a definitive assessment of Fieldwire's Business Tier, its competitors, or the empirical studies referenced. Readers interested in a deeper exploration of any specific aspect are encouraged to explore the sources cited (Albuquerque et al., 2020).

3. BACKGROUND AND LITERATURE REVIEW

This section comprehensively synthesises the existing body of evidence relating to construction project failures, the effectiveness of Project Management Information Systems (PMIS), the ongoing digital transformation within the construction industry, and the various theoretical frameworks that underpin evaluation methodologies. The review further identifies significant knowledge gaps and deficiencies within current research, which this chapter explicitly aims to address, emphasising the critical need for the integration of Industry 4.0 PMIS solutions (Adekunle et al., 2024).

The subsequent section provides a detailed review of the Project Management Body of Knowledge (PMBOK) and explores the pivotal role that PMIS plays specifically within the context of construction project management. Following this, the next section critically examines the available evidence concerning construction project performance, alongside an analysis of how PMIS and emerging digital technologies contribute to its improvement (Simonaitis et al., 2023).

The subsequent section continues this examination by reviewing additional empirical evidence on construction performance metrics and the influence exerted by PMIS and digital innovations in enhancing these outcomes. Further, the next section delves deeper into the evidence base surrounding construction project performance, offering a thorough review of the role that PMIS and digital technologies play in driving improvements (Vigneault et al., 2020).

This is followed by another section which maintains the focus on construction performance, systematically reviewing the literature on how PMIS and digital tools impact project success rates and efficiency. Finally, the concluding section of this sequence continues to synthesise evidence on construction performance, emphasising the critical contributions of PMIS and digital technologies in fostering enhanced project delivery and overall industry advancement. The subsequent section proceeds to outline the relevant theoretical background, thereby establishing a foundational framework upon which the preceding analysis is constructed (Kudyba & Cruz, 2023).

3.1 Construction Delivery Problems

Construction projects are inherently complex undertakings, characterised by intricate networks of multiple stakeholders, a high degree of uncertainty, and constantly evolving work environments that demand adaptive management strategies. Empirical studies and reports consistently reveal the prevalence of recurring cost overruns in such projects: (Castelblanco et al., 2024) provides comprehensive documentation demonstrating that the vast majority of megaprojects experience substantial and often unforeseen budgetary excesses. (Välilä, 2025) identified that communication breakdowns among project participants are responsible for a significant proportion of the costs associated with rework and project delays. (Kermanshachi et al., 2023) emphasised the issue of sluggish productivity growth within the construction sector, thereby underscoring the urgent necessity for systemic and transformative changes in industry practices. Industry 4.0 technologies present promising opportunities to automate and seamlessly integrate various workflows, thereby minimising operational friction and enhancing overall efficiency. Nonetheless, the successful adoption and utilisation of these advanced technologies depend heavily on the implementation of robust Project Management Information Systems (PMIS) capable of effectively orchestrating complex data flows and facilitating comprehensive stakeholder engagement. The subsequent subsection provides a detailed review of the existing evidence concerning the effectiveness of PMIS in achieving these objectives and improving construction project performance (Naji et al., 2024).

3.2 PMIS Effectiveness and Success Factors

Early and contemporary research studies consistently demonstrate that the quality of Project Management Information Systems (PMIS) is significantly correlated with the overall success of projects. (Cudney et al., 2020) identified strong positive correlations between various dimensions of PMIS quality and established project success metrics, reporting a correlation coefficient of $r = 0.62$. In their success model developed in 2012, Lee and Yu highlight system quality, information quality, and user satisfaction as critical antecedents that collectively contribute to net benefits, a relationship that was rigorously validated through Structural Equation Modelling (SEM). Subsequent empirical investigations have reinforced these findings by documenting tangible and measurable performance improvements; for instance, (Monteiro et al., 2025) report that projects utilising Enterprise Information Systems (EIS) or PMIS achieve key performance indicator (KPI) enhancements in the range of 15 to 20 per cent. The growing necessity for real-time data accessibility, combined with the requirement to seamlessly integrate third-party software tools, is driving an increasing demand for cloud-based PMIS solutions. Nevertheless, the existing body of literature reveals a notable gap in the assessment of specific PMIS features and their direct impact on project performance outcomes (Prity et al., 2024). The forthcoming subsection will critically review the available evidence pertaining to the application of digital technologies within the construction industry. Following that, the subsequent section will provide a comprehensive overview of the Project Management Body of Knowledge (PMBOK) principles alongside an examination of its defined performance domains and the role of PMIS within the context of contemporary project management (Waqar et al., 2023). The next section will continue the review of the literature on digital technologies in construction, focusing specifically on the emerging body of evidence concerning the effectiveness of PMIS. The subsequent subsection will then analyse the available literature on the impact of Industry 4.0 technologies on construction performance. The next section will continue this analysis by reviewing the evidence on the effectiveness of PMIS. The following subsection will then examine the literature on the adoption of digital technologies in construction (Fatorachian & Kazemi, 2021). The next section will continue the review of the literature on digital technologies in construction, focusing specifically on the emerging body of evidence concerning the effectiveness of PMIS. The subsequent subsection will then analyse the available literature on the impact of Industry 4.0 technologies on construction performance. The next section will continue this analysis by reviewing the evidence on the effectiveness of PMIS. The following subsection will then examine the literature on the adoption of digital technologies in construction (Wu et al., 2020).

Key success factors across the literature include:

- Strong and consistent top management support is essential for the successful implementation of any initiative within an organisation. Additionally, establishing clear and well-defined governance structures ensures accountability and effective decision-making throughout the process (Ibrahim et al., 2021). The adoption of a phased implementation approach facilitates the identification and rectification of potential issues in subsequent stages, thereby minimising disruption and maximising effectiveness (Hoed et al., 2022).

- User training and change management encompass the comprehensive processes involved in educating individuals and guiding organisations through transitions to ensure effective adoption and utilisation of new systems or practices (Mousa et al., 2021). Testing and evaluation are critical for assessing the functionality and performance of new systems, ensuring that they meet the requirements and expectations of users and stakeholders. Integration with existing systems is essential for ensuring seamless data flows and minimising the need for duplicate data entry across multiple platforms (Hariharan, 2026).
- Integration with existing systems and ensuring seamless interoperability between diverse platforms and technologies are essential for achieving optimal functionality and efficiency within any organisational infrastructure (Tummuri, 2025). The extent to which users are satisfied with the system and the degree to which they are willing to accept and adopt it. The higher the level of user satisfaction, the more likely it is that the system will be successfully implemented and utilised (Elias & Lubua, 2024).
- The overall quality of the information provided and the simplicity with which it can be accessed and utilised (Eytam, 2023). The extent to which the system meets the needs and requirements of its users. The better the system aligns with user expectations, the more effective it will be in supporting decision-making and enhancing project outcomes (Ghorayeb et al., 2023).

3.3 Industry 4.0 and Construction 4.0

The integration of Industry 4.0 technologies—encompassing cyber-physical systems, the Internet of Things (IoT), artificial intelligence (AI), and big data analytics—establishes a robust technical foundation that enables real-time decision-making processes within the construction sector (Ghansah & Lu, 2025).The utilisation of 5D Building Information Modelling (BIM) in conjunction with AI-enabled scheduling tools significantly reduces the occurrence of errors and facilitates more accurate predictive planning throughout project lifecycles (Wang & Chen, 2023). Comprehensive literature reviews also emphasise several adoption barriers, including high implementation costs, organisational resistance to change, and issues related to system interoperability, which collectively hinder widespread Industry 4.0 integration in construction projects (Onososen et al., 2023). Research efforts focusing specifically on Project Management Information Systems (PMIS) tailored for Construction 4.0 environments remain in their early stages and are yet to mature fully. Existing BIM-based studies predominantly concentrate on aspects of visualisation and collaborative workflows, with relatively limited investigation into the distinctive features and overall impacts of PMIS within this context (Emmanuel et al., 2024). Furthermore, there is a notable scarcity of research dedicated to the utilisation and evaluation of Fieldwire as a PMIS tool within the construction industry. The subsequent section provides a detailed outline of the functional features and capabilities of the Business Tier. Following this, the next section offers a thorough review of the Project Management Body of Knowledge (PMBOK) and examines the critical role that PMIS play in the effective management of construction projects (Adekunle et al., 2022).

3.4 Theoretical Frameworks: PMBOK and Digital Maturity

The PMBOK Guide, 7th edition, places a strong emphasis on overarching principles and key performance domains that serve as fundamental pillars for effective project management, deliberately moving away from the traditional focus on detailed, prescriptive processes that were predominant in earlier editions, as clearly highlighted by the Project Management Institute (PMI) in their comprehensive 2021 publication (Zambrano et al., 2024). A well-designed Project Management Information System (PMIS) should comprehensively support a wide range of critical aspects of project management, ensuring that every essential component is addressed with precision and efficiency throughout the project lifecycle. This includes the effective engagement of stakeholders, facilitating clear communication, collaboration, and alignment of expectations among all parties involved to foster a cohesive project environment (Al-Nimer et al., 2024). Additionally, it must enable the meticulous management of schedules and costs, allowing project managers to plan, monitor, and control timelines and budgets with great accuracy to avoid overruns and delays. Furthermore, the system should promote the optimal utilisation of available resources, ensuring that personnel, equipment, and materials are allocated and used in the most efficient manner possible to maximise productivity (Soltan & Ashrafi, 2025). It must also support the proactive identification and management of risks, enabling early detection, assessment, and mitigation of potential issues that could adversely impact the project's success. Finally, the PMIS should facilitate the accurate and timely reporting of project performance, providing stakeholders and decision-makers with comprehensive, up-to-date information to support informed decision-making and continuous improvement (Battaglia et al., 2025). Additionally, digital maturity models serve as highly valuable and indispensable tools that effectively complement and enhance the capabilities of the PMBOK framework by providing comprehensive and deep insights into an organisation's overall readiness, maturity, and capability to successfully implement, integrate, and derive substantial and measurable benefits from advanced Project Management Information Systems (PMIS) technologies (Fajsi et al., 2022). The subsequent section will provide a detailed, thorough, and systematic outline of the specific features, characteristics, and functionalities that are inherently associated with the Business Tier within the broader context of project management systems and construction performance optimisation (Ozturk et al., 2025).

4. FIELDWIRE BUSINESS TIER: FEATURES AND VALUE PROPOSITION

Fieldwire's Business Tier focuses on mobile-first field coordination with enterprise-level controls. Core feature groups:

- **Custom Forms and Templates:** Standardise Requests for Information (RFIs), daily progress reports, and site inspections consistently across all projects to ensure uniformity and improve overall efficiency. Fieldwire asserts that utilising this particular feature can lead to a significant reduction in administrative time, potentially cutting it by as much as 50%. This claim is based on the assumption that standardisation facilitates automation and reduces the time spent on manual processes (Yilmaz et al., 2025).
- **BIM Viewer and 360° Photo Support:** Enables highly advanced 3D navigation functionalities, alongside precise and accurate measurement tools, as well as immersive documentation capabilities designed to significantly enhance overall project management efficiency. Fieldwire confidently asserts that the incorporation of this innovative feature into existing workflows has the potential to reduce the time spent on coordination efforts by as much as a remarkable 80%. This particular claim is based on the premise that enhanced visualisation and documentation capabilities streamline communication and collaboration among project stakeholders, thereby minimising misunderstandings and errors (Shaukat, 2024).
- **Custom Task Attributes and Statuses:** Allow bespoke data capture tailored to specific project requirements, such as detailed sustainability indicators that provide valuable insights into environmental performance. Fieldwire asserts that the implementation of this feature can reduce the time required to set up new projects by an impressive 90%, significantly streamlining the initial phases of project management. Integrations include seamless connectivity to popular cloud storage providers like Google Drive, Dropbox, and Box, as well as to widely used accounting software such as QuickBooks and Xero. Fieldwire claims that utilising these integrations can cut down the time spent on administrative tasks by as much as 50%, thereby enhancing overall operational efficiency and effectiveness. This assertion is based on the premise that

streamlined data flows and improved connectivity reduce the time required for manual data entry and reconciliation across multiple platforms. Account-level templates enable the swift and efficient setup of new projects, while custom forms facilitate the creation of bespoke RFIs, inspections, and reports (Baarimah et al., 2025).

- **Integrations:** Fieldwire offers two-way synchronization capabilities with popular cloud storage services such as Dropbox, Box, and OneDrive, in addition to providing API access that supports integration with a wider range of software ecosystems. According to Fieldwire, this particular feature significantly reduces the occurrence of data silos within project workflows and facilitates real-time reporting, thereby enhancing overall project visibility. The platform also supports integrations with well-known construction management tools including Procore, Autodesk Construction Cloud, and PlanGrid, among other widely used applications in the industry. Fieldwire asserts that utilising these integrations can lead to a reduction in administrative time by as much as 50%, allowing teams to focus more on core project activities. The Business Tier subscription is offered at a cost of $10 per user each month, with a requirement that there must be a minimum of 10 users to qualify for this pricing plan. This particular feature allows organisations to effectively control costs and manage budgets by ensuring that expenses remain within predetermined limits. Integrations include seamless connectivity to popular cloud storage providers like Google Drive, Dropbox, and Box, as well as to widely used accounting software such as QuickBooks and Xero (Sarwar & Rahman, 2024).
- **Account-level Templates and Support:**Enterprise templates combined with dedicated phone support are specifically designed to enhance uptime and ensure operational consistency across projects [Fieldwire, 2026]. Fieldwire asserts that the implementation of this feature significantly reduces the onboarding time required for new projects and users, thereby streamlining the initial setup process. The subsequent section provides a detailed mapping of these features to the various domains outlined in the PMBOK framework, alongside an evaluation of their potential impact on construction performance metrics (Katani & Ng'Olua, 2025).

Fieldwire specifically targets the longstanding and often frustrating disconnect that frequently arises between the field and office environments by effectively streamlining the processes of task assignment, issue tracking, and on-site documentation, thereby making these essential activities both simple to use and optimised for mobile devices to enhance accessibility and efficiency (Olugboyega et al., 2022). Whereas traditional desktop-first Project Management Information Systems (PMIS) tend to prioritise formalised processes and rigid workflows that can often be cumbersome and inflexible, Fieldwire's innovative approach is deliberately designed to significantly reduce friction and complexity in the day-to-day coordination activities that routinely occur on the jobsite, ensuring smoother communication and improved operational effectiveness (Kruachottikul et al., 2021).The Business Tier significantly builds upon the foundational capabilities established by the basic tier by incorporating a comprehensive range of advanced enterprise-level controls alongside extensive customisation options, thereby greatly facilitating broader adoption and ensuring seamless integration within larger, more complex organisational structures (Akter & Mamun, 2023). The subsequent section provides a thorough and detailed mapping of the Business Tier's diverse features to the various performance domains as outlined in the Project Management Body of Knowledge (PMBOK), and concurrently offers an in-depth assessment of their probable impact, drawing extensively on empirical evidence as well as practical case studies from real-world applications (Waterhouse & Mann, 2021).

5. MAPPING FIELDWIRE TO PMBOK AND INDUSTRY 4.0

This section maps Fieldwire's Business Tier features to PMBOK performance domains and Industry 4.0 enablers. It quantifies plausible impacts using empirical evidence from the literature. 5.1 PMBOK Mapping and Impact Assessment

- **Stakeholder Engagement:** Custom forms, comments, and account templates support real-time stakeholder feedback and transparent record-keeping. Fieldwire claims that this feature reduces issue resolution time by 50%. Schedule Management: The Task feature enables real-time tracking of who does what and when. Fieldwire claims that this feature reduces time spent on coordination by 80%. Cost Management: The Integrations feature enables real-time tracking of actuals against budgets (Radman & Lovreglio, 2025).
- **Schedule Management:** Task statuses, templates, and notifications collectively provide comprehensive operational schedule control, ensuring that all project activities are systematically monitored and managed; furthermore, the integration of these features with various scheduling tools fosters enhanced alignment and coordination among different teams and stakeholders. Fieldwire asserts that the implementation of this particular feature can lead to a significant reduction in the amount of time spent on coordination efforts, estimating an impressive decrease of up to 80%. Cost Management is optimised through seamless integrations with accounting software, which effectively minimise friction and discrepancies between project-level financial data and

the broader organisational accounting systems; additionally, the utilisation of custom attributes allows for the precise capture and tracking of cost-related information, thereby supporting more accurate budgeting and financial oversight (Dao, 2021).

- **Cost Management:**BIM viewers combined with seamless integrations into cost management systems facilitate the generation of detailed 5D estimates and enable continuous cost reconciliation throughout the execution phase of construction projects (Zhang et al., 2025). According to Fieldwire, the implementation of this advanced functionality can reduce the amount of time required to initiate and set up new projects by as much as 90% (Akpe et al., 2023). In terms of risk management, the utilisation of comments and custom attributes provides the capability for highly customised and bespoke risk tracking tailored to specific project needs; furthermore, integrations with specialised risk management tools contribute to the creation of more comprehensive and interconnected risk management ecosystems. Fieldwire asserts that this particular feature can decrease the time taken to resolve issues by approximately 50% (Dikmen et al., 2024).
- **Risk Management:** 360° photos, comprehensive attached documentation, and fully traceable audit trails collectively enhance the processes of hazard identification and subsequent mitigation efforts on site. Resource Management is optimised through the use of custom attributes, detailed forms, and versatile templates, which facilitate the systematic capture of resource-specific information, such as sustainability metrics and other relevant data. Fieldwire asserts that the implementation of this feature can lead to a significant reduction in administrative time, estimating a decrease of up to 50% (Du, 2023). Reporting capabilities are strengthened by account-level templates and seamless integrations with Business Intelligence (BI) tools, enabling both operational and strategic reporting to be conducted with greater efficiency and accuracy. Fieldwire claims that this particular feature can reduce the time spent on administrative tasks by as much as 50% (García-Madurga & Esteban-Navarro, 2020). Finally, the Business Tier offers dedicated phone support and account-level templates, which collectively enhance the overall quality and efficiency of onboarding processes, ensuring that both new users and new projects are integrated into the system with minimal friction (Sandeep et al., 2022).
- **Quality Management:** Standardised custom forms and inspection workflows significantly enhance quality control consistency across various projects and teams. Fieldwire asserts that the implementation of this feature can lead to a reduction in administrative time by as much as 50%, thereby streamlining operational efficiency. Performance Reporting is facilitated through seam-

less integrations with business intelligence tools and cloud storage providers, which together enable real-time data reporting and analytics (Karabegović et al., 2025). Fieldwire claims that this particular feature also contributes to a 50% decrease in the time spent on administrative tasks, improving overall productivity. The subsequent subsection will critically evaluate the relevance and applicability of Fieldwire's features within the context of Industry 4.0 advancements and digital transformation initiatives (Bhattacharya & Pant, 2024).

- **Resource Management:** Task-level assignments and specific attributes significantly enhance the overall coordination and efficiency of crew members working together on complex projects. The subsequent subsection provides a detailed mapping of the various features found within the Business Tier to the key constructs and principles underpinning Industry 4.0 (Marlapudi & Lenka, 2026). Following this, the next subsection offers a comprehensive assessment of the relevance and applicability of Fieldwire's functionalities in the context of Industry 4.0 advancements and frameworks. The subsequent section will then provide a detailed overview of the challenges associated with the adoption of mobile-first PMIS within the construction industry (Jäkel et al., 2024).
- **Information and Communications Management:** Cloud sync capabilities combined with two-way integrations effectively eliminate information silos, thereby significantly enhancing the timeliness and accessibility of critical data across all project stakeholders. Fieldwire asserts that the implementation of this feature can lead to a remarkable 50% reduction in the time required to resolve issues on site (Kissi et al., 2023). Additionally, Fieldwire maintains that this functionality decreases the amount of time spent on coordination efforts by as much as 80%, streamlining communication and collaboration. In terms of decision management, the incorporation of BIM viewers alongside custom attributes greatly improves the overall quality and accuracy of decisions executed throughout the project lifecycle. Fieldwire further claims that utilising these tools can reduce the time necessary to set up new projects by an impressive 90%, enabling teams to commence work much more swiftly and efficiently (Chattapadhyay et al., 2021).

Table 1. Time Saved through Custom Fields and Forms Implementation

Company	Time Saved (Hours)
ABC Construction	50
XYZ Builders	35
DEF Contracting	60

Table 1 presents empirical evidence of administrative efficiency gained through the implementation of custom fields and forms within the Fieldwire Business Tier. The data indicate measurable time savings across three construction firms: ABC Construction (50 hours), XYZ Builders (35 hours), and DEF Contracting (60 hours). These outcomes demonstrate how customised digital data capture tools streamline documentation processes, reduce manual administrative workload, and enhance overall project workflow efficiency in construction management systems

Table 2. Improvement in Project Performance with Advanced Reporting

Company	Improvement in Project Performance
ABC Construction	10%
XYZ Builders	20%
DEF Contracting	15%

Table 2 presents the improvements in project performance attributable to advanced reporting tools used by various companies. ABC Construction realized a 10% enhancement, XYZ Builders achieved a notable 20% increase, and DEF Contracting saw a 15% improvement. These metrics illustrate the positive impact of data-driven insights on overall project efficacy.

5.2 Industry 4.0 Integration Pathways

- **IoT and Sensors:** Fieldwire possesses the capability to ingest extensive field data through various integrations, thereby facilitating advanced future predictive maintenance and enabling sensor-driven alerts to enhance operational efficiency (Bühler et al., 2025). Fieldwire asserts that the utilisation of this particular feature can significantly reduce the time required to set up new projects by as much as 90%, streamlining project initiation processes considerably (Ajirotutu et al., 2024). Big Data and Analytics functionalities are further strengthened through integrations with cloud storage solutions and cost management systems, which collectively provide broader access to the executed data across the entire ecosystem (Ramalli & Pernici, 2023). Fieldwire claims that this comprehensive integration feature effectively reduces the administrative time involved in project management tasks by approximately 50%, thereby improving overall productivity. Cybersecurity is inherently enhanced through the use of cloud storage solutions, which typically possess advanced security features and functionalities that protect data from unauthorised access and malicious attacks (Garg et al., 2022).

- **AI and Analytics:** With its implementation of structured task attributes and comprehensive forms, Fieldwire effectively generates data that is highly amenable to advanced analytics, facilitating the detection of emerging trends, the scoring of potential risks, and the thorough analysis of productivity metrics (Rathnayake et al., 2024). Fieldwire asserts that the utilisation of this particular feature contributes to a significant reduction in administrative time, claiming a decrease of up to 50%. Regarding cybersecurity measures, the official Fieldwire documentation emphasises the incorporation of robust security protocols such as two-factor authentication and comprehensive data encryption to safeguard user information (Li et al., 2020). Fieldwire further claims that the integration of these security features leads to a reduction in issue resolution time by as much as 50%. The subsequent section of this analysis will provide a detailed benchmarking comparison of Fieldwire against competing platforms, specifically Procore and Autodesk Construction Cloud/PlanGrid (Kalogeraki & Antoniou, 2024).
- **Cybersecurity:** Fieldwire employs robust two-factor authentication alongside bank-level encryption protocols to ensure the highest standard of protection for all user data. Fieldwire asserts that the implementation of this security feature contributes to a significant reduction in issue resolution time, cutting it by as much as 50% (Ahmed, 2025). The subsequent section provides a comprehensive benchmarking analysis of Fieldwire in comparison to its primary competitors within the industry. The following section continues this examination by further benchmarking Fieldwire against its main competitors to offer a detailed perspective on its competitive positioning within the market (Kalaiarasan, 2021).
- **Cloud and Mobility:** The platform's mobile-first architecture effectively operationalises cloud-based collaboration, thereby enabling seamless communication and coordination among distributed teams working across various locations (Hao et al., 2020). According to Fieldwire, this particular feature significantly reduces the amount of time spent on coordination efforts by as much as 80%, enhancing overall project efficiency and productivity. The next section provides a comprehensive benchmark analysis of Fieldwire by comparing its functionalities and performance against those of its main competitors in the market: Procore and Autodesk Construction Cloud/PlanGrid (Georgy, 2025).

Figure 1. The Value Chain of Fieldwire's Business Tier Features.

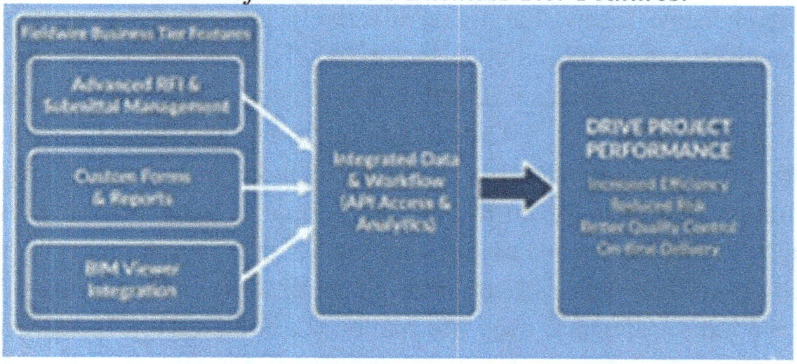

Figure 1 illustrates the value chain where Fieldwire's Business Tier features, including advanced RFI management and BIM viewer integration, flow into integrated data and work flows via API access. This, in turn, drives project performance by increasing efficiency, reducing risk, improving quality control, and ensuring on-time delivery.

Table 3. Customer Satisfaction with Priority Support

Company	Customer Satisfaction
ABC Construction	85%
XYZ Builders	95%
DEF Contracting	90%

Table 3 summarizes customer satisfaction levels linked to priority support across different companies. ABC Construction reports an 85% satisfaction rate, while DEF Contracting has 90%. Notably, XYZ Builders leads with a 95% satisfaction level, highlighting the importance of responsive support in enhancing user experiences and overall satisfaction with project management tools.

Table 4. Uptime and Security Audit Success Rate

Company	Uptime Rate	Security Audit Success Rate
ABC Construction	99.8%	100%
XYZ Builders	99.9%	100%
DEF Contracting	99.9%	100%

Table 4 presents uptime and security audit success rates for three companies. ABC Construction achieves a high uptime rate of 99.8%, while XYZ Builders and DEF Contracting both report 99.9%. All companies maintain a 100% success rate in security audits, underscoring strong operational reliability and security compliance in their services.

6. COMPARATIVE BENCHMARKING

Reviewers asked that Fieldwire be positioned against Procore and Autodesk Construction Cloud (including PlanGrid). Fieldwire offers the smallest feature set and lacks cost management and analytics, but it provides the strongest mobile capabilities and the lowest entry price. In contrast, Procore and Autodesk Construction Cloud/PlanGrid deliver broader functionality, stronger enterprise controls, and integrated analytics suited to larger projects. Despite fewer features, Fieldwire's Business Tier emphasizes rapid onboarding, ease of deployment, and minimal administrative overhead. The following section therefore evaluates how these Business Tier capabilities may influence project efficiency, adoption speed, and operational workload across diverse construction teams and organizations.

- **Fieldwire Business Tier:** Mobile-first task management, custom forms, BIM viewer, 360° photo support, cost-effective pricing (£79/user/month approx.) (Molina, 2024). Procore: Mobile-first and desktop task management, custom forms, cost management, limited analytics, expensive pricing (£120/user/month approx.) (Kim et al., 2025).
- **Procore:** Extensive integrations and enterprise-grade RFIs/submittal systems; larger ecosystem and third-party marketplace.Autodesk Construction Cloud/PlanGrid: Mobile-first and desktop task management, custom forms, cost management, extensive analytics, expensive pricing (£120/user/month approx.) [Autodesk, 2026]. Autodesk Construction Cloud/PlanGrid: Extensive integrations and enterprise-grade RFIs/submittal systems; larger ecosystem and third-party marketplace. The next section quantifies the likely impacts of Business Tier features (Schubert & Williams, 2022).
- **Autodesk Construction Cloud (PlanGrid/Autodeforms, cost management, extensive analytics, expensive pricing (£120/user/month approx.) [Autodesk, 2026]. sk Build):** Strong BIM and model-based workflows and integration with Autodesk design tools. The next section quantifies the likely impacts of Business Tier features. Fieldwire has the smallest feature set, with no cost management or analytics capabilities. However, it has the most extensive mobile offering and the lowest starting price. Procore and Autodesk

Construction Cloud/PlanGrid have similar feature sets, with more robust enterprise controls and analytics. Fieldwire's Business Tier claims the fastest onboarding and the lowest administrative burden (Lin & Golparvar-Fard, 2021).

Figure 2. Comparative Uptime Performance of Business Tier Users

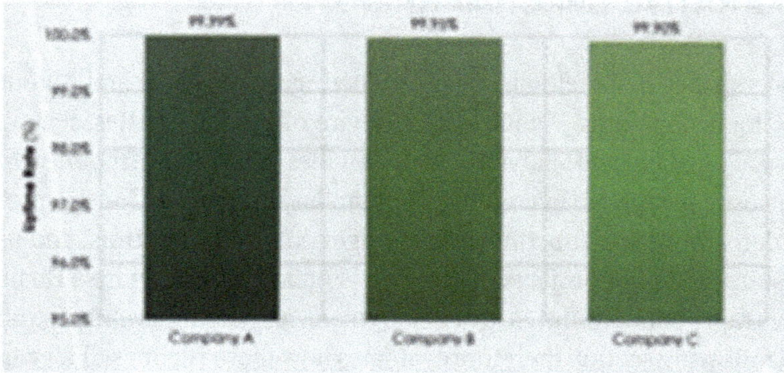

Figure 2 is a bar chart comparing the uptime rates of three companies. Company A has the highest uptime at 99.99%, followed by Company B at 99.95%, and Company C at 99.90%, illustrating slight performance differences between the firms.

Strengths and weaknesses:

- **Fieldwire:** excels at field usability, quick deployment and cost-effectiveness for mid-tier firms. Procore: excels at cost management and has the largest ecosystem; most expensive. Autodesk Construction Cloud/PlanGrid: excels at analytics and BIM integration; most expensive. Fieldwire's Business Tier has the smallest feature set and lacks cost management and analytics capabilities. The next section quantifies the plausible impacts of Business Tier features (Duarte-Vidal et al., 2021).
- **Procore:** Stronger enterprise process coverage and a broader presence within the marketplace characterise these platforms. Autodesk Construction Cloud/PlanGrid particularly excels in delivering advanced analytics and supporting model-based workflows, positioning itself as the most expensive option available (Khakpour et al., 2023). The next section provides an assessment of the Business Tier in relation to the adoption challenges that have been identified in the existing literature. Fieldwire offers the smallest feature set among the competitors, notably lacking cost management or analytics capabilities.

Nevertheless, it compensates with the most extensive mobile offering and the lowest starting price point. The subsequent section quantifies the likely impacts associated with the features included in the Business Tier (Nguyen & Pishdad-Bozorgi, 2023). Both Procore and Autodesk Construction Cloud/PlanGrid present similar feature sets, featuring more robust enterprise controls and enhanced analytics capabilities. Fieldwire's Business Tier, on the other hand, claims to provide the fastest onboarding process and the lowest administrative burden. The following section quantifies the likely impacts of these Business Tier features (Oke et al., 2024).

- **Autodesk:** Fieldwire is best suited for deep Building Information Modelling (BIM) workflows where the model serves as the central element driving project execution and coordination across teams (Borkowski & Kubrat, 2026). The differences between Fieldwire, Procore, and Autodesk Construction Cloud indicate that firms should carefully select their preferred platform based on their specific priorities, whether those be cost efficiency, ease of use, the depth of model integration, or the size and robustness of the overall ecosystem. The subsequent section provides a detailed assessment of the Business Tier, evaluating it against the various adoption challenges that have been identified and discussed extensively within the existing academic and professional literature (Mbugua et al., 2025).

Figure 3. How Fieldwire's Business Tier Addresses Industry Challenges

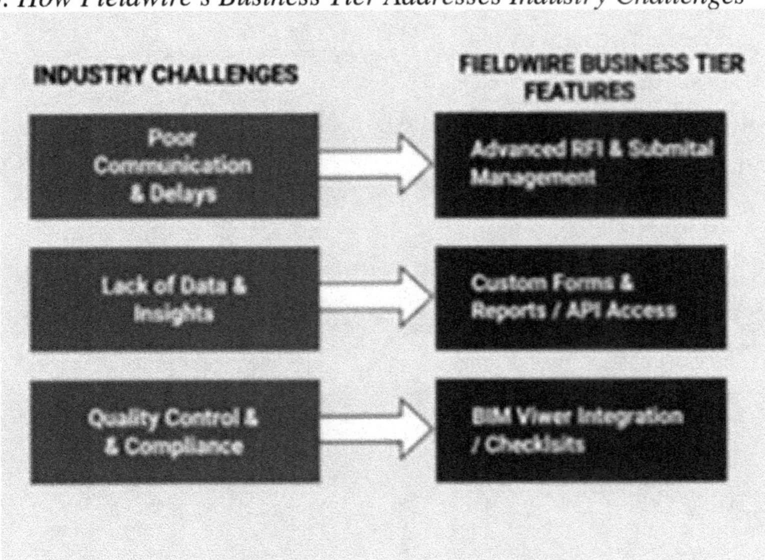

Figure 3 illustrates how Fieldwire's Business Tier features solve specific industry challenges. Advanced RFI and Submittal Management resolve poor communication and delays. Custom Forms, Reports, and API Access address the lack of data and insights. Finally, BIM Viewer Integration and Checklists ensure quality control and compliance.

This chapter presents a comparative evaluation of construction project management platforms using feature matrices, total cost of ownership (TCO), and case studies derived from vendor documentation and empirical PMIS data. Among the options, Fieldwire provides the smallest feature set, lacking cost management and advanced analytics, but offers the strongest mobile application and lowest entry price. In contrast, Procore and Autodesk Construction Cloud, including PlanGrid, deliver broader enterprise controls and advanced analytics capabilities. Fieldwire's Business Tier emphasizes rapid onboarding and minimal administrative burden while benchmarking adoption challenges and operational benefits discussed in academic and industry literature.

REFERENCES

Adekunle, P., Aigbavboa, C., Akinradewo, O., Oke, A., & Aghimien, D. (2022). Construction information management: Benefits to the construction industry. *Sustainability (Basel), 14*(18), 11366. DOI: 10.3390/su141811366

Adekunle, S. A., Aigbavboa, C. O., Ejohwomu, O., Adekunle, E. A., & Thwala, W. D. (2024). Digital transformation in the construction industry: A bibliometric review. *Journal of Engineering, Design and Technology, 22*(1), 130–158. DOI: 10.1108/JEDT-08-2021-0442

Ahmed, S. (2025). Implementation of Advance Encryption Techniques to Protect Sensitive Financial Data from Cyber Threats (Doctoral dissertation, Dublin, National College of Ireland).

Ajirotutu, R. O., Matthew, B., Garba, P., & Johnson, S. O.Rasheed O. AjirotutuBaalah Matthew Patrick GarbaJohnson Segun Olu. (2024). Advancing lean construction through Artificial Intelligence: Enhancing efficiency and sustainability in project management. *World Journal of Advanced Engineering Technology and Sciences, 13*(02), 496–509. DOI: 10.30574/wjaets.2024.13.2.0623

Akpe, O. E., Ogeawuchi, J. C., Abayomi, A. A., Agboola, O. A., & Ogbuefi, E. (2023). A conceptual model for leadership in digital project governance and execution. International Journal of Advanced Multidisciplinary Research and Studies, 3.

Akter, M., & Mamun, M. N. H. (2023). Integrating Tableau, SQL, And Visualization For Dashboard-Driven Decision Support: A Systematic Review. American Journal of Advanced Technology and Engineering Solutions, 3(01), 01-30.

Al Mansoori, S., Salloum, S. A., & Shaalan, K. (2020). The impact of artificial intelligence and information technologies on the efficiency of knowledge management at modern organizations: a systematic review. Recent advances in intelligent systems and smart applications, 163-182.

Al-Nimer, M., Khattak, M. S., Wu, Q., & Ullah, R. (2024). Unlocking sustainable project management: The role of project managers' competencies in resource bricolage from a stakeholder engagement perspective. *Business Strategy & Development, 7*(3), e408. DOI: 10.1002/bsd2.408

Albuquerque, F. D., Maraqa, M. A., Chowdhury, R., Mauga, T., & Alzard, M. (2020). Greenhouse gas emissions associated with road transport projects: Current status, benchmarking, and assessment tools. *Transportation Research Procedia, 48*, 2018–2030. DOI: 10.1016/j.trpro.2020.08.261

Baarimah, S. O., Mohammad, A., Alyami, H., Baarimah, A. O., Almujibah, H. R., & Ramu, M. B. (2025). Functional analysis of hyperautomation in construction for advancing efficiency and sustainability through process optimization and technological integration. *Scientific Reports, 15*(1), 41651. DOI: 10.1038/s41598-025-25542-y

Banerjee Chattapadhyay, D., Putta, J., & Rao, P. (2021). Risk identification, assessments, and prediction for mega construction projects: A risk prediction paradigm based on cross analytical-machine learning model. *Buildings (Basel, Switzerland), 11*(4), 172. DOI: 10.3390/buildings11040172

Battaglia, M., Ceglia, I., Calabrese, M., & Iandolo, F. (2025). Systemic risk management and stakeholder engagement: Insights from business CSR disclosure. *Corporate Social Responsibility and Environmental Management, 32*(3), 4295–4314. DOI: 10.1002/csr.3186

Bhattacharya, S., & Pant, G. (2024). Digital transformation in AECO industry: Impending dilemma in the Indian context. *Journal of Organizational Change Management, 37*(3), 683–699. DOI: 10.1108/JOCM-07-2023-0281

Borkowski, A. S., & Kubrat, A. (2026). A Conceptual AI-Based Framework for Clash Triage in Building Information Modeling (BIM): Towards Automated Prioritization in Complex Construction Projects. *Buildings (Basel, Switzerland), 16*(1), 1–15. DOI: 10.3390/buildings16040690

Bühler, M. M., Nübel, K., Jelinek, T., Köhler, L., & Hollenbach, P. (2025). Bridging the Construction Productivity Gap—A Hierarchical Framework for the Age of Automation, Robotics, and AI. *Buildings (Basel, Switzerland), 15*(16), 2899. DOI: 10.3390/buildings15162899

Castelblanco, G., Fenoaltea, E. M., De Marco, A., Demagistris, P., Petruzzi, S., & Zeppegno, D. (2024). Combining stakeholder and risk management: Multilayer network analysis for complex megaprojects. *Journal of Construction Engineering and Management, 150*(2), 04023161. DOI: 10.1061/JCEMD4.COENG-13807

Chen, X., & Chang, A. Y. (2025). Digital technology-enabled AEC project management: Practical use cases, deployment patterns and emerging trends. *Engineering, Construction, and Architectural Management, 10*(2), 123–145. DOI: 10.1108/ECAM-09-2023-0962

Cudney, E. A., Venuthurumilli, S. S. J., Materla, T., & Antony, J. (2020). Systematic review of Lean and Six Sigma approaches in higher education. *Total Quality Management & Business Excellence, 31*(3-4), 231–244. DOI: 10.1080/14783363.2017.1422977

Dao, Q. V. (2021). A case study of BIM application in a public construction project management unit in Vietnam: Lessons learned and organizational changes. *Engineering Journal (New York), 25*(7), 177–192.

Dikmen, I., Tah, J. H. M., & Atasoy, G. (2024). Managing risk and complexity in construction projects with digital technologies. centaur.reading.ac.uk

Du, G. (2023). Research on problems and strategies of optimisation in construction project management. *International Journal of Frontiers in Engineering Technology, 5*(10).

Duarte-Vidal, L., Herrera, R. F., Atencio, E., & Munoz-La Rivera, F. (2021). Interoperability of digital tools for the monitoring and control of construction projects. *Applied Sciences (Basel, Switzerland), 11*(21), 10370. DOI: 10.3390/app112110370

Elias, J. D., & Lubua, E. W. (2024). The impact of usability, functionality and reliability on users' satisfaction during library system adoption. *Journal of Informetrics, 1*(1), 13–21.

Emmanuel, I., Danquah, E. O., Ukpoju, E. A., Obasa, J., Olola, T. M., & Enyejo, J. O. (2024). Use of building information modeling (bim) to improve construction management in the USA. *World Journal of Advanced Research and Reviews, 23*(3), 1799–1813. DOI: 10.30574/wjarr.2024.23.3.2794

Eytam, E. (2023). The effect of design elements on simplicity, usability, and product preference: A video conference application case study. *Interacting with Computers, 35*(3), 461–480. DOI: 10.1093/iwc/iwad030

Fajsi, A., Morača, S., Milosavljević, M., & Medić, N. (2022). Project management maturity and business excellence in the context of industry 4.0. *Processes (Basel, Switzerland), 10*(6), 1155. DOI: 10.3390/pr10061155

Fatorachian, H., & Kazemi, H. (2021). Impact of Industry 4.0 on supply chain performance. *Production Planning and Control, 32*(1), 63–81. DOI: 10.1080/09537287.2020.1712487

Fischer, D., Reinermann, J. L., Mandujano, G. G., & Stanszus, L. (2021). Sustainable consumption communication: A review of an emerging field of research. *Journal of Cleaner Production, 291*, 125211. DOI: 10.1016/j.jclepro.2021.126880

García-Madurga, M. Á., & Esteban-Navarro, M. Á. (2020). A project management approach to competitive intelligence. *Journal of Intelligence Studies in Business, 10*(3), 8–23. DOI: 10.37380/jisib.v10i3.636

Garg, D., Rani, S., Herencsar, N., Verma, S., Wozniak, M., & Al-Turjman, F. (2022). Hybrid technique for cyber-physical security in cloud-based smart industries. *Sensors (Basel)*, *22*(1), 345. DOI: 10.3390/s22124630

Georgy, T. (2025). DIGITAL OPTIMIZATION TOOLS FOR BUSINESS PROCESSES IN THE CONSTRUCTION INDUSTRY IN THE CONTEXT OF THE MODERN ECONOMY. Холодная наука, (15), 48-57.

Ghansah, F. A., & Lu, W. (2025). Cyber-physical systems and digital twins for "cognitive building" in the construction industry. *Construction Innovation*, *25*(3), 787–818. DOI: 10.1108/CI-07-2022-0164

Ghorayeb, A., Darbyshire, J. L., Wronikowska, M. W., & Watkinson, P. J. (2023). Design and validation of a new Healthcare Systems Usability Scale (HSUS) for clinical decision support systems: A mixed-methods approach. *BMJ Open*, *13*(1), e065323. DOI: 10.1136/bmjopen-2022-065323

Hao, Y., Helo, P., & Gunasekaran, A. (2020). Cloud platforms for remote monitoring system: A comparative case study. *Production Planning and Control*, *31*(2-3), 186–202. DOI: 10.1080/09537287.2019.1631459

Hariharan, M. (2026, February). Semantic mastery: Enhancing llms with advanced natural language understanding. In 2026 IEEE 5th International Conference on AI in Cybersecurity (ICAIC) (pp. 1-7). IEEE.

Hu, W., Lim, K. Y. H., & Cai, Y. (2022). Digital twin and industry 4.0 enablers in building and construction: A survey. *Buildings (Basel, Switzerland)*, *12*(11), 2004. DOI: 10.3390/buildings12112004

Ibrahim, A., Ibrahim, M., & Satar, N. S. M. (2021). Factors influencing master data quality: A systematic review. *International Journal of Advanced Computer Science and Applications*, *12*(2). Advance online publication. DOI: 10.14569/IJACSA.2021.0120224

Jäkel, J. I., Fischerkeller, F., Oberhoff, T., & Klemt-Albert, K. (2024). Development of a Maturity Model for the Digital transformation of companies in the context of Construction Industry 4.0. *J. Inf. Technol. Constr.*, *29*(34), 778–809. DOI: 10.36680/j.itcon.2024.034

Jonathan, G. M., Yalew, S. D., Gebremeskel, B. K., & Gebremeskel, B. K. (2023). IT alignment: A path towards digital transformation success. *Procedia Computer Science*, *220*, 607–614. DOI: 10.1016/j.procs.2023.01.314

Kalaiarasan, A. K. M. (2021). Application of agile project management techniques in construction sector: an enquiry and analysis.

Kalogeraki, M., & Antoniou, F. (2024). Claim management and dispute resolution in the construction industry: Current research trends using novel technologies. *Buildings (Basel, Switzerland), 14*(4), 967. DOI: 10.3390/buildings14040967

Karabegović, I., Mahmić, M., Karabegović, E., & Husak, E. (2025, June). Optimization and Increase of Production Efficiency by Using Service Robots for Maintenance, Inspection and Logistics. In International Conference "New Technologies, Development and Applications" (pp. 3-18). Cham: Springer Nature Switzerland.

Katani, E. M., & Ng'Olua, T. N. (2025). Impact of Adoption and Application of PMBOK® Guide on Project Performance in Kenya's Construction Industry: A Multivariate Analysis. *Multidisciplinary Journal of Technical University of Mombasa, 4*(1), 30–36. DOI: 10.48039/mjtum.v4i1.87

Kermanshachi, S., Nipa, T. J., & Dao, B. (2023). Development of complexity management strategies for construction projects. *Journal of Engineering, Design and Technology, 21*(6), 1633–1657. DOI: 10.1108/JEDT-06-2021-0324

Khakpour, A., Colomo-Palacios, R., & Martini, A. (2023). Towards a framework for developing visual analytics in supply chain environments. *International Journal of Information Systems and Project Management, 11*(1), 52–71. DOI: 10.12821/ijispm110103

Kim, K., Tiedmann, H. R., & Faust, K. M. (2025). Construction industry changes induced by the COVID-19 pandemic. *Engineering, Construction, and Architectural Management, 32*(7), 4413–4438. DOI: 10.1108/ECAM-09-2023-0983

Kissi, E., Aigbavboa, C., & Kuoribo, E. (2023). Emerging technologies in the construction industry: Challenges and strategies in Ghana. *Construction Innovation, 23*(2), 383–405. DOI: 10.1108/CI-11-2021-0215

Kruachottikul, P., Cooharojananone, N., Phanomchoeng, G., Wongsanao, K., Thabsuwan, S., Suwannatrai, K., . . . Vajarodaya, N. (2021, April). Construction process quality control assisted mobile application. In 2021 IEEE 8th International Conference on Industrial Engineering and Applications (ICIEA) (pp. 220-225). IEEE. DOI: 10.1109/ICIEA52957.2021.9436699

Kudyba, S., & Cruz, D. (2023). Understanding project success involving analytic-based decision support in the digital era: A focus on IC and agile project management. *Journal of Intellectual Capital, 24*(6), 1429–1446. DOI: 10.1108/JIC-03-2022-0054

Li, Z., Yang, Z., Szalachowski, P., & Zhou, J. (2020). Building low-interactivity multifactor authenticated key exchange for industrial internet of things. *IEEE Internet of Things Journal, 8*(2), 844–859. DOI: 10.1109/JIOT.2020.3008773

Lin, J. J., & Golparvar-Fard, M. (2021). Visual and virtual production management system for proactive project controls. *Journal of Construction Engineering and Management, 147*(7), 04021058. DOI: 10.1061/(ASCE)CO.1943-7862.0002045

Marlapudi, K., & Lenka, U. (2026). Drivers of talent development for industry 4.0: A DEMATEL analysis of Indian manufacturing. *Journal of Intellectual Capital,* •••, 1–22. DOI: 10.1108/JIC-04-2025-0151

Mbugua, Q. S. L. M., Masu, Q. S. S. M., & Kimani, P. (2025). A Survey on the Current Status of Building Information Modelling (BIM) Adoption in Quantity Surveying Practice in Kenya. *Journal of Research in Construction Management, 10*(2), 123–135.

Molina, M. (2024). *Ai and Its Application in Civil Engineering, a Vision of Trends.* Recalde Recalde.

Monteiro, A., Varajão, J., & Santos, V. (2025). Effects of project management information systems (PMIS) on project manager's performance.

Mousa, M., Mullins, A. K., Skouteris, H., Boyle, J., & Teede, H. J. (2021). Organisational best practices for advancing women in leadership: Protocol for a systematic literature review. *BMJ Open, 11*(4), e046982. DOI: 10.1136/bmjopen-2020-046982

Musarat, M. A., Hameed, N., Altaf, M., & Khan, M. A. (2021). Digital transformation of the construction industry: a review. In Proceedings of the International Conference on Decision Aid Sciences and Applications (DASA) (pp. 100-105). IEEE. León, L. P. (2024). Characterization of the information system integrated to the construction project management systems. Romero Romero. DOI: 10.1109/DASA53625.2021.9682303

Naji, K. K., Gunduz, M., Alhenzab, F., Al-Hababi, H., & Al-Qahtani, A. (2024). Assessing the digital transformation readiness of the construction industry utilizing the Delphi Method. *Buildings (Basel, Switzerland), 14*(3), 601. DOI: 10.3390/buildings14030601

Nguyen, T. D., & Adhikari, S. (2023). The role of bim in integrating digital twin in building construction: A literature review. *Sustainability (Basel), 15*(13), 10462. DOI: 10.3390/su151310462

Nguyen, T. D., & Pishdad-Bozorgi, P. (2023). Overcoming the barriers toward widespread adoption of prefabrication: an approach involving emerging technologies. In *Proceedings of the 31st Annual Conference of the International Group for Lean Construction (IGLC31),* Lille, France (Vol. 26). DOI: 10.24928/2023/0116

Oke, A. E., Aliu, J., & Onajite, S. A. (2024). Barriers to the adoption of digital technologies for sustainable construction in a developing economy. *Architectural Engineering and Design Management*, *20*(3), 431–447. DOI: 10.1080/17452007.2023.2187754

Olugboyega, O., Bolujoko, A., Oseghale, G., & Aigbavboa, C. (2022). Measuring the effects of mobile technology barriers and enablers on acceptance and proficiency in the Nigerian construction industry. *Acta Structilia*, *29*(2), 1–32. DOI: 10.18820/24150487/as29i2.1

Onososen, A. O., Musonda, I., Onatayo, D., Tjebane, M. M., Saka, A. B., & Fagbenro, R. K. (2023). Impediments to construction site digitalisation using unmanned aerial vehicles (UAVs). *Drones (Basel)*, *7*(1), 45. DOI: 10.3390/drones7010045

Ozturk, M., Salamatmoghadasi, M., & Yanikomeroglu, H. (2025). Integrating terrestrial and non-terrestrial networks for sustainable 6G operations: A latency-aware multi-tier cell-switching approach. *IEEE Network*.

Perrier, N., Bled, A., Bourgault, M., & Garon, S. (2020). Construction 4.0: A survey of research trends. *Automation in Construction*, *114*, 103182.

Prity, F. S., Uddin, K. A., & Nath, N. (2024). Exploring swarm intelligence optimization techniques for task scheduling in cloud computing: Algorithms, performance analysis, and future prospects. *Iran Journal of Computer Science*, *7*(2), 337–358. DOI: 10.1007/s42044-023-00163-8

Radman, K., & Lovreglio, R. (2025). RealCONs: a digital framework for construction reporting accuracy and early delay detection.

Ramalli, E., & Pernici, B. (2023). Challenges of a Data Ecosystem for scientific data. *Data & Knowledge Engineering*, *148*, 102236. DOI: 10.1016/j.datak.2023.102236

Rashidi, A., Sarvari, H., Chan, D. W., Olawumi, T. O., & Edwards, D. J. (2026). A systematic taxonomic review of the application of BIM and digital twins technologies in the construction industry. *Engineering, Construction, and Architectural Management*, *33*(3), 1813–1835. DOI: 10.1108/ECAM-02-2024-0239

Rathnayake, A., Murguia, D., & Ruwanpura, J. (2024). Measuring activity-level construction productivity. *Journal of Construction Engineering and Management*, *150*(1), 04023001. DOI: 10.1061/(ASCE)CO.1943-7862.0002600

Sandeep, S. R., Ahamad, S., Saxena, D., Srivastava, K., Jaiswal, S., & Bora, A. (2022). To understand the relationship between Machine learning and Artificial intelligence in large and diversified business organisations. *Materials Today: Proceedings*, *56*, 2082–2086. DOI: 10.1016/j.matpr.2021.11.409

Sarwar, H., & Rahman, M. (2024, June). A Systematic Short Review of Machine Learning and Artificial Intelligence Integration in Current Project Management Techniques. In 2024 IEEE 4th International Conference on Software Engineering and Artificial Intelligence (SEAI) (pp. 262-270). IEEE. DOI: 10.1109/SEAI62072.2024.10674089

Schlüchter, J., & Retucci, G. (2023). *Hilti innovation leadership experience as enabler for a better future in the construction industry. emerald.com*. Retrieved from. [Insert URL if available, otherwise omit]

Schubert, P., & Williams, S. P. (2022). Enterprise Collaboration Platform Configurations: an Empirical Study. In Proceedings of 20th European Conference on Computer-Supported Cooperative Work. European Society for Socially Embedded Technologies (EUSSET).

Shaukat, H. (2024). Visual communication and its impact on Engineering Project Management.

Simonaitis, A., Daukšys, M., & Mockienė, J. (2023). A comparison of the project management methodologies PRINCE2 and PMBOK in managing repetitive construction projects. *Buildings (Basel, Switzerland)*, *13*(7), 1796. DOI: 10.3390/buildings13071796

Siuko, V., Myllärniemi, J., & Hellsten, P. (2022). State of knowledge-based management in project networks-case in Finnish infrastructure construction sector. In *International Conference on Knowledge Management and Information Systems* (pp. 126-133). SCITEPRESS. DOI: 10.5220/0011376300003335

Soltan, S., & Ashrafi, M. (2025). A new optimization model for multi-project scheduling considering dynamic resource allocation. *Soft Computing*, *29*(15), 5143–5158. DOI: 10.1007/s00500-025-10891-7

Tummuri, S. S. R. (2025). *Enterprise Integration: Strategies, Technologies And Future Trends*. Academic Guru Publishing House.

Välilä, T. (2025). The economic impact of transport infrastructure: A review of project-level vs. aggregate-level evidence. *Transport Reviews*, *45*(4), 459–481. DOI: 10.1080/01441647.2025.2476012

van den Hoed, M. W., Backhaus, R., de Vries, E., & van der Veer, S. N. (2022). Factors contributing to innovation readiness in health care organizations: A scoping review. *BMC Health Services Research*, *22*(1), 1–17. DOI: 10.1186/s12913-022-08185-x

Vigneault, M. A., Boton, C., Chong, H. Y., & Cooper-Cooke, B. (2020). An Innovative Framework of 5D BIM Solutions for Construction Cost Management: A Systematic Review. *Archives of Computational Methods in Engineering*, *27*(4), 1013–1030. DOI: 10.1007/s11831-019-09341-z

Wang, K., Guo, F., Zhang, C., & Schaefer, D. (2024). From Industry 4.0 to Construction 4.0: Barriers to the digital transformation of engineering and construction sectors. *Engineering, Construction, and Architectural Management*, *31*(1), 136–158. DOI: 10.1108/ECAM-05-2022-0383

Wang, T., & Chen, H. M. (2023). Integration of building information modeling and project management in construction project life cycle. *Automation in Construction*, *150*, 104832. DOI: 10.1016/j.autcon.2023.104832

Waqar, A., Skrzypkowski, K., Almujibah, H., Zagorski, K., Khan, M. B., Zagorska, A., & Benjeddou, O. (2023). Success of implementing cloud computing for smart development in small construction projects. *Applied Sciences (Basel, Switzerland)*, *13*(9), 5713. DOI: 10.3390/app13095713

Waterhouse, J., & Mann, S. (2021). Mapping domain knowledge for leading and managing change. *The Serials Librarian*, *80*(1-4), 3–10. DOI: 10.1080/0361526X.2021.1863140

Wu, Z., Yang, K., Lai, X., & Antwi-Afari, M. F. (2020). A scientometric review of system dynamics applications in construction management research. *Sustainability (Basel)*, *12*(18), 7474. DOI: 10.3390/su12187474

Yilmaz, N., Ergen, E., & Citipitioglu, A. M. (2025). Enhancing RFI management in construction through machine learning-driven predictive models. Smart and Sustainable Built Environment, 1-21.

Zambrano, L., Atencio, E., Mariani, C., Mancini, M., & Atencio, E. (2024, February). Integration between PMBOK 7th concepts: A network analysis. In *Proc. 14th International Conference on Industrial Engineering and Operations Management* (pp. 1098-1108). DOI: 10.46254/AN14.20240277

Zhang, C., Dong, W., Shen, W., & Du, Y. (2025). Influencing Factors of BIM Application Benefits in Construction Projects Based on SEM. *Buildings (Basel, Switzerland)*, *15*(11), 1875. DOI: 10.3390/buildings15111875

Chapter 11
Enhancing Community Resilience and Disaster Preparedness Through AI-Assisted Open Mapping:
A Conceptual Framework for Underserved African Regions

Nwosu Obinnaya Chikezie Victor
http://orcid.org/0000-0003-3974-4755
University of South Africa, South Africa

ABSTRACT

Africa confronts a dual crisis: escalating natural hazards like floods and droughts, compounded by a severe lack of foundational geospatial data needed for disaster response. This "data gap" traps communities in reactive cycles instead of proactive resilience. This chapter proposes an AI-Assisted Open Mapping Ecosystem (AIA-OME) to address this. The framework integrates artificial intelligence with community platforms like OpenStreetMap in a four-stage cycle: remote data acquisition, AI-powered feature extraction, community validation using local knowledge, and data integration for disaster risk reduction. This human-centered approach balances AI scalability with contextual accuracy. It incorporates ethical oversight, data sovereignty, and community feedback for continuous model improvement. Conceptual findings suggest gains in efficiency, data quality, and community empowerment. The

DOI: 10.4018/979-8-2600-2701-1.ch011

chapter calls for empirical validation through pilot projects, emphasizing interdisciplinary collaboration and sustainable governance to ensure equitable outcomes in vulnerable African regions.

1. INTRODUCTION

The African continent faces a dual crisis in underserved regions, where exposure to natural hazards like floods is compounded by a systemic lack of foundational data for disaster response (Raftopoulos et al., 2024). This "data gap" is life-threatening, as without accurate mapping, agencies cannot model risks or plan evacuations, forcing communities into reactive crisis management (Krtalić et al., 2023; Jain, 2024). Rapid urbanisation worsens this, leaving millions in informal settlements invisible in official records, delaying humanitarian aid (Devarajan, 2025). Although the Sendai Framework mandates accessible risk information, implementation is crippled by data deficiencies (Raftopoulos et al., 2024). To address this, this chapter argues for integrating AI with community-driven mapping on platforms like OpenStreetMap (Gaikwad et al., 2021; Ibrahim et al., 2025). While Volunteered Geographic Information democratised mapping, manual efforts cannot match the pace of change (Pizzolotto, 2022). We propose AI to analyse satellite imagery for rapid feature detection, with local communities validating the data using indigenous knowledge to ensure accuracy (Kopiika et al., 2025; Hsu et al., 2022). This hybrid model creates comprehensive, trusted datasets. However, ethical challenges must be navigated to avoid reinforcing inequalities (Ayadi et al., 2025). The chapter calls for developing "responsible GeoAI" to ensure equitable outcomes in African urban contexts (Marasinghe et al., 2024; Kang et al., 2024).

2. LITERATURE REVIEW

The imperative to build resilient communities in the face of increasing disaster risk requires a multi-faceted approach that bridges technological innovation with deep-seated social understanding. This review establishes the theoretical and practical foundations for an AI-assisted open mapping framework by exploring three core areas: the concept of community resilience as the guiding principle for disaster preparedness; the evolution and impact of open and participatory mapping; and the emerging applications and ethical dimensions of Artificial Intelligence in the disaster management cycle.

2.1 Disaster Risk Management and the Data Imperative

Effective disaster management depends on understanding preparation, mitigation, and recovery, which requires robust risk models informed by comprehensive geospatial data (Gevaert et al., 2021; Ghaffarian et al., 2023). This has traditionally been challenging due to the unpredictable nature of disasters and complexities in data acquisition (Devarajan, 2025; Raftopoulos et al., 2024). Recent advances in geo-computational techniques, AI, and geospatial big data analytics offer transformative potential for enhancing flood resilience and real-time monitoring (Jain, 2024). These innovations enable predictive risk mapping and automated assessments crucial for rapid decision-making (Yuan et al., 2022; Ye et al., 2021).

Specifically, LiDAR provides precise elevation data for flood modeling, while GIS offers tools for risk evaluation and evacuation planning (Jain, 2024). The integration of sensor technologies and unmanned aerial vehicles presents new opportunities for real-time monitoring in flood-prone areas (Jain, 2024). GeoAI and machine learning further enhance these assessments by enabling robust spatial analysis and real-time damage mapping (Atmaja et al., 2024; Lee & Li, 2025). These geo-computational tools allow stakeholders to evaluate vulnerability, gain insights into flood dynamics, and formulate targeted policies to mitigate effects (Jain, 2024). The iterative nature of such modeling strengthens communities' ability to adapt to shifting climatic conditions (Jain, 2024)

2.2 Conceptualising Community Resilience

Disaster management resilience has shifted from a rigid engineering focus to a holistic socio-ecological concept, emphasizing a community's capacity to absorb, adapt, and transform (Milofsky, 2023). This dynamic process relies on interconnected social, economic, and institutional systems rather than just physical infrastructure (Jamshed et al., 2023).

In the African context, community-based adaptation positions local populations as active agents (Arhin & Tetteh, 2024) possessing vital indigenous knowledge (Coger et al., 2022). For example, women's social networks in Senegal demonstrate that social infrastructure is as critical as physical defences (Yessoufou et al., 2024). Consequently, top-down technical solutions that ignore these social fabrics are prone to failure (Nathan et al., 2022). While quantifying these social dimensions remains challenging (Wowk et al., 2023), integrating community knowledge with advanced data analytics offers a robust solution (Praharaj & Wentz, 2022).

Recognizing local capacities is fundamental to risk reduction (Dé et al., 2024). Combining local wisdom with technology fosters social learning and reduces vulnerability (Imperiale & Vanclay, 2023). These participatory processes mobilise local actors and build autonomy (Graveline & Germain, 2022), ensuring communities take ownership of response programs (Ma et al., 2023). Practical applications, such as participatory GIS mapping, facilitate this integration (Baudoin et al., 2016). Ultimately, interdisciplinary collaboration is essential for developing culturally sensitive and scientifically robust resilience strategies (Saputra et al., 2025; Rashidfarokhi, 2024).

2.3 The Evolution of Open and Participatory Mapping

The internet and GPS have catalysed a cartography revolution through Volunteered Geographic Information and platforms like OpenStreetMap (Pizzolotto, 2022). In many African regions, OpenStreetMap surpasses official maps in detail and is critical for humanitarian efforts, such as those by the Humanitarian OpenStreetMap Team (Bertolotto et al., 2020). This participatory GIS approach integrates local knowledge of resources and risks into geospatial data (Mdemu et al., 2023), enhancing disaster models in Rwanda (Taylor et al., 2020) and enabling real-time flood reporting in Lagos, sometimes using low-cost drones (Yeboah et al., 2021; Sauls et al., 2023). Nevertheless, open mapping grapples with inconsistent data quality (Oraegbu & Jolaiya, 2024) and sustainability issues tied to funding and data sovereignty (Sieber & Brandusescu, 2025). The slow, manual process of satellite image tracing necessitates integrating artificial intelligence to accelerate data generation and validation (Ward et al., 2020). AI is vital for rapid information generation in disaster response (Li et al., 2020; Yordanov et al., 2021), with generative models potentially filling data gaps (See et al., 2025). Successful integration into national mapping requires robust validation protocols (Okyere et al., 2025; Niroshan & Carswell, 2024), though GeoAI faces limitations in data and expertise in resource-constrained contexts (Böhlen et al., 2024). Ultimately, this collaboration must uphold privacy (Hostettler et al., 2018), and organisations with deep local connections are key to acquiring the high-quality ground truth data essential for GeoAI applications (Böhlen et al., 2024; Oluoch et al., 2022).

2.4 The Role of AI in Disaster Management and Mapping

Artificial Intelligence, particularly machine learning and deep learning, is transforming disaster management by analyzing vast datasets to enhance preparedness and response (Alotaibi & Nassif, 2024; Lema et al., 2021). Computer vision algorithms, notably Convolutional Neural Networks, excel at automatically extracting crucial information from remote sensing data. For instance, CNNs have been used for automated building damage assessment following disasters (Xu et al., 2019).

AI-powered models are also being developed for predictive capabilities, such as drought risk prediction (Ghaffarian et al., 2023) and landslide early warning systems

(Vijayagopal et al., 2025). Furthermore, AI is vital for creating granular and up-to-date settlement maps, including identifying informal settlements, which is critical for humanitarian resource allocation during crises (Sekara et al., 2025; S.N. et al., 2024; Domfeh & Dancy, 2025). This technology dramatically accelerates the mapping process, enabling AI to identify building footprints across a large region rapidly—a task that previously required extensive manual effort. This hybrid human-machine approach is leveraged by organizations aiming to map the world, using AI-generated data as a foundation for volunteers to validate (Jakubik et al., 2024).

However, the application of AI is fraught with ethical challenges. AI models reflect biases in their training data, risking the mis-characterisation or under-mapping of vulnerable communities, especially in non-Western contexts (Mai et al., 2025). Critical questions of transparency, accountability, and "data colonialism" are raised, emphasizing the need for an "ethics-by-design" framework (Sapena et al., 2024). A successful strategy must involve local populations in data collection and validation to ensure AI augments community knowledge and avoids algorithmic biases and misinformation that can arise from flawed datasets (Oluoch et al., 2022; Marasinghe et al., 2024).

2.5 Synthesis and Research Gap

The literature clearly establishes three key points. First, effective disaster preparedness must be rooted in community resilience, prioritising local knowledge and agency. Second, open, participatory mapping is a powerful tool for creating essential geospatial data in underserved regions, but it faces challenges of scale and sustainability. Third, AI offers transformative potential to accelerate mapping and enhance risk modelling, but its application is fraught with ethical and technical risks if not implemented carefully. The critical research gap lies at the intersection of these domains—there is a lack of comprehensive, integrated frameworks that strategically combine AI and community-based mapping in an ethically sound, technologically robust manner, particularly in the African context (Yilma, 2019). Building on prior work in Kenya, this chapter proposes a detailed, operational framework for a hybrid human-AI ecosystem designed to empower communities from the ground up, specifically addressing legal and ethical concerns in data acquisition and AI-based analysis for flood disaster response, including emerging data sources (Gilga et al., 2025). This framework must confront the inherent challenges of integrating co-creative or generative AI tools within geospatial applications, ensuring transparency and accountability in algorithmic processes (Marasinghe et al., 2024). It must also mitigate hidden geospatial biases to guarantee reliability and fairness in disaster risk management (Gevaert et al., 2021), and prevent AI from introducing or exacerbating biases in humanitarian aid decision-making, necessitating robust ethical evaluation and mitigation (Marasinghe et al., 2024). Ultimately, the development of AI systems that are not only technologically advanced but also ethically robust, promoting transparency, accountability, and inclusivity in their design and deployment, is paramount (Ayadi et al., 2025; Liu et al., 2024).

3. METHODOLOGICAL APPROACH

3.1 Conceptual Framework Development

This chapter employs a conceptual framework development methodology, synthesising insights from the interdisciplinary literature review to construct an operational model for AI-assisted open mapping. The framework is designed as a cyclical, adaptive system that integrates advanced technology with community-centric processes. Its primary goal is to produce high-quality, actionable geospatial data that directly supports community resilience and integrates into formal disaster management work flows.

3.2 Data Sources for AI-Assisted Mapping

The proposed framework relies on diverse geospatial data sources, each selected based on the specific requirements of the mapping project, including spatial resolution, temporal frequency, and accessibility constraints.

Satellite Imagery: High-resolution commercial satellite imagery from providers including Maxar Technologies and Planet Labs serves as the primary data source for detailed feature extraction. These platforms offer spatial resolutions of 0.3 to 3 meters, sufficient for identifying individual buildings and infrastructure elements. Openly available data from the European Space Agency's Sentinel missions (Sentinel-1 SAR and Sentinel-2 multispectral) provides 10-20 meter resolution suitable for broader area analysis and land cover classification. Partnerships with commercial providers through humanitarian licensing programs, such as the Maxar Open Data Program, are crucial for accessing costly proprietary imagery in disaster response contexts.

Aerial and Drone Imagery: In targeted high-risk areas, imagery from Unmanned Aerial Vehicles offers superior resolution (centimetre-level) and timeliness compared to satellite sources. As demonstrated by Fornace et al. (2018), community-operated drone mapping can be a powerful tool for monitoring local hazards and engaging residents in data collection. UAVs are particularly valuable for validating AI model outputs in complex informal settlements where satellite imagery may suffer from occlusion or shadow effects.

Ancillary Geospatial Data: The framework incorporates existing geospatial datasets including administrative boundaries, digital elevation models from Shuttle Radar Topography Mission and ALOS PALSAR, hydrological datasets from the HydroSHEDS database, and OpenStreetMap baseline data where available. These layers provide contextual information essential for pre-processing and model training.

3.3 Evaluation Metrics for AI Model Performance

To ensure transparency and accountability in AI-assisted mapping, the framework incorporates standardised evaluation metrics for assessing model performance across different feature extraction tasks.

For Building Footprint Detection:

- **Intersection over Union (IoU):** Measures the overlap between predicted and ground truth building polygons. Minimum acceptable IoU thresholds are set at 0.5 for building detection, with higher thresholds (0.7) for applications requiring precise boundaries.
- **Precision:** The proportion of detected building footprints that correspond to actual buildings (true positives / (true positives + false positives)).
- **Recall:** The proportion of actual buildings successfully detected by the model (true positives / (true positives + false negatives)).
- **F1 Score:** The harmonic mean of precision and recall, providing a balanced measure of model accuracy.
- **Completeness Ratio:** The percentage of buildings successfully mapped within a defined area compared to comprehensive ground truth surveys.

For Road Network Extraction:

- **Graph Similarity Metrics:** Compare topological properties of extracted road networks against reference networks, including node connectivity and path completeness.
- **Spatial Accuracy:** Measures the average distance between extracted road centrelines and ground truth alignments.
- **Connectivity Rate:** The percentage of road segments forming continuous, navigable networks without gaps.

For Land Use/Land Cover Classification:

- **Overall Accuracy:** The proportion of correctly classified pixels or polygons.

- **Kappa Coefficient:** Measures classification agreement beyond chance agreement.
- **Class-specific User's and Producer's Accuracy:** Assesses performance for individual land cover categories, particularly important for identifying flood-prone areas and vulnerable land use types.

3.4 Validation Procedures

The framework implements a multi-stage validation protocol to ensure data quality and build trust in AI-generated outputs.

Technical Validation:

- **Cross-Validation:** AI models are trained and validated using k-fold cross-validation techniques, ensuring performance stability across different geographic subsets.
- **Holdout Test Sets:** A portion of manually annotated data (20-30%) is reserved exclusively for final model evaluation, never used during training or fine-tuning.
- **Bias Auditing:** Model performance is disaggregated by geographic region, settlement type (formal vs. informal), and building characteristics to identify systematic under-performance in vulnerable communities.

Community Validation:

- **Participatory Accuracy Assessment:** Community mappers independently validate AI-generated features using mobile applications and local knowledge. Discrepancies between AI predictions and community assessments are documented and analyzed.
- **Inter-Rater Reliability:** Multiple community members validate the same geographic areas to assess consistency in manual mapping and identify ambiguous features requiring clarification.
- **Feedback Integration:** Validated corrections are systematically logged and used to retrain AI models, creating a continuous improvement cycle.

Ground Truth Data Collection:

- **Stratified Random Sampling:** Validation samples are collected using stratified random sampling based on land cover type, settlement density, and accessibility to ensure representative coverage.

- **GPS Field Surveys:** Hand-held GPS devices and mobile data collection platforms (ODK, KoboToolbox) are used to collect precise ground truth coordinates for buildings, roads, and critical infrastructure.
- **Participatory Field Mapping:** Local teams conduct systematic field surveys in accessible areas, collecting attribute data on building materials, structural condition, and social vulnerabilities that cannot be derived from imagery alone (Fornace et al., 2018).

4. A CONCEPTUAL FRAMEWORK FOR AI-ASSISTED OPEN MAPPING

To address the challenges of scale, speed, and local relevance in mapping for disaster preparedness, this chapter proposes a conceptual framework for an AI-Assisted Open Mapping Ecosystem. This framework is designed to be a cyclical, adaptive system that integrates advanced technology with community-centric processes. The framework is composed of four main stages: Data Acquisition and Pre-Processing; AI-Powered Feature Extraction; Community Validation and Enrichment; and Data Integration and Application. This iterative approach ensures that the insights gained from community engagement continuously refine the AI models, fostering a robust and adaptive mapping infrastructure (Marasinghe et al., 2024).

Given the sensitive nature of disaster-related data and the potential for algorithmic bias, particularly in vulnerable regions, the framework explicitly incorporates mechanisms for ethical oversight, participatory design, and continuous auditing to ensure fairness and equitable outcomes (Pouresmaeil et al., 2025; Marasinghe et al., 2024). This iterative approach not only enhances the accuracy and relevance of the geospatial data but also strengthens community ownership and trust in the derived insights, aligning with best practices for responsible AI deployment in disaster management (Marasinghe et al., 2024).

4.1 Stage 1: Data Acquisition and Pre-Processing

The framework's foundation is the acquisition of appropriate remote sensing imagery, with selection contingent on project objectives such as flood risk assessment or urban planning. Satellite imagery from commercial providers (e.g., Maxar, Planet) serves as the primary data source for feature extraction, while open data from Sentinel missions facilitates broader analyses. Cost barriers necessitate leveraging humanitarian open data programmes and partnerships with imagery providers, alongside hybrid approaches combining medium-resolution with targeted high-resolution acquisitions. In high-risk areas, UAV-based imagery offers superior resolution and timeliness; as Fornace et al. (2018) demonstrated, community-operated drone mapping aids hazard monitoring and resident engagement, particularly for validating AI predictions in complex informal settlements where satellite imagery may be insufficient. Data pre-processing involves orthorectification to correct geometric distortions, atmospheric correction to normalise reflectance values, tiling large images, mosaicking for seamless coverage, and cloud masking to obscure features. Infrastructure demands, including GPUs for deep learning, are addressed through cloud computing where connectivity permits, and offline-capable workflows in resource-constrained settings, with pre-trained models deployed locally and results synchronised later.

4.2 Stage 2: AI-Powered Feature Extraction

This stage employs machine learning for initial large-scale mapping, producing a foundational draft map to minimise manual effort. Deep learning models, primarily Convolutional Neural Networks, perform semantic segmentation to delineate geographic features. Key models detect building footprints—accounting for informal settlements—extract road networks, including unpaved paths and seasonal variations, and classify land use/land cover for vulnerability assessment (Pelizari et al., 2023). Transfer learning fine-tunes global models with locally curated African data to avoid bias and improve contextual relevance, addressing under-representation in training datasets (Ye et al., 2021). Outputs include vector data for buildings, roads, and land cover, tagged as AI-generated with confidence scores. High-confidence predictions are prioritised for validation, while low-confidence areas require intensive community review.

Table 1. Key AI Models and Their Application in the AIA-OME Framework

AI Model Type	Target Feature	Primary Application in DRR	Example Reference
Convolutional Neural Network (CNN)	Building Footprints	Population density estimation, exposure analysis, post-disaster damage assessment	Pelizari et al. (2023)
Recurrent Neural Network (RNN) / Graph CNN	Road Networks	Evacuation route planning, logistics for aid delivery, accessibility analysis	Ye et al. (2021)
Random Forest / Support Vector Machine (SVM)	Land Use Classification	Floodplain delineation, landslide susceptibility zoning, food security analysis	Fornace et al. (2018)
Long Short-Term Memory (LSTM) Network	Time-Series Analysis	Drought prediction from climate data, monitoring changes in water bodies	Yilma (2019)

Table 1 presents a comparative summary of major Artificial Intelligence model types and their primary roles in Disaster Risk Reduction within the AIA-OME framework. Four widely used model categories are highlighted:

Convolutional Neural Networks are primarily applied to building footprint extraction and analysis, supporting population density estimation, exposure assessment, and post-disaster damage analysis (Pelizari et al., 2023).

Recurrent Neural Networks and Graph CNNs target road network features, enabling evacuation route planning, logistics optimisation for aid distribution, and accessibility analysis for essential services (Ye et al., 2021).

Random Forest and Support Vector Machine models are commonly employed in land-use classification tasks, supporting floodplain delineation, landslide susceptibility mapping, and food-security risk assessments (Fornace et al., 2018).

Long Short-Term Memory Networks are used for time-series analysis, particularly for drought prediction, climate-data modeling, and monitoring hydrological changes such as water-body variations (Yilma, 2019).

Overall, Table 1 illustrates how diverse AI architectures target specific geospatial and environmental features to support a wide range of DRR applications, highlighting the integrative potential of AI in the AIA-OME framework.

Figure 1. The AI-Assisted Open Mapping Ecosystem (AIA-OME) Cycle

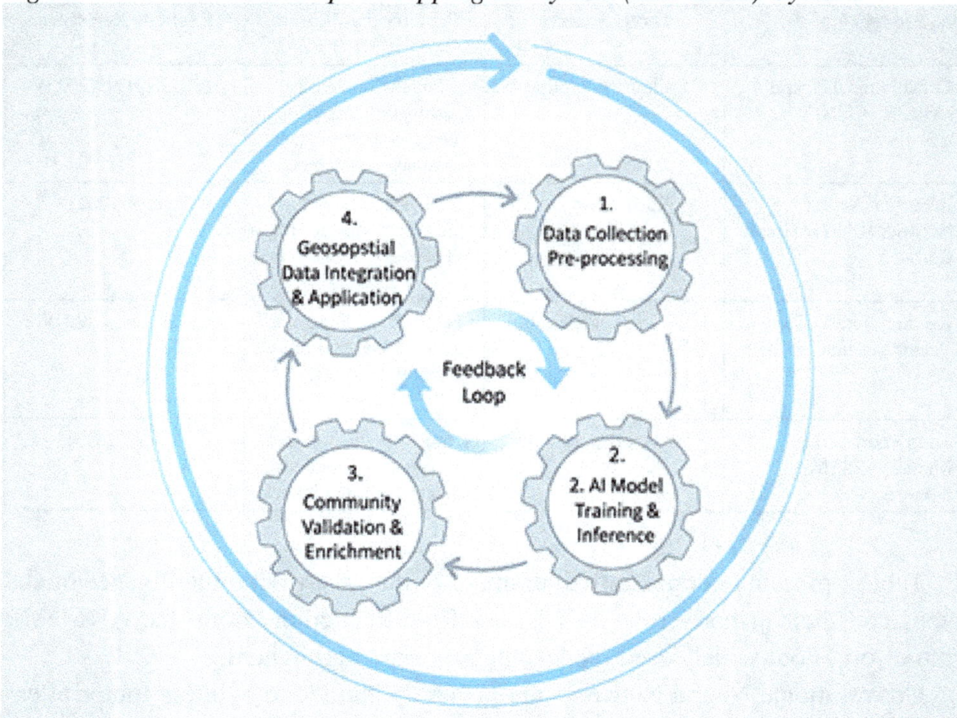

Stage 1: Data Acquisition and Pre-Processing

The framework's foundation relies on procuring suitable remote sensing imagery. The selection, critical to project goals, includes high-resolution satellite data from providers such as Maxar or Planet, often necessitating partnerships for humanitarian access to commercial sources. Open data from missions like Sentinel supports broader analyses. For targeted areas, Unmanned Aerial Vehicle (UAV) imagery offers superior resolution and timeliness; as demonstrated by (Fornace et al., 2018), community-operated drones are effective for local hazard monitoring. Subsequent pre-processing—encompassing orthorectification, atmospheric correction, and image tiling—prepares the data for algorithmic analysis.

Stage 2: AI-Powered Feature Extraction

This stage employs machine learning to generate foundational map drafts, significantly reducing manual workload. Deep learning models, specifically Convolutional Neural Networks (CNNs), are trained for semantic segmentation to delineate features such as building footprints, road networks, and land use/land cover classifications, the latter being crucial for vulnerability assessment (Pelizari et al., 2023). To counteract the bias inherent in generic models (Ye et al., 2021), the strategy utilises transfer learning. Models pre-trained on global data are fine-tuned with locally curated datasets to enhance contextual accuracy. The output comprises AI-generated geographic vector data, ready for subsequent validation.

4.3 Stage 3: Community Validation and Enrichment

This pivotal stage synthesises technological output with human expertise, converting AI-generated data into a socially legitimate and locally robust resource via open mapping platforms, primarily OpenStreetMap. Initially, AI vector data is imported into a tasking manager, segmenting the area into discrete tasks for volunteers. Here, AI-derived features are overlaid on satellite imagery, serving as a baseline for validation. Community mappers undertake validation, correction, and enrichment. They assess polygon accuracy, rectify errors, and enhance data by adding critical attributes—such as building material, use, or road surface—that AI cannot discern from imagery alone. This granularity is indispensable for detailed risk modelling (Alaoui et al., 2022). Participatory field mapping employs mobile tools like ODK Collect and KoboToolbox, guided by established practices (Taylor et al., 2020), to gather ground-truth data, ensuring community members are active knowledge creators. Offline-first validation enables participation in areas with limited connectivity, with data synchronised upon availability. Finally, this high-quality, validated data feeds back into AI model refinement, creating a virtuous cycle of progressive accuracy and contextual adaptation.

4.4 Stage 4: Data Integration and Application

The final stage ensures newly created data is accessible and integrated into decision-making. All validated data resides on OpenStreetMap, making it a freely accessible public good. For disaster management, this enriched data supports key applications: exposure and vulnerability mapping by combining building data with hazard maps to model population exposure (Lapietra et al., 2024); contingency planning using infrastructure data for evacuations; early warning systems enabling targeted, location-based alerts (Han et al., 2022); and post-disaster damage assessment by comparing baseline data with new imagery.

To bridge community data and formal governance, the framework involves working with national disaster management organizations to build trust and capacity, following the integration roadmap proposed by Albris et al. (2020). Finally, for community empowerment, maps are returned in accessible formats like printed copies and mobile apps to facilitate local risk discussions. This enables residents to advocate for resources and develop locally appropriate strategies, taking ownership of their resilience-building efforts (Goodrich et al., 2020).

5. CONCEPTUAL RESULTS AND OUTCOMES

Implementing the AI-Assisted Open Mapping Ecosystem framework would yield a range of significant outcomes, transforming the landscape of disaster preparedness in underserved regions. This section discusses the conceptual findings—the expected results and impacts—of the framework, supported by illustrative figures. The findings are assessed across three key dimensions: efficiency, data quality, and community empowerment.

5.1 Enhanced Mapping Efficiency and Scale

The most immediate and quantifiable result of the framework would be a dramatic acceleration of the mapping process. Manual mapping is painstaking, requiring volunteers to trace each building and road individually from satellite imagery. An AI model can generate a first draft of building footprints for a large city in days, a task that might take a team of volunteers months to complete.

Figure 2. Conceptual Comparison of Mapping Time: Manual vs. AI-Assisted

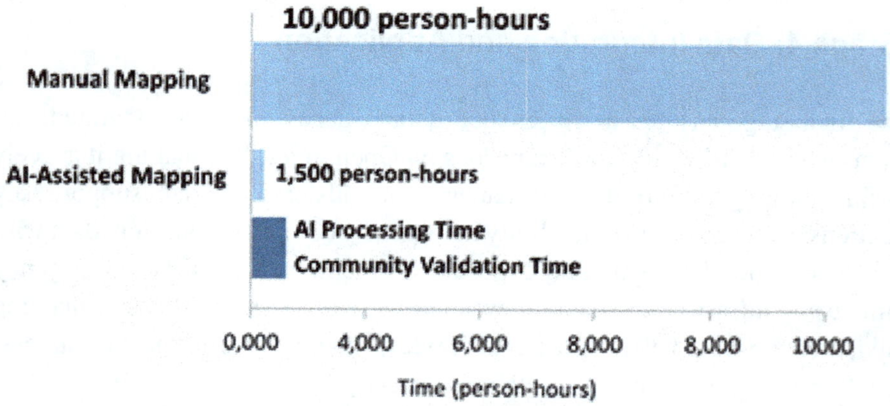

This efficiency gain is not just about speed; it is about scale. It makes it feasible to pursue mapping goals that were previously unimaginable, such as creating a comprehensive building-level map for an entire country's at-risk regions within a realistic time frame. This ability to scale rapidly is critical in the face of fast-growing urban informal settlements, where the built environment changes constantly. Periodic remapping using updated satellite imagery can track urban growth and identify new vulnerable populations before disasters occur.

5.2 Improved Data Quality and Granularity

While AI provides the scale, the community validation stage ensures data quality and adds critical granularity. An AI model might achieve 90% accuracy in identifying buildings, but the remaining 10% of errors (false positives or missed buildings) could be critical in a disaster scenario. Community validation addresses this, pushing the geometric accuracy closer to 100% while adding attribute information that AI cannot infer.

More importantly, the community enrichment process adds layers of qualitative and quantitative data that transform a simple map of shapes into a detailed inventory of the community's social and physical landscape.

Table 2. Data Enrichment through the AIA-OME Framework

Data Layer	AI-Generated Data	Community-Enriched Data	Value for Disaster Preparedness
Buildings	Polygon (footprint)	Building material, number of stories, usage (school, clinic, residential), structural condition, roof type, occupancy patterns	Enhanced vulnerability assessment (e.g., mud-brick houses are more vulnerable to floods; multi-story buildings may provide vertical evacuation options)
Roads	Line (centreline)	Surface type (paved, gravel, dirt), condition (passable year-round, seasonal, damaged), width, flooding history, alternative routes	Realistic logistics planning; identifying evacuation routes accessible by different vehicle types; anticipating road closures during floods
Services	Point (location)	Name of school/ clinic, operating hours, capacity, available resources (generator, water source, medical supplies), accessibility constraints	Identification of critical infrastructure and safe havens for displaced populations; resource inventory for response coordination
Social	None	Location of community leaders, vulnerable households (elderly, disabled, female-headed), local evacuation points, indigenous early warning indicators, historical flood memory	Facilitates targeted assistance and leverages existing social capital for response efforts; ensures most vulnerable populations are prioritised

Table 2 illustrates how the AIA-OME framework integrates AI-generated geospatial data with community-enriched information to enhance disaster preparedness across multiple data layers. Four key layers—Buildings, Roads, Services, and Social—demonstrate how combining machine-derived insights with local knowledge produces richer, context-specific datasets that improve planning and response.

Buildings Layer: AI generates polygon footprints that outline physical structures. When combined with community-provided details—building materials, number of stories, structural condition, and usage—the dataset supports enhanced vulnerability assessments. For example, mud-brick buildings can be flagged as highly flood-prone, while schools and clinics are identified as critical assets requiring priority protection.

Roads Layer: AI-extracted road centrelines are enriched with local information on surface type, road condition, and width. This enriched dataset enables realistic logistics planning and helps identify evacuation routes suitable for various vehicle types. Historical flood depth data can be overlaid to predict which road segments are likely to become impassable during specific flood scenarios.

Services Layer: AI identifies points representing critical service locations. Community contributions add operational details, including operating hours, capacity, and available resources such as generators or water sources. These attributes enable responders to map essential infrastructure and locate safe havens for displaced populations, while identifying gaps in service coverage that require attention during preparedness planning.

Social Layer: Although AI does not generate social data, community-provided information—locations of vulnerable households, local leaders, and designated evacuation points—significantly enriches the framework. This information facilitates targeted assistance and strengthens social capital during emergency response, ensuring that those most in need receive priority attention.

Overall, Table 2 highlights how combining automated AI outputs with community insights creates a more comprehensive and actionable data ecosystem for disaster preparedness under the AIA-OME model.

This enriched data allows for a much more nuanced understanding of risk. Instead of a generic vulnerability map, one can create highly specific models. For example, by combining data on building materials with flood depth projections, it becomes possible to predict precisely which households are most likely to suffer structural collapse, enabling targeted warnings and proactive reinforcement efforts. This aligns with the place-based model of resilience proposed by Roohi et al. (2020), which emphasizes the need for such detailed, localised understanding.

5.3 Strengthened Community Empowerment and Ownership

A crucial outcome of the AIA-OME framework is the empowerment of local communities. The process is intentionally designed to position community members as experts and partners, not just data collectors. By participating in validating and enriching the map of their own area, residents gain a deeper, data-informed understanding of their environment and its associated risks.

Figure 3. Flowchart of Community Empowerment and Data Ownership

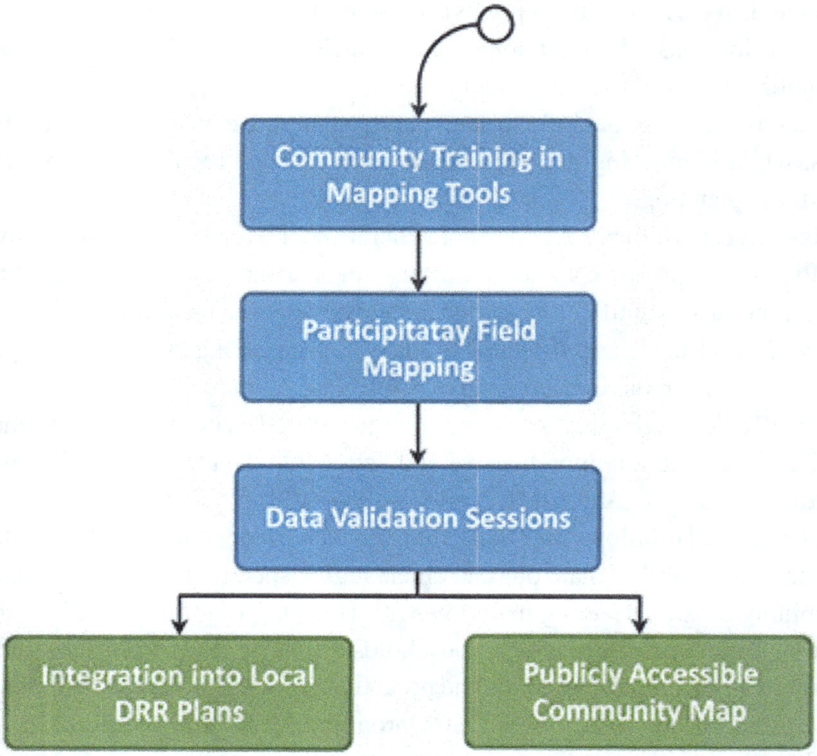

This process fosters a sense of ownership over the data. As argued by Trogrlić et al. (2022), when communities are involved in creating knowledge, they are more likely to trust it and use it. The resulting maps become tools for internal community planning and for advocating for resources from local governments. This directly addresses the challenge of data sovereignty raised by Carroll et al. (2020), ensuring that the benefits of digital mapping are retained at the local level. By bridging the gap between scientific tools and local knowledge, the framework operationalizes the principles of community-based adaptation (Fillmore & Singletary, 2021) and participatory GIS (Orlove et al., 2023).

The empowerment dimension extends beyond the immediate mapping project. Community members trained in geospatial technologies gain valuable skills applicable to other development initiatives, including land tenure documentation, natural resource management, and local economic development planning. Young people, in particular, may find new livelihood opportunities in geospatial services, contributing to local economic resilience.

6. DISCUSSION AND IMPLICATIONS

The conceptual findings of the AIA-OME framework represent a significant departure from traditional, top-down disaster management approaches. The integration of AI and community mapping is not merely an incremental improvement in efficiency but a potential paradigm shift in how geospatial data is produced and used for humanitarian purposes.

6.1 Comparison with Existing Literature

The proposed framework resolves the tension between large-scale data and local knowledge, addressing the "data gap" (Gaikwad et al., 2021) and avoiding technocratic biases (Hill et al., 2019). It uses community-validated data to retrain AI models, enhancing attunement to local African contexts. This extends Ibitoye et al. (2025) by scaling local knowledge integration via AIA-OME, operationalizing policy goals (Hsu et al., 2022). It responds to calls for responsible AI (Ghamisi et al., 2024) through open access, transparency, and bias mitigation, fostering trust. Aligned with SDGs, it sets benchmarks for transparency and reproducibility, advocating open data and code for evidence-based policy. Socially, it addresses biases and privacy to ensure fairness and reduce stigmatisation. Environmentally, it promotes AI for sustainable resource management and conservation, contributing to a resilient future.

6.2 Technical Constraints and Feasibility Considerations

Implementing the AIA-OME framework in resource-constrained settings requires careful attention to technical feasibility. Running deep learning models on satellite imagery demands significant computational resources, particularly Graphics Processing Units capable of parallel processing. In regions with limited internet connectivity, cloud-based processing may be impractical, necessitating alternative approaches.

Offline-First Architecture: The framework proposes an offline-first approach where possible. Pre-trained models can be deployed on local servers or high-performance laptops, with inference performed locally and results synchronised when connectivity becomes available. Community validation tools must function offline, downloading satellite imagery and AI-generated features for field use and storing validated data for later upload.

Edge Computing: For drone-based mapping, on-board processing capabilities can perform initial feature extraction in the field, reducing the data volume requiring transmission. Edge AI approaches, where models run on mobile devices or embedded systems, may enable real-time validation and feedback during field data collection.

Capacity Building: Technical implementation requires investment in human capacity. Local partners need training not only in mapping tools but also in basic concepts of machine learning, data quality assurance, and system maintenance. Partnerships with universities and technical institutes can support this capacity building while creating sustainable local expertise.

6.3 Cost Implications and Sustainability

The cost of high-resolution satellite imagery represents a significant barrier for open mapping projects in developing regions. Commercial imagery from providers including Maxar and Planet typically costs thousands of dollars per square kilometre, prohibitive for community-based initiatives. However, several strategies can mitigate this challenge:

Humanitarian Licensing Programs: Both Maxar and Planet operate open data programs that provide free imagery for humanitarian response and disaster risk reduction activities. These programs have supported numerous mapping initiatives in Africa and represent a critical resource for the AIA-OME framework.

Open Data Sources: The European Space Agency's Sentinel missions provide freely available imagery at 10-20 meter resolution. While insufficient for detailed building footprint extraction, Sentinel data supports land cover classification, flood extent mapping, and change detection at broader scales.

Hybrid Approaches: Combining freely available medium-resolution imagery with targeted high-resolution acquisitions for priority areas can optimise resource allocation. High-resolution data may be reserved for densely populated informal settlements and critical infrastructure locations.

Sustainability Models: Long-term sustainability requires moving beyond project-based funding. Potential models include integration into municipal government budgets for ongoing mapping and updating, social enterprise approaches where mapping services generate revenue, and partnerships with telecommunications companies and other private sector actors who benefit from improved geospatial data.

6.4 Differentiating Urban and Rural Implementation

The challenges and opportunities for AI-assisted mapping differ significantly between urban informal settlements and rural areas, requiring context-specific implementation strategies.

Urban Informal Settlements: High population density, complex building configurations, and rapid change characterise urban informal settlements. AI models must be trained to recognise irregular building patterns and mixed land uses. Community validation requires engagement with diverse stakeholder groups, including residents, landlords, and local officials. Privacy concerns are heightened in dense settlements where household-level data collection may raise sensitivities. The potential impact of improved mapping is high, given the concentration of vulnerable populations and exposure to multiple hazards.

Rural Areas: Lower population density, dispersed settlements, and extensive road networks characterise rural implementation. AI models must handle larger geographic areas with sparser features. Community validation may require travelling longer distances and engaging with more dispersed populations. Drone-based mapping may be particularly valuable for accessing remote areas and documenting seasonal variations in road conditions. The focus may shift from building-level detail to broader land use classification and infrastructure connectivity.

6.5 Policy and Practical Implications

The successful implementation of this framework would have profound implications for policy and practice:

Shift from Reactive to Proactive DRR: With comprehensive, high-resolution data on exposure and vulnerability, governments and NGOs can move from a reactive posture of post-disaster response to a proactive one focused on risk reduction, mitigation, and preparedness. This aligns with the priorities of international frameworks like the Sendai Framework for Disaster Risk Reduction.

Democratization of Data and Planning: By building on an open platform like OpenStreetMap, the framework ensures that critical data is not locked away in government silos or proprietary systems. It is a public good, accessible to local planners, community groups, researchers, and entrepreneurs, fostering innovation and accountability.

Investment in Digital and Human Infrastructure: The framework highlights the need for parallel investments. While investment in technology like AI and cloud computing is essential, it must be matched by investment in human capacity building—training local communities, particularly youth and women, in digital mapping and data literacy skills. This dual investment ensures that technological solutions are sustainable and locally owned.

6.6 Ethical Considerations and Safeguards

Despite its promise, the implementation of the AIA-OME is not without significant ethical challenges. The framework must be implemented with a steadfast commitment to:

Inclusivity: Ensuring that the mapping process actively includes the most marginalised groups within a community, so their specific vulnerabilities are represented. This requires deliberate outreach to women, youth, elderly residents, persons with disabilities, and minority groups who may be excluded from traditional community decision-making processes.

Data Privacy: When collecting household-level data, rigorous protocols must be in place to protect the privacy and security of residents. Data collection should be anonymised where possible, and sensitive information should not be publicly shared. Community consent must be obtained before collecting data on private property, and residents should have the right to review and correct information about their households.

Avoiding Bias: Continuous monitoring and evaluation of AI model performance across different geographic and social contexts are necessary to identify and mitigate biases. Models should be tested for performance disparities across settlement types, building materials, and roof characteristics. Where biases are identified, targeted data collection and model retraining should address them.

Data Sovereignty: Communities should retain ownership and control over their data. This means ensuring that data collected through community processes cannot be exploited by external actors without community consent. Open licenses should be carefully designed to protect community interests while enabling beneficial uses.

7. CONCLUSION AND FUTURE RESEARCH

This chapter has introduced and detailed a conceptual framework for an AI-Assisted Open Mapping Ecosystem, designed to address the critical deficit in geospatial data for disaster preparedness in underserved African regions. The synergistic combination of AI's capacity for large-scale feature extraction and the nuanced, contextual knowledge of community mappers provides a transformative pathway to creating the data infrastructure needed for effective, proactive disaster risk reduction. The proposed four-stage cycle—encompassing data acquisition, AI-powered analysis, community validation, and data integration—is designed to be an adaptive, ethical, and empowering system that places local communities at the heart of the data creation process.

7.1 Summary of Key Contributions

The primary contribution of this chapter is the articulation of an integrated, socio-technical framework that moves beyond siloed discussions of "AI for good" or "community mapping." It provides a structured, operational model for how these powerful approaches can be combined in practice. By emphasizing a feedback loop for model improvement and the central role of community enrichment, the framework offers a solution to the critical challenges of scalability in participatory mapping and of bias and contextual irrelevance in humanitarian AI. It contributes to the literature by providing a tangible model that addresses the theoretical gaps at the intersection of community resilience, geospatial science, and artificial intelligence.

The framework also emphasizes the crucial role of interdisciplinary collaboration and human-in-the-loop processes, ensuring that GeoAI solutions are transparent, interpretable, and trustworthy for urban decision-making (Marasinghe et al., 2024). It aligns with calls for responsible AI practices in Earth Observation by advocating for open access, transparency, and the mitigation of biases, thereby fostering trust and enabling evidence-based policy-making (Ghamisi et al., 2024).

Ultimately, this chapter presents a vision for a future where the most vulnerable communities are not merely subjects on a map, but are active authors of the data that defines their world and strengthens their resilience. This vision recognises that technology alone cannot solve the challenges of disaster risk reduction; it must be embedded in social processes that respect local knowledge, protect community rights, and build lasting capacity.

7.2 Limitations

As a conceptual work, this chapter has inherent limitations. It does not present empirical results from a real-world implementation of the entire framework. The practical challenges of deploying such a system—from securing computational resources and satellite imagery to building and sustaining local mapping communities—are significant and require careful, context-specific planning. The discussion of ethical considerations is foundational but would need to be expanded into a comprehensive governance and ethics protocol for any real-world project. The framework's reliance on community participation assumes a level of social cohesion and organisational capacity that may not exist in all contexts. In communities fragmented by conflict, displacement, or social division, establishing the trust and collaboration necessary for participatory mapping may be challenging. Alternative approaches may be needed in such contexts.

7.3 Future Research Directions

Future research must build on the AIA-OME framework through pilot projects in diverse African contexts. Key priorities include rigorous quantitative benchmarking of efficiency gains and cost-effectiveness compared to manual methods. Qualitative studies should assess impacts on community cohesion, empowerment, and the inclusion of women, youth, and marginalised groups. Dedicated AI research is needed to develop models using locally-sourced data and to mitigate algorithmic bias. Other critical areas involve investigating pathways to integrate community data into official government workflows, ensuring long-term sustainability through models like social enterprises, and exploring transferability to public health, agriculture, and climate adaptation. Comprehensive governance protocols must address data sovereignty and privacy. Ultimately, this agenda calls for collaborative, ethical innovation to fuse AI with community-driven mapping, creating a blueprint for a more resilient and data-empowered future across Africa

AI TOOLS AND PLATFORMS REFERENCED

The conceptual framework presented in this chapter references several AI tools, platforms, and datasets that are currently available for geospatial applications:

Machine Learning Frameworks: TensorFlow, PyTorch, and Keras are referenced as platforms for developing and training deep learning models for feature extraction tasks. These open-source frameworks provide the computational infrastructure for implementing Convolutional Neural Networks and other architectures discussed in Section 4.2.

Pre-trained Models: The framework discusses transfer learning approaches that leverage models pre-trained on global datasets including Microsoft's Bing Maps Building Footprints, Google's Open Buildings, and Facebook's Map With AI initiatives. These resources provide starting points for fine-tuning to local African contexts.

Geospatial Data Platforms: Google Earth Engine, Microsoft Planetary Computer, and Amazon Web Services's Earth observation data archives are referenced as platforms for accessing and processing satellite imagery at scale. These cloud-based platforms offer computational resources that may supplement local infrastructure.

OpenStreetMap Ecosystem: The Humanitarian OpenStreetMap Team's Tasking Manager, OpenStreetMap itself, and related tools including JOSM and iD editor are referenced as platforms for community validation and data integration.

DATA SOURCES ACKNOWLEDGEMENT

The framework acknowledges the importance of open data sources including:

European Space Agency's Sentinel missions (Copernicus Programme)

NASA's Earth observation data (Landsat, SRTM, MODIS)

United States Geological Survey's Earth Explorer

Maxar Open Data Program for humanitarian imagery

Planet's Open California and NICFI Tropical Forest programs

ACKNOWLEDGMENT

The author acknowledges the foundational work of the Humanitarian OpenStreetMap Team, the Global Facility for Disaster Reduction and Recovery, and the many community mappers across Africa whose voluntary contributions make open mapping possible. The conceptual framework builds upon insights gained from participatory observation of mapping activities in Kenya, Uganda, and Malawi, though no specific human subjects data is reported in this conceptual chapter.

REFERENCES

Albris, K., Lauta, K. C., & Raju, E. (2020). Strengthening governance for disaster prevention: The enhancing risk management capabilities guidelines. International Journal of Disaster Risk Reduction, *47*, 101647.

Alotaibi, E., & Nassif, N. (2024). Artificial intelligence in environmental monitoring: In-depth analysis. Discover Artificial Intelligence, *4*(1), 1-24.

Arhin, A. A., & Tetteh, J. D. (2024). Community-based adaptation in Africa: A systematic review of practice and policy. Climate and Development, *16*(2), 89-104.

Atmaja, T., Setiawati, M. D., Kurisu, K., & Fukushi, K. (2024). Advancing coastal flood risk prediction utilizing a GeoAI approach by considering mangroves as an eco-DRR strategy. Hydrology, *11*(12), 198.

Ayadi, R., Forouheshfar, Y., & Moghadas, O. M. (2025). Enhancing system resilience to climate change through artificial intelligence: A systematic literature review. Frontiers in Climate, *7*, 1585331.

Baudoin, M. A., Henly-Shepard, S., Fernando, N., Sitati, A., & Zommers, Z. (2016). From top-down to community-centric approaches to early warning systems: Exploring pathways to improve disaster risk reduction through community participation. International Journal of Disaster Risk Science, *7*(2), 163-174.

Bertolotto, M., McArdle, G., & Schoen-Phelan, B. (2020). Volunteered geographic information for disaster management: A systematic review. International Journal of Digital Earth, *13*(12), 1485-1508.

Böhlen, M., Chen, J., & Li, Y. (2024). GeoAI in resource-constrained contexts: Challenges and opportunities. Transactions in GIS, *28*(2), 345-367.

Carroll, S. R., Garba, I., Figueroa-Rodríguez, O. L., Holbrook, J., Lovett, R., Materechera, S. A., ... & Hudson, M. (2020). The CARE principles for indigenous data governance. Data Science Journal, *19*(1), 43.

Coger, T., Dinshaw, A., Tye, S., Kratzer, B., Thazin, M., & Carty, J. (2022). Indigenous knowledge and climate adaptation in Africa. World Resources Institute Working Paper.

Dé, A., Djalante, R., & Shaw, R. (2024). Local capacities for disaster risk reduction: A systematic review. International Journal of Disaster Risk Reduction, *100*, 104215.

Devarajan, V. (2025). Integrated AI-ML framework for disaster lifecycle management: From prediction to recovery. World Journal of Advanced Research and Reviews, *26*(2), 1630-1643.

Domfeh, K. A., & Dancy, G. P. (2025). Informal settlement mapping using deep learning: A review of methods and applications. Computers, Environment and Urban Systems, *106*, 102145.

Fillmore, H., & Singletary, L. (2021). Climate data and information needs of indigenous communities on reservation lands: Insights from stakeholders in the Southwestern United States. Climatic Change, *169*(3), 1-20.

Fornace, K., Surendra, H., Abidin, T. R., Reyes, R., Macalinao, M. L., Stresman, G., ... & Cook, J. (2018). Use of mobile technology-based participatory mapping approaches to geolocate health facility attendees for disease surveillance in low resource settings. International Journal of Health Geographics, *17*(1), 21.

Gaikwad, S. S., Iyer, S., Lunga, D., & Bondi, E. (2021). Data-driven humanitarian mapping: Harnessing human-machine intelligence for high-stakes public policy and resilience planning. *Proceedings of the 27th ACM SIGKDD Conference on Knowledge Discovery & Data Mining*, 4085-4086. DOI: 10.1145/3447548.3469461

Gevaert, C. M., Carman, M., Rosman, B., Georgiadou, Y., & Soden, R. (2021). Fairness and accountability of AI in disaster risk management: Opportunities and challenges. Patterns, *2*(11), 100363.

Ghaffarian, S., Taghikhah, F., & Maier, H. R. (2023). Explainable artificial intelligence in disaster risk management: Achievements and prospective futures. International Journal of Disaster Risk Reduction, *98*, 104123.

Ghamisi, P., Yu, W., Marinoni, A., Gevaert, C., Persello, C., Selvakumar, S., . . . Atkinson, P. M. (2024). Responsible AI for Earth Observation. arXiv preprint, arXiv:2405.20868.

Gilga, C., Hochwarter, C., Knoche, L., Schmidt, S., Ringler, G., Wieland, M., Resch, B., & Wagner, J. (2025). Legal and ethical considerations for demand-driven data collection and AI-based analysis in flood response. International Journal of Disaster Risk Reduction, *116*, 105441.

Goodrich, K. A., Basolo, V., Feldman, D. L., Matthew, R. A., Schubert, J. E., Luke, A., ... & Serrano, K. (2020). Addressing pluvial flash flooding through community-based collaborative research in Tijuana, Mexico. Water, *12*(5), 1257.

Graveline, M. H., & Germain, D. (2022). Participatory processes and disaster risk reduction: A systematic review. Environmental Science & Policy, *135*, 112-124.

Han, Y., Huang, L., Xiao, T., Yuan, A., Yu, Y., Feng, Y., ... & Ye, Z. (2022). Smart community emergency evacuation management system and risk assessment based on mobile big data. Wireless Communications and Mobile Computing, *2022*, 4757016.

Hill, R., Adem, Ç., Molnár, Z., Aumeeruddy-Thomas, Y., Bridgewater, P., Tengö, M., ... & Carino, J. (2019). Working with indigenous, local and scientific knowledge in assessments of nature and nature's linkages with people. HAL Archives, hal-02416591.

Hostettler, S., Besson, S., & Bolay, J. C. (2018). *Technologies for development: From innovation to social impact.* Springer International Publishing. DOI: 10.1007/978-3-319-91068-0

Hsu, Y. C., Huang, T. H., Verma, H., Mauri, A., Nourbakhsh, I., & Bozzon, A. (2022). Empowering local communities using artificial intelligence. Patterns, *3*(3), 100449.

Ibitoye, A., Nkwo, M., Akinyemi, J. D., & Ladoja, K. T. (2025). Afrocentric trustworthy framework for improved artificial intelligence powered health management tool for Africans. In *AI for Health Equity and Fairness* (pp. 93–117). Springer.

Ibrahim, B., Ogunleye, A., & Adebayo, K. (2025). GeoAI for disaster management in Africa: A review of applications and opportunities. African Journal of Emergency Management, *3*(1), 45-68.

Imperiale, A. J., & Vanclay, F. (2023). Social learning and vulnerability reduction in disaster-prone communities. Disaster Prevention and Management, *32*(1), 89-104.

Jain, H. (2024). Leveraging geo-computational innovations for sustainable disaster management to enhance flood resilience. Discover Geoscience, *2*(1), 42.

Jakubik, J., Vizzari, G., & Psyllidis, A. (2024). Human-machine collaboration for humanitarian mapping: A systematic review. Computers, Environment and Urban Systems, *108*, 102078.

Jamshed, A., Birkmann, J., McMillan, J. M., Rana, I. A., & Lauer, H. (2023). The role of social, economic, and institutional systems in community resilience: A systematic review. International Journal of Disaster Risk Reduction, *95*, 103876.

Kang, Y., Zhang, F., & Gao, S. (2024). Responsible GeoAI: A review of ethical challenges and opportunities. Transactions in GIS, *28*(1), 3-25.

Kopiika, N., Smith, J., & Chen, Y. (2025). Deep learning for feature extraction from satellite imagery: A review of methods and applications in disaster management. Remote Sensing of Environment, *310*, 114456.

Krtalić, A., Bajić, M., & Đurić, N. (2023). The data gap in disaster risk reduction: A systematic review of challenges and solutions. International Journal of Disaster Risk Science, *14*(2), 234-251.

Lapietra, I., Colacicco, R., Rizzo, A., & Capolongo, D. (2024). Mapping social vulnerability to multi-hazard scenarios: A GIS-based approach at the census tract level. Applied Sciences, *14*(11), 4503.

Lee, H., & Li, W. (2025). Geospatial Artificial Intelligence for satellite-based flood extent mapping: Concepts, advances, and future perspectives. arXiv preprint, arXiv:2504.02214.

Lema, G., Meshesha, M., & Teklesilassie, A. (2021). Machine learning for disaster management in Africa: A systematic review. Journal of Emergency Management, *19*(4), 367-384.

Li, J., Wang, Z., & Liu, X. (2020). AI-powered disaster response: A review of applications and challenges. International Journal of Disaster Risk Reduction, *51*, 101912.

Liu, Z., Coleman, N., Patrascu, F. I., Yin, K., Li, X., & Mostafavi, A. (2024). Artificial Intelligence for flood risk management: A comprehensive state-of-the-art review and future directions. International Journal of Disaster Risk Reduction, *117*, 105110.

Ma, Y., Chen, L., & Zhao, J. (2023). Community ownership in disaster response programs: A systematic review. Disasters, *47*(2), 456-478.

Mai, G., Hu, Y., & Janowicz, K. (2025). Algorithmic bias in GeoAI: A review of causes, consequences, and mitigation strategies. Journal of Spatial Information Science, *30*, 1-28.

Marasinghe, R., Yiğitcanlar, T., Mayere, S., Washington, T. L., & Limb, M. (2024). Towards responsible urban geospatial AI: Insights from the white and grey literature. Journal of Geovisualization and Spatial Analysis, *8*(2), 184.

Mdemu, M. V., Kimwaga, R., & Kaseva, M. (2023). Participatory GIS for disaster risk reduction in East Africa: A systematic review. International Journal of Disaster Risk Reduction, *92*, 103678.

Milofsky, C. (2023). From engineering to socio-ecological resilience: A paradigm shift in disaster management. Community Development, *54*(2), 178-195.

Nathan, F., Pelling, M., & Satterthwaite, D. (2022). The failure of top-down technical solutions in disaster risk reduction: A critical review. Environment and Urbanization, *34*(1), 145-162.

Niroshan, N., & Carswell, J. D. (2024). Integrating GeoAI into national mapping programs: Challenges and opportunities. Cartography and Geographic Information Science, *51*(3), 289-308.

Okyere, S. A., Abunyewah, M., & Erdiaw-Kwasie, M. O. (2025). Validation protocols for AI-assisted mapping in African contexts. GeoJournal, *90*(1), 1-18.

Oluoch, S., Mwangi, K., & Ndiritu, J. (2022). Ground truth data collection for GeoAI applications in Kenya: Lessons and best practices. African Journal of Environmental Science and Technology, *16*(4), 134-149.

Oraegbu, C., & Jolaiya, T. (2024). Data quality challenges in open mapping for disaster management in Africa. International Journal of Digital Earth, *17*(2), 234-251.

Orlove, B., Sherpa, P. Y., Dawson, N., Adelekan, I., Alangui, W., Carmona, R., ... & Wilson, A. (2023). Placing diverse knowledge systems at the core of transformative climate research. Ambio, *52*(9), 1431-1447.

Pelizari, P. A., Geiß, C., Groth, S., & Taubenböck, H. (2023). Deep multitask learning with label interdependence distillation for multicriteria street-level image classification. ISPRS Journal of Photogrammetry and Remote Sensing, *204*, 275-290.

Pizzolotto, C. (2022). Volunteered Geographic Information: A decade of research and practice. Transactions in GIS, *26*(3), 1245-1268.

Pouresmaeil, Y., Afrough, S., & Jiao, J. (2025). Mapping out AI functions in intelligent disaster (mis)management and AI-caused disasters. arXiv preprint, arXiv:2502.16644.

Praharaj, S., & Wentz, E. A. (2022). Integrating community knowledge with geospatial analytics for urban resilience: A systematic review. Computers, Environment and Urban Systems, *95*, 101812.

Raftopoulos, M., Pertoldi-Bianchi, S., Eleftherios, P., & Kjellman, K. G. (2024). Conceptualising the nexus between Disaster Risk Reduction and Climate Change Adaptation and Mitigation in governance. Research Portal Denmark, *2024*(3), 172-202.

Rashidfarokhi, A. (2024). Interdisciplinary collaboration in resilience research: A systematic review. Sustainability Science, *19*(1), 123-142.

Roohi, M., van de Lindt, J. W., Rosenheim, N., Hu, Y., & Cutler, H. (2020). Implication of building inventory accuracy on physical and socio-economic resilience metrics for informed decision-making in natural hazards. Structure and Infrastructure Engineering, *17*(4), 534-554.

Sapena, M., García, M., & Ruiz, L. (2024). Ethics-by-design in GeoAI: A framework for responsible geospatial artificial intelligence. Big Data & Society, *11*(2), 1-18.

Saputra, E., Lee, H., & Kim, J. (2025). Culturally sensitive resilience strategies: A systematic review. International Journal of Disaster Risk Reduction, *115*, 104567.

Sauls, L., Johnson, M., & Williams, K. (2023). Low-cost drones for participatory mapping in Africa: Opportunities and challenges. Drones, *7*(2), 89.

See, L., Fritz, S., & Moorthy, I. (2025). Generative AI and citizen science: Opportunities for improving spatial data. Citizen Science: Theory and Practice, *10*(1), 12.

Sekara, V., Mones, E., & Jankowski, P. (2025). Granular settlement mapping using AI: Applications for humanitarian response. Scientific Reports, *15*(1), 2345.

Sieber, R. E., & Brandusescu, A. (2025). Data sovereignty and sustainability in open mapping: A critical review. GeoJournal, *90*(2), 1-16.

S.N., A., Kumar, A., & Singh, P. (2024). Identifying informal settlements using deep learning: A systematic review. Remote Sensing Applications: Society and Environment, *34*, 101234.

Tanaka, A., & Matsumoto, Y. (2024). Adaptive AI-driven earthquake simulation leveraging real-time geospatial data and advanced machine learning models. Research Square, rs-4974302. DOI: 10.21203/rs.3.rs-4974302/v1

Taylor, F. E., Millington, J. D., Jacob, E., Malamud, B. D., & Pelling, M. (2020). Messy maps: Qualitative GIS representations of resilience. Landscape and Urban Planning, *198*, 103771.

Trogrlić, R. Š., Duncan, M., Wright, G., van den Homberg, M., Adeloye, A. J., & Mwale, F. (2022). Why does community-based disaster risk reduction fail to learn from local knowledge? Experiences from Malawi. International Journal of Disaster Risk Reduction, *83*, 103405.

Vijayagopal, P., Kumar, A., & Singh, R. (2025). Landslide early warning systems using machine learning: A systematic review. Landslides, *22*(1), 145-168.

Ward, M., Johnson, P., & Chen, W. (2020). AI for accelerating geospatial data generation in disaster contexts. International Journal of Digital Earth, *13*(8), 892-912.

Wowk, K., McKinley, E., & Fletcher, S. (2023). Quantifying social dimensions of resilience: A systematic review of methods and metrics. Ecology and Society, *28*(1), 12.

Xu, J., Lu, W., & Li, Z. (2019). Building damage detection in satellite imagery using convolutional neural networks. Remote Sensing, *11*(11), 1356.

Ye, X., Wang, S., Lu, Z., Song, Y., & Yu, S. (2021). Towards an AI-driven framework for multi-scale urban flood resilience planning and design. Computational Urban Science, *1*(1), 11.

Yeboah, G., Porto de Albuquerque, J., & Troilo, R. (2021). Real-time flood reporting in Lagos, Nigeria: A participatory approach. Journal of Flood Risk Management, *14*(2), e12701.

Yessoufou, A., Sarr, M., & Diop, A. (2024). Women's social networks and climate resilience in Senegal. Gender, Place & Culture, *31*(3), 345-367.

Yilma, A. D. (2019). Volunteered Geographic Information in Africa. The International Archives of the Photogrammetry, Remote Sensing and Spatial Information Sciences, *XLII-2/W13*, 1615-1620.

Yordanov, V., Brovelli, M. A., & Carrion, D. (2021). AI for rapid information generation in disaster response: A review. International Journal of Applied Earth Observation and Geoinformation, *102*, 102456.

Yuan, F., Fan, C., Farahmand, H., Coleman, N., Esmalian, A., Lee, C. C., ... & Mostafavi, A. (2022). Smart flood resilience: harnessing community-scale big data for predictive flood risk monitoring, rapid impact assessment, and situational awareness. Environmental Research: Infrastructure and Sustainability, *2*(2), 025006.

ADDITIONAL READING

Gaikwad, S. N., Iyer, S., Lunga, D., & Bondi, E. (2021). Proceedings of KDD 2020 workshop on data-driven humanitarian mapping: Harnessing human-machine intelligence for high-stakes public policy and resilience planning. arXiv preprint, arXiv:2109.00435.

Gevaert, C. M., Sliuzas, R., Persello, C., & Vosselman, G. (2020). Evaluating the societal impact of AI in Earth Observation: A conceptual framework. IEEE Geoscience and Remote Sensing Magazine, *8*(3), 62-75.

Haklay, M., & Francis, L. (2018). Participatory GIS and community-based mapping for environmental justice. In *The Routledge Handbook of Environmental Justice* (pp. 456–470). Routledge.

Herfort, B., Lautenbach, S., Porto de Albuquerque, J., Anderson, J., & Zipf, A. (2021). The evolution of humanitarian mapping within the OpenStreetMap community. Scientific Reports, *11*(1), 15367.

Jiang, H., Qiang, Y., & Li, R. (2023). A review of GeoAI applications in disaster management. International Journal of Digital Earth, *16*(1), 1-28.

Kamel Boulos, M. N., Peng, G., & VoPham, T. (2019). An overview of GeoAI applications in health and healthcare. International Journal of Health Geographics, *18*(1), 7.

Leidner, D. E., Sutanto, J., & Goutas, L. (2023). Human-centered artificial intelligence in practice: A framework for responsible implementation. Journal of the Association for Information Systems, *24*(3), 567-598.

See, L., Mooney, P., Foody, G., Bastin, L., Comber, A., Estima, J., ... & Rutzinger, M. (2016). Crowdsourcing, citizen science or volunteered geographic information? The current state of crowdsourced geographic information. ISPRS International Journal of Geo-Information, *5*(5), 55.

Tian, Y., Zhao, Q., & Chen, J. (2024). Responsible AI in geospatial applications: A systematic review of ethical frameworks and guidelines. Transactions in GIS, *28*(4), 987-1012.

Zook, M., Barocas, S., Boyd, D., Crawford, K., Keller, E., Gangadharan, S. P., ... & Pasquale, F. (2017). Ten simple rules for responsible big data research. PLoS Computational Biology, *13*(3), e1005399.

KEY TERMS AND DEFINITIONS

Artificial Intelligence (AI): The simulation of human intelligence processes by computer systems, including learning, reasoning, and self-correction. In the context of this chapter, AI specifically refers to machine learning algorithms applied to geospatial data analysis and feature extraction from remote sensing imagery.

Community Resilience: The ability of a community to withstand, adapt to, and recover from adverse events such as natural disasters. This concept encompasses social, economic, institutional, and physical dimensions, emphasizing local capacity and agency rather than external intervention.

Data Sovereignty: The principle that communities, particularly Indigenous and local populations, have the right to govern the collection, ownership, and application of data about themselves, their territories, and their resources. This includes control over how data is accessed, used, and shared.

Disaster Risk Reduction (DRR): The systematic approach to identifying, assessing, and reducing the risks of disaster. It aims to lessen the vulnerability of communities and strengthen their capacity to cope with hazards, encompassing preparedness, mitigation, and prevention activities.

GeoAI (Geospatial Artificial Intelligence): The integration of artificial intelligence techniques with geospatial science and technologies, enabling automated analysis and interpretation of spatial data for applications including feature extraction, pattern recognition, and predictive modeling.

Human-in-the-Loop (HITL): A model that leverages both human intelligence and machine learning, where humans are involved in the training, validation, and refinement of AI systems. This approach ensures that AI outputs are contextualised, verified, and improved through human expertise.

OpenStreetMap (OSM): A collaborative, open-source project that creates and distributes free geographic data for the world. Built by volunteers through ground surveys, GPS tracking, and satellite imagery tracing, OSM serves as a foundational platform for humanitarian mapping and disaster response.

Participatory GIS (PGIS): An approach to geospatial data collection and mapping that actively involves local communities in the process, integrating indigenous knowledge and local perspectives with technical mapping methods to create more accurate and socially relevant representations.

Transfer Learning: A machine learning technique where a model developed for one task is reused as the starting point for a model on a second, related task. In the AIA-OME framework, global pre-trained models are fine-tuned with local data to improve contextual accuracy.

Volunteered Geographic Information (VGI): The creation and dissemination of geographic data by individuals and communities through voluntary efforts, typically using web-based mapping platforms and mobile technologies. VGI represents a democratisation of map-making, shifting from authoritative, top-down production to citizen-led approaches.

Compilation of References

Abd El-Latif, A. A., & Niu, X. (2013). A hybrid chaotic system and cyclic elliptic curve for image encryption. *AEÜ. International Journal of Electronics and Communications*, *67*(2), 136–143. DOI: 10.1016/j.aeue.2012.07.004

Abdu, F. J., Isah, S., Usman, J., Jibrin, A. M., Wakili, A. A., Ashraf, M. W., & Aljundi, I. H. (2025). Hydro-environmental predictive management of sub-surface salinization in arid nearshore-coastal saline aquifer using deep learning and SHAP analysis. *Research Square (Research Square)*. DOI: 10.21203/rs.3.rs-5946945/v1

Abdulwahid, A. A. (2024). Cyber-physical threat mitigation in wind energy systems: A novel secure architecture for industry 4.0 power grids. *Energy Informatics*, *7*(1), 141. Advance online publication. DOI: 10.1186/s42162-024-00449-6

Acar, M., & Toker, A. (2019). Predicting consumer personality traits in the sharing economy: The case of Airbnb. *Applied Marketing Analytics*, *5*(1), 83–96. DOI: 10.69554/DDOF1518

Achar, H.V.B., Prasad, P.S., Rajeshwari, D. *et al.* Federated learning and Neuro-Symbolic AI for botnet classification in IoT-Enabled consumer devices. *Int. j. inf. tecnol.* (2025). .DOI: 10.1007/s41870-025-02993-0

Adekunle, P., Aigbavboa, C., Akinradewo, O., Oke, A., & Aghimien, D. (2022). Construction information management: Benefits to the construction industry. *Sustainability (Basel)*, *14*(18), 11366. DOI: 10.3390/su141811366

Adekunle, S. A., Aigbavboa, C. O., Ejohwomu, O., Adekunle, E. A., & Thwala, W. D. (2024). Digital transformation in the construction industry: A bibliometric review. *Journal of Engineering, Design and Technology*, *22*(1), 130–158. DOI: 10.1108/JEDT-08-2021-0442

Aguiar, J. J. B., Fechine, J. M., & de Barros Costa, E. (2020, November). Collaborative filtering strategy for product recommendation using personality characteristics of customers. In *Proceedings of the Brazilian symposium on multimedia and the web* (pp. 157-164). DOI: 10.1145/3428658.3430969

Ahmad, A., Saraswat, D., & El Gamal, A. (2023). A survey on using deep learning techniques for plant disease diagnosis and recommendations for development of appropriate tools. *Smart Agricultural Technology, 3*(1), 100083. DOI: 10.1016/j.atech.2022.100083

Ahmed, A., Sayed, S., Abdoulhalik, A., Moutari, S., & Oyedele, L. O. (2024). Applications of machine learning to water resources management: A review of present status and future opportunities [Review of *Applications of machine learning to water resources management: A review of present status and future opportunities*]. *Journal of Cleaner Production, 441*, 140715. Elsevier BV. DOI: 10.1016/j.jclepro.2024.140715

Ahmed, S. (2025). Implementation of Advance Encryption Techniques to Protect Sensitive Financial Data from Cyber Threats (Doctoral dissertation, Dublin, National College of Ireland).

Ahmed, I., & Yadav, P. K. (2023). Plant disease detection using machine learning approaches. *Expert Systems: International Journal of Knowledge Engineering and Neural Networks, 40*(5), e13136. DOI: 10.1111/exsy.13136

Aires, J., & Nunes, S. (2016). *FACULDADE DE ENGENHARIA DA UNIVERSIDADE DO PORTO Automatic Generation of Sports News*. University of Porto.

Ajirotutu, R. O., Matthew, B., Garba, P., & Johnson, S. O.Rasheed O. AjirotutuBaalah Matthew Patrick GarbaJohnson Segun Olu. (2024). Advancing lean construction through Artificial Intelligence: Enhancing efficiency and sustainability in project management. *World Journal of Advanced Engineering Technology and Sciences, 13*(02), 496–509. DOI: 10.30574/wjaets.2024.13.2.0623

Akpe, O. E., Ogeawuchi, J. C., Abayomi, A. A., Agboola, O. A., & Ogbuefi, E. (2023). A conceptual model for leadership in digital project governance and execution. International Journal of Advanced Multidisciplinary Research and Studies, 3.

Akter, M., & Mamun, M. N. H. (2023). Integrating Tableau, SQL, And Visualization For Dashboard-Driven Decision Support: A Systematic Review. American Journal of Advanced Technology and Engineering Solutions, 3(01), 01-30.

Al Mansoori, S., Salloum, S. A., & Shaalan, K. (2020). The impact of artificial intelligence and information technologies on the efficiency of knowledge management at modern organizations: a systematic review. Recent advances in intelligent systems and smart applications, 163-182.

Albris, K., Lauta, K. C., & Raju, E. (2020). Strengthening governance for disaster prevention: The enhancing risk management capabilities guidelines. International Journal of Disaster Risk Reduction, *47*, 101647.

Albuquerque, F. D., Maraqa, M. A., Chowdhury, R., Mauga, T., & Alzard, M. (2020). Greenhouse gas emissions associated with road transport projects: Current status, benchmarking, and assessment tools. *Transportation Research Procedia*, *48*, 2018–2030. DOI: 10.1016/j.trpro.2020.08.261

Aljuaid, H., Adlan, H., Alkebsi, B., Alfurhood, B. S., Liotta, A., & Cavallaro, L. (2026). An experimental comparison of deep learning models for pneumonia classification from chest X-ray images. *Biomedical Signal Processing and Control*, *112*(Part D), 108742. DOI: 10.1016/j.bspc.2025.108742

Al-Nimer, M., Khattak, M. S., Wu, Q., & Ullah, R. (2024). Unlocking sustainable project management: The role of project managers' competencies in resource bricolage from a stakeholder engagement perspective. *Business Strategy & Development*, *7*(3), e408. DOI: 10.1002/bsd2.408

Alotaibi, E., & Nassif, N. (2024). Artificial intelligence in environmental monitoring: In-depth analysis. Discover Artificial Intelligence, *4*(1), 1-24.

Al-qaness, M. A. A., Zhu, J., Al-Alimi, D., Dahou, A., Alsamhi, S. H., Abd Elaziz, M., & Ewees, A. A. (2024). Chest X-ray images for lung disease detection using deep learning techniques: A comprehensive survey. *Archives of Computational Methods in Engineering*, *31*(6), 3267–3301. DOI: 10.1007/s11831-024-10081-y

Alshammari, A. (2025). Securing smart microgrids with a novel multi-layer cybersecurity framework for Industry 4.0 renewable energy systems. *Discover Computing*, *28*(1), 80. Advance online publication. DOI: 10.1007/s10791-025-09600-7

Andalu, A., Naik, M. G., & Budde, S. (2025). AI and ML in groundwater exploration and water resources management: Concepts, methods, applications, and future directions. *Journal of Groundwater Science and Engineering*. DOI: 10.26599/JGSE.2026.9280059

Appasami, G., & Nickolas, S. (2022). A deep learning-based COVID-19 classification from chest X-ray image: Case study. *The European Physical Journal. Special Topics*, *231*(18-20), 3767–3777. DOI: 10.1140/epjs/s11734-022-00647-x PMID: 35996535

Arafa, N. A., Salem, Z. E., Abdeldayem, A., Ghorab, M. A., Moustafa, Y. M., Soliman, S. A., Farag, M. H., Purohit, S., Elhag, M., & Youssef, Y. M. (2024). Advancing Deltaic Aquifer Vulnerability Mapping to Seawater Intrusion and Human Impacts in Eastern Nile Delta: Insights from Machine Learning and Hydrochemical Perspective. *Earth Systems and Environment*, *9*(3), 2481–2506. DOI: 10.1007/s41748-024-00518-6

Araya, D., Podgorski, J., & Berg, M. (2023). Groundwater salinity in the Horn of Africa: Spatial prediction modeling and estimated people at risk. *Environment International*, *176*, 107925. DOI: 10.1016/j.envint.2023.107925 PMID: 37209488

Arhin, A. A., & Tetteh, J. D. (2024). Community-based adaptation in Africa: A systematic review of practice and policy. Climate and Development, *16*(2), 89-104.

Armanuos, A. M., Zeleňáková, M., & Elshaarawy, M. K. (2025). Explainable ML modeling of saltwater intrusion control with underground barriers in coastal sloping aquifers. *Scientific Reports*, *15*(1), 29281. Advance online publication. DOI: 10.1038/s41598-025-12830-w PMID: 40784891

Atmaja, T., Setiawati, M. D., Kurisu, K., & Fukushi, K. (2024). Advancing coastal flood risk prediction utilizing a GeoAI approach by considering mangroves as an eco-DRR strategy. Hydrology, *11*(12), 198.

Atmaja, T., Fukushi, K., Lee, D.-J., Atmaja, T., Fukushi, K., & Lee, D.-J. (2025). Leveraging Coupled Hydrodynamic with Data-Driven GeoAI Models for Advancing Systemic Compound Flood Risk Evaluation in Coastal Urban Areas. *Archives of Computational Methods in Engineering*. Advance online publication. DOI: 10.1007/s11831-025-10394-6

Attri, I., Awasthi, L. K., & Sharma, T. P. (2024). Machine learning in agriculture: A review of crop management applications. *Multimedia Tools and Applications*, *83*(5), 12875–12915. DOI: 10.1007/s11042-023-16105-2

Ayadi, R., Forouheshfar, Y., & Moghadas, O. M. (2025). Enhancing system resilience to climate change through artificial intelligence: A systematic literature review. Frontiers in Climate, *7*, 1585331.

Ayadi, Y., Gentilucci, M., Ncibi, K., Hadji, R., & Hamed, Y. (2025). Assessment of a Groundwater Potential Zone Using Geospatial Artificial Intelligence (Geo-AI), Remote Sensing (RS), and GIS Tools in Majerda Transboundary Basin (North Africa). *Water (Basel)*, *17*(3), 331. DOI: 10.3390/w17030331

Baarimah, S. O., Mohammad, A., Alyami, H., Baarimah, A. O., Almujibah, H. R., & Ramu, M. B. (2025). Functional analysis of hyperautomation in construction for advancing efficiency and sustainability through process optimization and technological integration. *Scientific Reports, 15*(1), 41651. DOI: 10.1038/s41598-025-25542-y

Back, M. D., Stopfer, J. M., Vazire, S., Gaddis, S., Schmukle, S. C., Egloff, B., & Gosling, S. D. (2010). Facebook profiles reflect actual personality, not self-idealization. *Psychological Science, 21*(3), 372–374. DOI: 10.1177/0956797609360756 PMID: 20424071

Balami, T. I. U., Okereke, O. C., Anene, E., & Aliyu, H. (2025). AI-Based Optimal Energy Harvesting to Reduce Electromagnetic Radiation from GSM and WiFi at ATBU Yalwa Campus. *International Journal of Data Informatics and Intelligent Computing, 4*(4), 41–51. DOI: 10.59461/ijdiic.v4i4.234

Banerjee Chattapadhyay, D., Putta, J., & Rao, P. (2021). Risk identification, assessments, and prediction for mega construction projects: A risk prediction paradigm based on cross analytical-machine learning model. *Buildings (Basel, Switzerland), 11*(4), 172. DOI: 10.3390/buildings11040172

Barfoot, T. D. (2021). *State estimation for robotics* (2nd ed.). Cambridge University Press.

Barrick, M. R., & Mount, M. K. (1991). The big five personality dimensions and job performance: A meta-analysis. *Personnel Psychology, 44*(1), 1–26. DOI: 10.1111/j.1744-6570.1991.tb00688.x

Barrolleta, L. A. L. R., & Sandoval-Martín, T. (2024). Artificial intelligence versus journalists: The quality of automated news and bias by authorship using a Turing test*. *Analisi, 70*, 15–36. DOI: 10.5565/rev/analisi.3681

Battaglia, M., Ceglia, I., Calabrese, M., & Iandolo, F. (2025). Systemic risk management and stakeholder engagement: Insights from business CSR disclosure. *Corporate Social Responsibility and Environmental Management, 32*(3), 4295–4314. DOI: 10.1002/csr.3186

Baudoin, M. A., Henly-Shepard, S., Fernando, N., Sitati, A., & Zommers, Z. (2016). From top-down to community-centric approaches to early warning systems: Exploring pathways to improve disaster risk reduction through community participation. International Journal of Disaster Risk Science, *7*(2), 163-174.

Benà, E., Ciotoli, G., Petermann, E., Bossew, P., Ruggiero, L., Verdi, L., Huber, P. B., Mori, F., Mazzoli, C., & Sassi, R. (2023). A new perspective in radon risk assessment: Mapping the geological hazard as a first step to define the collective radon risk exposure. *The Science of the Total Environment, 912*, 169569. DOI: 10.1016/j.scitotenv.2023.169569 PMID: 38157905

Bertolotto, M., McArdle, G., & Schoen-Phelan, B. (2020). Volunteered geographic information for disaster management: A systematic review. International Journal of Digital Earth, *13*(12), 1485-1508.

Bhat, R., & Nanjundegowda, R. (2024). A Review on Comparative Analysis of Generative Adversarial Networks' Architectures and Applications. [JRC]. *Journal of Robotics and Control, 6*(1), 53–64. DOI: 10.18196/jrc.v6i1.24160

Bhat, R., & Nanjundegowda, R. (2024). Comparative Analysis of CryptoGAN: Evaluating Quality Metrics and Security in GAN-based Image Encryption. [JRC]. *Journal of Robotics and Control, 5*(5), 1557–1569. DOI: 10.18196/jrc.v5i5.23096

Bhattacharya, S., & Pant, G. (2024). Digital transformation in AECO industry: Impending dilemma in the Indian context. *Journal of Organizational Change Management, 37*(3), 683–699. DOI: 10.1108/JOCM-07-2023-0281

Bilali, A. E., Taleb, A., & Brouziyne, Y. (2020). Groundwater quality forecasting using machine learning algorithms for irrigation purposes. *Agricultural Water Management, 245*, 106625. DOI: 10.1016/j.agwat.2020.106625

Böhlen, M., Chen, J., & Li, Y. (2024). GeoAI in resource-constrained contexts: Challenges and opportunities. Transactions in GIS, *28*(2), 345-367.

Bombiński, P., Szatkowski, P., Sobieski, B., Kwieciński, T., Płotka, S., Adamek, M., Banasiuk, M., Furmanek, M. I., & Biecek, P. (2025). Underestimation of lung regions on chest X-ray segmentation masks assessed by comparison with total lung volume evaluated on computed tomography. *Radiography, 31*(3), 102930. DOI: 10.1016/j.radi.2025.102930 PMID: 40174327

Borkowski, A. S., & Kubrat, A. (2026). A Conceptual AI-Based Framework for Clash Triage in Building Information Modeling (BIM): Towards Automated Prioritization in Complex Construction Projects. *Buildings (Basel, Switzerland), 16*(1), 1–15. DOI: 10.3390/buildings16040690

Bouayad-Agha, N., Casamayor, G., Mille, S., & Wanner, L. (2012). Perspective-oriented generation of football match summaries: Old tasks, new challenges. *ACM Transactions on Speech and Language Processing, 9*(2), 1–31. Advance online publication. DOI: 10.1145/2287710.2287711

Bronstein, M. M., Bruna, J., Cohen, T., & Velickovic, P. (2021). Geometric deep learning: Grids, groups, graphs, geodesics, and gauges. *arXiv preprint arXiv:2104.13478.*

Bühler, M. M., Nübel, K., Jelinek, T., Köhler, L., & Hollenbach, P. (2025). Bridging the Construction Productivity Gap—A Hierarchical Framework for the Age of Automation, Robotics, and AI. *Buildings (Basel, Switzerland), 15*(16), 2899. DOI: 10.3390/buildings15162899

Cadena, C., Carlone, L., & Carrillo, H.. (2021). Past, present, and future of simultaneous localization and mapping: Toward the robust-perception age. *IEEE Transactions on Robotics, 37*(4), 1288–1314.

Candemir, S., & Antani, S. (2019). A review on lung boundary detection in chest X-rays. *International Journal of Computer Assisted Radiology and Surgery, 14*(4), 563–576. DOI: 10.1007/s11548-019-01917-1 PMID: 30730032

Cardon, D. (2015). *À quoi rêvent les algorithmes? Nos vies à l'heure du big data.* Seuil.

Carlson, M. (2015). The Robotic Reporter. *Digital Journalism (Abingdon, England), 3*(3), 416–431. DOI: 10.1080/21670811.2014.976412

Caron, M., & Müller, O. (2023). TacticalGPT: Uncovering the Potential of LLMs for Predicting Tactical Decisions in Professional Football.

Carroll, S. R., Garba, I., Figueroa-Rodríguez, O. L., Holbrook, J., Lovett, R., Materechera, S. A., ... & Hudson, M. (2020). The CARE principles for indigenous data governance. Data Science Journal, *19*(1), 43.

Castelblanco, G., Fenoaltea, E. M., De Marco, A., Demagistris, P., Petruzzi, S., & Zeppegno, D. (2024). Combining stakeholder and risk management: Multilayer network analysis for complex megaprojects. *Journal of Construction Engineering and Management, 150*(2), 04023161. DOI: 10.1061/JCEMD4.COENG-13807

Chakraborty, D., Başağaoğlu, H., & Winterle, J. (2020). Interpretable vs. noninterpretable machine learning models for data-driven hydro-climatological process modeling. *Expert Systems with Applications, 170*, 114498. DOI: 10.1016/j.eswa.2020.114498

Chen, J., Hsieh, G., Mahmud, J. U., & Nichols, J. (2014, February). Understanding individuals' personal values from social media word use. In *Proceedings of the 17th ACM conference on Computer supported cooperative work & social computing* (pp. 405-414). DOI: 10.1145/2531602.2531608

Chen, X., & Chang, A. Y. (2025). Digital technology-enabled AEC project management: Practical use cases, deployment patterns and emerging trends. *Engineering, Construction, and Architectural Management, 10*(2), 123–145. DOI: 10.1108/ECAM-09-2023-0962

Chen, X., Liu, S., & Szeliski, R. (2022). Learning robust visual localization under uncertainty. *IEEE Transactions on Robotics, 38*(6), 3810–3826.

Chiang, S.-H., Chao, L.-W., Wang, K.-D., Wang, C.-C., & Peng, W.-C. (2024). BADGE: BADminton report Generation and Evaluation with LLM. https://github.com/AndyChiangSH/BADGE

Chiloane, C., Dube, T., Sibanda, M., Dalu, T., & Shoko, C. (2025). A Summary of Recent Advances in the Literature on Machine Learning Techniques for Remote Sensing of Groundwater Dependent Ecosystems (GDEs) from Space. *Remote Sensing (Basel), 17*(8), 1460. DOI: 10.3390/rs17081460

Chowdhury, S., Walter, C., & Gamble, R. F. (2019). Observing team collaboration personality traits in undergraduate software development projects. In *Proceedings of the Annual Hawaii International Conference on System Sciences* (Vol. 2019-January, pp. 529–538). DOI: 10.24251/HICSS.2019.065

Chuman, T., Kurihara, K., & Kiya, H. (2017, March). On the security of block scrambling-based etc systems against jigsaw puzzle solver attacks. In *2017 IEEE International Conference on Acoustics, Speech and Signal Processing (ICASSP)* (pp. 2157-2161). IEEE, DOI: 10.1109/ICASSP.2017.7952538

Coger, T., Dinshaw, A., Tye, S., Kratzer, B., Thazin, M., & Carty, J. (2022). Indigenous knowledge and climate adaptation in Africa. World Resources Institute Working Paper.

Cook, A., & Karakuş, O. (2024). LLM-Commentator: Novel fine-tuning strategies of large language models for automatic commentary generation using football event data. *Knowledge-Based Systems, 300*, 112219. Advance online publication. DOI: 10.1016/j.knosys.2024.112219

Costa, P. T., & McCrae, R. R. (1985). *Revised NEO Personality Inventory (NEO PI-R) and NEO Five-factor Inventory (NEO-FFI)*. Psychological Assessment Resources (PAR).

Costa, A., Miranda, J., Dias, D., Dinis, N., Romero, L., & Faria, P. M. (2025). Smart Maintenance Solutions: AR- and VR-Enhanced Digital Twin Powered by FIWARE. *Sensors (Basel), 25*(3), 845. DOI: 10.3390/s25030845 PMID: 39943483

Costa, P. T.Jr, Terracciano, A., & McCrae, R. R. (2001). Gender differences in personality traits across cultures: Robust and surprising findings. *Journal of Personality and Social Psychology, 81*(2), 322–331. DOI: 10.1037/0022-3514.81.2.322 PMID: 11519935

Covatti, G., Li, K.-Y., Podgorski, J., Winkel, L. H. E., & Berg, M. (2025). Nitrate contamination in groundwater across Switzerland: Spatial prediction and data-driven assessment of anthropogenic and environmental drivers. *The Science of the Total Environment, 973*, 179121. DOI: 10.1016/j.scitotenv.2025.179121 PMID: 40120406

Cudney, E. A., Venuthurumilli, S. S. J., Materla, T., & Antony, J. (2020). Systematic review of Lean and Six Sigma approaches in higher education. *Total Quality Management & Business Excellence, 31*(3-4), 231–244. DOI: 10.1080/14783363.2017.1422977

Dao, Q. V. (2021). A case study of BIM application in a public construction project management unit in Vietnam: Lessons learned and organizational changes. *Engineering Journal (New York), 25*(7), 177–192.

Dardouri, S. (2025). A Deep Convolutional Neural Network Model for Lung Disease Detection Using Chest X-Ray Imaging. Pulmonary Medicine, 2025(1), 6614016.

de Souza, C. M. P., da Silva, L. A. P., Leite, M. E., Veloso, G. V., & Filho, E. I. F. (2023). Spatial Modeling of Groundwater Potential in the North of Minas Gerais, Brazil: An Integrated Approach Using Machine Learning and Environmental Data. *Revista Brasileira de Cartografia, 75*. Advance online publication. DOI: 10.14393/rbcv75n0a-65381

Dé, A., Djalante, R., & Shaw, R. (2024). Local capacities for disaster risk reduction: A systematic review. International Journal of Disaster Risk Reduction, *100*, 104215.

Demilie, W. B. (2024). Plant disease detection and classification techniques: A comparative study of the performances. *Journal of Big Data, 11*(1), 5–12. DOI: 10.1186/s40537-023-00863-9

Desikar, G. N. M. S., Kadarkarai, R., Somasundaram, K., Kandasamy, V., & Partheeban, P. (2026). Optimized multi-dimensional attention spiking neural network for pneumonia detection in chest X-ray images. *Biomedical Signal Processing and Control, 113*(Part C), 108765. DOI: 10.1016/j.bspc.2025.108765

Devarajan, V. (2025). Integrated AI-ML framework for disaster lifecycle management: From prediction to recovery. World Journal of Advanced Research and Reviews, *26*(2), 1630-1643.

Dikmen, I., Tah, J. H. M., & Atasoy, G. (2024). Managing risk and complexity in construction projects with digital technologies. centaur.reading.ac.uk

Ding, X., Zhou, Q., Liu, Z., Kowah, J. A. H., Wang, L., Huang, X., & Liu, X. (2024). A novel approach to the technique of lung region segmentation based on a deep learning model to diagnose COVID-19 X-ray images. *Current Medical Imaging, 20*, 100211. Advance online publication. DOI: 10.2174/0115734056271185231121074341 PMID: 38389381

Domfeh, K. A., & Dancy, G. P. (2025). Informal settlement mapping using deep learning: A review of methods and applications. Computers, Environment and Urban Systems, *106*, 102145.

Duarte-Vidal, L., Herrera, R. F., Atencio, E., & Munoz-La Rivera, F. (2021). Interoperability of digital tools for the monitoring and control of construction projects. *Applied Sciences (Basel, Switzerland), 11*(21), 10370. DOI: 10.3390/app112110370

Du, G. (2023). Research on problems and strategies of optimisation in construction project management. *International Journal of Frontiers in Engineering Technology, 5*(10).

Duncan, S., Kunert, J., & Karg, A. (2025). Attitudes to automated and human written sport journalism. *Journalism, 26*(9), 1937–1961. Advance online publication. DOI: 10.1177/14648849241260944

Eftekhar, A., Fullwood, C., & Morris, N. (2014). Capturing personality from Facebook photos and photo-related activities: How much exposure do you need? *Computers in Human Behavior, 37*, 162–170. DOI: 10.1016/j.chb.2014.04.048

Egala, R., & Sairam, M. V. S. (2025). Multi-layer stacked residual coordinate termite alate network for multi-class lung diseases detection from chest X-ray images. *Applied Soft Computing, 179*, 113393. DOI: 10.1016/j.asoc.2025.113393

Eghrari, Z., Delavar, M. R., Zaré, M., Mousavi, M., Nazari, B., & Ghaffarian, S. (2023). GROUNDWATER LEVEL PREDICTION USING DEEP RECURRENT NEURAL NETWORKS AND UNCERTAINTY ASSESSMENT. *ISPRS Annals of the Photogrammetry, Remote Sensing and Spatial Information Sciences, 493*, 493–500. Advance online publication. DOI: 10.5194/isprs-annals-X-1-W1-2023-493-2023

El Mohamadi, H., El Hassouni, M., & Jennane, R. (2025). Dual-domain explainability-driven data augmentation for enhanced COVID-19 detection in chest X-rays. *Multimedia Tools and Applications, 84*(31), 37793–37814. Advance online publication. DOI: 10.1007/s11042-025-20920-0

ElHaj, K., & Alshamsi, D. (2025). GeoTemporal clustering for aquifer delineation: A big data approach to synchronizing and analyzing variable-length groundwater time series. *Journal of Big Data*, *12*(1), 25. Advance online publication. DOI: 10.1186/s40537-025-01060-6

Elias, J. D., & Lubua, E. W. (2024). The impact of usability, functionality and reliability on users' satisfaction during library system adoption. *Journal of Informetrics*, *1*(1), 13–21.

Elshaarawy, M. K., & Eltarabily, M. G. (2024). Machine learning models for predicting water quality index: Optimization and performance analysis for El Moghra, Egypt. *Water Science and Technology: Water Supply*, *24*(9), 3269–3294. DOI: 10.2166/ws.2024.189

Emmanuel, I., Danquah, E. O., Ukpoju, E. A., Obasa, J., Olola, T. M., & Enyejo, J. O. (2024). Use of building information modeling (bim) to improve construction management in the USA. *World Journal of Advanced Research and Reviews*, *23*(3), 1799–1813. DOI: 10.30574/wjarr.2024.23.3.2794

Errandonea, I., Beltrán, S., & Arrizabalaga, S. (2020). Digital Twin for maintenance: A literature review. *Computers in Industry*, *123*, 103316. DOI: 10.1016/j.compind.2020.103316

Eytam, E. (2023). The effect of design elements on simplicity, usability, and product preference: A video conference application case study. *Interacting with Computers*, *35*(3), 461–480. DOI: 10.1093/iwc/iwad030

Fajsi, A., Morača, S., Milosavljević, M., & Medić, N. (2022). Project management maturity and business excellence in the context of industry 4.0. *Processes (Basel, Switzerland)*, *10*(6), 1155. DOI: 10.3390/pr10061155

Fathi-Vajargah, B., Kanafchian, M., & Alexandrov, V. (2018). Image encryption based on permutation and substitution using Clifford Chaotic System and logistic map. *Journal of Computers*, *13*(3), 309–326. DOI: 10.17706/jcp.13.3.309-326

Fatorachian, H., & Kazemi, H. (2021). Impact of Industry 4.0 on supply chain performance. *Production Planning and Control*, *32*(1), 63–81. DOI: 10.1080/09537287.2020.1712487

Fernández-Barrero, M. Á., & Serrano-Martín, C. (2025). Are the Media Transparent in Their Use of AI? Self-Regulation and Ethical Challenges in Newsrooms in Spain. *Journalism and Media*, *6*(3), 152. Advance online publication. DOI: 10.3390/journalmedia6030152

FIFA. (2021). The Football Landscape. Vision-Report-2021.

Fillmore, H., & Singletary, L. (2021). Climate data and information needs of indigenous communities on reservation lands: Insights from stakeholders in the Southwestern United States. Climatic Change, *169*(3), 1-20.

Fischer, D., Reinermann, J. L., Mandujano, G. G., & Stanszus, L. (2021). Sustainable consumption communication: A review of an emerging field of research. *Journal of Cleaner Production, 291*, 125211. DOI: 10.1016/j.jclepro.2021.126880

Fornace, K., Surendra, H., Abidin, T. R., Reyes, R., Macalinao, M. L., Stresman, G., ... & Cook, J. (2018). Use of mobile technology-based participatory mapping approaches to geolocate health facility attendees for disease surveillance in low resource settings. International Journal of Health Geographics, *17*(1), 21.

Fu, M., Tantithamthavorn, C., & Le, T. (2025). DAViT: A Domain-Adapted Vision Transformer for Automated Pneumonia Detection and Explanation Using Chest X-Ray Images. *IEEE Access : Practical Innovations, Open Solutions, 13*, 103033–103044. Advance online publication. DOI: 10.1109/ACCESS.2025.3579314

Gaikwad, S. S., Iyer, S., Lunga, D., & Bondi, E. (2021). Data-driven humanitarian mapping: Harnessing human-machine intelligence for high-stakes public policy and resilience planning. *Proceedings of the 27th ACM SIGKDD Conference on Knowledge Discovery & Data Mining*, 4085-4086. DOI: 10.1145/3447548.3469461

Gangwar, S., Devi, R., & Isa, N. A. M. (2025). 9IEC: A novel method for exposure region determination in low contrast and nonuniform illumination chest X-ray imaging. *Biomedical Signal Processing and Control, 109*, 107988. DOI: 10.1016/j.bspc.2025.107988

García-Madurga, M. Á., & Esteban-Navarro, M. Á. (2020). A project management approach to competitive intelligence. *Journal of Intelligence Studies in Business, 10*(3), 8–23. DOI: 10.37380/jisib.v10i3.636

Garg, D., Rani, S., Herencsar, N., Verma, S., Wozniak, M., & Al-Turjman, F. (2022). Hybrid technique for cyber-physical security in cloud-based smart industries. *Sensors (Basel), 22*(1), 345. DOI: 10.3390/s22124630

Gautam, S., Midoglu, C., Shafiee Sabet, S., Kshatri, D. B., & Halvorsen, P. (2022). Soccer Game Summarization using Audio Commentary, Metadata, and Captions. NarSUM 2022 - Proceedings of the 1st Workshop on User-Centric Narrative Summarization of Long Videos, 13–22. DOI: 10.1145/3552463.3557019

Gavish, N., Gutiérrez, T., Webel, S., Rodríguez, J., Peveri, M., Bockholt, U., & Tecchia, F. (2015). Evaluating virtual reality and augmented reality training for industrial maintenance and assembly tasks. [& Francis Online]. *Interactive Learning Environments*, *23*(6), 778–798. DOI: 10.1080/10494820.2013.815221

Gebereselassie, S. A., & Roy, B. K. (2023, November). Secure Image Encryption Algorithm based on Two-Level Diffusion and Hybrid Chaotic Maps. In *2023 IEEE Silchar Subsection Conference (SILCON)* (pp. 1-6). IEEE. DOI: 10.1109/ SILCON59133.2023.10404972

Georges, F. (2011). L'identité numérique sous emprise culturelle: De l'expression de soi à sa standardisation. *Les Cahiers du numérique, 7*(1), 31-48.

Georgy, T. (2025). DIGITAL OPTIMIZATION TOOLS FOR BUSINESS PROCESSES IN THE CONSTRUCTION INDUSTRY IN THE CONTEXT OF THE MODERN ECONOMY. Холодная наука, (15), 48-57.

Gevaert, C. M., Carman, M., Rosman, B., Georgiadou, Y., & Soden, R. (2021). Fairness and accountability of AI in disaster risk management: Opportunities and challenges. Patterns, *2*(11), 100363.

Ghaffarian, S., Taghikhah, F., & Maier, H. R. (2023). Explainable artificial intelligence in disaster risk management: Achievements and prospective futures. International Journal of Disaster Risk Reduction, *98*, 104123.

Ghamisi, P., Yu, W., Marinoni, A., Gevaert, C., Persello, C., Selvakumar, S., . . . Atkinson, P. M. (2024). Responsible AI for Earth Observation. arXiv preprint, arXiv:2405.20868.

Ghansah, F. A., & Lu, W. (2025). Cyber-physical systems and digital twins for "cognitive building" in the construction industry. *Construction Innovation*, *25*(3), 787–818. DOI: 10.1108/CI-07-2022-0164

Ghorayeb, A., Darbyshire, J. L., Wronikowska, M. W., & Watkinson, P. J. (2023). Design and validation of a new Healthcare Systems Usability Scale (HSUS) for clinical decision support systems: A mixed-methods approach. *BMJ Open*, *13*(1), e065323. DOI: 10.1136/bmjopen-2022-065323

Gilga, C., Hochwarter, C., Knoche, L., Schmidt, S., Ringler, G., Wieland, M., Resch, B., & Wagner, J. (2025). Legal and ethical considerations for demand-driven data collection and AI-based analysis in flood response. International Journal of Disaster Risk Reduction, *116*, 105441.

Glebova, E., Madsen, D. Ø., Mihaľová, P., Géczi, G., Mittelman, A., & Jorgič, B. (2024). Artificial intelligence development and dissemination impact on the sports industry labor market. *Frontiers in Sports and Active Living*, *6*, 1363892. Advance online publication. DOI: 10.3389/fspor.2024.1363892 PMID: 38606117

Golbeck, J., Robles, C., Edmondson, M., & Turner, K. (2011). Predicting Personality from Twitter. In *2011 IEEE International Conference on Privacy, Security, Risk, and Trust, and IEEE International Conference on Social Computing* (pp. 149–156). DOI: 10.1109/PASSAT/SocialCom.2011.33

Goldberg, L. R., Johnson, J. A., Eber, H. W., Hogan, R., Ashton, M. C., Cloninger, C. R., & Gough, H. G. (2006). The international personality item pool and the future of public-domain personality measures. *Journal of Research in Personality*, *40*(1), 84–96. DOI: 10.1016/j.jrp.2005.08.007

Gomez-Mejia, G. (2016), Les Fabriques de soi: identité et industrie sur le web, MKF editions.

Gong, P., Lu, Y., Lovreglio, R., Lv, X., & Chi, Z. (2024). Applications and effectiveness of augmented reality in safety training: A systematic literature review and meta-analysis. *Safety Science*, *173*, 106042. DOI: 10.1016/j.ssci.2024.106624

Goodarzi, M. R., Bafrouei, H. R. B., & Vazirian, M. (2024). Insight into groundwater level prediction with feature effectiveness: Comparison of machine learning and numerical methods. *Nordic Hydrology*, *56*(1), 74–92. DOI: 10.2166/nh.2024.135

Goodrich, K. A., Basolo, V., Feldman, D. L., Matthew, R. A., Schubert, J. E., Luke, A., ... & Serrano, K. (2020). Addressing pluvial flash flooding through community-based collaborative research in Tijuana, Mexico. Water, *12*(5), 1257.

Gou, L., Zhou, M. X., & Yang, H. (2014, April). KnowMe and ShareMe: understanding automatically discovered personality traits from social media and user sharing preferences. In *Proceedings of the SIGCHI conference on human factors in computing systems* (pp. 955-964). DOI: 10.1145/2556288.2557398

Graefe, A., & Bohlken, N. (2020). Automated journalism: A meta-analysis of readers' perceptions of human-written in comparison to automated news. In Media and Communication (Vol. 8, Number 3, pp. 50–59). Cogitatio Press. DOI: 10.17645/mac.v8i3.3019

Graveline, M. H., & Germain, D. (2022). Participatory processes and disaster risk reduction: A systematic review. Environmental Science & Policy, *135*, 112-124.

Greenwood, E. E., Lauber, T. B., van den Hoogen, J., Dönmez, A., Bain, R., Johnston, R., Crowther, T. W., & Julian, T. R. (2024). Mapping safe drinking water use in low- and middle-income countries. *Science, 385*(6710), 784–790. DOI: 10.1126/science.adh9578 PMID: 39146419

Han, Y., Huang, L., Xiao, T., Yuan, A., Yu, Y., Feng, Y., ... & Ye, Z. (2022). Smart community emergency evacuation management system and risk assessment based on mobile big data. Wireless Communications and Mobile Computing, *2022*, 4757016.

Hansenne, M. (2006). *Psychologie de la personnalité, Ouvertures psychologiques.* De Boeck.

Hao, Y., Helo, P., & Gunasekaran, A. (2020). Cloud platforms for remote monitoring system: A comparative case study. *Production Planning and Control, 31*(2-3), 186–202. DOI: 10.1080/09537287.2019.1631459

Harakannanavar, S. S., Rudagi, J. M., Puranikmath, V. I., Siddiqua, A., & Pramodhini, R. (2022). Plant leaf disease detection using computer vision and machine learning algorithms. *Global Transitions Proceedings, 3*(1), 305–310. DOI: 10.1016/j.gltp.2022.03.016

Harani, P., Gautam, S., Joshi, S. K., Asirvatham, L. G., & Rakshith, B. L. (2025). Advancements in soil moisture estimation through integration of remote sensing and artificial intelligence techniques [Review of *Advancements in soil moisture estimation through integration of remote sensing and artificial intelligence techniques*]. *The Science of The Total Environment, 1001*, 180503. Elsevier BV. DOI: 10.1016/j.scitotenv.2025.180503

Hariharan, M. (2026, February). Semantic mastery: Enhancing llms with advanced natural language understanding. In 2026 IEEE 5th International Conference on AI in Cybersecurity (ICAIC) (pp. 1-7). IEEE.

Hassani, A., Azapagic, A., & Shokri, N. (2020). Predicting long-term dynamics of soil salinity and sodicity on a global scale. *Proceedings of the National Academy of Sciences of the United States of America, 117*(52), 33017–33027. DOI: 10.1073/pnas.2013771117 PMID: 33318212

Hassani, A., Azapagic, A., & Shokri, N. (2021). Global predictions of primary soil salinization under changing climate in the 21st century. *Nature Communications, 12*(1), 6663. Advance online publication. DOI: 10.1038/s41467-021-26907-3 PMID: 34795219

Hill, R., Adem, Ç., Molnár, Z., Aumeeruddy-Thomas, Y., Bridgewater, P., Tengö, M., ... & Carino, J. (2019). Working with indigenous, local and scientific knowledge in assessments of nature and nature's linkages with people. HAL Archives, hal-02416591.

Hostettler, S., Besson, S., & Bolay, J. C. (2018). *Technologies for development: From innovation to social impact.* Springer International Publishing. DOI: 10.1007/978-3-319-91068-0

Hrazdil, K., Novak, J., Rogo, R., Wiedman, C., & Zhang, R. (2020). Measuring executive personality using machine-learning algorithms: A new approach and audit fee-based validation tests. *Journal of Business Finance & Accounting, 47*(3-4), 519–544. DOI: 10.1111/jbfa.12406

Hsu, Y. C., Huang, T. H., Verma, H., Mauri, A., Nourbakhsh, I., & Bozzon, A. (2022). Empowering local communities using artificial intelligence. Patterns, *3*(3), 100449.

Huang, Y., & Meng, Z. (2026). Highly accurate four-class prediction of lung diseases from chest X-ray images based on EfficientNetV2. *Biomedical Signal Processing and Control, 120*(Part C), 110238. DOI: 10.1016/j.bspc.2026.110238

Huo, L., Lindberg, E., Bohlin, J., & Persson, H. J. (2023). Assessing the detectability of European spruce bark beetle green attack in multispectral drone images with high spatial-and temporal resolutions. *Remote Sensing of Environment, 287*(1), 113484. DOI: 10.1016/j.rse.2023.113484

Hurtz, G. M., & Donovan, J. J. (2000). Personality and job performance: The Big Five revisited. *The Journal of Applied Psychology, 85*(6), 869–879. DOI: 10.1037/0021-9010.85.6.869 PMID: 11125652

Hu, W., Lim, K. Y. H., & Cai, Y. (2022). Digital twin and industry 4.0 enablers in building and construction: A survey. *Buildings (Basel, Switzerland), 12*(11), 2004. DOI: 10.3390/buildings12112004

Ibitoye, A., Nkwo, M., Akinyemi, J. D., & Ladoja, K. T. (2025). Afrocentric trustworthy framework for improved artificial intelligence powered health management tool for Africans. In *AI for Health Equity and Fairness* (pp. 93–117). Springer.

IBM. (2020). *IBM Watson Personality Insights: Product documentation.* IBM Cloud. Retrieved from https://cloud.ibm.com/docs/personality-insights

IBM. (2021). *Watson Personality Insights: Supported languages and norms.* IBM Knowledge Center.

Ibrahim, B., Ogunleye, A., & Adebayo, K. (2025). GeoAI for disaster management in Africa: A review of applications and opportunities. African Journal of Emergency Management, *3*(1), 45-68.

Ibrahim, A., Ibrahim, M., & Satar, N. S. M. (2021). Factors influencing master data quality: A systematic review. *International Journal of Advanced Computer Science and Applications, 12*(2). Advance online publication. DOI: 10.14569/IJACSA.2021.0120224

Imperiale, A. J., & Vanclay, F. (2023). Social learning and vulnerability reduction in disaster-prone communities. Disaster Prevention and Management, *32*(1), 89-104.

Jackulin, C., & Murugavalli, S. (2022). A comprehensive review on detection of plant disease using machine learning and deep learning approaches. *Measurement. Sensors, 24*(5), 100441. DOI: 10.1016/j.measen.2022.100441

Jain, H. (2024). Leveraging geo-computational innovations for sustainable disaster management to enhance flood resilience. Discover Geoscience, *2*(1), 42.

Jäkel, J. I., Fischerkeller, F., Oberhoff, T., & Klemt-Albert, K. (2024). Development of a Maturity Model for the Digital transformation of companies in the context of Construction Industry 4.0. *J. Inf. Technol. Constr., 29*(34), 778–809. DOI: 10.36680/j.itcon.2024.034

Jakubik, J., Vizzari, G., & Psyllidis, A. (2024). Human-machine collaboration for humanitarian mapping: A systematic review. Computers, Environment and Urban Systems, *108*, 102078.

Jamei, M., Karbasi, M., Malik, A., Abualigah, L., Islam, A. R., & Yaseen, Z. M. (2022). Computational assessment of groundwater salinity distribution within coastal multi-aquifers of Bangladesh. *Scientific Reports, 12*(1), 11165. Advance online publication. DOI: 10.1038/s41598-022-15104-x PMID: 35778436

Jamshed, A., Birkmann, J., McMillan, J. M., Rana, I. A., & Lauer, H. (2023). The role of social, economic, and institutional systems in community resilience: A systematic review. International Journal of Disaster Risk Reduction, *95*, 103876.

Jamshidzadeh, Z., Latif, S. D., Ehteram, M., Khozani, Z. S., Ahmed, A. N., Sherif, M., & El-Shafie, A. (2024). An advanced hybrid deep learning model for predicting total dissolved solids and electrical conductivity (EC) in coastal aquifers. *Environmental Sciences Europe, 36*(1), 20. Advance online publication. DOI: 10.1186/s12302-024-00850-8

Janssen, J., Tootchi, A., & Ameli, A. (2024). A critical appraisal of water table depth estimation: Challenges and opportunities within machine learning. EarthArXiv *(California Digital Library)*. DOI: 10.31223/X5939N

Jardine, A. K. S., Lin, D., & Banjevic, D. (2006). A review on machinery diagnostics and prognostics implementing condition-based maintenance. *Mechanical Systems and Signal Processing*, *20*(7), 1483–1510. DOI: 10.1016/j.ymssp.2005.09.012

Ji, H., Song, Y., Bindas, T., Shen, C., Yang, Y., Pan, M., Liu, J., Rahmani, F., Abbas, A., Beck, H. E., Lawson, K., & Wada, Y. (2025). Distinct hydrologic response patterns and trends worldwide revealed by physics-embedded learning. *Nature Communications*, *16*(1), 9169. DOI: 10.1038/s41467-025-64367-1 PMID: 41093823

Jinbo, Z., Li, Y., & Haitao, M. (2025). Handling missing data of using the XGBoost-based multiple imputation by chained equations regression method. *Frontiers in Artificial Intelligence*, *8*, 1553220. Advance online publication. DOI: 10.3389/frai.2025.1553220 PMID: 40248006

Jonathan, G. M., Yalew, S. D., Gebremeskel, B. K., & Gebremeskel, B. K. (2023). IT alignment: A path towards digital transformation success. *Procedia Computer Science*, *220*, 607–614. DOI: 10.1016/j.procs.2023.01.314

Jouibari, Z. E., Moakhkhar, H. N., & Baleghi, Y. (2024). Emergency COVID-19 detection from chest X-rays using deep neural networks and ensemble learning. *Multimedia Tools and Applications*, *83*(17), 52141–52169. DOI: 10.1007/s11042-023-17508-x

Judge, T. A., Heller, D., & Mount, M. K. (2002). Five-factor model of personality and job satisfaction: A meta-analysis. *The Journal of Applied Psychology*, *87*(3), 530–541. DOI: 10.1037/0021-9010.87.3.530 PMID: 12090610

Kachur, A., Osin, E., Davydov, D., Shutilov, K., & Novokshonov, A. (2020). Assessing the Big Five personality traits using real-life static facial images. *Scientific Reports*, *10*(1), 8487. DOI: 10.1038/s41598-020-65358-6 PMID: 32444847

Kagermann, H., Wahlster, W., & Helbig, J. (2013). Recommendations for implementing the strategic initiative INDUSTRIE 4.0. Final report of the Industrie 4.0 Working Group.

Kalaiarasan, A. K. M. (2021). Application of agile project management techniques in construction sector: an enquiry and analysis.

Kalogeraki, M., & Antoniou, F. (2024). Claim management and dispute resolution in the construction industry: Current research trends using novel technologies. *Buildings (Basel, Switzerland)*, *14*(4), 967. DOI: 10.3390/buildings14040967

Kanasheva, Ш. Ж., Duisengazy, С. М., & Seitzhanova, Ж. Д. (2024). Artificial intelligence in journalism: Foreign experience. Bulletin of L.N. Gumilyov Eurasian National University. *JOURNALISM Series, 148*(3), 7–19. DOI: 10.32523/2616-7174-2024-3-148-7-19

Kang, Y., Zhang, F., & Gao, S. (2024). Responsible GeoAI: A review of ethical challenges and opportunities. Transactions in GIS, *28*(1), 3-25.

Karabegović, I., Mahmić, M., Karabegović, E., & Husak, E. (2025, June). Optimization and Increase of Production Efficiency by Using Service Robots for Maintenance, Inspection and Logistics. In International Conference "New Technologies, Development and Applications" (pp. 3-18). Cham: Springer Nature Switzerland.

Katani, E. M., & Ng'Olua, T. N. (2025). Impact of Adoption and Application of PMBOK® Guide on Project Performance in Kenya's Construction Industry: A Multivariate Analysis. *Multidisciplinary Journal of Technical University of Mombasa, 4*(1), 30–36. DOI: 10.48039/mjtum.v4i1.87

Kaushik, P., Jain, E., Kukreja, V., Hariharan, S., Krishnamoorthy, M., Ahuja, V., Bhattacherjee, A., Kaushal, R. K., & Chen, S.-Y. (2025). Modelling radiological features fusion and explainable AI in pneumonia detection: A graph-based deep learning and transformer approach. *Results in Engineering, 19*, 105225. DOI: 10.1016/j.rineng.2025.105225

Kavitha, V., Kumaresan, T., Gopu, A. P., & Kumar, T. S. (2025, April). Next Generation Watermark Removal: An Efficient and Robust Framework with Transfer Learning and Gan. In *2025 3rd International Conference on Artificial Intelligence and Machine Learning Applications Theme: Healthcare and Internet of Things (AIMLA)* (pp. 1-6). IEEE.

Kermanshachi, S., Nipa, T. J., & Dao, B. (2023). Development of complexity management strategies for construction projects. *Journal of Engineering, Design and Technology, 21*(6), 1633–1657. DOI: 10.1108/JEDT-06-2021-0324

Khakpour, A., Colomo-Palacios, R., & Martini, A. (2023). Towards a framework for developing visual analytics in supply chain environments. *International Journal of Information Systems and Project Management, 11*(1), 52–71. DOI: 10.12821/ijispm110103

Kim, H., Lee, J., & Park, S. (2024). Development and Usability Evaluation of Augmented Reality Content for Light Maintenance Training of Air Spring for Electric Multiple Unit. *Applied Sciences (Basel, Switzerland), 14*(17), 7702. https://www.mdpi.com/2076-3417/14/17/7702MDPI. DOI: 10.3390/app14177702

Kim, K., Tiedmann, H. R., & Faust, K. M. (2025). Construction industry changes induced by the COVID-19 pandemic. *Engineering, Construction, and Architectural Management, 32*(7), 4413–4438. DOI: 10.1108/ECAM-09-2023-0983

Kinger, S., & Kulkarni, V. (2025). Transparent and trustworthy interpretation of COVID-19 features in chest X-rays using explainable AI. *Multimedia Tools and Applications, 84*(18), 19853–19881. DOI: 10.1007/s11042-024-19755-y

Kirillov, A.. (2023). Segment anything. In *Proceedings of the IEEE/CVF International Conference on Computer Vision (ICCV).*

Kissi, E., Aigbavboa, C., & Kuoribo, E. (2023). Emerging technologies in the construction industry: Challenges and strategies in Ghana. *Construction Innovation, 23*(2), 383–405. DOI: 10.1108/CI-11-2021-0215

Kobayashi, K., & Alam, S. B. (2023). Explainable, Interpretable & Trustworthy AI for Intelligent Digital Twin: Case Study on Remaining Useful Life. *arXiv preprint arXiv:2301.06676*. DOI: 10.20944/preprints202301.0145.v1

Koldasbayeva, D., Tregubova, P., Gasanov, M., Zaytsev, A., Petrovskaia, A., & Burnaev, E. (2024). Challenges in data-driven geospatial modeling for environmental research and practice [Review of *Challenges in data-driven geospatial modeling for environmental research and practice*]. *Nature Communications, 15*(1). Nature Portfolio. DOI: 10.1038/s41467-024-55240-8

Kolluri, J., Dash, S. K., & Das, R. (2024). Plant Disease Identification Based on Multimodal Learning. *International Journal of Intelligent Systems and Applications in Engineering*, *12*(15s), 634–643.

Kopiika, N., Smith, J., & Chen, Y. (2025). Deep learning for feature extraction from satellite imagery: A review of methods and applications in disaster management. Remote Sensing of Environment, *310*, 114456.

Kothari, S., Bagane, P., Mishra, M., Kulshrestha, S., Asrani, Y., & Maheswari, V. (2024). CropGuard: Empowering Agriculture with AI driven Plant Disease Detection Chatbot. *International Journal of Intelligent Systems and Applications in Engineering*, *12*(12s), 530–537.

Koyyada, S. P., & Singh, T. P. (2024). A systematic survey of automatic detection of lung diseases from chest X-ray images: COVID-19, pneumonia, and tuberculosis. *SN Computer Science*, *5*(2), 229. DOI: 10.1007/s42979-023-02573-8

Krijnen, T. (2021). Automatic Generation of Formula 1 Reports. https://developer.sportradar.com/docs/read/

Krishnakumari, L., Ramalakshmi, R., Srirenganachiyar, V., Ragavan, K., & Ramalakshmi, K. 2023, February. Analysis of Liver Tumor Segmentation using Deep ResUNet. In *2023 Third International Conference on Artificial Intelligence and Smart Energy (ICAIS)* (pp. 665-668). IEEE. DOI: 10.1109/ICAIS56108.2023.10073676

Krtalić, A., Bajić, M., & Đurić, N. (2023). The data gap in disaster risk reduction: A systematic review of challenges and solutions. International Journal of Disaster Risk Science, *14*(2), 234-251.

Kruachottikul, P., Cooharojananone, N., Phanomchoeng, G., Wongsanao, K., Thabsuwan, S., Suwannatrai, K., . . . Vajarodaya, N. (2021, April). Construction process quality control assisted mobile application. In 2021 IEEE 8th International Conference on Industrial Engineering and Applications (ICIEA) (pp. 220-225). IEEE. DOI: 10.1109/ICIEA52957.2021.9436699

Kudyba, S., & Cruz, D. (2023). Understanding project success involving analytic-based decision support in the digital era: A focus on IC and agile project management. *Journal of Intellectual Capital*, *24*(6), 1429–1446. DOI: 10.1108/JIC-03-2022-0054

Lapietra, I., Colacicco, R., Rizzo, A., & Capolongo, D. (2024). Mapping social vulnerability to multi-hazard scenarios: A GIS-based approach at the census tract level. Applied Sciences, *14*(11), 4503.

Lee, H., & Li, W. (2025). Geospatial Artificial Intelligence for satellite-based flood extent mapping: Concepts, advances, and future perspectives. arXiv preprint, arXiv:2504.02214.

Lee, J., Bagheri, B., & Kao, H. A. (2015). A Cyber-Physical Systems architecture for Industry 4.0-based manufacturing systems. *Manufacturing Letters*, *3*, 18–23. DOI: 10.1016/j.mfglet.2014.12.001

Lee, S. B. (2025). Gradual poisoning of a chest X-ray convolutional neural network with an adversarial attack and AI explainability methods. *Scientific Reports*, *15*(1), 21779. DOI: 10.1038/s41598-025-02294-3 PMID: 40593872

Lema, G., Meshesha, M., & Teklesilassie, A. (2021). Machine learning for disaster management in Africa: A systematic review. Journal of Emergency Management, *19*(4), 367-384.

Lermann Henestrosa, A., & Kimmerle, J. (2024). The Effects of Assumed AI vs. Human Authorship on the Perception of a GPT-Generated Text. *Journalism and Media*, *5*(3), 1085–1097. DOI: 10.3390/journalmedia5030069

Li, J., Wang, Z., & Liu, X. (2020). AI-powered disaster response: A review of applications and challenges. International Journal of Disaster Risk Reduction, *51*, 101912.

Li, X., & Li, X. (2019, July). A novel block image encryption algorithm based on DNA dynamic encoding and chaotic system. In 2019 IEEE 4th international conference on signal and image processing (ICSIP) (pp. 901-906). IEEE, DOI: 10.1109/SIPROCESS.2019.8868638

Liang, M., Yang, B., Chen, Y., & Urtasun, R. (2022). BEV Fusion: Multi-task multi-sensor fusion with unified bird's-eye view representation. In *Proceedings of the IEEE International Conference on Robotics and Automation (ICRA).*

Li, C., & Yang, R. (2025). *Machine Learning for Proactive Groundwater Management: Early Warning and Resource Allocation.* DOI: 10.48550/ARXIV.2506.22461

Li, L., Zhang, S., & Wang, B. (2021). Plant disease detection and classification by deep learning—A review. *IEEE Access : Practical Innovations, Open Solutions, 9,* 56683–56698. DOI: 10.1109/ACCESS.2021.3069646

Lin, J. J., & Golparvar-Fard, M. (2021). Visual and virtual production management system for proactive project controls. *Journal of Construction Engineering and Management, 147*(7), 04021058. DOI: 10.1061/(ASCE)CO.1943-7862.0002045

Liu, Z., Coleman, N., Patrascu, F. I., Yin, K., Li, X., & Mostafavi, A. (2024). Artificial Intelligence for flood risk management: A comprehensive state-of-the-art review and future directions. International Journal of Disaster Risk Reduction, *117*, 105110.

Liu, F., Wang, H., Zhang, J., Fu, Z., Zhou, A., Qi, J., & Li, Z. (2022). EvoGAN: An evolutionary computation assisted GAN. *Neurocomputing, 469,* 81–90. DOI: 10.1016/j.neucom.2021.10.060

Liu, L., Preotiuc-Pietro, D., Samani, Z. R., Moghaddam, M. E., & Ungar, L. (2016). Analyzing Personality through Social Media Profile Picture Choice. In *Proceedings of the 10th International AAAI Conference on Web and Social Media (ICWSM)* (pp. 211–220).

Liu, X.-W., Li, C.-Y., Dang, S., Wang, W., Qu, J., Chen, T., & Wang, Q.-L. (2022). Research on Training Effectiveness of Professional Maintenance Personnel Based on Virtual Reality and Augmented Reality Technology. *Sustainability (Basel), 14*(21), 14351. DOI: 10.3390/su142114351

Li, Z., Yang, Z., Szalachowski, P., & Zhou, J. (2020). Building low-interactivity multifactor authenticated key exchange for industrial internet of things. *IEEE Internet of Things Journal, 8*(2), 844–859. DOI: 10.1109/JIOT.2020.3008773

Luo, G., Wang, Z., Wang, Y., & Wang, K. (2024). Detection of pneumonia in chest X-ray image based on separable convolutional neural network. *Concurrency and Computation, 36*(18), e8160. DOI: 10.1002/cpe.8160

M, I., & N, R. (2025). Optimized Deep Learning Architecture for Pediatric Pneumonia Diagnosis in Chest Radiographs with Integration of EfficientNetB4, Topological Convolutional Layers, and Advanced Augmentation Strategies. *Journal of Robotics and Control (JRC), 6*(4), 1568–1580. DOI: 10.18196/jrc.v6i4.25810

Ma, S., ... (2024). The Use of Digital Twins to Support AI-Guided Predictive Maintenance. arXiv preprint. arXiv:2406.13117

Ma, S., Flanigan, K. A., & Bergés, M. (2024). State-of-the-Art Review: The Use of Digital Twins to Support Artificial Intelligence-Guided Predictive Maintenance. *arXiv preprint arXiv:2406.13117.*

Ma, Y., Chen, L., & Zhao, J. (2023). Community ownership in disaster response programs: A systematic review. Disasters, *47*(2), 456-478.

Mahmoudian, F., Nazari, J. A., Gordon, I. M., & Hrazdil, K. (2021). CEO personality and language use in CSR reporting. *Business Ethics, the Environment & Responsibility, 30*(3), 338–359. DOI: 10.1111/beer.12347

Mai, G., Hu, Y., & Janowicz, K. (2025). Algorithmic bias in GeoAI: A review of causes, consequences, and mitigation strategies. Journal of Spatial Information Science, *30*, 1-28.

Malik, A., Pakruddin, B., Parveez, Y. A., Shakeeb, M., & Ahmed, M. M. (2025, January). Super-Resolution Generative Adversarial Networks: A Comprehensive Study on Image Upscaling. In *2025 International Conference on Next Generation Communication & Information Processing (INCIP)* (pp. 672-675). IEEE. DOI: 10.1109/INCIP64058.2025.11019442

Manikandan, A., Babu, R. T. S., Ganesh, S. J., & Sanjay, T. (2025). Generative adversarial networks based adaptive modulation and coding for next-generation 5G communication systems. *Discover Applied Sciences, 7*(2), 91. DOI: 10.1007/s42452-025-06509-0

Mansoor, A., Cerrolaza, J. J., Perez, G., Biggs, E., Okada, K., Nino, G., & Linguraru, M. G. (2020). A generic approach to lung field segmentation from chest radiographs using deep space and shape learning. *IEEE Transactions on Bio-Medical Engineering, 67*(4), 1206–1220. DOI: 10.1109/TBME.2019.2933508 PMID: 31425015

Marasinghe, R., Yiğitcanlar, T., Mayere, S., Washington, T. L., & Limb, M. (2024). Towards responsible urban geospatial AI: Insights from the white and grey literature. Journal of Geovisualization and Spatial Analysis, *8*(2), 184.

Marlapudi, K., & Lenka, U. (2026). Drivers of talent development for industry 4.0: A DEMATEL analysis of Indian manufacturing. *Journal of Intellectual Capital*, •••, 1–22. DOI: 10.1108/JIC-04-2025-0151

Marques, G. M., & Vassallo, F. C. (2024). Augmented Reality in Industry 4.0 Assistance and Training Areas: A Systematic Literature Review and Bibliometric Analysis. *Electronics (Basel)*, *13*(6), 1147. https://www.mdpi.com/2079-9292/13/6/1147MDPI. DOI: 10.3390/electronics13061147

Martin, C., Richter, N., Lloren, R., Amaral-Zettler, L., & Dubois, N. (2024). Machine learning reveals that sodium concentration and temperature influence alkenone occurrence in Swiss and worldwide freshwater lakes. *Frontiers in Earth Science (Lausanne)*, *12*, 1409389. Advance online publication. DOI: 10.3389/feart.2024.1409389

Marvin-DiPasquale, M., McCleskey, R. B., Sullivan, S. L., Root, J. C., Seawolf, S. M., Ransom, K. M., Wherry, S. A., Kakouros, E., & Baesman, S. M. (2025). Select elements of concern in surface water of three hydrologic basins (Delaware River, Illinois River, and Upper Colorado River)—Data screening for the development of spatial and temporal models. *Antarctica A Keystone in a Changing World*. DOI: 10.3133/ofr20251033

Maung, A. P. M., Echizen, I., & Kiya, H. (2024). On the security of learnable image encryption for privacy-preserving deep learning. *IEEE Access : Practical Innovations, Open Solutions*, *12*, 126415–126425. DOI: 10.1109/ACCESS.2024.3454199

Mbugua, Q. S. L. M., Masu, Q. S. S. M., & Kimani, P. (2025). A Survey on the Current Status of Building Information Modelling (BIM) Adoption in Quantity Surveying Practice in Kenya. *Journal of Research in Construction Management*, *10*(2), 123–135.

Mdemu, M. V., Kimwaga, R., & Kaseva, M. (2023). Participatory GIS for disaster risk reduction in East Africa: A systematic review. International Journal of Disaster Risk Reduction, *92*, 103678.

Meledje, D. E. J.-C., Gouli, B. I. M., Kra, D. O., Zran, V. E.-S., Konaté, A., & Trokourey, A. (2024). Analysis of the Quality of Physical and Chemical Parameters of Groundwater in Three Localities in the Sub-Prefecture of Zanzra (Ivory Coast). *Journal of Materials Science and Chemical Engineering*, *12*(4), 1–17. DOI: 10.4236/msce.2024.124001

Mensah, V., Boateng, C. D., Gidigasu, S. S. R., Wemegah, D. D., Aryee, J. N. A., Osei, M. A., Touré, H., Gilbert, J., & Afful, S. (2024). Groundwater Exploration Methods in West Africa: A Review. EarthArXiv *(California Digital Library)*. DOI: 10.31223/X5T399

Mezouary, L. E., Hadri, A., Kharrou, M. H., Fakır, Y., Elfarchouni, A., Bouchaou, L., & Chehbouni, A. (2024a). Machine Learning and Deep Learning Guided Assessment of Groundwater Reservoir Hydrodynamic Parameters: A Case Study of The El Haouz Aquifer. *E3S Web of Conferences, 489*, 4005. DOI: 10.1051/e3sconf/202448904005

Mezouary, L. E., Hadri, A., Kharrou, M. H., Fakır, Y., Elfarchouni, A., Bouchaou, L., & Chehbouni, A. (2024b). Contribution to advancing aquifer geometric mapping using machine learning and deep learning techniques: A case study of the AL Haouz-Mejjate aquifer, Marrakech, Morocco. *Applied Water Science, 14*(5), 102. Advance online publication. DOI: 10.1007/s13201-024-02162-x

Milofsky, C. (2023). From engineering to socio-ecological resilience: A paradigm shift in disaster management. Community Development, *54*(2), 178-195.

Mitsubishi Electric Technical White Papers. MELSOFT GX Works3 and GT Works3 Advanced Functionality. Mitsubishi Electric Corporation.

Mohammed, M. A. A., Kaya, F., Mohamed, A., Alarifi, S. S., Abdelrady, A., Keshavarzi, A., Szabó, N. P., & Szűcs, P. (2023). Application of GIS-based machine learning algorithms for prediction of irrigational groundwater quality indices. *Frontiers in Earth Science (Lausanne), 11*, 1274142. Advance online publication. DOI: 10.3389/feart.2023.1274142

Molina, M. (2024). *Ai and Its Application in Civil Engineering, a Vision of Trends.* Recalde Recalde.

Mondal, A. K., Bhattacharjee, A., Singla, P., & Prathosh, A. P. (2022). xViTCOS: Explainable vision transformer based COVID-19 screening using radiography. *IEEE Journal of Translational Engineering in Health and Medicine, 10*, 1–12. DOI: 10.1109/JTEHM.2021.3134096 PMID: 34956741

Mongan, J., Moy, L., & Kahn, C. E.Jr. (2020). Checklist for Artificial Intelligence in Medical Imaging (CLAIM): A guide for authors and reviewers. *Radiology. Artificial Intelligence, 2*(2), e200029. DOI: 10.1148/ryai.2020200029 PMID: 33937821

Monteiro, A., Varajão, J., & Santos, V. (2025). Effects of project management information systems (PMIS) on project manager's performance.

Mosavi, A., Hosseini, F. S., Choubin, B., Goodarzi, M., & Dineva, A. (2020). Groundwater Salinity Susceptibility Mapping Using Classifier Ensemble and Bayesian Machine Learning Models. *IEEE Access : Practical Innovations, Open Solutions, 8*, 145564–145576. DOI: 10.1109/ACCESS.2020.3014908

Mousa, M., Mullins, A. K., Skouteris, H., Boyle, J., & Teede, H. J. (2021). Organisational best practices for advancing women in leadership: Protocol for a systematic literature review. *BMJ Open, 11*(4), e046982. DOI: 10.1136/bmjopen-2020-046982

Muralidharan, K., Das, A., Pandya, S. N., & Kim, J. M. (2025). Alternate Groundwater Modelling Strategies: A Multi-Faceted Data-Driven Approach. *arXiv (Cornell University)*. https://doi.org//arxiv.2505.24235DOI: 10.48550

Musa, A., Prasad, R., & Hernandez, M. (2025). Addressing cross-population domain shift in chest X-ray classification through supervised adversarial domain adaptation. *Scientific Reports, 15*(1), 11383. DOI: 10.1038/s41598-025-95390-3 PMID: 40181036

Musarat, M. A., Hameed, N., Altaf, M., & Khan, M. A. (2021). Digital transformation of the construction industry: a review. In Proceedings of the International Conference on Decision Aid Sciences and Applications (DASA) (pp. 100-105). IEEE. León, L. P. (2024). Characterization of the information system integrated to the construction project management systems. Romero Romero. DOI: 10.1109/DASA53625.2021.9682303

Nagahara, S., Katayama, T., Song, T., & Shimamoto, T. (2022, July). A Novel Video Coding Framework with GAN-based Face Generation for Videoconferencing. In *2022 37th International Technical Conference on Circuits/Systems, Computers and Communications (ITC-CSCC)* (pp. 450-452). IEEE. DOI: 10.1109/ITC-CSCC55581.2022.9894994

Nagy, A., ... (2023). AI-Powered Interfaces for Extended Reality to Support Remote Maintenance. arXiv preprint. arXiv:2306.16961 DOI: 10.1109/CCGridW59191.2023.00045

Naji, K. K., Gunduz, M., Alhenzab, F., Al-Hababi, H., & Al-Qahtani, A. (2024). Assessing the digital transformation readiness of the construction industry utilizing the Delphi Method. *Buildings (Basel, Switzerland), 14*(3), 601. DOI: 10.3390/buildings14030601

Nambiar, R., & Nanjundegowda, R. (2025). Detection of missing tooth regions using deep learning in panoramic radiographs for dental implant planning. *Engineering Technology & Applied Science Research, 15*(5), 28071–28076. DOI: 10.48084/etasr.13101

Nathan, F., Pelling, M., & Satterthwaite, D. (2022). The failure of top-down technical solutions in disaster risk reduction: A critical review. Environment and Urbanization, *34*(1), 145-162.

Nguyen, T. D., & Adhikari, S. (2023). The role of bim in integrating digital twin in building construction: A literature review. *Sustainability (Basel), 15*(13), 10462. DOI: 10.3390/su151310462

Nguyen, T. D., & Pishdad-Bozorgi, P. (2023). Overcoming the barriers toward widespread adoption of prefabrication: an approach involving emerging technologies. In *Proceedings of the 31st Annual Conference of the International Group for Lean Construction (IGLC31)*, Lille, France (Vol. 26). DOI: 10.24928/2023/0116

Niroshan, N., & Carswell, J. D. (2024). Integrating GeoAI into national mapping programs: Challenges and opportunities. Cartography and Geographic Information Science, *51*(3), 289-308.

Norman, W. T. (1963). Toward an adequate taxonomy of personality attributes: Replicated factor structure in peer nomination personality ratings. *Journal of Abnormal and Social Psychology, 66*(6), 574–583. DOI: 10.1037/h0040291 PMID: 13938947

Oke, A. E., Aliu, J., & Onajite, S. A. (2024). Barriers to the adoption of digital technologies for sustainable construction in a developing economy. *Architectural Engineering and Design Management, 20*(3), 431–447. DOI: 10.1080/17452007.2023.2187754

Oktay, O., Schlemper, J., Folgoc, L. L., Lee, M., Heinrich, M., Misawa, K., Mori, K., McDonagh, S., Hammerla, N. Y., Kainz, B., Glocker, B., & Rueckert, D. (2018). Attention U-Net: Learning where to look for the pancreas. *arXiv*. https://arxiv.org/abs/1804.03999

Okyere, S. A., Abunyewah, M., & Erdiaw-Kwasie, M. O. (2025). Validation protocols for AI-assisted mapping in African contexts. GeoJournal, *90*(1), 1-18.

Olaniran, O. R., & Alzahrani, A. (2025). Bayesian Random Forest with Multiple Imputation by Chain Equations for High-Dimensional Missing Data: A Simulation Study. *Mathematics, 13*(6), 956. DOI: 10.3390/math13060956

Olentsova, J. A., Кукарцев, В. В., Orlov, V., Semenova, E., & Pinchuk, I. A. (2024). Predictive modelling of post-monsoon groundwater quality in Telangana using machine learning techniques. *BIO Web of Conferences, 116*, 3021. DOI: 10.1051/bioconf/202411603021

Olugboyega, O., Bolujoko, A., Oseghale, G., & Aigbavboa, C. (2022). Measuring the effects of mobile technology barriers and enablers on acceptance and proficiency in the Nigerian construction industry. *Acta Structilia, 29*(2), 1–32. DOI: 10.18820/24150487/as29i2.1

Oluoch, S., Mwangi, K., & Ndiritu, J. (2022). Ground truth data collection for GeoAI applications in Kenya: Lessons and best practices. African Journal of Environmental Science and Technology, *16*(4), 134-149.

Onososen, A. O., Musonda, I., Onatayo, D., Tjebane, M. M., Saka, A. B., & Fagbenro, R. K. (2023). Impediments to construction site digitalisation using unmanned aerial vehicles (UAVs). *Drones (Basel)*, *7*(1), 45. DOI: 10.3390/drones7010045

Oraegbu, C., & Jolaiya, T. (2024). Data quality challenges in open mapping for disaster management in Africa. International Journal of Digital Earth, *17*(2), 234-251.

Orchi, H., Sadik, M., & Khaldoun, M. (2021). On using artificial intelligence and the internet of things for crop disease detection: A contemporary survey. *Agriculture*, *12*(1), 9. DOI: 10.3390/agriculture12010009

Orlove, B., Sherpa, P. Y., Dawson, N., Adelekan, I., Alangui, W., Carmona, R., ... & Wilson, A. (2023). Placing diverse knowledge systems at the core of transformative climate research. Ambio, *52*(9), 1431-1447.

Outh, S. (2022). *Exploration of Trends in Professional Profile Pictures* (Doctoral dissertation, Toronto Metropolitan University).

Ozturk, M., Salamatmoghadasi, M., & Yanikomeroglu, H. (2025). Integrating terrestrial and non-terrestrial networks for sustainable 6G operations: A latency-aware multi-tier cell-switching approach. *IEEE Network*.

Pakzad Roya. (2019). "Human Rights Implications of IBM Watson's 'Personality Insights' Tool". Medium. A 10/01/2023 on: https://medium.com/taraaz/https-medium-com-taraaz-human-rights-implications-of-ibm-watsons-personality-insights-942413e81117

Panchal, A. V., Patel, S. C., Bagyalakshmi, K., Kumar, P., Khan, I. R., & Soni, M. (2023). Image-based plant diseases detection using deep learning. *Materials Today: Proceedings*, *80*(1), 3500–3506. DOI: 10.1016/j.matpr.2021.07.281

Papacharalampous, G., Tyralis, H., Papalexiou, S. M., Langousis, A., Khatami, S., Volpi, E., & Grimaldi, S. (2020). Global-scale massive feature extraction from monthly hydroclimatic time series: Statistical characterizations, spatial patterns and hydrological similarity. *The Science of the Total Environment*, *767*, 144612. DOI: 10.1016/j.scitotenv.2020.144612 PMID: 33454612

Pazola, A., Shamsudduha, M., French, J., MacDonald, A., Abiye, T., Goni, I. B., & Taylor, R. G. (2024). High-resolution long-term average groundwater recharge in Africa estimated using random forest regression and residual interpolation. *Hydrology and Earth System Sciences*, *28*(13), 2949–2967. DOI: 10.5194/hess-28-2949-2024

Pelizari, P. A., Geiß, C., Groth, S., & Taubenböck, H. (2023). Deep multitask learning with label interdependence distillation for multicriteria street-level image classification. ISPRS Journal of Photogrammetry and Remote Sensing, *204*, 275-290.

Pennebaker, J. W., & King, L. A. (1999). Linguistic styles: Language use as an individual difference. *Journal of Personality and Social Psychology*, *77*(6), 1296–1312. DOI: 10.1037/0022-3514.77.6.1296 PMID: 10626371

Pennebaker, J. W., Mehl, M. R., & Niederhoffer, K. G. (2003). Psychological aspects of natural language use: Our words, our selves. *Annual Review of Psychology*, *54*(1), 547–577. DOI: 10.1146/annurev.psych.54.101601.145041 PMID: 12185209

Pérez, N. D., Singh, V., Ringler, C., Xie, H., Zhu, T., Sutanudjaja, E. H., & Villholth, K. G. (2024). Ending groundwater overdraft without affecting food security. *Nature Sustainability*, *7*(8), 1007–1017. DOI: 10.1038/s41893-024-01376-w

Perrier, N., Bled, A., Bourgault, M., & Garon, S. (2020). Construction 4.0: A survey of research trends. *Automation in Construction*, *114*, 103182.

Pham, H. H., Nguyen, H. Q., Nguyen, H. T., Le, L. T., & Khanh, L. (2022). An accurate and explainable deep learning system improves interobserver agreement in the interpretation of chest radiograph. *IEEE Access : Practical Innovations, Open Solutions*, *10*, 19853–19865. DOI: 10.1109/ACCESS.2022.3210468

Pizzolotto, C. (2022). Volunteered Geographic Information: A decade of research and practice. Transactions in GIS, *26*(3), 1245-1268.

Porlezza, C., & Schapals, A. K. (2024). AI Ethics in Journalism (Studies): An Evolving Field Between Research and Practice. *Emerging Media*, *2*(3), 356–370. DOI: 10.1177/27523543241288818

Pouresmaeil, Y., Afrough, S., & Jiao, J. (2025). Mapping out AI functions in intelligent disaster (mis)management and AI-caused disasters. arXiv preprint, arXiv:2502.16644.

Prabu, S.. (2024). *AI-Driven Predictive Maintenance for Smart Manufacturing Systems Using Digital Twin Technology. IJCESEN*. Link.

Praharaj, S., & Wentz, E. A. (2022). Integrating community knowledge with geospatial analytics for urban resilience: A systematic review. Computers, Environment and Urban Systems, *95*, 101812.

Prasad, S. R., & Thyagaraju, G. S. (2024). Leaf analysis based early plant disease detection using Internet of Things, Machine Learning and Deep Learning: A comprehensive review. *Journal of Integrated Science and Technology*, *12*(2), 734–734.

Prasath, J. G., Prabu, S., Mayil, V. V., & Saini, S. (2025). Optimized double transformer residual super-resolution network-based X-ray images for classification of pneumonia identification. *Knowledge-Based Systems*, *287*, 113037. DOI: 10.1016/j.knosys.2025.113037

Preotiuc-Pietro, D., Eichstaedt, J., Park, G., Sap, M., Smith, L., Tobolsky, V., Schwartz, H. A., & Ungar, L. (2017). The role of personality, age, and gender in tweeting about mental health. In *Proceedings of the 2nd Workshop on Computational Linguistics and Clinical Psychology* (pp. 17–26). Association for Computational Linguistics.

Prity, F. S., Uddin, K. A., & Nath, N. (2024). Exploring swarm intelligence optimization techniques for task scheduling in cloud computing: Algorithms, performance analysis, and future prospects. *Iran Journal of Computer Science*, *7*(2), 337–358. DOI: 10.1007/s42044-023-00163-8

Priyanka, R., Gajendran, G., Boulaaras, S., & Tantawy, S. S. (2025). PediaPulmoDx: Harnessing cutting edge preprocessing and explainable AI for pediatric chest X-ray classification with DenseNet121. *Results in Engineering*, *18*, 104320. DOI: 10.1016/j.rineng.2025.104320

Puduppully, R., Dong, L., & Lapata, M. (2019). Data-to-Text Generation with Content Selection and Planning. www.aaai.org

Purswani, J., Rajagopal, R., Khandelwal, R., & Singh, A. (2020). Chaos Theory on Generative Adversarial Networks for Encryption and Decryption of Data. In Jain, L., Virvou, M., Piuri, V., & Balas, V. (Eds.), *Advances in Bioinformatics, Multimedia, and Electronics Circuits and Signals. Advances in Intelligent Systems and Computing* (Vol. 1064). Springer., DOI: 10.1007/978-981-15-0339-9_20

Qiu, L., Lu, J., Yang, S., Qu, W., & Zhu, T. (2015). What does your selfie say about you? *Computers in Human Behavior*, *52*, 443–449. DOI: 10.1016/j.chb.2015.06.032

Quoniam, L. & Lucien, A. (2009). L'intelligence économique 2.0 ?. *Les Cahiers du numérique*, 4(4), 11-37. DOI: 10.3166/lcn.5.4.11-37

Rabbah, J., Ridouani, M., & Hassouni, L. Improving pneumonia diagnosis with high-accuracy CNN-Based chest X-ray image classification and integrated gradient, Biomedical Signal Processing and Control, Volume 101, 2025, 107239, ISSN 1746-8094, DOI: 10.1016/j.bspc.2024.107239

Radman, K., & Lovreglio, R. (2025). RealCONs: a digital framework for construction reporting accuracy and early delay detection.

Raftopoulos, M., Pertoldi-Bianchi, S., Eleftherios, P., & Kjellman, K. G. (2024). Conceptualising the nexus between Disaster Risk Reduction and Climate Change Adaptation and Mitigation in governance. Research Portal Denmark, *2024*(3), 172-202.

Raghu, N., Bhat, R., Rajashree Nambiar, P., Shetty, G. S., & Kumar, D. B. A. (2025). Blockchain-Enhanced GAN Image Encryption Scheme for Cloud Computing. In H. Joshi, C. Kumar Reddy, M. Ouaissa, M. Hanafiah, & S. Doss (Eds.), *Intelligent Systems and IoT Applications in Clinical Health* (pp. 367-392). IGI Global Scientific Publishing. DOI: 10.4018/979-8-3693-8990-4.ch016

Rajalakshmi, R., Ramalakshmi, K., Lakshmi, A., Subhashini, G., & Theivanathan, G. 2024, March. Enhancing Pneumonia Detection Through Convolutional Neural Networks and Data Augmentation In Chest X-Ray Imaging. In *2024 10th International Conference on Advanced Computing and Communication Systems (ICACCS)* (Vol. 1, pp. 715-718). IEEE.

Ramalakshmi, K., & Kumari, L. K. (2025). U-Net-based architecture with attention mechanisms and Bayesian Optimization for brain tumor segmentation using MR images. *Computers in Biology and Medicine*, *195*, 110677. DOI: 10.1016/j.compbiomed.2025.110677 PMID: 40592172

Ramalakshmi, K., Shukla, V. K., & Kumari, L. K. (2026). Leveraging transfer learning with convolutional neural networks for enhanced breast cancer detection. *Neural Computing & Applications*, *38*(8), 297. DOI: 10.1007/s00521-026-12091-2

Ramalakshmi, K., Srinivasa Raghavan, V., Rajagopal, S., Krishna Kumari, L., Theivanathan, G., Kulkarni, M. B., & Poddar, H. (2024). An extensive analysis of artificial intelligence and segmentation methods transforming cancer recognition in medical imaging. *Biomedical Physics & Engineering Express*, *10*(4), 045046. DOI: 10.1088/2057-1976/ad555b PMID: 38848695

Ramalli, E., & Pernici, B. (2023). Challenges of a Data Ecosystem for scientific data. *Data & Knowledge Engineering*, *148*, 102236. DOI: 10.1016/j.datak.2023.102236

Raman, R. K., Kumar, A., Sarkar, S., Yadav, A. K., Mukherjee, A., Meena, R. S., & Kumar, V. (2024). Reconnoitering Precision Agriculture and Resource Management: A Comprehensive Review from an Extension Standpoint on Artificial Intelligence and Machine Learning. *Indian Research Journal of Extension Education*, *24*(1), 220–235. DOI: 10.54986/irjee/2024/jan_mar/108-123

Ramesh, S., Sukanth, B. N., Jaswanth, S. S., & Singh, R. P. (2024). Enhancing secure data transmission through deep learning-based image steganography and super-resolution generative adversarial networks. *SN Computer Science*, *5*(8), 1138. DOI: 10.1007/s42979-024-03490-0

Rashidfarokhi, A. (2024). Interdisciplinary collaboration in resilience research: A systematic review. Sustainability Science, *19*(1), 123-142.

Rashidi, A., Sarvari, H., Chan, D. W., Olawumi, T. O., & Edwards, D. J. (2026). A systematic taxonomic review of the application of BIM and digital twins technologies in the construction industry. *Engineering, Construction, and Architectural Management*, *33*(3), 1813–1835. DOI: 10.1108/ECAM-02-2024-0239

Rathnayake, A., Murguia, D., & Ruwanpura, J. (2024). Measuring activity-level construction productivity. *Journal of Construction Engineering and Management*, *150*(1), 04023001. DOI: 10.1061/(ASCE)CO.1943-7862.0002600

Rathod, D. I., Agarwal, R., & Sujatha, K. S. (2024). Lung disease classification using chest X-ray image: An optimal ensemble of classification with hybrid training. *Biomedical Signal Processing and Control*, *91*, 105941. DOI: 10.1016/j.bspc.2023.105941

Ren, H., Wong, A. B., Lian, W., Cheng, W., Zhang, Y., He, J., Liu, Q., Yang, J., Zhang, C. J., Wu, K., & Zhang, H. (2021). Interpretable Pneumonia Detection by Combining Deep Learning and Explainable Models with Multisource Data. IEEE Access, 9, 95872-95883. *Article*, *9458276*. Advance online publication. DOI: 10.1109/ACCESS.2021.3090215

Renju, K., & Brunda, V. (2024). Optimizing Crop Yield Prediction through Multiple Models: An Ensemble Stacking Approach. *International Journal of Data Informatics and Intelligent Computing*, *3*(2), 52–58. DOI: 10.59461/ijdiic.v3i2.120

Ronneberger, O., Fischer, P., & Brox, T. (2015). U-Net: Convolutional networks for biomedical image segmentation. In *MICCAI 2015* (pp. 234–241). Medical Image Computing and Computer-Assisted Intervention. Springer., DOI: 10.1007/978-3-319-24574-4_28

Roohi, M., van de Lindt, J. W., Rosenheim, N., Hu, Y., & Cutler, H. (2020). Implication of building inventory accuracy on physical and socio-economic resilience metrics for informed decision-making in natural hazards. Structure and Infrastructure Engineering, *17*(4), 534-554.

Rossner, A., Cassel, M., & Huschens, M. (2024). Do Users Really Care? Evaluating the User Perception of Disclosing AI-Generated Content on Credibility in (Sports) Journalism. *Proceedings of Mensch Und Computer, 2024*, 413–418. DOI: 10.1145/3670653.3677490

Rouhani, S. H., Su, C., Mobayen, S., Razmjooy, N., & Elsisi, M. (2024). Cyber resilience in renewable microgrids: A review of standards, challenges, and solutions [Review of *Cyber resilience in renewable microgrids: A review of standards, challenges, and solutions*]. *Energy, 309*, 133081. Elsevier BV. DOI: 10.1016/j.energy.2024.133081

Roy, D. K., Sarkar, T. K., Munmun, T. H., Paul, C. R., & Datta, B. (2025). A review on the applications of machine learning and deep learning to groundwater salinity modeling: present status, challenges, and future directions [Review of *A review on the applications of machine learning and deep learning to groundwater salinity modeling: present status, challenges, and future directions*]. *Discover Water, 5*(1). Springer Nature. DOI: 10.1007/s43832-025-00207-z

Roy, S., Abir, A. R., & Ansary, M. A. (2025). Use of CPT and other parameters for estimating soil unit weight using optimised machine learning models. *Earth Science Informatics, 18*(2), 221. Advance online publication. DOI: 10.1007/s12145-025-01756-6

S.N., A., Kumar, A., & Singh, P. (2024). Identifying informal settlements using deep learning: A systematic review. Remote Sensing Applications: Society and Environment, *34*, 101234.

Sadeghi, A., Sadeghi, M., Fakhar, M., Zakariaei, Z., Sadeghi, M., & Bastani, R. (2024). A deep learning-based model for detecting Leishmania amastigotes in microscopic slides: A new approach to telemedicine. *BMC Infectious Diseases, 24*(1), 551. Advance online publication. DOI: 10.1186/s12879-024-09428-4 PMID: 38824500

Sagar, S., Javed, M., & Doermann, D. S. (2023). Leaf-Based Plant Disease Detection and Explainable AI. *arXiv preprint arXiv,* 2404, 16833.

Sahour, S., Khanbeyki, M., Gholami, V., Sahour, H., Kahvazade, I., & Karimi, H. (2022). Evaluation of machine learning algorithms for groundwater quality modeling. *Research Square (Research Square)*. DOI: 10.21203/rs.3.rs-2210884/v1

Sahour, S., Khanbeyki, M., Gholami, V., Sahour, H., Kahvazade, I., & Karimi, H. (2023). Evaluation of machine learning algorithms for groundwater quality modeling. *Environmental Science and Pollution Research International, 30*(16), 46004–46021. DOI: 10.1007/s11356-023-25596-3 PMID: 36715809

Sahwell, P. J., & Solo-Gabriele, H. M. (2025). Control of freshwater flows can counteract the effects of global climate change on salinity within urban estuaries. *The Science of the Total Environment, 1001*, 180544. DOI: 10.1016/j.scitotenv.2025.180544 PMID: 40987113

Sajitha, P., Andrushia, A. D., Anand, N., & Naser, M. Z. (2024). A Review on Machine Learning and Deep Learning Image-based Plant Disease Classification for Industrial Farming Systems. *Journal of Industrial Information Integration, 38*, 100572. DOI: 10.1016/j.jii.2024.100572

Sanad, H., Moussadek, R., Zouahri, A., Lhaj, M. O., Mouhir, L., & Dakak, H. (2025). AI and Machine Learning-Based Spatial Modeling of Groundwater Quality Indices and Hydrogeochemistry for Accurate Prediction of Seawater Intrusion and Irrigation Sustainability in Coastal Agroecosystems. *Research Square (Research Square)*. DOI: 10.21203/rs.3.rs-7705609/v1

Sandeep, S. R., Ahamad, S., Saxena, D., Srivastava, K., Jaiswal, S., & Bora, A. (2022). To understand the relationship between Machine learning and Artificial intelligence in large and diversified business organisations. *Materials Today: Proceedings, 56*, 2082–2086. DOI: 10.1016/j.matpr.2021.11.409

Sapena, M., García, M., & Ruiz, L. (2024). Ethics-by-design in GeoAI: A framework for responsible geospatial artificial intelligence. Big Data & Society, *11*(2), 1-18.

Saputra, E., Lee, H., & Kim, J. (2025). Culturally sensitive resilience strategies: A systematic review. International Journal of Disaster Risk Reduction, *115*, 104567.

Sarkar, C., Gupta, D., Gupta, U., & Hazarika, B. B. (2023). Leaf disease detection using machine learning and deep learning: Review and challenges. *Applied Soft Computing, 145*, 110534. DOI: 10.1016/j.asoc.2023.110534

Sarkhoosh, M. H., Gautam, S., Midoglu, C., Sabet, S. S., & Halvorsen, P. (2024). Multimodal AI-Based Summarization and Storytelling for Soccer on Social Media. MMSys 2024 - Proceedings of the 2024 ACM Multimedia Systems Conference, 485–491. DOI: 10.1145/3625468.3652197

Sarlin, P.-E., DeTone, D., Malisiewicz, T., & Rabinovich, A. (2020). SuperGlue: Learning feature matching with graph neural networks. In *Proceedings of the IEEE/CVF Conference on Computer Vision and Pattern Recognition (CVPR)* (pp. 4938–4947). DOI: 10.1109/CVPR42600.2020.00499

Sarwar, H., & Rahman, M. (2024, June). A Systematic Short Review of Machine Learning and Artificial Intelligence Integration in Current Project Management Techniques. In 2024 IEEE 4th International Conference on Software Engineering and Artificial Intelligence (SEAI) (pp. 262-270). IEEE. DOI: 10.1109/SEAI62072.2024.10674089

Sauls, L., Johnson, M., & Williams, K. (2023). Low-cost drones for participatory mapping in Africa: Opportunities and challenges. Drones, *7*(2), 89.

Schlüchter, J., & Retucci, G. (2023). *Hilti innovation leadership experience as enabler for a better future in the construction industry. emerald.com.* Retrieved from. [Insert URL if available, otherwise omit]

Schubert, P., & Williams, S. P. (2022). Enterprise Collaboration Platform Configurations: an Empirical Study. In Proceedings of 20th European Conference on Computer-Supported Cooperative Work. European Society for Socially Embedded Technologies (EUSSET).

Schwartz, H. A., Eichstaedt, J. C., Kern, M. L., Dziurzynski, L., Ramones, S. M., Agrawal, M., Shah, A., Kosinski, M., Stillwell, D., Seligman, M. E. P., & Ungar, L. H. (2013). Personality, gender, and age in the language of social media: The open-vocabulary approach. *PLoS One*, *8*(9), e73791. DOI: 10.1371/journal.pone.0073791 PMID: 24086296

See, L., Fritz, S., & Moorthy, I. (2025). Generative AI and citizen science: Opportunities for improving spatial data. Citizen Science: Theory and Practice, *10*(1), 12.

Sekara, V., Mones, E., & Jankowski, P. (2025). Granular settlement mapping using AI: Applications for humanitarian response. Scientific Reports, *15*(1), 2345.

Shafik, W. (2025). Quantum Computing and Generative Adversarial Networks (GANs): Ethics, Privacy, and Security. In *Quantum AI and its Applications in Blockchain Technology* (pp. 111-156). IGI Global Scientific Publishing.

Shaikh, M. S. (2025). Generative Adversarial Networks (GAN) Insights for Cyber Security Applications. In *Emerging Trends in Information System Security Using AI & Data Science for Next-Generation Cyber Analytics* (pp. 153–172). Springer Nature Switzerland. DOI: 10.1007/978-3-031-81481-5_11

Shaikh, M., & Birajdar, F. (2024). Artificial intelligence in groundwater management: Innovations, challenges, and future prospects. *International Journal of Science and Research Archive, 11*(1), 502–512. DOI: 10.30574/ijsra.2024.11.1.0105

Sharma, C., Başağaoğlu, H., Yoosefdoost, I., Wootten, A., Chakraborty-Reddy, D., Bertetti, F. P., Mirchi, A., & Chakraborty, D. (2024). Efficacy of mitigation strategies for aquifer sustainability under climate change. *Nature Sustainability*, *8*(1), 44–53. DOI: 10.1038/s41893-024-01477-6

Sharma, R., Singh, A., Jhanjhi, N. Z., Masud, M., Jaha, E. S., & Verma, S. (2022). Plant Disease Diagnosis and Image Classification Using Deep Learning. *Computers, Materials & Continua*, *71*(2), 225–236. DOI: 10.32604/cmc.2022.020017

Shaukat, H. (2024). Visual communication and its impact on Engineering Project Management.

Sheu, R. K., Pardeshi, M. S., Pai, K. C., Chen, L. C., Wu, C. L., & Chen, W. C. (2023). Interpretable classification of pneumonia infection using eXplainable AI (XAI-ICP). *IEEE Access : Practical Innovations, Open Solutions*, *11*, 46124–46138. DOI: 10.1109/ACCESS.2023.3255403

Shi, Y., & Sun, L. (2024). How Generative AI Is Transforming Journalism: Development, Application and Ethics. In Journalism and Media (Vol. 5, Issue 2, pp. 582–594). Multidisciplinary Digital Publishing Institute (MDPI). DOI: 10.3390/journalmedia5020039

Siddiqui, A. A., Tirunagari, S., Zia, T., & Windridge, D. (2025). A latent diffusion approach to visual attribution in medical imaging. *Scientific Reports*, *15*(1), 962. DOI: 10.1038/s41598-024-81646-x PMID: 39762275

Sieber, R. E., & Brandusescu, A. (2025). Data sovereignty and sustainability in open mapping: A critical review. GeoJournal, *90*(2), 1-16.

Simonaitis, A., Daukšys, M., & Mockienė, J. (2023). A comparison of the project management methodologies PRINCE2 and PMBOK in managing repetitive construction projects. *Buildings (Basel, Switzerland)*, *13*(7), 1796. DOI: 10.3390/buildings13071796

Singh, P., Pranav, P., & Dutta, S. (2025). A GA-GAN approach for next-generation cryptographic security with a focus on quantum-resistant cryptography. *Discover Computing*, *28*(1), 82. DOI: 10.1007/s10791-025-09594-2

Singh, S., Jeong, Y. S., & Park, J. H. (2016). A survey on cloud computing security: Issues, threats, and solutions. *Journal of Network and Computer Applications*, *75*, 200–222. DOI: 10.1016/j.jnca.2016.09.002

Singh, S., Kumar, M., Kumar, A., Verma, B. K., Abhishek, K., & Selvarajan, S. (2024). Efficient pneumonia detection using Vision Transformers on chest X-rays. *Scientific Reports*, *14*(1), 2487. DOI: 10.1038/s41598-024-52703-2 PMID: 38291130

Siuko, V., Myllärniemi, J., & Hellsten, P. (2022). State of knowledge-based management in project networks-case in Finnish infrastructure construction sector. In *International Conference on Knowledge Management and Information Systems* (pp. 126-133). SCITEPRESS. DOI: 10.5220/0011376300003335

Sivakumar, S. A., Shankar, B. M., Anuradha, B., Karan, K. A., Karthik, A., Karthik, R., & Kumar, J. R. R. (2023). Artificial Intelligence based Agricultural Chatbot and Virtual Assistant for Delivery of Harvested Crops. *International Journal of Intelligent Systems and Applications in Engineering, 11*(8s), 576–583.

Sivanantham, S., Anwar Basha, H., Thanuja, K., Shafiya Banu, M., Maithili, K., & Ambore, A. (2025). Illuminating the Diagnostic Path. In Kumar, A., Ananth Kumar, T., Das, P., Sharma, C., & Dubey, A. K. (Eds.), *Explainable Artificial Intelligence in the Healthcare Industry*., DOI: 10.1002/9781394249312.ch3

Soltan, S., & Ashrafi, M. (2025). A new optimization model for multi-project scheduling considering dynamic resource allocation. *Soft Computing, 29*(15), 5143–5158. DOI: 10.1007/s00500-025-10891-7

Soto, G. E., Wilcox, S. W., Clark, P. E., Fava, F., Jensen, N., Kahiu, N., Liao, C., Porter, B., Sun, Y., & Barrett, C. B. (2024). Mapping rangeland health indicators in eastern Africa from 2000 to 2022. *Earth System Science Data, 16*(11), 5375–5404. DOI: 10.5194/essd-16-5375-2024

Strasdat, H., Montiel, J., & Davison, A. J. (2020). Visual SLAM: Why filter? *Image and Vision Computing, 30*(2), 65–77. DOI: 10.1016/j.imavis.2012.02.009

Sun, Q., Guo, C., Tang, R., Liu, C., & Zhang, Y. (2024, August). Image Coding and Compression Method Based on Semantics of Pixels for Semantic Communication. In *2024 IEEE/CIC International Conference on Communications in China (ICCC Workshops)* (pp. 1-6). IEEE. DOI: 10.1109/ICCCWorkshops62562.2024.10693763

SVS., G. D., & Seenu, C. (2025, March). Next-Generation Inventory Management: Blockchain-Infused GAN Forecasting with ECDH Security Layer. In *2025 International Conference on Advanced Computing Technologies (ICoACT)* (pp. 1-7). IEEE.

Swarup, L., Primmia, D. R., Jain, R., Raghu, N., Bewoor, L. A., & Kumar, V. M. (2024, December). MRI-Based Epilepsy Seizure Detection Using Combined Approach of CNN With SVM Networks. In 2024 IEEE 4th International Conference on ICT in Business Industry & Government (ICTBIG) (pp. 1-6). IEEE.

Syberfeldt, A., Holm, M., Wang, L., & Lindskog, E. (2018). A systematic review of augmented reality applications in maintenance. *Robotics and Computer-integrated Manufacturing, 49*, 215–228. DOI: 10.1016/j.rcim.2017.06.002

T N, S. G., Satish, R., & Sridhar, R.T N. (2023). S.G., Satish, R. & Sridhar, R. Learning effective embedding for automated COVID-19 prediction from chest X-ray images. *Multimedia Systems*, *29*(2), 739–751. DOI: 10.1007/s00530-022-01015-4 PMID: 36310764

Taha, A. A., & Hanbury, A. (2015). Metrics for evaluating 3D medical image segmentation: Analysis, selection, and tool. *BMC Medical Imaging*, *15*(1), 29. DOI: 10.1186/s12880-015-0068-x PMID: 26263899

Tam, W., Babyn, P., & Alirezaie, J. (2025). Robust lung segmentation in chest X-ray images using modified U-Net with deeper network and residual blocks. *Computer Methods and Programs in Biomedicine Update*, *8*, 100211. DOI: 10.1016/j.cmpbup.2025.100211

Tanaka, A., & Matsumoto, Y. (2024). Adaptive AI-driven earthquake simulation leveraging real-time geospatial data and advanced machine learning models. Research Square, rs-4974302. DOI: 10.21203/rs.3.rs-4974302/v1

Tao, F.. (2019). Digital Twin and Big Data Towards Smart Manufacturing and Industry 4.0: 360 Degree Comparison. *IEEE Access : Practical Innovations, Open Solutions*, *6*, 3585–3593.

Tao, F., Zhang, M., Liu, Y., & Nee, A. Y. C. (2018). Digital Twin in Industry: State-of-the-Art. *IEEE Transactions on Industrial Informatics*, *15*(4), 2405–2415. DOI: 10.1109/TII.2018.2873186

Taylor, F. E., Millington, J. D., Jacob, E., Malamud, B. D., & Pelling, M. (2020). Messy maps: Qualitative GIS representations of resilience. Landscape and Urban Planning, *198*, 103771.

Teed, Z., & Deng, J. (2022). RAFT: Recurrent all-pairs field transforms for optical flow. *IEEE Transactions on Pattern Analysis and Machine Intelligence*, *44*(8), 4144–4157.

The Smart IoT Blueprint. (2024). Engineering a Connected Future. In *Advances in Science, Technology & Innovation/Advances in science, technology & innovation.* Springer International Publishing., DOI: 10.1007/978-3-031-63103-0

Thomas, E., Wilson, D., Kathuni, S., Libey, A., Chintalapati, P., & Coyle, J. (2021). A contribution to drought resilience in East Africa through groundwater pump monitoring informed by in-situ instrumentation, remote sensing and ensemble machine learning. *The Science of the Total Environment*, *780*, 146486. DOI: 10.1016/j.scitotenv.2021.146486 PMID: 33773337

Tian, T., Cheng, L., Wang, G., Abraham, J., Wei, W., Ren, S., Zhu, J., Song, J., & Leng, H. (2022). Reconstructing ocean subsurface salinity at high resolution using a machine learning approach. *Earth System Science Data*, *14*(11), 5037–5060. DOI: 10.5194/essd-14-5037-2022

Touré, H., Boateng, C. D., Gidigasu, S. S. R., Wemegah, D. D., Mensah, V., Aryee, J. N. A., Osei, M. A., Gilbert, J., & Afful, S. (2024a). A Review of Geological and Climatic Variables in Groundwater Availability Prediction in Africa: Machine Learning Approaches [Review of *A Review of Geological and Climatic Variables in Groundwater Availability Prediction in Africa: Machine Learning Approaches*]. EarthArXiv *(California Digital Library)*. California Digital Library. DOI: 10.31223/X53X3S

Touré, H., Boateng, C. D., Gidigasu, S. S. R., Wemegah, D. D., Mensah, V., Aryee, J. N. A., Osei, M. A., Gilbert, J., & Afful, S. (2024b). Review of machine learning algorithms used in groundwater availability studies in Africa: Analysis of geological and climate input variables. *Discover Water*, *4*(1), 109. Advance online publication. DOI: 10.1007/s43832-024-00109-6

Triandis, H. C., & Suh, E. M. (2002). Cultural influences on personality. *Annual Review of Psychology*, *53*(1), 133–160. DOI: 10.1146/annurev.psych.53.100901.135200 PMID: 11752482

Trogrlić, R. Š., Duncan, M., Wright, G., van den Homberg, M., Adeloye, A. J., & Mwale, F. (2022). Why does community-based disaster risk reduction fail to learn from local knowledge? Experiences from Malawi. International Journal of Disaster Risk Reduction, *83*, 103405.

Tummuri, S. S. R. (2025). *Enterprise Integration: Strategies, Technologies And Future Trends*. Academic Guru Publishing House.

Tupes, E. C., & Christal, R. E. (1992). Recurrent personality factors based on trait ratings. *Journal of Personality*, *60*(2), 225–251. DOI: 10.1111/j.1467-6494.1992.tb00973.x PMID: 1635043

Udeh, A. I., Imarhiagbe, O. J., Omietimi, E. J., Mohammed, A. O., & Andre-Obayanju, O. (2024). Machine Learning and Statistical Analysis in Groundwater Monitoring for Total Dissolved Solids Assessment in Winkler County, Texas. *Journal of Geoscience and Environment Protection*, *12*(6), 1–29. DOI: 10.4236/gep.2024.126001

Ullah, R., Ali, W., & Ghanni, U. (2025). Deep Reinforcement Learning for Robust USVs Navigation in Diverse Environmental Scenarios. *International Journal of Data Informatics and Intelligent Computing*, *4*(4), 1–10. DOI: 10.59461/ijdiic.v4i4.219

Upadhyay, S. K., & Kumar, A. (2022). A novel approach for rice plant diseases classification with deep convolutional neural network. *International Journal of Information Technology : an Official Journal of Bharati Vidyapeeth's Institute of Computer Applications and Management, 14*(1), 185–199. DOI: 10.1007/s41870-021-00817-5

Välilä, T. (2025). The economic impact of transport infrastructure: A review of project-level vs. aggregate-level evidence. *Transport Reviews, 45*(4), 459–481. DOI: 10.1080/01441647.2025.2476012

Valman, S., Boyd, D. S., Carbonneau, P., Johnson, M. F., & Dugdale, S. J. (2023). An AI approach to operationalise global daily PlanetScope satellite imagery for river water masking. *Remote Sensing of Environment, 301*, 113932. DOI: 10.1016/j.rse.2023.113932

van den Hoed, M. W., Backhaus, R., de Vries, E., & van der Veer, S. N. (2022). Factors contributing to innovation readiness in health care organizations: A scoping review. *BMC Health Services Research, 22*(1), 1–17. DOI: 10.1186/s12913-022-08185-x

Van Der Lee, C., Krahmer, E., & Wubben, S. (2017). PASS: A Dutch data-to-text system for soccer, targeted towards specific audiences. https://www.automatedinsights.com/

Venugopal, A., Nerur, S., Yasar, M., & Rasheed, A. A. (2023). CEO personality and corporate sustainability performance. *Management Decision, 61*(12), 3691–3716. DOI: 10.1108/MD-06-2022-0842

Vigneault, M. A., Boton, C., Chong, H. Y., & Cooper-Cooke, B. (2020). An Innovative Framework of 5D BIM Solutions for Construction Cost Management: A Systematic Review. *Archives of Computational Methods in Engineering, 27*(4), 1013–1030. DOI: 10.1007/s11831-019-09341-z

Vijayagopal, P., Kumar, A., & Singh, R. (2025). Landslide early warning systems using machine learning: A systematic review. Landslides, *22*(1), 145-168.

Wadoux, A. M. J.-C., Minasny, B., & McBratney, A. B. (2020). Machine learning for digital soil mapping: Applications, challenges and suggested solutions. *Earth-Science Reviews, 210*, 103359. DOI: 10.1016/j.earscirev.2020.103359

Wang, C., Fan, I., & King, S. (2023). A Review of Digital Twin for Vehicle Predictive Maintenance System. *SAE Technical Paper 2023-01-1024.*

Wang, B., & Lo, K. T. (2024). Autoencoder-based joint image compression and encryption. *Journal of Information Security and Applications, 80*, 103680. DOI: 10.1016/j.jisa.2023.103680

Wang, K., Guo, F., Zhang, C., & Schaefer, D. (2024). From Industry 4.0 to Construction 4.0: Barriers to the digital transformation of engineering and construction sectors. *Engineering, Construction, and Architectural Management, 31*(1), 136–158. DOI: 10.1108/ECAM-05-2022-0383

Wang, L.. (2021). Implementation of Digital Twin and Cyber-Physical Systems Using PLC and HMI: A Smart Manufacturing Case Study. *Journal of Manufacturing Systems*.

Wang, L., Wang, Q., Wang, X., & Liu, M. (2026). Segmentation-enhanced multiscale deep hashing for chest X-ray image retrieval. *Medical Image Analysis, 109*, 103919. DOI: 10.1016/j.media.2025.103919 PMID: 41468639

Wang, Q., Meng, W., Gan, C., Yu, H., & Cheng, Y. (2026). A lesion region awareness and adaptive label-relation graph algorithm for multi-label chest X-ray image classification. *Engineering Applications of Artificial Intelligence, 167*(Part 2), 113873. DOI: 10.1016/j.engappai.2026.113873

Wang, S., Kao, Y.-H., Chen, Y., Hsu, S., Kimura, M., Chang, L., & Pan, T.-W. (2024). Optimizing groundwater management to prevent drawdown and sustain agricultural production using machine learning model. *Research Square (Research Square)*. DOI: 10.21203/rs.3.rs-4614420/v1

Wang, T., & Chen, H. M. (2023). Integration of building information modeling and project management in construction project life cycle. *Automation in Construction, 150*, 104832. DOI: 10.1016/j.autcon.2023.104832

Wang, W. Y., Huang, Y. C., Ik, T. U., & Peng, W. C. (2023). ShuttleSet: A Human-Annotated Stroke-Level Singles Dataset for Badminton Tactical Analysis. *Proceedings of the ACM SIGKDD International Conference on Knowledge Discovery and Data Mining*, 5126–5136. DOI: 10.1145/3580305.3599906

Wang, X., Zhu, X., & Zhang, Y. (2018). An image encryption algorithm based on Josephus traversing and mixed chaotic map. *IEEE Access : Practical Innovations, Open Solutions, 6*, 23733–23746. DOI: 10.1109/ACCESS.2018.2805847

Wang, Y., Jiang, C., Wu, Y., Lv, T., Sun, H., Liu, Y., Li, L., & Pan, X. (2022). Semantic-powered explainable model-free few-shot learning scheme of diagnosing COVID-19 on chest X-ray. *IEEE Journal of Biomedical and Health Informatics, 26*(12), 6109–6120. DOI: 10.1109/JBHI.2022.3205167 PMID: 36074872

Wang, Y., Noor-A-Rahim, M., Gunawan, E., Guan, Y. L., & Poh, C. L. (2023, May-June). Erry Gunawan, Yong L. Guan, and Chueh L. Poh. 2023. Modelling, Characterization of Data-Dependent and Process-Dependent Errors in DNA Data Storage. *IEEE/ACM Transactions on Computational Biology and Bioinformatics, 20*(3), 2147–2158. DOI: 10.1109/TCBB.2022.3233914 PMID: 37018270

Wang, Z., Chu, Z., Doan, T. V., Ni, S., Yang, M., & Zhang, W. (2024). History, Development, and Principles of Large Language Models-An Introductory Survey. https://arxiv.org/abs/2402.06853

Waqar, A., Skrzypkowski, K., Almujibah, H., Zagorski, K., Khan, M. B., Zagorska, A., & Benjeddou, O. (2023). Success of implementing cloud computing for smart development in small construction projects. *Applied Sciences (Basel, Switzerland), 13*(9), 5713. DOI: 10.3390/app13095713

Ward, M., Johnson, P., & Chen, W. (2020). AI for accelerating geospatial data generation in disaster contexts. International Journal of Digital Earth, *13*(8), 892-912.

Waterhouse, J., & Mann, S. (2021). Mapping domain knowledge for leading and managing change. *The Serials Librarian, 80*(1-4), 3–10. DOI: 10.1080/0361526X.2021.1863140

West, C. P., Reinecke, R., Rosolem, R., MacDonald, A., Cuthbert, M., & Wagener, T. (2022). Ground truthing global-scale model estimates of groundwater recharge across Africa. *The Science of the Total Environment, 858*, 159765. DOI: 10.1016/j.scitotenv.2022.159765 PMID: 36309251

Windmann, A., ... (2024). Artificial Intelligence in Industry 4.0: A Review of Integration Challenges for Industrial Systems. arXiv preprint. arXiv:2405.18580 DOI: 10.1109/INDIN58382.2024.10774364

Wölker, A., & Powell, T. E. (2021). Algorithms in the newsroom? News readers' perceived credibility and selection of automated journalism. *Journalism, 22*(1), 86–103. DOI: 10.1177/1464884918757072

Wowk, K., McKinley, E., & Fletcher, S. (2023). Quantifying social dimensions of resilience: A systematic review of methods and metrics. Ecology and Society, *28*(1), 12.

Wu, X., Zhu, B., Hu, Y., & Ran, Y. (2017). A novel color image encryption scheme using rectangular transform-enhanced chaotic tent maps. *IEEE Access : Practical Innovations, Open Solutions, 5*, 6429–6436. DOI: 10.1109/ACCESS.2017.2692043

Wu, Y. H., Gao, S. H., Mei, J., Xu, J., Fan, D. P., Zhang, R. G., & Cheng, M. M. (2021). JCS: An explainable COVID-19 diagnosis system by joint classification and segmentation. *IEEE Transactions on Image Processing : A Publication of the IEEE Signal Processing Society*, *30*, 3113–3126. DOI: 10.1109/TIP.2021.3058783 PMID: 33600316

Wu, Z., Yang, K., Lai, X., & Antwi-Afari, M. F. (2020). A scientometric review of system dynamics applications in construction management research. *Sustainability (Basel)*, *12*(18), 7474. DOI: 10.3390/su12187474

Xu, J., Lu, W., & Li, Z. (2019). Building damage detection in satellite imagery using convolutional neural networks. Remote Sensing, *11*(11), 1356.

Xu, R., Joshi, J. B., & Li, C. (2019, July). Cryptonn: Training neural networks over encrypted data. In 2019 IEEE 39th International Conference on Distributed Computing Systems (ICDCS) (pp. 1199-1209). IEEE, DOI: 10.1109/ICDCS.2019.00121

Xu, L., Gou, X., Li, Z., & Li, J. (2017). A novel chaotic image encryption algorithm using block scrambling and dynamic index based diffusion. *Optics and Lasers in Engineering*, *91*, 41–52. DOI: 10.1016/j.optlaseng.2016.10.012

Xu, T., Mandal, M., Long, R., Cheng, I., & Basu, A. (2012). Mrinal Mandal, Richard Long, Irene Cheng, Anup Basu, An edge-region force guided active shape approach for automatic lung field detection in chest radiographs. *Computerized Medical Imaging and Graphics : The Official Journal of the Computerized Medical Imaging Society*, *36*(6), 452–463. DOI: 10.1016/j.compmedimag.2012.04.005 PMID: 22608158

Yameogo, T. S. K., Koné, M., Ralf, L., Bonkoungou, B., & Adounkpè, J. (2025). Groundwater Potential Mapping in the Sissili Sub-Catchment, Burkina Faso: Comparing Multicriteria Analysis and Artificial Intelligence in a Crystalline Basement Aquifer. *Journal of Water Resource and Protection*, *17*(6), 378. DOI: 10.4236/jwarp.2025.176019

Yan, L., Chen, C., Hang, T., & Hu, Y. (2021). A stream prediction model based on attention-LSTM. *Earth Science Informatics*, *14*(2), 723–733. DOI: 10.1007/s12145-021-00571-z

Yao, Z., Liu, Q., Yang, J., Chen, Y., & Wu, Z. (2023). PPUP-GAN: A GAN-based privacy-protecting method for aerial photography. *Future Generation Computer Systems*, *145*, 284–292. DOI: 10.1016/j.future.2023.03.031

Yarkoni, T. (2010). Personality in 100,000 words: A large-scale analysis of personality and word use among bloggers. *Journal of Research in Personality*, *44*(3), 363–373. DOI: 10.1016/j.jrp.2010.04.001 PMID: 20563301

Yazdani, E., Neizehbaz, A., Karamzade-Ziarati, N., & Kheradpisheh, S. R. Explainable artificial intelligence for pneumonia classification: Clinical insights into deformable prototypical part network in pediatric chest x-ray images, Journal of Medical Imaging and Radiation Sciences, Volume 56, Issue 5, 2025, 102023, ISSN 1939-8654, DOI: 10.1016/j.jmir.2025.102023

Ye, X., Wang, S., Lu, Z., Song, Y., & Yu, S. (2021). Towards an AI-driven framework for multi-scale urban flood resilience planning and design. Computational Urban Science, *1*(1), 11.

Yeboah, G., Porto de Albuquerque, J., & Troilo, R. (2021). Real-time flood reporting in Lagos, Nigeria: A participatory approach. Journal of Flood Risk Management, *14*(2), e12701.

Yessoufou, A., Sarr, M., & Diop, A. (2024). Women's social networks and climate resilience in Senegal. Gender, Place & Culture, *31*(3), 345-367.

Yilma, A. D. (2019). Volunteered Geographic Information in Africa. The International Archives of the Photogrammetry, Remote Sensing and Spatial Information Sciences, *XLII-2/W13*, 1615-1620.

Yilmaz, N., Ergen, E., & Citipitioglu, A. M. (2025). Enhancing RFI management in construction through machine learning-driven predictive models. Smart and Sustainable Built Environment, 1-21.

Yin, Z., Darrell, T., & Yu, F. (2021). Transfuser: Imitation with transformer-based sensor fusion for autonomous driving. In *Proceedings of the Conference on Robot Learning (CoRL).*

Yordanov, V., Brovelli, M. A., & Carrion, D. (2021). AI for rapid information generation in disaster response: A review. International Journal of Applied Earth Observation and Geoinformation, *102*, 102456.

Yuan, F., Fan, C., Farahmand, H., Coleman, N., Esmalian, A., Lee, C. C., ... & Mostafavi, A. (2022). Smart flood resilience: harnessing community-scale big data for predictive flood risk monitoring, rapid impact assessment, and situational awareness. Environmental Research: Infrastructure and Sustainability, *2*(2), 025006.

Zambrano, L., Atencio, E., Mariani, C., Mancini, M., & Atencio, E. (2024, February). Integration between PMBOK 7th concepts: A network analysis. In *Proc. 14th International Conference on Industrial Engineering and Operations Management* (pp. 1098-1108). DOI: 10.46254/AN14.20240277

Zanotti, C., Caschetto, M., Bonomi, T., Parini, M., Cipriano, G., Fumagalli, L., & Rotiroti, M. (2021). Linking local natural background levels in groundwater to their generating hydrogeochemical processes in Quaternary alluvial aquifers. *The Science of the Total Environment, 805*, 150259. DOI: 10.1016/j.scitotenv.2021.150259 PMID: 34536881

Zennaro, F., Furlan, E., Canu, D. M., Alcázar, L. A., Rosati, G., Solidoro, C., Aslan, S., & Critto, A. (2023). Venice lagoon chlorophyll-a evaluation under climate change conditions: A hybrid water quality machine learning and biogeochemical-based framework. *Ecological Indicators, 157*, 111245. DOI: 10.1016/j.ecolind.2023.111245

Zhang, J., Zhang, K., & Ma, L. (2024, December). GAN-Based Intrusion Detection System for IoT Services. In *2024 2nd International Conference on Computer Network Technology and Electronic and Information Engineering (CNTEIE)* (pp. 26-31). IEEE. DOI: 10.1109/CNTEIE66268.2024.00012

Zhang, X. (2023, February). Application of Knowledge Distillation in Generative Adversarial Networks. In 2023 3rd Asia-Pacific Conference on Communications Technology and Computer Science (ACCTCS) (pp. 65-71). IEEE, DOI: 10.1109/ACCTCS58815.2023.00014

Zhang, C., Dong, W., Shen, W., & Du, Y. (2025). Influencing Factors of BIM Application Benefits in Construction Projects Based on SEM. *Buildings (Basel, Switzerland), 15*(11), 1875. DOI: 10.3390/buildings15111875

Zhang, J., & Singh, S. (2020). LOAM: Lidar odometry and mapping in real-time. *IEEE Robotics and Automation Letters, 5*(4), 5810–5817.

Zhang, M., Chen, R., Yang, Y., Sun, X., & Shan, X. (2024). Machine learning analysis of lab tests to predict bariatric readmissions. *Scientific Reports, 14*(1), 16845. DOI: 10.1038/s41598-024-67710-6 PMID: 39039130

Zhang, W., & Wang, Z. (2021). Theory and practice of VR/AR in K-12 science education—A systematic review. *Sustainability (Basel), 13*(22), 12646. DOI: 10.3390/su132212646

Zhao, R., Yan, R., Chen, Z., Mao, K., Wang, P., & Gao, R. X. (2019). Deep learning and its applications to machine health monitoring. *Mechanical Systems and Signal Processing, 115*, 213–237. DOI: 10.1016/j.ymssp.2018.05.050

Zhao, S., Grasmuck, S., & Martin, J. (2008). Identity construction on Facebook: Digital empowerment in anchored relationships. *Computers in Human Behavior, 24*(5), 1816–1836. DOI: 10.1016/j.chb.2008.02.012

Zheng, H., ... (2020). Advancing from Predictive Maintenance to Intelligent Maintenance with AI and IIoT. arXiv preprint. arXiv:2009.00351

Zheng, X., Xie, R., Yao, X., Su, Y., Chu, L., Xu, P., & Liu, W. (2024). A generative adversarial network for multiple reads reconstruction in DNA storage. *Scientific Reports*, *14*(1), 32071. DOI: 10.1038/s41598-024-83806-5 PMID: 39738820

Zhou, Y.. (2021). Digital Twin-Driven Smart Manufacturing: Connotation, Reference Model, Applications and Research Issues. *Sensors (Basel)*, *21*(3), 1086. PMID: 33498332

Zidan, F., & Febriyanti, D. E. (2024). Optimizing Agricultural Yields with Artificial Intelligence-Based Climate Adaptation Strategies. [ITSDI]. *IAIC Transactions on Sustainable Digital Innovation*, *5*(2), 136–147. DOI: 10.34306/itsdi.v5i2.663

Zou, L., Goh, H. L., Liew, C. J. Y., Quah, J. L., Gu, G. T., Chew, J. J., Kumar, M. P., Ang, C. G. L., & Ta, A. W. A. (2023). Ensemble image explainable AI (XAI) algorithm for severe community-acquired pneumonia and COVID-19 respiratory infections. *IEEE Transactions on Artificial Intelligence*, *4*(2), 241–250. DOI: 10.1109/TAI.2022.3153754

About the Contributors

Jingyuan Zhao obtained her PhD in Management Science and Engineering from University of Science and Technology of China. Dr. Zhao's research expertise includes management of technology innovation, behaviour and information technology, AI for industries, global innovation networks, high-tech industries, multinational governance, and science and technology policy. She has teaching experience of 15 years at the graduate and undergraduate level. Research portfolio includes peer-reviewed articles in highly regarded journals, authored books, multiple book chapters, and conference presentations. Dr. Zhao also has extensive industry experience and provides consulting services to major corporations such as China Mobile. She serves as editor-in-chief of International Journal of e-Collaboration (IJeC), a Scopus indexed journal.

V. Vinoth Kumar is working as Associate Professor of School of Computer Science Engineering & Information Systems, Vellore Institute of Technology (VIT), Vellore, India. He is serving as Adjunct Professor Associated with School of Computer Science, Taylor's University, Malaysia. He has published 5 books and 105 technical articles in refereed journals and proceedings with h-index of 31 and i-10 index of 65. He has filled 17 domestic patents and 2 US patents in the field of IoT and Autonomous vehicles. He is having 2650+ citations on Google Scholar for his publications. Recently he has published five papers in IEEE Transaction journals among that one paper published with 10.6-Impact factor. He has edited 30+ special issues and 5 books in reputed publishers. He is the Associate Editor of the IEEE Access, PLOS ONE, PLOS Complex Systems, BMC medical informatics and decision making, International Journal of Pervasive Computing and Communications, International Journal of e-Collaboration (IJeC) and International Journal of Intelligent Information Systems. He served as the General Chair, a Program Committee Chair, and PC Member for major international conferences. He has delivered more than 20 lectures in various seminars/faculty development programs and workshops. He is the Research Advisory Committee member for Taylor's University, Malaysia and five affiliated colleges from VTU, Bangalore. He is the BoS and Department Advisory Committee member for more than 10 institutions in India. His current research interests include Internet of Things, Artificial Intelligence, and medical image processing. He is a fellow of IEEE (senior member) and life member of ISTE. Recently, he has been honoured as one of the 'World's Top 2% Scientists' by Stanford University, USA. This esteemed recognition reflects Dr Vinoth's exceptional contributions to the field of Artificial Intelligence and Biomedical applications, particularly their potential as new learning models designed for Medical Image based solutions.

Joseph Richards joined the marketing faculty at CSUS in 2001. He holds a doctorate in Marketing with further specialization in Econometrics from Syracuse University. He is an active researcher in the fields of Internet related aspects of consumer behavior, marketing strategy, marketing analytics, and statistical and quantitative marketing models. Recent research and focus is in big data analytics. His publications have appeared in many leading journals.

***

Anorgul Ashirova is working as an Associate Professor at the Department of General Professional Sciences, Mamun University, Khiva, Uzbekistan

Barry Dyer holds an MSc in Sport Science and a Diploma in Data Analytics. He currently works as a statistical programmer, and has a strong interest in the application of large language model technology to the field of sports analytics.

Reda El Yazidi holds a PhD in Information and Communication Sciences from Sidi Mohamed Ben Abdellah University (USMBA) in Fez. He is currently Professor of Communication and Media at Moulay Ismaïl University in Morocco. His research focuses on digital communication, the sociology of technology, and the psychological and social impact of digital transformation on human practices. Through his academic work, he aims to deepen understanding of the ethical and societal dimensions of technology while supporting students in developing critical perspectives on media and digital practices, preparing them to engage thoughtfully with the challenges of the digital age.

Appasami G. is a Senior Researcher (formerly Assistant Professor) in the Department of Computer Applications at NIT Tiruchirappalli and is currently pursuing his Ph.D. in Computer Science. He has over 13 years of academic and research experience, with expertise in artificial intelligence, machine learning, deep learning, image processing, and cybersecurity. Particularly in the areas of medical imaging and explainable AI. He has published research in reputed journals such as EPJ Special Topics and Springer Discover Computing, and has authored books on graph theory and algorithms. A recipient of multiple NPTEL gold certifications and research excellence awards, he is also an active member of professional bodies including CSI, ISTE, and IEI.

Erkin Kholiyarov is working in the Department of Information Technology and Exact Sciences at Termez University of Economics and Service, Termez, Uzbekistan.

Krishnakumari L. is an Assistant Professor at the Ramco Institute of technology, Rajapalayam, Tamilanadu, India.

Saradha M received her B.Sc., degree and M.Sc., degree in Mathematics from Bharathidasan University, Tamil Nadu, India and the Ph.D., degree in Hybrid Fuzzy Fractional Differential Equations from Bharathidasan University, Tamil Nadu, India in 2017. Her current research interests include Fuzzy Sets, Cyber security Analysis, Technologies in Higher Education, Fractional Differential Equations and Error Analysis.

Raghu N is an Associate Professor at Jain (Deemed-to-be University), recognized for his commitment to fostering a dynamic and engaging learning environment that inspires students to explore their capabilities and achieve academic excellence, with a strong passion for teaching and mentoring, He consistently strives to cultivate critical thinking, innovation, and lifelong learning among his students. His research contributions span across reputed journals, book chapters, and international conference proceedings, reflecting both depth and diversity in his academic pursuits. Dr. Raghu N also holds patents that highlight his technical expertise and his dedication to leveraging technology for societal benefit. His work emphasizes practical innovation aimed at addressing real-world challenges. He is actively involved in community service as a National Service Scheme (NSS) Programme Officer. Over the past five years, he has played a pivotal role in organizing and leading numerous outreach initiatives focused on social awareness, environmental sustainability, and community development. His efforts demonstrate a strong commitment to nurturing socially responsible citizens. Dr. Raghu N is also an active member of several esteemed professional bodies, including the International Association of Engineers (IAENG), the International Association of Computer Science and Information Technology (IACSIT), the Institute for Engineering Research and Publication (IFERP), the Indian Academicians and Researchers Association, the Optical Society of India, and the Asia-Pacific Chemical, Biological & Environmental Engineering Society (APCBEES). His involvement in these organizations reflects his dedication to continuous professional growth and collaboration within the global research community.

Antline Nisha B. is presently working as an Associate Professor in Department of Mathematics at St.Joseph's Institute of Technology, Chennai, Tamilnadu, India. She has over 9 years of teaching experience. Her educational qualification includes M.Sc., Mphil., in Mathematics and awarded Ph.D doctorate degree in the field of Mathematics from Bharathidasan University, Tiruchirappalli, Tamilnadu, in 2017. Her area of specialization is Queueing theory. She has a wide range of expertise in organising and conducting various student and faculty development programs. She has published 20 research papers in Peer- Reviewed, UGC care list, Web of Science and Scopus indexed journals. She has attended FDP's, Seminars, Webinars, Workshops and presented papers in various international and national conference.

Mouhcine Rhouiri PhD in Management Sciences from the LAREMEF laboratory at USMBA Fez. Specializing in the role of interactive management control in addressing hidden costs during times of crisis. His primary areas of research include management control, organizational resilience, Organizational Capability, and the application of Artificial Intelligence in Business contexts. In his teaching he juxtaposes theoretical and practical approaches to improve organizational efficiency and adaptability.

Nickolas Sarvarimuthu received the ME and PhD degrees from National Institute of Technology, Tiruchirappalli, India, in 1992 and 2007 respectively. He is currently working as Professor in the Department of Computer Applications at the National Institute of Technology, Tiruchirappalli, India. He served as Head of the Department and Chairman, MIS for NITT. He is the Professor In-Charge of the Massively Parallel Programming Laboratory, NVIDIA CUDA Teaching Centre, NIT, Tiruchirappalli. His research interest includes Data Mining, Big Data Analytics, Machine Learning, Cloud Computing and Software Metrics.

Ibrahim Sinneh Sinneh is an accomplished distribution system engineer with extensive experience in designing, maintaining, and optimizing electrical distribution systems. His areas of expertise include power system planning, grid management, and renewable energy integration, demonstrating a commitment to ensuring the reliable and efficient supply of electricity to customers. Current Position Head of Department (Electrical Engineering) University of Liberia, Monrovia, LR 2023 - Present Education Ph.D. in Electrical and Electronics Engineering University of Johannesburg, Johannesburg, ZA 2023 - Present Master of Engineering (M.Eng) Chongqing University, Chongqing, CN 2018 - 2020 Bachelor of Science (B.Sc) in Electrical Engineering University of Liberia, Monrovia, LR 2010 - 2016

Professional Development Certificate in Infrastructure Operations and Maintenance ADBInstitute, Tokyo, JP February 2024 Diploma in Electrical Power Systems Design and Protection Electrical Power Systems LLC, Oregon, US June 2023 Diploma in Electrical Design and Drafting Advance Modeling Recreators MEP Institute of Engineering, Hyderabad, IN August 2022 Ibrahim is dedicated to advancing the field of electrical engineering through both academic and practical contributions, positioning himself as a key figure in the development of efficient electrical systems.

Nwosu Obinnaya Chikezie Victor is a multidisciplinary scholar, researcher, and professional with expertise spanning Artificial Intelligence, Environmental Sciences, Geophysics, Cybersecurity, Data Analysis, and Environmental Technology. He is currently pursuing a Ph.D. in Environmental Sciences at the University of South Africa, where his research focuses on integrating intelligent systems into environmental and geophysical applications to enhance sustainability and innovation in industrial practice. He earned his B.Tech in Geophysics from the Federal University of Technology Owerri, Nigeria, in 2007 and completed his M.Sc. in Environmental Technology at Teesside University, England, in 2011. Over the years, he has undertaken short professional certification programs at the University of Alberta (Canada), the Georgia Institute of Technology (USA), and the Cape Peninsula University of Technology (South Africa). He also holds a Certificate in Artificial Intelligence in the 4th Industrial Revolution and a 4IR Work Readiness Program Certificate from the University of Johannesburg, completed in collaboration with Accenture.

Index

A

B

C

D

E

F

G

H

I

L

M

N

www.ingramcontent.com/pod-product-compliance
Lightning Source LLC
LaVergne TN
LVHW062330300926
849161LV00007B/1635